The Cambridge Companion to the Musical

Tracing the development of the musical both on Broadway and in London's West End, this updated *Companion* continues to provide a broad and thorough overview of one of the liveliest and most popular forms of musical performance. Ordered chronologically, essays cover the history of the genre from the American musical of the nineteenth century through to the most recent productions, and the book also includes key information on singers, audience, critical reception and traditions. All of the chapters from the first edition remain – several in updated forms – and five new chapters have been added, covering ethnic musicals in the United States; the European musical; Broadway musicals in revival and on television; the most recent shows; and a case study of the creation of the popular show *Wicked* based on interviews with its creators. The *Companion* also includes an extensive bibliography and photographs from key productions.

William A. Everett is Associate Professor of Musicology at the University of Missouri–Kansas City.

Paul R. Laird is Professor of Musicology at the University of Kansas.

The Cambridge Companion to the
MUSICAL

. . . .

SECOND EDITION

EDITED BY
William A. Everett and Paul R. Laird

 CAMBRIDGE
UNIVERSITY PRESS

CAMBRIDGE UNIVERSITY PRESS
Cambridge, New York, Melbourne, Madrid, Cape Town, Singapore, São Paulo, Delhi

Cambridge University Press
The Edinburgh Building, Cambridge CB2 8RU, UK

Published in the United States of America by Cambridge University Press, New York

www.cambridge.org
Information on this title: www.cambridge.org/9780521680844

First published 2002
Second edition 2008
Reprinted 2009

Printed in the United Kingdom at the University Press, Cambridge

A catalogue record for this publication is available from the British Library

Library of Congress Cataloguing in Publication data

The Cambridge companion to the musical / edited by William A. Everett and Paul R. Laird. – 2nd edn.
     p. cm.
Includes bibliographical references (p. 372) and index.
ISBN 978-0-521-86238-7 (hardback) – ISBN 978-0-521-68084-4 (pbk.)
1. Musicals–History and criticism.   2. Musical theater–History.   I. Everett, William A., 1962–
II. Laird, Paul R.   III. Title.

ML2054.C35 2008
782.1′4–dc22   2007053042

ISBN 978-0-521-86238-7 hardback
ISBN 978-0-521-68084-4 paperback

Contents

List of illustrations [*page* vii]
Notes on contributors [ix]
Preface to the second edition [xiv]

Part I • Adaptations and transformations: before 1940

1 American musical theatre before the twentieth century *Katherine K. Preston* [3]

2 Non-English-language musical theatre in the United States *John Koegel* [29]

3 Birth pangs, growing pains and sibling rivalry: musical theatre in New York, 1900–1920 *Orly Leah Krasner* [54]

4 American and British operetta in the 1920s: romance, nostalgia and adventure *William A. Everett* [72]

5 Images of African Americans: African-American musical theatre, *Show Boat* and *Porgy and Bess John Graziano* [89]

6 The melody (and the words) linger on: American musical comedies of the 1920s and 1930s *Geoffrey Block* [103]

Part II • Maturations and formulations: 1940–1970

7 'We said we wouldn't look back': British musical theatre, 1935–1960 *John Snelson* [127]

8 The coming of the musical play: Rodgers and Hammerstein *Ann Sears* [147]

9 The successors of Rodgers and Hammerstein from the 1940s to the 1960s *Thomas L. Riis and Ann Sears* [164]

10 Musical sophistication on Broadway: Kurt Weill and Leonard Bernstein *bruce d. mcclung and Paul R. Laird* [190]

Part III • Evolutions and integrations: after 1970

11 Stephen Sondheim and the musical of the outsider *Jim Lovensheimer* [205]

12 Choreographers, directors and the fully integrated musical *Paul R. Laird* [220]

13 From *Hair* to *Rent*: is 'rock' a four-letter word on Broadway? *Scott Warfield* [235]

14 The megamusical: the creation, internationalisation and impact of a genre *Paul Prece and William A. Everett* [250]

15 'Something borrowed, something blue': the marriage of the musical and Europe *Judith Sebesta* [270]

16 New horizons: the musical at the dawn of the twenty-first century *Bud Coleman* [284]

Part IV • Legacies and transformations

17 Why do they start to sing and dance all of a sudden? Examining the film musical *Graham Wood* [305]

18 Revisiting classic musicals: revivals, films, television and recordings *Jessica Sternfeld* [325]

19 The creation of a Broadway musical: Stephen Schwartz, Winnie Holzman, and *Wicked Paul R. Laird* [340]

Notes [353]
Select bibliography [372]
Index [386]

Illustrations

1 Scenic design for Act 2 from Emma Abbott's production of the opera *Paul and Virginia* by Victor Massé (1872) showing the interior of the plantation home of Mons. St. Crois on 'a picturesque island off the coast of Africa'. Tams-Witmark Collection, University of Wisconsin-Madison [*page* 23]

2 'A Brivele dem Taten' (A Little Letter to Papa) (1911). Words and music by Solomon Smulewitz (1868–1943), arranged by Joseph Rumshisky (1881–1956) [41]

3 Libretto cover from 'Klein-Deutschland' (Little Germany) (1897) by Adolf Philipp [46]

4 Editorial cartoon concerning the popularity of *The Merry Widow* from *The Evening American*, 1909 [62]

5 The original New York production of *The Student Prince* with Ilse Marvenga and the Male Chorus. Photo courtesy of The Shubert Archive [78]

6 A production of *Show Boat*, c. 1938 at the St Louis Municipal Opera. Photo courtesy of the Municipal Theatre Association of St Louis [100]

7 Gertrude Lawrence with the doll that George Gershwin gave her to hold while singing 'Someone to Watch Over Me' in *Oh, Kay!* Photo courtesy of New York Public Library, Billy Rose Theatre Collection [121]

8 Programme cover from original production of *Twenty to One* (12 November 1935, Coliseum). Photo from private programme collection of John Snelson [128]

9 Programme cover from the 1945 revival at the Victoria Palace of *Me and My Girl* (original premiere 16 December 1937, Victoria Palace). The design is the same as the original cover and Lupino Lane starred in both productions. Photo from private programme collection of John Snelson [136]

10 Programme cover from the original production of *Bless the Bride* (26 April 1947, Adelphi Theatre). Photo from private programme collection of John Snelson [136]

11 Programme cover from original production of *Gay's the Word* (16 February 1951, Saville Theatre). Photo from private programme collection of John Snelson [136]

12 Programme cover from *Expresso Bongo* (23 April 1958, Saville Theatre). Photo from private programme collection of John Snelson [136]

13 Shirley Jones as Maria with the children in the 1977 production of *The Sound of Music* at Starlight Theatre, Kansas City, Missouri. Photo courtesy of Starlight Theatre, Kansas City, Missouri [161]

14 Carol Channing in the 1977 production of *Hello, Dolly!* at Starlight Theatre, Kansas City, Missouri. Photo courtesy of Starlight Theatre, Kansas City, Missouri [187]

15 Lotte Lenya performing the song 'Pirate Jenny' with Leonard Bernstein conducting during concert production of *The Threepenny Opera* at Festival of the Creative Arts, Brandeis University, 1952. Photo courtesy of The Kurt Weill Foundation for Music [191]

16 Production of *Company* in 2001 at the Missouri Repertory Theatre. Photo courtesy of Kansas City Repertory Theatre [209]

17 Ann Reinking, P. J. Mann and Christine Colby Jacques in 'Stout-Hearted Men', a dance number from Bob Fosse's *Dancin'*, in 1979. Photo courtesy of TimePix, Martha Swope Collection [227]

18 The original production of *Hair* in 1968. Photo by Dagmar [238]

19 The original London cast of *Les Misérables*, Palace Theatre, 1985. © Donald Cooper, Photostage [252]

20 Sarah Brightman and Michael Crawford in *The Phantom of the Opera*, Her Majesty's Theatre, 1986. © Donald Cooper, Photostage [262]

21 German production of *Elisabeth*, courtesy of Stage Entertainment, Inc. Photographer: Karen Stuke, Theaterfotografie, Bielefeld [278]

22 Imperial Theatre marquee featuring *The Boy from Oz*, summer 2004. Photograph by William A. Everett [288]

23 *Chicago* at the Ambassador Theatre, New York, summer 2004. Photograph by William A. Everett [327]

24 *Playbill* cover for *Wicked* [346]

Contributors

Geoffrey Block, Professor of Music History at the University of Puget Sound in Tacoma, Washington, is the author of *Charles Ives: A Bio-Bibliography* (1988), a Cambridge Music Handbook on Ives's *Concord Sonata* (1996), and *Enchanted Evenings: The Broadway Musical from 'Show Boat' to Sondheim* (1997), the co-editor of *Charles Ives and the Classical Tradition* (1996), and the editor of *The Richard Rodgers Reader* (2002). His most recent book is *Richard Rodgers* (2003), the inaugural volume of Yale Broadway Masters, a series for which Block serves as General Editor.

Bud Coleman is Associate Professor at the University of Colorado at Boulder and Chair of the Department of Theatre and Dance. A former dancer with Les Ballets Trockadero de Monte Carlo, Fort Worth Ballet, Kinesis, and Ballet Austin, he has directed/choreographed *Seussical, A Grand Night for Singing, Pippin, Wonderful Town, Songs in the Key of . . . Caffeine* (also librettist), *A Funny Thing Happened on the Way to the Forum, The Mikado, Into the Woods, Merrily We Roll Along, Lysistrata, Dames at Sea, Hair, Six Degrees of Separation,* the opera *Being of Sound Mind,* and numerous other productions. Coleman has a PhD in Theatre History and Criticism from the University of Texas at Austin, and his publications have appeared in the *St. James Press Gay & Lesbian Almanac, qlbtq.com, New York Native, Theatre History Studies, The Austin American-Statesman, Theatre InSight,* and *Choreography and Dance.* With co-editor Judith Sebesta, he published *Women in American Musical Theatre: Essays on Lyricists, Writers, Arrangers, Choreographers, Designers, Producers, and Performance Artists* (2007).

William A. Everett is Associate Professor and Area Coordinator of Musicology at the University of Missouri–Kansas City Conservatory of Music and Dance. His research interests include the American musical theatre, particularly operetta, and the relationship between music and national identity. He is the author of *The Musical: A Research and Information Guide* (2004) and *Sigmund Romberg* (2007), a volume in Yale Broadway Masters. He co-authored, with Paul R. Laird, *The Historical Dictionary of the Broadway Musical* (2007), and his book on Rudolf Friml is forthcoming from the University of Illinois Press.

John Graziano is Professor in the Graduate Center of the City University of New York, where he holds appointments in the departments of Music and American Studies. Currently he also serves as president of the Society for American Music. Among other studies, Graziano has edited (with Michael Rophino Lacy, arranger) Rossini's *Cinderella* in English (1994); edited (with Joanne Swenson-Eldridge) Charles Hommann's *Chamber Music for Strings* (1998); and co-edited (with Susan Porter) *Vistas of American Music: Essays and Compositions in Honor of William K. Kearns* (1999). Other recent work has appeared in the *Journal of the American Musicological Society* and *Black Music Research Journal.*

John Koegel is Associate Professor of Music (Musicology) at California State University, Fullerton. He investigates topics relating to the musical life of different immigrant groups in the United States (Spanish-speaking, German, French), as well as music in Mexico, with an emphasis on musical theatre. He also researches musical life in California. His most recent articles include 'Adolf Philipp and Ethnic Musical Theater in New York's Little Germany' in *American Music*, 'Mexican Musicians in California and the United States, 1910–1950' in *California History*, and 'Músicos mexicanos y cubanos en Nueva York, c. 1880–1920' (Mexican and Cuban Musicians in New York, 1880–1920) in *Historia mexicana*. His book *Music in German Immigrant Theater: New York City, 1840–1930* will appear in the Eastman Studies in Music series.

Orly Leah Krasner is an independent scholar living in New York City. She received her PhD in Musicology from the City University of New York. Dr Krasner has written extensively about turn-of-the-century musical theatre and lectured both in America and Europe; her edition of Reginald de Koven's *The Highwayman* appears in *Nineteenth-Century American Musical Theater* (1994). She has also contributed to the *New Grove Dictionary of Opera* and *New Grove Dictionary of Music and Musicians*, *College Music Symposium* and *Current Musicology*. Dr Krasner has been visiting scholar at the Université de Rouen (where she taught a course on the Broadway musical), Boston University, Fordham University and Franklin & Marshall College. She is currently Adjunct Associate Professor at Hofstra University and also teaches at City College, CUNY.

Paul R. Laird is Professor of Musicology at the University of Kansas. He completed his PhD in Musicology at the University of North Carolina at Chapel Hill. In addition to being co-editor of both editions of *The Cambridge Companion to the Musical*, Laird is the author of *Towards a History of the Spanish Villancico* (1997), *Leonard Bernstein: A Guide to Research* (2002), *The Baroque Cello Revival: An Oral History* (2004), and *Leonard Bernstein's Chichester Psalms* (forthcoming). With William A. Everett, he is the co-author of *The Historical Dictionary of the Broadway Musical* (2007).

Jim Lovensheimer is Assistant Professor of Music History and Literature at Vanderbilt University's Blair School of Music, where he has been a faculty member since 2002. His MA and PhD are from The Ohio State University; he also studied musical theatre performance at the University of Cincinnati College–Conservatory of Music and earned a BM in music history from the University of Tennessee, graduating *summa cum laude*. Currently at work on a monograph on the cultural and creative contexts of Rodgers and Hammerstein's *South Pacific*, he has also written on Stephen Sondheim, disco, Scott Joplin and other topics in American music, and his current research concerns constructs of masculinity in the American musical. The recipient of several teaching awards, he lectures on topics in American music in general and the American musical theatre in particular. In addition to his academic career, he has worked in the professional theatre as an actor, musical director, accompanist, and arranger; and he continues to coach singer-actors.

bruce d. mcclung is Associate Professor of Musicology at the University of Cincinnati's College–Conservatory of Music. His articles on the music theatre works of

Kurt Weill may be found in *A Stranger Here Myself: Kurt Weill Studien*, *Kurt Weill Newsletter*, *Pipers Enzyklopädie des Musiktheaters*, *Playbill* and *Theater*. He co-edited *Lady in the Dark: A Sourcebook* (Kurt Weill Foundation) and acted as music/text consultant for the first London production of *Lady in the Dark* (National Theatre). He is the author of *Lady in the Dark: Biography of a Musical* (2007), winner of the Kurt Weill Prize (2007) and the Theatre Library Association's Special Jury Prize (2006) and is editing *Lady in the Dark* for the Kurt Weill Edition.

Paul Prece is Professor and Chair of the Theatre Department at Washburn University in Topeka, Kansas where he directs and teaches performance, directing, dramatic literature, history, theatre for children and youth and musical theatre. He has directed over 150 productions ranging from classic to contemporary and from the musical theatre repertoire. He holds a BA from Catholic University and an MFA from Florida State University, and is currently a PhD candidate in Theory and Criticism at the University of Kansas.

Katherine K. Preston is the David N. and Margaret C. Bottoms Professor of Music at the College of William and Mary in Williamsburg, Virginia. Her area of scholarly specialisation is the history of music and musical culture in nineteenth-century America; she is particularly interested in the performance and reception history of all types of musical theatre. Among her books are *Opera on the Road: Traveling Opera Troupes in the United States, 1825–1860* (1993/2001) and *Irish-American Theater*, Volume X in the series *Nineteenth-Century American Musical Theater* (1994), which she edited. She is currently working on two large projects: *George F. Bristow's Symphony No. 2 ('Jullien'): A Critical Edition* for the series *Music of the United States of America (MUSA)*, and a study of the performance and reception history of English-language opera, *Against the Grain: Prima Donna/Impresarios of English Language Opera Companies in the United States, 1860–1900* (working title). She recently agreed to serve as a member of the Advisory Board for the second edition of *The New Grove Dictionary of American Music*.

Thomas L. Riis has served as Professor of Musicology and Director of the American Music Research Center at the University of Colorado at Boulder since 1992. His previous publications devoted to American musical theatre include the first complete edition of Will Marion Cook's 1902 musical comedy, *In Dahomey*, and *Just Before Jazz: Black Musical Theater in New York, 1890 to 1915*, which received an ASCAP–Deems Taylor Award in 1995. He lectures widely on African-American performers and their performances in the US and abroad, as well as many other topics in American popular and classical music. In 2005 he served as a Fulbright Senior Scholar at the University of Lüneburg, Germany. His most recent project is *Frank Loesser* (2007), a volume in Yale Broadway Masters.

Ann Sears is Professor of Music and Director of Performance at Wheaton College in Norton, Massachusetts, where she teaches piano and courses in American music. She currently holds Wheaton's Mary Heuser Endowed Chair for the Arts. She has degrees from the New England Conservatory of Music, Arizona State University, and The Catholic University of America, where her doctoral dissertation was about American art song in turn-of-the-century Boston. She appears as pianist on three compact discs of African-American song for Albany Records: *Deep River: The*

Songs and Spirituals of Harry T. Burleigh, with bass Oral Moses; *Fi-yer! A Century of African-American Song*, with tenor William Brown; and *Swing Time: The Songs of Will Marion Cook*, also with tenor William Brown.

Judith Sebesta teaches theatre theory, history and criticism at the University of Missouri–Columbia. Her essays on musicals have appeared in such publications as *Studies in Musical Theatre, Contemporary Theatre Review, New England Theatre Journal, Theatre Annual, Baylor Journal of Theatre and Performance*, and *The Sondheim Review*. She currently serves as Secretary of the Association for Theatre in Higher Education. Her co-edited anthology on women in musical theatre is forthcoming from McFarland Press, and she also is co-author of a digital textbook for Theatre Appreciation courses forthcoming from Allyn & Bacon. Sebesta was the recipient of the College of Fine Arts Outstanding Teacher Award for 2004–5 where she previously taught at the University of Arizona.

John Snelson is Commissioning Editor at the Royal Opera House, Covent Garden, writing and researching across the broad field of the lyric stage. He has a special interest in musical theatre and its British repertory, and holds a PhD from the University of Birmingham, UK, writing his thesis on the West End musical 1947–54. He was a Senior Internal Editor, with responsibility for musical theatre and popular music, for *The New Grove Dictionary of Music and Musicians* (2nd edition), and wrote *Andrew Lloyd Webber* (2004) for Yale Broadway Masters. Among other writings, he contributed the article on Ivor Novello to *The Oxford Dictionary of National Biography* and has written on the musical for *The Oxford Companion to Music*. His work in opera includes lectures, articles and the book *The Ring: An Illustrated History of Wagner's Ring at the Royal Opera House* (2006). He has also worked in musical theatre as a musical director, arranger and répétiteur, and his piano duet arrangements of the overtures to the Savoy operas are published by Peters Edition.

Jessica Sternfeld earned her PhD in musicology from Princeton University in 2002, and currently serves as an Assistant Professor of Music at Rhode Island College. Her research and teaching interests include the history and cultural contexts of musical theatre, opera, various pop genres, and western Classical and Romantic musics. She is the author of *The Megamusical* (2006). A lifelong musical theatre performer and choral singer/conductor, she now serves as the music director and conductor for musicals at Rhode Island College, where she also runs the music history division of the Department of Music, Theatre, and Dance.

Scott Warfield holds a PhD from the University of North Carolina at Chapel Hill, where he wrote his dissertation on Richard Strauss's first tone poem, *Macbeth*. His articles and reviews have appeared in *Fontes Artis Musicae, Journal of Musicological Research, Kurt Weill Newsletter*, MLA *Notes, Nineteenth-Century Music Review*, and *Richard Strauss-Blätter*, and he has also contributed a chapter and the bibliography essay to *The Richard Strauss Companion* (2003). He is currently the classical music critic for the Orlando *Sentinel*, and he also writes frequently as a programme annotator. Since 2002, he has been on the faculty of the University of Central Florida; previously he taught at Centre College in Danville, Kentucky, Nebraska Wesleyan University, and several colleges in North Carolina.

Graham Wood is Associate Professor of Music at Coker College in Hartsville, South
Carolina where he teaches music history, world music, film music and the history
of Broadway and Hollywood musicals. He is also coordinator of the musical theatre programme at Coker and regularly produces and conducts musical theatre
productions and showcases. He has been a clinician and guest lecturer at the South
Carolina Governor's School for Science and Math and is currently a member of
the editorial board of *Studies in Musical Theater*. A native of England, he has a
BA in music from the University of Newcastle-upon-Tyne, and an MA and PhD
in musicology from the University of Minnesota. An earlier version of his chapter in this book appears in the first edition of *The Cambridge Companion to the
Musical*. His doctoral dissertation 'The Development of Song Forms in the Broadway and Hollywood Musicals of Richard Rodgers, 1919–1943' explores how the
construction of songs, and in particular their chorus patterns, function in larger
dramatic-narrative frameworks and also in broader cultural scenarios.

Preface to the second edition

A great deal has happened in the realm of musical theatre and musical theatre scholarship since the first edition of *The Cambridge Companion to the Musical* appeared in 2002. *Les Misérables* closed on Broadway only to be revived three and a half years later; a new Lloyd Webber musical, *The Woman in White*, while successful in London, failed in New York; and the genre of the film musical has experienced a significant renaissance. In the media domain, PBS produced and broadcast *Broadway: The American Musical*, which it subsequently released on DVD along with a companion book; the film *Broadway: The Golden Age*, consisting of interviews with seminal musical theatre personalities, played across the US and was issued on DVD; and three volumes of *Broadway's Lost Treasures*, DVDs with clips from musicals originally aired on the Tony Awards, have appeared. Yale University Press inaugurated its Yale Broadway Masters series, and studies that address the musical theatre from a variety of perspectives have likewise been published by major academic and commercial presses.

The second edition of *The Cambridge Companion to the Musical*, like the first, offers an array of essays intended to illuminate particular areas of the genre. It is not intended to be an all-inclusive history or survey. Neither do all authors take the same approach – some offer overviews while others emphasise seminal works or significant themes.

Most chapters from the first edition appear in either their original form or with slight alterations and updating. Two, however, have undergone significant changes: William Everett's essay on operetta (chapter 4) and Graham Wood's on the film musical (chapter 17). Everett incorporates recent research on American operetta in his chapter, while Wood shifts his focus to film musicals from the early twenty-first century.

The first edition strongly emphasised English-language musical theatre traditions. While this repertory remains central to the present volume, two chapters devoted to musical theatre in languages other than English have been added. John Koegel addresses non-English traditions in the United States before World War II (chapter 2) while Judith Sebesta surveys approaches to the musical in continental Europe since that time (chapter 15).

New concepts and developments in the genre in the early twenty-first century led to the commissioning of three other new essays for the second edition. Bud Coleman discusses new shows and their places in the rich tapestry of contemporary theatre (chapter 16). Additionally, the musical is finding new life through screen adaptations conceived for theatrical release, television broadcast or DVD. Jessica Sternfeld addresses these transformations, along with revivals and studio recordings (chapter 18). The volume concludes with Paul Laird's chronicle of a case study in the development of Stephen Schwartz's *Wicked,* one of the most significant musicals to appear in the early twenty-first century (chapter 19).

The editors wish to thank the contributors to the volume and the staff at Cambridge University Press, especially Victoria Cooper, who not only oversaw the first edition but also encouraged us to create the second edition, for their support and enthusiasm.

William A. Everett
Paul R. Laird

PART I

Adaptations and transformations: before 1940

1 American musical theatre before the twentieth century

KATHERINE K. PRESTON

The history of musical comedy begins in confusion.[1] EDITH BORROFF

Most histories of American musical theatre give short shrift – at best – to the 'origin of the species', to use Edith Borroff's apt phrase. Despite lofty ambitions (titles that claim coverage 'from the beginning to the present'), most authors are content to offer a brief essay about the antecedents of musical comedy, usually including definitive identification of 'the first American musical' (*The Black Crook*, *Little Johnny Jones*, *Evangeline*, *Show Boat*, *The Beggar's Opera*, *The Wizard of the Nile* or any number of other works), before turning, with an almost discernible sigh of relief, to musical theatre of the twentieth century. The reasons for the brevity and for the disagreement on the 'first' musical become readily apparent as soon as one attempts to sort out the myriad different types of musical theatrical forms that materialised, metamorphosed, became popular, disappeared, re-emerged and cross-fertilised prior to the twentieth century. To put it simply, for the scholar in search of a clear lineage to the forms of the twentieth century, musical theatre in the eighteenth – and even more so in the nineteenth – century was a tangled, chaotic mess. This was not the impression at the time, of course. To the contrary, a nineteenth-century American, especially the resident of a large city like New York, found musical theatrical life during the time to be gloriously rich, varied and ever-changing; it was a world that was entertaining, interesting, exciting and innovative to an extent that should elicit a twinge of envy from the modern reader. But the job of the historian is to clarify and attempt to put into some kind of order the messiness of a bygone era. And the richness of that period makes the job both difficult and important.

What follows, then, is a carefully guided and succinct tour of the American musical-theatrical world of the eighteenth and nineteenth centuries. To some readers – especially those anxious to reach the more familiar terrain of the twentieth century – the description of musical life of the earlier eras will be a little puzzling, primarily because this essay will describe genres that have since been removed from the general category of 'musical theatre'. But the varied musical forms that Americans enjoyed in the late eighteenth and early nineteenth centuries (including opera, pantomime, melodrama, minstrelsy and dance) developed, changed and influenced each other to a remarkable degree. The wealth of earlier musical styles evolved into the wonderfully diverse, rich and confusing jumble that was the American musical-theatrical world of the last third of the nineteenth century, which many scholars agree was the birthplace of the twentieth-century musical. It is important, then, to examine the whole picture – albeit in summary fashion – in order to comprehend the foundations of this truly American musical form.

The eighteenth century

There is scattered evidence of theatrical activity in the American colonies in the seventeenth century, but the real history of musical theatre commences in the eighteenth. The first opera mounted in English-speaking America was the ballad opera *Flora, or, Hob in the Wall,* performed in Charleston, South Carolina in 1735; two weeks prior to that, the same theatre had offered a different work that was equally musical in nature: the pantomime *The Adventures of Harlequin and Scaramouche,* performed as an afterpiece.[2] From the 1730s until the Revolution, Americans – especially those living in the urban centres of the Northeast or the market towns of the rural Southeast – witnessed a constant stream of theatrical offerings imported from the British Isles. Many thespians of this period were associated with itinerant or 'strolling' companies, formed by players (frequently family members) who performed in return for shares of the box-office take. Women performers, in particular, were all but obliged by the mandates of society to tour with male family members, in order to preserve any semblance of reputation already made suspect by public performance. The first permanent such strolling troupe in the colonies was Lewis Hallam's Company of Comedians, which arrived from London in 1752, renamed itself the American Company, and gave its first performance in Williamsburg, Virginia.[3] This company and others like it travelled from town to town and city to city on regular circuits (primarily via horse-drawn vehicles) during the mid-eighteenth century; they eventually built theatres in larger towns from which they branched out – especially during the summer – to perform in smaller towns and villages located within a reasonable distance from the hub city. This *modus operandi* was similar to that in the British Isles, where London was the principal hub, cities like Manchester, Birmingham, Edinburgh and Dublin were smaller hubs, and other towns and villages were served by itinerant troupes that used theatres in the larger urban areas as seats of operation.

To a great extent, then, strolling theatrical troupes active in America were transatlantic extensions of the provincial theatrical circuit of Great Britain; American theatres were essentially part of the London cultural sphere.

In 1774 professional theatrical activity in the colonies officially stopped (although dramatic performances continued, mostly under the guise of 'concerts'), when the Continental Congress passed a resolution that prohibited activities that were distracting to the Revolution. After the War, the banished strolling companies resumed activities. Hallam's troupe, now proudly called the Old American Company, returned from Jamaica in 1784, re-established its circuit and enjoyed a virtual monopoly until the early 1790s. During that decade American theatrical life underwent significant change, as urban areas in the new nation increased sufficiently in size to allow the establishment of permanent theatres with resident stock companies. Important theatres were built (especially in the 1790s) in New York, Philadelphia, Boston, Charleston, Baltimore and other cities on the East Coast. Resident stock companies, complete with orchestras and musical directors, were hired; their performances frequently included the assistance of 'gentlemen amateurs', which reflects a continuing – and growing – active interest in the theatre among American city-dwellers. Since theatres traditionally offered permanent work to musicians, this spate of theatre-building helped to attract to America a whole coterie of musicians from Europe. These musicians – most of whom arrived in the 1790s – included Alexander Reinagle (1756–1809), Rayner Taylor (1747–1825), Benjamin Carr (1768–1831) and James Hewitt (1770–1827) from Scotland and England, Victor Pelissier (c. 1740/50–c. 1820) from France, and Gottlieb Graupner (1767–1836) from Germany.

The repertory of all theatres during this period relied heavily on music; the historian Julian Mates asserts that by the beginning of the nineteenth century fully half of the repertory on the American stage was musical in nature.[4] Every theatre had an orchestra, and a typical evening, in the words of William Brooks, consisted of 'an encyclopedia of entertainment, a potpourri of performance', much of which required orchestral accompaniment.[5] The evening's activity generally commenced with a short concert of 'waiting music' played by the orchestra, followed by first a prologue and then the principal dramatic work (the mainpiece), which – in turn – was followed by a shorter work, usually a farce or pantomime (the afterpiece). Between the mainpiece and the afterpiece, the orchestra would play several selections, and during both dramatic works the actors would interpolate songs or dances as *divertissements* or changes of pace. The evening's entertainment – which frequently lasted four or five hours – would conclude with diverse amusements such as singing, dancing, further works performed by the orchestra, or possibly a short epilogue; sometimes the choice of repertory was in response to requests from audience members.[6] Audience behaviour at such entertainments was not unlike that typical of twentieth-century sporting events: members of the audience would come and go, eat and drink, talk among themselves, applaud wildly, heckle the actors mercilessly, or sing along with the performers. The 'dramatic' evening just described is one that featured a drama; when the mainpiece consisted instead of a ballad opera or a comic opera (both, on the American stage, essentially plays with songs), the percentage of music performed was even greater. It should be clear that during this period the terms 'theatre' and 'musical theatre' were essentially synonymous.

For the most part, the American theatre during the final decades of the eighteenth century remained firmly British in orientation: American theatres became important competitors with provincial English theatres for actors, actresses, and even pantomimists, most of whom were French (but who arrived via England).[7] Costumes and scenery were either imported outright or copied from productions in England, and theatrical repertory was also, by and large, from London – imported either as manuscripts, as prompt books or as published music in keyboard or vocal format.[8] One of the principal tasks for a theatre's musical director was the re-orchestration (frequently from keyboard reduction) of musical accompaniment to dramatic or operatic works; musical directors also composed new incidental music, and – increasingly – musical-theatrical works of their own. The most popular musical works performed on the American stage between 1790 and 1810, according to Susan Porter, included such standard London fare as the comic operas *The Poor Soldier* (1783) and *Rosina* (1782) by William Shield; *The Children in the Wood* (1793) and *The Mountaineers* (1793) by Samuel Arnold; and *No Song, No Supper* (1790) by Stephen Storace.[9] During the last decade of the eighteenth century, however, American theatre-goers could increasingly witness musical-theatrical works written in America, usually by the recent musical immigrants mentioned above. These included such works as Victor Pelissier's *Edwin and Angelina* (1791), operas by James Hewitt (*Tammany; or, the Indian Chief,* 1794) and Benjamin Carr (*The Archers,* 1796), and music for pantomimes by composers such as Pelissier, Reinagle, Hewitt and Taylor. Melodrama (introduced from France by way of England) also became part of the American theatrical repertory in the 1790s; it would become one of the dominant forms of musical theatre in the nineteenth century. The music from all of these shows increasingly permeated American society by means of sheet music; it was both imported and published by American firms, snapped up from music store shelves, and played on fortepianos in American parlours all over the country.

The nineteenth century: 1800–1840

By the first decades of the nineteenth century, theatrical production in the United States was accomplished almost exclusively by established theatres with resident stock companies. Itinerant theatrical troupes (like the earlier 'strolling' players) were still active in the less settled parts of the country (and would remain so, moving ever further west with the frontier); the 'star system', under which a visiting dramatic star (usually from England) would visit different theatres in turn, taking the starring roles of plays mounted by the stock companies, had just been introduced from Great Britain. For the most part, however, theatrical performances in Federal-period America were mounted by the stock companies of local theatres, with musical accompaniment by the theatres' orchestras. For repertory during this period, American theatres for the most part continued to rely on London for their material. With an ever-growing critical mass of skilled actors, playwrights and composers resident in the United States, however, these imported materials, more frequently than not, were extensively modified (mostly in subject matter) for American audiences.

Melodrama

Melodrama, which would (arguably) become the most important and popular dramatic and musical genre in America during the nineteenth century, emerged in full force during the first decades. Originally a French technique from the mid-eighteenth century, melodrama – the use in drama of short musical passages to heighten emotional affect, either in alternation with or underlying spoken dialogue – came to America, as had pantomime, from the British popular theatre.[10] The first melodrama presented in America was probably *Ariadne Abandoned by Theseus in the Isle of Naxos*, with music (now lost) by Victor Pelissier, performed in New York in 1797. Early melodramas used music quite sparingly; this, as we shall see, would change later in the century.

Few instrumental 'melos' (snippets of 'hurry music', 'diabolical music', 'sorrow', 'pursuit', etc.) survive from before 1850; it was rare for such manuscripts to be published, and most perished in the fires that regularly consumed theatres in the nineteenth century. But specific directions indicated in prompt books, in conjunction with information from the few scores that do survive, suffice to provide a clear indication of the nature of melodrama. Two early works merit some mention. Victor Pelissier's complete orchestral score to William Dunlap's *The Voice of Nature* (1803) is the earliest extant musical score for a complete dramatic work written for the American theatre.[11] It includes several composed pieces (marches, a dance, choruses); musical cues in the first and third acts indicate clearly where the music is to be inserted.[12] Dunlap's score is actually a good illustration of contemporary *incidental* music, for – although sometimes referred to as such – *The Voice of Nature* is not technically a melodrama, since the music neither alternates with nor underlies spoken dialogue.[13] The first extant score to a melodrama that is closer to the mark (and the only extant American score for melodrama prior to 1850) is J. N. Barker and John Bray's *The Indian Princess, or, La belle sauvage* (1808), which is identified on the title page of the published score as an 'operatic melo-drame'.[14] As a hybrid, *The Indian Princess* is more than 'a mixed drama of words and ten bars of music' (Dunlap's description of melodrama), for it has both vocal music (songs, glees and choruses) and passages of instrumental melodramatic music that underlie mimed dramatic action.[15] Music used to accompany action was borrowed from the world of pantomime; small dances and closed-form songs (usually seen at the beginnings of scenes) were traditions from *opéra-comique* and ballad opera.[16] Most of the melodramas popular on the American stage prior to 1850 were from London (or France via London); most probably had new music composed by American theatre composers, and none survives.[17]

One final insight into the popularity of early melodramas in America comes from an examination of the careers of French dancers who toured the United States during the period. One such is Madame Celeste Keppler Elliott (b. 1810), a French actress and dancer. Like other French dancers who visited during this period, Madame Celeste originally performed in 'ballets' (in her case, in New York after her arrival in 1827), but very quickly switched to melodramas such as *The French Spy; or, the Siege of Constantina* (with music by Daniel François-Esprit Auber), in part because of the popularity of the form, in part because the lead female role in the melodrama is mute (her spoken English was weak). Madame Celeste eventually used as performance vehicles some dozen mimed melodramatic works (including an adaptation of James Fenimore Cooper's *The Wept of Wish-Ton-Wish*); as a 'melodramatic artist' she mounted several lucrative tours of America from the late 1820s to the early 1840s.[18] Presumably the music to many of the works in which she and other dancers so successfully appeared was composed, as was normal, by musicians associated with American theatres. The performances of such dancers in both ballets and melodramatic works suggests a clear overlap between the two styles of dramatic art; Madame Celeste's remarkable success on the American stage, furthermore, is additional evidence of the popularity of melodrama.

Itinerant singers and vocal stars

In the 1810s a new kind of musical performer began making the rounds of theatres in the United States; they were the musical counterparts of the theatrical 'stars' who had begun to visit in the 1790s. These vocal stars began to arrive individually in 1817; they performed in concert and in operas with stock companies, all of which still included in their standard repertories English operatic works by such composers as Thomas Arne, Charles Dibdin, William Shield and Thomas Linley.[19] These early vocal stars were followed in the 1820s by a whole host of (mostly) British singers, who toured on the American theatrical circuit in the company of such British *theatrical* stars as Edmund Kean, William Charles Macready, Junius Brutus Booth, Peter Richings, and Charles Kemble. The most important early vocal stars were Elizabeth Austin (toured 1827–35) and Joseph and Mary Anne Paton Wood (1833–6, second tour in the 1840s), who opened the floodgates for additional singers in the 1830s and early 1840s. Vocal stars who banded together into small 'vocal-star troupes' in the late 1830s included Jane Shirreff (1811–83), John Wilson (1801–49) and the husband-and-wife team of Anne (?1809–88) and Edward (Ned) (1809–52) Seguin, all of whom arrived in 1838. These singers toured up and down the East Coast, utilising the expanding steam (rail and water) transportation system to take them to large cities as well as to the smaller towns and hamlets in between. These (and many other) singers – whether touring alone or as duos or trios – became a regular part of American popular musical theatre; they electrified American audiences, who flocked to performances and who purchased reams of arias 'as sung by' the vocalists, whose images were engraved on sheet music covers. The singers took the starring roles in standard English comic operas such as those mentioned above, with stock company performers singing secondary roles and functioning as the chorus. They also introduced to American audiences more opera from the *bel canto* and French schools (in English adaptation), including works by Auber, Boieldieu, Rossini, Bellini and Mozart.[20] These translated operas fitted readily into an American theatrical repertory that already included English comic and ballad operas, pantomime and melodrama. But the introduction of the more difficult *bel canto* operas – made possible by the higher-calibre performances of the itinerant vocalists – thrilled American audiences of all economic classes; as a result, Americans developed an almost insatiable appetite for Italian operatic music. The enthusiastic reception of the newer operatic repertory opened the door both for larger English opera troupes (starting in the 1840s) and for foreign-language opera companies. The singing by the women vocal stars, in particular, spurred a fondness among Americans for 'bird-like' vocal gymnastics that would continue throughout the century.

In 1825 the Spanish tenor Manuel García (1775–1832) visited New York City with his family (including his daughter María Malibran), where they mounted the first American seasons of opera in Italian.[21] Two years later John Davis's French Opera Company of New Orleans embarked on an East

Coast tour, the first of six annual tours (1827–33) during which they performed opera in French in various East Coast cities.[22] Throughout the 1830s numerous itinerant Italian opera companies (mostly based in New York) attempted to capitalise on the growing American taste for this particular flavour of musical theatre; they met with varying degrees of success, but built the foundation for many more – and more successful – Italian opera troupes that would follow in the 1840s.[23] It is worth reminding the reader that during this period both English and foreign-language opera fitted easily into the American theatrical repertory. Opera had not yet been segregated from the regular theatre, nor did Americans readily make a distinction between 'theatre' and 'musical theatre'.

The nineteenth century: c. 1840–1865

By the 1840s the infrastructure to support the theatre in America was firmly in place. The increase in population in the country (fuelled, in part, by a phenomenal immigration rate) was such that there were now numerous towns and cities large enough to support at least one – and frequently more than one – theatre with a resident stock company. These theatres now hosted on a regular basis increasing numbers of theatrical and musical 'stars', who utilised the ever-expanding steam-powered transportation system.[24] The stock companies – with or without the 'stars' – performed repertory that continued to be heavily musical in nature. Added to the mix of visiting stars were specialised musical-theatrical performers who likewise traversed the theatrical circuit in ever-increasing numbers: blackface minstrel troupes; English, Italian and French opera companies; acrobats, dancers and pantomimists – each of these will be discussed below. The 'star' system would eventually destroy the stock company system (and the fault lines were already readily apparent during the 1850s and 1860s); it would be replaced in the last decades of the century by the combination system, of which these itinerant 'specialty' companies already proliferating in the 1840s and 1850s were forerunners. During the period 1840–65, however, the dominant *modus operandi* for theatrical production was still the local stock company, augmented by 'stars' and supplanted, for weeks at a time, by visiting troupes of minstrels, opera singers or specialty acts.[25]

The theatrical offerings available to American town- or city-dwellers in the 1840s and 1850s changed regularly – usually weekly or bi-weekly – and (by modern standards) varied wildly. To antebellum Americans, going to the theatre was the modern equivalent of going to the multiplex cinema, and the range of diversity represents a certain degree of catholicity of taste among the middle and upper middle classes. By the 1850s there were already apparent seeds of the breakdown in theatrical tastes that eventually would result in a more socially and economically stratified audience; during this period, however – especially in non-East Coast towns that supported fewer theatres – that stratification was not yet a *fait accompli*. Americans went to the theatre regularly and enjoyed a wide array of different kinds of entertainments, most of which could be considered, by the standards of later centuries, musical.

Stock company repertory: melodrama and plays with songs

Melodrama continued its dominance of the American theatrical repertory during this period. By the 1850s, the earlier technique of alternating speech and music had given way to more specialised use of music within the drama: to draw attention to – and heighten the emotional impact of – specific scenes or portions of scenes. As Shapiro points out, instrumental music was now used to heighten 'strong emotional moments of the play when speech was inadequate or even – as in a fight scene – realistically impossible'.[26] It was also during this period that the term melodrama came to refer not to a technique but rather to a particular kind of drama (whether or not it included music). This stereotype (of characters, clearly good or evil, involved in an action-filled plot where evil temporarily succeeds but is eventually defeated by good) is the popular definition of melodrama today (Snidely Whiplash and Dudley Do-Right of Rocky and Bullwinkle fame come immediately to mind); its dramatic style clearly provides much opportunity to use music to express emotion.

Few scores have been found for melodramatic pieces from this period, but those that are extant indicate that there were generally some thirty or forty 'melos' per drama, and that they were composed (not improvised) for full theatre orchestra. Evidence from prompt books also suggests that the melodramatic music was used in tight coordination with scenic and lighting effects to create the heightened mood. Pantomimic techniques such as short snippets of 'hurry music' were employed regularly to underscore quick action or to indicate emotional agitation.[27] In its impact on audience members the music was probably similar to film scores today: extremely successful in terms of underscoring dramatic emotion, but almost completely unnoticed by most auditors.

By mid-century the use of instrumental music for melodramatic effect had become so accepted a theatrical practice that it was not uncommon for such music to be added to non-melodramatic plays. Dramatised versions of Harriet Beecher Stowe's *Uncle Tom's Cabin* are instructive. The novel, which became an immediate best-seller after its publication in 1852, was adapted to the stage within the year. Extant programmes, prompt books and playbills suggest clearly that music was central to the performances. One published version includes some two dozen cues for instrumental music to undergird particularly emotional scenes (Eliza's escape, Simon Legree's whipping of Uncle Tom or Eva's assumption).[28] Stage productions also included hymns, minstrel tunes and sentimental songs; some were composed specifically for adaptations of the novel, others were simply popular songs interpolated into particular productions. This insertion of vocal music into stage productions was by no means unusual performance practice for the period and is further evidence of the important role of music in the American theatre at mid-century.

Blackface minstrelsy

Blackface minstrelsy, the most important American musical-theatrical development of the antebellum period, would quickly come to rival melo-drama in popularity. Ostensibly, the form burst upon the American theatri-cal scene in 1843, with the inaugural appearance of the Virginia Minstrels in New York City. In reality, the four performers who banded together to form the troupe simply codified performance traditions and techniques – including blackface – that had been seen on the American stage for decades; they also incorporated sensibilities, such as burlesque of the powerful, that had been part of western culture for centuries.[29]

The Virginia Minstrels' format quickly became the standard for other early minstrel troupes: four or six performers, all male and all in blackface, would stand on stage facing the audience in a line or a shallow semicircle; 'Mr Bones' (who played a rhythmic 'instrument' fashioned from animal bones) and 'Mr Tambo' (who played a tambourine) would be on either end, with the 'Interlocutor' in the middle. The performance was divided into two halves, and included a wide variety of entertainment modes, including singing, skits, jokes, dancing and stand-up comedy; the first half focused on the stereotype of the urban dandy, the second 'portrayed' plantation life. The minstrel songs and dances at first were inspired by the emerging fiddle-tune tradition, but quickly came to be influenced by other popular-song traditions, including sentimental songs, glees, and the four-part harmony of itinerant singing families.[30] Minstrelsy, at bottom, was a musical experience; excepting the skits and comedy routines, the entire performance was musical in nature, with song accompaniments and dances alike performed by the minstrel band, which consisted of fiddle, banjo, tambo and bones.

Blackface minstrel troupes quickly joined the other 'specialty' musical-theatre companies on the circuit in the 1840s and 1850s, attracting audiences of varied social and economic classes.[31] With the increased commerciali-sation of the form during the late 1840s, minstrel troupes became more streamlined and the format more formulaic. By the late 1850s the first sec-tion had become more of a song concert (of genteel and sentimental songs), and a middle section – called the 'olio' – had been added; this latter featured blackface songs and burlesque skits, mocking everything from Shakespeare, to singing families, to opera. The third and final part remained the core of the show, with its 'depictions' of extended plantation scenes. The whole theatrical extravaganza ended with a finale called a 'walk-around', in which the entire company would parade around the stage, singing and accompanied by the minstrel band.[32] The increased commercialisation of the form is also evident in minstrels' exploitation of the growing technology of popular culture. Minstrels – like other contemporary theatrical companies – utilised the expanding American transportation network to travel all over the Eastern United States; they published song-books containing the words of their latest tunes, and sheet music of the sentimental ballads featured in their performances; they corresponded with musical or theatrical journals of national circulation, which published reports of their comings and goings; they advertised upcoming performances in local newspapers prior to arrival in town. Exploitation of such tools helped rapidly to create a large audience for this new musical-theatrical form.

To a great extent the minstrel show – which would continue to evolve and change after the Civil War – was a condensation of various elements of American popular musical theatre during the period. Essentially a variety show (a musical-theatrical form that would become increasingly popular), minstrelsy featured dancing, singing and irreverence; undergirding it all was an emphasis on burlesque, which was an elemental aspect of nineteenth-century American humour.

Pantomime, ballet, spectacle and extravaganza

The pantomime tradition on the American stage had changed significantly by mid-century: the earlier English mode was replaced by a style of visual theatre best exemplified by the family of Gabriel Ravel – exponents of the 'French style' of pantomime, and entertainers *extraordinaires* during the 1840s and 1850s. The four Ravel brothers, who combined physical virtuosity and sophisticated stage machinery with the visual narrative of pantomime (all to musical accompaniment), arrived in America with their entourage in 1832 and toured all over the country (including California) before returning to France in 1858. (Some members of the family returned to the States in the 1860s.[33]) Nor were the Ravels the only performers in their genre; other troupes – both foreign and domestic – likewise traversed the American theatrical circuit at mid-century and dazzled their audiences with feats of physical prowess. A typical Ravel Family programme consisted of several parts: a pantomime, physical feats (tightrope tricks, balancing, military and sporting skills, and exhibitions of tableaux), and a ballet (e.g. the first act of a contemporary ballet, such as Paul Taglioni's *La sylphide*, including a *grand pas de deux*, a quickstep, a Grand Tableau and 'The Flight of the Sylphide').[34] The strength of the Ravel Company was its mixture of repertory: ballet, gymnastic skills and (most important) pantomime. The latter category – especially the combination of physical virtuosity, pantomimic narrative, and stage machinery and scenery – would evolve into a form that several decades later would be termed 'spectacle' or 'extravaganza'.

American theatre-goers during this period also witnessed many itinerant European dancers who were the successors to Madame Celeste. The Austrian ballerina Fanny Elssler (1810–84) was the most prominent visitor of the 1840s; she toured from 1840 to 1842 and provoked an outpouring of near-hysterical adulation from American audiences. Many individual dancers and entire troupes (such as the Rousset sisters, the Montplaisir Ballet Troupe, Natalie Fitzjames, the Ronzoni Ballet Company and others) toured the United States in the 1850s and 1860s; they frequently performed either as part of or in conjunction with opera troupes. Their repertories included *divertissements* or portions of nineteenth-century ballets such as *La sylphide* (music by Herman Løvenskiold), *Le dieu et la bayadère* (Auber) and *La sonnambule* (Ferdinand Hérold).

Very little research has been conducted on companies like the Ravels or on ballet troupes that toured America in the nineteenth century; as a result, we have almost no knowledge of the music that accompanied these performances.[35] Both types of performers (and their music), however, were ubiquitous; as such, they must be included in a discussion of the antecedents of the modern musical. Furthermore, it should be clear that both 'pantomimic acrobats' and dancers had an important role in the formation of 'spectacle' and 'extravaganza', two closely related musical-theatrical forms that would become popular in the second half of the century. Another important proponent of American 'spectacle' and 'extravaganza' was Laura Keene, whose shows – which combined burlesque, music, ballet, transformation scenes, and spectacular scenery and costumes – were among the most popular theatrical works in New York during the 1860s.[36] All of these theatrical forms (burlesque, pantomime, ballet and drama), accompanied by music and augmented by lavish costumes and scenery, commingled and cross-fertilised during the second half of the century; all had a role in the eventual formation of the twentieth-century American musical.[37]

Burlesque

The American theatrical burlesque in the early and mid-nineteenth century was a dramatic production of a satirical and humorous nature (the form would only later become a variety show with striptease as its major component). By the mid-nineteenth century, the form had adopted some of the characteristics of extravaganzas – in particular, whimsical humour presented in pun-filled verses full of double and triple entendres and oblique humorous word-play. Burlesques also began during this time to include a significant amount of music.[38] Poking fun at someone or something – whether German or Irish immigrants, the pretensions of the wealthy, African Americans, or the latest entertainer to catch the public's fancy – was so much a part of American humour in the nineteenth century that the popularity of a musical-theatrical form of this nature was inevitable. Hundreds of burlesques or burlesque-extravaganzas (mostly one-act farces or afterpieces) were written for the American stage in the 1840s and 1850s; as already mentioned, the technique was also employed by blackface minstrel troupes in the 'olio' sections of their performances.

In New York the burlesque was raised to new heights by the actor/manager William Mitchell at his Olympic Theatre starting in the late 1830s; Mitchell's competitor, the actor and playwright John Brougham (1810–80), followed Mitchell's successful example and wrote and acted in numerous burlesques from 1842 until 1879.[39] The best example of Brougham's burlesques (and one of the most popular of the century) was *Po-ca-hon-tas; or, the Gentle Savage* (1855), a parody on Indian plays that were currently the rage. The music, which occupies over a third of the show, was arranged by New York theatre composer James G. Maeder; it ranges from simple contrafacta (to the tunes of 'Rosin the Bow', 'Widow Machree' and 'The King of Cannibal Islands', all identified in the script) to complicated extended pieces constructed by patching together tunes from sources as widely divergent as 'Old Folks at Home' and 'Là ci darem la mano' from *Don Giovanni*. The long-lasting popularity of *Po-ca-hon-tas* would keep it – and its example as a successful merging of burlesque and music – before the American public for decades.[40] From the 1860s onwards, burlesques often functioned as the framework for elaborate spectacles and extravaganzas, the characteristics of which have already been discussed.

Opera: English, French and Italian

By the 1840s, the vocal stars that had been such an important part of the American stage had all but disappeared, replaced by English opera companies performing repertory that had become firmly established as popular theatre. The Seguin Opera Company, a troupe that was both wildly popular and enormously successful, had a virtual monopoly on English opera performance during the 1840s. They – like other English troupes that began to appear later in the decade – performed repertory that included works by British composers (Wallace, Balfe and Rooke) as well as translations of operas by French (Auber and Adam), German (Weber and Mozart) and Italian composers (Bellini, Donizetti, Mercadante, and Rossini). In the 1850s English opera began to be considered old-fashioned, as increasing numbers of large skilled Italian troupes performed on the American theatre circuit. Despite the competition, several English troupes – including the Pyne and Harrison, the Anna Bishop, and the Lyster and Durand English opera companies – managed to mount very successful tours in the United States and maintained a strong presence within the repertory of American popular theatre.

French opera during this period was firmly established in New Orleans, but was represented in the rest of the country primarily by the performance of translations of French repertory (by Auber, in particular), usually by English opera companies. In the 1840s and 1850s a handful of French opera companies – some from New Orleans and some from France – toured America, but the heyday of French opera would arrive only in the 1860s, with the influx of the operettas of Jacques Offenbach and companies to perform this repertory.[41]

The major thrust for operatic development during the middle decades of the century was in the arena of Italian-language opera. Various incarnations of the Havana Opera Company visited occasionally during the 1840s (performing in New Orleans, Pittsburgh and Cincinnati, and on the East Coast), and numerous transient New York-based Italian companies imported from Europe appeared and performed repertories of works by Rossini, Bellini, Donizetti and – increasingly – Verdi. The overall picture of Italian operatic activity in the 1840s and 1850s is one of growth: larger and more polished companies, more extensive itineraries and repertories, and more troupes. Furthermore, many of the imported Italian singers remained in America after the completion of their companies' tours; by the early 1850s there were enough Italian singers living in New York (and teaching music there) to make possible the formation of locally based Italian opera companies. Because of this development, impresarios such as Bernard Ullman, Max Maretzek, Maurice Strakosch and Max Strakosch could circumvent the logistical and financial difficulties inherent in recruiting an entire company from abroad and could now concentrate recruiting efforts (and funds) on big-name stars. As a result, impresarios could engage higher-calibre performers, which contributed to the established trend: heightened audience expectations and subsequent engagement of even more highly skilled musicians. The list of stellar singers who appeared in various companies in the States during the period includes some of the best vocalists of Europe: Marietta Alboni, Henriette Sontag, Teresa Parodi, Giovanni Matteo Mario, Giulia Grisi, Lorenzo Salvi and many others. It is important to reiterate that although Italian-language opera was beginning, by the 1850s, to become associated with the elite and wealthy, this change in the opera audience was still new and limited primarily to the East Coast. The appearance of an Italian opera company during the 1850s in a theatre in, say, St Louis or Cincinnati was regarded as a special event (similar to the visit of a major dramatic star); it was not yet regarded as an 'exclusive' engagement that appealed only to the elite or wealthy. Italian opera was still entertainment; as such, it was still a part of the constantly changing potpourri of American popular musical theatre at mid-century. Furthermore, music from the operatic stage, by this time, had completely infiltrated the American soundscape, and many Americans attended operatic performances to hear music that was readily familiar. Americans danced to quadrilles and lanciers fashioned from tunes from the most popular continental operas; they heard brass bands playing these same tunes in open-air concerts; theatre orchestras performed operatic selections as entr'acte music or overtures; piano benches all over America overflowed with piano variations, arrangements of operatic 'gems' and sheet-music adaptations of the most popular arias. Musical theatre, then, was not limited to theatres; it permeated American life.

The nineteenth century: c. 1865–1900

The last third of the nineteenth century was a period during which musical theatrical forms on the American stage proliferated to the point of rank confusion. Most of the styles already discussed (burlesque, minstrelsy, opera, melodrama, pantomime, dance and plays with songs) continued to be performance vehicles, but these older styles mutated, expanded and cross-fertilised each other. Furthermore, new styles were introduced: operetta (including *opéra-bouffe*, Austrian and British operetta, and 'light operas' by American composers), farce-comedy, spectacle/extravaganza and the expansions of variety (including the early revue and the shows of Harrigan and Hart).

By this time many of the local stock companies of earlier decades had disappeared; most theatres now relied exclusively on the itinerant 'combination' companies that performed everything from drama and opera/operetta to variety and farce-comedy. Itinerant musical-theatrical companies now toured all over the United States, including – after the opening of the transcontinental railroad in 1869 – the interior of the far West. Although many of the theatrical innovations of this period can be covered by an examination of developments in New York City, this should not mislead the reader; travelling performers were able to exploit fully a well-developed transportation system that criss-crossed the United States and they took their performances to city and hamlet alike. During this period there also emerged the theatrical syndicate – a central managerial office (usually in New York, Boston or Chicago) that controlled both local theatres and the itinerant troupes that visited them.[42] This centralisation of control exemplifies another element of the coming-of-age of the theatrical business.

Scheduling was much less haphazard; managers also exploited the national and local press for purposes of advertising and publicity and collaborated with publishing houses to ensure that 'hit' songs from popular shows would be readily available to consumers in sheet-music format.

Added to the rank confusion of musical-theatrical forms of the time was an imprecision of terminology that can drive a codifier mad: the same show might be called a 'farce-comedy', a 'revue' or an 'extravaganza'; many shows exhibited characteristics of numerous categories. The first use of the term 'musical comedy' dates from this period, but there is general disagreement about which show, precisely, the name was first bestowed upon; some of the candidates include *The Pet of the Petticoats* (1866), *Evangeline* (1874) and *The Gaiety Girl* (1894).[43] The American musical stage was beginning to come of age during this thirty-year period: metaphorically, it was a gangly and untidy adolescent experiencing a magnificent growth spurt; this diverse yet contradictory youngster would eventually mature into the twentieth-century American musical.

Spectacles, extravaganzas and burlesques

During the post-Civil War period terms such as 'extravaganza', 'burlesque' and 'spectacle' were frequently used interchangeably or in combination. The theatrical works in this style were clearly based on forms that had been familiar to American theatre-goers for some years, but shows of this nature became more prominent and numerous during the last third of the century.

The Black Crook (1866), with music by Thomas Baker, is frequently cited as the first real precursor to the twentieth-century musical. A combination of many of the forms already discussed, the five-and-a-half-hour extrava-ganza (performed at Niblo's Gardens in New York City) included elements of melodrama and fantasy (inspired in part by Carl Maria von Weber's opera *Der Freischütz* and Goethe's *Faust*), ballet (performed by a troupe of one hundred French female dancers, in tights), spectacular scenery and costumes, and transformation scenes made possible by sophisticated stage machinery.[44] The play, although not particularly novel (it was constructed of many elements already familiar to American theatre-goers), became aston-ishingly popular, achieving a run of 474 performances over the course of sixteen months. It remained a mainstay of the American theatre until almost the end of the nineteenth century. In addition to the music written by Baker for the original production, there were many additional compositions writ-ten for interpolation later.[45]

The success of *The Black Crook* (coupled with the popularity of the Ravels' and Laura Keene's productions) inevitably resulted in a spate of additional extravaganzas and spectacles, including the unsuccessful sequel to *The Black Crook*, *The White Fawn* (1868). The two decades after the Civil

War marked the height of popularity for American spectacle, which – as we have seen – combined elements from a variety of familiar theatrical forms and in which music played an important role as unifying accompaniment.[46] The burlesque-spectacles mounted by Lydia Thompson and her 'British blondes', who arrived from London in 1868, are good examples of this admixture of elements. Thompson first appeared in New York in a full-length burlesque, *Ixion, or the Man at the Wheel*, which boasted of a pun-heavy script, topical references to and burlesques upon contemporary events and people, *opéra-bouffe*-like songs, spectacle, transformation scenes, gags and dances.[47] Thompson and her troupe, furthermore, were responsible for injecting into burlesque the element of the 'girlie show' that eventually would become closely associated with the genre. This overt exploitation of stage women as the object of the male gaze represents an important development in the role of women performers on the musical stage; it would have major repercussions early in the twentieth century, in particular with the revue style developed by Florenz Ziegfeld.

Edward Everett Rice's *Evangeline; or the Belle of Acadie* (1874), to words by John Cheever Goodwin, is another excellent example of the cross-fertilisation typical of late-century musical-theatrical forms: from spectacle it took elaborate costumes, sets and stage machinery (a spouting whale, a balloon trip to Arizona); from burlesque it borrowed a rhyming text full of puns and topical references, and ostensibly with a literary basis (it was originally a burlesque on Longfellow's poem, although Goodwin's version has little to do with its plot); from variety show and minstrelsy it took skits, gags and specialised 'acts'; from comic opera it borrowed spoken dialogue, a romantic plot, and a musical score of songs, dances, ensemble numbers and choruses.[48] There were also elements of melodrama and pantomime in the work, which was the only nineteenth-century musical production to rival the popularity of *The Black Crook*; it was mounted all over the country for the next thirty years.[49]

Three years after the premiere of *Evangeline*, there emerged another style of burlesque, called farce-comedy. *The Brook* (1877), created by Nate Salsbury and first performed by his troupe in St Louis, was a parody of musical-theatrical conventions, although it was not a burlesque in the standard definition of the form (Salsbury called it a 'laughable and musical extravaganza').[50] *The Brook* featured music that was borrowed and arranged;[51] it was also a simple show with a small cast: it was neither an extravaganza nor a spectacle, and it required no chorus, ballet dancers, pantomime, transformation scenes, extravagant costumes or spectacular scenery. From the variety stage and the British music hall, *The Brook* incorporated the concept that a theatrical work could be casual and natural. The simplicity (and success) of *The Brook* guaranteed immediate imitations;

farce-comedies remained popular in New York for only five years, but itinerant companies (called 'combinations') toured North America for the rest of the century.[52] The most popular successor to *The Brook* was *A Trip to Chinatown* by Charles H. Hoyt (music by Percy Gaunt); this show opened in 1890 and ran for a record 650 performances in its first engagement. Loosely constructed with an extremely thin plot (typical of a farce-comedy) and incorporating elements from vaudeville (such as specialty act appearances by artists like dancer Loie Fuller), the work featured a score that included some popular tunes that are still known today, e.g. 'The Bowery' and 'Reuben and Cynthia'.

Melodrama

By the last third of the century, the technique of using instrumental 'melos' as dramatic cues had become almost ubiquitous in musical-theatrical (and many dramatic) forms of all kinds. Melodrama itself also continued its domination of the American stage; the popularity of full-length melodramatic plays would not begin to wane until the twentieth century.[53] Continued popularity in the late nineteenth century was enhanced by the use of more elaborate scenery, better lighting and more sophisticated stage machinery to increase the sense of realism; the overlap with spectacle and extravaganza should be obvious.[54] The continued importance of music to melodramatic presentation – and hence the significance of melodrama as one of the precursors of the twentieth-century American musical – is sometimes ignored. As the theatre historian David Mayer points out, however, 'nowhere is the use of musical accompaniment more pervasive . . . from ten years before the start of the nineteenth century until well after the First World War, than in the melodrama'.[55]

Scores to melodramatic works are rare, even from the second half of the nineteenth century; there are perhaps a dozen known scores to such plays in the United States and some thirty in collections in Great Britain.[56] One of the most important examples of melodramatic music from this period is for the play *Monte Cristo* (1883), an adaptation by Charles Fechter of Alexandre Dumas's 1844 romance novel *Le Comte de Monte-Cristo*, first produced in the United States in 1870. The twenty-eight melos in the manuscript score, for the most part, are extremely brief, but this music was greatly augmented by overtures and entr'acte music, played before and between the acts. Some of the melos in *Monte Cristo* are used almost as leitmotifs, not only to indicate entrances and exits of important characters, but also to signify emotional and psychological developments in the *dramatis personae*. Other non-melo music used in melodramatic plays, however, did not differ significantly from interpolated songs and incidental music performed in many 'straight' dramatic plays of the period, indicating both the continued importance of music to most theatrical works and the ubiquitous overlap among different 'distinct' forms on the American stage in the late nineteenth century. The subsequent impact of these well-developed (and familiar) melodramatic musical techniques at the turn of the century was twofold. On the one hand, the pervasive use of music for dramatic purposes clearly influenced those individuals who – consciously or unconsciously – were writing the works that would be the immediate precursors to the early musical. On the other hand, melodramatic music would inevitably influence the adaptation of similar melos for use in the early 'silent' cinema; the primary difference, of course, was that the musical accompaniment for film had to be continuous instead of intermittent.[57]

Minstrelsy; black musical theatre

By the final decades of the century the 'Golden Era' of blackface minstrelsy (1840s–70s) had almost run its course. During the 1870s minstrel troupes grew ever larger, sometimes including as many as thirty performers. Known as 'mastodon' or 'giant' minstrel troupes, these companies grew in order to compete with the burgeoning forms and styles of entertainment emerging during the period.[58] Minstrel troupes also began to employ other 'hooks': all-female minstrel troupes, all-black minstrel troupes. The first important example of the latter, called the Georgia Minstrels, appeared in 1865; this company (managed by a white man) was followed, in turn, by numerous other troupes, some of them managed by African Americans.[59]

The advent of black minstrel companies marked the beginning (in the final decades of the nineteenth century) of a great influx of African-American performers onto the American stage. Minstrelsy, minstrelsy-influenced vaudeville (or variety) and the craze for 'coon' songs all offered to African Americans an entrée into a hitherto all-white world; Allen Woll, in fact, notes that a majority of African-American actors enumerated in the 1890 census identified themselves as minstrels.[60] The Hyers Sisters represent the first attempt by blacks to produce dramatic shows with songs. The sisters' combination company produced musical plays starting in the late 1870s and lasting well into the 1880s.[61] The influx of African Americans into the theatrical world led, inevitably, to the creation of black 'musicals'. *The Creole Burlesque Co.* (1890), produced for the burlesque stage, was very much a minstrel-flavoured entertainment. It was followed by *Octoroons* (1895), which included a hit Tin Pan Alley 'coon' song, 'No Coon Can Come Too Black for Me'.[62] Two shows of 1898 were closer to what we think of as 'musical comedy': *Clorindy, or the Origin of the Cakewalk* (Will Marion Cook) and *A Trip to Coontown* (Bob Cole) were both vaudeville-like – rather than book-like – musical theatrical works; the latter was the first musical written, directed and performed by black performers.[63]

Opera and operetta

During the last thirty years of the nineteenth century, foreign-language opera performance in America gradually became ever more closely associated both with the elite and with immigrant communities. In mainstream America, it was also gradually removed from the domain of the popular theatre, in part because of this increased sense of 'exclusivity', in part because of the tendency in the theatre towards the concept of 'niche marketing': as the American population grew, it became increasingly possible for theatres devoted to a particular repertory to be economically viable, especially in large cities. In the 1880s and 1890s theatres devoted primarily to the performance of opera were found in the larger American cities (New York, Boston, Philadelphia, Washington DC, Chicago and San Francisco); even many of these houses, however – such as Albaugh's Opera House in Washington, DC, the Academy of Music in Philadelphia and Crosby's Opera House in Chicago – also hosted productions of musical comedy, operetta drama and other entertainments in addition to grand opera. It is also important to mention that opera companies – even the New York Metropolitan (founded in 1883) – continued to travel throughout America for the remainder of the century and to perform, for the most part, in normal theatres rather than in houses limited to opera production. As a result, there persisted an ambiguity about the place of foreign-language opera within the spectrum of American musical theatre during the last decades of the century.

English-language opera continued to appeal to a broadly based musical theatre audience during this period; its popularity would inevitably have a major impact on the development of the twentieth-century American musical. Much of the repertory consisted of translations of the Italian and German operas that were increasingly associated with the upper classes; this contributes (in retrospect) to the aforementioned sense of ambiguity in relation to opera reception. English-language troupes continued to tour the United States regularly in the 1870s, 1880s and 1890s, headed by Italian-opera impresarios and by prima donnas such as Caroline Richings (daughter of the British actor Peter Richings mentioned earlier; active 1863–74), Euphrosyne Parepa-Rosa (active in the US 1865–74) and Clara Louise Kellogg (active in English opera 1873–7). These troupes performed English translations of Italian and German operas as well as operas written in English; many of them billed their productions as 'opera for the people', clearly as an attempt to counter the growing perception of opera as an elite pastime. Emma Abbott (active 1879–91), known as 'the people's prima donna', headed a troupe that opened some thirty-five different opera houses in the far West and introduced this musical-theatrical form to many Americans; her sudden death (of pneumonia) while on tour in Utah provoked a national outpouring of grief from her supporters. Emma Juch, a successful performer with

Plate 1 Scenic design for Act 2 from Emma Abbott's production of the opera *Paul and Virginia* by Victor Massé (1872) showing the interior of the plantation home of Mons. St. Crois on 'a picturesque island off the coast of Africa'.

Italian troupes, was also known as a crusader for English opera for 'regular' Americans. Dozens of other English-language troupes were active in the United States during this period; they performed a mixed repertory of operas and operettas by composers who wrote in English (Balfe, Wallace, Benedict, Eichberg and Sullivan), French (Auber, Meyerbeer, Lecocq, Thomas, Offenbach, Gounod, Planquette and Bizet), Italian (Mozart, Bellini, Rossini, Donizetti, Verdi, Puccini, and – later – Mascagni and Leoncavallo) and German (Mozart, Weber, Beethoven and Wagner).[64] The spectacularly unsuccessful American Opera Company, established by Jeanette Thurber in 1885 in an attempt to establish English opera in America, should be noted, but its failure was anything but typical.

Many of the English-language companies were increasingly influenced by the growing American enthusiasm for operetta, and many operetta troupes also performed standard repertory. The Boston Ideals, for example – founded in 1879 to perform Gilbert and Sullivan operettas – regularly performed such typical fare as *The Bohemian Girl* (Balfe), *The Marriage of Figaro* (Mozart), *Fra Diavolo* (Auber), *Martha* (Flotow) and *L'Elisir d'amore* (Donizetti), in addition to 'lighter' operettas like *The Pirates of Penzance* and *Fatinitza*.[65] Operetta had first been introduced to American audiences in the 1860s, in the form of the *opéras-bouffes* of Jacques Offenbach. *La Grande Duchesse de Gerolstein* was first performed in New York (in French) in 1867. Several troupes mounted this and other works in New York and elsewhere, with great success. The 1870s, in fact, were a heyday of *opéra-bouffe* production in the United States; performances of operettas by Offenbach, Lecocq, Audran, Hervé and Planquette – in English, French and German – were widespread.[66] As a result of the new-found craze for French opera, the number of French companies that toured widely in the United States increased during this time; these included the French Opera Company of New Orleans and troupes formed in support of the *opéra-bouffe* sopranos Marie Aimée and Lucille Tostée. Offenbach himself visited the United States in 1876 and conducted performances in Philadelphia and New York. As this repertory became more popular, an increasing number of troupes performed the *opéra-bouffe* repertory in English translation; this, paradoxically, led to a decrease in the popularity of these works, as more Americans understood and were offended by the double entendres and compromised sexual situations of the plots. German companies (notably in New York, Cincinnati, Chicago and Milwaukee) also performed translations of this repertory, but primarily for the large German immigrant populations of those cities.[67] The French light opera repertory was augmented during the 1870s and 1880s by Viennese operettas, including works by Franz von Suppé (*Fatinitza*), Karl Millöcker (*The Black Hussar* and *The Beggar Student*) and Johann Strauss (*The Merry War* and *The Queen's Lace Handkerchief*).

The most successful operettas on the American stage during the last third of the nineteenth century were by W. S. Gilbert (1836–1911) and Arthur Sullivan (1842–1900). Scholars generally agree that the 1878 Boston premiere of *HMS Pinafore* marks a turning point in the history of American musical theatre.[68] Within a year the work had become the most frequently performed operetta in America, with more than ninety *Pinafore* companies touring the United States. In 1879 Gilbert, Sullivan and the company of Rupert d'Oyly Carte travelled to the United States to perform *Pinafore* and to mount the world premiere of *The Pirates of Penzance* (in order to secure the American copyright). Neither *Pirates* nor *The Mikado* (1885) achieved the popularity of *Pinafore*, but the level of performance of the D'Oyly Carte company greatly influenced American operetta and English opera companies, and the format of the Gilbert and Sullivan shows – the inoffensiveness of the humour (especially in comparison with burlesque, vaudeville or even *opéra-bouffe*), the witty satire at the expense of the British establishment, and Sullivan's skilful melodies – appealed mightily to American audiences. The shows would remain popular for the rest of the century. British operetta clearly had a profound impact on the future course of American musical comedy; Gerald Bordman, in fact, claims that *Pinafore* itself 'determined the course and shape of the popular lyric stage in England and America for the final quarter of the nineteenth century'.[69] Part of the astonishing success of *Pinafore* can be attributed to the operetta's unprecedented assimilation into American mass popular culture; a veritable mushroom-crop of amateur theatrical companies – devoted to the performance of *Pinafore* – sprang up all over America in the late 1870s and early 1880s.

American composers also found a voice in operetta, although most operetta and English opera companies preferred to perform European imports. Julius Eichberg's *Doctor of Alcantara*, which was premiered in Boston in 1862, was an attempt by that German immigrant to emulate the success of Offenbach. The show, which was referred to in the contemporary press as an 'opera', 'operetta', 'opera of the comic order', 'comic operetta', 'opera bouffa' and 'light operatic entertainment', entered the repertories of numerous troupes in the 1860s and 1870s and made Eichberg the most successful American operetta composer during the 1860s.[70] Other Americans followed in Eichberg's footsteps, including the opera impresario Maretzek (*Sleepy Hollow, or the Headless Horseman*, 1879) and J. S. Crossey (*The First Life Guards at Brighton*, 1879). Willard Spencer's *The Little Tycoon* (1886) was almost the only American comic opera to enjoy any popular success in the 1880s. John Philip Sousa, who wrote some fifteen operettas, was clearly influenced by the works of Gilbert and Sullivan, but suffered from inadequate librettos. Although his works held their own against foreign operettas in the late 1880s and early 1890s, his only true success was *El Capitan* (1896).[71] Ludwig Engländer (1853–1914) also enjoyed some success as a composer of comic operas, primarily in the 1890s. George Whitfield Chadwick, a more 'classical' composer, also tried his hand at the genre, with *Tabasco* (1894). Two late-century American composers of comic opera enjoyed greater success than the others. Reginald de Koven (1859–1920) wrote several operettas in the late 1880s, including *The Begum* (1887), described as a cross between *La Grande Duchesse* and *The Mikado*.[72] De Koven relied heavily on Gilbert and Sullivan for his only major success, *Robin Hood*, premiered by the Bostonians (formerly the Boston Ideals) in 1890. Victor Herbert (1859–1924), who also wrote for the Bostonians (and for other English opera companies), was by far the most successful and skilled American comic opera composer of the late nineteenth century. Most of his best known works – characterised by dramatic and memorable melodies and skilful orchestrations – are twentieth-century works; several of his operettas, however, were premiered in the 1890s, including *The Wizard of the Nile* (1895), *The Serenade* (1897) and *The Fortune Teller* (1898).

Vaudeville and variety show

Variety shows came of age on the American stage during the final years of the nineteenth century. Many concert saloons had begun offering 'light' varied entertainment in the 1850s as inducement to drink; the amusement was similar to that of the English music hall and included a bill of songs (comic and sentimental), instrumental solos, comic skits, dancing, juggling and acrobatics of various sorts. Americans, of course, were already readily familiar with the format through minstrelsy. By the mid-1860s, concert saloons and their style of entertainment were common all over the country; after the Civil War the format moved from saloons into theatres.[73] Variety theatres became commonplace during the 1880s and 1890s; as such they – like opera houses – are another example of the increasing numbers of theatres catering to specific audiences. For the most part variety entertainment was considered disreputable (because of the association with saloons and the prevalence of objectionable material). Managers of variety theatres or 'théâtres comiques' (including, most notably, Tony Pastor and B. F. Keith in New York) attempted to attract family audiences by cleaning up the content of their shows, professionalising the performances, banning drink and changing the name of the entertainment form to 'vaudeville', a term already used in Europe for variety-like entertainment.[74] Playbills from American variety theatres from the last two decades of the century illustrate the diversity of programming: an evening's entertainment might consist of a full-length vaudeville show, burlesque skits, revues, magic shows and minstrelsy; most of these performances were to musical accompaniment.[75] It is also during this period that many variety entertainers began fruitful collaboration with music publishers to 'plug' particular songs. This combination of musical theatre and music publishing illustrates another aspect of an emerging music business that occurred during the early Tin Pan Alley era; it also suggests the important role of musical theatre in that coming of age.

In the 1870s many variety shows – like minstrel shows – included extended comic skits. One variety performer who eventually transformed his skits into something much closer to an extended musical-theatrical show was the actor, lyricist and playwright Edward Harrigan (1844–1911), who in 1871 teamed up with the actor Tony Hart (Anthony Cannon, 1855–91) to form the variety team of Harrigan and Hart. In the same year Harrigan also commenced a fruitful collaboration with the established theatre composer Dave Braham (1834–1905); the partnership eventually produced a whole series of comical musical plays that relied heavily on burlesque and ethnic humour (caricaturing Irish and German immigrants as well as African Americans). The first version of *The Mulligan Guard*, from 1873, was a ten-minute sketch typical of variety-show fare: it contained three or four songs, dialogue, and 'gags and business'.[76] Encouraged, Harrigan and

Braham continued to expand upon the theme; eventually the sketch evolved into a full-length play that, in turn, spawned an entire cycle of related 'Mulligan' musical plays that were performed (in New York and elsewhere) throughout the 1880s and into the 1890s.[77] The evolution of the Mulligan series is a perfect example of the transformations and cross-fertilisations characteristic of the American stage: a variety show song-and-dance routine developed into a full-length musical entertainment that incorporated elements of variety, burlesque, melodrama and minstrelsy. Furthermore, the growing importance of Dave Braham's music – the increased number of songs and the greater reliance on incidental music as dramatic cues (in the style of melodrama) – points clearly towards the close integration of music and drama that is the hallmark of the mature American musical comedy.[78]

In the 1890s variety continued to be popular on the American stage; many other individuals important to the development of American musical theatre cut their performance teeth in vaudeville. One of the most notable was George M. Cohan (1878–1942), whose play *Little Johnny Jones* (1904) is frequently cited as the first American musical. Cohan grew up a member of his family's itinerant vaudeville troupe ('The Four Cohans'). The company's first musical comedy, *The Governor's Son* (1901) – like Ned Harrigan's works of twenty years earlier – was an elaboration of a vaudeville sketch. This show was an immediate failure, but the dramatic and musical seeds were sown and would result, three years later, in Cohan's more integrated *Little Johnny Jones*.

Another style of entertainment that would have an impact on twentieth-century musical theatre also emerged in the 1890s on the vaudeville stage. 'Revues', a style of entertainment that had become popular in Paris, were introduced in New York in the early 1890s. The first successful American example of this genre, *The Passing Show* (1894, Ludwig Engländer), was called a 'topical extravaganza' and combined burlesque, satire, specialty acts, minstrelsy, dance, a scantily clad female chorus and *tableaux vivants*; in essence it was a variety show in the best of the American tradition.[79] The revue as a form would have a profound impact on musical theatre of the early twentieth century; the 'follies' and 'scandals' of Florenz Ziegfeld and George White (for which composers such as Irving Berlin, George Gershwin and Cole Porter wrote music) were outgrowths of this Parisian style.

Conclusion

In the eighteenth and nineteenth centuries the theatrical realm was not so clearly separated from normal life as it is now; elements of the stage permeated American life during this period – especially the last several decades of the nineteenth century – to an extent almost unimaginable today. Americans were readily conversant with songs from theatrical venues as widely divergent as opera and variety show; their dance cards were full of music from the stage; they played arrangements of show tunes on their parlour pianos, mounted amateur productions of operettas and listened to concerts by the local brass band playing arrangements of music of operas, operettas and variety shows. Furthermore many Americans of varied social and economic standing attended musical-theatrical performances with a matter-of-fact regularity foreign to us today. The variety of musical-theatrical repertory available then is approximated two centuries later only in the largest of American cities, or in the local multiplex.

It is also impossible, for most of the nineteenth century, to view the repertory of 'musical theatre' as different and distinct from the repertory of the 'theatre'. It is true that by the final decades of the century the concept of the 'legitimate' stage – a style of drama that did *not* include music – had begun to emerge. But as the theatre historian David Mayer points out, this development – which modern theatre-goers take for granted as the natural order of things – was an aberration and clearly marked a change from long-standing tradition.[80] A thorough understanding of the antecedents of the American musical, then, must include an examination of a wide variety of different types of musical-theatrical styles and genres, including many that today are not included in the modern definition of 'musical theatre'.

Finally, it is important to realise that our modern preference for clear distinctions between musical-theatrical forms even in the twentieth century is sometimes artificial and counterproductive. Well into the twentieth century American 'musical theatre' continued to be varied and changeable, with a rich and valuable tradition of cross-fertilisation; as Joel Kaplan notes in his introduction to a study of the Edwardian theatre, it is precisely this 'interplay of forms or genres that seems, to late twentieth-century eyes, one of the most remarkable features of pre-[World War I] entertainment'.[81] It is clear that during at least the first third of the twentieth century composers and performers moved readily between variety, film musicals, burlesque, revues and book musicals. Recognition of this is essential in any attempt to understand the development of the American musical; it also illustrates a healthy continuation – into the twentieth century – of many of the musical-theatrical traditions of the nineteenth.

2 Non-English-language musical theatre in the United States

JOHN KOEGEL

Immigrant groups from all parts of Europe, several Latin American countries and Asia staged musical theatre works in their native languages that reflected their particular concerns and experiences. Audiences attended musicals of various sorts brought from the homeland as well as new pieces created in the United States. Such works constitute the core repertory of America's many immigrant musical stages from the late eighteenth century to World War II. While non-English-language stages were always open to outsiders, they functioned primarily for the entertainment and cultural education of the ethnicities that produced them.

Transplanted foreign-language musical theatre (especially French, German, and Italian opera and operetta) also existed in the United States. These works, however, were representative of foreign cultures and did not directly reflect the immigrant experience; instead, they were geared toward diverse audiences that spoke a variety of languages and came from multiple backgrounds. French opera in New Orleans (a dominant theatrical form in the Crescent City from at least 1796 until 1919) and Spanish-language theatre in long-lived Hispano and Latino communities in the American Southwest (practised there since the early seventeenth century) constitute yet another dimension of the history of non-English-language musical theatre in the United States. While musical stage repertories were mostly imported to New Orleans or Santa Fe, the French- and Spanish-speaking residents of Louisiana and New Mexico were more frequently long-established residents than recently arrived immigrants.

The various foreign-language houses that flourished in the United States from the nineteenth century to World War II emphasised different forms of musical theatre. They mirrored Broadway musical theatre tradition with its emphasis on operetta, musical revue, variety/vaudeville and musical comedy, but also featured opera, politically oriented musical revues, comic plays and farces with many songs, folk plays with extensive music, and other musical theatre pieces. While the spoken drama (classic or popular, comic or serious) was a very significant aspect of immigrant and transplanted non-English-language stages, it was popularly oriented music theatre in its various guises that regularly attracted large audiences to the 'ethnic' theatre.[1]

Professional groups (German, Mexican, Chinese, Yiddish, Cuban, Italian, and French theatre, operetta and opera companies) artistically dom-inated dramatic life in their respective communities. Other immigrant groups (such as the Portuguese, Norwegians, Finns, Swedes, Armenians, Poles, Slovaks and Baltic peoples) primarily supported an amateur or semi-professional theatre tradition that was led by a relatively small number of professional directors, actors and musicians brought from the home-land (or already resident in the United States), and featured enthusiastic and talented amateur local performers. A representative but not exhaus-tive listing of some of the dominant ethnic theatre traditions in the United States demonstrates the wide geographic spread of this theatrical world (see Table 2.1).

The vast quantity of musical theatre activity on the large number of immigrant or transplanted stages hardly figures in the current scholarship on the American musical theatre, except in the case of foreign-language opera and comic opera for English speakers. Hence, it requires a compara-tive analysis here, supported by important examples of both common and divergent trends and features. Likewise, an expansive rather than restric-tive definition of musical theatre is integral to this chapter, given the often hybrid nature of the repertory, which, among other theatrical forms (all with extensive music), included German *Volksstücke* (folk plays with music), *Pos-sen* (farces with songs), operetta and opera; French *opéra-bouffe*, vaudeville, *opéra comique* and opera; Italian opera, operetta, *caffè-concerto* (music hall) and *macchiette* (sketches); Spanish, Mexican and Cuban *zarzuela* (operetta) and *revista* (musical revue); Finnish and Swedish musical comedy and folk plays; and Chinese opera. American vaudeville also had a direct impact on most ethnic stages.

The groups represented here – Spanish-speaking (Mexican, Cuban, Spanish, Puerto Rican), French (including New England's Franco-Americans and Louisiana's Cajuns and Creoles), Italian, German, Scan-dinavian, Finnish, Chinese, Yiddish – hardly comprise the entirety of the extensive history of immigrant and transplanted foreign-language musical theatre, but they are certainly representative of this tradition and documen-tation on their activities is more or less readily available.[2] The performance spaces, performers and managers, immigrant themes, theatrical repertories, recordings, individual stage works and songs, practices, and commercial enterprises discussed in this chapter serve as examples that illuminate larger trends.

Other theatrical traditions not discussed here are nevertheless important to a complete history. Native American ritual dance (usually with sacred

Table 2.1 *Ethnic Theatres in the United States*

STATE, CITY OR TOWN	Chinese	Czech	Finnish	French/Franco-American	German	Italian	Polish	Portuguese	Spanish	Mexican	Cuban	Puerto Rican	Swedish	Yiddish
ARIZONA–Douglas										X				
ARIZONA–Nogales										X				
ARIZONA–Phoenix										X				
ARIZONA–Tucson										X				
CALIFORNIA–Fresno										X				
CALIFORNIA–Los Angeles	X				X	X?			X	X	X			X
CALIFORNIA–Oakland	X				X	X?		X		X				
CALIFORNIA–San Diego					X					X				
CALIFORNIA–San Francisco	X			X	X	X		X		X			X	X
CALIFORNIA–San Jose					X					X				
CALIFORNIA–San Juan Bautista										X (El Teatro Campesino, bilingual)				
CALIFORNIA–Santa Barbara	X?									X				
COLORADO–Denver					X					X				
COLORADO–Leadville					X									
COLORADO–Pueblo					X					X				
COLORADO–Trinidad										X				
FLORIDA–Miami											X			
FLORIDA–Tampa (and Ybor City)									X		X			
HAWAII–Honolulu	X							X				X?		
ILLINOIS–Chicago	X?				X		X			X			X	X
INDIANA–Evansville					X									
INDIANA–Fort Wayne					X									
INDIANA–Indianapolis					X									
INDIANA–New Albany					X									
IOWA–Davenport					X									

(*cont.*)

Table 2.1 (*cont.*)

STATE, CITY OR TOWN	Chinese	Czech	Finnish	French/Franco-American	German	Italian	Polish	Portu-guese	Spanish	Mexican	Cuban	Puerto Rican	Swedish	Yiddish
IOWA–Denison					X									
IOWA–Des Moines					X									
IOWA–Dubuque					X									
KANSAS–Leavenworth					X									
KANSAS–Lindsborg													X	
KANSAS–Wilson		X												
KENTUCKY–Louisville					X									
LOUISIANA–Lafayette				X										
LOUISIANA–New Orleans				X	X									
LOUISIANA–St. Martinville				X										
MAINE–Lewiston				X										
MARYLAND–Baltimore					X									X
MASSACHUSETTS–Boston				X?	X									X
MASSACHUSETTS–Fall River								X						
MASSACHUSETTS–Fitchburg			X											
MASSACHUSETTS–Gloucester								X						
MASSACHUSETTS–Holyoke				X										
MASSACHUSETTS–Lawrence				X										
MASSACHUSETTS–New Bedford								X						
MASSACHUSETTS–Provincetown								X						
MASSACHUSETTS–Quincy			X											
MASSACHUSETTS–Worcester			X	X										

	1	2	3	4	5	6	7	8
MICHIGAN–Detroit	X			X		X		X
MICHIGAN–Saginaw				X		X		X
MINNESOTA–Duluth						X		X
MINNESOTA–Mankato						X		
MINNESOTA–Minneapolis/St. Paul		X				X		
MINNESOTA–New Ulm						X		
MINNESOTA–Red Wing						X		
MINNESOTA–Rochester						X		
MINNESOTA–Stillwater						X		
MINNESOTA–Winona						X		
MISSOURI–Boonville						X		
MISSOURI–Cape Girardeau						X		
MISSOURI–Hannibal						X		
MISSOURI–Hermann						X		
MISSOURI–Jefferson City						X		
MISSOURI–Kansas City						X		
MISSOURI–St. Joseph						X		
MISSOURI–St. Louis	X					X		
MISSOURI–Ste Genevieve						X?	X?	
MISSOURI–Washington						X		
NEBRASKA–Omaha						X		
NEW HAMPSHIRE–Manchester							X	
NEW JERSEY–Camden						X		
NEW JERSEY–Hoboken					X	X		
NEW JERSEY–Jersey City						X		
NEW JERSEY–Newark					X	X		
NEW JERSEY–Patterson					X			
NEW MEXICO–Albuquerque			X					
NEW MEXICO–Belen			X					
NEW MEXICO–Las Cruces			X					

(cont.)

Table 2.1 (*cont.*)

STATE, CITY OR TOWN	Chinese	Czech	Finnish	French/Franco-American	German	Italian	Polish	Portu-guese	Spanish	Mexican	Cuban	Puerto Rican	Swedish	Yiddish
NEW MEXICO–Las Vegas										X				
NEW MEXICO–Santa Fe										X				
NEW MEXICO–Socorro										X				
NEW MEXICO–Taos										X				
NEW YORK–Buffalo					X		X							
NEW YORK–Jamestown													X	
NEW YORK–New York City (Manhattan, Brooklyn, Queens, Bronx)	X	X	X	X	X	X	X	X	X	X	X	X	X	X
NEW YORK–Poughkeepsie					X									
NEW YORK–Rochester					X									
NEW YORK–Troy					X									
OHIO–Cincinnati					X									
OHIO–Cleveland					X		X							X
OHIO–Columbus					X									
OHIO–Put-in-Bay					X									
OHIO–Toledo					X									
OREGON–Astoria			X											
OREGON–Portland			X					X						
PENNSYLVANIA–Allegheny					X									
PENNSYLVANIA–Allentown					X (PA German)									
PENNSYLVANIA–Erie					X			X						
PENNSYLVANIA–Philadelphia				X	X	X								X
RHODE ISLAND–Providence					X			X						
RHODE ISLAND–Woonsocket				X										

Location				
SOUTH CAROLINA–Charleston		X	X	
TEXAS–Austin		X	X	X?
TEXAS–Brownsville			X	
TEXAS–El Paso		X	X	
TEXAS–Fredricksburg			X	
TEXAS–Galveston		X	X	
TEXAS–Houston		X	X	
TEXAS–Laredo		X		
TEXAS–Matamoros		X		
TEXAS–New Braunfels			X	
TEXAS–New Bremen			X	
TEXAS–San Antonio		X	X	
UTAH–Salt Lake City			X	
WASHINGTON–Seattle	X			
WASHINGTON, D.C.			X	
WEST VIRGINIA–Wheeling			X	
WISCONSIN–La Crosse			X	
WISCONSIN–Manitowoc			X	
WISCONSIN–Milwaukee	X		X	

connections), always accompanied by song, represents the confluence of music, spirituality and theatricality. Neither an immigrant nor transplanted theatrical practice, it is indigenous. Additionally, various forms of Asian (non-Chinese) theatre with music, such as Indonesian *wayang kulit* (shadow puppet plays accompanied by gamelan) or Japanese *noh* or *kabuki* drama, are imported traditions that have appeared in the United States in recent years.

The history of the ethnic theatre in the United States relates directly to at least eight repeating patterns of cultural maintenance, conflict and accommodation: 1) migration, 2) the establishment of immigrant neighbourhoods, 3) the creation of societies and institutions for the good of these communities, 4) the encouragement of literacy through language maintenance and the establishment of language schools and newspapers, 5) the development of institutionally complete societies in which most artistic, economic, and social needs were provided for within the community, 6) the institutionalisation of ritualised festivals, 7) rejection and ultimately acceptance by 'mainstream' society, and 8) acculturation and/or assimilation.

The more immigrant groups maintained a sense of their own ethnicity and community in new circumstances the more they eased their transition to American life in places such as Swede Town (Chicago), Little Germany (New York), Over-the-Rhine (Cincinnati) and the German Athens (Milwaukee). Other geographic examples include Mexican Sonoratown (Los Angeles) and Mexican communities in Tucson and San Antonio, the Yiddish-speaking Lower East Side (New York), Finn Town (Astoria, Oregon), Chinatown (San Francisco, New York and Los Angeles) and Little Italy (New York). Despite this tremendous amount of creative activity, the ethnic stage represented a parallel theatrical world that was hidden in plain view to outsiders. Those not from the individual ethnic community were often unaware of or uninterested in drama and musical theatre from outside their own experience. Language barriers could also discourage attendance by outsiders.

Notable exceptions occurred. Non-Chinese audiences flocked to Beijing opera star Mei Lanfang's performances in New York in 1930.[3] American composers Harry Partch and Lou Harrison were intrigued by the Chinese opera they attended in San Francisco's Chinatown. Non-German opera lovers attended the premieres in New York of some of Wagner's operas in Klein Deutschland's Stadttheater on the Bowery in the mid-nineteenth century. Some Anglo-American writers, such as Hutchins Hapgood, author of the influential book *The Spirit of the Ghetto* (1902), gave fascinating and sympathetic accounts of the Yiddish theatre in New York. Mexican Americans made up a sizeable portion of the audience for the United States premiere of Puccini's *La Bohème* in Los Angeles on 14 October 1897, given by an Italian opera troupe travelling to California directly from Mexico. New York society matrons avidly attended performances of Shakespeare in Italian by famed actor Tommaso Salvini in the late nineteenth century. These and similar examples point to a complex situation that defies easy categorisation.

Establishment of the ethnic musical theatre

Over the course of the history of the ethnic stages in the United States, certain events occurred more or less in similar ways, though with somewhat different results, in most or all of these traditions. Amateur dramatic companies were established soon after the arrival of a core group of immigrants sufficient in number to provide the performers and audiences for theatre. These amateur, and later professional, performers wished to recreate a theatrical experience – almost always with music – that they had known in their homeland (*patria, patrie, Heimat*). Long after the introduction of French opera and vaudeville in eighteenth-century New Orleans (established earlier in Saint-Domingue, modern-day Haiti) and the performance of Christmas shepherds' plays with music in Spanish and Mexican New Mexico, California and Texas (*La pastorela* or *Los pastores*), German-Americans regularly produced a wide variety of non-English-language musical theatre pieces beginning in the 1840s in New York's Klein Deutschland. These performances included operatic excerpts, folk plays and farces with integrated songs and later complete operas and operettas – all in German. At first, the theatrical forms prevalent in the immigrants' homelands were stressed, and only somewhat later did comic and serious plays with a large number of songs about the local immigrant experience appear. Many of these concerned the Greenhorn, or recently arrived, naive immigrant. In most ethnic theatre traditions, a conflict between high and popular art was continually present; lowbrow entertainment alternated with highbrow art.

Critics and intellectuals wanted the theatre to emphasise the classical drama of Goethe, Schiller, Lessing, Shakespeare (in translation) or their foreign equivalent. Working-class immigrant audiences, and often their middle-class counterparts, favoured lighter fare originally written in their own languages, usually with a strong musical component. They especially wanted to attend performances of operettas and musical comedies, as well as plays and melodramas with liberal doses of song.

Non-English-language socialist theatre (usually with music) stressed social causes and included themes of strong immediacy to working-class audiences (for example, the Triangle Factory Fire of 1911, the Patterson, New Jersey Strike of 1917, or the ills of tenement life). This type of theatre developed strongly in ethnic communities, including the German ones in New York and Chicago, the Italian and Yiddish-speaking areas in New York and the Finnish enclave in Duluth, Minnesota – the Helsinki of America.

Musical theatre in its myriad forms was used to address social and political questions as well as to provide popular entertainment.

Audience acceptance of the immigrant stage cut across language, as well as cultural and generational divides. The first generation of immigrants generally supported theatre in the language of their homeland. The second generation – born and raised in the United States – had a somewhat conflicted relationship and alternately either embraced or rejected its own ethnic theatre in favour of the mainstream, or supported it sporadically. The third generation, with the frequent loss of ability in the language of the homeland, was often unaware of or uninterested in the tradition. However, groups that experienced continued waves of immigration lasting over several decades, or a century or more (including Germans, Mexicans and Chinese) maintained interest in ethnic theatre. Many traditions lasted fifty to a hundred years and reflected the growth and assimilation patterns of the individual immigrant groups. Most traditions were in decline or defunct by the time of World War II, if not earlier. Few of the earlier live theatrical traditions exist today; exceptions include the Spanish-language stage (Chicano, Latino, and Puerto Rican/Nuyorican) and the Yiddish Folksbiene Theatre (New York). However, new theatrical experiences emerged that reflect the lives of the descendants of immigrants (albeit in an English-language context), such as the Asian-American theatre companies active in California.

Immigration themes represented in song

Many of the experiences that immigrants and their families actually lived through were represented as themes in songs sung on the ethnic musical stage: the comic experiences of the Greenhorn newly arrived at Ellis Island or in New York City, the sadness of the parent left behind in Europe, the joy at the promise of a better life in the new world, the fond thoughts of the old homeland, disillusionment about conditions in the new homeland. Every ethnic theatre tradition in the United States that created a new musical theatre repertory based on the immigrant experience represented these and other themes on stage. Solomon Smulewitz's Yiddish song 'A Brivele der Mamen' (A Little Letter to Mother) tells the story of the mother forgotten by the son who has left for America, where he has become rich. She only asks him to write her a little letter, but he will not even do that. Before she dies, in poverty, she writes again asking that he say Kaddish (prayers for the dead) for her. Smulewitz's famous (and still well-known) song tapped into a well of deep feeling about the sense of loss that many immigrants felt. Smulewitz's later song, 'A Brivele dem Taten' (A Little Letter to Papa) tells the story of the dutiful son rather than the hard-hearted and forgetful son of

'A Brivele der Mamen.' In 'A Brivele dem Taten', the sad father writes to his son in America that his mother has died and asks him to write a letter that will drive away his loneliness. The dutiful son saves the money to send for his father, who arrives in New York but is too ill to be admitted. The father and son can only see each other through a fence at Ellis Island before the father is sent back to Europe. The Statue of Liberty on the sheet music cover is a bittersweet symbol for the father and son rather than the representation of freedom and a new life experienced by so many other immigrants. (See Plate 2.)

'A Brivele dem Taten'
(A Letter to Papa)
Words and music by Solomon Smulewitz
Arranged by Joseph Rumshisky

Verses

Ich ken dich kind nit zwingen mehr	My child, I can no longer force you
In armuth do mit mir zu bleiben,	to stay here with me in poverty.
Sol sein mit glik, nor shwer mir, shwer,	Good fortune be with you, but it's hard for me, hard;
A Brivele dem Taten shreiben.	write a letter to papa.
Dien Muter hot der todt geraubt.	Death has taken your mother,
Mein besten freind von mir entrisen.	torn my best friend away from me.
Hob ich, mein Kind, in dir geglaubt	My child, I believed that you
Du vest mein leben mir versisen.	will sweeten my life.
Zum sof bleib ich, mein kind, alein,	I'll remain alone to the end, my child,
Wie mich geboren wird a stein,	as if a stone had been born to me,
Mein einzig treist, auch du, must gehn, oi!	my single consolation; you too must go, my son, oi!

Refrain

A brivele dem Taten solstu shreiben,	You should write a letter to your papa,
Yede woch a beigele papier,*	every week a little sheet of paper,
Dos wet mir mein einsamkeit zutreiben,	that will drive away my loneliness,
Elend bin ich kindele ohn dir,	I'm miserable without you, child,
Meine broches solstu mit sich fihren.	[but] take my blessings with you.
Greich die hechste stuffe von progress,	Reach for the highest rung of progress,
Doch wie un wos mit dir wet jetzt pasieren,	but however and whatever things happen to you,
A brivele dem Taten solstu shreibe.	you should write a letter to papa.

Verses

Der sun gehalten hot sein wort,	The son kept his word,
Mit geldt gestitzt ihm, brief geshreiben,	helped him with money, wrote letters,
A shifkart auch geshikt fun dort,	even sent him a ship ticket from there,
Jetzt fohrt er zu sein suhn dem lieben.	and now he travels to his dear son.
Van elend sein bald nehmt an ek.	His misery soon turned a corner.
Der alter fihlt sich hechst zufrieden;	The old man felt most content;
Un er derzehlt in zwishen-deck	and he shared his happiness with all
Sein simche dort far ale Yiden.	the Jews in steerage.
Vernichtet seinen meine leid	All my sorrows are gone,
Ich fohr zu mein lieb kind mit freid;	I'm travelling with joy to my child;
Es hot gewirkt dem tatens reid, oi!	the old man's advice was successful, oi!

Repeat refrain
Verses

In Ellis Island verurteilt is	On Ellis Island they decided
Der alter man zurik zum shiken,	to send the old man back,
Ihm fehlt die kraft zu sein a riez	he didn't have the strength to be a giant
Derfar is aus mit seine glicken.	and so his good fortune is at an end.
Men lost sein kind zu ihm nit zu,	They didn't allow his child to go to him;
Die herzer bluten bei sei beiden;	both of their hearts bled;
Es helft kein trehren, kein shum mihe	tears were of no help, no amount of effort [worked].
Auf eibig musen sei sich sheiden.	They had to part forever.
Dem altens broch is skreklich grois,	The old man's grief is enormous,
Dos freie land treibt ihm are's	the land of freedom drives him away,
Un fun die grates shreit er aus, oi!	and from behind the iron gate he cries out, oi!

Repeat refrain
* Note: 'a beigele papier' = 'a little sheet of paper' and 'a banknote'
Translation by Lee Gilbert

Plate 2 'A Brivele dem Taten' (A Little Letter to Papa) (1911).

Performance spaces

The performance spaces used by the multitude of non-English-language theatre troupes varied as much as the groups themselves. Theatres ranged in size
from small, intimate spaces that held only fifty to a hundred people to those
that could seat thousands, and included both indoor and outdoor venues.
Spaces could be modest, average or luxurious in their comfort, furnishings
and decoration. This depended upon a variety of factors, including the size
of the performance space, its intended purpose, the financial resources of
the owner of the building and its lessees, the repertory performed and the
relative affluence of the audience. The fact that some theatrical companies
were peripatetic (the Mexican Esperanza Iris Viennese Operetta Company)
while others were located in fixed venues for long time periods (New York's
Irving Place Theatre, in continuous existence as a German house between
1893 and 1918) added to the multifaceted nature of the performance venues.
For special occasions, some groups rented large theatres that catered primarily to English-speaking audiences (for example, German performers

leasing New York's Academy of Music or Madison Square Garden). Others performed on particular days of the week in 'American' theatres (as did Ottilie Genée's German troupe in San Francisco during the 1870s and 1880s). Relatively few groups or individuals built their own theatres; rather, they usually adapted and/or remodelled previously existent theatre buildings, or else leased theatres that they renamed, often after themselves. (David Kessler's Thalia Theatre in New York was the Yiddish incarnation of the former English-language Bowery Theatre and the German-language Thalia.[4])

There were notable exceptions. New Orleans' several successive French opera houses (1790s–1919) were all purpose-built for this musical-dramatic art (and for dancing after the opera). The Merced Theatre (Teatro Mercedes) in Los Angeles (1870) and the García Opera House in Socorro, New Mexico (1886) were built for use by Mexican and Mexican-American, as well as English-speaking, performers.[5] Milwaukee's famous Pabst Theatre, built by Frederick Pabst (of the Pabst Brewery) in 1895 for his German company, was a theatrical jewel of the Midwest (and is still in use as a theatre). In 1912, Adolf Philipp built his own Adolf Philipp Theatre on East 57th Street in New York for his German-American musical comedies (see below). Detroit's Fredro Theatre opened in 1913 and was intended solely for Polish-language productions. Several Yiddish theatres in New York and Detroit were built by Jewish impresarios as Yiddish playhouses.

Halls owned by social and civic organisations, such as Swedish American Hall in San Francisco[6] and Dania Hall in Minneapolis, often included spaces for theatrical performances. Countless German *Turnvereine* (gymnastic societies) and *Gesangvereine* (singing societies) maintained concert halls, theatres, or performance spaces (for example, Liederkranz Hall and Turn Hall in New York and Tivoli Turnhalle in Denver[7]). These were used by German and non-German organisations, both amateur and professional. Socialist halls (Finnish, German, Italian) were situated in various parts of the country and were leased to different socialist immigrant musical and theatrical groups.

Civic and town halls and courthouses also provided performance spaces. The Opera House in the Town Hall in the summer resort of Put-in-Bay, South Bass Island, Ohio (on Lake Erie) hosted performances by German professional players of German farces with songs in July 1900.[8] One of the earliest theatres in Los Angeles was located in the Los Angeles City Hall and Courthouse, erected in 1859, where in 1865 the Gerardo López del Castillo Company from Mexico performed operatic excerpts and Spanish musical theatre pieces.[9]

Roman Catholic 'national' (i.e. non-English-language) parishes often had halls that provided space for amateur and itinerant theatrical companies:

Franco-American in New England; Mexican-American in the Southwest; Polish-American in New York, Illinois and Michigan; and Italian-American in New York and New Jersey. Lydia Mendoza (1916–2007), the famous Texas-Mexican singer, appeared in such parish halls in the 1930s while on tour in South Texas with her family's stage act.

Performers and repertory

This was primarily a performer's theatre, and the star system that helped propel the English-language stage forward also existed on many non-English-language immigrant stages. At the same time, most of these theatres existed because of the core group of resident performers that formed the basis for their existence. The Yiddish, German, Italian, Chinese, Finnish, Swedish, Mexican and other stages all had their stars. While many leading actors and musicians visited from abroad (Austrian operetta superstar Marie Geistinger and Mexican *zarzuela* and operetta performer Esperanza Iris, for example), many of the principal performers of the ethnic stage resided in the US. Boris Thomashefsky, Jacob P. Adler, Bertha Kalich, Rudolf Schildkraut and Molly Picon played in the Yiddish theatres on New York's Bowery and Second Avenue, while Adolf Philipp, Rudolf Christians, Max Lube, Eugenie Schmitz and Bernhard Rank appeared in New York's German Irving Place and Germania Theatres. Romualdo Tirado, Rodolfo Hoyos and Beatriz Escalona were stars of the Mexican-American stage in Los Angeles and San Antonio.

Audience acceptance was crucial to the survival of ethnic musical theatre. These immigrant or transplanted stages did not receive outside or civic subsidies, except for the rare support of a few wealthy individuals such as piano manufacturer William Steinway, and restaurant owner August Luchow, who financially supported New York's Irving Place Theatre. (Both men were prominent members of the German-American business elite and were well-known throughout New York.) Audience patronage made performance possible and theatre-goers knew this. Because most individual ethnic communities usually supported one or just a few professional companies in any given city, there was often a limited audience base from which to draw – especially when compared with English-language theatre. The largest ethnic communities naturally had the largest number of theatres in any single city. This was especially true of the Yiddish theatres in New York, the Mexican venues in Los Angeles and San Antonio, and the German houses in New York and Chicago. Consequently, a repertory system that presented a quickly changing and varied theatrical bill of fare was established in almost all non-English-language theatres. One notable exception was the German-American musical comedies of Adolf Philipp, whose long runs lasted up to an entire season in one theatre (see below). A constant parade of plays, musical farces, musical comedies and operettas, as well as individual songs, comic sketches, dance numbers (including folk dances), instrumental solos, recitations and monologues appeared in many ethnic theatres, with performances often followed by balls or dances.

Three theatrical worlds – German, French, and Franco-American – serve to illustrate the common and divergent patterns related to the repertory of ethnic stages. The primary aspects of these three traditions are representative of almost all immigrant and transplanted stages: 1) the varied nature of the repertory; 2) the wide geographical spread of performance venues, though New York was the one city in which all ethnic theatres seem to have converged; 3) the tension between popular and high art forms; and 4) the importance of music in the theatrical experience.

Distinct differences existed between the Franco-American and French theatres in the United States. The former was primarily an amateur stage situated in parish, high school and town auditoriums in French-Canadian immigrant communities in New England (such as Holyoke, Worcester and Lawrence, Massachusetts; Manchester, New Hampshire; Lewiston, Maine; and Woonsocket, Rhode Island). Significant growth occurred over time. Between 1868 and 1870 there were seven dramatic circles, while eighteen groups functioned between 1870 and 1880. By around 1930 there were 150 active troupes.[10] As with other ethnic stages, this growth was due to the rise in immigration, in this case of French-Canadians. French drama dominated the repertory, but several favourite nineteenth-century comic operas were performed, including Charles Lecocq's *Giroflé, Giroflá* and Edmond Audran's *La Mascotte*. (The English-language farce *Charley's Aunt* was also popular in translation.) French companies from New York, Paris or Canada occasionally visited these Franco-American communities.

Professional French theatre existed in New Orleans, New York, Philadelphia and San Francisco, and touring companies took *opéra-bouffe* and French opera throughout the country in the nineteenth century. With the exception of some theatrical pieces written by Francophone playwrights in New Orleans, the French theatre focused primarily on European repertory: French opera and Italian opera in French translation, French plays (but few classic tragedies), French vaudeville (comic plays with songs, or what might be considered musical comedies), and *opéra-comique* and *opéra-bouffe* by Offenbach and his predecessors and contemporaries. The influence of French drama was also strongly felt on the Broadway stage, for many plays, farces and comic operas performed in English-language theatres were translations or adaptations of French originals.

The German theatre flourished throughout the country for about a century beginning in the late 1830s, with an interruption during World War I, until the mid-1930s, depending on location. As with all other immigrant stages, a strong amateur dramatic component was continually present, but unlike many other ethnic stages, the German-American theatre had assumed a fully professional existence as early as the 1850s. While the cities with the greatest amount of activity were New York, Milwaukee, Philadelphia, St Louis, and Chicago, most American cities had German theatre of some sort (see Table 2.1). From its very beginning, music was an integral component of this tradition.

While much of the repertory of operas, comic operas, operettas, musical comedies, *Possen* and *Volksstücke* with extensive music was imported from Germany and Austria, several German-American theatre composers and playwrights made significant contributions with original *Volksstücke* based on the immigrant experience in addition to new European-themed operettas. Chief among them was the actor-singer-composer-playwright-director-manager Adolf Philipp (1864–1936), author and star of numerous New York German-American *Volksstücke* (really musical comedies). His extensive work list includes such pieces as *Der Corner Grocer aus der Avenue A* (1893), *Der Pawnbroker von der Eastside* (1894), *Der New Yorker Brauer und seine Familie* (The New York Brewer and His Family, 1894), *Der Butcher aus der Erste Avenue* (The Butcher from First Avenue, 1895), *New York in Wort und Bild* (New York in Word and Picture, 1895), *New York bei Nacht* (New York at Night, 1896) and *Klein-Deutschland* (Little Germany, 1897). All of these works were performed in Philipp's own Germania Theatre (the third with this name) on 8th Street in New York's Lower East Side.[11] Another very important figure was composer-conductor Adolf Neuendorff (1843–97), manager of the first and second Germania Theatres in New York in the 1870s and 1880s, whose operetta *Die Rattenfänger von Hameln* (The Ratcatcher of Hameln, 1880) was very successful on both American and German stages. Neuendorff also wrote the German-language operettas *Don Quixote* (1882), *Prinz Waldmeister* (1887) and *Der Minstrel* (1892) expressly for performance in the United States, as well as the New York *Volksstück*, *Der Pawnbroker von Harlem* (1882).[12]

In addition to Philipp and Neuendorff, a succession of performer-manager-impresarios helped determine the direction of New York's German-American stage just as they did in other American (and German) cities. Those who were most active in New York included, in chronological birth order: Otto Hoym (1823–76), Gustav Amberg (1844–1921), Mathilde Cotrelly (1850–1933), Heinrich Conried (1855–1909), and Rudolf Christians (1869–1921). Each was exceptional in different ways and all had

Plate 3 Libretto cover from 'Klein-Deutschland' (Little Germany) (1897) by Adolf Philipp.

as their principal goal the encouragement of the German-American stage, though they varied considerably in their purposes and methods.

Composers and librettists (such as Philipp and Neuendorff) of German-American musical *Lokalstücke* (theatre pieces geared specifically to the German-speaking population) emphasised the centrality of popular song within the context of plays based on the immigrant experience. The tears shed by German-American theatre audiences in response to nostalgic or pathetic songs, or the hearty laughter in answer to comic or satirical songs, represented a tremendous release from the cares of a daily existence in an alien land, despite America's promise of freedom and worldly prosperity. Composers and playwrights used German humour, folklore and music in ways familiar to their audiences – but with New World references – in order to create a theatrical experience that was both meaningful to Klein Deutschland and profitable to artists and managers. The creators of this theatrical tradition took care to balance sentiment and harsh reality, achieving this especially through the medium of song. Once the trials of 'becoming' American were lessened over time, and even after German-Americans had moved away from the old neighbourhood in the Lower East Side of Manhattan, the first generations of immigrants returned to Klein Deutschland's stages to remember their youth and to instruct their children in the traditions of the homeland.

Another important European musical theatre repertory that was represented on the ethnic stage was the Savoy operas of Gilbert and Sullivan. The widespread popularity of these works spilled onto some non-English-language stages, though the brilliant wit of Gilbert's lyrics did not always come across as well in translation as in the original. Nevertheless, various theatrical groups produced G & S works. For example, the German company at the German-language Thalia Theatre on the Bowery in New York presented *The Mikado* in the 1880s,[13] the same decade in which *HMS Pinafore* was performed in Pennsylvania Dutch (Pennsylvania German) in Lancaster, Allentown, Bethlehem, Reading, Altoona, Scranton and other Pennsylvania cities.[14] Yiddish versions of *The Pirates of Penzance* (*Die Yom Bonditten*) and *HMS Pinafore* (*Der Shirtz* (The Apron)) were arranged in the 1950s for all-female casts.[15] The main characters in *The Pirates of Penzance* became Feivel (Frederic), Der Yom Bondit (The Pirate King), Zlotka (Ruth), Malke (Mabel), and Der General (Major General) in Yiddish. These 1950s Yiddish G & S productions provided the impetus in the 1980s for the creation of The Gilbert and Sullivan Yiddish Light Opera Company, based on Long Island, New York, which performs and has recorded *Der Yiddisher Pinafore*, *Der Yiddisher Mikado*, and *Di Yam Gazlonim* (Pirates of Penzance).[16] These Yiddish versions succeed because the plots have been changed to reflect Jewish sensibilities and humour instead of precisely following the original story or attempting to offer a literal translation of Gilbert's text, although the new lyrics have been fitted carefully to Sullivan's sparkling music.

Recordings

The large number of commercial recordings of musical works in a multitude of languages from America's myriad of immigrant communities, including many musical theatre songs, dates from the earliest days of the recording industry in the United States in the 1890s.[17] This aspect of the entertainment business is important to an understanding of how the music of the immigrant and transplanted stages was disseminated in the United States. In many cases, recordings provide some of the only available musical documentation of ethnic musical theatre in the United States.

Among the first non-English-language popular recordings were those by three Cuban-American singers: María Godoy (b. c. 1872) – one of the first ever to make Spanish-language recordings, if not the very first, c. 1896–7; baritone Emilio de Gogorza (1872–1949); and soprano Rosalía Chalía (1864–1948). Other recording artists from this era include Eugenia Ferrer (originally from San Francisco) and the now-unknown baritone Antonio Vargas and similarly now-obscure tenor Arturo Adamini.[18] These six singers collectively made many hundreds of recordings of Spanish-language songs (including numerous pieces from Spanish *zarzuela* and continental European operetta in Spanish translation) in addition to opera arias and duets at the turn of the twentieth century.[19] Following this initial Spanish-language theatrical and popular song recording activity (and the increase in recordings of Italian, French and German operatic excerpts after 1900), the major American recording companies (Victor, Columbia, Edison and later Brunswick and Vocalion, among others) pursued active programmes of recording ethnic music, including theatre songs. Though most ethnic groups present in the United States were represented by commercial recordings of their own musical repertories, the greatest number of recordings were made by and for those groups that had the largest populations. Many of these groups recorded their own theatre songs. The largest number of recordings by far was of Spanish-language musical repertories from Latin America, the Caribbean and Spain, as well as the United States' Latino populations. This was followed by German, Italian, Jewish (especially Yiddish) and Polish works. Richard K. Spottswood includes recordings by thirty-five non-English-language immigrant groups in his important discography of ethnic recordings made in the United States before World War II.[20]

The high point of this recording activity in terms of musical theatre, when singers recorded the songs they introduced on stage, coincided with the height of immigration during the early decades of the twentieth century. Major Yiddish theatre stars such as Boris Thomashefsky (c. 1868–1939), Molly Picon (1898–1992), Maurice Schwartz (1890–1960), Ludwig Satz (1891–1944), Bertha Kalich (1874–1939) and David Kessler (c. 1863–1920) are among those whose legacies are preserved in this fashion. One of the most notable was Molly Picon, whose recordings included Joseph Rumshisky's 'Yankele' (her signature song from the musical of the same name), 'Dus Zigainer Madel' (The Gypsy Girl) and 'Molly Dolly'. Among the Italian performers working in American recording studios in the early decades of the twentieth century was Eduardo Migliaccio (1882–1946), known as Farfariello, who recorded many comic or satirical songs and *macchiette* about the Italian-American experience between 1907 and 1935, for which he wrote most of the song lyrics and dialogue.[21] Others include the famous stage and film actress Mimi Aguglia (1884–1970), who sang periodically, and Giovanni de Rosalia (1864–1934), who recorded a large number of Sicilian-American sketches about his signature character of Nofrio and his comic encounters with modern American life.[22] Hjalmar Peterson (1886–1960), the Swedish peasant comedian with the straw-coloured wig and blackened-out front tooth, whose stage name was Olle I Skratthult (Olle from Laughtersville), often sang in his native Vårmland dialect, and appealed to both Swedish and Norwegian audiences in the United States.[23] His recording of the comic song 'Nikolina', a best-seller in the Scandinavian-American community, exudes a sense of theatricality in its tale of the young man who asks for the hand of Nikolina, only to have her father object so strongly that he thrashes the young man with his cane. Nikolina and her lover wait for her father's death so that they can be together and plant the cane on the father's grave in 'remembrance'.[24]

Somewhat strangely, especially given the large size of the German-American community, recordings of German musical theatre songs made in the United States are relatively rare in comparison to the large number of recordings of German, Swiss, and Austrian folk, ersatz-folk, and popular German songs. However, singer Ernest Balle recorded a number of German-American songs and song sketches, the titles of which reveal theatrical connections. Among these are 'Ein Reise nach der alten Heimat' (A Trip to the Old Country) and 'Die Ankunft der Grünhorner' (The Arrival of the Greenhorn). Seppel Burger recorded theatre songs by the famous German stage humorist Otto Reutter (1870–1931), whose songs and sketches (still well-known today in Germany) evoked and parodied turn-of-the-century German urban life. Some of the German members of the Metropolitan Opera recorded selections from the continental German operetta and operatic repertory, including Wagnerian bass Carl Braun (1886–1960) and baritones Otto Göritz (1873–1929) and Robert Leonhardt (1877–1923). Perhaps one reason why comparatively few recordings of German operetta and musical comedy songs from Berlin and Viennese stages were made in the United States is that the latest recordings of this repertory were imported directly from Europe. Also curious is the fact that relatively few recordings were made of German-American *Lokalstücke* (musical comedies with local American references), especially given the number of similar pieces recorded from the Yiddish, Italian-American, and Mexican-American traditions.

Spanish-speaking musicians, especially Mexican singers and instrumentalists, recorded a large number of theatrical works in the United States before World War II. During the 78-rpm era, a wide range of performing styles and theatrical genres was offered to the US's Latino, Latin-American and Spanish record-buying public. These included continental operettas in translation such as Franz Lehár's *El conde de Luxemburgo* (Der Graf von Luxemburg/The Count of Luxembourg) and Oscar Straus's *El soldado de chocolate* (Der Tapfere Soldat/The Chocolate Soldier),[25] songs from erotic or politically satirical Mexican *revistas* sung by María Conesa (?1892–1978) and recordings of the standard Spanish and (less commonly recorded) Mexican and Cuban *zarzuela*. Internationally known touring musicians such as director-composers Carlos Curti (1861–1926) and Miguel Lerdo de Tejada (1869–1941) in addition to singers Esperanza Iris (1884–1962) and Felipe Llera (1879–1924) made recordings of theatrical repertory.

Several examples illustrate the wide range of Spanish-language recording activity, especially of songs with theatrical connections, and the versatility of Mexican performers. Mexican-American baritone Rodolfo Hoyos (1896–1980), a long-time resident of Los Angeles, appeared in standard nineteenth-century Italian and French operas in the United States and Mexico, led a *zarzuela* troupe that toured throughout the United States, and hosted radio music programmes. He was as proficient in singing Mexican *corridos* and *huapangos* and other folk-style musical pieces as he was in performing the current theatrical songs and the romantic popular songs by important Mexican songwriters such as María Grever, Mario Talavera and Jorge del Moral. Hoyos also recorded Spanish-language versions of English-language popular songs in a crooning style, in addition to comic theatrical song sketches. His recordings were released by most of the major American record labels of the 78-rpm era (Victor, Columbia, Edison, Brunswick, Vocalion and OKeh).

Other Latin American performers recorded popular songs and sketches with a direct theatrical connection in the United States. Among the most important are the group Los Hermanos Areu (The Areu Brothers), who recorded 'Escándalos en la Cámara de Diputados y en las calles de la Ciudad de México' (Scandals in the Chamber of Deputies and in the Streets of Mexico City), and Beatriz Escalona (1903–79), known professionally as La Chata Noloesca,[26] who recorded 'Amores chicanos' (Chicano Loves), 'Mi compadre en Santa Anita' (My Godfather in Santa Anita) and 'Chismitos de vecindad' (Neighborhood Gossip) with Los Hermanos Areu. Recordings also survive of comic sketches by actor and director Romualdo Tirado (1880–1963).[27]

Throughout the first half of the twentieth century, the major American record companies strongly promoted ethnic popular and theatre music recordings. Following a hiatus during World War II, ethnic recording activity was resumed on a smaller scale, primarily within ethnic communities, as the major record labels seemed less interested than before in releasing this material.[28] Today, however, multinational corporations heavily promote popular music within certain ethnic communities, particularly the Spanish-speaking market.

Film musicals

For more than a decade, beginning in 1929, musical (and dramatic) films in languages such as Spanish, French and Yiddish were made in the United States for both American and foreign audiences. The greatest amount of activity occurred in the Cine Hispano, the Spanish-language film units of Hollywood studios (including MGM, Paramount, Fox, Universal, RKO, Columbia, Warner Brothers and some minor, short-lived companies), which released musical films featuring such well-known Mexican performers as operatic tenor José Mojica (1899–1974), singing actor Ramón Novarro (1899–1968) and popular tenor and actor Tito Guízar (1908–99). The Cine Hispano was followed in activity by the New York-centred Yiddish film industry.[29] To the 1930s theatre-going public, these musical films – based on stage pieces, English-language films or original ideas – enriched and in some cases supplanted live ethnic musical theatre.

Producer-directors such as Joseph Green (1900–96) and Edgar G. Ulmer (1904–72) directed major Yiddish theatre stars such as Molly Picon, Ludwig Satz, Leo Fuchs (1911–94) and Moishe Oysher (1907–58) in sentimental and comic musical films that had a strong appeal to the first and second generations of Yiddish speakers. As in the live immigrant musical theatre, English dialogue was increasingly inserted into Yiddish musical films, such as Ulmer's *Amerikaner Shadkhn* (American Matchmaker) of 1940, starring Fuchs and set in New York City. Filmed in 1936 on location in Poland and with an Old World setting, *Yidl mitn fidl* (Yiddle with a Fiddle), reportedly the greatest commercial success of the Yiddish film industry, stars Picon, who dresses as a boy to join a group of travelling musicians, thus providing the opportunity to incorporate numerous songs and instrumental pieces into the plot.

Two foreign national musical film traditions – German and Mexican – had an especially strong impact in the United States in immigrant communities. The continental German film mostly replaced live German-American theatre for German speakers in American urban areas by the mid-1930s, and film versions of romantic operettas such as Johann Strauss's *Der Zigeunerbaron* (The Gypsy Baron, 1935) and Karl Millöcker's *Gasparone* (1937) or musical films such as *Du bist mein Glück* (You Are My Happiness, 1936), starring Italian operatic tenor Beniamino Gigli, played in German motion picture houses in Manhattan's German Yorkville and elsewhere in the country up to World War II.[30]

Despite the general success of the Hollywood musical films made by Mojica and Guízar, the true lasting legacy of Spanish-language musical films for Spanish-speaking audiences in the United States relates to the history of the Golden Age of Mexican Cinema (1936–56), best represented by the singing *charro* (horseman) films of Jorge Negrete (1911–53) and Pedro Infante (1917–57), as well as by other Mexican musical films of this time. Negrete and Infante became the idols of Mexico and the Mexican community in the United States through their (separate) appearances in Mexican films. Negrete appeared in such films as *El fanfarrón* (The Braggart, 1938), *La valentina* (1938), *¡Ay Jalisco . . . no te rajes!* (Jalisco, Don't Back Down, 1941), and *Me he de comer esa tuna* (I Have to Eat That Prickly-Pear, 1944), which use contemporary urban popular songs, albeit often in rural settings, as well as folk material. In his film roles Negrete played characters similar to his own public persona (the *charro* character); consequently, the Mexican or Mexican-American public rarely saw the real man beneath the large *charro* hat. Infante, *ranchera* singer, pop icon, film actor and daredevil pilot, was the bad boy of Mexican popular culture in the 1940s and 1950s. He sang the *ranchera* songs he made famous in many of the more than sixty films in which he appeared, including *Jesusita en Chihuahua* (1942) – named after the famous polka of the same title – *Los tres García* (The Three Garcías, 1946), and the film biography of composer Juventino Rosas, *Sobre las olas* (Over the Waves, 1950). To many Mexicans, Infante represents *lo mexicano* (the Mexican spirit) and machismo.

Afterthought

Immigrants and their descendants maintained interest in the theatrical and musical impulses of their individual cultures. But from the earliest days of the American film industry, immigrants, like other Americans, eagerly attended the English-language cinema, which often provided them with insights into their new homeland, albeit viewed through the lens of a theatrical experience. From the early days of commercial radio, immigrant groups had their own musical programmes, but they also listened to English-language musical shows. For many immigrants today, television musical programmes, music videos and other forms of popular mass entertainment take the place of live musical theatre. While today numerous musical programmes are imported from Korea, China or Japan, many non-English-language television programmes are also produced in the United States. Thus the dichotomy between the immigrant and transplanted live theatre of an earlier age is mirrored in contemporary popular culture in many recent immigrant groups – Vietnamese, Indian, Filipino and others. Many of the issues faced by recent immigrant groups and their connections to and engagement with popular theatrical and musical culture are repeating processes that were experienced by earlier immigrant groups. The languages and homelands may change, but the principal themes of migration, cultural maintenance, conflict, assimilation and accommodation do not. These issues are as immediate and politicised today as they were fifty, a hundred, or a hundred and fifty years ago.

3 Birth pangs, growing pains and sibling rivalry: musical theatre in New York, 1900–1920

ORLY LEAH KRASNER

It has been a matter of regret with many music lovers that we have had so few really good comic operas during the past few years . . . the so-called comic opera stage has degenerated hopelessly of late.[1]

Critics in every generation lament the dearth of good material on the Broadway musical stage, but these lines, published in *Musical America* in 1906, do not actually sound the death-knell of a genre. The first two decades of the twentieth century were a period of great foment during which producers, performers, librettists and composers grappled with the notion of a single genre that could combine the best of all worlds into a unified, coherent whole. The problem of varied and inconsistent terminology, implied in the phrase 'so-called comic opera', was a legacy from the nineteenth century that continued to plague critics in the early decades of the twentieth. Musically well-educated writers often adopted a highbrow stance and treated anything lighter than opera with disdain while other critics, reviewing the same work, might praise it as a cut above similar fare. Composers in the dawning century struggled to reconcile their inheritance with the evolution of a new and uniquely American art-form: what we now blithely call the Broadway Musical. Several things had to happen in order to establish the book show as the norm. Librettists had to create plots that chimed with the rhythms and concerns of contemporary experience; this eventually caused a shift from the politically tinged satires of Gilbert and Sullivan and Offenbach to the sentimental romances of Herbert and Romberg. Composers had to discard or integrate remnants of hand-me-down imported musical vocabularies into a language that embraced American vernacular idioms in song and dance. 'Broadway' has always had room for multiple genres playing simultaneously – operetta and musical comedy, spectacle and revue, burlesque and vaudeville – although the specific characteristics, names, and relative audience support for each continues to shift.

The first tremors of change could be felt already in 1903 when a critic for the *New York Times* pointed out that 'the name of comic opera, as well as the thing itself, has fallen into disfavor'.[2] From the audience's vantage-point, however, the scene was hardly so dire. Gustav Luders' *The Prince of Pilsen* had its New York debut on 17 March 1903 and became a perennial favourite (in

London and Australia as well as in the United States). Victor Herbert's *Babes in Toyland* opened in the autumn and played 192 performances before its road tour began. Later that year Herbert's *Babette* and Reginald de Koven's *The Red Feather* opened within a week of each other; for several seasons these two composers had works running in competition. Comic opera was not dead yet, but it was indeed changing.

Vaudevillian roots

In 1904, George M. Cohan (1878–1942) toddled toward the future with *Little Johnny Jones*, the show that is often credited with being the first American musical. Its brisk plot was inspired by the recent adventures of Tod Sloane, an American jockey who rode in the English Derby. Cohan wrote the book, lyrics and music, and also played the title character; Ethel Levy, Cohan's wife, co-starred. Although he had played violin in the pit orchestra for his family's vaudeville act as a child, Cohan was essentially an untrained musician. His vaudevillian roots nourished him in ways that set him apart from his more classically tutored contemporaries. Fast-paced dialogue, streetwise humour and the vernacular slant of his lyrics approximated the ordinary speech of his audiences at a time when other Broadway writers, still in thrall to the poly-syllabic rhymes of W. S. Gilbert, often wrote grammatically awkward, inane texts filled with overblown imagery. Cohan's melodic writing was direct and uncomplicated; its simple harmonies and undemanding vocal ranges have made many of his over five hundred songs standards of the repertoire. Cohan wrote and occasionally starred in musical comedies until the 1920s when Jerome Kern would continue to cater to this new American taste.

Little Johnny Jones opened at the Liberty Theatre on 7 November 1904. Its first Broadway run lasted only fifty-two performances, but Cohan continued to tinker with it during its road tour. When he brought it back to New York the following year, it amassed over two hundred performances. The score contains two of Cohan's most unforgettable numbers: 'Give My Regards to Broadway' and 'The Yankee Doodle Boy'.

Cohan was not the only vaudevillian to make the transition to the legit-imate stage. In 1904, the famous partnership of Joseph Weber (1867–1942) and Lew Fields (1867–1941) disbanded. The pair had a long association both on stage and off. On stage, they were known as a Dutch-dialect duo whose sketches featured a thickly accented broad comedy. Off stage, they administered the Weber and Fields Music Hall. When their partnership dis-solved after nearly twenty years together, Weber continued to manage their theatre, mounting vaudevilles and burlesques. Fields hoped to move into a higher class of theatrical entertainment as a producer and actor.

Fields joined with producer Fred Hamlin and director Julian Mitchell to organise the Lew Fields Stock Company. Hamlin and Mitchell had been involved with two hits from 1903: *The Wizard of Oz* and *Babes in Toyland*. Mitchell's directorial career covered the full high–low spectrum from Herbert's comic opera *The Fortune Teller* starring Alice Nielsen, to Ziegfeld's *Papa's Wife*, to spectacle-revues such as *Hoity-Toity*, *Twirly-Whirly* and *Whoop-de-Doo* at the Weber and Fields Music Hall. To his new venture, Fields brought the knowledge that rapid pacing, topical references, catchy tunes, and visual splendour – both scenic and feminine – kept audiences engaged. Tired of his foreign-accented, low-comedy stage roles, Fields wanted to act in a vehicle that would 'reconcile the era's two most popular forms of stage entertainment, vaudeville and operetta'.[3] For the first production in the Lew Fields Theatre, under construction by Oscar Hammerstein, Fields hired the composer Victor Herbert.

Victor Herbert (1859–1924)

Dublin-born Victor Herbert always took great pride in his Irish heritage, even though he was brought up and educated in Germany. He began his musical career as an orchestral cellist in Stuttgart. In 1886, he and his wife, the soprano Therese Foerster, left for New York and their new positions with the Metropolitan Opera House, she on stage and he in the orchestra pit. Herbert readily joined New York's musical life as solo cellist, orchestral conductor and bandmaster; he began his Broadway career in the 1890s, and remained close to it for the rest of his life.

Although the plots of his shows are extremely diverse, they all share happy endings and stereotypical characters. Herbert is usually discussed as a composer of operettas, but the scores of his works, like those of his contemporaries, carry a variety of genre designations. Many of Herbert's best numbers, unlike Cohan's, lie beyond the technical capabilities of amateur performers; his rich, dense harmonies support melodies that demand a wide and flexible range. In spite of its homegrown popularity, surprisingly little of Herbert's substantial oeuvre travelled outside the United States. By comparison, *The Belle of New York*, a now-forgotten work by Gustave Kerker (1857–1923), became a West End hit – it played nearly seven hundred performances at the Shaftesbury – and did well on tour in Australia, Hungary, Germany, Austria and France. Herbert also composed two cello concertos, the film score (now lost) to *The Fall of a Nation*, and two operas, *Natoma* (1911, starring Mary Garden) and the one-act *Madeleine* (1914).

For his Lew Fields show, Herbert worked with Glen MacDonough (1870–1924), an association that had already produced *Babes in Toyland*. On

5 December 1905, the Lew Fields Theatre opened its doors for *It Happened in Nordland*; Cohan's *Little Johnny Jones* was playing half a block away.

It Happened in Nordland takes place in a fictitious Central European court. Queen Elsa, on the brink of an arranged marriage, has disappeared. Katherine Peepfogle (played by Marie Cahill), the new American diplomat, just happens to resemble the missing monarch. Katherine agrees to impersonate her and, as temporary queen, irons out the various wrinkles in the plot, one of which is the arrival of Katherine's long-lost brother, played by Lew Fields. Herbert's score, in addition to its lyrical waltzes, contained marches, ragtime and comic numbers (including a coon song routine) – enough stylistic variety to please any audience. The women were given plenty of opportunity to dance and look gorgeous in extravagant costumes.

Marie Cahill (1870–1933) could command star billing; her stage presence, similar to Marie Dressler's and May Irwin's, was plump, robust rather than pretty, and strong voiced – in essence, a 'coon shouter'. Backed by her husband and manager Daniel V. Arthur, Cahill insisted on diva treatment, which included the right to interpolate whatever material she chose. It was common at the time for stars to interpolate songs into a show, either to puff up the role or freshen a long-running vehicle. This was also a useful marketing trick since sheet-music covers could then tout in bold letters 'as sung by' so-and-so in such-and-such a production. However, at a time when composers were striving to create ever greater coherency between song, dance and book, such extraneous material was clearly detrimental. Herbert, who was active in the political fight to establish suitable copyright protection for music, usually included a no-interpolation clause in his contracts, but inexplicably neglected to do so in his new one with Hamlin, Mitchell and Fields. Conflict was inevitable. Cahill, who had no understudy, threatened to quit if management refused to acquiesce to her dialogue changes. Herbert, who was also the conductor, refused to include her demanded musical interpolations; in an initial compromise, Herbert handed over his baton to the musical director for any added numbers. Then Hamlin, the producer, died just before the New York premiere, delaying the opening by a few days. The fateful showdown occurred during the last New York performance before the summer road tour. Cahill presented Fields with an ultimatum: either she or Herbert would appear in Boston, but not both. Fields backed composer over star, and Cahill was replaced.

It Happened in Nordland was musically strong enough to hold up without a star on tour, but when it returned to Broadway for a second season (still alongside *Little Johnny Jones*), Fields signed Blanche Ring (1877–1961), another temperamental actress known for her interpolations. An ex-vaudevillian, Ring couldn't resist the habit of breaking character to address her fans from the stage. This was precisely the sort of behaviour that had driven Fields to leave vaudeville and he was not about to tolerate it from Ring. After another showdown, Ring quit, taking her costumes with her. A frantic call to the understudy ensued. When the curtain came up an hour later, a poised young Pauline Frederick – her three-octave soprano clearly superior to that of either of her predecessors – delivered a performance that (foreshadowing *42nd Street*) launched her on a sturdy career. In spite of all the backstage whoop-de-doo, *It Happened in Nordland* garnered 154 performances in New York before its summer tour and another hundred after its autumnal return.

Herbert then scored two successive hits with *Mlle Modiste* and *The Red Mill*, both with librettos by Henry Blossom (1866–1919). *Mlle Modiste* starred Fritzi Scheff in the role of the milliner Fifi. The Viennese-born Scheff (1879–1954) had trained as an opera singer and performed at the Metropolitan Opera House before decamping to Broadway where she first appeared in the title role of Herbert's *Babette* (1903). Herbert's score for *Mlle Modiste* included the waltz 'Kiss Me Again', part of Fifi's first act *tour de force* 'If I Were on the Stage', and the bass-baritone standard, 'I Want What I Want When I Want It'. Scheff's career had its ups and downs, but she remained identified with her early triumph; she reprised the role of Fifi at the age of fifty, in 1929.

The Red Mill was an instant success after its premiere at the Knickerbocker Theatre on 24 September 1906; after 274 performances in New York, it continued to do good business on tour. Blossom's libretto contained all the requisite features of comic opera, but integrated them into a scenario far better than most. Two penniless American tourists, the low-comedy pair Con Kidder and Kid Conner (played by Fred Stone and David Montgomery), arrive in the Dutch town Katwyk-ann-Zee where they lodge at an inn with a view of the old red mill. The innkeeper's daughter, Tina, is the soubrette. The Burgomaster (comic authority figure) refuses to let his daughter Gretchen (soprano) marry the man of her choice, Captain Doris Van Damm (tenor). They are ultimately united when it is revealed that the Captain is heir to a heretofore-undisclosed large fortune.

Herbert's score characterised the Americans Kid and Con by invoking popular ragtime rhythms in numbers such as the duet 'Good-a-bye, John!' and the quartet 'Go While the Goin' Is Good'. The plot complications allowed the pair to adopt various disguises, including Sherlock Holmes and Dr Watson, and Herbert gave them ample opportunity for stage business, such as the spirited, syncopated dance that concludes each of the three verses in the trio 'Whistle It'. *The Red Mill*, labelled a 'Musical Play in Two Acts', also contains some of Herbert's most enduring music, including 'Every Day Is Ladies' Day with Me' and the waltz 'The Streets of New York'.

Reginald de Koven (1859–1920)

Audiences who had already seen Herbert's newest works could compare them with plenty of others, including those by Reginald de Koven. For over a decade, Herbert and de Koven had works running simultaneously on Broadway. De Koven was born in Middletown, Connecticut, but was Oxford-educated and had studied music in Europe. A trio of English-inspired successes secured his reputation in the 1890s – *Robin Hood* (1891), *Rob Roy* (1894) and *The Highwayman* (1897), which was also the subject of a Weber and Fields burlesque, *The Wayhighman*. In addition to the roles of composer and conductor, de Koven was a music critic and socialite. His many press statements made explicit his aim to elevate and improve audience taste through his music. Unfortunately, de Koven was not always able to sugar-coat his pill. His theatrical output, like Herbert's, ran the gamut of genres, but he became increasingly uncomfortable catering to the musical demands at the lower end. De Koven's works after 1900 met with a varied reception, and at the end of his career, he composed two operas, *The Canterbury Pilgrims* (1917) and *Rip Van Winkle* (1920), in an attempt to reach audiences whose vision of the theatre matched his own.

De Koven's *Happyland*, set in the congenial kingdom of Elysia, ran concurrently with Herbert's *It Happened in Nordland* and Cohan's *Little Johnny Jones*. King Ecstaticus, played by De Wolf Hopper (1858–1935) – one of the preeminent comic actors of the day – is bored by excessive happiness, so he orders everyone to get married. The work, which was produced by the Shubert brothers, struggled to achieve its 136 performances.

The Student King, labelled a 'Romantic light opera', opened on Christmas Day, 1906 and played alongside *The Red Mill*. In Prague, at carnival time, Francis, a university student, is elected king for a day according to tradition. The Tyrolean princess Ilsa is promised to the real king, but while disguised as Anne, falls in love with Francis. All is resolved when, using a favourite Gilbert and Sullivan ploy, Francis is revealed as the King of Bohemia's long-lost son. A similar story, the bittersweet product of nostalgic Ruritania, would eventually become one of Sigmund Romberg's crowning achievements, but de Koven's *Student King* was deposed after forty performances. The rousing student songs and large male choral ensembles at the heart of *The Student King* were something of a novelty, but its plot devices were familiar and audiences perceived its massive choral writing as too operatic. The critic Rennold Wolf, writing in the *New York Telegraph*, suggested that perhaps this was the best that could be expected given the state of theatrical entertainments at the time.[4]

At this point in his career, de Koven may not have been the best that critics could expect from the theatre, but his works nevertheless exhibited a certain level of craftsmanship over uninspired material. Industry buzz and the word on the street, however, were beginning to hint at another imminent change. While Cohan's shows were establishing a taste for vigorous Americana, and de Koven and Herbert were making their first tenuous moves toward sentimental romances set in mythic European locales, continental operetta was on the brink of entering a second golden age. Just as imported operettas by Strauss and others transformed the American musical stage at the end of the nineteenth century, so, too, would these new imports revitalise it at the start of the twentieth.

The Merry Widow

On 30 December 1905, a Viennese audience at the Theater an der Wien attended the premiere of Franz Lehár's three-act operetta *Die lustige Witwe*.[5] Its libretto, written by Victor Léon and Leo Stein, was based on Henri Meilhac's four-act play, *L'attaché d'ambassade* (1861). The plot revolves around Hanna Glawari, a rich, young widow from Pontevedro – a transparent disguise for the Balkan Montenegro. Her countrymen fear that she will marry a foreigner while visiting Paris, thus withdrawing her millions from the national bank and bankrupting the country. The Pontevedran delegation to Paris hopes to convince her to remarry a loyal fellow countryman, Count Danilo, who prefers associating with Margot, Lolo, Dodo, Clo-Clo, Jou-Jou and Frou-Frou – the grisettes at Maxim's. The flirtation between an amorous Frenchman and the 'highly respectable wife' of the Pontevedran ambassador provides a comic foil for the relationship between Danilo and Hanna.

Lehár exploited pseudo-Balkan, Parisian and Viennese colour for his score. Act 2, for example, opens with a Pontevedran dance, followed by 'Vilja' – a counterfeit folk tale from the widow's homeland. Danilo's number in praise of Maxim's captures the sparkle of Parisian nightlife. Most importantly there are the waltzes, which achieve a new prominence by assuming a psychological importance in portraying romance and sexual tension.[6] They are no longer just vocal numbers in triple metre labelled 'à la valse' – these waltzes are meant to be danced as well as sung, thus raising the choreography above mere spectacle and integrating dance into the book. At a remove of nearly a century, Lehár's masterpiece may seem sentimental and nostalgic. In its day, it was daring and risqué.

By the end of the 1906–7 season, *Die lustige Witwe* was all the rage throughout the German-speaking theatrical world. Having seen the work during its first few months in Vienna, English-speaking impresarios made immediate plans to transport it. The translation by Basil Hood and with lyrics by Adrian Ross remained, for its day, remarkably faithful to the original. In its transformation from 'Witwe' to 'Widow', the locale was changed from Pontevedro to the equally fictional Marsovia, and some of the characters' names were altered, most notably Hanna to Sonia, Njegus to Nisch, and Baron Mirko Zeta to Popoff. Lehár's score was left virtually intact. When *The Merry Widow* opened at London's Daly Theatre on 8 June 1907, no one anticipated that it would run for an unprecedented 778 performances; King Edward VII himself attended four of them.

On 21 October 1907, *The Merry Widow* finally waltzed into Broadway's New Amsterdam Theatre. Although the Marsovian millions were nightly made safe, real-life finances were precarious. Within days of the premiere, the Knickerbocker Trust Company closed its doors, precipitating a wave of bank closures. It was the third financial panic in fourteen years. But it was not the only hysteria sweeping the nation. 'Merry Widow Madness' had also begun.[7]

Savvy entrepreneurs quickly applied the words 'Merry Widow' to a wide range of products as a marketing gimmick. In particular, Ethel Jackson's broad-brimmed, feather-trimmed hat created a fashion furore. The *Oxford English Dictionary* credits the earliest written use of the phrase 'Merry Widow hat' to July 1908, but spoken usage would have likely predated the written.[8] Within months of the New York premiere, vendors peddled readily available sheet music on street corners for a nickel a copy.[9] Several touring companies further disseminated its waltzes throughout the country, and there were even competitions for the best Sonia–Danilo couple.[10] The ensuing social-dance craze would soon open the door for Vernon and Irene Castle, and later Fred and Adele Astaire, who were then children dancing in vaudeville.

As part of the hype preceding *The Merry Widow*'s arrival in New York, *Musical America* quoted an excerpt from the London *Daily Graphic* in which an unidentified critic declared that 'Musical comedy being dead, . . . and comic opera not yet resuscitated, [. . . *The Merry Widow* is] something between the two and partaking of the character of both'.[11] Terminological indecision was not unique to the American side of the Atlantic. What is particularly important here, however, is the shared perception of a moribund genre on the brink of revivification.

The New York reviews of Lehár's operetta were unanimously laudatory, but they also show distinct differences in tone. The extensive, but unsigned, opening night review in the *New York Sun* was probably written by W. J. Henderson (1855–1937), the musically literate, Princeton-educated son of a theatrical manager. He predicted that *The Merry Widow*

> will undoubtedly remain in West Forty-second street for many a long day to gladden the spirits of a town which has been bored to death with lamentable rot and debasing rubbish wearing the outward guise of 'comic opera'. . . .
>
> Although it has been run through the sieve of honorable British censorship, all the bewitching diablerie of this operetta has not been

Plate 4 Editorial cartoon concerning the popularity of *The Merry Widow* from *The Evening American*, 1909.

eliminated, for the London book carpenter has done no serious wrong to the essentially Austrian comedy and the music of Franz Lehár remains intact. The story is excellent comedy and there are scenes and incidents calling for the exhibition of genuine acting ability instead of for acrobatic buffoonery on the American plan. This is a great joy.

Henderson also rhapsodised about the 'expression' of the dances, particularly 'the irresistible seduction of the Viennese waltz, the dance of dances, that steals men's souls out by way of their toes'.[12]

The uncredited review in the *New York Times* was probably penned by Richard Aldrich (1863–1937), a Harvard graduate who had studied music with John Knowles Paine. Under the headline '"The Merry Widow" Proves Captivating', Aldrich wrote that Ethel Jackson 'comprehends the verve and joy of the part, as well as its seductiveness. She makes the waltz the dramatic moment in the action, as it should be'.[13]

The curmudgeonly critic for the *New York Tribune*, however, was the noted champion of Wagner, Henry E. Krehbiel (1854–1923). His review, which appears between two columns of obituaries, is sedately headed 'Music. "The Merry Widow"'. With measured enthusiasm, Krehbiel proclaimed: 'At length a real operetta, one that does not filch the appellation, but fits it and fills it and does it credit.' He did not mention the work's seductiveness, but commented twice on its lack of vulgarity. As for the waltz, he conceded that it 'takes on the color of emotionality in the climax of the dramatic situation'.[14]

Perhaps the most patrician stance was taken by the *Musical Courier*. Unlike *Musical America*, it adopted the attitude of its cultivated readership, and there were neither preliminary publicity notices for *The Merry Widow* nor a formal review. On 30 October 1907, however, an item about Lehár with no headline was buried on page 22.

> 'The Merry Widow' … by the way, in the first week of her visit to New York has danced herself deeply into the affections of the metropolitan public and bids fair to be welcome here for an unbroken run of two seasons at least … It is admitted on every side that Lehár is not a genius like Strauss, Offenbach, Genée, Lecoq, Sullivan, Milloecker, etc., but nevertheless 'The Merry Widow' has been performed thousands of times everywhere in Europe. With no wish to detract in the slightest degree from the great charm of Lehár's popular work, nevertheless that great popularity demonstrates how poor was most of the light opera stuff which our transatlantic cousins had been getting – and exporting to us – for the past decade or so. Up to date, Lehár has made over $250,000 in royalties, which places him in the record ranks, together with the composers of 'Robin Hood' and 'The Belle of New York'.[15]

These other two record-holding composers were the German-born Gustave Kerker whose *The Belle of New York* opened in 1897, and Reginald de Koven.

Having recently rejoined the staff of the *New York World*, de Koven attended the premiere of *The Merry Widow* and wrote that

> The dramatic purpose and coherency, the artistic sincerity . . . shown in
> 'The Merry Widow' last night, came like water in the desert after the tawdry
> musical inanities which have pervaded and infested Broadway for some years
> . . . [B]ook and music are welded together into an organic, artistic whole, and it
> is this artistic unity in purpose and dramatic treatment that is the controlling
> factor in the success which the opera has obtained the world over.[16]

His praise hardly seems self-interested, especially when Victor Herbert seconded this idea of renewal. *Musical America,* on 26 October 1907, ran a bold front-page headline: 'American Public's Taste Is Improved'. Printed in slightly smaller type beneath it was: 'Victor Herbert Sees Good Signs in Success of "The Merry Widow" in New York.'[17]

Contemporary writers implied that Lehár's *Merry Widow* was raising audience standards when, in fact, they were only indulging America's historically conferred inferiority complex toward native creativity. Critics had for years been insinuating that American composers should strive to unify book and score into coherent structures that subjugated comedic elements to romance. The immediate popularity of *The Merry Widow* affirmed and validated these indigenous efforts. American operettas composed after Lehár's New York triumph were not substantially different from those that preceded it, but their creators gained cachet from the association. Just as the operettas of Strauss, and Gilbert and Sullivan, had invigorated the musical stage at the end of the nineteenth century by creating a touchstone against which American works might be judged, so too *The Merry Widow* revitalised American operetta by reinstating a foreign standard. Perhaps the best testament of *The Merry Widow*'s popularity were the burlesques that opened in its wake.

Burlesque

Burlesques, with their emphasis on broad comedy, are generally considered lowbrow works, but even if there were clear distinctions along the continuum of genres, no such divisions can be made among audiences. A parody is funniest, and therefore most successful, in direct proportion to the audience's familiarity with the original being spoofed. Less than three months after *The Merry Widow* first appeared in New York, Lew Fields's former partner brought *The Merry Widow and the Devil* into Weber's Music Hall (2 January 1908). It lasted 156 performances and worked from a new script by the prolific George V. Hobart (1867–1926); the Lehár score was used by permission of Henry Savage.[18] Joe Weber appeared as Disch, the embassy's janitor, while Fonia was played by Lulu Glaser (1874–1958), best known for her starring role in Julian Edwards's *Dolly Varden* (1902). (Glaser eventually ceded the role of Fonia to Blanche Ring.) Charlie Ross as Prince Dandilo 'contributed at moments a touch not of burlesque but of imitation, raising now and then his songs into the atmosphere of the real "Merry Widow"'.[19] The critic Acton Davies referred to Ross's performance as 'legitimate – in fact, it was too legitimate. That was the trouble with certain scenes of the whole performance.'[20]

This apparent blurring of boundaries between burlesque and legitimate product bothered critics. Hazy nomenclature was not limited to works at the highbrow end of the spectrum.

> A burlesque this transplanted 'Merry Widow' can hardly be called, because there never was a musical comedy yet serious enough to offer the contrast needed for real burlesque. You can burlesque grand opera – or Victor Herbert can if you can't, but not operetta.[21]

Herbert did, in fact, have experience in this arena. A few years earlier, Herbert had written a two-in-one entertainment for Joe Weber called *Dream City* and *The Magic Knight* (25 December 1906). The first half was a hilarious two-act operetta; *The Magic Knight* parodies Wagner's *Lohengrin*. Jealous, perhaps, of his former partner's success with *It Happened in Nordland*, 'Weber waxed desirous of purveying a show of higher class. Who but Herbert should supply the necessary music?'[22] With 102 performances, *Dream City* and *The Magic Knight* lasted as long as or longer than many 'legitimate' works.

Operetta after *The Merry Widow*

According to Charles Hamm,

> The immense popularity of European operetta resulted from its appeal to a number of different groups: recent immigrants from Europe and first- or second-generation Americans enjoying a fairytale view of their ancestral culture; the upwardly mobile, who wished to associate themselves with a more sophisticated form of musical theatre than the minstrel show or vaudeville, but were unwilling or unable to derive pleasure from opera in foreign languages; and the urban middle class who responded to effective and well-crafted stage pieces produced by talented writers and composers.[23]

Tempted by the profitability of *The Merry Widow*, American producers imported more than twenty-five different operettas from Vienna and Berlin over the next decade. These often came by way of London, including Leo Fall's *The Dollar Princess* (1909), Oscar Straus's *The Chocolate Soldier* (1909) and Lehár's *The Count of Luxembourg* (1912). New American works continued to compete with the imports, and several of Herbert's later works have become repertory staples of today's light opera companies. *Naughty Marietta* (1910), for example, starred the Italian prima donna Emma Trentini (1878–1959). Composing for singers of operatic calibre led Herbert to create many of his finest numbers for this score, including the marching-song 'Tramp! Tramp! Tramp!', the waltz 'I'm Falling In Love With Someone', 'Italian Street Song', and the dreamy duet 'Ah! Sweet Mystery of Life'. In spite of its triumphant Broadway run, *Naughty Marietta* remained virtually unknown outside America until Jeanette MacDonald and Nelson Eddy's 1935 film version popularised it abroad. Herbert's 1913 *Sweethearts* had a silly plot reminiscent of the Savoy shows, but it did uniformly well on Broadway, on the road and in revivals; it, too, became an Eddy–MacDonald film.

The imminent upheavals of World War I prompted several European composers to emigrate to the United States, most notably Sigmund Romberg (1887–1954) and Rudolf Friml (1879–1972), both of whom continued to write operettas in the new world. Friml's first American work was *The Firefly* (1912), designed as a second vehicle for Emma Trentini. Arthur Hammerstein had offered Otto Harbach's book to Victor Herbert, but when Herbert declined to work again with the temperamental Trentini, the task fell to Friml. *The Firefly* ran for 120 performances on Broadway and was produced throughout the United States; its substantial coverage in recording and radio ensured the composer's reputation in his new country. (Trentini was ultimately less fortunate. Having started her career in opera, she eventually worked her way down to vaudeville. In 1919, she appeared in the London revue *Whirlygig* and eventually retired to oblivion in her native land.)

At one and the same time, Lehár's *Merry Widow* crystallised two opposing trends. Producers who once used skeletal plots as a framework on which to hang hit songs, revealing costumes and dazzling effects, either moved toward better integrated, symbiotic relationships or unabashedly accepted the flimsiest scenario as a pretext for seductive scenery. Furthermore, with anti-German sentiment on the rise because of the war, many potentially profitable European works needed to have their books cooked into a dish more palatable to current American taste. Several talented youngsters served their apprenticeship in this kitchen alongside their more established peers.

Follies and *Scandals*

Florenz Ziegfeld Jr (1867–1932) epitomised all that was luxurious and alluring on Broadway. His near-mythic career began with musical productions showcasing his bride, the petite Polish-born, French-bred Anna Held

(1873–1918). Several of Ziegfeld's early confections for her were adaptations of French works, such as *Papa's Wife* – an amalgam of Hervé's *La Femme à Papa* and *Mam'zelle Nitouche*. The composite *Papa's Wife* was nominally the work of Reginald de Koven (interpolations were plentiful!) and his long-time librettist Harry B. Smith (1861–1936), whose librettos served virtually every composer of the era, including Herbert, Kerker, Julian Edwards, Ludwig Engländer, Jerome Kern, Irving Berlin and Sigmund Romberg. *Papa's Wife* opened on 13 November 1899 and ran for 147 performances. Several of de Koven's numbers were topical songs using novelty to good theatrical advantage, such as 'The Automobile Song' celebrating the imported French vehicle in which Miss Held made her sensational entrance. Another opulent production used the same creative team to remake the French *Niniche*, and *The Little Duchess* opened in New York on 14 October 1901 using its music to halo wasp-waisted women in chic couture. The score suffered so many successive interpolations that a programme for a performance a year after the opening warned audiences that due 'to the length of the performance the plot has been eliminated'.

In July 1907, Ziegfeld launched the first of a series of summertime diversions. The *Follies of 1907* boasted a bevy of 'Anna Held Girls' whose presence was supported by Harry B. Smith's book, Julian Mitchell's direction, and the financial clout of Klaw and Erlanger, the powerful and generally disliked Broadway producer syndicate. Over the next twenty years, Ziegfeld refined his presentation of feminine pulchritude, parading an average of sixty belles in each revue. He also had an eye for talent, and many legendary figures – Fanny Brice (1891–1951), Eddie Cantor (1892–1964), W. C. Fields (1879–1946) and Ed Wynn (1886–1966), among others – had their start under Ziegfeld's aegis. The 1910 edition, for example, featured three notable *Follies* first-timers who exemplify the ethnic humour endemic to the genre. Fanny Brice rendered Irving Berlin's unpublished (and now lost) Yiddish novelty song 'Good-Bye Becky Cohen'. More importantly perhaps, Ziegfeld was willing to break the colour barrier for the sake of his show, and *The Follies of 1910* highlighted the black comedian Bert Williams (1874–1922), formerly part of a minstrel team with George Walker (d. 1911).

Ziegfeld's formula consisted of balancing comedy and songs with gorgeous girls in lavish and revealing costumes. As the popular ideal of feminine beauty shifted, partly in response to new celluloid images, Ziegfeld's girls grew slimmer, their skirts shorter and their skin barer – even to the point of allowing bare midriffs. In 1915, the striking art deco set designs of Joseph Urban upgraded the look of the shows and added a new dimension to their spectacular nature. It was also the year of W. C. Fields's *Follies* debut, and he would continue to appear in them until 1921. Ziegfeld produced his *Follies* until 1927, but not without competition from other regular series of revues.

From 1912 to 1924, the influential Shubert brothers produced an annual series of *Passing Shows* that rarely surpassed Ziegfeld in either extravagance or artistry (even though their dance roster included Fred and Adele Astaire). The *George White Scandals* appeared regularly from 1919 to 1927, and sporadically thereafter until the final *Scandals 1939–40*. George White, a vaudeville dancer as a child, had partnered Ann Pennington in several *Follies* dance routines. If Ziegfeld's series exemplified pre-war elegance and expansiveness, then White's *Scandals* harnessed the streamlined energy of the roaring twenties. White was attuned to the subtle changes in the post-*Merry Widow* dance craze from the refined tango and maxixe to quick-stepping dances with gimmicky names like the turkey trot or grizzly bear. He envisioned a fast-paced show with harder colours (instead of nostalgic pastels) and edgier topical skits – a leaner post-war style suited to the age of Prohibition, gangsters and jazz. George Gershwin (1898–1937) composed the music for five of White's annuals, 1920–4, which included pop standards like 'I'll Build a Stairway to Paradise' and 'Somebody Loves Me'.

Irving Berlin (1888–1989)

Establishing one's reputation as a songwriter was an important first step toward a life in the theatre, and Irving Berlin was no exception. Berlin's early career consisted of interpolating songs – often ethnic novelty numbers – into the likes of Weber and Fields shows and Ziegfeld *Follies*. 'Alexander's Ragtime Band', published in 1911, first brought him worldwide fame. Its popularity sealed the rhythms of ragtime into the American imagination, and Berlin used this to good advantage in his first full Broadway score, *Watch Your Step*. Any weaknesses of plot were overshadowed by the fact that this was the first full-length book musical to have a score written entirely in the style of syncopated dance music.[24] *Watch Your Step* starred Vernon and Irene Castle, and was produced by C. B. Dillingham (1868–1934). It ran for 175 performances after opening on 8 December 1914 at the New Amsterdam Theatre and had a successful London run as well.

A sidelight of Berlin's early years was the 1916 revue *The Century Girl*, jointly produced by Dillingham and Ziegfeld. On the principle that two would be better than one, they asked the twenty-eight-year-old Berlin to share the score with the considerably more senior Victor Herbert. In no way a collaboration, each composer worked independently, and a star-studded cast brought the whole to life against a dazzling set by Joseph Urban that included the trademark Ziegfeld staircase. A year later, Dillingham and Ziegfeld asked Herbert and Jerome Kern to team up with Bolton and Wodehouse for *Miss 1917*, a successor to *The Century Girl*. In spite of rave reviews for a cast that included Lew Fields and Irene Castle, and sets by Urban, *Miss 1917* folded after six weeks.

Given the length of his career, the number of song standards emanating from Berlin's pen should hardly be surprising; several of them date from these early years. The short-lived army vaudeville *Yip, Yip, Yaphank* (1918) included a *Follies* burlesque and left posterity the song 'Oh, How I Hate to Get Up in the Morning'. 'A Pretty Girl Is Like a Melody' aptly hails from the *Ziegfeld Follies of 1919*.

In 1921, Berlin joined forces with the producer Sam H. Harris (1872–1941) who had recently ended his long alliance with George M. Cohan. Harris had produced *Little Johnny Jones* and many of Cohan's later pieces, including *The Little Millionaire* (1911), and the 1912 revival of *Forty-Five Minutes from Broadway* (1906). The new partnership resulted in the Music Box Theatre, an intimate playhouse smaller than the venues currently housing the *Follies*, *Scandals* or *Passing Shows*. Although there were only four editions of the *Music Box Revues*, starting in the 1921–2 season, Gerald Bordman refered to them as 'forty-carat flawless gems of the revue form'.[25] *The Music Box Revue of 1923–1924* included the song 'What'll I Do?'.

Jerome Kern (1885–1945)

A similarly jewel-like venue also featured prominently in the early career of Jerome Kern. Kern had a thorough Tin Pan Alley apprenticeship as a shipping clerk, song plugger and rehearsal pianist. He spent several years working in London, and, like Berlin, was one of Broadway's busiest interpolators before becoming a successful composer in his own right. Many of his incidental songs found their way into European operettas revamped for the London or Broadway stage, including Emmerich Kálmán's *The Gay Hussars* (1909) and Leo Fall's *The Dollar Princess* (1909). Kern's first billing as a show's principal composer (along with Frank Tours) was *La Belle Paree* which inaugurated the Shubert's Winter Garden Theatre on 20 March 1911. The show ran for 104 performances, largely on the strength of its debut performer, Al Jolson (1886–1950).

The year 1915 was a busy and decisive one in Kern's career since it marks his first joint effort with Guy Bolton (1884–1979). Along with lyricist Harry B. Smith, the three wrote *Ninety in the Shade*, which starred Marie Cahill in what would be her last Broadway role. The show was mounted by Daniel V. Arthur, Cahill's husband and sole producer ever since her unfortunate earlier contretemps with Victor Herbert. Although *Ninety in the Shade* quickly folded (driving the Arthurs into bankruptcy and Marie back to vaudeville), Kern salvaged most of his best numbers for later reuse, often as interpolations into his own or others' shows. Bolton became one of his most important collaborators, and with the fortuitous addition of P. G. Wodehouse (1881–1975) as lyricist, the trio was poised to rescue and redeem Broadway's smallest theatre.

The Princess Theatre was built at the edge of the theatre district in 1912 with a seating capacity of 299. When the one-act plays by up-and-coming new dramatists for which the house was originally intended failed to attract enough attention, management called in Elisabeth Marbury, the respected theatrical agent, for advice. She suggested musicals. What followed would be a series of shows synthesising the sophistication of European operetta with the pacing and verve of Cohan's American musical style.

The 'Princess Shows' offered audiences a theatrical experience the polar opposite of what Ziegfeld, Dillingham or White presented. The tiny house provided an intimate setting for a necessarily elitist gathering since it had limited inexpensive balcony seating. The orchestra held fewer than a dozen players and the stage not many more. Bolton's stories relied on situational humour; audiences laughed not at the mistaken identities of the characters, but rather at the mistaken relationships between them – familiar upper-middle-class figures caught in everyday situations gone awry. Wodehouse's lyrics captured the flow of natural speech while still turning a neat phrase or inventive rhyme, and they allowed the characters such scope for change as is practicable within the genre. Kern suffused the whole with musical warmth, wit and panache.

The success of works like *Oh, Boy!* (1917), which ran for 463 perfor-mances, left Kern with ample time to compose songs for other projects, including the revamping of another import. Klaw and Erlanger produced *The Riviera Girl* in 1917, an adaptation of Kálmán's *Die Czárdásfürstin* by Bolton and Wodehouse with additional music by Jerome Kern. It closed after seventy-eight performances. European operetta, in the decade before the war, spurred both action and reaction in American creativity but was slowly losing sway to the native product as the war drew to a close.

One work crowns Kern's career before *Show Boat*, bringing together the most important names of its time. *Sally* is essentially a Cinderella story of an orphaned dishwasher turned *Follies* star. Bolton wrote the book; Wode-house was one of four lyricists. The score, including 'Look For the Silver Lining', was Kern's, but Victor Herbert contributed 'The Butterfly Ballet'. Ziegfeld dictated the production values and *Sally* featured Marilyn Miller who had starred in his *Follies of 1918* and *1919* (and, after his divorce from Anna Held, in his heart, too). *Sally* became one of the longest-running and highest-grossing shows of its day after 570 Broadway performances, 387 performances at the Winter Garden in London, substantial road tours in the United States and Australia, and several Hollywood film versions.

Conclusion

If the critics are to be believed, Broadway at the threshold of the twentieth century provided yet one more example of Dickens's 'best and worst of times'. At the distance of a century, musical theatre has proved to be a hardy organism. Some fruits withered on the vine, others were cross-pollinated, grew new roots and scattered the seeds that are flourishing today. If vaudeville has slipped into the realm of late-night television, burlesques can be found in *Forbidden Broadway*. Follies à la Ziegfeld may not be politically correct in today's society, but revues flourish in works like *Riverdance*, *Smokey Joe's Café* and *Mamma Mia!*, not to mention seasonal extravaganzas like the Radio City Music Hall Christmas shows. Contemporary production values take full advantage of modern technology to dazzle audiences with more and more spectacular effects. Using the 'Merry Widow' to sell hats and cocktails is not all that dissimilar to the logos of today like the *Cats* eye and the *Phantom*'s demi-mask. Shows travel in both directions across the Atlantic, and 'Broadway' no longer seems limited to New York. Composers and choreographers continue to adapt their styles to the current vernacular of their audiences, exploring rock and roll, Latin, and increasingly, non-western idioms (*Bombay Dreams*). With *Sweeney Todd* just as likely to show up in the opera house, writers continue to deliberate over the parameters of the genre while critics wonder pessimistically if this is as good as it gets. In the final analysis, however, these are all secondary considerations. Audiences know what they like.

4 American and British operetta in the 1920s: romance, nostalgia and adventure

WILLIAM A. EVERETT

Operettas from the 1920s, the titles, music and lyrics of which evoke romantic images of times and places far away, enjoy a continued popularity that stems directly from their very nature of being 'old-fashioned'. Shows such as *The Student Prince*, *Rose Marie* and *Bitter Sweet* are as nostalgic in the early twenty-first century as they were at the time of their creation. Their inherent sense of sentiment and escapism, deeply rooted in romantic innocence, has been both their ultimate blessing and paramount curse. But many of these works, including *The Desert Song*, *The Three Musketeers* and *The New Moon*, are also filled with adventure and swashbuckling heroes who achieve victory over some sort of political tyranny or oppression while still managing to find time to fall in love.

In nineteenth- and early twentieth-century Vienna, operetta was envisaged as a popular form of entertainment set in some sort of fictionalised Ruritania – a Central European (usually Balkan) domain with nobles and peasants suspended in an eternal nineteenth century. Even the name 'Ruritania', the setting of Anthony Hope's 1894 novel *The Prisoner of Zenda*, evokes a sense of familiar exoticism.[1] Audiences adored such entertainments with plots in which characters interacted with each other in humorous and amorous ways while dressed in fanciful costumes amidst lavish sets. The action took place against a glorious musical score replete with waltzes, marches and tour-de-force solos and duets.

This stylised version of Viennese operetta found tremendous favour with American audiences in the early years of the twentieth century, and nothing could match the success of Franz Lehár's *The Merry Widow* when its English-language version waltzed into New York in 1907.[2] Following on the heels of *The Merry Widow* were numerous shows hoping to achieve success in its wake: Oscar Straus's *A Waltz Dream* (1908) and *The Chocolate Soldier* (1909), Paul Rubens' *The Balkan Princess* (1911) – a London import – and Felix Albini's *Baron Trenck* (1912), to name but a few.

With World War I, as would be expected, fondness for Central European operetta fell dramatically among English-speaking audiences, who did not want to visit mythical Balkan kingdoms with overt German overtones in their theatrical escapements. It would take time for audiences to desire a return to Ruritania, and when they did, it could not be to its pre-war archetypes. Operetta had to be redefined on several levels if it was going to survive.

The influence of Tin Pan Alley and other forms of musical theatrical entertainments provided the catalyst through which such necessary transformations could take place. In New York, the immigrant composers Rudolf Friml (1879–1972) and Sigmund Romberg (1887–1951) emerged as the leading creators of operetta during the 1920s. The success of the genre during this decade (and beyond, in various manifestations) was astounding. Of the eleven longest-running musicals of the 1920s, six of them – just over half – were operettas by either Romberg or Friml.[3] Post-war audiences craved the escapist nature of the operetta. In many ways the works represented the opulence of the era – wealth and splendour were clearly evident. This was the Gilded Age of F. Scott Fitzgerald's *The Great Gatsby* – a time when people had money and were travelling to Europe in great numbers. Here was a type of theatrical entertainment filled with characters of affluence, many of whom were European.

The escapist nature of the genre was an integral part of its appeal. While musical comedies centred on contemporary characters (almost always New Yorkers) in comic situations, operettas by definition needed to take place in some remote time and/or place. Since Ruritania and Germany were no longer satisfactory sites, other locales had to be discovered, and the decade's fascination with exoticism, in terms of both Orientalism and Native Americans, provided the solution to the dilemma. New worlds could be created through a judicious combination of plot, costumes and of course music.

Friml and Romberg: transforming operetta

Rudolf Friml, born in Prague, studied piano with Josef Jiranek and composition with Antonín Dvořák at the Prague Conservatory before moving to the US and settling in New York in 1906. Desiring to be a romantic virtuoso in the spirit of Chopin or Liszt, he achieved fame as a soloist and composer of miniature works for solo piano. In 1912 Friml benefited greatly from Victor Herbert's last-minute decision to break his contract to write *The Firefly*. This came after Herbert stormed off the podium during a performance of *Naughty Marietta* when the leading lady, Emma Trentini, demanded an encore and the conductor-composer refused. Herbert vowed never again to work with the diminutive soprano, and since *The Firefly* was to be a vehicle for her, producer Arthur Hammerstein suddenly found himself needing to find a new composer. His gamble on the young Czech proved successful, and Friml had a major star appearing in his first Broadway score.

The Firefly, with book and lyrics by Otto Hauerbach (who later changed his name to Otto Harbach) concerns an Italian street singer in New York who disguises herself as a cabin boy on board a ship bound for Bermuda in order to be with the man she loves. The score featured coloratura numbers for Trentini such as 'Gianina Mia' and 'Love Is Like a Firefly', but the show's resounding hit was a waltz for the secondary leads, 'Sympathy'.

Friml continued to write moderately successful shows during the teens, including the farce *High Jinks* (1913), set in a French spa where the resident physician prescribes an opiate-filled perfume for his clients, and the musically eclectic *Katinka* (1915), a complex tale of mistaken identities with Viennese, Arabian and American characters. *Katinka* included the popular 'Allah's Holiday', whose largely pentatonic melody gives it an Orientalist flavour.

Though often paired together, Friml and Romberg had substantially different beginnings and early careers. Whereas Friml grew up in a poor Catholic family and had formal Conservatory training, Romberg came from a relatively well-to-do Jewish family and lacked an advanced formal musical education. Romberg, born in Nagykanizsa, Hungary, spent his youth in Belišće and Osijek, today in Croatia. He completed studies at the secondary music school in Osijek and eventually made his way to Vienna. There, in the capital of both the Austro-Hungarian Empire and the Operetta Kingdom, Romberg befriended people such as Victor Heuberger and Franz Lehár while working at the Theater an der Wien, a house known for its operetta productions.

Romberg arrived in New York City in 1909 and eventually found work as a pianist in various restaurants. He formed and conducted a small orchestra at Bustanoby's, a venue frequented by the theatrical crowd, including the impresario J. J. Shubert. The Shubert Theatrical Corporation soon engaged Romberg to contribute to their revues, most notably *The Passing Show* series, write songs for their musical comedies (including the Al Jolson vehicles *Robinson Crusoe, Jr.* and *Sinbad*, although the star never sang any of Romberg's music but instead interpolated songs by other composers), and adapt Central European operettas for American audiences. It was while working for the Shuberts that Romberg acquired his knowledge of contemporary American popular song and dance styles, especially those derived from ragtime. This practical education in Broadway musical idioms was of tremendous benefit to the young composer.

Of these assignments, the adaptations had the strongest impact on Romberg's future musical development. The three most important of them were *The Blue Paradise* (1915), a version of Edmund Eysler's *Ein Tag im Paradis*; *Maytime* (1917), based on Walter Kollo's *Wie einst im Mai*; and *Blossom Time* (1921), a fictionalised account of the life of Franz Schubert taken from

Berté's *Das Dreimäderlhaus*. Romberg's music appeared alongside that of Eysler in *The Blue Paradise*, but in *Maytime* the score was entirely new. This was Romberg's first complete operetta score and, like Friml's *The Firefly*, it was a monumental success. The meteoric rise to fame continued with *Blossom Time*, a work in which the twentieth-century New York producers Shubert (without the 'c') capitalised on the fame of the nineteenth-century Viennese composer Schubert (with the 'c') in all of their publicity materials.

In these three shows, Romberg solidified the first of his two basic operetta paradigms. Developed with the Shuberts, who understood audience tastes, these operettas all have unhappy, or at least compromise, endings. The romantic leads who sing glorious music all evening are not together at the final curtain. In *The Blue Paradise* and *Maytime*, a successive generation of lovers realise the unfulfilled romance of their ancestors, but in *Blossom Time*, Schubert, the romantic lead, dies, leaving his Eighth Symphony unfinished. (Historical license is indeed invoked!) From a musical perspective, each score is unified through a recurring waltz duet: 'Auf Wiedersehn' in *The Blue Paradise*, 'Will You Remember?' (also known as 'Sweetheart, Sweetheart') in *Maytime* and 'Song of Love' (based on the second theme of the first movement of Schubert's Eighth Symphony) in *Blossom Time*. Romberg equates the waltz with nostalgia and loss, for in each case these principal refrains conclude the operetta with a reminder of what *could* have been. These waltzes function as centrepieces around which other musical styles, ranging from marches to syncopated vaudeville-style numbers, provide musical and dramatic foils for the tales of ill-fated love.

And so we arrive at the pivotal year of 1924, when two of the most important and most successful musicals of the decade appeared: *Rose Marie* (opened 2 September) and *The Student Prince* (opened 2 December). These were the most frequently performed operettas during the 1920s in New York and remain works against which all future operettas are compared. (See Table 4.1.)

Rose Marie (music by Rudolf Friml, book and lyrics by Oscar Hammerstein II and Otto Harbach) played for an impressive 557 performances in its initial New York run. In the operetta, the title character, who may be part Native American (the libretto is ambiguous on this central issue), is a singer at Lady Jane's Hotel, a small lodge in the Canadian Rockies. She loves Jim Kenyon, who is accused of murdering Black Eagle and goes into hiding in the Canadian woods. His accuser is Ed Hawley, who has his eye on Rose Marie. It turns out that Wanda, Black Eagle's wife, is the killer, and Rose Marie and Jim are reunited at the plot's denouement.

Several musical styles and influences are evident in *Rose Marie*, including a concerted waltz ('The Door of My Dreams'), a rousing march ('The Mounties'), a Tin Pan Alley love song ('Rose Marie'), Indianist numbers ('Indian

Table 4.1 *Numbers of performances of significant Friml and Romberg operettas in New York and London*

Much of the data in this table comes from Kurt Gänzl, *The Musical: A Concise History* (Boston, 1997), p. 196.

	New York	London
The Student Prince in Heidelberg (1924) (Romberg)	608	96
Rose Marie (1924) (Friml)	557	851
Blossom Time (1921) (Romberg)	516	–
The Vagabond King (1925) (Friml)	511	480
The New Moon (1928) (Romberg)	509	148
The Desert Song (1926) (Romberg)	471	432
The Three Musketeers (1928) (Friml)	318	240
My Maryland (1927) (Romberg)	312	–

Love Call' and 'Totem Tom Tom') and aspects of melodrama (Finaletto sequence in Act 2). Central to this discussion are the waltz – an homage to the Viennese operetta heritage, the heroic march – in a style which emerged as a staple of 1920s American operetta, and the Indianist numbers – demonstrations of the genre's fascination with exoticism.

The waltz's association with sentiment appears in the Act 2 'The Door of My Dreams', sung by Rose Marie as she is about to marry Hawley, whom she does not love. She tries to convince herself that she does indeed want to be with him, but her thoughts, expressed through the graceful waltz refrain, are with Jim.

The opening of the primary march of the show, 'The Mounties', includes the stage direction that it is to be sung by 'Mounties off stage at great distance', adding to the ominous power of the number through its disembodied choral sound. The middle section, accompanied by a shift to the minor mode, is a solo (with off-stage choral interjections) for Malone, leader of the Mounties, in which he warns of the impending arrival of the singing constabulary. Especially significant in the number is the careful attention to the spatial relationship between on-stage and off-stage voices. Malone, in addition to being a Mountie, is also a suitor of the title character. His psychological allegiances are divided and this dichotomy is presented to the audience through the staging of the number. He is not completely at one with his male colleagues, for his attentions lie elsewhere, namely with Rose Marie.

Created Native Americans were nothing new (consider Victor Herbert's *Natoma* (1911)) when *Rose Marie* appeared, and Friml employed many of the typical Indianist identifiers of the period in the operetta. In 'Indian Love Call', chromaticism is especially evident in the opening phrase, and drone fifths appear in the accompaniment at the words 'When the lone lagoon stirs in the spring' and again at various points in the underscoring for 'That means I offer my love to you to be your own'. In the woefully politically incorrect 'Totem Tom Tom', not only do Indianist musical clichés such as drone fifths and the incessant repetition of distinctive rhythmic motifs dominate the sound world, but the text promotes an image of Native Canadians as drunkards who only dance and sleep. Led by the murderess Wanda, the number was the show-stopping spectacle that preceded the first-act finale.

Three months to the day after the premiere of *Rose Marie*, Romberg's *The Student Prince* (book and lyrics by Dorothy Donnelly), appeared on Broadway and ran for a decade record of 608 performances. In the musical version of Wilhelm Meyer-Foerster's play *Alt Heidelberg* (Old Heidelberg), Karl Franz, prince of mythical Karlsberg, is in love with Kathie, a waitress at the Inn of the Golden Apples. The operetta continues the Romberg–Shubert paradigm of unhappy endings, for the work ends when Karl Franz, after entering an arranged marriage with Princess Margaret, returns to Heidelberg to bid farewell to Kathie and the days of his youth. The score's defining recurring waltz duet is 'Deep in My Heart, Dear', an expansive number with four distinct sections in its verse.

The Student Prince was not only the pinnacle of Romberg's unhappy ending, waltz-dominated approach to operetta but also heralded a new feature in his work: the large male chorus. In *The Student Prince*, they are Heidelberg students whose rousing music includes the diegetic 'Drinking Song' and the fast-paced 'Students' Marching Song'. They also accompany Karl Franz in his pursuit of Kathie's heart, both dramatically and musically, in the show's immortal 'Serenade' ('Overhead the moon is beaming'). (Friml also included a large male chorus, the Mounties, in *Rose Marie*.)

Nostalgia runs deep in the show about young love in Old Heidelberg. Romberg continues his association of the waltz with nostalgia in 'Golden Days', introduced by the Prince's tutor Engel and later reprised by the Prince himself. Both men recall the happiness of youth and their fond memories as they realise, in a somewhat bittersweet fashion, that recollections are all they can possess.

After the success of *The Student Prince*, Romberg began to fashion a new approach to operetta – one that had plots with happy endings and scores that included dramatically significant reprises of songs that were not waltzes. The male chorus that proved so successful in *The Student Prince* became a standard feature of these works, the most famous of which were *The Desert Song* (1926; book by Harbach, Hammerstein and Frank Mandel, lyrics by Hammerstein), *My Maryland* (1927; book and lyrics by Donnelly) and *The New Moon* (1928; book by Hammerstein, Mandel, and Laurence Schwab, lyrics by Hammerstein). In addition to romance, heroism was a key dramatic element in these works.

Plate 5 The original New York production of *The Student Prince* with Ilse Marvenga and the Male Chorus.

Capitalising on the popularity of Rudolf Valentino, Lawrence of Ara-bia and the actual Riff Wars in North Africa, the libretto of *The Desert Song* included overt references to contemporary events and popular cul-ture. The exoticism and intrigue of French Morocco replaced the nostalgia of Ruritania. The story is one of dual identity and, extending the definition of 'operetta', is set wholly in the present day: the Red Shadow (a.k.a. the awk-ward Pierre) helps the North African natives resist their French oppressors. Margot, daughter of the French governor, is in love with the mystique of the Red Shadow, and Pierre is in love with her. Not until the end of the operetta does Margot realise the dual identity of the person with whom she has been singing rapturous music for nearly the entire evening.

The score includes some of Romberg's most operatic music, includ-ing 'The Desert Song', 'The Riff Song', 'The Sabre Song', 'One Alone' and 'Romance'. In the score, Romberg employs different modes to distinguish between the Arab and the European characters. The music of the Moroccans tends to be in the minor while that of the Europeans sits firmly in the major. For example, when the heroic male Riff chorus sings the opening chorus, 'The Riff Song', they begin in the minor mode and the tune's augmented seconds intensify the march's exotic flavour. This same male chorus becomes

French and subsequently sings assertively in the major in 'French Marching Song'. Likewise, in the concerted scene 'Eastern and Western Love', where Ali Ben Ali and the Red Shadow (Pierre) compare views on women, the Moroccan view, 'One Flower Grows Alone in Your Garden', is minor while the French perspective, 'One Alone', is major. This modal characterisation is also evident in the title waltz, introduced by the male lead. When he is serenading Margot as the mysterious Red Shadow, the music is largely pentatonic and is harmonised in the minor. But when he expresses his true feelings as a Frenchman at the beginning of the refrain, he shifts to the major mode.

As part of Romberg's new operetta paradigm, *The Desert Song* includes a musically, dramatically and structurally significant duple-metre ballad, 'One Alone'. The Red Shadow initially sings it as his ode to monogamy (in the 'Eastern and Western Love' sequence), but the song assumes increasing dramatic significance throughout the show. This culminates in the final scene as Margot recognises Pierre's dual identity when the supposedly milquetoast leading man begins the refrain and she joins him in the final reprise.

Romberg continued to refine his post-*Student Prince* approach to operetta in the following years. Four works appeared in 1927, each of which was set in a different time and place: *Cherry Blossoms* in Japan, *My Maryland* during the American Civil War, *The Love Call* in Arizona and *My Princess* in contemporary New York City. Of these, only *My Maryland* was a critical and commercial success. A re-tooling of the Civil War legend of Barbara Fritchie, the Confederate woman who protects the Union officer she loves, *My Maryland* included the stirring male-choral march 'Your Land and My Land', which ends with a quotation from 'The Battle Hymn of the Republic', and a flowing waltz duet, 'The Same Silver Moon'. In 1928, Romberg and George Gershwin co-wrote the score to *Rosalie*, Florenz Ziegfeld's vehicle for 'the queen of musical comedy', Marilyn Miller. The plot concerned the romance of Princess Rosalie of Romanza and an American pilot. Romberg contributed marches and other music to evoke the Ruritianian domain of Romanza while Gershwin wrote music in the 'up-to-date' (i.e. musical comedy) style of 1920s America.

Romberg was unable to complete the entire score for *Rosalie* because of another project, *The New Moon* (book by Hammerstein, Mandel and Laurence Schwab, lyrics by Hammerstein). This operetta shared its setting with Victor Herbert's *Naughty Marietta* (1910), but also included parts that took place aboard the ship *The New Moon* and on an island in the Caribbean, recalling Friml's *The Firefly*. The story of Robert Misson, an escaped French aristocrat who wants to rid France of its monarchy, and Marianne Beaunoir, daughter of a Royalist landowner in Louisiana, provided the romantic backdrop against which the libretto unfolded. Romberg's score included the obligatory waltzes and marches, but his handling of musical material, including a sophisticated use of underscoring, surely shows the influence of the previous year's *Show Boat*. After the initial try-out of *The New Moon* in December 1927, work was suspended on the operetta so that Hammerstein could spend more time preparing *Show Boat*, another show that included shipboard scenes, for its release from dry dock.

The New Moon was the last of the great 1920s operettas and, like *The Desert Song* before it, demonstrated Romberg's new operetta paradigm. Robert and Marianne are together at the final curtain, and a duple-metre ballad, 'Lover, Come Back To Me', has the same musical prominence as any of the score's exquisite waltzes. Furthermore, the energetic male chorus is present, this time bellowing Romberg and Hammerstein's well-known call against tyranny and oppression, 'Stout-Hearted Men' ('Give me some men who are stouthearted men').

Whereas Romberg employed mode to distinguish between character types in *The Desert Song* (Arab and European), in *The New Moon* he used metre as a musical signifier of gender. Women, including the heroine Marianne, waltz, while the men march and dance in duple metre. Marianne's concerted waltz in the Act 1 finale, 'One Kiss', is a luxurious waltz, while duple metre numbers such as 'Stout-Hearted Men' and the jaunty 'Marianne' showcase the various talents of the male chorus.

In addition to these overt examples of metre being associated with gender, Romberg employs the technique in far more subtle ways. Duval, Marianne's cretinous suitor, sings 'Interrupted Trio'. Duval is not the man Robert is; he is somewhat effeminate and hence sings a waltz. Since he cannot sing in duple metre, he is not 'masculine' enough to be with the leading lady. In the show's primary love duet, 'Wanting You', the refrain is in 12/8 – a fusion of the male-associated duple metre (four beats per measure) and the female-related waltz (each beat divided into three parts). Robert and Marianne integrate their metric languages, just as they do their differing views on love and life, and the synthesis works.

Romberg also alludes to various popular music styles in *The New Moon*. 'Gorgeous Alexander' is a fast-paced revue-style number featuring the comic leads Alexander and Julie, while 'Softly, as in a Morning Sunrise' evokes the style of a tango. In 'Softly', Hammerstein's lyric alludes to the *tango canción*, a particular type of tango text focusing on unrequited or ill-fated love. Romberg sets the song for tenor, a direct homage to Carlos Gardel (1890–1935), the Argentinian pop icon who popularised the *tango cancion* in New York City. Thus, Philippe, Robert's compatriot who sings 'Softly', is both a musical foil for Robert's baritone and a dramatic one, for Robert focuses on the appealing aspects of love rather than the tragic ones.

Just as Romberg refocused his approach to operetta after the stunning success of *The Student Prince*, Friml turned away from North American plots (*Rose Marie*) and toward French ones in his next shows, *The Vagabond King* (1925) and *The Three Musketeers* (1928). These two works capitalised on the Francophilia prevalent in 1920s America. France and French culture were paramount during the decade: glamour magazines promoted French style, and in classical music circles, composers such as Edgard Varèse and members of Les Six were held in extremely high regard.

The Vagabond King (lyrics by Brian Hooker, book by Hooker, Russell Janney, and W. H. Post) had an impressive 511 performances in its initial run. The libretto, based on the play *If I Were King* by Justin McCarthy, related a fictitious tale of the real François Villon, a fifteenth-century Parisian poet. King Louis XI dubs Villon king for a day, during which time he must woo Katherine or be beheaded. Villon succeeds in his romantic efforts. Meanwhile, the Duke of Burgundy invades Paris, and Villon must gather his fellow vagabonds to defeat the assailants.

Heroism and love are the driving features in the plot, and the music accentuates these dimensions. 'Song of the Vagabonds' is another heroic march, a call for action against oppression, and its middle section is in the minor mode, recalling *Rose Marie*'s 'The Mounties'. Sentimental highlights include the lilting duple-metre ballad 'Only a Rose' and the languid waltz 'Love Me Tonight'.

The Three Musketeers (lyrics by P. G. Wodehouse and Clifford Grey, book by William Anthony McGuire) featured scenes from Alexandre Dumas's novel of swashbuckling adventure. The score included such arresting numbers as 'Ma Belle', 'One Kiss', 'My Dreams', 'My Sword and I' and the heroic 'March of the Musketeers'. The Queen's 'My Dreams' is a lilting duple-metre ballad in which the first note of each phrase begins one step lower than its predecessor, paralleling the character's descent into sleep.

In the decade following World War I, heroic marches equalled sentimental waltzes in importance when it came to American operetta scores. Numbers such as 'The Riff Song', 'Your Land and My Land', 'Stout-Hearted Men', 'Song of the Vagabonds' and 'March of the Musketeers' captivated audiences every bit as much as the more sentimental numbers. America's place as a world power was growing in the 1920s and the nation's reputation as a protector of democracy was promoted on Broadway through these rousing operetta marches.

This was not enough to keep stage operetta alive after the 1929 Stock Market Crash and subsequent Great Depression, however. Audiences preferred to laugh, not cry, when they went to the theatre for entertainment. Additionally, the costs of mounting operettas with their lavish sets, costumes and casts became prohibitive, though several impressive operettas appeared in the 1930s, including Friml's *Luana* (1930) and Romberg's *East Wind* (1930), *Nina Rosa* (1931) and *May Wine* (1935). Although its lustre on Broadway had faded, operetta found continued popularity through road tours (many of which were done on extremely small budgets), productions by light opera companies, and perhaps most importantly, film adaptations.

Hollywood versions of operettas

With the advent and growth of the sound motion picture industry in the late 1920s, film versions of classic operettas formed a significant part of the Hollywood industry. While space does not permit a thorough investigation of each of the fourteen full-length film adaptations of 1920s stage operettas, the fact that these films exist confirms the popularity of the genre. (See Table 4.2.) In these adaptations, plots and music were often radically transformed in order to keep the time of the film to less than two hours (substantially shorter than the stage originals) or to give all the great songs to the singing stars.

This model was certainly not the only approach. In fact, the first full-length, full-sound film version of an operetta, the 1929 *The Desert Song*, remained extremely faithful to the stage production. Every scene in the film is underscored, a carry-over from the 'silent' film era, where live musicians played throughout a film.

Two other versions of *The Desert Song* also exist: a 1943 version with Dennis Morgan and Irene Manning and the classic 1953 release starring Gordon MacRae and Kathryn Grayson. The plot for the 1943 version was altered to include Nazis in the North African desert and the hero becomes an American, making this a wartime propaganda film, while the MacRae–Grayson rendition remained closer to the original stage play.

Whereas the 1929 film of *The Desert Song* adhered to the stage libretto, the 1930 screen incarnation of *The New Moon*, called *New Moon*, did not. Starring renowned opera singers Grace Moore and Lawrence Tibbett, the film includes some extremely fine performances of Romberg's music. In the film's radically altered plot, which takes place in Tsarist Russia, a military hero (Tibbett) is in love with an aristocrat (Moore). The colossal alterations were likely due to financial considerations at the beginning of the Great Depression. MGM had just filmed *The Rogue Song*, also starring Tibbett, and could reuse the sets and costumes rather than manufacturing new ones. The trimmed-down musical score retained only four songs from the original: 'Wanting You', 'Lover Come Back to Me', 'One Kiss' and 'Stout-Hearted Men'. In an effort to create Russian atmosphere, a 'vulgar' gypsy song, 'The Farmer's Daughter' (by MGM music director Herbert Stothart), appears early in the film and a balalaika is added to the orchestration for 'Lover

Table 4.2 *Full-length film adaptations of 1920s operettas*

Bitter Sweet
1933, British and Dominion Film Corporation
Anna Neagle, Fernand Gravet
1940, MGM
Jeanette MacDonald, Nelson Eddy

The Desert Song
1929, Warner Brothers
John Boles, Carlotta King
1943, Warner Brothers
Dennis Morgan, Irene Manning
1953, Warner Brothers
Gordon MacRae, Kathryn Grayson

Maytime
1937, MGM
Jeanette MacDonald, Nelson Eddy

New Moon
1930, MGM
Lawrence Tibbett, Grace Moore
1940, MGM
Jeanette MacDonald, Nelson Eddy

Rose Marie
1928 (silent), MGM
Joan Crawford
1936, MGM
Jeanette MacDonald, Nelson Eddy
1954, MGM
Ann Blyth, Fernando Lamas, Howard Keel

The Student Prince
1954, MGM
Ann Blyth, Edmund Purdom (dubbed by Mario Lanza)

The Vagabond King
1930, Paramount
Dennis King, Jeanette MacDonald
1956, Paramount
Oreste Kirkop, Kathryn Grayson

Come Back to Me'. The subsequent 1940 version with Jeanette MacDonald and Nelson Eddy returned to French New Orleans, but with a modified plot.

It was the legendary team who appeared in the 1940 film of *The New Moon*, MacDonald (1903–65) and Eddy (1901–67), that epitomised the genre of the operetta film. In their eight film collaborations – *Naughty Marietta* (1935), *Rose Marie* (1936), *Maytime* (1937), *The Girl of the Golden West* (1938; music by Romberg, lyrics by Gus Kahn), *Sweethearts* (1938; their first colour film), *New Moon*, *Bitter Sweet* (1940) and *I Married an Angel* (1942; music by Richard Rodgers, lyrics by Lorenz Hart) – they not only provided legions of audiences with hours of entertainment but also became models for aspiring young singers. The duo repeatedly appeared as the romantic lovers who, though adversities plague them because of either their own doings or those of others, always end up together at the end. MacDonald played the aristocrat who is placed in circumstances uncomfortable for a person of her upbringing, while Eddy was often clad in a military uniform, a symbol of his masculinity. Stage plots were discarded and replaced by ones that resembled, but were not identical to, the originals. For example, in *Rose Marie*, the title character (MacDonald) falls in love with a Canadian Mountie (Eddy) rather than protecting her lover from one. In addition to their prescribed character types, MacDonald and Eddy had individual musical tropes. Mac-Donald typically sang a coloratura number, often an operatic interpolation, early in the film, and Eddy's first on-screen appearance frequently had him leading a freedom-fighting male chorus in a rousing operetta march.

In the 1950s, MGM produced a series of musical films that included screen versions of three beloved operettas, *Rose Marie*, *The Student Prince* and *The Vagabond King*. Full-colour visual opulence delighted the eye while songs were given new, lush orchestrations. Magnificent mountain scenery provided the visual backdrop for *Rose Marie* and seemingly hundreds of singing male students ran through the streets of Old Heidelberg in *The Student Prince*. Maltese tenor Oreste Kirkop made his one and only Hollywood musical appearance in a spectacle-filled version of *The Vagabond King* that featured a young Rita Moreno as the prostitute Huguette.

The British scene: from *Chu Chin Chow* to *Bitter Sweet*

With the arrival of the 1920s in London, two operettas whose lives began in the previous decade were still playing: *Chu Chin Chow* and *The Maid of the Mountains*. The exotic nature of these works set the stage for subsequent developments in the decade.

When *Chu Chin Chow* (1916; music by Frederic Norton, book and lyrics by Oscar Asche) first appeared at His Majesty's Theatre on 31 August 1916, Britain was in the midst of World War I. The retelling of the tale of Ali Baba and the Forty Thieves was filled with spectacular sets and appealing music.[4] The show's author and director, Oscar Asche, played the title character, the villainous Arab Abu Hasan whose first appearance is as the disguised Chinaman Chu Chin Chow, while his wife, the noted actress Lily Brayton, played Zahrat, the slave girl who brings justice to the criminals. The show reflected both general aspects of Orientalism and specific notions of British foreign policy in the Middle East.

Chu Chin Chow ran for an impressive 2,235 performances and closed in 1921, after playing for nearly five years. It inaugurated the concept of the long-running West End musical. The show was advertised throughout the

Home Counties and attending a performance of it often became a reason to journey by train into Central London. Furthermore, Asche kept revising the show during its run, adding scenes and creating increasingly spectacular sets as a means of getting people who had already seen the show to come and experience it again and again.

Norton's score included the fine ballads 'Any Time's Kissing Time' and 'I Love Thee So' as well as the bass-baritone favourite 'The Cobbler's Song'. Other highlights included the unison choral march 'Robbers of the Woods', with its distinctive chromatic bass line, and the title character's pentatonic signature tune, 'I Am Chu Chin Chow of China'.

The other big hit of the war, *The Maid of the Mountains* (1917; music by James Tate, lyrics by Harry Graham, book by Frederick Lonsdale), was set in the high mountains of a brigand land. The story centred on Teresa, the 'maid of the mountains', who is arrested by General Malona, the Governor of Santo. Malona has promised her release only if her lover, the outlaw Baldasarre, is captured. Complications ensue, Baldasarre is jailed, and Teresa succeeds in engineering her lover's release. Jose Collins played the heroine and introduced the evergreen 'Love Will Find a Way' with its luxurious waltz refrain. The operetta played for a total of 1,352 performances in its initial London run and enjoyed continued popularity as a vehicle for amateur operatic societies.

Operetta did not enjoy the same sense of native popularity in Britain that it did in America during the 1920s. Much of this certainly had to do with the post-war sentiment towards things Central European. The original operettas that did appear were decidedly non-Ruritanian. *The Rose of Araby* (1920; music by Merlin Morgan, book by Harold Simpson) and *Cairo* (1920, New York; 1921, London; music by Percy Fletcher, mime by Oscar Asche) both capitalised on the Arabian-nights exoticism of *Chu Chin Chow*. Their success and the accepted exoticism of North Africa certainly was at least partly responsible for the tremendous popularity of *The Desert Song* among British audiences.

Adaptations of German-language operettas were not completely unknown, however. *The Lady of the Rose* (1922, music by Jean Gilbert), an adaptation of *Die Frau im Hermelin*, played for nearly fifteen months, and *Lilac Time* (1922, music arranged by Heinrich Berté and G. H. Clutsam, book and lyrics by Adrian Ross), an adaptation of *Das Dreimäderlhaus*, enjoyed an eighteen-month run in London before entering the domain of touring productions and revivals. *Lilac Time* shared its source material with the Romberg–Donnelly *Blossom Time*, but the two shows are substantially different – *Lilac Time* is not a British version of the Romberg operetta.

As would happen again in the 1940s, American imports dominated much of the British musical scene. *Rose Marie*, with 851 performances,

The Vagabond King, with 480 performances, and *The Desert Song*, with 432 performances, found great favour among London audiences. Significantly, none of these works had Ruritanian settings – when *The Student Prince* appeared in London, it played for a mere ninety-six performances. Its German story and German-born star (Ilse Marvenga, reprising her Broadway role as Kathie) certainly militated against its acceptance seven years after the end of World War I.

A Ruritanian operetta, but one with a decidedly modern twist, appeared at the end of the decade, however. *Bitter Sweet* (1929), with book, music and lyrics by Noël Coward (1899–1973), was its creator's first major musical triumph. Told in flashback, the story takes place in nineteenth-century Vienna, the bastion of sentimental operetta. It is the tale of Sarah, Marchioness of Shayne, previously known as Sari, who was to have married a socially appropriate young man but instead ran off with her music teacher, Carl Linden. After the wedding, Linden worked as a conductor in a Viennese café where Sari sang. A lustful soldier tried to seduce Sari, and Carl died trying to protect her honour. Although Sari became a successful singer and had numerous romantic liaisons that culminated in marriage to a British Marquis, it is her faithfulness to Carl that rules her heart. Her tale is both bitter and sweet, reflected in the two-word title of the show, *Bitter Sweet*. Coward's mastery of various song styles is already strongly evident and the score includes some of the composer-lyricist's most beloved numbers. The effervescence of 'Ta-Ra-Ra-Boom-De-Ay' and the wittiness of the male quartet 'Green Carnations' aptly complement the Viennese waltzes 'Zigeuner' and 'I'll See You Again' and the plaintive 'If Love Were All'.

The legacy of operetta

The 1920s American operetta influenced popular culture throughout the twentieth century. Through innumerable road tours, New York and London revivals and other productions (from high schools to professional opera companies and everything in between), operetta continues to delight audiences and performers. In 2003, New York City Center's *Encores!* mounted *The New Moon* with opera stars Rodney Gilfry and Christiane Noll in the lead roles. Summer companies such as Ohio Light Opera have staged Friml's *Rose Marie*, *The Vagabond King* and *The Firefly* and Romberg's *Maytime* and *The Desert Song* in the early twenty-first century, introducing these seminal works to a new generation of audiences and performers.

Operettas from the early decades of the twentieth century also provide tremendous source material for imitation in either pastiche or parody. The continued popularity of the repertory allows this to happen, for if audiences did not understand the original reference, the derivative treatment would lose its meaning.

Aspects of the genre and specific works served as direct models for several musical theatre works and numbers in the latter part of the twentieth century. 'One More Kiss' from Stephen Sondheim's *Follies* (1971) is a pastiche of a quintessential operetta waltz for coloratura soprano. Stephen Banfield suggests Romberg influences in two songs from the Disney animated film (and subsequent stage musical) *Beauty and the Beast* (1991; music by Alan Menken, lyrics by Howard Ashman). 'The Mob Song' is a cinematic recreation of Nelson Eddy's nocturnal march 'Stout-Hearted Men' in the 1940 film of *The New Moon*, while 'Gaston' is a homage to 'Drinking Song' from *The Student Prince*.[5]

Rose Marie inspired the operetta parody *Little Mary Sunshine* (1959; music, lyrics and book by Rick Besoyan). Set in the Colorado Rockies, the plot concerns Mary Potts and Captain 'Big Jim' Warrington of the Forest Rangers. Their rapturous love duet is the 'Colorado Love Call', and other numbers in the show, such as 'Do You Ever Dream of Vienna?' and 'Naughty, Naughty Nancy', recall the quintessence of the genre.[6] Besoyan created another operetta parody, *The Student Gypsy* (1963), this one set in Ruritanian climes.

In addition to its overall concept, *Rose Marie* contains two specific numbers that live in parody: 'Indian Love Call' and 'The Mounties'. Among the most significant reappearances of 'Indian Love Call' is Slim Whitman's rendition that causes Martian heads to explode (literally) in the film *Mars Attacks!* (1996). The overt masculinity of Canadian Mounties promoted in 'The Mounties' is lampooned in Monty Python's 'The Lumberjack Song' – complete with the physical separation of the soloist and the chorus.

Other references to the genre include the insertion of 'Ah, Sweet Mystery of Life' from Victor Herbert's *Naughty Marietta* in Mel Brooks' film *Young Frankenstein* (1974). The song appears to great comic effect at several of the film's climactic moments. References to operetta are not limited to the entertainment industry, however, for Heidelberg College in Tifflin, Ohio has as its mascot none other than 'The Student Princes'.

Operetta is a genre whose legacy has endured well beyond the decade during which it was at its peak, the 1920s. It played an important role in the English-language musical theatre from mid-century onwards not only because of stage revivals, film versions and parodies but also because it provided the fundamental dramatic model for the musical plays of creators such as Rodgers and Hammerstein. It was the same Oscar Hammerstein II, after all, the wordsmith for shows such as *The Desert Song* and *The New Moon*, who crafted the texts for *Oklahoma!*, *South Pacific* and other classic shows in his collaboration with Richard Rodgers (see chapter 8). Operetta's worlds of romance – domains such as nineteenth-century Heidelberg, the Canadian Rockies, medieval Paris, French Morocco and eighteenth-century Louisiana – provided opportunities for audiences to escape to times and places filled with expansive amorous waltzes and stirring socially minded marches, locales where love and heroism could reign together in supreme harmony.

5 Images of African Americans: African-American musical theatre, *Show Boat* and *Porgy and Bess*

JOHN GRAZIANO

Soon after the end of slavery, African Americans formed musical troupes to sing, dance and act in a variety of shows. One of the first black companies was the Georgia Slave Troupe Minstrels, which was organised in April 1865 by a white manager, W. H. Lee. Another Georgia Minstrels company was organised in Indianapolis, under the management of a black performer, Charles B. Hicks; his company was to achieve fame as the foremost African-American minstrel troupe of the latter part of the nineteenth century. In these shows, African Americans followed the practice of established white troupes: they darkened their faces with burnt cork; staged burlesques on popular operas and operettas of the time, such as Jacques Offenbach's *The Grand Duchess of Gerolstein*; performed farces, such as *Mr Jinks*; pranced through eccentric and grotesque dances; and sang dialect, plantation and well-known minstrel songs both as solos and as ensemble pieces. The novelty of the black minstrel show was the race of the performers – the Georgia Minstrels, for example, advertised that in their shows the black performers were offering audiences a glimpse of 'genuine' plantation music and dance.[1]

Not all black troupes during the 1870s and 1880s, however, were of the burnt cork minstrel variety. The Hyers sisters, Anna Madah (1855–1920s) and Emma Louise (1857–?99), performed operatic excerpts, art and parlour songs, and jubilee songs and spirituals during their concert tours in the first half of the 1870s. From 1876 to 1883 the sisters performed as part of the 'Hyers Sisters Combination', managed by their father, Samuel B. Hyers.[2] Their repertory of musicals included *Out of Bondage*, written by the white playwright Joseph Bradford; *Urlina, the African Princess*, by E. S. Getchell; and a dramatisation of Harriet Beecher Stowe's *Uncle Tom's Cabin*. In the first of these shows, which is subtitled *Before and After the War*, the company demonstrates how life has changed for African Americans after emancipation. In Act 1, audiences see a Southern slave family at dinner, eating possum, drinking home-made whiskey and singing spirituals and plantation songs. The action of the second act takes place outside the cabin, with dancing and the singing of popular songs. As the act ends, Union troops arrive to battle the Southern soldiers. After the family is liberated, several former slaves decide to go north to seek their fortunes. Five years later, in Act 3, the family is reunited in Boston. Uncle Eph and Aunt Naomi, who had elected to stay on their family farm, discover that the four young people who left the plantation are now professional vocalists, who live and work in a society that treats them as equals. During this final act, the sisters, along with their singing co-stars, John Luca and Wallace King, sang operatic excerpts by Verdi, Flotow and Balfe, among others.

Urlina, the African Princess touched on a theme – life in Africa – that was to be reinvestigated by African Americans during the first decade of the twentieth century. Although the plot of *Urlina* is not concerned with African Americans who want to return to the lands of their birth, it does reflect nineteenth-century interest in the 'exotic', as seen in operas such as Giacomo Meyerbeer's *L'Africaine* (1864) and Léo Delibes's *Lakmé* (1883), and in operettas and comic operas that include James Barnes's *Chow Chow, or A Tale of Pekin* (1872) and Gilbert and Sullivan's *The Mikado* (1885). Advertised as an 'operatic bouffe extravaganza', the plot concerns a princess whose rights as successor to her father's throne have been usurped by another king. The latter's son, Prince Zurleska, falls in love with a picture of the princess, and decides to rescue her. After several attempts, the prince is successful in freeing Princess Urlina and overthrowing his father, the usurper. In their production of the musical, the Hyers sisters appeared in the two leading roles: Anna Madah, a soprano, played the Princess Urlina, while Emma Louise, a contralto, was the Prince. Others in the cast included a female impersonator, Willie Lyle, who played the maid, and the great comedian Billy Kersands (1842–1915), who was featured in several comic roles, including an Irish missionary, a pigtailed Puritan and a Christian Chinaman. The production of *Urlina* was an important milestone for African-American performers, because it demonstrated that they could appear successfully on the stage in works that were devoid of the stereotypes of minstrelsy. Although there were broadly comic scenes in the musical, there were also serious moments that placed *Urlina* squarely in the tradition of the musical theatre. That tradition was virtually ignored in African-American theatre for the remainder of the nineteenth century.

The Hyers sisters' 1880 production of *Uncle Tom's Cabin* was also groundbreaking. Prior to their performances, the major roles in the dramatic versions of Stowe's anti-slavery novel were usually performed by white actors in blackface. In casting their show, the sisters chose white actors to play the white parts and black actors to play the black parts. As was the case with *Urlina,* the company appears to have preferred to offer a musical that did not rely solely on minstrel-show stereotypes; rather, it portrayed blacks realistically on the American stage before mixed audiences.

During the 1880s, black minstrel shows, still tremendously popular with the public, were seen in large and small cities and towns across the United States as well as in England, Scotland and Wales. Several 'double' companies, with black and white performers, toured during the latter part of the 1880s and through much of the 1890s. In 1890 a new type of minstrel show was unveiled by Sam Lucas (1840–1916), another of the legendary African-American comedians who helped to shape black musical theatre, and Sam T. Jack, the white proprietor of several theatres in the Chicago area. Their extravaganza, the *Creole Burlesque Co.*, added women to the traditional all-male minstrel show. The show, in its first version, followed the usual tripartite format of the minstrel show. In the first part of the show, 'Tropical Revelries', the semicircle included women as well as men. The Interlocutor, who stood in the middle and attempted to bring order to the proceedings, was a woman in male attire, while Tambo and Bones were the usual male comedians and punsters. The company alternated with the featured singers, elocutionists, dancers and comedians in their solo turns. Following the opening chorus, there was a female 'conversationalist', a team of male punsters, who probably doubled as the endmen, and a sister act that specialised in 'sweet songs'. After the next song by the company, there were two more acts – a second conversationalist and a different pair of comedians. Two additional acts, with yet another conversationalist and a pair of 'courtiers', followed the third ensemble performance. The company then concluded that part of the programme. In the traditional minstrel show, the second part was called the 'olio'; it consisted of a series of solos by the stars of the troupe, and was usually followed by an afterpiece, which was a brief sketch that combined comedy, pathos, suspense, song and dance. In the *Creole* show, a burlesque, 'The Beauty of the Nile, or Doomed by Fire', began the second part. While there is no information concerning the plot of this burlesque, we can assume from the names of the characters in the programme that it was in the tradition of those brief song and dance sketches that were expected by knowledgeable minstrel-show audiences. At the conclusion of the sketch, the *Creole* olio was seen; for the finale of the show, the women of the company were once again spotlighted in a 'Grand Amazonian March'. The *Creole Burlesque Co.* toured the country and was very successful with the public; during the summer of 1893, it was seen in Chicago at one of Jack's theatres not far from the Columbian Exposition, and continued touring in new 'editions' for several more seasons. While the format of *Creole Burlesque Co.* was clearly derived from the minstrel show, it transcended the limitations of the genre, allowing African Americans to demonstrate a wide range of talents in many areas. It also provided employment and served as a training ground for a number of male and female performers who would be in the forefront of black musical theatre during the first decade of the twentieth century.

The success of the *Creole Burlesque Co.* led to the development of several competing shows. John W. Isham, who was an advance man for Sam Jack, formed his own company, the *Octoroons*, in 1895. While one can note that the format of the minstrel-show is still underlying the show, there are significant differences as well. The minstrel-show semicircle with Interlocutor, Tambo and Bones has disappeared, and the afterpiece now opens the show. The olio with star specialties still begins the second part of the show, but replacing the afterpiece is a musical extravaganza, '30 Minutes Around the Operas', in which the whole cast performs well-known excerpts such as 'The Anvil Chorus' from popular operas and operettas.

The opening sketch, 'The Blackville Derby', is set at a racetrack; the main characters are Lucky Bill, Good Thing Jackson, a Bookmaker and a variety of betting 'belles' and 'swells'. The plot is slim (as were the plots of most musicals of the time), and turns on an unlikely race between several horses and a mule, which the mule wins. Lucky Bill has beat the odds in all three races and has won enough money to invite all his friends to accompany him to Coney Island for the evening. As with most musicals, song and dance interrupt the plot. There is an opening chorus, a solo number, 'The Sporty Coon', for Lucky Bill at his first appearance, several special dances including 'The Milkmaid's Flirtations' and a Spanish ballet, songs for most of the remaining leads and a grand finale for the whole company.

In contrast to the musicals presented by the Hyers sisters, in which characters were seen to be moving upwards on the socio-economic-cultural ladder, Isham's show portrays the stereotype of the lazy, cunning, non-working black and his tough and possibly dishonest friends. Lucky Bill is a professional gambler who tells the crowd that he has been on a winning streak for several days; his invitation to the crowd to join him at Coney Island conjures up the image of a big spender who, when he is flush, will spend all the money he has. Bill is certainly not a member of the middle class who goes to church every week; when he comments on the possibility that his good luck won't last, he invites the crowd to come to see him baptised because he's going to join a church when his luck starts to go. Ike, the bully, is another representative of the lower class, and his entry in the race is the mule. In general, the characters in 'The Blackville Derby' do not represent African Americans at their best. They do not represent the hard-working upwardly-mobile 'New Negro'; instead the Bookmaker happily exclaims that he is as willing to take money from the ladies at the races as he would from their husbands. These are ladies of leisure, who are wealthy enough to gamble. No doubt these characterisations were frowned upon by church-going and intellectual African Americans, who saw this type of sketch as demeaning to the race.

Isham's *Octoroons* was a great success; not only did he launch a second touring company in the autumn of 1896, but he also formed a new company, *Oriental America*. Its opening sketch, 'Madame Toussante L'Ovature's Reception', takes place in a hotel on the south Florida coast. Here well-to-do African Americans are attending an anniversary party. Because of labour problems, Mr Waldorf, the proprietor of the hotel, has to ask his guests to cook and serve the tables. To mollify his guests, Waldorf provides some unusual entertainment: first, four Japanese maidens; second, the men of the Magnolia Golf Club and ladies of the Grove Lawn Tennis Club; and finally, the Twentieth Century Bicycle Maids, who wear bloomers when they cycle, and their 'dudes', who call themselves Manhattan sports. Waldorf's servant complains that this last group is not up to the standard of the establishment. This sketch, while still a farce, is clearly delineating a higher class of blacks; there are no gamblers, touts, bullies or bookmakers here. Indeed, these cultivated people, members of golf and lawn tennis clubs, are attending a society gathering, and if 'Waldorf' has not got his party to go without a flaw, he and his guests represent an upwardly-mobile segment of African-American society that even frowned on women wearing bloomers in public. The music heard in these shows included ragtime songs, generally referred to at that time as 'coon' songs, as well as sentimental songs that audiences would have been familiar with from vaudeville, and descriptive songs (such as Dave Marion's 'Still the World Goes On'), which for many years had been featured in popular entertainments. Isham's companies were extremely popular with both black and white audiences. During 1897 and 1898, two of his three companies travelled all over the United States, while the third sailed for Great Britain, where it toured for a year.

Each season, Isham's touring shows opened with a new farce. During the 1897–8 season, the *Octoroons* company's sketch was 'Darktown Outing at Blackville Park', the following season 'A Tenderloin Coon', and in the 1899–1900 season '7–11–77'. While these shows were obviously popular with audiences, they were not generally booked into first-run theatres in the larger cities and they were performed before segregated audiences in many parts of the country. In addition to Isham's and Jack's companies, another important troupe was the *Black Patti's Troubadours* company, which toured the country from 1896 to 1915. For the first ten years, the *Troubadours* presentation was similar to *Octoroons* and *Oriental America*; each show opened with a one-act farce, followed by solo turns by the stars. It concluded with an appearance of Sissieretta Jones (1868–1933), the 'Black Patti', who sang opera and operetta selections with the entire company.

In the summer of 1898, however, a black show finally reached Broadway. *Clorindy, or the Origin of the Cakewalk*, with a script and lyrics by Paul Laurence Dunbar (1872–1906) and music by Will Marion Cook (1869–1944), was seen as part of a late evening entertainment on the roof garden of the Casino Theatre. Unlike the shows produced by Jack and Isham, which had eclectic scores with songs by both black and white composers, *Clorindy* was the first black show to have music by a single African-American composer. It was a stunning success; critics were enthusiastic in their praise for the novelty of the music and dancing, and audiences kept it running through most of the summer. Cook's music was primarily of the coon song variety, with titles such as 'Who Dat Say Chicken in Dis Crowd?' and 'Darktown Is Out Tonight'. Although *Clorindy* was probably conceived as a full-length show, when it finally reached Broadway as the finale of the late-night entertainment, most of Dunbar's script had been eliminated in favour of extended song and dance numbers that featured ragtime and eccentric dancing, with a cast headed by one of the leading African-American composer-performers, Ernest Hogan (1859–1909), who referred to himself as the 'unbleached American'.

Until the success of *Clorindy*, ragtime 'coon' songs had been heard primarily in vaudeville and in the few black shows that were produced by Jack and Isham. By 1898, they had been heard on Broadway in only a few shows; the white comedienne and 'coon shouter' May Irwin (1862–1938) had first featured several coon songs in her show *The Widow Jones* (1895) and the following year in *Courted into Court*. Thus, when *Clorindy* achieved its great public success, the difference to audiences was that these syncopated songs, and the dances associated with them, were once again being performed authentically by African Americans. Ragtime had long been associated with establishments that catered to immoral pursuits; Scott Joplin and Eubie Blake both played rags in bordellos early in their careers. Over the next two decades, syncopated music was to become a mainstay of American popular song, but in 1898, it was still enough of a novelty and a representative of lower-class immorality to cause consternation among the general public. Compared to the patter, genteel and sentimental songs that were the basis of most Broadway shows prior to *Clorindy*, the new music was catchy and representative of the modern period. So too was the cakewalk, an African-American dance probably deriving from the plantation dance in antebellum America, where slaves held dance competitions. The popularity of the cakewalk with white audiences was so great that it appeared in most African-American shows for the next five years.

While *Clorindy* captivated audiences, another show, *A Trip to Coontown*, was touring the eastern seaboard without the same recognition, though it travelled for four seasons in various versions. This full evening's entertainment starred Robert (Bob) Cole (1868–1911) and Billy Johnson (1858–1916); the plot, derived in part from minstrelsy, followed a predictable pattern. A con man, Jim Flimflammer (played by Johnson), tries to take a $5,000 pension from an old man, Silas Green (played by Sam Lucas). Willie Wayside, a tramp (played by Cole), saves the pension for Green by exposing the Flimflammer's schemes. Here again, audiences saw some black stereotypes in the characters of Flimflammer and Green. Willie Wayside, however, occupies a rare place in these shows; he is selfless and honest and is looking to protect innocent gullible people from the schemes of crooks. Though the character of Wayside is sympathetic, Flimflammer is not. And more often than not, his type of unsavoury and dishonest character appeared in the musicals that followed.

The next major black musical seen on Broadway was *Sons of Ham* (1901), which starred the up-and-coming team of Bert Williams (1876–1922) and George Walker (1872–1911). By the time of their appearances on Broadway, Williams and Walker had perfected their act. Williams, who appeared in blackface, played the slow gullible type (later personified by Stepin Fetchit), a dupe for the shenanigans that ensued, while Walker played the dude (descended from minstrelsy's 'Zip Coon'), fast-talking and usually looking to enrich himself at another's expense. In *Sons of Ham,* they play Tobias Wormwood (Williams) and Harty Lafter (Walker), who go to the house of Hampton J. J. Flam, masquerading as his sons, whom he has not seen for six years. The old man is fooled by the impostors until the final minutes of the show when his real sons, Aniesta Babdola and Jeneriska Hassambad, known as Annie and Jennie, arrive to inform him that it was all a joke. Toby and Harty, in the interim, have taken two packages of clothes that were delivered to Ham's house, and have disguised themselves so others will not realise that they are impostors. While in disguise, Harty tells the assembled guests that Toby is the renowned Professor Skinnerbunch, 'a palmist, phrenologist, ocultist [sic], chropodist [sic], odontologist, dentist, florist, ahem-ist, mind reader, and fortune teller', who can tell the past, present, and future, as long as he is paid. Harty's introduction leads into a song, 'The Phrenologist Coon', which is sung by Bert Williams; his sly but knowing delivery was so well received that he recorded it for Victor soon after the show opened. As with all black shows of this period, scripts merely served as outlines for the actual performance, which changed according to the actors available during the tour. In the script for *Sons of Ham,* as in other African-American musicals of the time, minstrelsy and racial pride coexist uncomfortably. The names of the characters, such as Professor Skinnerbunch, Professor Nicholas Switchem (who has difficulty making up his mind) of Riske College, Willie Wataboy, Gabby Slangtry ('an advocate of Modern English'), Tobias Wormwood and Harty Lafter, recall the punning repartee associated with minstrelsy. Still, the young people who populate this show are college students who represent a new educated black America. Though Ham's sons, Jennie and Annie, are involved in high jinks to fool their father, he has worked hard to pay for their education, sending them to Riske Industrial School for six years. For black audiences at the turn of the twentieth century, the farce that parodied them and their ethnicity also painted a brighter future by demonstrating that they were becoming part of the educated middle class.

Williams and Walker's next show, *In Dahomey* (1902), was their first big hit.[3] After fifty-three performances on Broadway, it travelled to England, where it was well received by audiences and critics. As in *Sons of Ham*, there is an underlying reality beneath the clowning and pratfalls of the characters; in this show, it is the romance of returning to Africa, which was being hotly debated in the African-American community during the first decade of the twentieth century. Most of *In Dahomey* takes place in Florida, where Williams, as Shylock Homestead, and Walker, as Rareback Pinkerton, pretend to be detectives so they can hoodwink Cicero Lightfoot to collect a $500 reward and join the African Colonisation Society. When Lightfoot finds a pot of gold, however, he decides to take all his friends to Dahomey so they can see the homeland for themselves. The final act, mostly in pantomime with dance, begins with a jungle scene. As all the Americans arrive, they are expected to adapt to the strange customs of Dahomey. Eventually, they all decide to return to Florida and the 'good life'. Cook once again provided most of the score; significant among his songs in the show are the chorus 'Swing Along', which highlights black pride ('We'll a swing along, yes, a swing along An' a lif a' yo' heads up high, Wif' pride and gladness beamin' from yo' eye'), and 'On Emancipation Day', which celebrates post-Civil war festivities ('On Emancipation day, All you white folks clear de way, Brass ban' playin' sev'ral tunes, Darkies eyes look jes' lak moons, Marshall of de day a struttin', Lord but he is gay'). Although the show was generally viewed as a comedy, there were moments of seriousness where the characters spoke to blacks in the audience.

The African theme appears once again in Williams and Walker's next musical, *Abyssinia* (1906). Having won a lottery, Rastus Johnson (Walker) decides to take his relatives and a friend, Jasper Jenkins (Williams), to Europe. After some difficulties in France, the group goes to Abyssinia where they meet the Grand Emperor, Menelik. As in *Sons of Ham*, the use of an abbreviated name, in this case, 'Ras' for Rastus, leads the Americans into trouble. The Emperor believes that Ras is a prince, since 'Ras' in Abyssinian means 'prince'. As in their earlier play, mistaken identities lead to complications that are resolved at the last moment by the intervention of an Abyssinian princess. After the two friends are freed, they decide to return to America. Much of the play contrasts the cultural and social differences between Americans and Abyssinians, with the Africans depicted as the more enlightened of the two. Cook once again wrote most of the score, though Bert Williams contributed several numbers, one of which, 'Nobody', was to become his signature song.

Contemporary with Williams and Walker's musicals were those of Cole and the Johnson brothers, James Weldon (1871–1938) and J. Rosamond (1873–1954). Their two shows, *The Shoo-Fly Regiment* (1907) and *The Red*

Moon (1909), avoided many of the stereotypes noted above. In the former show, the plot revolves around a black regiment sent to the Philippines, where a Tuskegee Institute graduate, Hunter Wilson, leads his men in an attack on an enemy fortress. On his victorious return to the United States, his sweetheart, who had broken off their engagement, readily agrees to marry him. In the latter show, Cole and the Johnsons explore the interactions of African Americans and Amerindians. Minnehaha is the half-black, half-Indian daughter of Chief Low Dog, who abandoned her and her black mother when she was an infant. He suddenly returns after fifteen years to bring Minnehaha back to his reservation. She is rescued by Slim Brown and Plunk Green, her boyfriend, who, after some comic situations at the reservation, bring her back to Virginia, where she and Green are married and Chief Low Dog is reunited with his wife. Rosamond Johnson's music for the show utilises native Indian tunes that he and Cole heard while travelling the vaudeville circuit through the western United States. Although a few of the songs are still reflective of the earlier ragtime genre, many are written as art-songs, similar to those written by Amy Beach, George W. Chadwick and Reginald de Koven, making *The Red Moon* more of an operetta than a musical comedy.

At the end of the decade, African-American musical theatre suffered a tremendous setback with the deaths of Hogan in 1909 and Walker and Cole in 1911. Bert Williams joined Ziegfeld's *Follies*,[4] where he became a regular headliner, and Johnson joined briefly with several other performers, but did not seem to find a partner who was equal to Cole. In 1915 he became the director of the Music School Settlement in Harlem, which was funded by the white philanthropist David Mannes.

During the second decade of the twentieth century, several younger performers continued to write musicals, but few of their efforts attracted mixed audiences to the same degree as the earlier shows. *Dr Beans from Boston* by Sherman H. Dudley (1873–1940) reverted to stereotypes. An ex-minstrel, Gymnasium Butts, who has taken the identity of Dr Beans, and his sidekick, Bill Simmons, purchase a drug store in which a love potion is stored. Butts gives it, in a large dose, to Susie Lee, to win her affection. The real Dr Beans arrives and is hit over the head by Butts; he loses his memory and Butts is able to conclude his scheme successfully. Another veteran of the stage, J. Leubrie Hill (1873–1916), who was a member of the Williams and Walker repertory company, wrote and starred in *Darktown Follies* (1914), a revue that mirrored Ziegfeld's popular show. While the show did not succeed in drawing the large black audiences that Hill expected, the rights for several of the musical numbers, including 'Rock Me in the Cradle of Love' and 'At the Ball, That's All', were purchased by Ziegfeld for use in his *Follies* revue. The brothers J. Homer Tutt (?1870s–?1930s) and Salem Tutt Whitney

(1869–1934) wrote numerous musicals during the decade. While most of their shows included slapstick, the characters they portrayed were usually representative of up-to-date African-American culture and devoid of caricature. In *How Newtown Prepared* (1916), for example, George Washington Bullion, played by Whitney, hears about the fight between Mexican troops and the Tenth Cavalry, which was a black unit. He takes his volunteer army to join the fight, but owing to a number of mishaps, his soldiers are captured by the Turks. Eventually the company is rescued by an American man-o'-war. In *The Children of the Sun* (1919), the Dean of Howard University finds an archaeological document that establishes the origins of the Negro race. After adventures in Japan, Persia, India and Egypt, Abe and Gabe Washington (played by the brothers) reach Ethiopia, which is the original site where the race began. To judge by the titles of the songs heard in these shows, they were a mixture of various genres that appeared in most musicals of the period. Because most of Tutt's songs were not published, they have probably not survived.

In 1921 *Shuffle Along* arrived on upper Broadway. It created a sensation with audiences and critics and ushered in a new period of black musicals on Broadway. The book of *Shuffle Along*, by Flournoy Miller (1887–1971) and Aubrey Lyles (1883–1932), was neither groundbreaking nor representative of the 'New Negro' position that was central to the writings of W. E. B. DuBois, Alain Locke and others. Rather, it was a continuation of the stereotypical representation of African Americans that had been seen twenty years earlier. Miller and Lyles had created the comic characters of Steve Jenkins and Sam Peck at the Pekin Theatre in Chicago more than a decade earlier. They had written a number of short and full-length skits around these characters, including 'The Mayor of Dixie', which were then refined over the years.

The plot of *Shuffle Along* relates the comic struggles of Jenkins and Peck to become mayor of the southern town of Jimtown. Through some dishonest dealings, which include stealing money from the grocery store that they jointly own, Jenkins becomes mayor, to the dismay of the honest candidate, Harry Walton, who can marry the daughter of the richest man in town only if he is elected. After the election, Jenkins goes back on his campaign promises, refusing to name Peck his Chief of Police. There is a boxing match – one of their famous set pieces – between the partners, which Peck wins. Jenkins appoints him and Peck quickly assumes authority and begins to arrest as many townspeople as the jail will hold. But a New York detective uncovers their misdeeds; Walton becomes the new mayor and is able to marry his sweetheart, and the partners are allowed to return to their grocery store without punishment.

While the plot did not demonstrate the kind of originality that would catch the attention of the public, the music and lyrics of Noble Sissle

(1889–1975) and James Hubert 'Eubie' Blake (1883–1983) were first-rate, up-to-date, and varied enough to guarantee a long Broadway run.[5] There are more than twenty numbers in the show; they run the gamut from blues ('Gypsy Blues', 'Lowdown Blues' and 'Serenade Blues'), jazz ('I'm Just Simply Full of Jazz') and African-American songs ('Pickaninny Shoes', 'Old Black Joe and Uncle Tom' and 'If You've Never Been Vamped by a Brownskin') to ballads ('Everything Reminds Me of You' and 'Love Will Find a Way') and up-tempo numbers ('I'm Just Wild about Harry'). Although Sissle was a member of the cast, he appeared out of character towards the end of the show when he and Blake appeared on stage in tuxedos for 'A Few Minutes with Sissle and Blake', which recreated their vaudeville act. In this instance, they were following the example of Bob Cole and J. Rosamond Johnson, who had pioneered a high-class act almost two decades earlier.

The immense popularity of *Shuffle Along* kept it on Broadway for 504 performances. The book musicals that ensued were, for the most part, copies of Sissle and Blake's blockbuster; even revues, such as *From Dixie to Broadway* and the various editions of Lew Leslie's *Blackbirds*, which became increasingly popular during the decade, alternated antebellum plantation scenes with current social problems, such as rent parties.[6] Many shows also included cemetery scenes, with ghostly apparitions and stereotypical humour, and farcical scenes that satirised African-American social issues, such as weddings and gambling. Jungle scenes, which had been seen in *In Dahomey* and *Abyssinia,* became popular once again, with music and costumes that were much more suggestive than those seen in the earlier shows.[7]

The publication of Edna Ferber's *Show Boat* in 1926, both in serialised form and as a book, raised serious issues about relationships between the races. The mixed cast of characters were real people; there was no intended stereotyping of African Americans. The novel, which quickly became a bestseller, traces the lives and fortunes of a riverboat family, their troupe of actors and their deck crew through several generations; Ferber addresses difficult social issues, such as 'passing' and miscegenation. A little more than one year later, in December 1927, a musical by Jerome Kern (1885–1946) and Oscar Hammerstein (1895–1960) based on the novel opened in New York City. Although Hammerstein changed some aspects of Ferber's novel, he retained these two issues that are so central to the plot.

Show Boat was not the first Broadway musical to employ a multiracial cast; several companies had mixed-cast productions of *Uncle Tom's Cabin,* and *The Southerners,* with music by Will Marion Cook, had a brief run in 1904. But the popularity of Hammerstein and Kern's musical brought these sensitive issues to the forefront of public attention. Instead of the caricatures that populated most black musicals of the Harlem Renaissance, Hammerstein offered a serious and sympathetic portrayal of African Americans. The

Plate 6 A production of *Show Boat*, c. 1938 at the St Louis Municipal Opera.

problems faced by blacks during the last quarter of the nineteenth century are dealt with directly. Julie, one of the actresses in the troupe, is passing for white; Hammerstein and Kern give the first hint that something is amiss in a scene that is not part of the novel, when Queenie, the cook of the Cotton Blossom, comments that the song Julie is singing, 'Can't Help Lovin' Dat Man', is associated with black folks. A bit later, when Julie's true origins are discovered, she and her white husband, Frank, are forced to leave the show boat. Though *Show Boat* is a Broadway musical in the grand tradition, Hammerstein did not try to evade these issues. His forthrightness was a shock to audiences that were accustomed to lightweight plots that did not ask them to think.

Kern's music for the show is a pastiche. In addition to Julie's number, there is a spiritual, 'Misery', that is sung by the black chorus, and 'Ol' Man River', which is Kern's version of a work song. Ravenal and Julie, however, sing a Viennese waltz, 'Make Believe'. And because *Show Boat* is an epic, Kern composed music in a number of styles to represent different time periods – the 1880s, 1893 (at the time of the Columbian Exposition in Chicago), 1906 and 1927. For the New Year's Eve scene in the second act, Kern even uses well-known pieces of the 1880s and 90s, including 'After the Ball', an 1892 waltz-ballad by Charles K. Harris, John Philip Sousa's 'Washington Post

March' (1889), Joseph Howard's 'Goodbye My Lady Love' (1904) and Kerry Mills' 'At a Georgia Camp Meeting' (1897), to lend authenticity to the score. The success of *Show Boat*, however, did not lead others to write dramatic musicals. *Show Boat*'s serious treatment of social issues was not matched until *West Side Story*.

George (1898–1937) and Ira (1896–1983) Gershwin's opera, *Porgy and Bess*, provides a different view of African Americans. Based on the novel and play *Porgy* by Dorothy (1890–1961) and [Edwin] DuBose (1885–1940) Heyward, the opera depicts the residents of Catfish Row, a tenement on the waterfront in Charleston, South Carolina. Heyward's depiction of the community focuses on its general despair and the violent nature of life there. His characters include a bully, Crown; his woman, Bess; a cripple, Porgy; a ne'er-do-well, Sportin' Life, who offers Bess some 'happy dust'; and the various residents of the tenement. Heyward opens the story with a scene of nightlife in Catfish Row; there is dancing, a mother sings a lullaby to her baby, and some of the men are playing a crap game. When Crown commits murder as a result of an argument at the crap game, the tone for the rest of the drama is set. Although the play as a whole tends towards melodrama and operatic exaggeration, Heywood attempted to provide realism through his use of local colour, such as a picnic on one of the Charleston area's well-known barrier islands, Kitiwah (or Kiawah), where Bess is confronted by Crown, who is hiding from the police. A hurricane provides a symbolic background for the confrontation scene over Bess between Porgy and Crown, while the frightened residents of Catfish Row sing spirituals to try to appease the fury of the storm.

In spite of his Charlestonian background and his knowledge of the Gullah language and tenement life, Heyward's depiction of African Americans has been controversial, with some critics asserting that he was dealing only with stereotypes and did not understand the black character. This negative appraisal of his work began soon after the play was seen on Broadway in 1927 and reached its zenith after the Civil Rights movement was established. Seen in the context of the 1920s, however, Heyward's serious attempt to delineate poor urban Southern black life was far removed from the efforts of black writers of musicals such as Miller and Lyles in their Broadway shows, or Billy King (1875–1936) in Chicago, whose stereotypical depictions included malapropisms, knockabout humour, and portrayals of cheating and other dishonest practices.

Gershwin's music for the drama is eclectic. There are hit songs, such as 'Summertime', 'Oh, I Got Plenty O' Nuttin'' and 'It Ain't Necessarily So'. There are also operatic ensembles that demand a style of singing usually not required in a Broadway musical. When Serena and the chorus sing 'My Man's Gone Now' in the second scene of Act I, the tessitura of the solo requires that Serena sings an octave and a fifth, from e′ to b″, a range that is suitable for an operatic singer but not for most Broadway performers. Gershwin's use of sung recitative as a replacement for spoken dialogue also separates his opera from the usual musical comedy.

Although the Metropolitan Opera was eager to produce a Gershwin opera,[8] Gershwin chose to have the Theatre Guild produce *Porgy and Bess* on Broadway. His decision was certainly pragmatic. Undoubtedly, he was concerned about the problem of casting: would the Met have allowed an all-black ensemble to perform in repertory during the regular season? Another concern was the number of performances the opera might have received during the season. The most successful American opera premiered during the 1930s was Deems Taylor's *Peter Ibbetson*, which received sixteen performances over three seasons. By deciding to have *Porgy and Bess* produced on Broadway, Heyward and the Gershwins' opera received 124 performances. By Broadway standards, its run was not exceptional. By operatic standards, however, it would have to be considered most successful.

From its beginnings after emancipation, African-American musical theatre pursued two contradictory goals – to entertain and to enlighten. As a primary and necessary economic goal, it had to entertain audiences. Its dependence on white patronage may have imposed some of the stereotypes of minstrelsy on the scripts and music of most shows, though this cannot be stated unequivocally; at the same time, some show scripts included brief scenes or dialogue that, to those who were listening carefully, heralded the arrival of the African-American middle class, symbolised by the New Negro. While black minstrel stereotypes continued to be prominent during the Harlem Renaissance (and beyond), a few musicals attempted to portray African Americans with enlightened realism. Several Tutt and Whitney shows, as well as a few by other African-American authors, endeavour to address serious issues; among white-authored musicals, *Show Boat* falls into that category also. *Porgy and Bess* is likewise realistic – but only when viewed within the conventions of late nineteenth-century opera. It attempts, however, to offer a non-stereotypical view of African Americans, and, in doing so, joins the small group of musical works that present theatrically realistic characterisations of black people and their lives.

6 The melody (and the words) linger on: American musical comedies of the 1920s and 1930s

GEOFFREY BLOCK

Setting the stage

The period under surveillance in this chapter divides with discomforting accuracy into two vastly contrasting national moods. America in the 1920s, retrospectively tagged as the Jazz Age (from F. Scott Fitzgerald's 1931 essay, 'Echoes of the Jazz Age'), the Roaring Twenties or, more euphemistically, Prohibition, experienced a decade of unprecedented prosperity and self-confidence. Republican presidents, for whom the business of America was business, led the country. Immigration, which had in the previous generation brought the parents of future songwriters to America, came to a virtual halt, and isolationism reigned as the prevailing sentiment. Women voted for the first time in the election of 1920 and the Smart Set began to explore social freedoms as well, such as public smoking, reading sex and confession magazines, applying make-up, bobbing their hair and wearing short skirts. As further manifestation of what contemporary social historian Frederick Lewis Allen called 'a revolution in manners and morals', both men and women sharply increased their alcohol consumption, imbibing in thousands of newly sprouting metropolitan speakeasies in Prohibition America.[1] By the end of the decade radio became a family ritual, and sound films revolutionised an already popular entertainment and created new opportunities for musicals, both adapted from the stage and original. The 1920s introduced an exceptional generation of American playwrights (Eugene O'Neill, Maxwell Anderson), novelists (Sinclair Lewis, Ernest Hemingway, Fitzgerald), classical composers (Edgard Varèse, Aaron Copland) and jazz artists (Louis Armstrong, Duke Ellington). It was also a period, not unlike the present, when a news event (e.g. the plight of Floyd Collins trapped in a Kentucky mine for a month in 1925 or Charles Lindbergh's transatlantic solo flight in 1927) could transfix and dominate national attention to the exclusion of all else.

In sharp contrast, the 1930s were marked by economic despair, disastrously high unemployment and a social unrest that fell dangerously close to cultivating the kind of political upheavals that demoralised much of Europe and the Far East. Broadway was not immune to the austere economic conditions that overshadowed the decade, conditions that prompted all of the songwriters featured in this chapter – with varying degrees of commitment and success – to heed the siren call of the more lucrative, if less artistically free, Hollywood film milieu. In contrast to the 1920s, where ten book shows ran for more than five hundred performances on Broadway (including four musical comedies), in the 1930s only three book shows (all musical comedies) lasted more than four hundred performances (*Of Thee I Sing*, *Anything Goes* and *DuBarry Was a Lady*). Nothing seemed to cure Broadway's woes, not even the repeal of Prohibition in 1933 or President Franklin D. Roosevelt's alphabet soup of social programmes. In the 1933–4 season only thirteen new musicals of any type appeared, and most of these failed. Two seasons later the total was reduced still further to twelve, five book shows and seven revues, and of these, only Richard Rodgers and Lorenz Hart's *On Your Toes* made a clear profit (although their *Jumbo* and Cole Porter's *Jubilee* were imaginative and musically rich, and George and Ira Gershwin's and DuBose Heyward's *Porgy and Bess* was soon recognised as one of America's great artistic treasures). For most of the first month that *I'd Rather Be Right* played (November 1937), Rodgers and Hart's only competition was their own *Babes in Arms*, which for a time during the previous July (of course, without air-conditioning) was the only show then running on Broadway. This relative inactivity presents a sober contrast to the largesse of the 1920s, in which *No, No, Nanette* (Vincent Youmans, Irving Caesar and Otto Harbach), *Dearest Enemy* (Rodgers and Hart), *The Vagabond King* (Rudolf Friml and Brian Hooker) and *Sunny* (Jerome Kern and Oscar Hammerstein II) all had their debuts during one seven-day period in 1925. The 1927–8 season witnessed over fifty new musicals among a record-breaking total of possibly 270 theatrical offerings (264 according to *Variety*), most notably *Good News!*, *A Connecticut Yankee*, *Funny Face* and *Show Boat*, all of which arrived between September and December (see Table 6.1).

Musical comedies early in the 1920s favoured Cinderella stories in modern urban America such as the long-running *Irene* that opened in November 1919 and *Sally* (December 1920). Topical subjects later in the decade included bootlegging (*Oh, Kay!*), the Florida land boom and land speculation (*Tip-Toes* and *The Cocoanuts*), the Lindbergh flight (*Rosalie*) and sports, the last most systematically in the B. G. DeSylva–Lew Brown–Ray Henderson trilogy that revolved around popular sports crazes: football (*Good News!*), boxing (*Hold Everything!*) and golf (*Follow Thru*). In the 1930s several musicals, for example, Porter's *Red, Hot and Blue!* and Rodgers and Hart's *On Your Toes* (both from 1936), and also Kern and Hammerstein's 1931 operetta, *The Cat and the Fiddle*, grappled with an alleged aesthetic gulf between popular and classical music, the former coming out ahead in each case. *Anything Goes* targeted celebrity criminals such as Baby Face Nelson and celebrity evangelists like Aimée Semple McPherson.

Table 6.1 *Selected American and British musical comedies of the 1920s and 1930s*

	Kern	Gershwin (lyrics: I. Gershwin)	Porter	Rodgers (lyrics: L. Hart)	Others
1920	*The Night Boat* (313) (Caldwell) *Sally* (570) (Bolton; L: Grey, et al.)				
1921	*The Cabaret Girl* (361) (Grossmith, Wodehouse; L: Wodehouse) [London] *Good Morning Dearie* (347) (Caldwell)				*Shuffle Along* (504) (Miller, Lyles; L: Sissle; music: Blake)
1922					
1923	*The Beauty Prize* (213) (Grossmith, Wodehouse) [London] *The Stepping Stones* (241) (Burnside, Caldwell; L: Caldwell)				
1924	*Sitting Pretty* (95) (Bolton, Wodehouse; L: Wodehouse)	*Sweet Little Devil* (120) (Mandel, Schwab; L: DeSylva) *Lady, Be Good!* (330) (Bolton, Thompson) *Primrose* (225) (Grossmith, Bolton; L: Carter) [London]			
1925	*Sunny* (517) (Harbach, Hammerstein)	*Tell Me More!* (100) (Thompson, Wells; L: DeSylva, I. Gershwin) *Tip-Toes* (194) (Bolton, Thompson)		*Dearest Enemy* (286) (Fields)	*No, No, Nanette* (321) Harbach, Mandel; L: Caesar; music: Youmans) *The Cocoanuts* (276) (Kaufman; L: Berlin; music: Berlin)

(cont.)

Table 6.1 (*cont.*)

	Kern	Gershwin (lyrics: I. Gershwin)	Porter	Rodgers (lyrics: L. Hart)	Others
1926	Criss-Cross (206) (Harbach, Caldwell)	Oh, Kay! (256) (Bolton, Wodehouse)		The Girl Friend (301) (Fields) Lido Lady (259) (Bolton, Kalmar, Ruby) [London] Peggy-Ann (333) (Fields) Betsy (39) (Caesar, Freeman)	
1927		Funny Face (244) (Thompson, Smith)		A Connecticut Yankee (418) (Fields)	Hit the Deck (352) (Fields; L: Grey, Robin; music: Youmans) Good News! (551) (Schwab, DeSylva; L: DeSylva, Brown; music: Henderson)
1928	Blue Eyes (276) (Bolton, John; L: John) [London]	Rosalie (335) (Wodehouse; music: Romberg, G. Gershwin) Treasure Girl (68) (Thompson, Lawrence)	Paris (195) (Brown)	She's My Baby (71) (Bolton, Kalmar, Ruby) Present Arms (155) (Fields) Chee-Chee (31) (Fields)	Hold Everything! (413) (DeSylva, McGowan; L: DeSylva, Brown; music: Henderson)
1929		Show Girl (111) (McGuire; L: Kahn, I. Gershwin)	Wake Up and Dream (263) (Hastings) Fifty Million Frenchmen (254) (Fields)	Spring Is Here (104) (Davis) Heads Up! (144) (McGowan, Smith)	Follow Thru (403) (Schwab, Mandel; L: DeSylva, Brown; music: Henderson)
1930		Strike Up the Band (191)(Ryskind) Girl Crazy (272) (Bolton, McGowan)	The New Yorkers (168) (Fields)	Simple Simon (135) (Wynn, Bolton) Ever Green (254) (Levy) [London]	Flying High (357) (McGowan, DeSylva, Brown; L: DeSylva, Brown; music: Henderson)
1931		Of Thee I Sing (441) (Kaufman, Ryskind)		America's Sweet-Heart (135) (Fields)	Fine and Dandy (255) (Stewart; L: James; music: Swift)

Year				
1932			Gay Divorce (248) (Taylor)	Face the Music (165) (M. Hart; L: Berlin; music: Berlin), Take a Chance (243) (DeSylva, Schwab, Silvers; L: DeSylva; music: Whiting, Brown, Youmans)
1933	Pardon My English (46) (Fields), Let 'Em Eat Cake (90) (Kaufman, Ryskind)	Roberta (295) (Harbach)	Nymph Errant (154) (Brent) [London]	
1934		Three Sisters (72) (Hammerstein)	Anything Goes (420) (Lindsay, Grouse)	
1935			Jubilee (169) (M. Hart)	Jumbo (233) (Hecht, MacArthur)
1936			Red, Hot and Blue! (183) (Lindsay, Crouse)	On Your Toes (315) (Rodgers, L. Hart, Abbott); Johnny Johnson (68) (Green; music: Weill), The Cradle Will Rock (19) (Blitzstein) [1938: 104 perf.]
1937				Babes in Arms (289) (Rodgers, L. Hart), I'd Rather Be Right (290) (Kaufman, M. Hart)
1938			You Never Know (78) (Leigh), Leave It to Me! (291) (B. &S. Spewack), DuBarry Was a Lady (408) (Fields, DeSylva)	I Married an Angel (338) (Rodgers, L. Hart), The Boys from Syracuse (235) (Abbott); Knickerbocker Holiday (168) (Anderson; music: Weill)
1939	Very Warm for May (59) (Hammerstein)			Too Many Girls (249) (Marion)

Numbers in parentheses refer to first-run performances. Unless otherwise indicated the names in parentheses refer to librettists and lyricists. L: = lyrics.

Although the politicisation of the musical has been overstated, overt political themes and musicals with social commentary proliferated in the 1930s, affecting virtually everyone in addition to Kern and Hammerstein, who had daringly explored racial politics the previous decade in *Show Boat*.[2] Between 1930 and 1933 the Gershwin brothers, along with George S. Kaufman and Morrie Ryskind, offered a political trilogy that satirised war in *Strike Up the Band*, the vapidity of political campaign themes (and nearly everything else) in *Of Thee I Sing*, and even political revolution in the latter's more acerbic sequel *Let 'Em Eat Cake*. In *Face the Music* (February 1932) Irving Berlin, working with Moss Hart and Kaufman, satirised police corruption and eerily foreshadowed the scandals that would force New York City Mayor James Walker out of office a few months later. Rodgers and Hart made President Roosevelt the central character in *I'd Rather Be Right* (with a book by Kaufman and Hart), in which Roosevelt was impersonated by Broadway legend George M. Cohan in his last Broadway hurrah. The same year, 1937, Rodgers and Hart effectively spoofed socialism in the character Peter from *Babes in Arms*, a socialist who advocates money and property sharing until he acquires instant wealth. Porter's main contribution in this vein was *Leave It to Me* (1938; book by Bella and Samuel Spewack), the story of an ambassador to Russia abruptly recalled when he presents a plan for world peace. The first American musical comedies of Kurt Weill offered a satire on war in the parable about a pacifist during World War I, *Johnny Johnson* (1936; book and lyrics by Paul Green), and a play about the despot Governor Peter Stuyvesant in colonial New York in *Knickerbocker Holiday* (1938; book and lyrics by Maxwell Anderson), a parable that suggested the modern potential for similar abuses.[3] Marc Blitzstein created a musical that paralleled real-life union struggles amidst the larger theme of metaphorical prostitution and selling out in *The Cradle Will Rock*, which, when banned from its theatre for its uncompromising leftist leanings in June 1937, made front-page news in its own time and inspired a popular political movie in ours.[4] Two of the decade's most highly acclaimed revues, Irving Berlin and Moss Hart's *As Thousands Cheer* and Harold Rome's *Pins and Needles*, were also based on political themes, from the gently satirical (Rome's 'Doing the Reactionary') to the profoundly disturbing song about the lynching of African Americans (Berlin's 'Supper Time'). At the end of the decade, when war became an imminent reality, the political musical disappeared. Thus in 1939, two years after *I'd Rather Be Right*, Rodgers and Hart offered the college musical *Too Many Girls*; one year after *Leave It to Me* Porter wrote the apolitical *DuBarry Was a Lady*.

By 1920, America, in the aftermath of the Great War, indisputably a world political, economic, and nascent cultural power, had long since begun extricating itself from the courtly muses of Europe to develop its own dramatic and musical identity. After two decades of American vernacular jingoism on the one hand (the musicals of Cohan) and musicals either imported directly from Europe or closely modelled on European products on the other (Franz Lehár's *The Merry Widow,* Victor Herbert's *Naughty Marietta*), a new generation had arrived. Several years before the new decade Berlin, Kern and Gershwin had each composed a major hit song, Berlin's Tin Pan Alley song 'Alexander's Ragtime Band' (1911), Kern's interpolation in *The Girl From Utah*, 'They Didn't Believe Me' (1914) and Gershwin's 'Swanee' (added for Al Jolson in the road tour of Sigmund Romberg's *Sinbad* in 1919). By 1920 Berlin, Kern and Gershwin had also composed Broadway scores of their own, Kern's *The Red Petticoat* (1912) and a series of historic and widely praised shows now known for the theatre, the Princess, that housed several of them, Berlin's 'ragtime' musical *Watch Your Step* (1914) and Gershwin's *La! La! Lucille* (1919). Porter saw his first Broadway musical, *See America First* (1916), quickly close, moved to Europe, and would not compose his next complete show for another twelve years. In 1919 Rodgers and Hart heard their first song, 'Any Old Place with You', interpolated in a Broadway show; the following year, the new team shared half a score of *Poor Little Ritz Girl* with the established prince of operetta, Sigmund Romberg.[5]

In 1924, the year Kern tried unsuccessfully to create an enlarged Princess-type show in the musically rich *Sitting Pretty* (with Princess collaborators Guy Bolton and P. G. Wodehouse), musical comedy seemed to change direction. Possible catalysts for this change, marked musically in the perceptible transition from ragtime to jazz, were the extended solo appearance of Armstrong in New York City with the Fletcher Henderson Orchestra and Gershwin's popular adaptation of jazz into the concert world in *Rhapsody in Blue*, both events occurring also in 1924. In musical comedy the change is readily apparent from even a superficial comparison between *Sitting Pretty* and *Lady, Be Good!*, the latter inaugurating, again in 1924, the collaboration of George and Ira Gershwin in a show that captured both the fashion and spirit of a new kind of jazz syncopation ('Fascinating Rhythm', 'Little Jazz Bird' and the title song), and contemporary dance rhythms such as the Charleston ('I'd Rather Charleston') added when the show was exported to London in 1926.

In the 1920s and 1930s distinctions between home-grown musicals, i.e. musical comedies, and musicals that conspicuously revealed their debt to European themes and styles, operettas, were sharper and more easily recognised than they would be in future generations. One such distinction is that American musical comedies, in addition to the romantic ballads common to both genres, also featured vernacularly inflected rhythms and melody. With increased frequency the duty of composing both types of songs were combined in a single composer and a single show (e.g. Kern's *Roberta* has the romantic 'Smoke Gets In Your Eyes' and the jazzy 'I'd Be Hard to Handle'). By the end of the decade the decision to join the vernacular Gershwin (then, unlike the Rodgers of *Poor Little Ritz Girl*, at the height of his fame) with the Ruritanian Romberg in *Rosalie* (1928) was unusual. Musical comedies normally utilised contemporary American urban settings with matching dialogue and music (e.g. ragtime, blues, jazz and, after 1930, swing).[6]Operettas were customarily set in exotic locations or fabled early Americana and tended to emphasise the trappings of opera, including operatic voices, contrapuntal duets and choruses, and more elaborate and frequent sections with continuous music. Occasionally, perhaps most notably with *Show Boat*, a musical that successfully balances musical comedy and operetta, or musical comedies like *Of Thee I Sing* and *Let 'Em Eat Cake*, operetta characteristics gradually intruded on musical comedy turf sufficiently to pose a taxonomic challenge. Throughout the era the formats of both operettas and musical comedies called for spoken dialogue and occasional choruses mixed with solos and duets, the latter often harmonised in operettas.

The role stars played in the success of musical comedies of the 1920s and 30s is analogous to the fame and high salaries enjoyed by the film stars of today. In both eras certain performers consistently ensured box-office success. The 1920s featured several stars, perhaps most notably Marilyn Miller, who possessed an invariable ability to entrance live audiences (*Sally, Sunny* and *Rosalie*). Her recordings do not reveal the secret to her strong stage persona and appeal. Fortunately, a star comedian, the ever-bumbling Victor Moore, first seen in Cohan musicals as early as 1906 (*Forty-Five Minutes from Broadway*) and in the 1920s and 30s most memorably in *Oh, Kay!* (1926), *Funny Face* (1927), *Of Thee I Sing* (1931), *Anything Goes* (1934) and *Leave It to Me!* (1938), can be enjoyed in at least one film musical, Berlin's *Top Hat* (1935).

Generations of movie audiences continue to appreciate the comic persona of Bert Lahr, the man for whom *Flying High* (1930) was designed, as the Cowardly Lion in *The Wizard of Oz*, a film musical released the same year Lahr sang 'Friendship' with Ethel Merman in *DuBarry Was a Lady* (1939). Merman, whose recording and film legacy has preserved the memory of one of the last major stars who did not need amplification, went on to have some of her biggest successes after 1940 (*Annie Get Your Gun, Call Me Madam* and *Gypsy*), but she was also one of the great singing actresses of the 1930s, from her auspicious debut singing 'I Got Rhythm' in *Girl Crazy* (1930), to *Anything Goes* (1934), *Red, Hot and Blue* (1936) and *DuBarry*. On the other hand, the stage charisma of William Gaxton, a successful leading man in *A Connecticut Yankee* (1927) and *Fifty Million Frenchmen* (1929) before teaming with Moore in the 1930s, is not evident from the few films he made between 1943 and 1945. Other factors must be considered, including the musical scores, of course, but it is probably not a coincidence that the four most popular musical comedy successes of the 1930s featured Gaxton, Lahr, Merman or Moore, usually in combination: *Flying High* (Lahr), *Of Thee I Sing* (Gaxton and Moore), *Anything Goes* (Gaxton, Merman, and Moore) and *DuBarry* (Lahr and Merman). Some stars today can still launch or maintain a new show or a revival. The 1920s and 1930s contained a firmament of stars that could start (and stop) a show.

Although the stars of these shows deserve praise (the other unequivocal high point, the songs, will be discussed shortly), it must be said that musicals during this period were and remain accused of lacking strong books, especially by the standards set by the Rodgers and Hammerstein model. Surprisingly, unless the memory of earlier shows with still weaker books lingered, critics, even when they noted the failings of musical comedy books, did not seem too disturbed about it. Audiences, who were not unaware of well-made contemporary plays, did not mind either. For the most part the stories remained plausible, coherent and well crafted, presented a welcome series of opportunities to feature songs, dances and stars, and purposely contrasted with the integrated plot narratives found in contemporary American plays.

Because their books seemed so dependent on improvising comedy teams, even today such bona fide musical comedies as Flournoy Miller and Aubrey Lyles' *Shuffle Along* (1921) and the Marx Brothers' *The Cocoanuts* (1925) are commonly mistaken for a third type of musical, the revue. In contrast to musical comedies and operettas, genres that also acquired their initial identity and prominence in the 1890s, revues feature intentionally loose and autonomous skits that exploit the idiosyncratic talents of star comedians, production numbers with beautiful girls, and, most memorably from a later perspective, songs – qualities that were by no means strangers to musical comedy or operetta. Revues may be organised around a unifying theme such as travel (*At Home Abroad*) or newspaper headlines (*As Thousands Cheer*), or they may reflect more generally the stylistic imprint of a producer such as Florenz Ziegfeld or George White. As the 1920s began, revues were the most popular form of musical theatre. In fact, before 1924 revues were the exclusive venue of Berlin (*Ziegfeld Follies* and *Music Box Revues*), Gershwin (*George White's Scandals*) and Porter (*Hitchy-Koo, Greenwich Village Follies*), while Rodgers, who spent these years writing amateur shows, made his hit debut in *The Garrick Gaieties*, a Theatre Guild revue from 1925 that introduced 'Manhattan'. By mid-decade, operettas and musical comedies vied for hegemony, with the former claiming seven of the decade's ten most popular shows (see chapter 3). In the 1930s musical comedy would eclipse both operetta and revues in quantity and popularity and could boast nine of the fifteen most popular shows (although the two longest-running shows of the decade, *Hellzapoppin'* and *Pins and Needles*, were revues).

Music and words

For most readers of this volume the central legacy of musical theatre of all types during this period remains the songs. Contemporary critics and audiences may have been willing to overlook the fact that musical comedy books lacked the qualities expected of the best plays, but a musical comedy score in the 1920s or 1930s without at least one notable song quickly disappeared. Every successful show, and the majority of those otherwise forgotten, offered one or more songs that continued with a life of its own. The Broadway and film songs of Berlin, Gershwin, Kern, Porter and Rodgers, among others, are still with us, frequently sung and increasingly revered. Even when heard in instrumental versions in shopping centres, lifts and cafés, many retain at least a recognisable association with their original verbal messages.

Several sociological and musical characteristics link the major songwriters, who shared lyricists, librettists, producers and stars, and knew, respected, and learned from each other – sometimes, as in the unlikely friendship of Berlin and Porter, genuinely enjoying each other's company. All were born between 1885 (Kern) and 1902 (Rodgers), nearly all in one of the New York City boroughs. Most were the sons of recent Jewish immigrants from Central and Eastern Europe or from Russia. Only Berlin, who arrived from Temun, Russia when he was five years old, was not born in America. The geographical and ethnic exception was Porter, a Protestant who grew up in Peru, Indiana, but who by the 1920s was self-consciously trying to emulate what he perceived to be Jewish melodic and harmonic characteristics.[7] Economic status ranged from poor (Berlin) to affluent or relatively affluent (Kern, Porter, Rodgers). Before establishing their careers, Kern, Porter and Rodgers received at least some formal musical education in theory and composition. At the age of eighteen Kern studied piano, counterpoint, harmony and composition at the New York College of Music. One year after graduating from Yale University, Porter enrolled for a year in Harvard's music department and several years later continued his studies in composition, counterpoint, harmony and orchestration with Vincent d'Indy at the Schola Cantorum in Paris. At the age of twenty-one Rodgers studied harmony with the noted theorist Percy Goetschius at the Institute of Musical Art (renamed the Juilliard School of Music in 1946). Gershwin studied the piano, performing professionally as a song plugger from the age of fifteen and later as a rehearsal pianist and professional performer of his own music, and for the rest of his life absorbed what he needed from a sporadic procession of theorists and composers, including Edward Kilenyi, Joseph Schillinger and Arnold Schoenberg. Berlin alone was self-taught and barely capable of notating or playing his own songs. The songwriters in this short list quickly absorbed early ragtime and blues as well as operetta models and eventually incorporated 1920s jazz and 1930s swing styles into their musical language, harmonically conservative by modernist standards but often strikingly original.

The majority of their songs fitted a standard framework, widely known as thirty-two-bar song form. In most cases the main part of the song, the chorus, was prefaced by a verse, a sometimes independent, sometimes thematically linked introductory section stylistically somewhere between speech and song, a bridge between spoken dialogue and a fully developed melody. Although a famous song such as Gershwin's 'The Man I Love' began its life as a verse, most verses lack the tunefulness or even the rhythmic regularity of the chorus, the portion that gives most songs their primary identity. On rare occasions, most famously in Kern and Harbach's 'Smoke Gets In Your Eyes' and 'Yesterdays', both from *Roberta*, verses are absent altogether. Popular and jazz artists and revivals that took up the song frequently removed verses also (or like Fred Astaire, sang them *after* introducing his recordings with the more familiar chorus), but most songs included verses when they made their musical comedy stage debuts. The thirty-two bars of each chorus were most frequently divided into four phrases of eight bars each, with an AABA scheme ('My Heart Stood Still' from *A Connecticut Yankee* is an example) making up the vast majority of songs. Numerous songs favoured the format ABAC (e.g. 'Embraceable You' from *Girl Crazy*). A related but distinctly different song form that had begun to wane by 1925 offers a more parallel eight-bar periodisation of the thirty-two bars with a complete break in the middle: AB // AB (as in 'Thou Swell' from *A Connecticut Yankee*) or AB // AC (as in 'My Romance' from *Jumbo*).[8] For the most part, the songwriters featured in this chapter shared Rodgers' view that he 'never felt restricted but rather enjoyed the challenge of coming up with something fresh within the prescribed regulations'.[9]

Early in their careers the major songwriters developed idiosyncratic musical characteristics. Gershwin often favoured pentatonic melodies ('I Got Rhythm'), blue notes ('I'll Build a Stairway to Paradise' and 'Somebody Loves Me' in *George White's Scandals*, and throughout *Porgy and Bess*), and a predilection for repeated notes, for example the release or B section of 'I Got Rhythm' (an AABA song) and the 'no, no, they can't' portion of 'They Can't Take That Away'. Characteristically, as in the last-named song, Gershwin changes the harmony on each repeated note. Other harmonic features in Gershwin songs are the delayed resolution of the central key ('Slap That Bass') and the use of harmony for expressive textual purposes (the

harmonically imaginative chord that fits the phrase 'just imagine someone' in 'Nice Work If You Can Get It'). These latter characteristics become
increasingly prevalent in Gershwin's film songs, more than half of which
also display at least one section that is either longer (or in one case shorter)
than eight measures. Although they are almost invariably disregarded by
the thousands of jazz musicians who play the 'I Got Rhythm' chord progressions (known as the 'rhythm changes'), two additional bars originally
belonged to the final A section of this song.

Porter exhibits a strong predilection throughout his career for the juxtaposition of major and minor modes ('Night and Day'), release sections
that closely parallel the main A sections ('Let's Do It' and 'Night and Day'),
and exotic beguine and other Latin rhythms ('Begin the Beguine'). Rodgers'
nearly ubiquitous trademark is the simple scale, either ascending or descending, both with Hart and later with Hammerstein, out of which he manages to
develop a staggering melodic variety (from 'Mountain Greenery' to 'Do-Re-
Mi'). 'My Heart Stood Still', yet another variation of this technique, consists
of an ascending series of three-note descending scales that carefully avoid
the climactic note until the word 'thrill' in the final A section. Among other
prominent Rodgers trademarks are the intentionally surprising notes at the
ends of phrases[10] and a long and impressive series of memorable waltzes
from 'Falling in Love with Love' to 'Do I Hear a Waltz?'

Although subject matter varies enormously and includes numerous
songs of social and political significance, the central subject in the vast
majority of musical comedy songs is romantic love. Within this convention
the lyricists Berlin, Ira Gershwin, Hammerstein, Hart and Porter manage to
convey an impressive variety of individual responses and attitudes. Although
their lyrical versatility and range defy comfortable generalisations, some
characteristics did emerge during the course of their careers. Hart's lyrics
tend to ponder the bittersweetness of unrequited love ('Glad to Be Unhappy')
or even love as a sickness ('It's Got to Be Love' and its sequel 'This Can't
Be Love'). Porter focuses more on the direct approach ('Let's Do It'). Philip
Furia notes that Ira Gershwin 'situated most of his songs at the moment of
falling in love'.[11] John Clum explores a possible gay subtext in Hart's lyrics
and the more transparent references to homosexuality in Porter's.[12]

From the Rodgers and Hammerstein era onwards, lyrics typically came
first, but in the 1920s and 1930s it was nearly always the music, unless, as
with Berlin and Porter, the composer and lyricist resided in the same person.
It may be constructive to compare the compositional methods of some of
the leading songwriters. Early in his career Berlin summarised his lifelong
working methods in the following succinct terms: 'I get an idea, either a
title or a phrase or a melody, and hum it out to something definite.'[13] In a
1936 interview Porter described a related working procedure: 'First I think

of an idea for a song and then I fit it to a title. Then I go to work on a melody, spotting the title at certain moments in the melody. Then I write the lyric – the end first – that way it has a strong finish.'[14] In the same interview Porter also disclosed that he tried to pick rhymes for which he could assemble a long list with the same ending. Kern, the Gershwins and Rodgers and Hart almost invariably began with the music, often after a title had been determined. A rare if not unprecedented exception to Kern's music-first rule created shortly after the time period encompassed in this chapter is the song 'The Last Time I Saw Paris', the Academy Award-winning song that the composer set at Hammerstein's request for the film *Lady Be Good* (1941). No extant documentation reveals that Rodgers ever set a Hart lyric for a full chorus.[15] But just as Berlin and Porter frequently begin their compositional process with a title, so did the Gershwins and Rodgers and Hart. When Rodgers composed 'My Heart Stood Still', for example, he was setting a title that formed the central starting point for Hart's future lyrics.[16] In this very real sense, the words, or at least arguably the most important words, did indeed come first. What is remarkable, to continue with this famous song, is Hart's unusual sensitivity to Rodgers' music. The line 'my heart stood still' may have been a given, but Hart knew to pick a climactic word ('thrill') that corresponded perfectly to Rodgers' climactic melodic note (attached with a harmonic surprise, the IV chord).[17] In an interview that appeared in 1925 Hart offered a valuable insight about his working methods.[18] Hart's normal starting point was 'the most distinctive melodic phrase' of a Rodgers tune. The example he used was the musical phrase set to the word 'adorable' in the opening line, 'Here in my arms, it's adorable', from the song 'Here In My Arms' (*Dearest Enemy* (1925)).[19] This pivotal musical phrase also inspired a series of prominent multi-syllabic rhymes ('adorable/deplorable' and 'kissable/permissible' in the first stanza and 'affable/laughable' in the second). Many Gershwin songs began with an untitled (and unfinished) melodic fragment. In the case of 'Fascinating Rhythm', for example, something in the song eventually yielded a title and a rhyme scheme, i.e. a set of lyrics to match the fascinating musical rhythms.[20]

According to Stephen Banfield's theory of melopoetics, by the end of the songwriting process, and usually at the beginning, the music and words form a symbiotic, if not always inseparable, union.[21] This principle remains applicable, even in the songs of Rodgers and Hart with their striking opposition of soaring music and languishing and acerbic words. This is, of course, part of the secret of many great songs, whether by Schubert or by Berlin, but for the Broadway songwriters the creative process almost invariably serves both the union and the purposeful contrasts. This generality holds even when new lyrics are created for a song, either unused (a so-called trunk song) or recycled from a failed or otherwise abandoned show. Since the song is the staple of the show in the 1920s and 30s, it is probably unfair to deride a song for stopping the show, its avowed purpose. Like Mozart's arias, songs were often conceived to show off the strengths and minimise the vocal limitations of particular stars. Even if most of the books lack the integration of the Rodgers and Hammerstein era, they usually manage to place their characters in believable, if silly, dramatic situations, and they express the feelings and intellect of their characters. Nearly all the songs of Kern, the Gershwins, Rodgers and Hart, and Porter were conceived or revised for specific characters in specific situations, and contrary to the standard perception, do not characteristically arise meaninglessly out of nowhere.

Legacies: stage revivals, film adaptations, and reconstructed recordings

Soon after *Oklahoma!* (1943), cast albums became common and then a required by-product for nearly every show. Song selections and in many cases relatively complete vocal scores became available for most shows, and by the 1950s aficionados could usually purchase scripts as well. Many shows from the Rodgers and Hammerstein era have been recreated – sometimes slavishly – in film versions, occasionally with the original stars (Rex Harrison in *My Fair Lady*, Robert Preston in *The Music Man*). More recently, some shows have been filmed in staged versions (Sondheim's *Sweeney Todd, Sunday in the Park With George, Into the Woods* and *Passion*). It is also the norm rather than the exception that post-Rodgers and Hammerstein shows appear in reasonably faithful staged revivals. Thanks to these developments the idea of an American musical as an integral unit, still a novel notion in the 1940s, is now an established standard by which musical theatre audiences, critics and even scholars embrace or dismiss a particular show. Although the primary concern of modern practitioners, like their predecessors, is the reaction of opening-night audiences, after *Oklahoma!* those responsible for creating musicals realised that their products had a potentially longer shelf life than in previous decades.

In contrast to the well-preserved monuments of the post-Rodgers and Hammerstein era, the legacies of American musicals of all types from the 1920s and 30s pose difficult, occasionally insurmountable problems. Shows that lasted only three months could earn a profit; the lives of popular shows were extended by a national tour, a London production or a film adaptation. Complete, even representative recordings of shows from this earlier era are therefore rare, although the situation improves if one considers London cast recordings of Broadway exports.[22] Saleable songs were published individually in sheet-music format, but scripts and complete scores appeared only sporadically.[23] Revivals and film versions as a rule altered either the stories, the scores or both, occasionally beyond recognition. In many cases no one now alive can remember what the shows looked like, how they worked, the indefinable dimension of star appeal, what words were spoken, how they were sung, or why audiences could not stay away. Despite our lack of familiarity with most of this repertory, in any form, American musical comedies of the 1920s and 30s have nonetheless left their mark through three frequently distorted yet valuable legacies, namely revivals, films and reconstructions, and one indestructible remnant – the songs.

For a variety of reasons, few of even the most popular musical comedies before *Oklahoma!* have made successful comebacks, at least in their original form. Consider the fate of the four musical comedies of the 1920s to receive over five hundred performances, *Sally* (1920), *Shuffle Along* (1921), *Sunny* (1925) and *Good News!* (1927). The decade's first hit show, *Sally* (book by Bolton, lyrics by Clifford Grey, among others), enjoyed successful runs in London and Sydney and inspired the making of two films, both featuring the huge star who played the original Sally, Marilyn Miller. Perhaps the most lasting memory of the show is Judy Garland's performance of 'Look for the Silver Lining' (lyric by DeSylva), playing Miller in the hemidemisemi-biographical film about Kern's life, *Till the Clouds Roll By* (MGM, 1946). The 1948 revival, in which nearly half of the score was recycled from other Kern shows, closed after thirty-six performances. *Shuffle Along* (lyrics by Noble Sissle and music by Eubie Blake) which introduced 'I'm Just Wild About Harry', Harry Truman's campaign song of 1948, and interpolated 'How Ya' Gonna Keep 'Em Down on the Farm' (music by Walter Donaldson), was a runaway hit of 1921. It is also credited as the launching pad of the Harlem Renaissance and the careers of several distinguished African Americans from Florence Mills in the replacement cast to Josephine Baker, Paul Robeson and Adelaide Hall in the chorus, and inspired a long list of imitators for more than a decade.[24] Three attempts to revive the show with new material, *Shuffle Along: Keep Shufflin* (1928), *Shuffle Along of 1933* (1932), and *Shuffle Along* (1952), however, all quickly closed. Kern's second 1920s hit, *Sunny*, also with Miller, fared slightly better than *Sally*. Although it too vanished after its tour, *Sunny* at least left a fine representative period recording of eight songs from the London cast, including two songs not heard in New York. It also marked the beginning of a collaboration with Hammerstein that would lead to *Show Boat* two years later. Again, its most lingering memory is a song, 'Who', featured in the *Sunny* sequence from *Till the Clouds Roll By*, sung and to some extent danced by Garland, then pregnant with Liza Minnelli.[25]

The fourth hit musical comedy of the 1920s, *Good News!* (lyrics by DeSylva and Brown, music by Henderson), alone managed to have a future on the wicked stage, albeit radically transformed. Thus the 1974 revival altered the setting, plot and book, raided other DeSylva, Brown and Henderson shows for formerly popular songs that a fresh audience might enjoy to join 'The Best Things In Life Are Free' and the 'The Varsity Drag', yet still closed after sixteen performances. In the 1990s Wayne Bryan and Mark Madama wrote another new libretto, which according to the notes that accompany the recording 'streamlines the romantic complications into a unified, fast-moving farce, whose characters have believable backgrounds and motivations', i.e. a musical that follows the Rodgers and Hammerstein model.[26]

The new *Good News!* exemplifies the *modus operandi* of revivals for the past fifty years. Even when the integrity of the earlier scores is largely preserved, as in the revival of *No, No, Nanette* in 1971 that successfully resuscitated hoofers from an earlier era and lasted for two years, and the impressive 1983 Broadway restoration of George Balanchine's choreography and Hans Spialek's orchestrations in *On Your Toes*, the books are invariably revised or rewritten in response to real and imagined modern dramatic expectations and sensitivities.[27] As with *Good News!* the most familiar practice is to invade other scores by the composer at hand and find a way in a new book to include as many familiar songs by that composer as possible. Among the most successful embodiments of this approach are *My One and Only* from 1983, a reworking of Gershwin's *Funny Face* (and other Gershwin shows), the 1962 off-Broadway and 1987 Broadway revivals of Porter's *Anything Goes*[28] and in 1992, *Crazy for You*, a major overhaul of Gershwin's *Girl Crazy* that ran for an astonishing 1,622 performances.

Good News! provides a useful starting point to introduce another lasting legacy of 1920s and 30s musical comedies: films. The second film incarnation of *Good News!* (MGM, 1947), which starred June Allyson, Peter Lawford and Mel Tormé, illustrates a familiar pattern. On this occasion the studio commissioned a new book by Betty Comden and Adolph Green, retained six songs from the 1927 score (about half), some with new lyrics, and added two songs by other composers. Film adaptations of other shows present a range of fates, none of which includes fidelity to the staged originals. Even though the original creators were more likely to still be around to protest, however ineffectually, the general practice in film adaptation closely paralleled the distortions of future stage revivals. Retentions usually (but not always) included the basic storyline, typically half or fewer of the songs, and occasionally only one (e.g., 'Night and Day' in *The Gay Divorce*, *Divorcée* on film, or 'Strike Up the Band' in the 1940 musical film of that title). Sometimes the original composer and lyricist added one or more new songs expressly for the film; in other cases new composers under studio contract were brought in for this purpose. The creative control that Broadway composers had begun to exert in the 1920s was largely absent when it came to film adaptations. Original film musicals fared considerably better.

A few examples will illustrate representative adaptive possibilities. *The Cocoanuts* (Broadway, 1925; Paramount, 1929), the first in a long and popular series of films with the Marx Brothers and Margaret Dumont, was perhaps the only significant contemporary film setting of a 1920s musical comedy. Most of the original songs from the 1925 score were dropped, and the film added a new love ballad, 'When My Dreams Come True'. Surprisingly, *The Cocoanuts* film preserves extensive portions of Kaufman's published script (including Groucho's puns and other silly business) and presents a serious challenge to those who want to believe that the zaniness was mainly improvised.[29] The plot of Youmans's *Hit the Deck* (1927) was freely adapted in the Fred Astaire and Ginger Rogers film, *Follow the Fleet* (RKO, 1936). Additionally, the film offered an entirely new score, not by Youmans, but by Berlin – it was a fine film perhaps, but not quite the *Hit the Deck* Broadway audiences came to see in 1927. Two decades later a second film, now called *Hit the Deck* (MGM, 1955), dutifully used seven of Youmans's ten songs (including 'Hallelujah' and 'Sometimes I'm Happy'), but still managed to completely disregard the original book by Herbert Fields. Although the filming of *Funny Face* (Broadway, 1927; MGM, 1957) was delayed by thirty years, it managed to offer one of its original stage stars, Astaire. The film *Funny Face* also used a new screenplay, retained five songs, including 'How Long Has This Been Going On?', cut from the original score, reintroduced a familiar Gershwin tune originally from *Oh, Kay!* ('Clap Yo' Hands'), and added three new songs by studio composers Leon Gershe and Roger Edens. With *Rosalie* (Broadway, 1928; MGM, 1937) the original double story (Lindbergh flight/Queen of Romania visit) was preserved, but the composite Gershwin/Romberg score was replaced by an all-new one by Porter.

Freewheeling adaptation practices would continue with musicals that first appeared in the 1930s. From the trio of Gaxton, Moore and Merman, only Merman remained in the first filming of *Anything Goes* two years later (Broadway 1934; Paramount, 1936). The film used Merman's songs, the title song, 'You're the Top', 'I Get a Kick Out of You', and 'Blow, Gabriel Blow', but only two songs of those originally sung by others, 'All Through the Night' and 'There'll Always Be a Lady Fair'. For the 1956 remake, starring Bing Crosby in the role introduced by Gaxton, now teamed with Mitzi Gaynor and Donald O'Connor, the story was more drastically altered. The film version of *Babes in Arms* (Broadway, 1937; MGM, 1939), starring Judy Garland and Mickey Rooney, preserved the basic story and spirit of Rodgers and Hart's Broadway show, but omitted the significant political and racial component and retained only two songs, the title song and 'Where or When', from a score that is widely regarded as one of the richest of any decade.[30] *The Boys from Syracuse* (Broadway, 1938; Universal, 1940) with comedians Martha Raye and Joe Penner retained the basic story and four songs and added two new ones by Rodgers and Hart. When *Jumbo* (Broadway 1935; MGM 1962) was finally filmed, the story was considerably rewritten but nonetheless recognisable: half the original score and the original Jimmy Durante were preserved (along with his 'Elephant? What elephant?' routine); the film also pilfered two vintage Rodgers and Hart songs from other shows, 'Why Can't I?' from *Spring Is Here* (1929) and 'This Can't Be Love' from *The Boys from Syracuse* (1938).

Roberta (Broadway, 1933; RKO, 1935) stands out as perhaps the finest contemporary film of a staged musical comedy.[31] It also demonstrates how it is possible to retain a storyline while at the same time adapting roles for new stars, especially if the stars are Astaire (as Huck Haines, now dancing in the formerly non-dancing role played on stage by newcomer Bob Hope) and Rogers (as Countess Tanka Schwarenka, impersonating the stage Countess Lyda Roberti's Polish-Hungarian accent). The original score, which included 'Yesterdays', 'Smoke Gets In Your Eyes', 'Let's Begin', 'I'll Be Hard to Handle', 'Something Had to Happen', 'The Touch of Your Hand', and 'You're Devastating', was already one of the most memorable of the 1930s. The film dropped the three last-named titles as song numbers, but retained the melodies of the last two to underscore the fashion-show sequence. On stage, 'Yesterdays' was sung by Aunt Minnie (Fay Templeton); in the film 'Yesterdays' joins 'Smoke Gets In Your Eyes' as Stephanie's (Irene Dunne's) second major song, leaving non-singing Helen Westley (Parthy in Universal's 1936 *Show Boat* classic) songless, a net gain. The combination of European elegance represented by Dunne and the addition of two new swing dance numbers for Astaire and Rogers, 'I Won't Dance' (reworked by Dorothy Fields and Jimmy McHugh from Kern's recent London flop with Hammerstein, *Three Sisters*) and 'Lovely to Look At' (composed expressly for the film by Kern and Fields), captures the best of both worlds and the best of what musical comedy of the 1930s has to offer modern audiences, even if viewers are asked to swallow the outrageous notion of an exiled Russian princess living in Paris in 1935, the 'Gee, that's swell' persona of the non-singing Randolph Scott and the unsightly fashions.

The third prominent modern legacy of the musical is the series of reconstructed recordings, sometimes referred to as 'restorations'. Among the chief and most knowledgeable instigators of this practice are the conductor John McGlinn (*Sitting Pretty, Show Boat, Anything Goes*), and Tommy Krasker, the archivist and administrator for the Ira and Leonore Gershwin Trusts. Taking advantage of such invaluable rediscoveries as the Warner Brothers materials in Secaucus Warehouse in 1982 and Tams Witmark Music Library in 1987, McGlinn and Krasker have been able to resurrect the original

Plate 7 Gertrude Lawrence with the doll that George Gershwin gave her to hold while singing 'Someone to Watch Over Me' in *Oh, Kay!*

orchestrations by Hans Spialek and Robert Russell Bennett and salvaged even whole scripts and songs previously considered lost. Casts have been carefully chosen to parallel the original vocal types as closely as possible, and performing styles and tempos are carefully observed, when known. The end result may give present and future students of the 1920s and 30s their most reliable opportunities to hear relatively complete versions of these scores as New York audiences first heard them, along with musical numbers discarded on try-out tours and during the early stages of their Broadway runs.

Those who wish to explore this literature should be advised, however, that the restorations sometimes recreate versions that no first-night, or any night, audiences may have heard or seen. In some cases scholars such as McGlinn and Krasker are motivated by a desire to preserve an imagined pristine pre-Broadway integrity. For example, the song 'Buddy Beware' was cut from the first production of *Anything Goes* at the request of Merman in favour of a reprise of 'I Get a Kick Out of You'. The McGlinn reconstruction restores it.[32] With *Fifty Million Frenchmen*, Krasker's restoration revised Herbert Fields's script in order to recycle several songs dropped during the pre-Broadway try-out ('I Worship You', 'Please Don't Make Me Be Good', 'The Queen of Terre Haute', and 'The Tale of the Oyster'). Another song dropped before Broadway, 'Down with Everybody But Us', however, is absent from the album. Early during the Broadway run 'Let's Step Out' replaced 'The Boy Friend Back Home'; both are included in the restored recording, albeit in different acts.[33]

Restorations commonly favour the initial vision of those that created the songs and tend to dismiss the practical concerns that led to pragmatic decisions by directors and producers and anyone under time constraints. To take one example among many, Krasker's restoration of *Oh, Kay!* returns to the way the show looked before its excessive length forced some cutting.[34] At the Philadelphia premiere the first three songs audiences heard were 'The Moon Is On the Sea', 'Don't Ask' and 'Someone to Watch Over Me', the last written for Gertrude Lawrence, the show's star and namesake. A fourth song, 'When Our Ship Comes Sailing In', originally placed between 'Moon' and 'Don't Ask', had been dropped during the rehearsals. At least in part as a solution to the excessive length, 'The Moon Is On the Sea' was dropped (along with 'Ain't It Romantic?' and the Finaletto to Act 2, scene 1 from later in the show). 'A Woman's Touch' was relocated to start the show followed by 'Don't Ask', and 'Someone to Watch Over Me' became the first song of Act 2. The shift of Lawrence's hit song created some dramatic problems that have not gone unnoticed. In a national televised broadcast Leonard Bernstein pointed out the silliness that results from the line 'Haven't found him yet' after Kay has already made it clear in the first act that she has in fact found the man whose initial she would like to add to her monogram. Bernstein interprets this incongruity as a sign that neither Broadway songwriters nor their audiences cared about dramatic credibility and nuance: 'As they said in the mad, gay Twenties, what's the diff?'[35] Bernstein's assessment is accurate in that the song 'doesn't *quite* fit the situation in which it was sung', and Ira Gershwin either did not notice or chose not to adjust his lyrics to the new situation. As originally conceived, however, the song did fit dramatically. Thus Krasker restored the appropriateness of a lyric, which depicts Kay looking for a man she had not only met but also saved from drowning the previous summer. Since one intention in a restored recording is to present as much of the original score as possible (and length is no longer an issue on a compact disc), listeners might welcome a return to the more substantial pre-Broadway concept. But what is being restored does not necessarily correspond to the solution agreed to by the original creators of the show (e.g. the inclusion of 'When Our Ship Comes Sailing In', a song dropped before the try-outs).[36]

The shortened *Oh, Kay!* became, after *Lady, Be Good!*, Gershwin's second biggest hit of the 1920s. On the other hand, Gershwin's penultimate musical comedy, *Pardon My English* (1933), never recovered from numerous cast changes and endlessly revised scripts and songs. At forty-six performances, it failed in its own time, and it remains little known today beyond the songs 'Isn't It a Pity?' and 'My Cousin in Milwaukee'. It also poses extremely difficult reconstruction problems. The only extant Fields/Ryskind script is a draft that dates from 15 November 1932, two weeks prior to its Philadelphia try-out, making a Broadway version unsalvageable beyond a reconstruction of song order. After reviewing the earlier script and what is known about the changes in Philadelphia, Boston and Brooklyn over the next few months, Krasker's decision to use the Philadelphia song line-up as the starting point was arguably more felicitous than the decision to restore the rehearsal and try-out versions of *Oh, Kay!*[37] Even if Krasker's restoration does not represent a version that any audience heard in 1932 or 1933, it does successfully rescue most of the extant music from an exceptionally fine Gershwin score. That's something to sing about.

Despite their liabilities and the perhaps inevitable fact that they reveal as much about a later time as they do about the 1920s and 30s, revivals, films, and reconstructions offer indispensable as well as more than occasionally entertaining glimpses into this unknown territory, a territory which extends far beyond *Show Boat* and *Porgy and Bess*. With the right casting and sense of period style, producers and directors might be surprised at the revivability of an undoctored *No, No, Nanette*, *Lady, Be Good!*, and *Oh, Kay!* in the 1920s, or *Anything Goes*, *On Your Toes*, *Babes in Arms*, *The Boys from Syracuse*, *Johnny Johnson*, *Knickerbocker Holiday*, and *The Cradle Will Rock* in the 1930s. Like most of the forgotten comic operas of the past 250 years, musical comedies, belonging perhaps more to their time than serious operas, music dramas, operettas or the integrated musical plays that began in earnest on Broadway in the 1940s, appear more susceptible to the ravages of time than more obliquely topical genres. This is as true today as it was in 1920. The shows of the 1920s and 30s may have ended but their melodies and words linger on. And to match these catchy tunes and clever lyrics, these musical comedies – however ephemeral and difficult to recapture – offer unsung dramatic treasures.

PART II

Maturations and formulations: 1940–1970

7 'We said we wouldn't look back': British musical theatre, 1935–1960

JOHN SNELSON

Between the early Edwardian musical comedies of the Gaiety Theatre and the recent megamusicals of Andrew Lloyd Webber is a largely forgotten era in the history of the British musical of some twenty-five years. Between 1935 and 1960, 127 new British musicals were presented in the West End, but only a handful have survived into today's active repertory. *Me and My Girl* (1937; music by Noel Gay) was neglected for decades until it received a major London revival in 1984 and successfully transferred to Broadway. *The Boy Friend* (1953–4; Sandy Wilson), itself a tribute to an earlier style of show, has achieved an international prominence while *Salad Days* (1954; Julian Slade) has found popularity predominantly in Britain. Some individual songs from shows of this period are still favourites in the light music repertory – particularly those by Ivor Novello and Noël Coward – but almost always the songs have been divorced from any knowledge of the original shows. Based on this scant evidence, any view of British musical theatre in the mid-twentieth century is likely to be strange.

So what happened to all of the other shows? Why did most of them never receive more than one original professional production? Were they really so bad as to be better forgotten or did other factors lead to their neglect? This chapter will look at the major works of the period and provide some answers as to why this part of the British musical theatre has been and continues to be largely ignored.[1]

1935–1939

In 1935 there were seven new British musicals in the West End, including the 'sporting farce' of *Twenty to One* (music by Billy Mayerl), *Love Laughs – !*, (music by Noel Gay) and *Please Teacher!* (music by Jack Waller and Joseph Tunbridge). However, the show that was to have the most lasting effect on the West End and made 1935 a significant year for British musical theatre was *Glamorous Night*, the first of a series of musicals by Ivor Novello (1893–1951). Novello dominated British musical theatre of the 1930s and 1940s with an extraordinary series of popular stage works that had huge national appeal, and yet almost never travelled beyond Britain. At

Plate 8 Programme cover from original production of *Twenty to One*
(12 November 1935, Coliseum).

the time of his sudden death in 1951 he was one of the most loved figures
of British theatre and a household name. Half a century later he is largely
forgotten.

Born David Ivor Davies, Ivor Novello formed his professional name
from his own middle name and that of his mother, Clara Novello Davies;
he changed his name formally to Ivor Novello by deed poll in 1927. Novello
first came to public prominence with his music for the song 'Keep the Home
Fires Burning', which fast became an anthem of World War I. In 1916 he
was co-composer with Jerome Kern on *Theodore & Co*; in contemporary
British terms Novello was the big name and Kern the newcomer. Novello
wrote a series of musical shows and revues in the rest of that decade, but
his contributions to such works in the 1920s were increasingly subject to his

diversions into silent film as a romantic actor. After becoming the country's foremost matinée idol on film he began to develop a similar presence in the theatre, one that took over from film in the early 1930s. When the Theatre Royal, Drury Lane needed something spectacular to revive its fortunes in 1935, Novello's combination of musical, theatrical and performing skills made him the ideal choice for a big new work.

The resulting show, *Glamorous Night*, was a strange concoction of operetta, musical comedy and ballet, with a plot that combined old and new in the romance of a Ruritanian princess and a television inventor. But it was most notable for its scale. Everything about it was indulgent: lines of royal guards, a horse-drawn carriage and a gypsy wedding made the show spectacular. Most strikingly, through the hydraulics of the huge Drury Lane stage, the sinking of a passenger liner was simulated, and photographs of the show reveal how like film was the whole approach. And this is where Novello innovated: he brought the visual, geographical and temporal potential of film to the stage. He followed *Glamorous Night* with *Careless Rapture* (1936), *Crest of the Wave* (1937) and *The Dancing Years* (1939), which reinforced the image of a 'Novello' show as overtly emotive in music, romantically idealised in plot and rich in visual impact.

Today, the reputation of Novello stands in sharp contrast to his contemporary Noël Coward (1899–1973). In many ways their careers are similar. Both occupied the roles of playwright, film and stage actor, composer and (though to a limited extent with Novello) lyricist. They were both icons of their time, with Coward as the urbane sophisticate and Novello as the male romantic ideal. Yet any discussion of British musical theatre keeps returning to Novello as a pivotal figure, while Coward is largely incidental, in opposition to their more general theatrical reputations. Novello's eight shows were produced consistently between 1935 and 1951, with a common identifiable quality that allows his name to be used as an adjective for that style. Coward's musical theatre output in the same period constantly changed direction, through *Operette* (1938), *Pacific 1860* (1946), *Ace of Clubs* (1950) and *After the Ball* (1954), but continually failed to regain the public appeal of his first 'operette' *Bitter Sweet* (1929). While individual songs, often comic, from Coward's shows have found a life in cabaret, the lack of a common identity through his diverse stage works has left no sense of a distinct Coward musical theatre style. Coward now has an international profile whereas Novello is barely remembered nationally, although professional revivals of the musicals of both men are almost completely unknown. Despite the temporary boost to Novello's reputation through his (historically questionable) portrayal in Robert Altman's film *Gosford Park* (2001), it is only the British music industry's annual Ivor Novello Awards that now give his name any significant public prominence.

Today, however, the most widely known British musical of the 1930s, through a modern reworking, is not by either Novello or Coward. *Me and My Girl* (1937) became an immediate success through both its accessible, tuneful score and a storyline designed to showcase the performer Lupino Lane. The central character of Bill Snibson, a working-class cockney, was developed for the musical *Twenty to One* (1935), with music by Billy Mayerl (1902–59), who is now best remembered for his syncopated piano style and accompanying piano schools.[2] *Me and My Girl* was written to capitalise on the success of the Snibson character as performed by Lane, and with Gay's score became a success with hit songs. Of its numbers, 'Leaning on a Lamp-post' is characteristic of Gay's ability to write simple, instantly appealing melodies while the success of the cockney march 'The Lambeth Walk', complete with dance steps, gave the name to the film of the show (1939) and achieved remarkable fame. The show ran for 1,646 performances at the Victoria Palace, successfully toured and had West End revivals in 1941, 1945 and 1949. It was a much less sophisticated style of show than that of the Novello romances, relying on a farcical plot, slapstick humour, specialty dances, even audience vocal participation in 'The Lambeth Walk', all of which reveal links with the peculiarly British form of the pantomime, whose influence on the British understanding of the musical has generally been neglected.

Novello's best remembered and most performed show is *The Dancing Years,* which opened at the Theatre Royal, Drury Lane in March 1939. In the plot the composer Rudi Kleber (the leading male role, played, as usual, by Novello himself) is in love with the opera singer Maria Ziegler (Mary Ellis), but their affair is thwarted through misunderstandings. It was also a political musical, despite the operetta naivety of much of the on-stage world, as Novello made his central character an Austrian Jew in order to bring in overt criticism of the Nazi regime. While much of this theme was included in the production, the management tried to remove it on the grounds that it was inappropriate for a musical. It proved to be all too appropriate for the time: as Coward had used the comparison of different ages and their ideals of love in *Bitter Sweet*, so Novello used a similar chronological contrast between the romantic Austria of operetta and the real effects of German political aspirations of the 1930s.

The music of the show is some of Novello's finest, and includes a number of stylistic references that root the work in European operetta while incorporating the later American developments of the 1920s. Viennese operetta is referenced in the waltzes (the song 'Waltz of My Heart' remains one of his most frequently performed and best-known songs) and through many deliberate allusions to Lehár's *Die lustige Witwe* (*The Merry Widow*), which, in its original London production, had been a formative influence on Novello. In *The Dancing Years*, for example, the opening section of the concerted number 'Lorelei' is based on an inversion of the melody and an exact repetition of the rhythm of the opening chorus of the first act of Lehár's classic operetta. The solos 'My Heart Belongs to You', 'I Can Give You the Starlight' and 'My Dearest Dear' are expansive 4/4 melodies that show the later influence of Romberg, while the pastiche 'Primrose', in the style of an Edwardian musical comedy number, is an acknowledgement of Novello's youth and the musical theatre with which he grew up. The shifting time periods of the plot, the range of musical influences and the references to contemporary European politics provided a broad base for audience appeal. Yet a cursory glance at listings of long-running shows does not fully indicate the popularity of *The Dancing Years*. Special circumstances conspired to make Novello's most long-lived show the least successful if viewed only from the evidence of such raw statistics. Its initial London production ran for only 187 performances, closing on 1 September 1939.

Wartime

As soon as war was declared in September 1939 all the West End theatres shut down in anticipation of immediate bombing and more pressing priorities. Within a few weeks they opened again. In fact, throughout the war, the theatre benefited from something of a revival of fortunes. There was a high demand for live entertainment to raise morale and the number of professional actors consequently swelled considerably, so much so that, after war's end, British Actors' Equity felt obliged to discuss methods of regulating entry into the profession in order to counter this influx of inadequately trained performers. Not surprisingly there were very few new works in the first years of the war, and the revivals included many operetta-style works. These included such comfortingly familiar favourites as *The Desert Song*, *Chu Chin Chow* (which began its initial record-breaking run during World War I), *Maid of the Mountains*, *Rose-Marie*, *Show Boat* and *The Merry Widow*. Musical comedy revivals included *Twenty to One* and *Me and My Girl*. In 1943, however, two West End successes were the new shows of *Old Chelsea*, with music by the singer Richard Tauber, and *The Lisbon Story*, with music by Harry Parr Davies (1914–55), more familiar at that time as Gracie Fields's regular accompanist. The latter show involved British spies and the French resistance and had its heroine killed on stage at the end. It was tuneful, indulgently dramatic, and just sufficiently removed in location and events to tread a fine line between reflecting wartime concerns and providing a diversion from them. Novello had one of his few near-misses in 1943 with *Arc de Triomphe*, a biographical musical based on the life of Mary Garden, but reworked as the story of an imaginary French singer, Marie

Forêt. For other West End composers it would have been considered a fair run, but 222 performances for Novello was well below his usual expectations. Yet an omnipresent feature of musical theatre around the whole country and in the West End during the war was his earlier show *The Dancing Years*. It had been deprived of the Theatre Royal, Drury Lane at the start of the war when the theatre was taken over as the headquarters of ENSA (Entertainments National Service Association). There was no other sufficiently large theatre available in the West End to which it could move. After a year's delay, it was launched as a national tour in September 1940, finally returning to the Adelphi in the West End in March 1942 and playing there until July 1944. It was revived again in 1947, filmed in 1950 and entered the amateur dramatic repertory, where it still receives the occasional airing. A television version was broadcast in 1981, which was a rare honour indeed for a British musical. Its presence in the musical theatre world was consequently much greater than the length of its short initial run in London would indicate.

In April 1945, just before peace was declared in Europe, Novello launched his next show at the Hippodrome. Drury Lane was still occupied by ENSA and the association of Novello with that theatre was broken in practice if not in the mind of the public. *Perchance to Dream* followed an affair through reincarnations of the lovers over three eras: Regency (1818), Victorian (1843) and contemporary ('193–?'). Novello was able to revel in period costumes, and romantic figures such as the masked highwayman, familiar to audiences through the style of films from the Gainsborough Studio and from the novels of Georgette Heyer and Daphne du Maurier. The show was further decorated with a 'singing ballet' called 'The Triumphs of Spring', while the music included the waltzes 'Love Is My Reason' and 'Highwayman Love', and a hugely popular pastiche of a Victorian parlour ballad, 'We'll Gather Lilacs'.

It was Noël Coward who relaunched Drury Lane after the war, perhaps remembering his great success in that theatre at the start of the 1930s with the celebratory pageant *Cavalcade*. The resulting work, *Pacific 1860*, which opened on 19 December 1946, is remembered as something of a disaster, set against a background of an unready and unheated theatre in the middle of a fearsome winter aggravated by fuel shortages, and dominated by the miscasting of Mary Martin in the leading role of Elena Salvador. (Serious miscasting also blighted Coward's 1954 show, *After the Ball*, in which his nostalgic remembrance of Mary Ellis's singing proved as out-of-date as the show itself.) As Coward represented an important strand of British theatrical continuity across the divide of World War II, the faltering of such a high-profile work as *Pacific 1860* in London's leading theatre for musicals made it a symbol of perceived British musical theatre decline. In retrospect the judgements of the time on *Pacific 1860* seem harsh. There is some wonderfully luxurious music in the score which, although not seeming as much of a whole as *Bitter Sweet*, still showed Coward to be inventive, and the work is no more indulgent or old-fashioned than the first American show that had opened in London after the war in March 1946, *Song of Norway*.

1947 and the 'American invasion'

The war changed the content and perception of West End musical the-atre. A wartime combination of revivals of shows from up to thirty-five years previously with an absence of newer Broadway shows had held British musical theatre in a time-warp of its own. London saw few new American musicals between 1939 and 1946, and contemporary Broadway was thus principally represented by Cole Porter (*Let's Face It* and *DuBarry Was a Lady*, both 1942, and *Panama Hattie*, 1943). The first new American shows to be produced after the end of the war were the contrasting demotic com-edy of *Follow the Girls* (1945), led in his own distinctive performing style by British comedian Arthur Askey, and *Song of Norway* (1946), whose subject matter, musical style, geographical setting, operetta influences and British casting made it seem anything but an American show. Consequently the impact of the first distinctively American show after the war – Rodgers and Hammerstein's *Oklahoma!* in 1947, some four years after Broadway – was significantly heightened. The British public, worn down by years of war and deprivation, principally responded to the escapist image of vigorous youth, but at the same time incorporated other qualities of *Oklahoma!* to form the notion of a 'post-*Oklahoma!*' musical, a phrase much used at the time but never explicitly defined. Opening shortly after *Oklahoma!* was Irving Berlin's *Annie Get Your Gun*, with Dolores Gray in the role created on Broadway by Ethel Merman. Again it was rapturously received as the new type of Amer-ican show and, as with *Oklahoma!*, the energy and style of performance were emphasised in reviews. In terms of construction and staging these two American shows were far apart: Berlin's show was an old-fashioned star vehicle using front cloths for scene changes and a ball in Act 2 that is reminis-cent of a British pantomime walk-down finale; Rodgers and Hammerstein's work was more evenly balanced and tightly structured. Crucially in the West End, *Oklahoma!* began with an almost exclusively American cast with the perceived authentic spirit of youthful America. As the long run progressed, the casting gradually shifted to British performers but with no detriment to the show. *Annie Get Your Gun* only had two American performers from the start, Dolores Gray as Annie Oakley and Bill Johnson as Frank Butler. So, the performing energy may have been American in spirit but was very much British in execution.

Such distinctions matter. The arrival of *Oklahoma!* and *Annie Get Your Gun* created a sense of an 'American invasion' and the term is increasingly applied in the late 1940s as indicative of successful, integrated, modern musicals from America driving out of the West End the old-fashioned and feeble British shows. In fact, it was not until 1953 that the production of new British musicals collapsed, principally because of the increasing lack of confidence of West End producers who preferred proven Broadway shows to the financial risks of unknown British ones. The idea that 'British = old' and 'American = new' was given a further spur into being by the long presence in the West End of a British work that had opened just a few weeks before *Annie Get Your Gun. Bless the Bride*, with book and lyrics by A. P. Herbert and music by Vivian Ellis (1904–96), was hugely successful and challenged the notion of an 'American invasion'; equally and paradoxically it probably also helped to form the concept.

In one sense, *Bless the Bride* seems to reinforce the idea that British musicals in the mid-1940s were old-fashioned. It tells the story of a young English girl, Lucy, in the Victorian England of 1870–1, during the lead-up to and outbreak of the Franco-Prussian war. She falls in love with a dashing Frenchman, Pierre, and elopes with him on the morning of her intended marriage to a stereotypical upper-class Englishman, the Honourable Thomas Trout. At the outbreak of the war Pierre joins the French army and Lucy returns to England, distraught. In the last act Pierre, previously thought lost in action, returns and they are reunited. The show capitalised on the period costumes and imagery of its Victorian setting, while Vivian Ellis's music adopts a Gilbert and Sullivan idiom, considerably more 'old-fashioned' than his work for shows before the war, but appropriate to the setting. The show dealt with the consequences of war, but through a sufficiently distant time to dilute the pain of the all-too-recent events, yet contemporary relevance was expressed through, for example, the maiden swept away by the foreign stranger (for which could be read GI), a song to Lucy from her nanny on the eve of her wedding that has more in common with the words of a mother to her son leaving for war, suspicion of foreigners, and the eventual return from the dead of a loved one lost in action. Its concerns were specifically (but not exclusively) British, and A. P. Herbert made much of the ambiguous relationship between England and France in witty asides and exaggerated posturing in the script.

Vivian Ellis supported the themes of Herbert's libretto through music that built up its own patterns of national identity. The English are portrayed in foursquare rhythms and four-part harmony, suggesting a communal and socially rigid character, while the French are given freer melismatic lines in dance rhythms suggesting individuality and freedom. Two examples illustrate the point. The opening of the first act presents a croquet game on the lawn, set to a relaxed 6/8 pastorale, but the following introduction of the foreign game of 'tennis' (with licentious implications for the prudish British) is set to the equally foreign dance form of the polka. Later, when Pierre seduces Lucy in the shrubbery it is to another continental dance form, that of the waltz in the song 'I Was Never Kissed Before', again with sexually charged overtones, and contrasts strongly with the preceding constraint in Lucy's observations on her own engagement to Thomas Trout. With Trout she acts out of duty and the music is formal and restrained; with Pierre she is driven by emotion and her vocal line becomes increasingly free as the waltz number progresses under the encouragement of Pierre. Such contrasts throughout the work play subtly on British self-image and confidence in the face of Europe and the world. On the surface the show appears to be extremely dated yet it had strong contemporary undercurrents for a British audience. If the West End taste had changed towards American shows then *Bless the Bride* should have failed quickly. Instead, it was hugely popular; but the production was taken off after more than two years while still playing to capacity houses because the theatre impresario C. B. Cochran wanted to try something new with the same creative team of Herbert, Ellis and Toye. The subsequent work, *Tough at the Top*, was not the success for which Cochran had hoped.

The contrast of the plot, musical style and period design of *Bless the Bride* with those of *Annie Get Your Gun* and *Oklahoma!* was striking and reinforced the notion of 'English = old' and 'American = new'. Yet the appeal of the American works in the West End was escapist, while that of the British ones was a subtle reflection of matters still very close to the public psyche. *Bless the Bride* would have had different resonances on Broadway and was never transferred; the concerns of the show are those on an axis between Britain and Europe, not Britain and the USA. To juxtapose *Oklahoma!* and *Annie Get Your Gun* with *Bless the Bride* is thus to compare shows that were through subtext not intended to be on the same continent. However, the received reputation of *Bless the Bride* from some sixty years on is that of a 'Victorian' show failing to reach the length of run of the American import through its dated style and content. A London fringe revival in 1999 was rewritten and restructured by an American director to make the work more accessible. In fact, it removed precisely those elements which gave the work its initial appeal and dramatic motivation. The context of the show is both its strength as a theatrical work and its weakness in entering a contemporary active repertory.

The biggest indication that the West End and Broadway markets were not the same and that there was a peculiarly British tradition of musical theatre received its best expression immediately after the war in *King's Rhapsody*

Plates 9–12 (9) Programme cover from the 1945 revival at the Victoria Palace of *Me and My Girl* (original premiere 16 December 1937, Victoria Palace). The design is the same as the original cover and Lupino Lane starred in both productions. (10) Programme cover from the original production of *Bless the Bride* (26 April 1947, Adelphi Theatre) (11) Programme cover from the original production of *Gay's the Word* (16 February 1951, Saville Theatre). (12) Programme cover from *Expresso Bongo* (23 April 1958, Saville Theatre).

(1949), the last of Novello's musical romances. It included everything that was against the spirit of the 'American invasion' yet was a great success. Set in the Ruritanian country of 'Krasnia', it concerned princes, kings, marriages, mistresses and abdications. The music was lush, with 'Someday My Heart Will Awake' in the best Novello waltz-song tradition, and the set pieces included a dramatic coronation scene as the finale of the show. Importantly, it concerned one dominating feature of the British social structure, a focal point at the time of war and an institution that provided a sense of national unity: royalty. Central to *King's Rhapsody* is the prince with the foreign mistress who gives up his throne rather than lose her, and the abdication of Edward VIII was a recent memory in the late 1940s. In addition, reference to living people was restricted under the Lord Chamberlain's censorship of the stage at the time, while the portrayal of royalty of the past couple of centuries was forbidden. Consequently, the use of the royal settings of European operetta had become one of the ways in which the British could see expressed on stage issues relating to royalty, and anything that presented the emotions and personal lives of these revered and distant figures was thus tantalising.[3] This aspect of the show's appeal is peculiarly British and it is hardly surprising from this perspective that one of the great West End successes of the immediate post-war years was never considered a candidate for Broadway.

King's Rhapsody maintained its popularity throughout its two-and-a-half-year run, with Novello playing the central character of Prince Nikki up until his sudden death from a heart attack just hours after his performance on Monday, 5 March 1951. Obviously the presence of Novello in the cast was a huge draw, but it ran for a further seven months after Novello's death with his role played by another West End legend, Jack Buchanan. At the time of the show's eventual closure, box-office receipts confirm that a steady public interest had been maintained at near capacity despite this substitution in the central role. The show could have run in the West End for much longer, but went on tour from October 1951 until June 1952, still to great acclaim. A film was made in 1955 with Errol Flynn, past his best, in the Novello role. The music was altered so that no number was heard in full and the dubious talents of Anna Neagle did little for the role of the mistress. To compare this with the remarkably faithful and painstaking adaptation to screen of *Oklahoma!*, released in the same year, is to appreciate how much the British repertory has suffered through an ongoing inaccessibility due to a lack of good – or indeed any – significant screen adaptations until those of *Oliver!* and *Half a Sixpence*. While key works of the American repertory are available today at the local video store there is no similar access to British works of the same period.

In the 1940s and 1950s America represented to the British the escapist, the optimistic, the future, all in strong contrast to the daily bleak reality of the after-effects of the war. Not surprisingly British writers of musicals addressed their home audience through the home concerns of the day, particularly those of post-war recovery and sometimes the perceived lack of it. This introversion not only accounts for the impenetrability of some shows at the time to foreign visitors, but also explains their increasing irrelevance to more modern generations. Such domestic concerns, although present as subtext *(Bless the Bride,* for example), were also presented explicitly. In 1949 Cicely Courtneidge starred in the musical play *Her Excellency* as a woman ambassador to a South American country, whose main purpose was to secure a meat supply contract for Britain. In many respects the plot foreshadows that of *Call Me Madam*, but whereas a British audience could understand many of the topical references to American financial imperialism towards Europe in Howard Lindsay and Russell Crouse's American book the British topical references in Archie Menzies and Harold Purcell's book defeated American understanding.

The subplot of *Her Excellency* involves the selling of British furniture to Latin America as part of the British export drive, while the main plot revolves around the British ambassador beating the American ambassador in securing the beef supply contract. Some of the jokes are still funny but, as much of the script was concerned with topical reference, the show cannot be understood outside the context of food rationing, which had been introduced soon after the start of the war and was only completely discontinued in 1954.[4] The particular circumstances of 1947–8 inspired the context of the show as the meat ration hit its lowest level since the start of wartime rationing. The direct supply of beef to Britain from Argentina and not via the canning factories of the USA (as a part of Lend-Lease) was thus a theme of strong practical and symbolic value to a British audience in 1949. The language of the show also invokes symbols of England, with the song 'Sunday Morning in England' evoking a national image that played on both a strong and proud past and a tired and run-down present. A crisis of confidence in the country comes through in many British shows of the period as they seek to address the long-term effects of World War II, particularly in the patriotic bolstering of national spirit. For example, *Tough at the Top* portrays a European princess enamoured of all things English (especially an attractive boxer) and who sings that 'England Is a Lovely Place'; in 1954 Harry Parr Davies's setting and Christopher Hassall's lyrics emote 'I Leave My Heart in an English Garden' (*Dear Miss Phoebe*, 1954). While these expressions of patriotism were hardly new – Ivor Novello's 'Rose of England' from *Crest of the Wave* is perhaps the best example of all – the grim aftermath of the war required an additional dose of them.

Such nationalistic sentiment does not chime well with a modern audience, set against the tainting of patriotism with the racist and bigoted overtones of recent decades and the increasingly ambiguous position of the United Kingdom in relation to mainland Europe. Again, the contemporary strength of these works has proved a latter-day handicap. Generally the judgement of West End musicals after World War II has been viewed from a Broadway-led agenda which has denied these British shows their own home character, yet it is precisely this character that explains why British shows such as *Bless the Bride*, *Her Excellency* and *King's Rhapsody* could be successful despite being apparently so out of step with the prevailing notion of a modern 'post-*Oklahoma!*' musical.

The 1950s

Any retrospective look at the West End musical in the first half of the 1950s makes for uncomfortable reading from a British perspective. Contrasted with the American imports of *Carousel*, *Kiss Me, Kate*, *South Pacific*, *Call Me Madam*, *Guys and Dolls*, *The King and I* and *Pal Joey*, *Wonderful Town* and *Kismet* are indigenous shows such as *Ace of Clubs* (Coward), *Golden City* (John Toré), *Dear Miss Phoebe* (Harry Parr Davies), *Gay's the Word* (Novello), *Zip Goes a Million* (George Posford), *Wild Thyme* (Donald Swann), *The Water Gipsies* (Vivian Ellis) and *A Girl Called Jo* (John Pritchett). Nothing of this British repertory has survived, while the American imports are mostly 'classics'.

There was an awareness at the time of a difference in style between British and American musicals and two British shows in particular adapted American models in response. In *Golden City* (1950) John Toré wrote a work that was essentially a copy of *Oklahoma!*, adapted to suit the different cultural resonances of a London audience. In the place of the Oklahoman frontier was that of South Africa; instead of farmers and cowboys there were the opposing groups of farmers and miners; the rustic dance of 'The Farmer and the Cowman' became the communal barbecue of 'Braavleis'. The music also used the features of contemporary American shows: 'It's Love, My Darling, It's Love' is a clear copy of the ideas and style of *Oklahoma!*'s 'People Will Say We're In Love', *Annie Get Your Gun*'s 'The Girl That I Marry' was transmuted into 'The Prettiest Girl in the Town', while the 'Oklahoma!' chorus itself became 'It's a Great Occasion', complete with high sustained chords for the women's voices, and the chanting of 'trekkin', ridin'' to match the now familiar rhythmic 'Ok-la-ho-ma' of that title song's arrangement. In *Gay's the Word* (1951) Novello changed direction by writing for Cicely Courtneidge rather than himself (he was still performing in *King's Rhapsody*), and this provided an opportunity to adopt a different style, one through which he made the perceived contrasts between British and American shows the substance of the show itself. His ultimate conclusion as presented in *Gay's the Word* was that a confident style of presentation and energy in performance were lacking in British musical theatre at the time, a state further aggravated by a lack of respect for the individuality of British theatrical history. These were far more significant concerns than any notion of changing content. By creating for Courtneidge the character of Gay Daventry, a middle-aged musical comedy star, he was able to juxtapose images of bad old shows and good new shows as part of the dramatic construction. He also surprised his audiences through music that adopted a more popular American idiom, so much so that distinct models can be found for most of the numbers: the show's theme song 'Vitality' is clearly related to 'Another Op'nin', Another Show', the romantic ballad 'If Only He'd Looked My Way' shares crucial similarities of melody and harmony with 'Some Enchanted Evening', while the Novello waltz 'A Matter of Minutes' is not the expected broad sweeping melody but adopts a fast, short-phrased and repetitive structure indebted to Richard Rodgers. As with the theme of rationing in *Her Excellency*, the subject matter of *Gay's the Word* was not suited to export. While a battle between indigenous British musicals and imported American ones became a topic of some heat in the West End, it was an irrelevance for Broadway at that time. In addition to the show's strictly contemporary theme, its reliance on the skills of one unique comic performer and the current ambiguity of the title have contributed to the difficulties for any attempt at revival.

In 1953, however, the effects of an 'American invasion' were felt most strongly, with only two new British shows, one a disaster called *Happy as a King*, led by the much-loved comedian Fred Emney, and a musical pageant *The Glorious Days* which capitalised on the fervour of coronation year by having Anna Neagle play Nell Gwynn and Queen Victoria (both young and old). The Lord Chamberlain was sympathetic towards a slight relaxation of the conventions governing the presentation of royal personages on stage in the year that Elizabeth II became Queen, and justified Neagle's portrayals in this show on the grounds that the drama took place in the imagination of a girl who had been knocked out during an air raid, and so was an imagined not actual portrayal of the Queen![5] The American productions that opened in the same year were *Paint Your Wagon*, *Guys and Dolls*, *The King and I* and *Wish You Were Here*, although most of their leading performers were British, in contrast to the position of some five years before. Only *Guys and Dolls* relied on leading American performers, with Isobel Bigley, Sam Levene and Stubby Kaye recreating their Broadway roles.

The effect of censorship on British writers is shown indirectly by comparison through the response of the Lord Chamberlain's office to the production of the American show *Wish You Were Here* and in a lesser way to

Call Me Madam. The reader for the Lord Chamberlain completely missed
the point of the social setting of the former work by Harold Rome, Arthur
Kobler and Joshua Logan, equating it with the British family holiday camp
of Butlins rather than an exclusive setting for priapic American youth. The
only change required by the Lord Chamberlain prior to production was
the replacement of a reference to the Duke of Windsor with an alternative.
The need to remove his name was simply because of its existence. There
was nothing in its context that was in any way offensive; it was, if anything,
complimentary to the Duke by including him in a list of famous and influential world figures. Four months after the show opened a single complaint
from a member of the public over its supposed decadent nature prompted
a visit from a representative of the Lord Chamberlain's office, whose report
makes for humorous reading today as each piece of dubious or suggestive
movement is described in excessive detail.[6] The presentation of the show
was subsequently toned down by order. In *Call Me Madam* a reference to
Princess Margaret Rose had to be removed (simply because it existed) while
the representation in the show of the real American congressman Dean
Acheson was allowed on the grounds that it had not been objected to in
America. In Britain the representation of real people was often prohibited, especially where offence could be taken by foreign powers, and such
restrictions provided a challenge to the development of satire. By effectively
banning the presentation of a real monarchy, political figures and any sense
of sex (as opposed to idealised romance) the British musicals were inevitably
behind the times when compared with the American ones whose censorship
in London was more limited through a lack of understanding (as with *Wish
You Were Here*) or a bending of rules.[7] American writers for the musical
stage were more free to represent contemporary life than British counterparts who existed in a long-established culture of compliance in which
rules of censorship were subconsciously learned or actively considered at
an early stage of writing. The play, rather than the musical, was generally
the battle ground for contentious matters. It was only after the challenges
to the Lord Chamberlain through straight theatre in the second half of
the 1950s that the British musical began to escape this self-censorship, and
with *Expresso Bongo* (discussed below) jumped forward decades in a single
show.

What was perceived as a strike back at the American repertory began in
1954 with *The Boy Friend* (Sandy Wilson, b. 1924) and *Salad Days* (music by
Julian Slade, 1930–2006; book and lyrics by Slade and Dorothy Reynolds).
Both musicals were conceived as small-scale works for the specific companies
of the Players' Theatre and the Bristol Old Vic respectively. In their different
ways they present a particular sense of archetypal Britishness. In the case
of *The Boy Friend*, although primarily a tribute to musical comedies of

the 1920s, finishing schools, debutantes, aristocrats in disguise all played to notions of class, particularly upper-class, behaviour. *Salad Days* drew on the rarefied idyll of a Cambridge college, the select world of undergraduates, and family connections that extended to Whitehall. Both shows are also sexless, although sexuality through the codified language of a gay subculture casts a subtle shade. While *Wish You Were Here* was overtly displaying a cast of mostly sexually rampant semi-clad youths, the British response was to summarise romantic relations with a chaste kiss or two. One of the most well-known songs in *Salad Days* declares that 'We Said We Wouldn't Look Back', yet it is gently ironic in that the reminder not to be nostalgic prompts in the lyrics exactly that which it aspires to eschew. This duality of view, the present as interpreted through the past, is a common strand in British musicals, and *Salad Days* and *The Boy Friend* did look back in both musical and dramatic ways. *Salad Days* was conceived as an entertaining, ephemeral diversion, at the heart of which is a nostalgic innocence conjuring up an affectionate cartoon of certain English stereotypes. Whereas the passion of *West Side Story* invokes death, the 'romance' of *Salad Days* remains chaste. The lyrics of *Salad Days* are equally one-dimensional while its music is inoffensive, with diatonic (often pentatonic) melodies, simple harmony and the most straightforward of verse–refrain structures.

The Boy Friend was revised and extended from an original one-act version and eventually entered a mainstream West End theatre at Wyndhams in January 1954, running there for a month over five years; *Salad Days* went into the Vaudeville in August 1954 and stayed there until 1960. Consequently, for the second half of the 1950s, the most enduring image of the British musical was of something with the parochial virtues of the village hall in *Salad Days* or the over-refined, nostalgic atmosphere of a fictitious and glamorised 1920s in *The Boy Friend.* For an American audience on Broadway in the mid-1950s – or, for that matter, all through the USA by virtue of extensive touring – *The Boy Friend* represented the only contact with contemporary British musical theatre, so reinforced the perception of a dated and retrospective British style. Nearly five years after *Salad Days* had opened at the Vaudeville theatre Jerome Robbins sat in foggy Manchester for the out-of-town try-outs of the first British production of *West Side Story.* An interviewer told him the plot of London's longest-running musical and quoted a few of its lyrics. After a short silence Robbins' response was a stunned 'You're kidding!' How could you explain to one of the creators of such a socially aware show as *West Side Story* that its main London British rival, seen by some five million people by then, concerned a magic piano that made people dance? Yet *The Boy Friend* and *Salad Days* are about all that remains active of the British musical theatre repertory of the 1950s. Their continuing popularity is partly accounted for by their dramatic lightness, adaptability for performance and inoffensive natures, making them safe for school productions and amateurs. Both have received very occasional professional revivals, but only *The Boy Friend* has achieved an international dimension to its fame.

That *The Boy Friend* has been taken to be a leading example of the British musical in the 1950s is, however, in one sense particularly apt. The music of the show is derivative, using – albeit most skilfully – older styles. This approach is a constant one in British musical theatre. Novello consciously borrowed from a range of sources including classical music, Viennese operetta and certain characteristics of Richard Rodgers. Vivian Ellis's later works adopted period styles appropriate to their dramatic settings, while Coward relied strongly on Victorian parlour music and music-hall styles throughout his works. There was no specific sound that characterised the West End. The search for that distinctive voice brought about the chameleon-like shifts of Coward and the last change of direction (or return to his musical youth in one sense) for Novello.

Despite the impression given by the longest-running British musicals, the second half of the 1950s was a lively period for British theatre as a whole. John Osborne's play *Look Back in Anger* (1956) has become a symbol for the beginning of a move towards greater realism in theatre, although subject to some of the same over-stressed importance that *Oklahoma!* has received. The inoffensive styles of Slade and Wilson in their first big successes contrasted with the increasingly serious intent of other contemporary theatre works, especially those of the more politically driven theatre as characterised by Joan Littlewood's theatre company at Stratford East whose demotic show of 1959 (note that *Salad Days* ran until 1960), *Fings Ain't Wot They Used T'Be*, contrasted an East End working class complete with resident prostitute with *Salad Days'* middle-class 'niceness'. Yet for all the supposed realism of *Fings Ain't Wot They Used T'Be*, it shared with the Slade and Wilson shows a common naivety towards characters (as with the camp interior designer) and a certain predictability in the music. *Fings* extended the reputation of the up-and-coming songwriter Lionel Bart (1930–99) and only shortly preceded his international success *Oliver!* in 1960. Julian Slade followed up *Salad Days* with another escapist work, *Free as Air* (1957), but the conditions that had made inconsequential escapism a surprise hit in 1954 were sufficient only to sustain an existing reputation, not to support a new one. Wilson's attempt to adapt the novellas of Ronald Firbank as *Valmouth* (1959) became a cult success, although the baroque excesses of Firbank's characters proved too strange for a wider audience.

A further contemporary antidote to any British nostalgia was provided in *Grab Me a Gondola* (1956, with music by James Gilbert), whose central character was based on the British 'sex-bomb' Diana Dors. More significantly, David Heneker and Monty Norman's *Expresso Bongo* (1958) laid into the world of the pop singer and teenage heart-throb, bringing contemporary pop styles into the theatre along with the first electric guitar in a West End pit orchestra. (Amplified acoustic guitars had been in use at least since 1950.) *Expresso Bongo* is remarkable for the cynicism of its characterisations, which include the pelvis-thrusting singer Bongo Herbert, 'Me' who is a crooked agent ripping off Bongo's strictly limited talent and a predatory older actress keen to boost her own flagging career through some fame by association. One number proclaims that 'There's nothing wrong with British youth today', while comprehensively listing all the problems created in the world (most notably the atom bomb) caused by their own parents. It was compared to *Pal Joey* in the unpleasant range of its characters and hailed as the show in which the British musical grew up. The film version (1959) had Cliff Richard in the role of the pop idol, but the plot and style were so diluted as to undermine the thrust of the whole show, and the most punchy of the musical numbers were cut from the film's release. Again, the future was deprived of a suitable advocate for an innovative show. The Lord Chamberlain's office worked overtime to tease out every innuendo it could from the book and lyrics, but ultimately failed to dilute the central message. The sexual puns in *Pal Joey* had not been censored for the West End in 1954 (although the 'Den of Iniquity' scene was cut when Princess Margaret visited a performance), but four years later *Expresso Bongo* had to fight over many lines. An air of deference to the Lord Chamberlain was fast being replaced by a cheeky rebellion, such that the alternative suggested by the authors to the censored line 'Go and stuff herself' was 'Go and screw herself'. They ended up with 'Get lost', which was not exactly at the hard edge of realism.

Expresso Bongo opened in the West End in the same year as *My Fair Lady*. It did not run as long and it has hardly been seen since, but its gritty cynicism, contemporary setting and pop score gained it many fans. It was voted Best British Musical of the Year in a *Variety* annual survey of shows on the London stage, with a ballot result far ahead of *My Fair Lady*, and was referred to in general as 'the other musical' to distinguish it from Lerner and Loewe's work. A London view of the musical in 1958 reverses the usual historical assumption in that the new American success was a costume and period work whereas the new British success was utterly contemporary in its characters, setting, plot, language and music.

Conclusion

World War II interrupted the development of British musical theatre and led to a post-war dichotomy between the need to take up again and develop the interrupted past as an assertion of continuity and the need to embrace change in a world that could not be the same again. In musical theatre the British writers understandably tended to address the former need, while the imported American shows addressed for a British audience the latter. The focus of America was on America, the focus of Britain was on Britain. Not surprisingly the traffic in shows across the Atlantic was almost exclusively one-way as the British works had a social and political dimension alongside a general national mood that was not interesting or even comprehensible to a Broadway audience. Furthermore, the different aspirations of homegrown and imported West End shows were judged by the same criteria although fulfilling different functions, and the consequence of this approach towards their contemporary and subsequent interpretation and comparison has been seen in a reinforcement of an American-led musical-theatre canon in Britain. In 1956 Vivian Ellis was moved to head an article for *Plays and Players* 'Give Us a Chance', which was 'an eloquent plea for the British composer, who is generally denied all the opportunities open to his American rival'.[8] In addition, the repertory has remained inaccessible owing to a lack of quality films of British stage shows and to a more limited representation on record than American ones; subsequent transfers from 78 to LP have been negligible, and CD releases followed only in the mid-2000s as copyrights expired. This lack of exposure has prevented the development of an easy familiarity with some of the best works, and the resulting lack of opportunity to learn the canon has in turn reinforced its undeserved obscurity.

The heritage of the period still persists, partly through a distinctive British characteristic in musicals of retrospection. Constant reference to the past is found through plots, but also often through the remnants of music-hall and revue styles. The famous comic songs of Coward are from a music-hall tradition from the start of the century and subject to very little stylistic change throughout his life; David Heneker drew on music-hall sing-along styles in 'Flash-Bang-Wallop' (*Half a Sixpence*) as did Lionel Bart in 'Oom Pah Pah' (*Oliver!*) and the title song of *Fings Ain't Wot They Used T'Be*, itself indicative to some of a British state of mind. Coward's tendency towards allusion and clever lyrics often comes to the fore in British musicals, most directly in the works of Sandy Wilson who has followed this epigrammatic approach in lyrics at least. The style of Novello has been continued by Andrew Lloyd Webber, whose works exhibit the same predilections, often with the large-scale and the visual as strong components. Musically they have much in common in adaptable musical styles that reference classical elements and a tendency to go for the 'big tune' – 'Waltz of My Heart', 'Rose of England', 'Someday My Heart Will Awake' for Novello and 'Memory' or 'Music of the Night' for Lloyd Webber.

Knowledge of the past is important to the understanding of both the content and the appeal of the British musical mid-century, and the reassertion of its individuality as distinct from Broadway is a revealing consequence of this. Although 'we said wouldn't look back', in the case of this particular repertory, maybe we should.

8 The coming of the musical play: Rodgers and Hammerstein

ANN SEARS

Broadway was an exciting place to be in the 1920s, as many new voices were heard in American musical theatre. One important voice was that of jazz; other new voices included the composers George Gershwin, Vincent Youmans, Arthur Schwartz, Ray Henderson and, of course, the team of Richard Rodgers and Lorenz Hart. Rodgers (1902–79) and Hart (1895–1943) began their twenty-five-year collaboration during college productions at Columbia University. Their professional productions began with *Poor Little Ritz Girl* in 1920, and they attracted considerable critical and popular attention with their hit song 'Manhattan' in *The Garrick Gaieties* in 1925. By the end of the 1920s, several more of their shows had appeared on Broadway: *Dearest Enemy* (1925); *The Girl Friend*, a second *The Garrick Gaieties*, *Peggy-Ann* and *Betsy* (1926); *A Connecticut Yankee* (1927); *She's My Baby*, *Present Arms* and the disastrous failure *Chee-Chee* (1928); and *Heads Up!* (1929). By the end of the decade Rodgers and Hart counted among the most popular songwriters in America, but after the start of the Depression and with the arrival of sound in motion pictures, they turned to the promising opportunities of writing film scores in Hollywood.

Hollywood proved to be financially rewarding, and Rodgers and Hart created some of their most enduring songs for films produced in the early to mid-1930s, such as 'Isn't It Romantic', 'You Are Too Beautiful', and 'Easy to Remember'. However, the waiting game of writing a few songs for a film over which they had little artistic control was not for this energetic pair. They returned to Broadway in 1935 with *Jumbo*, an extravaganza staged by Billy Rose. The 233 performances of *Jumbo* began a five-year series of hit shows for Rodgers and Hart, and at one point they had three shows running simultaneously.[1] Most of these shows from the late 1930s were very successful and later appeared in film versions, including, for example, *On Your Toes* (1936), *Babes in Arms* (1937), *The Boys from Syracuse* (1938) and *Pal Joey* (1940). When their masterpiece *Pal Joey* appeared, Rodgers and Hart were at the peak of their creative partnership. The play's seamy plot and characters provoked much criticism, but by the time of its revival in 1952, *Pal Joey* was acknowledged as the most important work produced by Rodgers and Hart. The most integrated of all their musicals, *Pal Joey* is probably the only one of their shows that can be easily revived today.

By the 1940s Hart's lifelong battle with alcoholism and related problems had made meeting theatre deadlines extremely stressful. When the Theatre Guild directors Theresa Helburn and Lawrence Langner approached Rodgers about transforming Lynn Riggs' play *Green Grow the Lilacs* into a musical, the situation came to a head. Hart did not believe the play could be adapted successfully, and he refused to work on the project, even though Rodgers confronted him with the possibility of finding another lyricist. Rodgers had already discreetly spoken to the man he thought might replace Hart – Oscar Hammerstein II.

Hammerstein (1895–1960) came from a family with theatrical traditions in its bones. His grandfather Oscar Hammerstein I founded the Manhattan Opera Company in 1906, giving the American premieres of several important operas and featuring many famous singers. In 1910 he sold his interests in the Manhattan to the Metropolitan Opera.[2] Oscar I's sons William and Arthur were also successful producers and theatre managers. Although William's son Oscar II had promised his father that he would never become involved in show business, like Rodgers and Hart, he was drawn to amateur productions while at Columbia University; during law school at Columbia, he began working for his Uncle Arthur. Eventually he became a writer, collaborating with his mentor Otto Harbach on works by Vincent Youmans (*Wildflower*, 1923), Rudolf Friml (*Rose Marie*, 1924), Sigmund Romberg (*The Desert Song*, 1926, and *The New Moon*, 1928), and most importantly, Jerome Kern (*Sunny*, 1925). In 1927, Kern and Hammerstein wrote *Show Boat*, a groundbreaking show often considered to be the 'prototype for the "musical play" – the singularly American type of operetta which was popularised by Hammerstein and Richard Rodgers'.[3] Hammerstein's great success with *Show Boat* was followed by two other successful shows with Kern, *Sweet Adeline* (1929) and *Music in the Air* (1932). Like many others, Hammerstein was drawn to Hollywood during the 1930s, contributing screenplay or lyrics to ten films.

However, for most of the 1930s Hammerstein's career was an odd patchwork of frustration and gratification. His stage works during the early 1930s had very short runs. *The Gang's All Here* (with Louis E. Gensler) opened to very mixed reviews and closed after only twenty-three performances. *East Wind* (with Romberg) also closed after twenty-three performances, and *Free for All* (with Richard A. Whiting) after a dismal fifteen. Two productions enjoyed respectable runs (*Ball at the Savoy*, London, 1933, 148 performances; and *May Wine*, with Romberg, 1935, 213 performances), and the 1936 film version of *Show Boat*, for which Hammerstein wrote the screenplay and some new songs, was an instant critical and popular success; but several later stage shows were disappointments (including *Very Warm for May* with Kern, 1939, fifty-nine performances). The early 1940s were likewise uneven. Although Hammerstein had written some of his most memorable lyrics in the years following *Show Boat* ('I've Told Every Little Star' from *Music in the Air*; 'When I Grow Too Old to Dream' from *The Night Is Young*; or 'All the Things You Are' from *Very Warm for May*), it seemed to most of the musical theatre world, and perhaps to Hammerstein himself, that his best work was behind him.

Having no specific commitments to either Hollywood or Broadway, Hammerstein turned to a project he had first contemplated in 1934 after hearing a concert performance of Bizet's opera *Carmen* at the Hollywood Bowl. He had tried to interest MGM in a film version of an opera, but they never followed through on the idea. Nonetheless, in 1942, listening to a recording of *Carmen* and with his career at a watershed point, Hammerstein began the transformation of Bizet's nineteenth-century Spanish gypsies into African Americans from the American South during World War II. By July 1942, he had completed the entire libretto of *Carmen Jones*. Condensing the original four-act libretto into two acts and moving the location from a cigarette factory in Seville, Spain, to a parachute factory near a southern town, Hammerstein set his new lyrics to the original music of the opera. He eliminated the recitatives from the opera, restoring Bizet's original balance of spoken dialogue and arias, and as closely as possible kept to the original order of the music.

Opening only a few months after *Oklahoma!*, *Carmen Jones* (502 performances) further signalled the return of the Oscar Hammerstein who had written works such as *The Desert Song*, *Show Boat* and *The New Moon*. The lyrics captured both the opera's tempestuous love story and the unique character of African-American culture. Critics noted how well Hammerstein had matched his words to Bizet's music and story. *Variety* stated that 'Hammerstein is now at the peak of his career.'[4] With such accolades pouring in and two successful Broadway runs launched, Hammerstein's career was reborn. Thus, both Rodgers and Hammerstein brought many years of theatrical experience to their new collaboration, each was intent on having the plot, music and lyrics closely knit together to form a coherent whole, and each was strongly influenced by the operetta tradition. As collaborators, Rodgers and Hammerstein reversed the writing process Rodgers had used with Hart. Rodgers usually wrote music first to which Hart then set lyrics. Now, however, after lengthy discussions about the play, the characters, and the function and placement of the songs, Hammerstein would carefully craft his lyrics, then turn them over to Rodgers, who in turn composed the music. Hammerstein had learned from the unhurried, concentrated writing of *Carmen Jones* that he did his best work when he took plenty of time to polish it. Having accommodated Hart for many years, Rodgers found the reliable, meticulous Hammerstein a comfortable partner.

The result of their initial efforts together was *Oklahoma!*, which exploded on Broadway in 1943 with unprecedented critical and popular acclaim that would have been unimaginable in previous decades. Even Hammerstein was surprised, having written to his son William that while 'here is the nearest approach to *Show Boat* that the theatre has attained' and 'it is comparable in quality', he didn't think that 'it has as sound a story or that it will be as great a success'.[5] Although the opening-night performance in New York was not sold out, by the next day long lines waited at the box office. *Oklahoma!* ran for 2,243 performances on Broadway and toured for fifty-one weeks. A national company toured for ten years through over 150 cities, and the international companies included a USO unit in the Pacific that entertained American troops. The London production at the Drury Lane Theatre was the longest run in the history of that theatre. The show won a special Pulitzer Prize for Drama in 1944. The film version was made in 1955, winning two Oscars: Best Scoring of a Musical Film and Best Sound Recording.[6]

As he wrote the book and lyrics for *Oklahoma!*, Hammerstein aimed to keep the character of the original play, even quoting Lynn Riggs' opening paragraph:

> It is a radiant summer morning several years ago, the kind of morning which, enveloping the shapes of earth – men, cattle in a meadow, blades of the young corn, streams – makes them seem to exist now for the first time, their images giving off a golden emanation that is partly true and partly a trick of the imagination, focusing to keep alive a loveliness that may pass away.[7]

In the stage play, the story takes place in the Indian Territory of Oklahoma around 1900. Laurey, a young, innocent girl, lives on a farm with her widowed Aunt Eller. She falls in love with Curly, a cowboy. They are shy with each other, and to provoke Curly, Laurey agrees to attend a box social with Aunt Eller's farmhand, Jeeter Fry, whom she fears. At the social, Jeeter and Laurey argue, and Jeeter leaves. Soon after, Laurey and Curly are married. During the shivaree on their wedding night, Jeeter appears and dies after falling on his own knife while fighting with Curly. Aunt Eller convinces the authorities to let Curly spend one night with Laurey before he is sent to jail.[8] Traditional folk songs were sung throughout the play.

Hammerstein used much of the original play and kept Riggs' arrangement of two acts, each with three scenes. However, he changed the second act considerably, compressing it and writing a new ending in which Jud (formerly Jeeter) Fry's death from his own knife while fighting with Curly is declared self-defence. Laurey and Curly can leave on their honeymoon. Additionally, Hammerstein created a secondary, comic love triangle by redefining Ado Annie and inventing her suitors, neither of whom is in Riggs' play. The shy, quiet Ado Annie of the original becomes a brash, irrepressible girl who cannot resist men. The cowboy Will Parker and the Persian pedlar Ali Hakim both attempt to woo her. Hammerstein expands the traditional pairs of lovers, observed so frequently in opera, to pairs of love triangles.

As Rodgers and Hammerstein translated the play to a musical setting, they indeed took the musical in a new direction. While Broadway composers of the day might typically have placed an ensemble number early in the show, preferably with a bevy of beautiful girls singing and dancing, *Oklahoma!* opens with Aunt Eller alone on stage churning butter. The leading man, Curly, begins singing 'Oh, What a Beautiful Mornin'' off-stage and without accompaniment. The western setting dictated costumes that were rather homespun compared to the glittering revues and witty comedies of previous eras. No one believed that Rodgers and Hammerstein could sell a death in the second act, not even the accidental death of so disagreeable a character as Jud Fry. Rodgers and Hammerstein themselves joked about why the show could flop: 'the chorus girls didn't appear until the curtain had been up for forty minutes; the first act had no plot except a girl deciding which young man to go to a dance with; there were virtually no important new numbers in the second act; and so on.'[9] There were further examples of a new approach: the combination of ballet and vernacular American dance used as a narrative element; long musical scenes and thoughtful use of song reprises; a plot about ordinary people and their ordinary, yet deeply dramatic lives; and the unusual way the romantic couple interact and fall in love. It all worked together to form a show that, like *Show Boat*, became a milestone, so that later historians writing about important moments in twentieth-century musical theatre would begin to identify eras according to their relationship to *Oklahoma!*, for example 'Act I: Before Rodgers and Hammerstein' and 'Act II: The Broadway Musical After *Oklahoma!*'[10]

Hammerstein's decision to follow the play's original arrangement of three scenes that developed character followed by three scenes more centred around the plot enabled him to create characters of such depth that the audience empathised with them at once. By the end of Act 1 Aunt Eller is established as a wise woman and earth mother. Laurey has revealed both her love for Curly and her fear of Jud Fry. Ado Annie is ripe for Will Parker's ultimatum about marriage, and the pedlar Ali Hakim is bound to be caught by some enterprising young woman. Jud Fry is obviously the villain, but touchingly so, because we know from 'Lonely Room' and 'Pore Jud Is Daid' just how miserable he is. All the action of Act 2 follows from the emotions and events set up in Act 1: Laurey and Ado Annie making choices about their love relationships, the resolution of conflicts between their men, the sad end of the villain, and the community moving towards statehood.

The flow of the dramatic action is helped along by the way Rodgers and Hammerstein use song reprises. For example, the two renditions of 'The Surrey with the Fringe on Top' in scene 1 are the first steps in the relationship between Laurey and Curly. As Curly begins to describe the beautiful surrey in which he will take Laurey to the dance that night, he is really telling her how much he wants to spend a romantic evening with her. Following the song, he discovers that she has agreed to attend the dance with Jud Fry. She realises that the wonderful surrey is not just in Curly's imagination; rather, he has really rented it to drive her to the dance. The reprise of 'The Surrey with the Fringe on Top' is Curly's opportunity to tell her what she has missed, and it prompts her to reconsider her feelings for him. The last song in Act 1, scene 1, 'People Will Say We're in Love', functions similarly; in the rendition that ends Act 1, scene 1, an interaction is begun that must be completed later. After the anxiety set up by 'The Surrey with the Fringe on Top', 'People Will Say We're in Love' lets us see the first blossoming of serious romantic love between Laurey and Curly. Not until Act 2, scene 2 do we hear the reprise of 'People Will Say We're in Love' and know that Laurey and Curly have sorted out their differences and agreed to marry, releasing the tension held from Act 1, scene 1. The resulting organic unfolding of the plot gives *Oklahoma!* a dramatic unity and momentum that had hardly been present in American musical theatre before 1943, and thus announces the arrival of the 'musical play'.

Although the self-effacing Hammerstein claimed that his lyrics were a result of a predilection for 'a more primitive type of lyric',[11] in fact, his fresh, romantic approach to poetry matched the tone of *Oklahoma!*'s story and frontier location perfectly. The repetition of lines in 'Oh, What a Beautiful Mornin'' captured the hushed, suspended serenity of morning in the country before the world was permeated by traffic noise. Country life was also echoed in the patterns of 'The Surrey with the Fringe on Top', where the first two lines are composed of a series of one-syllable words followed by two-syllable words at the end of the line, reminiscent of the true-to-life sounds of clip-clopping horses' hooves and the chicken yard, still familiar to many people in the 1940s. The patterns of his judicious use of western dialect add to the depth of characterisation. Special characters and tender moments are delineated by leaving off the dialect, for example, in Laurey's songs and in Curly's songs about his relationship with Laurey. When Curly sings with or about other characters, such as about Jud Fry in 'Pore Jud Is Daid', the dialect reappears. Hammerstein also disproved critics who thought he could only write sweet, sentimental, inspirational lyrics. Precisely matching his lyrics to Jud Fry's interior landscape he created a dark, introspective picture of

Oklahoma!'s most sinister character, who describes his bleak world in the song 'Lonely Room'.

The music Rodgers wrote for *Oklahoma!* matched and amplified the brilliant characterisations of Hammerstein's lyrics. Curly's repeated opening lines ('There's a bright golden haze on the meadow' and 'Oh, what a beautiful mornin', Oh, what a beautiful day') are paralleled by repeated musical phrases. The repeated notes on 'looks like it's climbin' clear up to the sky' along with the other repetitions reinforce the environment of the Oklahoma territory: wide-open spaces, long days and repetitive tasks, and the deliberate unfolding of a daily life marked by occasional festivities. The hesitant steps Laurey and Curly take towards each other are mirrored in their songs, 'The Surrey with the Fringe on Top' and the 'almost love song' (also a 'list song'), 'People Will Say We're in Love'. Compelling characterisations and music are also given to the minor characters. For example, Will Parker's 'Kansas City' simultaneously introduces Will Parker and the context of the show to the audience. Ado Annie is given some of the most interesting characterisation in the show through her song 'I Cain't Say No', which leaves the audience with a crystal-clear understanding of what motivates her. 'Lonely Room' particularly shows Rodgers' ability to describe character through music. The dissonant intervals of a second that murmur through much of the accompaniment to the song also begin and end the vocal part, mirroring the pain within Jud's psyche and his dysfunctional relationship with the world around him.

The dances in *Oklahoma!* were choreographed by Agnes de Mille, fresh from her triumphs of choreographing and dancing in Copland's ballet *Rodeo* with the Ballet Russe de Monte Carlo in 1942. The choice of de Mille seemed natural in view of the western theme and set of *Rodeo.* Her mixture of vernacular American dance and ballet turned out to be just right for *Oklahoma!*, continuing the character illustration and plot propulsion already inherent in the book, lyrics, and music. Will Parker's dance following 'Kansas City' uses a new social dance, the two-step, tap dancing with references to ragtime, and occasional square dance steps. It sums up the potpourri of popular culture at that time, neatly paralleling the dialect in which Will both speaks and sings. For the 'Dream Ballet' at the end of the first act, de Mille used ballet, flavoured with turn-of-the-century costumes, to reveal Laurey's psychological state and her fear of Jud Fry. While all kinds of dance had been incorporated in the shows of earlier eras, the profound connection of the 'Dream Ballet' to the plot of *Oklahoma!* revolutionised the use of dance in musical theatre. As her fellow choreographer Jerome Robbins said about the use of ballet to tell a story, 'Agnes made it stick.'[12]

There were many obvious innovations in *Oklahoma!* – the importance of the story; songs growing seamlessly out of the plot and characters; the complexity of the strong women characters; the use of lengthy musical scenes; the striking simplicity of the opening; the 'almost love song'; the narrative use of multiple dance styles; and the forthright approach to moral and social issues. Nearly all these elements had appeared to some extent in the work of Rodgers and Hart, who had always considered the integration of story and music a crucial factor in a successful show. For example, Rodgers and Hart had incorporated dance significantly in their shows, showcasing George Balanchine's ballets. As Hammerstein had in 'People Will Say We're in Love', Lorenz Hart often approached love-song lyrics obliquely, sometimes even speaking of love more as a disease than an emotional state ('This can't be love because I feel so well'). Some aspects of the Rodgers and Hammerstein collaboration had been important in Hammerstein's earlier work as well. Hammerstein had tried the western theme in *Rainbow* (1928), and moved towards longer musical scenes in *Show Boat* with Kern. However, with Rodgers and Hammerstein these ideas coalesced, and their innovations would become the recipe for a series of Rodgers and Hammerstein hits. Part of *Oklahoma!*'s immediate success, along with the freshness and coherence of the production itself, was its appearance at the mid-point of World War II, a crucial time in the nation's history. In the context of a devastating world war, the outcome of which appeared far from certain, *Oklahoma!*'s story transmitted a powerful message about the American spirit to its audiences. After Hitler's advance through Europe, the shock of Pearl Harbor, and two brutal years of war, *Oklahoma!*'s celebration of the indomitable pioneer spirit was just what Americans needed to hear. The book, lyrics, costumes and music (especially 'Oklahoma', the 'song about the land' that closes the show) reflected currents in American art, music and popular culture that looked at American life past and present through a haze of romanticism and nostalgia.

Shortly after *Oklahoma!* was launched, Hammerstein wrote the screenplay and lyrics for Twentieth Century-Fox's remake of *State Fair*, returning to the nostalgia of rural America. Rodgers and Hammerstein wrote two of their most memorable songs for the film, 'It's a Grand Night for Singing' and 'It Might as Well Be Spring', which won the Academy Award for Best Song that year. These songs and the title song continued the Rodgers and Hammerstein strategy of using songs to move the plot and explicate character. As the film opens, the title song 'State Fair' functions as an exposition of the story, carrying the action as the song is handed from one character to another, with each giving his or her description of the chief delights of attending the fair. 'It's a Grand Night for Singing' also moves the plot along as the characters hand this song back and forth while they move through the fair. The soliloquy 'It Might as Well Be Spring' provides the most personal, intimate observation of any character in this film, as we see a young girl learning about love between men and women. The making of *State Fair* was a better experience than most of either Rodgers' or Hammerstein's early Hollywood work, and it may have influenced them later to consider film adaptations of their stage productions.

Knowing that it would be difficult to surpass or even equal the triumph of *Oklahoma!*, Rodgers and Hammerstein carefully weighed possibilities for a new show. When the Theatre Guild suggested adapting Ferenc Molnár's play *Liliom*, they refused. After all, 'common knowledge' said that Molnár had refused even Puccini permission for an opera setting.[13] Furthermore, they thought that the Hungarian setting and the bitterness of the second act presented insoluble difficulties. The first challenge was met by having Molnár see *Oklahoma!* for himself, after which he happily gave permission for a musical setting. The other obstacle was overcome by moving the play to the coast of Maine in 1873, turning the leading lady into a wife rather than a mistress, and finding a more acceptable approach to the ending. Inspired by the carnival theme of *Liliom*, they called the new show *Carousel*.

The musical version begins without the customary overture; rather Rodgers settled on a 'Prologue (The Carousel Waltz)' that is an integral part of Act 1. As the waltz plays (its orchestration reminiscent of genuine carnival music), a pantomime unfolds in which the two most important characters are introduced. The body of the play explores the relationship between Billy and Julie, who fall in love, marry and are expecting a child, and the moral choices they make. Julie's friend Carrie marries Mr Snow, providing a stable family story against which Billy and Julie's tragedy is counterposed. Having been fired from the carnival by Mrs Mullin, Billy is unable to support his family. He and his friend Jigger contemplate a robbery, during which Billy is killed. The celestial Starkeeper allows him to return to earth for one day, during which he tells Julie he loved her and encourages his daughter Louise to believe in herself, because she is not alone.

Many ingredients from the smash hit *Oklahoma!* reappeared in *Carousel*, including the use of long musical scenes and reprises. Dance was still an important element, with ensemble numbers for the whole cast and a ballet introducing Billy and Julie's troubled child, Louise. The 'almost love song' ('If I Loved You') appeared in an even more integrated way, emerging seamlessly from the dialogue. Moral choices were more realistically addressed, as conflicted leading man Billy Bigelow struggled with issues such as work and responsibility, domestic abuse, and whether to turn to a life of crime. Julie and Carrie joined Aunt Eller, Laurey and Ado Annie in the Rodgers and Hammerstein pantheon of strong, individualistic women characters. Rodgers and Hammerstein also added an element that would appear in all their subsequent shows: important child characters and issues concerning children.

Musically, the Rodgers and Hammerstein approach became even more organic. Many critics have noticed that 'The Carousel Waltz' of the 'Prologue' provides much of the musical material for the songs in the show.[14] Borrowing from melodrama, *Carousel*'s characters frequently speak over music, a technique that Hammerstein previously used in *Rose Marie*, *Show Boat* and *The New Moon*. The greater complexity of all the characters, whose stories often involve conflict and resolution within themselves, is reflected in their music, particularly in Billy Bigelow's 'Soliloquy', an episodic song that moves far away from the traditional AABA form of the typical Broadway song and through several keys, and the reprise of 'If I Loved You' in Act 2, in which Billy Bigelow finally allows himself to admit his love for Julie.

Like *Oklahoma!*, *Carousel* was produced by the Theatre Guild and supervised by Theresa Helburn and Lawrence Langner. The superb integration of all the show's elements was carefully overseen by a production team almost transplanted from *Oklahoma!*, headed by director Rouben Mamoulian. Agnes de Mille again choreographed the dances, and Miles White designed the costumes. Although some critics found the second act too slow and the ending peculiar, the opening reviews were generally enthusiastic. A few reviewers liked *Carousel* even more than *Oklahoma!*. Anticipating Richard Rodgers' own opinion, Robert Garland wrote that 'when somebody writes a better musical play than "Carousel", written by Richard Rodgers and Oscar Hammerstein, Richard Rodgers and Oscar Hammerstein will have to write it.' Later Rodgers admitted that *Carousel* was his favourite of all his musicals, saying: 'Oscar never wrote more meaningful or more moving lyrics, and to me, my score is more satisfying than any I've ever written. But it's not just the songs: it's the whole play. Beautifully written, tender without being mawkish, it affects me deeply every time I see it performed.'[15] Certainly Rodgers and Hammerstein reached a more profound level of integration and dramatic sensitivity in *Carousel*.

Following *Carousel*, Rodgers and Hammerstein began a pattern of producing other work in between writing and producing their own. In 1946 they produced *Annie Get Your Gun* with a score by Irving Berlin, which went on to have successful runs in New York and London, and throughout Europe. By 1946 Hammerstein had running simultaneously on Broadway a string of hits that included *Oklahoma!*, *Carousel*, *The Desert Song* (with *Carmen Jones* to follow), *Show Boat* and two shows that he and Rodgers co-produced, *I Remember Mama* and *Annie Get Your Gun*. Rodgers and Hammerstein had become two of the most influential men in American musical theatre, and with theatre receipts and royalties flowing in steadily, two of the most affluent.

Their next show, *Allegro* (1947), is perhaps Rodgers and Hammerstein's most experimental work, but its 315-performance run could not compare to their first two outings. Based on the life story of a doctor from birth to the age of thirty-five, the show illustrates stages of his life through a 'Greek chorus', various lighting effects, lantern slides and rear-screen projections, short scenes, dances and songs. The idealistic doctor, Joe Taylor, marries a hometown girl, becomes corrupted by money and power, and loses his healing connection to his patients. Eventually his friend Charlie and Emily, a nurse who loves Joe, help him face his life and leave his unfaithful wife. They return to their hometown and their ideals of medicine. There is much speculation about the so-called 'failure' of *Allegro*. It was the first show Rodgers and Hammerstein created from scratch, whereas their previous two successful productions were based on strong literary sources. Agnes de Mille, who directed, found the play uneven. She thought the first act so beautiful that she cried when she first read it, but she felt that the second act, which Hammerstein wrote under time pressure, did not match the first act, either in quality of lyrics or in continuity of story. *Allegro* marked de Mille's directorial debut, and she struggled to direct, choreograph and manage the complicated, multi-level sets plus a large cast of forty-one principals and almost a hundred dancers and chorus singers. After a frantic rehearsal period and many revisions, *Allegro* opened to mixed reviews. Its forty-week run and thirty-one-week tour might have been a success had the production not been so expensive. However, the artistic failure distressed Rodgers and Hammerstein more than the financial loss. While some praised the show as 'unconventional' and 'a musical play without any of the conventions of form', Hammerstein knew that he had not written the story he really wanted to convey.[16] The commentary of the 'Greek chorus' seemed too moralistic, and it sapped the vitality of the characters and the action. The attempt to make characters less important while emphasising the other elements of the show – dancers, the chorus, the abstract set, the lighting effects – was lost on most people. Some people thought that Rodgers and Hammerstein's styles did not match well enough in the innovative *Allegro*, which may have been the first concept musical, and that Rodgers' music was too conventional for the book and lyrics Hammerstein had written.[17] In any case, the failure of *Allegro* was a misfortune for the world of musical theatre, because Rodgers and Hammerstein never again ventured into so radical a project. The rest of their collaboration was devoted to 'refining the dramatic musical play until they took their particular brand of it as far as it could go'.[18] However, Hammerstein retained an affection for *Allegro*, and was rewriting the musical for television when he died.

Returning to the successful approach that had produced *Oklahoma!* and *Carousel* required finding the right literary property to adapt. When Joshua Logan suggested James Michener's *Tales of the South Pacific*, both Rodgers and Hammerstein were enthusiastic. A series of short stories about World

War II in the South Pacific, the book included many characters and episodes. Hammerstein settled on 'Fo Dolla', the story Logan had first mentioned, and combined it with 'Our Heroine'. The resulting play revolved around two couples: Liat, a young Tonkinese girl, and Lt Joe Cable, an American from an aristocratic Philadelphia family; and Nellie Forbush, a young nurse from Arkansas, and Emile de Becque, a middle-aged French planter. Each couple faces the obstacle of racial prejudice. Lt Cable cannot imagine taking Liat back to America, and Nellie hesitates to marry de Becque after learning of his children born to his late native wife. Cable tells Liat he cannot marry her and leaves on a reconnaissance mission, during which he is killed. De Becque returns from the same mission to discover that Nellie has transcended her learned racism and awaits him with the children. Since having two serious romantic couples was unusual, two important, high-energy characters provided comedy: Bloody Mary, a native trader and Liat's mother, and Luther Billis, an entrepreneurial enlisted man.

Early in the writing of *South Pacific*, Rodgers and Hammerstein engaged Ezio Pinza, a bass with the Metropolitan Opera, and Mary Martin, whom they had wanted but could not get for *Oklahoma!*. Having two major stars in the show created tremendous publicity, and the show's entire try-out week in New Haven was sold out. The Boston try-out was also well received, leading one critic to call the show 'South Terrific, and then some!' With such enthusiastic advance press, the New York opening on 7 April 1949 was equally triumphant.[19] *South Pacific* went on to run for 1,925 performances in New York, winning nine Donaldson awards, eight Tonys, and the coveted Pulitzer Prize for Drama. Many of its songs became familiar to the general public. The original cast album sold over one million copies, and in 1957 a film version appeared, directed by Joshua Logan.

Rodgers and Hammerstein's stamp was on every aspect of the production. They created another pair of strong female characters: nurse Nellie Forbush, who proves her spirit by overcoming her prejudices, and the irascible, incorrigible Bloody Mary. The spotlight on child characters begun in *Carousel* continued with Emile de Becque's two children. Furthermore, the children open and close the show with their song 'Dites-moi', illustrating their pivotal importance in the plot. The old device of a show-within-a-show appeared as a variety show for the troops. The show contained several stellar examples of Rodgers and Hammerstein's extraordinary ability to suggest a locale or a setting, from the exotic flavour of the beautiful, mysterious island described in 'Bali Ha'i' to the rowdy, slightly shady world of 'Bloody Mary' and the soldiers' world of 'There Is Nothin' Like a Dame' and 'Honey Bun'.

The refinements of their evolving formula were apparent in the dramatic use of two romantic couples, and the character-tailored music that fitted the vocal and acting talents of the two stars so well. A new level of dramatic maturity was noticeable in the social commentary of 'You've Got to Be Carefully Taught'. *South Pacific* also ventured into more adult territory with the sexual relationship between Liat and Lt Cable, engineered by Bloody Mary with the hope that Cable will marry her daughter.

Their next show would be an adaptation of Margaret Landon's 1943 *Anna and the King of Siam*, about British widow Anna Leonowens and her stint in the 1860s as tutor to the children of King Mongkut of Siam. The show featured the brilliant actress Gertrude Lawrence, who was not a particularly accomplished or reliable singer, but who had a wonderfully magnetic stage presence. Again the Rodgers and Hammerstein formula would be extended and refined; and again the expansion of the recipe would create a hit show. *The King and I* enjoyed a 1,246-performance Broadway run, toured for eighteen months and ran for 926 performances in London. After capturing three Tonys and five Donaldson awards as a stage production, the 1956 film version won six Academy Awards.

The charm of the show was obvious from the beginning, often in a way predictable from their previous three big shows. The fascination of the exotic time and place was gloriously emphasised by opulent sets and costumes designed after authentic models. Rodgers incorporated enough pentatonic melodies and Thai percussion motifs to imply a genuinely Oriental environment. Three significant songs featured adorable children of various ages: 'Getting to Know You', 'I Whistle a Happy Tune' and the 'March of the Siamese Children'. Jerome Robbins' imaginative ballet, 'The Small House of Uncle Thomas', retold the story of Harriet Beecher Stowe's controversial novel *Uncle Tom's Cabin*, pinpointing several important social issues, such as slavery and gender inequality. Dance and the 'almost love song' combined in 'Shall We Dance?'. Strong women characters abounded in this show: Anna, Lady Thiang and Tuptim.

The real story of *The King and I* was the relationship between Mrs Anna and the King. Bit by bit through the show, the audience observes the gradual understanding established between these two strong-willed characters, reaching towards each other across an enormous cultural abyss. Despite their political and philosophical differences, they grow to love and depend on each other. Their love is never overtly expressed, though coming close in 'Shall We Dance', when they talk about relationships and connect physically in the polka. As they gaze at each other breathlessly after dancing, the audience knows that the love between them hovers on the brink of speech. The tension is broken, not by spoken words of affection, but by the announcement that Tuptim has been found by the police. Any further progression of their feelings is prevented by the King's death, and the 'almost love song' becomes part of a compelling 'almost love story'.

With a fourth huge hit show behind them, Rodgers and Hammerstein had established a nearly infallible relationship with the theatre-going public. Consequently their next two shows managed respectable runs (*Me and Juliet*, 1953, 358 performances; *Pipe Dream*, 1955, 246 performances), but were far from their finest critical successes or best financial windfalls. As with *Allegro*, *Me and Juliet* was an original story by Hammerstein, in this case springing from Rodgers' desire to do a show about life in the theatre. Despite George Abbott's experienced direction, Irene Sharaff's costumes, and Jo Meilziner's ingenious set, the public did not respond to the story. *Pipe Dream* fared still less well, even with a story by John Steinbeck and glamorous opera star Helen Traubel in the cast. Unfortunately, Steinbeck's story and characters were closer to the world of Rodgers and Hart's *Pal Joey* than to the usual Rodgers and Hammerstein recipe. The failure of the production to recreate the earthy atmosphere of Steinbeck's novel and Helen Traubel's unsuitability in the role of whorehouse madam led to the shortest run of a Rodgers and Hammerstein show.

Despite the disappointments of *Me and Juliet* and *Pipe Dream*, Rodgers and Hammerstein forged ahead into new enterprises in the early 1950s. Rodgers wrote the music for a thirteen-hour television documentary series, *Victory at Sea* (1952), which covered important naval battles of World War II. Still popular today, the documentary is available in video format. The film version of *Oklahoma!* released in 1953 was the first film version of one of their shows, and they gave it careful attention, producing it themselves. A close reworking of the stage numbers, except for the omission of 'It's a Scandal! It's an Outrage!' and 'Lonely Room', the film repaid the time and money that went into it, winning two Academy Awards and becoming a screen favourite. They also wrote a well-received version of *Cinderella* (1957) for television that featured a young Julie Andrews, and assisted with producing film versions of *Carousel* (1956) and *South Pacific* (1958). Their new show *Flower Drum Song* began a six-hundred-performance run in March of 1958. Both films and *Flower Drum Song* won Gold Records for their respective cast recordings and soundtracks, and *South Pacific* won an Oscar for Best Sound Recording.

As the 1950s closed, Rodgers and Hammerstein began a new show based on the story of the von Trapp family and their escape from Nazism. Early in the show's preparations, Hammerstein became ill and was diagnosed with stomach cancer. Nonetheless, they were able to write one of their most memorable works. Perhaps the best-known of all their shows because of the immense popularity of the film version, *The Sound of Music* was the epitome of the Rodgers and Hammerstein musical play. The components that had guaranteed the success of the first big shows appeared in force in *The Sound of Music*: tightly integrated book, lyrics, and music with significant dramatic

Plate 13 Shirley Jones as Maria with the children in the 1977 production of *The Sound of Music* at Starlight Theatre, Kansas City, Missouri.

use of song reprises; an atypical love story; important child characters; strong women (a whole abbey of them, along with Maria von Trapp!); narrative use of dance, for example the 'Ländler' during which Captain von Trapp and Maria fall in love; the trademark 'almost love song'; and a brilliant depiction of the story's environment through poetic, musical and design elements. Hammerstein wrote some of his simplest, most heartfelt lyrics.

With memories of World War II and the Nazis' rise to power still vivid and reinforced by the spread of communism in Europe, and well-publicised stories about attempted escapes from communist countries in the American press, audiences took the singing von Trapp family to their hearts and made the show a hit. The artistic acclaim for the show meant even more to Rodgers and Hammerstein. Though some critics found it 'sticky with sweetness and light', many others considered it 'the full ripening of these two extraordinary talents'. Six Tonys, a Gold Record and a Grammy for the cast album, a *Variety* Critic Poll Award for Best Score, and a National Catholic Theatre Conference Award were indisputable evidence of the show's immediate success. A two-year American tour and a 2,385-performance London run were followed by the film version (1965) which carried away five Academy Awards, a Golden Globe, a Gold Record for the cast album and various other awards. Although Hammerstein did not live to know of the remarkable popularity of this show and its film version, in many ways it was a most appropriate capstone to his career and in particular his collaboration with Richard Rodgers. Often decried as overly sentimental, Hammerstein's story and lyrics encoded his own values and principles that he thought audiences found important and believable. Over the years, his continued insistence on writing what he found authentic led to his development as a writer of great maturity, and combined with Richard Rodgers' musical and theatrical genius, produced a series of musical plays that revolutionised post-1943 American musical theatre.

Facing the certainty of his imminent death, Hammerstein encouraged Rodgers to find new projects and continue working with other lyricists. A second television documentary, *Winston Churchill – The Valiant Years* (1960), garnered Rodgers a second Emmy, and his television version of *Androcles and the Lion* (1967; book by Peter Stone, music and lyrics by Rodgers) was generously reviewed. Several new shows had impressive runs: *No Strings* (1962; 580 performances, book by Samuel Taylor, music and lyrics by Rodgers); *Do I Hear a Waltz?* (1965; 220 performances, book by Arthur Laurents, lyrics by Stephen Sondheim); and *Two by Two* (1970; 343 performances, play by Peter Stone, lyrics by Martin Charnin). While he proved his ability to write his own lyrics when necessary, Rodgers continued working with various writers. However, he never found a third collaborator who matched his own innate gifts so well as Hart or Hammerstein. Compared with most of his earlier work, his final two shows (*Rex*, 1976, forty-nine performances, and *I Remember Mama*, 1979, 108 performances) were failures.

Rodgers and Hammerstein's legacy rests on an astonishing body of work, first with other partners, and secondly on their collaborations, particularly their five best shows: *Oklahoma!, Carousel, South Pacific, The King and I* and *The Sound of Music.* All these shows had lengthy if not record-breaking Broadway runs, received significant Broadway show awards, and were issued in film versions. A long list of songs from their shows have become standard popular songs, heard around the world in a dizzying array of arrangements and contexts. Much of popular and even critical perception of their work is based primarily on knowledge of the film versions of their shows, sometimes softened and sweetened for accessibility. However, viewing stage versions, hearing original recordings or reading the plays makes clear the fundamental integrity and power of the shows, and Rodgers and Hammerstein's best work retains its significance at the dawn of a new century.

The vitality of the musical play that Rodgers and Hammerstein developed remains undiminished. Performances of their works in both amateur and professional theatres are ongoing, and the shows continue to find new venues. *Oklahoma!, The King and I* and *South Pacific* all enjoyed important London revivals in the late 1990s and early 2000s. A television version of *South Pacific* starring Glenn Close appeared in spring 2001; and *The*

Sing-along Sound of Music has become the latest Rodgers and Hammerstein rage. We cannot know what Rodgers and Hammerstein might have thought about seeing long lines of movie-goers in their favourite characters' costumes from *The Sound of Music*, but the movie-goers' opinion is quite obvious: the Rodgers and Hammerstein phenomenon is alive and well! Various opinions have been offered as to the reason for Rodgers and Hammerstein's enduring popularity. Irving Berlin said that 'of all the Broadway lyricists, Hammerstein was the only one who was a poet'.[20] Oscar's own words about what he wanted to write may be the best description of his and Rodgers' work and its evergreen presence on the stage: 'The good and the simple and the true are alone eternal.'[21]

9 The successors of Rodgers and Hammerstein from the 1940s to the 1960s

THOMAS L. RIIS AND ANN SEARS

Musical comedies that are recognisably American in tone or theme predate the opening of *Oklahoma!* by many years. At the turn of the century, critics applauded the shows of George M. Cohan for the original, furiously quick-paced action and vernacular dialogue that were his trademarks. Other non-operatic popular plays of the era with appealing music began to feature more kinetic staging, homespun and believable (if often silly) characters, and an air of optimism and headstrong abandon. The singing and dancing actors of Cohan's type, masters and mistresses of the Triple Threat,[1] bespoke a special brand of native entertainment as early as 1902. Fresh, clean, full of slangy humour and catchy songs, with plots loose enough to allow virtually any kind of specialty act to be inserted, truly American musical comedies like *The Belle of New York* (1897), *Little Johnny Jones* (1904; featuring the hit number 'Yankee Doodle Boy'), or *In Dahomey* (1903; the first major African-American musical comedy to put ragtime songs on Broadway) established a type that became the standard through the 1920s.

Nevertheless, in the mid-twentieth century *Oklahoma!*, not merely a hit but an indisputable blockbuster of remarkable coherence, presented a new thematic direction and dramatic formula that marked yet another turning point for musical theatre and would be widely emulated. *Oklahoma!*'s popularity signalled a turn away from the contemporary and topical subjects preferred during the Depression Era in favour of a more sentimental style and subject. Historical subjects, especially nostalgic or patriotic American ones, could and would be portrayed on stage in a manner that avoided farce or parody. The legacy of *Oklahoma!* and successive hits by Rodgers and Hammerstein was multifaceted, but one of its most important elements was the book, or the story. Before *Oklahoma!*, the term 'book show' meant little more than the bare outlines of a plot with a serviceable script about a more or less chronological set of events. Afterwards, it implied a story that was well made, capable of serious dramatic goals, and liable to stimulate the audience with genuine emotions other than laughter.

The Rodgers and Hammerstein approach advocated earnestness and honesty of expression, and it was hardly ever gruesome or visibly violent. Rarely was it sexually explicit, and of course, no overt nudity was permitted. It minimised slapstick antics and pun-saturated wit. Song lyrics and dialogues were romantic and thoughtful; they built storylines and, most crucially, they developed characters. Even dancing could be integrated into the movement of the play, becoming more than merely a diverting interlude. For example, Laurey's 'Dream Ballet' at the end of *Oklahoma!*'s first act permitted the exploration of deep feelings far more effectively than dialogue could ever do. Rodgers' musical language was conventional, but occasionally it included modern sounds to achieve pointed dramatic effect. His musical subtleties were not lost on his successors. Hammerstein's serious lyrics were often about something other than the ubiquitous subject of young love and romance, although certainly love songs are to be found in good supply. The critical element was primarily Rodgers and Hammerstein's integration of words, music, dance and story. This valued coherence had been a long-sought goal of operettas and even some Broadway productions in earlier decades, but it was achieved infrequently during the doldrums of the 1930s. Despite some remarkable works, such as George Gershwin's uniquely appealing folk opera *Porgy and Bess* (1935) and Rodgers and Hart's innovative dance show *On Your Toes* (1936), the 1930s favoured the revue format, in part because of its relatively modest production costs. However, after *Oklahoma!* the integrated show came into fashion again with a vengeance. This integration became one of the most prized aspects of the modern musical.

Oklahoma! also indicated to Broadway producers that certain formulas could be avoided without losing the audience. A full chorus of leggy women did not have to raise the first curtain. Mixed choruses could dance and even sing in parts – before this a style usually reserved for shows with serious operatic pretensions. Indeed, the use of an intelligent plot with a string of beautiful songs opened the door to many other sophisticated innovations, which could be slipped in without offending taste or inducing boredom. More flexibility in the creation of scenarios and even occasional violence resulting in an on-stage killing could be included, if the deserving characters were saved or exonerated in the end (as in both *Oklahoma!* and *Carousel*), thus raising the possibility of a fully formed musical with a tragic ending such as *West Side Story*.

Finally, *Oklahoma!* also reinforced other equally well-understood Broadway conventions that could *not* be discarded without careful consideration. By looking backwards in a few respects, it cleared the space for future experiments while underlining the need to retain always some elements of familiarity and contact for the audience. Like countless melodramas before it, the show's action is dominated by the activities and songs of two couples (one serious and one comic), one ethnic comedian and one villain. The plot's progress from character exposition to complications whereby the lovers are alienated from one another and then reconciled is its most obvious cliché.

Oklahoma!'s seemingly endless run (2,212 performances over six years at the St James Theatre), the continuing productivity of Rodgers and Hammerstein through the late 1950s, and the team's involvement in the production end of the business with shows other than their own all guaranteed that their influence would be profound. But their first and most important contribution was the works themselves, solidly built on universally understood themes with a wide appeal to people of all social and economic classes in mid-twentieth-century America. These works greatly shaped Rodgers and Hammerstein's contemporaries and, more significantly, became models for the succeeding generations of musical theatre composers and lyricists.

The 1940s

Musical theatre in the 1940s faced enormous difficulties, but there was also a resurgence of creative energy. Despite the economic challenges of getting new productions on stage during the 1930s and the resulting exodus of Broadway's best composers to Hollywood's more financially rewarding film opportunities, Broadway began to recover from the Depression by the late 1930s and early 1940s. Along with the old-guard writers Irving Berlin, Richard Rodgers and Lorenz Hart, Cole Porter, Arthur Schwartz and Howard Dietz, and Harold Arlen, a new generation of composers and lyricists either appeared on Broadway for the first time or produced their first important shows, including such writers as Alan Jay Lerner and Frederick Loewe, Jule Styne, Robert Wright and George Forrest, and Frank Loesser. The extraordinary efforts of America to mobilise for the war effort and the concurrent welling up of patriotic feeling throughout the country may have provided some impetus for the material of Rodgers and Hammerstein's *Oklahoma!*, and the wartime atmosphere certainly created a climate in which a show about the American frontier spirit was welcomed and could remain a hit for years to come. While the social and technological changes spurred by the war created an open atmosphere for new ideas and experimentation, the acceptance of innovation in theatrical works was balanced by an appreciation of American life and history, both present and past. Revues, shows exploring the usual romantic relationships (for example, Wright and Forrest's *Song of Norway*, 1944, or Cole Porter's *Kiss Me, Kate*, 1948) and shows based on fantasy (Lerner and Loewe's *Brigadoon* and Harburg and Lane's *Finian's Rainbow*, both opening in 1947) appeared during the 1940s; and an astonishing number of shows centred around Americans' experiences at home and abroad and around American military life opened on Broadway in the 1940s and 1950s (Berlin's *This Is the Army*, 1942, Bernstein's *On the Town*, 1944, Harold Rome's *Call Me Mister*, 1946). With an almost uncanny understanding of the public's state of mind, Rodgers and Hammerstein combined the nostalgia for early American rural life with dramatic innovation to produce *Oklahoma!*, the biggest hit and most influential show of the 1940s.

The initial impact of *Oklahoma!* was felt almost immediately with the E. Y. Harburg/Harold Arlen show *Bloomer Girl* in 1944, featuring the story of the Civil War crusader for comfortable women's clothing, Amelia ('Dolly') Bloomer. Set safely in the colourful past, with a dance choreographed by Agnes de Mille focusing on women's personal anguish as the men go off to war – a transparent reference to the ongoing world war – and introducing the subject of slavery into the plot, *Bloomer Girl* captured in song and story many elements from the Rodgers and Hammerstein prototype, even using its star dancer, Joan McCracken, and its comic singer, Celeste Holm, who had played Ado Annie. Although Herzig and Saidy's libretto was less seamless than Hammerstein's, Arlen's music is undeservedly neglected. A romantic duet, 'Right as the Rain', the character Jefferson Calhoun's song to his love, 'Evelina', and the black servant's plea for racial harmony, 'The Eagle and Me', make a good effect. The show has seldom been revived; although it emphasised the most important social issues of the Civil War period, the book came across as 'superficial and somewhat silly', and certainly not comparable to *Oklahoma!*'s 'artistic cohesiveness'.[2]

Arlen's second show, this time with lyricist Johnny Mercer, was *St Louis Woman* (1946), with an all-black cast featuring such well-known artists as the Nicholas Brothers, Harold and Fayard, Pearl Bailey, Rex Ingram and Juanita Hall. Although the score contained some beautiful songs, such as 'Come Rain or Come Shine' and 'I Had Myself a True Love', the weak libretto foretold a brief run. The writer, Countee Cullen, died before the show made it to New York. Not even the extensive revisions of the replacement director, Rouben Mamoulian, who had directed the original productions of both Gershwin's *Porgy and Bess* (1935) and Rodgers and Hammerstein's *Oklahoma!*, could sustain the show beyond 113 performances, but the original cast album made later in 1946 eventually led to the critical recognition the fine score deserves. *St Louis Woman* was in many ways a worthy successor to some striking stage works focusing on African-American life and culture during the 1930s and early 1940s, among them *The Green Pastures* (1930), *Porgy and Bess*, *Cabin in the Sky* (1940) and Oscar Hammerstein's *Carmen Jones* (1943). Both of Arlen's first two Broadway shows reflected his long-standing interest in African-American music and his understanding of the issues facing African Americans in the United States. Having written arrangements for Fletcher Henderson's band and music for Cotton Club Revues from 1930 to 1934, Arlen had thoroughly absorbed the melodic, harmonic and rhythmic elements of black music, particularly the blues form.

His ability to synthesise blues, jazz and Tin Pan Alley styles in popular song form gave his music a strong individual stamp as well as an unmistakably American identity, but his score has been lost for posterity because of the poor book. *St Louis Woman* never returned to Broadway, but the music later appeared in an operatic version in Amsterdam (1959) and Paris.

If one way to define the Rodgers and Hammerstein formula was simply operetta plus Americana, *Up in Central Park* (1945) fitted the bill perfectly, with a book by the experienced brother and sister team Herbert and Dorothy Fields, and music by the veteran operetta composer Sigmund Romberg. Complete with an American hero in the form of a journalist battling the corrupt politician Boss Tweed and Tammany Hall, it is set well back from modern times in New York of the 1870s. Although critical opinion of this show suggests that it failed to live up to the highest standards of its creators, its relatively lengthy run of 504 performances (and later preservation on film in 1947 with Deanna Durbin and Dick Haymes) implies that the writers and composer were giving the public what it wanted. A sumptuous production by Mike Todd and choreography by the emerging Helen Tamiris, who would later go on to stage the dances for the revival of *Show Boat* in 1946 and the original production of *Annie Get Your Gun* (1948), also helped to guarantee its warm reception, but the show is little known today.

Irving Berlin's *Annie Get Your Gun* (1946) did not seek to imitate Rodgers and Hammerstein in its details, although the team produced the show. The third-longest-running musical of the 1940s, it demonstrated that even after *Oklahoma!* and *Carousel*, good songs well performed could still make for a Broadway smash hit. The liveliness of the historical title character played by the triumphant Ethel Merman helped as well. Herbert and Dorothy Fields's book, while not strictly adhering to the facts of sharpshooter Annie Oakley's life, at least avoided the hackneyed melodrama of days gone by, and if Berlin's melodies are easily extractable from the show, they are no less worthy for that. The perennial creator of American popular song produced a string of superb numbers for the show, such as 'Doin' What Comes Natur'lly', 'Anything You Can Do', and 'They Say It's Wonderful'. The classic 'There's No Business Like Show Business', which entices Annie to join Buffalo Bill's Wild West Show, simply brings down the curtain better than any other song ever written for Broadway. The show has played in many countries and its revival on Broadway in the late 1990s with Bernadette Peters – succeeded in the role by actors such as Cheryl Ladd, Reba McEntire and Crystal Bernard – demonstrates its continuing popularity.

Miss Liberty, Robert Sherwood and Irving Berlin's show of 1949 (with director Moss Hart and choreographer Jerome Robbins), once again invoked a patriotic theme, this time about the search for a girl to pose as the model for the Statue of Liberty, and an old-fashioned setting from 1885. Because of advance sales, the show played for over three hundred performances; however, the tuneless score and heavy-handed libretto with its shocking failure to provide a final love interest for the 'girl next door' character put off audiences from the outset. Even with its all-star production team, the only memorable number from the show is the final hymn-like setting of the popular poem inscribed on the statue's base, 'Give Me Your Tired, Your Poor'.

Jule Styne (1905–94) had received classical training, made a success of himself in Hollywood song-writing and was a practised vocal arranger. Long before he reached Broadway in 1947, Styne had collaborated successfully with good lyricists such as Frank Loesser and Sammy Cahn on scores for over fifty films. He mixed writing and producing all through his career, and at his peak (1959–67) wrote music for television and the live stage, as well as popular songs. Over the years it became apparent that he possessed a discerning eye for talented women and was adept at making vehicles for them. (Styne also boosted Ethel Merman, Barbra Streisand and Mary Martin, and he had even coached Shirley Temple and Alice Faye years before.) Carol Channing became a star after her first important Broadway role in Styne's *Gentlemen Prefer Blondes* (1949), where 'Diamonds Are a Girl's Best Friend' became her anthem. Like many American musicals, the show enjoyed runs in London and Germany as well. It was revived as *Lorelei* in 1973, again with Channing as the star, a production that reached Broadway the following year. The importance of a star like her in the show is underscored by the short-lived revival at the Lyceum in 1995.

High Button Shoes (1947) was Styne's first foray onto Broadway after working in Hollywood. He was assisted by Sammy Cahn's lyric writing and considerable rewriting by the noted director George Abbott. The book is formulaic and all the specialties (separate acts featuring the talents of individual performers but not contributing to a plot) of the show collectively make up its main attraction. These included the fresh comedy of Phil Silvers, the duo dancing of Nanette Fabray and Jack McCauley in 'Papa, Won't You Dance with Me', and an elaborate chase scene/ballet, choreographed by Jerome Robbins. Styne and Cahn's score was well liked and the sum total of these parts spelled a hit even as Rodgers and Hammerstein were experimenting with one of their least successful vehicles, *Allegro*. (*Allegro* opened on the day after *High Button Shoes* but enjoyed fewer than half as many performances on Broadway – 315 versus 727.) Both shows avoided colourful features of American history or operetta. Further versions of *High Button Shoes* have included two for American television in 1956 and 1966 and several regional productions. Styne's Broadway career was only beginning, but it was taking off at a time when the standard expectations for both song lyrics and quality of book were reaching an extraordinarily high level. With the clever literary texts of Lorenz Hart or Ira Gershwin fresh in people's minds, along with the production savvy of the Rodgers and Hammerstein team, a young musical newcomer like Styne could only benefit from close observation of the shows around him.

In *Gentlemen Prefer Blondes* (1949) the true genius of Jule Styne began to emerge. Rarely has a musician been more perfectly attuned to a medium than Styne was to the Broadway stage. He understood the larger-than-life quality of live theatre, the flair required to put over a song, the graphic gestures needed to make comedy convincing and the visible tear to evoke sympathy. Speaking in purely musical terms, Styne melodically derives from Irving Berlin, who always demanded a radically simple match between tune and text. Styne's love of show-business razzle-dazzle and his ability to bring filmic intensity to the live stage mirrored the widespread passion of Broadway denizens in his time. Just as so many Hollywood musicals are really about the process of making a show, so Styne's Broadway creations reflect the obsessions connected with the experience of putting a story with music and dance on stage. Styne was also involved in producing musicals, and until the late 1950s occupied himself with directing the revival of Rodgers and Hart's *Pal Joey* (1952) and Jerry Bock's *Mr Wonderful* (1956), a vehicle designed to introduce Sammy Davis Jr to the musical theatre stage.

With *Brigadoon* (1947), their third show and first hit together, Alan Jay Lerner (1918–86) and Frederick Loewe (1901–88) easily established themselves as the heirs apparent to the Rodgers and Hammerstein tradition. Although Lerner and Loewe had written two earlier musicals, in *Brigadoon* they settled on a style which followed Rodgers and Hammerstein in its combination of a well-written book with elements of operetta, for example, an exotic location, operetta-influenced music which demanded well-trained voices, and the incorporation of ballet. Loewe further reflected Rodgers' influence in writing idiomatically for the voice and effectively capturing the flavour of the faraway locale in music. Like Rodgers and Hammerstein, they had a series of hit shows produced during a partnership over a decade long (*Paint Your Wagon*, 1951; *My Fair Lady*, 1956; *Camelot*, 1960; and the film *Gigi*, 1958). Also like Rodgers and Hammerstein, Lerner and Loewe wrote in a 'words first, music second' fashion. After extensive discussions about the book, character development and placement of songs, Lerner sketched lyrics that Loewe then set to music. Revisions were done in a collaborative fashion, often working together. *Brigadoon* ran for 581 performances, a successful show in comparison to other shows on Broadway that year, even though it was not quite an '*Oklahoma!*'. Set in the misty Scottish Highlands, the story concerns two American tourists who happen on a town that only awakens every hundred years. It begins rather simply, again recalling *Oklahoma!*. As the plot unfolds, three love stories must work themselves out, and the visitors must decide whether to remain in the enchanted village or return to New York. Lerner's eloquent lyrics and Loewe's music were complemented by the brilliant choreography of Agnes de Mille. The reviews exceeded Lerner and Loewe's wildest hopes: Brooks Atkinson of the *New York Times* praised their work as a 'major achievement on the musical stage', noting that 'it is impossible to say where the music and dancing leave off and the story begins in this beautifully orchestrated Scottish idyll'.[3] With such acclaim, Lerner and Loewe were well launched on their Broadway careers, and if they did not quite overturn Rodgers and Hammerstein's domination of American musical theatre, they did loom large over most of their contemporaries during the late 1940s and 1950s. As authors of three shows that have had frequent revivals, Lerner and Loewe remain one of Broadway's most important creative teams.

Burton Lane and E. Y. 'Yip' Harburg's *Finian's Rainbow* (1947) opened shortly before *Brigadoon*. It was the third of Burton Lane's stage musicals written in the 1940s, interspersed among his highly successful assignments for the Hollywood films that were the primary focus of his career from 1933 to 1954. Academy Award nominations for Best Song for 'How About You' from *Babes on Broadway* (1941) and 'Too Late Now' from *Royal Wedding* (1951; starring Fred Astaire) indicated Lane's standing in film music, but musical theatre was his real interest, and he returned to New York in 1955 to concentrate on Broadway productions. Like *Brigadoon*, *Finian's Rainbow* was based on a fantasy story and featured a lush score. Its 725-performance run outlasted *Brigadoon*, but in any case both shows proved that when well done, fantastic and imaginative settings were viable topics for Broadway. *Finian's Rainbow*'s bittersweet ending did not detract, and the gems in the score carried the show, for example, 'How Are Things in Glocca Morra', 'Look to the Rainbow' and 'Old Devil Moon'. The show has been revived several times, including at the City Center in 1955, 1960 and 1967. The 1960 production was moved to the 46th Street Theater, but it folded after twelve performances.

Cole Porter's *Kiss Me, Kate* (1948) is considered by many to be the masterwork of his output. Similar to Kern's and Gershwin's experience, Porter's career began in 1915 writing songs for interpolation into musicals. His first success with a complete score came with *Fifty Million Frenchmen* (1929), followed by *The Gay Divorce* (1932; starring Fred Astaire), and *Anything Goes* (1934) and *Panama Hattie* (1940) with Ethel Merman. By the 1940s he had a firmly established reputation. The seven shows Porter wrote in the 1940s encountered mixed success, but *Kiss Me, Kate* opened to rave reviews and ran for 1,070 performances. Based on Shakespeare's *The Taming of the Shrew*, with a brilliant book by Samuel and Bella Spewack, the story of *Kiss Me, Kate* cleverly paralleled the lives of Shakespeare's characters Petruchio and Katharine with the lives of a pair of divorced actors who play their parts in the show-within-the-show. As the Shakespeare play proceeds with the feuding divorced couple reciting Shakespeare's lines, the actors make up, just as do Petruchio and Kate, and they are reunited in the end. A secondary actor/actress couple also work out their difficulties throughout the show. As usual, Porter wrote both his own lyrics and the music. Porter's sophisticated lyrics matched the ebullience of Shakespeare's play, and the elegance of the entire production assured that it became the fourth-longest-running musical of the 1940s, quite a record considering that Rodgers and Hammerstein's *Oklahoma!* swept all attendance records for the entire decade. Furthermore, Porter's show has remained popular, as is shown in the important recent productions in both New York and London in 2000 and 2001. It has also played in Australia, Germany, Austria and France, among other countries. *Kiss Me, Kate* was a departure from the musical comedies Porter wrote earlier in his career, proving that he too had learned important lessons from such shows as *Oklahoma!* and *Carousel*. The theatre historian Gerald Bordman notes that in *Kiss Me, Kate*, 'all the ideals that musical plays had been striving for were triumphantly realized'. He points to the 'remarkably lifelike, believable protagonists, with every character having a sensible and important bearing on the plot, with every song perfectly related to the action and more often than not advancing it', and lyrics and dialogue 'that remained literate and witty or touching throughout'.[4] Many songs from *Kiss Me, Kate* became popular, including 'Another Op'nin', Another Show', another actors' anthem, much in the spirit of Irving Berlin's 'There's No Business Like Show Business'; 'Wunderbar', a waltz that even Richard Rodgers might have been proud of and a brief echo of the operetta tradition; and 'So in Love', a slow but passionate ballad.

The 1950s

Irving Berlin's next show, *Call Me Madam* (1950), was a far cry from Rodgers and Hammerstein in its tone of parody, and its wit and music kept it running on Broadway for well over a year. Similar in attitude to political shows of the 1930s, it managed to be both modern and old-fashioned. Its plot arose directly from President Harry Truman's decision at the time to appoint Washington hostess Perle Mesta as Ambassador to Luxembourg. In the musical, the socialite Sally Adams, played by the ever-popular Ethel Merman, is the new minister to the mythical country of Lichtenburg. Love interests and complications ensue. American gaucherie is played off against European sophistication, reminiscent of operetta situations a half-century before. Berlin's songs were hailed and a movie, also starring Merman, was made in 1953. The show has seen a few revivals, including one at the Victoria Palace in London in 1983.

Call Me Madam was directed by the legendary George Abbott (1887–1995), who was as essential as anyone in creating what is often described as the 'Rodgers and Hammerstein type' of musical. His first musical was Rodgers and Hart's circus show *Jumbo* (1935), with the score realised by Paul Whiteman's orchestra. Having a great deal of experience from the legitimate theatre and film arenas in the 1920s and 1930s, Abbott was highly regarded on Broadway by mid-century. He believed in well-constructed plots, attentive actors who gave clear and crisp line delivery, and well-planned stage movement, rather than improvised business. His method was formulaic but extremely effective and required a high degree of precision. While he demanded efficiency and eschewed excess, he was not afraid of innovation, especially when it came to twists in theme, plot or choreography. He made his mark permanently on the acting style of the genre. From the 1940s until nearly the end of his long life, Abbott wrote, produced and directed shows with many of the greatest composers and lyricists of American musical theatre, including Irving Berlin, Leonard Bernstein, Comden and Green, Jule Styne, Frank Loesser, Arthur Schwartz, Adler and Ross, Bob Merrill, Jerry Bock, and Stephen Sondheim. The title 'show doctor' is perhaps more appropriately applied to him than almost any other figure in recent Broadway history.

Frank Loesser (1910–69), like Jule Styne, had extensive experience in writing songs for motion pictures before arriving on Broadway, although almost all of that experience came with writing only lyrics. Doing both words and music for his wartime hit 'Praise the Lord and Pass the Ammunition' inspired him to expand his horizons, and he joined George Abbott, who wrote the book and directed, to rework the classic English farce *Charley's Aunt* into the musical *Where's Charley?*. The first of Loesser's five complete Broadway scores, the show was a slow starter, but ultimately became a successful vehicle for dancer Ray Bolger, who returned to Broadway in 1951 for forty-eight performances and appeared in the 1952 film version.

Loesser's masterpiece, *Guys and Dolls* (1950), reflects a debt to Rodgers and Hammerstein in its recognition of the essentially collaborative nature of modern musical theatre. The team coordination brought about by Loesser, who wrote music and lyrics, and Abe Burrows, the book-writer who developed the script from Damon Runyon's tales of New York City's underworld, tells much about how to do it right. The producers, Cy Feuer and Ernest Martin, were inspired by the unusual love interest represented by Nellie and Emile in *South Pacific*. In light of that show's success, the unlikely pairing of the earnestly evangelical Sarah Brown and the high-rolling sportsman Sky Masterson in Runyon's 'The Idyll of Miss Sarah Brown' seemed at least plausible in a popular musical context. However, Loesser and Burrows put their own stamp on *Guys and Dolls* only after realising that they needed to deviate from the serious emphasis of *South Pacific* and give the comic aspect of the story free play in both dialogue and situation. Since Loesser had already written the songs, Burrows was presented with the unique challenge of writing a comic script to surround fully composed music. Unburdened by previous experience in writing for Broadway, Burrows succeeded brilliantly. *Guys and Dolls* was a perfect blend of romantic fun and funny romance. Even better, the floating crap game and the Save-a-Soul Mission were both located in the heart of the city, close to Broadway itself, that most American of thoroughfares. George M. Cohan would have loved it, and audiences have continued to applaud the show, one of the most frequently revived from the period. It has done very well in English-speaking countries, but has proved less popular elsewhere.

Guys and Dolls together with Rodgers and Hammerstein's *Carousel*, *South Pacific* and *The King and I* represent especially well the new blend of moods possible within the well-written script of the time. Both romance and comedy not only coexisted in different characters and situations but could be expressed – along with a generally wider range of emotions – at times by the *same* character. The music placed characters in a new realm outside the spoken play and hence could express what was otherwise unsayable within the typical serious drama. The inarticulate, abusive Billy Bigelow could be a touching optimist as he soliloquised about his unborn child. The brutal and arbitrary King of Siam can express 'A Puzzlement' and vulnerability in song when confronting the equally formidable but tender-hearted Anna.

Loesser's other Broadway hits did not equal his triumph with *Guys and Dolls*, but they represent a continuing willingness to deviate from stock dramatic scenarios filled with besotted but otherwise uninteresting young lovers. In *The Most Happy Fella* (1956) in particular, the ageing winemaker Tony, betrothed to the ultimately unfaithful but realistically frustrated and passionate waitress Rosabella, is reminiscent again of the ages and personal issues that divide *South Pacific*'s Nellie Forbush and Emile de Becque. *The Most Happy Fella* also represents a vote for musical integrity and seriousness but without reverting to operetta in the old style or trying to appeal to an audience beyond a typical Broadway crowd. Loesser's *How to Succeed in Business Without Really Trying* (1961) as a parody of corporate climbing and opportunism was about as far from a Rodgers and Hammerstein *theme* as could be imagined. Yet the quality of its book, only the fourth ever to win a Pulitzer Prize for drama – the previous winners had been *Of Thee I Sing* (1931), *South Pacific* (1949) and *Fiorello!* (1959) – indicated that the creative team, essentially the group that had confected *Guys and Dolls*, all subscribed to Lehman Engel's dictum that great musicals begin with great books, a principle Engel had derived from his observations of and participation in the shows of Rodgers and Hammerstein from the conductor's podium. *How to Succeed in Business* became a successful film, played well in other English-speaking countries, and reappeared in a successful Broadway production in the 1990s with Matthew Broderick as the star.

Lerner and Loewe's first Broadway offering of the decade was *Paint Your Wagon* (1951), a Gold Rush story inspired by Lerner's reading of Bret Harte's rough-and-ready frontier tales. The show was beset with problems from its very beginning: Loewe had to be coaxed to work on it; the production team argued over casting choices; and by Lerner's own admission, he struggled to create a coherent musical play that combined the realism of actual frontier life and robust entertainment. Despite the contributions of the experienced producer Cheryl Crawford and the choreographer Agnes de Mille, the popularity of several memorable songs (for example, 'I Talk to the Trees' and 'They Call the Wind Maria') and a run of 289 performances, the show lost money. Indicating Rodgers and Hammerstein's continued sway over Broadway, critics described Lerner's lyrics in contrast to Hammerstein's (they lacked his 'honest sentiment'); and they compared Loewe to Rodgers as well as Loesser (Loewe had written the 'most accomplished music Broadway had fallen heir to since *The King and I* and *Guys and Dolls*').[5] *Paint Your Wagon* and its ambivalent reviews in no way prepared either audiences or critics for Lerner and Loewe's next production, *My Fair Lady*, which became their biggest success, while *Paint Your Wagon* has fallen into relative obscurity.

My Fair Lady (1956) began as the brainchild of film producer Gabriel Pascal, who originally approached Rodgers and Hammerstein to write the musical adaptation of George Bernard Shaw's *Pygmalion*. Unable to solve the problems presented by Shaw's insistence that *Pygmalion* was not a love story, Hammerstein withdrew from the project.[6] Interested by the story, Lerner and Loewe began working on the book, and Pascal signed an agreement for production with the Theatre Guild. After a few months, Lerner and Loewe admitted defeat as had Rodgers and Hammerstein; Pascal was subsequently refused by Noël Coward, Cole Porter, Schwartz and Dietz, and Fred Saidy and E. Y. Harburg. After half-hearted efforts on a number of new show possibilities and writing the screenplay for the successful film of *Brigadoon* (1954), Lerner read in the newspaper that Pascal had died, leaving a complicated estate that included the rights to *Pygmalion*. Lerner and Loewe went to work, resolved to 'do Pygmalion simply by doing Pygmalion',[7] while their attorney sorted out the legalities. The musical was a very faithful adaptation, changing little of the play except the addition of three scenes, including the Ascot Racetrack Scene and the ending: in the original play, Eliza walks out on Higgins but in a postlude Shaw suggests that she might have married young Freddie; in the musical, she returns to the irascible Higgins. Lerner retained as much of the dialogue as he could, blending his own dialogue and lyrics almost flawlessly with Shaw's own words. He and Loewe aimed to 'musicalise' the play with 'fresh expressions' of the conventions of 'the balance of the score, the proper distribution of solos, ensemble singing, and choreography', so the 'characters arrive at the emotional moment that demands the right kind of music to balance the score'.[8] Loewe's charming music, if redolent of the operetta of an earlier day, added to the lavish, stunning period costumes designed by Cecil Beaton. A superb cast, headed by Rex Harrison as Higgins, included a young, radiant Julie Andrews as Eliza and veteran character actor Stanley Holloway as Eliza's father. The night of the opening in New Haven, Connecticut, a blizzard struck, and nervous about his foray into musical theatre, Rex Harrison announced that he was not yet ready to appear in the role. Yet, after a few changes in New Haven and a second try-out period in Philadelphia, *My Fair Lady* opened in New York to unanimously glowing reviews, one of which said, 'Don't bother reading this review now. You'd better sit right down and send for those tickets to *My Fair Lady*. First things first.'[9] Acknowledging that the Shavian story was an atypical Broadway approach to romance, critics praised the thoughtful use of Shaw's original play, the brilliance of the lyrics, and Loewe's well-integrated score. Brooks Atkinson wrote in the *New York Times* that 'in taste, intelligence, skill and delight, *My Fair Lady* is the finest musical play in years.' *My Fair Lady* was undoubtedly the 'most influential musical of the Fifties'.[10] The cast album was a best-seller, and the 1964 film starring Rex Harrison and Audrey Hepburn won Academy Awards for Best Picture, Best Actor and Best Director. Even with the memory of distinctive performances of the original cast, the show has remained a favourite in revivals in many countries, including anniversary productions on Broadway in 1976 and 1981, the latter again starring Rex Harrison. Like all the important Rodgers and Hammerstein shows, *My Fair Lady* succeeded partially because it was based on an original literary work of the highest quality. Lerner and Loewe's smash hit further harked back to Rodgers and Hammerstein's latest big show *The King and I* in its half-sung/half-spoken part for the hero, more overtones of romance between the leading couple than in the source material, and Loewe's operetta-flavoured music. Apparently, the Rodgers and Hammerstein formula still provided a framework for artistic and commercial success.

As Rodgers and Hammerstein continued their march across musical theatre history and the careers of Lerner and Loewe peaked, something of an era ended when Cole Porter returned to Broadway in the 1950s for his last two musicals, *Can-Can* (1953) and *Silk Stockings* (1955), his fifth and sixth musicals with French settings. *Can-Can* is set in Paris in 1893, telling two stories side by side. A young judge investigates the scandalous can-can dancing at a café, but falls in love with the café owner and then helps legalise the dance. One of the dancers is pursued by a sculptor and an art critic, who attacks the sculptor's work. Of course, all ends happily. Like many of Porter's scores, *Can-Can* was poorly received initially, but became a hit with five new standards, among them 'I Love Paris'. The show was helped along by the sizzling dancing of the young Gwen Verdon in her first major Broadway role. It was revived at the City Center in 1962, but critics found the book dated in a 1982 production at the Minskoff, despite Abe Burrows' revision of his original text. *Silk Stockings* was inspired by the 1939 film *Ninotchka*, starring Greta Garbo. The story is about Ninotchka, a beautiful but icy Russian woman official seduced both by the luxuries of western culture and by a talent scout who wants a Soviet composer to write the score for a movie version of *War and Peace*. When the composer opts to stay in Paris, Ninotchka is sent to bring him home. Pursued to Russia by the talent scout, she returns with him to the West. Full of clever allusions to the ongoing Cold War, the lyrics are Porter's usual polished, topical, erudite work; and the score of *Silk Stockings* contained some of his favoured Latin-influenced, beguine-like melodies. The show has rarely been revived, and the story remains best known in the original film version.

Among the most conventional of successful musicals in the post-*Oklahoma!* decade was *Kismet*, which had its premiere on 3 December 1953 at the Ziegfeld Theatre and ran for nearly six hundred performances. The secret of its success lay in the use of thoroughly romantic and exotic music by the Russian composer Alexander Borodin (1833–87) matched to a gaudy story of magic and adventure set in ancient Baghdad. Robert Wright and George Forrest added the lyrics for 'Stranger in Paradise' and 'Baubles, Bangles, and Beads' to Borodin's instrumental works ('Polovtsian Dances' from his opera *Prince Igor* and the second string quartet, respectively). Charles Lederer and Luther Davis rewrote the play based on the 1911 Oriental chestnut by Edward Knoblock. The make-believe operetta world that *Kismet* inhabits is seldom absent from Broadway for long – one can see traces at least as far back as *The Black Crook* of 1866. But the show's appeal, during an otherwise unremarkable Broadway season, underscored the basic need for both musical and dramatic solidity within an idiom that audiences readily understood. The classical music was put together with the same building blocks that Rodgers and others used so well in their songs. *Kismet* remains among the shows from the period that have been revived, playing in New York in 1962, 1965 and 1976. The 1976 production appeared in London the following year.

The appropriateness of Borodin's music, with a vocabulary that serves the tonal world of much nineteenth-century classical music as well as Tin Pan Alley, begs a further comment on Rodgers' stylistic legacy, which claims both a classical and a popular resonance. Rodgers was nothing if not flexible, and his ability to generate and maintain an overall sound was crucial to his success in so many shows with his principal collaborators, Hart and Hammerstein. In *South Pacific*, *The King and I* and *Flower Drum Song*, despite the harmony or instrumentation of a vaguely or superficially Asian nature, the main tunes come unmistakably from Rodgers' pen, using the song formulas that he uses in the other non-ethnic shows as well. The most talented musicians who created scores for shows between 1945 and 1970, such as Irving Berlin, Cole Porter, Kurt Weill, Leonard Bernstein, Harold Arlen, Frank Loesser, Jule Styne, Frederick Loewe and Charles Strouse, were similarly adaptable.

A host of neophytes led by the Broadway giant George Abbott created *The Pajama Game* in 1954. With a little bit of politics blended with the required romantic story, a healthy dose of comedy and several good songs, the vehicle ran efficiently for over a thousand performances at the St James Theatre before hitting the road. Richard Adler and Jerry Ross wrote their first songs for a book show, including 'Hey, There, You With the Stars in Your Eyes', 'Hernando's Hideaway' and 'There Once Was a Man'. Co-director with Abbott was the young Jerome Robbins. The cast included the veterans John Raitt, Janis Paige, and Eddie Foy Jr, as well as the newcomer Shirley MacLaine. Hal Prince, Frederick Brisson and Robert Griffith produced their first major show. The twenty-six-year-old choreographer Bob Fosse created his first big Broadway dance for 'Steam Heat', rich with the jazzy and angular gestures that would become his signature moves.

In 1955 virtually the same creative team followed up on *The Pajama Game* with the equally successful *Damn Yankees*, this time featuring the lithe and youthful Gwen Verdon (as Lola, the devil's assistant who typically gets what she wants). Ray Walston played the Tempter himself, the character called Mr Applegate, who transforms a middle-aged baseball fan into the youthful sports star Joe Hardy, played by Stephen Douglass, in exchange for his soul. Since devils and seductive temptresses had been appearing on stage since the Middle Ages, a certain sense of familiarity was inevitable, but the baseball-centred theme and Fosse's choreography added zip to the whole Faustian affair. Ross's death from leukaemia in 1955 (at the age of twenty-nine) ended what would undoubtedly have been a far more extended career on Broadway. Both of his musicals have been revived, including *The Pajama Game* in New York in 1973 and at the New York City Opera in 1989, and both often play in regional theatres.

Harold Arlen appeared on Broadway in his last musical theatre endeavours in the 1950s, beginning with *House of Flowers* (1954). Based on Truman Capote's short story about a bordello in Port-au-Prince, Haiti (which he himself had frequented), it tells the story of two competing houses of pleasure. The House of Flowers run by Madame Fleur features employees with flower names; the rival house is run by Madame Tango. When sailors bring a mumps epidemic and consequent financial ruin to the House of Flowers, Madame Fleur contemplates selling her employee 'Violet', but Violet prefers to marry her sweetheart. Despite a kidnapping plot, the sweethearts are married, but the House of Flowers survives when Madame Tango's entire establishment sails away on a world cruise. The high points of the show were the beautiful sets by Oliver Messel and Arlen's wonderfully atmospheric score. The sets and score did not carry the show, however, and it ran for a barely respectable 165 performances.

Arlen's 'Caribbean companion' to *House of Flowers* was *Jamaica* (1957). Koli, a poor fisherman on an island off the coast of Jamaica, loves the ravishing Savannah, who wants to live in New York. She is tempted by a city-slicker pearl broker, but after Koli saves her little brother's life, she chooses to remain with the simple fisherman. In a clear reference to *Oklahoma!*, she visits New York in a 'dream ballet'. Lena Home's appearance in the leading role and in eleven of the twenty-one numbers of the show guaranteed the show a remunerative run of 558 performances, but critics agreed that the score was derivative at best.[11] *Saratoga* (1959), Arlen's final show of the 1950s, was a period piece adapted from Edna Ferber's novel of the same name, and closed after only ten weeks. Despite stage and revue successes and the many popular songs from those efforts, and a thorough biography available, Arlen remains most famous for his work in musical films, especially the ubiquitous *The Wizard of Oz* (1939). Although his musical style is innovative and original, and the catalogue of his works extensive, Arlen's lack of name recognition even now indicates that he has not yet found his rightful place in American musical theatre history.[12] None of his Broadway shows remains in the popular consciousness.

Bells Are Ringing (1956) marked the first full-blown musical of Betty Comden and Adolph Green with Jule Styne. It also became their longest-running collaborative effort, with over nine hundred performances at the Shubert Theatre. (The team had made the composer's professional acquaintance during their work together on *Peter Pan* and worked with him on eight shows in all.) The story, a modern romance between a telephone switchboard operator and a playwright, was intended as a vehicle for Comden and Green's friend and earlier performing partner Judy Holliday. Two great songs, 'Just in Time' and 'The Party's Over', along with spirited dancing, snappy list-making lyrics, a New York setting and the personal charisma of Holliday gave this show an old-fashioned, but well-made quality. The show is still sometimes seen, for example in the 2001 Broadway revival starring Faith Prince, but it is now overshadowed by a number of more famous musicals from the decade. It has played in several foreign countries.

Styne's magnum opus was *Gypsy* (1959). Key to its success was the coming together of many phenomenal talents – lyricist Stephen Sondheim, choreographer Jerome Robbins, Arthur Laurents as author of the book (just two years after all three helped create the classic *West Side Story*), together with David Merrick and Leland Hayward to produce and Ethel Merman at her brassy, belting best. Merman insisted that someone more experienced than the young Sondheim create the music. Enter Jule Styne. It was immediately obvious from its opening that the show was a vehicle for the player of Mama Rose (rather than the title role, Gypsy Rose Lee), and in revival *Gypsy* has enjoyed success with good actresses, including Angela Lansbury and Tyne Daly, in that part. However, *Gypsy* is one of those rare shows in Broadway history whose quality in the eyes of critics has changed for the better over time, chiefly because of the surprising durability of both Laurents's book, with its concentration on the inner turmoil of a middle-aged mother, and Styne's enhancing music. The prospects for future revivals are high, especially as burlesque, the genre in which Gypsy Rose Lee perfected her striptease entertainments, becomes more and more distant, a quaint rather than lurid bit of our theatrical past.

Meredith Willson's *The Music Man* (1957) – set in the genteel Midwest of 1912 – was a startling contrast to the other big hit show of the year, *West Side Story* (see pp. 200, 224 below). A charismatic con man plans to sell musical instruments to school children and then skip town, but is found out by, and enamoured of, the town librarian. Forced to stay in River City, Iowa, and teach the children, although he cannot read music himself, Hill leads the climactic parade. Though a dreadful din, it sounds wonderful to the loving parents and enthusiastic townspeople. Willson, who had grown up in Iowa, authentically captured the nostalgia and sentimental sweetness of a bygone era. Several appealing songs from the show became popular ('Seventy-Six Trombones', 'Good-Night, My Someone', and 'Till There Was You'), and the show ran for almost twice as long as the gritty, realistic *West Side Story*. It remains popular for revivals in summer stock and schools, and has played in many other countries as well.

Jerry Bock's *Fiorello!* (1959) was based on a ten-year period of the colourful New York politician Fiorello La Guardia's life before he became mayor of New York City. Covering such events as La Guardia's election to Congress before World War I, his joining the Air Force, his first race for mayor against the seemingly invincible James J. Walker, the death of his first wife, a financial scandal and preparations for the successful 1933 campaign, the show included various styles of music. *Fiorello!*'s Pulitzer Prize award inevitably invited comparison with George and Ira Gershwin's Pulitzer Prize-winning political satire, *Of Thee I Sing* (1931); however, *Fiorello!* did not quite measure up to the humour, wit and unity of the earlier musical. The Pulitzer

Prize notwithstanding, *Fiorello!* has hardly been seen since its original production. Bock would create his most important work a few years later with *Fiddler on the Roof.*

The 1960s

Most Americans of the 1960s, certainly the vast majority of Broadway habitués, intuitively understood the Rodgers and Hammerstein synthesis, at least in its broadest strokes, and they took it for granted. In 1967 the conductor and composer Lehman Engel hailed the arrival of the modern musical, which he linked to *Pal Joey* and *Oklahoma!*, for representing models of dramatic maturity, formal integrity and artistic excellence.[13] (He then expanded on his thesis by discussing eleven shows in detail, including three others by Rodgers and Hammerstein.) Any would-be achievers on Broadway in this period had to begin with what Rodgers and Hammerstein had done. As always, young newcomers could seek to introduce further innovations of the proven formulas, but the basic template was clear.

Bye Bye Birdie (1960), with book by Michael Stewart, choreography by Gower Champion, music by Charles Strouse and lyrics by Lee Adams, was a hit in the year of Oscar Hammerstein's death, and perhaps symbolically represents a passing of the torch to a new generation. *Bye Bye Birdie* is unquestionably a show of its era, an observation that could be taken as either a compliment or a criticism. Its talky-teens-in-middle-America theme guaranteed instant identification across the land. *Birdie* was the first full Broadway show by its young creative team. Strouse wrote many excellent tunes ('Put On a Happy Face', 'A Lot of Livin' to Do', 'Kids'), an uproarious 'Shriners' Ballet', and a charming love ballad ('Baby, Talk to Me'). The show ran for over six hundred performances, and several of its stars – Dick Van Dyke, Paul Lynde, Kay Medford, Michael Pollard, Chita Rivera – went on to more exciting careers as a result of their exposure here. The parodic quality of *Bye Bye Birdie*, however, while never flagging in sharpness and energy, imparted a second-hand feeling to the show, whose intensity will likely increase over time. The show's use of teenagers and its youthful spirit have made it a favourite for high school productions, and in 1991 a major touring production starred Tommy Tune and Ann Reinking.

Because of its subject matter, the imminent departure of a rock star for the military (a spoof on the early rock icon Elvis Presley), *Birdie* was widely sold as a rock 'n' roll musical. In fact, the musical idiom is traditional Broadway through and through. Conrad Birdie only appears as the image of Elvis, not as the real thing. Attempted revivals have not been especially successful, and the show has travelled poorly outside the United States.

In retrospect *Bye Bye Birdie* closely resembles the ubiquitous college-kid musicals of the 1920s, blessed with charming melodies, a few clever lyrics, a dose of inventive dance and staging, with teens on the telephone in 'The Telephone Hour', and a harmless and relatively fast-moving plot. Strouse, of course, went on to write several more shows, but only *Applause* (1970) and *Annie* (1977) had the drawing power of *Bye Bye Birdie*. Like Frank Loesser, with whom he worked in the 1950s, Charles Strouse possesses prodigious musical gifts, showing a technical command of musical language that allows him to recreate nearly any period style or sound. Trained by several greats of the classical world, including Aaron Copland, Nadia Boulanger and David Diamond, he has written many songs for television and the movies, as well as live theatre, without always being recognised as an individual voice.

Strouse and Adams's only other major show of the 1960s was *Golden Boy* (1964), a remake of the Clifford Odets play of 1937, with one inspired twist sanctioned by the author, namely changing the name and race of the main character, a conflicted and doomed prize-fighter, from that of an Italian American to an African American. A considerable amount of the plot of the original script was deleted when the show was made into a musical. Strouse's songs were unexceptional, but with Sammy Davis Jr in the main role, the show ran for a year and a half at the Majestic Theatre. By creating a musical play focused on a substantial social issue, albeit with a certain amount of character complexity removed, Strouse and Adams once again invoked the spirit of Rodgers and Hammerstein. The jazzy score did not much resemble Rodgers in style, but Donald McKayle's choreography – especially in the final concluding boxing match – was widely hailed for its poetic appropriateness, a distant echo of Agnes de Mille in *Oklahoma!* and *Carousel*. *Golden Boy* has never been revived on Broadway, but a revised version played in Brooklyn, Florida and Connecticut in 1985 and 1991.

The Fantasticks also premiered in 1960, the year after *The Sound of Music* triumph. Probably no musical could be less like a Rodgers and Hammerstein show on the surface – with simple sets and a virtual annihilation of local colour – yet its perennial popularity can be linked to the values of Hammerstein in particular. The first act features an old-fashioned love story of thwarted meetings between two naifs and idealistic marriage triumphant. There is plenty of worldly-wise comedy provided by the fathers of the two lovers who at first obstruct, then engineer their children's romance. This obvious manipulation is carried off with great charm and sweet music. In the second act, reality sets in. Only in boring lives, filled with unrealised potential, do things ever proceed 'happily ever after'. The Candide-like moral, 'without a hurt the heart is hollow', confirms what we suspect all along, that new life and strength can only come out of pain and experience with the wider world. The mask of tragedy does not cover up a clearly optimistic tone that still manages to avoid strident preaching or rosy unreality. The barebones nature of the sets and costumes for *The Fantasticks*, the most obviously unspectacular feature of the show, is precisely the thing that maintained its appeal for off-Broadway audiences, not to mention innumerable high school, college and community productions.

The music is fully up to the standards of Rodgers and Hammerstein, and there is a kind of simplicity and universality about *The Fantasticks* that has aided its popularity in tens of thousands of performances in thousands of productions in dozens of countries. The direct appeal of a romantic situation bound up with issues of families experiencing seasonal changes of the sort that occur everywhere is close to the centre of *The Fantasticks'* incomparable success. Its humour wears well also. This kind of appeal can be found in many Rodgers and Hammerstein vehicles, most obviously in *Carousel* and *The Sound of Music*. Because of the restraint required in production of *The Fantasticks*, the warmly emotional text and tune of 'Try to Remember', for example, does not tumble into an embarrassing or cloying sentimentality. Harvey Schmidt's music matches Tom Jones's lyrics in much the same way that Rodgers was able efficiently and delicately to complement Hammerstein's poetry.

Lerner and Loewe's last collaboration, *Camelot*, opened late in 1960, almost as a last gasp of the Rodgers and Hammerstein type of musical play. Anxiously awaited by theatre-goers and critics alike, it was Lerner and Loewe's first show since *My Fair Lady*. Based on T. H. White's novel, *The Once and Future King*, *Camelot* told the story of the medieval King Arthur, his marriage to fair Guenevere, the creation of the idealistic Round Table, Guenevere's romance with Lancelot, and the villain Mordred's revelation of the illicit affair in order to provoke the destruction of Arthur's dream. With his Round Table in shambles and war raging in France, Arthur charges the young boy Tom to flee the battle, but always to remember and work to rebuild the ideals of Camelot. The king's final ringing soliloquy reminded many of the young, inspirational President Kennedy (elected in 1960) and his glamorous wife, Jacqueline. The public's willingness to associate a new Broadway show with a contemporary presidency reveals the extent to which America was attuned to New York's theatrical life in its heyday. Much of the group that assured *My Fair Lady*'s immense success joined Lerner and Loewe for *Camelot*, including Julie Andrews (leading actress), Moss Hart (director) and Oliver Smith (designer). Rex Harrison's leading-man counterpart in *Camelot* was the British actor Richard Burton, noted for dramatic roles. Opulent sets, elegant costuming and Lerner and Loewe's lyrics and music made a splendid vehicle, and several hit songs became very popular, especially 'If Ever I Would Leave You'. However, despite its 873-performance run, a successful touring company and at least three New York revivals, for most critics, *Camelot* was a disappointment after the delights of *My Fair Lady*, which was the pinnacle of Lerner and Loewe's work together. It was ironic that both the Lerner and Loewe collaboration and the Rodgers and Hammerstein creative and business partnership ended the same year, one pair having essentially begun the move towards the integrated musical play and the second pair having helped close that chapter of American musical theatre history.

The last show to open on Broadway in 1960 (on 26 December) was Garson Kanin's music industry satire about the selling of jukeboxes, *Do Re Mi*. Comden and Green provided the lyrics with Jule Styne's music, and the show enjoyed a good run of four hundred performances, owing primarily to its clownish stars, Phil Silvers and Nancy Walker, and the beautiful tunes of Styne, especially 'Make Someone Happy'.

By the 1960s the time was ripe for new ideas. The final proof of the power of the status quo was the vehemence with which newcomers struggled to break from patterns that Rodgers and Hammerstein had relied on so often. One example of interesting innovation was Bob Merrill's *Carnival* (1961), based on a current film about Lili, an orphan who joins a carnival, falls in love with the magician Marco the Magnificent and ends up with the carnival's crippled, bitter puppeteer. Forgoing the use of any stage curtain and having performers entering and exiting through aisles, the director and choreographer Gower Champion staged some of the most exciting dances Broadway had seen in years. *Carnival* swept theatre awards that year and ran for seven hundred performances, and was revived by the City Center in 1968.

Apparently unstoppable, Richard Rodgers continued to work after the death of Oscar Hammerstein, writing both music and lyrics for *No Strings* (1962). He created a show about Barbara Woodruff, an African-American fashion model, and David Jordan, a Pulitzer Prize-winning author from Maine, who meet in Paris and fall in love. They travel to exotic locales together, but part when the writer decides to return to Maine in order to resume writing. Barbara declines to accompany him, aware of the prejudice they would meet. They part, their time together having been spent with 'no strings attached'. Rodgers' work was innovative: the orchestra sat backstage, musicians accompanied singers on-stage, principals moved scenery and props in view of the audience, and the orchestra contained no string instruments. Although Rodgers was admitted to be 'still a magician of the musical theater' and his score full of 'enchanted music', *No Strings* received very mixed reviews. Nonetheless, the show ran for 580 performances and enjoyed both successful tours and a London production in 1963. Rodgers continued his efforts with *Do I Hear a Waltz?* (1965), this time leaving the lyric writing to Stephen Sondheim. Since Sondheim had been a protégé of

Oscar Hammerstein, many in the theatrical world had assumed that Rodgers and Sondheim might work together at some point. The bleak story concerns American spinster Leona Samish, who has an intense but hopeless affair with a married merchant in Venice. Sondheim's lyrics, described by Gerald Bordman as 'competent', the gloomy plot and a slow-moving production limited the run of *Do I Hear a Waltz?* to 220 performances, the shortest run of a Rodgers show during the entire decade.

Harvey Schmidt and Tom Jones's *110 in the Shade* (1963), based on the successful play by N. Richard Nash, *The Rainmaker* (1954), played for a creditable 330 performances on Broadway, but its songs never caught on once removed from the stage production. Despite a superficial resemblance to *Oklahoma!* in the show's western setting, use of a shady character (the rainmaker Starbuck) and focus on the romantic dreams of a young woman, the show sets its own tone. Starbuck, a far cry from *Oklahoma!*'s Jud, is saved from exposure by the miraculous arrival of rain, but heroine Lizzie Curry still resolves her wanderlust by opting for her dependable boyfriend, Sheriff Fife, rather than the handsome stranger.

The ability of many of Rodgers and Hammerstein's songs to fly on their own was, of course, harder to imitate than their stage conventions. If it was difficult to write a new show that would succeed like *Oklahoma!* at a time when everyone alive knew the formula, it has always been challenging to write a great popular song that could stand on its own. *110 in the Shade* had no such song, and Schmidt and Jones's final collaboration of the sixties, *I Do! I Do!*, had only one. Produced by David Merrick and Gower Champion, and starring Robert Preston and Mary Martin, *I Do! I Do!* is a monothematic play tracing the fifty years of married life of the two characters. A work of taste, charm and sweet sentiment, it looked more towards the concept shows of the years to come. The show's intimacy and small staging demands have encouraged later productions in England, Australia and Germany.

Bob Merrill and Jule Styne's *Funny Girl* ran for 1,348 performances at the Winter Garden starting on 26 March 1964. The 'funny girl' referred to in the title was the vaudevillian, film and radio comedienne and torch singer Fanny Brice (1891–1951). The show illustrates some of the problems associated with using a historical figure in the relatively recent past as a focus, as opposed to merely a period setting. Life and art sometimes conflict, and audiences notice. Stanley Green reports several changes of production personnel and no fewer than forty rewrites of the final scene required before the show was deemed ready for an official premiere. On the other hand, *Funny Girl* benefited from the quite conscious parallels attempted with Styne's earlier woman-centred show, *Gypsy*. *Funny Girl* was also the show that made Barbra Streisand's stage career. The song 'People' became a runaway hit even before the opening. (Sondheim was first approached to write the story of Fanny Brice, but turned it down.) The show became a worthwhile film and it has remained in the popular consciousness, playing regularly in regional theatres in several English-speaking countries.

Jerry Bock's most spectacular show, *Fiddler on the Roof* (1964), was his greatest success and became the first Broadway musical to run for more than three thousand performances.[14] The theatre historian Gerald Bordman has described the show as the 'last of the great masterworks of the era'.[15] Based on Sholom Aleichem's short stories, 'Tevye and His Daughters', it relates the experiences of a Jewish family in Russia around 1905 trying to survive poverty and religious persecution in a too quickly changing world. The story entwined issues of family relationships with romantic love interests to create a plot that appealed to a wide and diverse audience. The title and the fiddler who plays off and on throughout the show were inspired by the Russian artist Marc Chagall's painting 'The Green Violinist', in which a fiddler appears to be dancing on the roofs of a village.[16] Although the plot, lyrics and music are at times overwhelmingly sentimental and nostalgic, the realisation that the story mirrored genuine experiences of Jewish immigrants from the *shtetls* of the Ukraine gave the production unique credibility and power. Several songs from the show became standards almost overnight (such as 'Tradition', 'Matchmaker, Matchmaker', 'If I Were a Rich Man', and 'Sunrise, Sunset'). An impressive production team assembled the show: Hal Prince produced, Jerome Robbins directed and choreographed, and Zero Mostel, who played Tevye, displayed a phenomenal range of acting ability from the poignant to the comic. *Fiddler on the Roof* exhibits much of Rodgers and Hammerstein's recipe for success: a compelling, original literary source; a well-written libretto with intelligent theatrical pacing; beautifully written songs, many of which spring naturally from the action and contribute to character development; and sentiment that is natural and genuine enough to convince the audience this show is well worth seeing again. It is still produced in various types of venues throughout the world.

Jerry Herman's first Broadway show, *Milk and Honey* (1961), was set in Israel and told the story of American tourists and their desert romance. The show ends with the married but separated man aiming for a divorce in order to marry his new love. The song 'Shalom' became a hit, and Herman won a Tony award, but even better times were ahead for him when *Hello, Dolly!* opened in 1964, ran for 2,844 performances and won ten Tony awards. The title song, recorded by Louis Armstrong, was a staple on the song charts that year, greatly adding to the popularity of the show. The story had a long history, first appearing on the London stage in 1835, and eventually appearing as Thornton Wilder's play *The Matchmaker*. The plot centres around Dolly Levi, an 1890s New York matchmaker who sets her cap for her client

Plate 14 Carol Channing in the 1977 production of *Hello, Dolly!* at Starlight Theatre, Kansas City, Missouri.

Horace Vandergelder and entraps him for herself with some high jinks along the way, including a riotous evening at the Harmonia Gardens restaurant where she is welcomed by the staff ('Hello, Dolly!'). Neither innovative nor unusual in any way, it succeeded as a brilliant spectacle. Direction by the gifted Gower Champion and tasteful, turn-of-the-century-influenced sets provided a backdrop against which a long list of Broadway's most glamorous leading ladies played Dolly. Carol Channing made the role very much her own, and she was succeeded by the likes of Ginger Rogers, Martha Raye, Betty Grable, Pearl Bailey, Phyllis Diller and even the redoubtable Ethel Merman, who had turned down the invitation to create the role. Channing returned to the part several times during her career, and remains closely identified with both the character and the title song. It is no surprise that *Hello, Dolly!* remains exceedingly popular with the theatre-going public and has been produced in several languages. Herman scored another coup with *Mame* (1966), which received the Tony as best musical of the year and ran for 1,508 performances. The story of zany Auntie Mame and the adventures of her nephew as she raises him (amid the stock-market crash, an attempt to break into musical theatre, subsequent marriage to a rich man who is killed while climbing the Alps, and then helping her nephew find the proper mate) gave Angela Lansbury the same kind of opportunity *Hello, Dolly!* had given

Carol Channing, and she too became an important Broadway star through a Herman show. However, a revival of *Mame* with Lansbury in the summer of 1983 failed.

Several other significant shows opened in the mid-1960s. Mitch Leigh's only big hit, *Man of La Mancha* (1965), resembled Herman's two big shows of the 1960s in that it depended on the leading character for much of its energy. *Man of La Mancha* was a show-within-a-show production, where the novelist Cervantes is imprisoned for debts during the Spanish Inquisition and tells his fellow prisoners the story of Don Quixote, his faithful servant Sancho Panza and Aldonza, a servant girl whom Quixote sees as an idealistic 'Dulcinea' and for whom he is willing to fight any battle. By the end of the show, Aldonza/Dulcinea believes in Quixote's 'The Impossible Dream', too. The show is still produced often around the world and has been revived on Broadway.

Burton Lane and Alan Jay Lerner collaborated to write *On a Clear Day You Can See Forever* (1965), from which the title song became a long-remembered favourite, but the libretto was loosely constructed and the fantasy theme involving extra-sensory perception proved awkward. The title song is still well known, but the seldom-seen show is far better recognised from the 1970 film featuring Barbra Streisand.

A few other important collaborators also contributed their most important work to Broadway during the 1960s. Bricusse and Newley's *Stop the World – I Want to Get Off* (1962) and *The Roar of the Greasepaint – The Smell of the Crowd* (1965), and Sherman Edwards's *1776* (1969) enjoyed successful runs. The latter has proven most popular in regional and community theatres, especially around 1976, the year of the American Bicentennial, but its appeal outside the US has been limited. One of the most important new partnerships of the 1960s was formed by John Kander and Fred Ebb, whose first musical, *Flora, the Red Menace* (1965), provided Liza Minnelli with her first Broadway role. Their second show, *Cabaret* (1966), was set in the Kit Kat Klub of Berlin during the Nazis' rise to power. The love relationship between the American actress Sally Bowles and the aspiring young American writer Clifford Bradshaw, and Cliff's doomed friendship with the German Ernst Ludwig, who befriends Cliff and smuggles to help the Nazi cause, unfold amid conflicts related to anti-Semitism, social justice, personal freedom and abortion. The ironic, Brecht–Weill-influenced score, the clever unifying use of the Master of Ceremonies character, brilliantly played by Joel Grey, and the bitter undercurrents of the story made *Cabaret* an unusually powerful theatrical piece. It remains an utterly convincing show, although revivals are hampered by the strong identification of Joel Grey's masterly delineation of decadence captured in the well-adapted film version. Liza Minnelli's Sally is undoubtedly her best work on film.

A considerable part of Rodgers and Hammerstein's constructive legacy extends to the choice and formation of books, although here the point is one of general procedure on the road to achieving a script rather than the use of specific themes or techniques. As Lehman Engel and others have observed, nearly all successful musicals written between *Pal Joey* and *A Chorus Line* originated in a previous form, whether dramatic, literary or filmic. The challenge of developing a completely 'original' libretto has been met occasionally in a concept musical, such as *Company* (see p. 207 below), and even in an old-fashioned book show like *Bye Bye Birdie*. However, beginning with someone else's play, poem, short story or biography seems to be the surer road to success. Rodgers and Hammerstein's ill-fated *Allegro* of 1947 and the successful but flawed *Me and Juliet* in 1953, coming amidst so many other successes for the team, seem to prove the rule.

The achievements of the major Broadway artists working between 1943 and 1970 transformed virtually all elements that make up what is known today as the American musical. Rodgers and Hammerstein led the way in the deft construction of plots, the invention of brilliantly singable poetry, the provision of consistently attractive music and the devising of stylised choreography for an entire evening's entertainment. Besides calculating the balance of forces and combining all elements to evoke a deep emotional response from a large and diverse audience in individual shows, they also paved the way for an era. Most remarkably, they succeeded in navigating the zone in which one could create with artistic integrity without sacrificing accessibility and popular appeal.

10 Musical sophistication on Broadway: Kurt Weill and Leonard Bernstein

BRUCE D. MCCLUNG AND PAUL R. LAIRD

> What a marvellous sight, looking out the window during the rehearsal and seeing the students sitting around listening, some even singing the 'Moritat' ['Mack the Knife'] already. I don't think I will ever hear the music played as beautifully as when Lenny did it. It was so magical and effortless.[1] LOTTE LENYA

So recalled Kurt Weill's widow about the performance of *The Threepenny Opera* at Brandeis University's Festival of the Creative Arts on 14 June 1952. The concert featured Bertolt Brecht and Weill's 1928 work, *Die Dreigroschenoper*, in an English translation by Marc Blitzstein, who also served as narrator. Nearly five thousand people filled the new Adolph Ullman Amphitheatre, and Lenya stopped the concert cold with her rendition of 'Pirate Jenny' (see Plate 15). The following year, a fully staged *Threepenny Opera* opened at the Theater de Lys in Greenwich Village. It ran for ninety-six performances, but closed because of a previous booking at the theatre. Reopening the following season, *The Threepenny Opera* ran for 2,611 performances to become (for a time) the longest-running musical in American history.[2] Lenya won the Tony for best featured actress in a musical, and the production garnered a special Tony, highly unusual for an off-Broadway show.

The conductor for the 1952 concert performance of *The Threepenny Opera* had been Leonard Bernstein, then a Brandeis faculty member. The concert proved a turning point for both Weill's and Bernstein's careers. Weill, who died in 1950 at the age of fifty, had fled Germany in 1933 and emigrated to the United States two years later. The Brandeis concert ushered in the so-called 'Weill renaissance' and the rediscovery of his German works by American audiences. *The Threepenny Opera*'s 'Mack the Knife', in renditions by Louis Armstrong, Dick Hyman, Bobby Darin, Frank Sinatra and Ella Fitzgerald, successively climbed the hit parade to sell over ten million records. As for Bernstein, his first opera, *Trouble in Tahiti*, had premiered at Brandeis two days before the *Threepenny Opera* concert. Although his conducting career was firmly established, the period following the *Threepenny Opera* concert was devoted to the stage: *Wonderful Town* opened on Broadway in 1953, *Candide* in 1956 and *West Side Story* in 1957.

Plate 15 Lotte Lenya performing the song 'Pirate Jenny' with Leonard Bernstein conducting during concert production of *The Threepenny Opera* at Festival of the Creative Arts, Brandeis University, 1952.

When asked in an interview about Weill's possible influence on Bernstein, Lenya responded:

> I think surely Leonard Bernstein knows every note of Kurt Weill. I'm sure he does. Oh, he knows more than *The Threepenny Opera*. And he is the one who took up after Weill's death. I think Leonard Bernstein is the closest to Kurt Weill.[3]

Indeed, both composed in cultivated forms, such as the symphony and chamber music, and in vernacular genres, such as film scoring and the musical. Today both are regarded as prototypical 'crossover' composers who exploited the respective technologies of radio and television to reach broader audiences. Both drew musically on their Jewish heritage in such large-scale works as Weill's Biblical epic, *The Eternal Road* (1937), and Bernstein's Third Symphony ('Kaddish'), in vocal settings of the liturgy (the 'Kiddush' for Weill, the 'Hashkiveinu' and 'Yidgal' for Bernstein) and in settings of Hebrew folk songs. Although they arrived on Broadway from different avenues (via experimental drama for Weill, via modern dance for

Bernstein), both brought a new level of musical and dramatic sophistication to the genre.

When Weill arrived in New York in 1935, economics were squeezing Broadway: the Depression had diminished investors' capital for new shows, the film industry had lured away the most talented writing teams, top ticket prices had been driven down from $6.60 to $4.40, and Hollywood 'talkies' and radio were giving live entertainment a run for its money. The only two musicals to run for more than five hundred performances during the 1930s were topical or escapist revues: *Pins and Needles* (1937) and *Hellzapoppin* (1938). Despite the grim outlook for the book musical, the first show Weill saw on Broadway was probably a rehearsal of *Porgy and Bess* (1935).[4] This exposure to one of Broadway's most unusual and lofty offerings of the 1930s exerted a profound influence on the composer.

The Group Theatre, the noted company associated with Harold Clurman, recruited Weill for what became his first American stage work. Known for its leftist leanings, the Group brought Weill together with playwright Paul Green for a play with music entitled *Johnny Johnson* (1936). The story follows the adventures and psychological downfall of Johnny, an ordinary soldier who opposes the war he finds himself fighting. An example of how Weill creates intra-textual allusions in a score full of parody and musical quotations is 'Johnny's Song', which closes the show and attempts to encapsulate its pacifist message. Green recalled Weill telling him, 'If we can send the audience out humming a melody . . . it will be like a leitmotif.'[5] Weill included the melody of 'Johnny's Song' at critical junctures in the drama, foreshadowing its full statement at the denouement. One tabloid reporter described 'Johnny's Song' as 'the one song that is haunting everybody, that is hummed, sung and whistled on streets, in subways, in bathtubs and on terraces from one end of this comely island to the other'.[6] Nevertheless, *Johnny Johnson* failed to find an audience for its satire and closed after sixty-eight performances.

Weill's next collaborator was Maxwell Anderson, winner of the 1936–7 Critics' Circle Award for *High Tor*. As Weill had done in Germany, he was involving leading dramatists in musical theatre:

> One of the first decisions I made was to get the leading dramatists of my time interested in the problems of the musical theatre. The list of my collaborators reads like a good selection of contemporary playwrights of different countries: George Kaiser and Bert Brecht in Germany, Jacques Deval in France, Franz Werfel, Paul Green, Maxwell Anderson, Moss Hart . . . in America.[7]

Together Weill and Anderson fashioned a musical version of Washington Irving's *The History of New York by Diedrich Knickerbocker*. Although now primarily remembered for 'September Song', *Knickerbocker Holiday* (1938) gently lampooned Roosevelt's New Deal while telling a traditional love story. Weill's score is closest to operetta, with twenty-eight musical numbers invoking models from Gilbert and Sullivan to Sigmund Romberg. Weill bucked many of Broadway's conventions, chief among them that of entrusting his scores to professional orchestrators. (This was remarkable, but not unprecedented: Victor Herbert had orchestrated his own operettas.) Weill described the gruelling schedule of orchestrating his own shows:

> You sleep about two hours a night for the four weeks that it takes, but it's fun. Not until the rehearsals get under way can you start your orchestrating . . . since until you know who the singers are going to be you can't tell what key to put each number in.[8]

In his *New York Times* review, Brooks Atkinson described *Knickerbocker Holiday* as 'vigorous composing for the modern theatre, superior to Broadway songwriting without settling in the academic groove'.[9] *Knickerbocker Holiday* played for 168 performances, but failed to recoup its investment.

Lady in the Dark (1941) provided Weill with his proverbial big break. The musical play, which dramatised a woman undergoing psychoanalysis, brought together playwright Moss Hart (author of a string of comedies with George S. Kaufman), lyricist Ira Gershwin and Weill. Sam Harris's production was strictly first class. Gertrude Lawrence signed for the title role at a minimum of $2,000 per week against 15 per cent of the box office. To enable nearly instantaneous scene changes, Harry Horner placed *Lady* on four hand-operated turntables. With a cast of fifty-five, a twenty-member orchestra, and a stage crew of forty-one, the musical's budget grew to an astronomical $127,715. *Lady* played for two seasons on Broadway and toured ten cities with a Broadway re-engagement for a total jackpot of 777 performances. The crush for seats helped to establish the practice of advance sales on Broadway, while Paramount Pictures' $285,000 bid broke the previously held record paid for film rights.

Lady in the Dark's commercial success, however, did not overshadow its revolutionary form. Music was restricted to three through-composed dream sequences, which articulate the heroine's subconscious. Although primarily confined to these sequences, music was also at the centre of the plot: the key to the 'lady's' neurosis was the recollection of a childhood song ('My Ship') of which a fragment recurs in her nightmares. Weill expanded the leitmotivic technique of *Johnny Johnson* not only to create a web of allusions, but also to provide a musical analogue for the drama. The first two phrases of 'My Ship' are tonally ambiguous, arpeggiating a complex of notes whose constituents are D minor and F major triads. Weill worked out this musical riddle over the course of the drama: the 'incorrect' minor sub-mediant giving way to the 'correct' major tonic to parallel the heroine's psychoanalytical treatment.[10] Such sophisticated techniques caused Atkinson in a *Times* review of *Lady*'s second season to deem Weill 'the best writer of theatre music in the country'.[11]

Weill's next offering was as close as he ever came to a regulation musical comedy, and, perhaps not coincidentally, it enjoyed the longest continuous Broadway run of his American shows (567 performances before heading out on tour). His collaborators included lyricist Ogden Nash and Marx Brothers' scriptwriter S. J. Perelman. Based on F. Anstey's 1885 novella *The Tinted Venus* (a remake of the Pygmalion/Galatea myth), *One Touch of Venus* (1943) told the story of a barber, Rodney Hatch, who slips his fiancée's ring on a statue of Venus. The goddess comes miraculously to life, and, much to Rodney's panic, sets out to win him away from his sweetheart. *One Touch of Venus* starred Mary Martin, who popularised 'That's Him' and 'Speak Low'. Agnes de Mille's two ballets capitalised on her previous success with *Oklahoma!* (see chapters 8 and 12). *One Touch of Venus* provided escapist fare during the war, made Mary Martin a star and saw 'Speak Low' climb to the top of the charts.

In 1944 Weill and Ira Gershwin reunited for a musical version of Edwin Justus Mayer's 1924 play, *The Firebrand*, about Benvenuto Cellini. Weill's intentions, preserved in a letter to Gershwin, were to turn it into a 'smart, intelligent, intimate romantic-satirical operetta for the international market'.[12] At the Boston tryout, George S. Kaufman attempted his renowned play doctoring, but to no avail. *The Firebrand of Florence* (1945), despite an astronomical budget of $225,000, closed on Broadway after a mere forty-three performances and represents Weill's only full-fledged American flop. *Song of Norway* (1944), presented earlier that season, may have captured the best vocalists and audience, and *Firebrand*'s production may have been leaden, but in any case, the latter's closing signalled that European operetta's brief renaissance on Broadway was nearly over.[13] Despite its shortcomings, *The Firebrand of Florence* was the lengthiest of Weill's scores for the American theatre to date, sprawling to some 650 pages of orchestral score. The opening scene of Cellini's near-execution and pardon was remarkable on Broadway: twenty minutes of continuous music incorporating recitative, aria, choruses and dances.

Street Scene (1947) fulfilled two of Weill's dreams. The first, evidently sparked by *Porgy and Bess*, was to write an American opera. The second was to create 'a special brand of musical theatre which would completely integrate drama and music, spoken word, song and movement'.[14] Elmer Rice's Pulitzer Prize-winning play of 1929 contained all the necessary ingredients, as Weill explained:

> It was a simple story of everyday life in a big city, a story of love and passion
> and greed and death. I saw great musical possibilities in its theatrical
> device – life in a tenement house between one evening and the next
> afternoon. And it seemed like a great challenge to me to find the inherent
> poetry in these people and to blend my music with the stark realism of the
> play.[15]

Weill and Rice collaborated on the adaptation of the play, and poet Langston
Hughes provided the lyrics. Rather than unify the score through a single
idiom, Weill chose as an analogue for the melting pot a disparity of musical
styles: 'I discovered that the play lent itself to a great variety of music, much
as the streets of New York themselves embrace the music of many lands and
many people.'[16]

Street Scene's diverse score reveals something about each of the characters: the heightened musical language of late nineteenth-century Italian
opera tells the central story of betrayal and murder in the Murrant family.
Other inhabitants of the brownstone sing in their respective idioms: a blues-
inspired number for the black janitor, a jitterbug for the nightclub hoppers, a
children's game-song for the young people, etc. 'Opera was a way people lost
money' on Broadway, quipped Oscar Hammerstein II. Consequently, *Street
Scene* was billed as a 'dramatic musical'. Lest anyone be fooled, the two dramatic leads were cast from the Metropolitan Opera and a thirty-five-piece
orchestra filled the pit. Olin Downes, the *New York Times*'s music critic,
called it 'the most important step towards significantly American opera' to
date.[17] Although *Street Scene* had an impressive opening, it was not able to
hold its own against that season's *Finian's Rainbow* and *Brigadoon.* It closed
after 148 performances – a disappointing run for a 'dramatic musical', but
an impressive record for 'An American Opera', as it was subtitled when the
piano-vocal score was published.

Never one to repeat himself, Weill's next show was worlds away from
opera. He conceived with Alan Jay Lerner what was to become the prototypical 'concept musical'. Subtitled 'A Vaudeville', *Love Life* (1948) carried
an explanatory note in its playbill regarding its unusual form:

> *Love Life* is presented in two parts, each consisting of a series of acts. The
> sketches, which start in 1791 and come up to the present day, are presented
> in the physical style of the various periods. The four main characters, Susan
> and Sam Cooper, and their children, Johnny and Elizabeth, who present the
> story, do not change in appearance as time moves on. The vaudeville acts
> which come between each sketch are presented before a vaudeville drop and
> are styled and costumed in a set vaudeville pattern.

The book scenes record economic effects on the Coopers' marriage: from the
transition of an agrarian to an industrial economy, through the halcyon days

of the 1920s to the post-war period. Intervening vaudeville acts comment on the book scenes and keep the audience from getting too emotionally involved with the Coopers.

Love Life, with its book scenes of the Coopers' marriage in six periods (from 1791 to the 'today' of 1948), adumbrates the concept musical through its series of vignettes. The vaudeville acts prefigure the use of the Kit Kat Klub numbers of *Cabaret* and the comment songs in *Company*. All the disciplines of the production reflected the overriding concept of the economic effect on the institution of marriage. Lerner, credited with book and lyrics, recalled, 'What made writing *Love Life* so much fun was discarding a lot of old rules and making up your own as you went along. We knew what we wanted to say. The problem was finding a way to tell our story.'[18] *Love Life* paved the way for such later concept musicals as *Cabaret* (1966), *Company* (1970), *A Chorus Line* (1975), *Chicago* (1975) and *Assassins* (1991). Weill's score ran to 738 pages – a full two hours of music. *Love Life*, starring Nanette Fabray and Ray Middleton, chalked up a sturdy run of 252 performances.

Weill's last musical for Broadway was an adaptation of Alan Paton's anti-apartheid novel, *Cry the Beloved Country*. Weill and Maxwell Anderson planned a 'musical tragedy' (an inversion of 'musical comedy') with the chorus as the central musical element. On top of this layer, they fashioned a handful of songs for individual characters. Weill scored the work for twelve instrumentalists, which gives it a transparent, chamber texture. After *Lost in the Stars* (1949) opened, Olin Downes wrote a letter to Weill complaining about the use of numbers in American popular song form (AABA) in a work with such operatic power. In response, Weill defended his use of the form:

> Personally, I don't feel that this represents a compromise because it seems to me that the American popular song, growing out the American folk-music, is the basis of an American musical theatre (just as the Italian song was the basis of Italian opera), and that in this early stage of development, and considering the audiences we are writing for, it is quite legitimate to use the form of the popular song and gradually fill it with new musical content.[19]

Lost in the Stars, despite a strong opening, struggled to find an audience. The stress exacerbated Weill's hypertension, hastening a heart attack. Anderson and he had begun work on a new musical (*Huckleberry Finn*), but Weill did not live to see it completed. In eulogising Kurt Weill, composers, critics and collaborators attempted to sum up his contributions to the American musical theatre. Virgil Thomson wrote in the *New York Herald Tribune*, 'every new work was a new model, a new shape, a new solution of dramatic problems'.[20] The *New York Times* obituary quoted Brooks Atkinson's 1941 review, 'He is not a song writer but a composer of organic music that can bind the separate elements of a production and turn the underlying motive into a song.'[21] Maxwell Anderson in *Theatre Arts* magazine wrote, 'We have had no other rounded and complete composer, able to help on the book and lyrics, consummate as arranger and orchestrator, bubbling with original and unhackneyed melodies.'[22] Nine days after *Lost in the Stars* closed (after a run of 281 performances), ten thousand people attended a Kurt Weill Memorial Concert at Lewisohn Stadium. Olin Downes, in previewing the concert, concluded, 'He has written for the stage with a technic and imagination and heart which make him one of the central figures in the development of an American form of opera.'[23]

Leonard Bernstein's stage career overlapped with that of Weill by only six years, and the only musical he wrote before Weill died was *On the Town* (1944). Despite its success, Bernstein did not return to Broadway for almost a decade. Except for his three musicals in the 1950s – *Wonderful Town*, *Candide* and *West Side Story* – Bernstein was an irregular presence on Broadway, in part because of his many other activities, but his importance comes in the prominence of these four shows. From the time of his appointment as assistant conductor of the New York Philharmonic in 1943, Bernstein was seldom far from a podium, making his compositional activity sporadic. His interest in the stage had begun as a teenager when he put on versions of Gilbert and Sullivan operettas and Bizet's *Carmen* with friends. While still at Harvard he had directed Marc Blitzstein's *The Cradle Will Rock* (1937), taking the composer's famous role as pianist and narrator. Blitzstein had attended the production and was most impressed, launching his long-term friendship with Bernstein.

Bernstein's entrance into the Broadway musical came through modern dance. Jerome Robbins, a young dancer with the American Ballet Theatre, sought a composer to score a wartime ballet concerning three sailors on leave in New York City. He found Bernstein, who took to the idea and the vernacular dance music that Robbins wanted in the score. The ballet *Fancy Free* (1944) is a delightful romp through many twentieth-century styles, including blues, big band jazz, and Russian neo-classicism. It became a hit, and the ballet's set designer, Oliver Smith, and his business partner Paul Feigay saw the makings of a good Broadway musical. They convinced Robbins and Bernstein, who insisted that his friends Betty Comden and Adolph Green write the book and lyrics. The addition of veteran director George Abbott helped secure funding, including some from MGM in return for the film rights. All agreed that the show should reflect Broadway's recent move towards the integration of plot, music and dance, exemplified the previous season by *Oklahoma!*.[24] Abbott asserted creative control and moulded the play, songs and dances through many cuts and changes. After a Boston tryout, the show opened at New York's Adelphi Theatre on 28 December 1944.

The cast included only two noted personalities: Sono Osato, formerly a featured dancer in Weill's *One Touch of Venus*, and comedienne Nancy Walker. Comden and Green played roles in addition to their writing duties. *On the Town*'s story surged forward breathlessly in locales all over New York City, propelled by Abbott's excellent sense of pacing, Robbins' energetic dances and Bernstein's eclectic score. The show included six dance sequences – often accompanied by the complex music associated with modern dance – and songs that more or less fitted into Broadway types. *On the Town*'s dances each helped advance the plot. Their importance has been recognised by Denny Martin Flinn: 'In one startling night . . . and 436 subsequent performances, *On the Town* created and established the greatest of all American contributions to the stage arts: American theatre dance.'[25]

Bernstein composed the music for the dance numbers himself, a job often assigned to a dance arranger, but unlike Weill, he did not do all of his own orchestrations and received assistance from Hershy Kay, Don Walker, Elliott Jacoby, Bruce Coughlin and Ted Royal.[26] Three of the dances are heard in Bernstein's symphonic work *Three Dance Episodes from 'On the Town'*: 'The Great Lover Displays Himself', a lively swing movement from the dream ballet in Act 2; 'Lonely Town: Pas de Deux', an arrangement reminiscent of Copland (following the ballad's performance in Act 1); and 'Times Square: 1944', a jaunty exploration of 'New York, New York' that serves as the finale of Act 1. *On the Town*'s songs demonstrate Bernstein's witty manipulation of American vernacular music. 'I Feel Like I'm Not Out of Bed Yet' includes prominent use of blues notes, and 'New York, New York' includes a surprisingly dissonant fanfare, jazz rhythms, and canonic imitation. The raucous 'Come Up to My Place' is a dialogue with Chip and Hildy, singing, respectively, with boogie-woogie and blues references. 'Carried Away' is a quasi-operatic duet in an unexpected minor key. The ballad 'Lonely Town' is perhaps the most typical Broadway song in the show, with a bluesy melody and an AABA form. 'Carnegie Hall Pavane (Do-Do-Re-Do)' begins stiffly classical, but becomes a parody of the Andrews Sisters.

Bernstein's next score on Broadway was incidental music and songs for J. M. Barrie's *Peter Pan*, followed in 1952 by his one-act opera *Trouble in Tahiti*, which ran for forty-eight performances on Broadway in 1955. *Wonderful Town*, somewhat in the mould of *On the Town*, provided Bernstein, Comden and Green with another hit. The musical was based upon stories by Ruth McKenney about two sisters who move from Ohio to New York, further popularised by Joseph Fields and Jerome Chodorov in their play *My Sister Eileen* (1940). They had adapted the play as a musical and producers Robert Fryer and George Abbott held an option on Rosalind Russell to star in the show. When the first team hired to write the score failed to do so, Abbott asked Bernstein, Comden and Green to join the project before losing the option on Russell. They completed the score in just five weeks in late 1952.

Wonderful Town was essentially a musical comedy with songs strategically placed in the plot. The show included important dance numbers choreographed by Donald Saddler (with unattributed assistance from Jerome Robbins[27]), such as Russell's hilarious 'Conga!' with Brazilian sailors and the 'Ballet at the Village Vortex', but the songs carried the evening. Comden and Green's evocations of 1930s culture, such as the questions that Ruth asks the Brazilian sailors in 'Conga!', helped set the time and place, and Bernstein captured the era through music. 'Christopher Street' opens the show with a tour of Greenwich Village, spiced with delightful blues references and rich tempo and mood changes. 'One Hundred Easy Ways' balances musical interest and clever lyrics while working around Russell's limited singing ability. 'Swing!' evokes music of the 1930s and 'Wrong Note Rag' brings rhythmic and harmonic complexity to the service of comedy, one of Bernstein's greatest compositional gifts. *Wonderful Town* ran for 559 performances, with Carol Channing replacing Russell near the end of the run. The *Times*'s Olin Downes was among those who found the show a major step forward:

> This is an opera made of dance, prattle and song . . . We are coming to believe that when American opera created by a composer of the stature of the Wagners and Verdis of yore does materialize, it will owe much more to the robust spirit and the raciness of accent of our popular theater than to the efforts of our emulators . . . of the tonal art of Bartok, Hindemith, and Stravinsky.[28]

Bernstein's next Broadway projects came in collaboration with the dramatist Lillian Hellman, starting with incidental music for Hellman's *The Lark* (1955), a translation of Jean Anouilh's French play on Joan of Arc. In *Candide* (1956) Hellman and Bernstein set out to demonstrate in the McCarthy era that the United States was not 'the best of all possible worlds'. The long search for a lyricist included early work with James Agee, Dorothy Parker and John LaTouche before they found Richard Wilbur.[29] Unfortunately, the collaborators never agreed what *Candide* was: Hellman wrote heavy-handed satire, and Bernstein and Wilbur produced an operetta. The show's director was the famous Tyrone Guthrie. Much has been written about the difficulty of the collaboration and concept. Guthrie emerges as a believable source when he calls *Candide* 'wildly pretentious'. He notes Hellman's disadvantage because they had to cast singers rather than actors and writes that his own direction 'skipped along with the effortless grace of a freight train heavy-laden on a steep gradient'.[30] Despite a sumptuous production and some positive notes from Brooks Atkinson and other critics,

Candide never found an audience and closed after seventy-three performances.

But *Candide*, of course, did not die in the 1950s. Bernstein's score is a charming romp through many European dance forms and genres with several unforgettable numbers, inspiring several revivals, including Hal Prince's so-called 'Chelsea' version of 1973, where Hellman's book was replaced by one from Hugh Wheeler, and new versions in the 1980s. Bernstein fashioned the score basically without his usual jazz and blues influences. He mined other musical traditions and produced a Broadway score of rare sophistication and range. Among the gems in *Candide* are the rollicking Overture, the gavotte 'Life is Happiness Indeed', Candide's laments, the witty 'Auto-da-fé', the laughing-song 'Glitter and Be Gay', the tango 'I Am Easily Assimilated', the schottische 'Bon Voyage', and the inspiring, Copland-like finale, 'Make Our Garden Grow'.

Where *Candide* failed in the collaborative process, *West Side Story* (1957) succeeded because its four main creators – director and choreographer Jerome Robbins, writer Arthur Laurents, Bernstein and lyricist Stephen Sondheim – worked together to make the dancing, script, music and lyrics an artistic whole. The show's integration and use of dance is considered in chapter 11; here we explore Bernstein's unification of the score through recurring musical styles and intervals. Bernstein employs various musical styles in *West Side Story* to describe different groups in the story. Complex rhythms and mixed metres capture the violence of the gangs, heard in the 'Prologue', 'Jet Song', 'Cool' and 'The Rumble'. Latin rhythms evoke the background of the Puerto Rican gang, the Sharks. Bernstein included Latin dances in 'The Dance at the Gym' and 'America' and used hemiola in the accompaniment of 'Something's Coming', a *tresillo* (3+3+2) bass line for 'Maria', and a beguine accompaniment for 'Tonight'. More traditional Broadway fare such as lyrical ballads and waltzes appear in songs involving the lovers Tony and Maria. Ballads include 'Maria', 'Tonight', and 'Somewhere'. 'One Hand, One Heart' is a slow waltz, but 'I Feel Pretty' is faster and perhaps infused with the spirit and rhythms of the Aragonese *jota*. *West Side Story*'s various styles come together dramatically in 'A Boy Like That/I Have a Love', where Anita's unpredictable, violent song is vanquished by Maria's sweet statement of devotion to Tony.

A number of commentators have noted Bernstein's structural use of an interval to unify the score (similar to how Weill tonally organised *Lady in the Dark*).[31] The opening motive of *West Side Story*, an ascending perfect fourth followed by an ascending tritone, announces the latter interval's importance. The tritone is the first interval heard in the melodies of 'Maria' and 'Cool', and occurs early in 'Something's Coming'. It figures prominently in the accompaniment of a number of other songs. The 'Dance at the Gym' includes a number of obvious tritones, especially when Tony first sees Maria, and then the melody of the song 'Maria', with its tritone, sounds in the 'Maria Cha Cha'. The minor seventh is less important in the score, but its strong association with the song 'Somewhere' allows for several satisfying moments of dramatic unity, not unlike a leitmotif in Wagner's operas.

About the time *West Side Story* opened, Bernstein assumed co-directorship of the New York Philharmonic with Dimitri Mitropoulos. The orchestra soon named Bernstein music director. During Bernstein's sabbatical in 1964–5 he tried to adapt Thornton Wilder's *The Skin of Our Teeth* as a musical with Robbins, Comden and Green, but the effort failed.[32] In 1968 another project with Robbins that came to naught was an adaptation of Bertolt Brecht's play *The Exception and the Rule.*[33] *Mass* (1971), composed for the opening of the Kennedy Center in Washington, DC, included elements from Broadway, but is an entirely different sort of work.

Weill's and Bernstein's careers metaphorically crossed one last time through their collaborations with lyricist Alan Jay Lerner. For Bernstein, this was his last musical, *1600 Pennsylvania Avenue* (1976), with book and lyrics by Lerner. The show was a strident plea for racial tolerance, including both white and black occupants of the White House: presidents and first ladies, slaves and servants. As was the case with the prototypical concept musical *Love Life* (1948) by Weill and Lerner, *1600 Pennsylvania Avenue* was based on a central concept and exchanged a linear narrative for a series of vignettes in different historical eras. The show, however, suffered from a cumbersome book, and many urged Bernstein and Lerner to revise it or cancel the project. The show opened on Broadway on 4 May 1976 and closed after seven performances. Bernstein's score fared better in reviews than the book, but its reception was at best mixed, and Bernstein refused to allow an original cast album. In subsequent years some have praised Bernstein's use of nineteenth-century musical styles and such songs as 'Duet for One' and 'Take Care of this House'. Bernstein's estate issued a concert version in 1997 called *A White House Cantata.* It was first performed at London's Barbican Centre on 8 July 1997 and has since been recorded.[34]

Weill and Bernstein shared similar approaches to the Broadway musical, both making fresh use of vernacular musical styles and bringing a musical sophistication unusual for Broadway. As Lotte Lenya suggested, it was Bernstein who continued Weill's trajectory as a composer of dramatic music on Broadway in the 1950s. In an age when many were content to follow the lead established by the success of Rodgers and Hammerstein, Weill, Bernstein and their collaborators continued to challenge Broadway's prevailing norms and produce some of the more artistically influential musicals of the 1940s and 1950s.

PART III

Evolutions and integrations:
after 1970

11 Stephen Sondheim and the musical of the outsider

JIM LOVENSHEIMER

In a *New York Times Magazine* interview with Frank Rich, Stephen Sondheim (b. 1930) told an anecdote as revealing as it was charming. Reminiscing about the New Haven opening of *Carousel* in 1945, when he was fifteen, the composer/lyricist recalled the emotional impact of the first act's closing moments. 'I remember how everyone goes off to the clambake at the end of Act One and Jigger just follows, and he was the only one walking on stage as the curtain came down. I was sobbing.'[1] In the next paragraph, however, Sondheim displays a more characteristic caginess when considering why *Carousel* is his second favourite score. (*Porgy and Bess* is his favourite.) After suggesting that he might be drawn to *Carousel* 'because it's about a loner [the protagonist Billy Bigelow] who's misunderstood', Sondheim dismisses the thought, calling it 'psychobabble'.[2] Later in the interview, he returns to this somewhat defensive argument, noting that, after all, 'the outsider is basic to a lot of dramatic literature. This country's about conformity. And so nonconformity is a fairly common theme.'[3]

Non-conforming outsiders are indeed inherent in much dramatic literature. American musicals, however, have generally avoided them, and certainly their presence as protagonists in musicals before *Carousel* is rare. Even their existence as important supporting characters is unusual. Notable exceptions exist, of course. They include the mulatto Julie in *Show Boat* (1927), the discovery of whose racial heritage results in her dismissal from the showboat company and her subsequent tragedy, and Jud Fry in *Oklahoma!* (1943), whose angry isolation is voiced in the disturbing number 'Lonely Room'. With the possible exceptions of *Pal Joey* (1940) and the opera-derived *Carmen Jones* (1943), however, musicals before *Carousel* were not about these outsiders. Instead, these were secondary characters whose conflict with society usually resulted in society's triumph. Interestingly, each of these rather atypical works, with the exception of *Pal Joey*, had book and lyrics by Oscar Hammerstein II, Sondheim's mentor and close personal friend. Only after *Carousel*, which was also written by Hammerstein, do we find the outsider increasingly cast as the principal figure in a musical, particularly a musical with a score by Stephen Sondheim. Perhaps, as Sondheim acknowledges, this is because the non-conformity of the outsider is 'obviously something I feel, belonging to a number of minorities'.[4] (Sondheim is Jewish and gay.) Or perhaps such observations really are psychobabble. Either way, Sondheim's body of work for the musical theatre thus far suggests that his early emotional reaction to a work about a disenfranchised member of society, a non-conformist, was an indication of the theme upon which he since has written many variations, each of them in a distinct personal style. He seems always to have been attracted to characters whose actions place them outside mainstream society. Neuroses are plentiful in these musicals, and they are found in characters whose complexities often recall the loner who troubled and moved the young Sondheim.

Sondheim's first Broadway shows were *West Side Story* (1957) and *Gypsy* (1959), for which he provided the lyrics to Leonard Bernstein's and Jule Styne's scores, respectively, and even they are concerned with outsiders and/or the disenfranchised. Already Sondheim's lyrics create sharply drawn characters who express, among other feelings, a frustration with, or even contempt for, mainstream society. *West Side Story*, for example, concerns several layers of social ostracism: a white gang (the Jets) aggressively treats a Puerto Rican gang (the Sharks) as outsiders from American society, and the Sharks deeply resent and violently challenge that status; both gangs are disenfranchised from society in general (in the clever lyrics of the number 'Gee, Officer Krupke!', the Jets chronicle their misfit status); and the lovers Tony and Maria are rejected by both gangs because of their relationship. Sondheim's lyrics for the show create an expressive vernacular that emphasises the strained social relationships between the two gangs. *Gypsy*'s Mama Rose thumbs her nose at 'respectable' bourgeois society: 'they can stay and rot', she sings, 'but not Rose'. Only at the end of the show, when Rose breaks down in 'Rose's Turn', does the audience see the toll that this disenfranchisement has taken. Furthermore, both early works also feature a motive common to several of the later works: the outsider's ability, or at least hope, to escape reality through dreams or dreamlike fantasy. *West Side Story* contains a dream ballet in which the two principal characters imagine a life in which none are outsiders; and *Gypsy* is full of Rose's leitmotif 'I had a dream', with which she confronts various crises. Many of Sondheim's subsequent outsiders also express themselves in or through dreams, or in dreamlike detachments from reality. In *Follies*, for instance, the neurotic and emotionally frazzled characters take turns performing acts in an imaginary and nightmarish vaudeville. Much of the action of *Company* (1970) occurs in a timeless and dreamlike suspension of reality in which Robert, an emotionally detached bachelor, comes to grips with what he really wants from life. In the second act of *Sunday in the Park with George* (1984), the twentieth-century George is consoled and inspired by the dreamlike apparition of Dot, a character from another century (and another act), and in *Assassins*

(1991), the characters fervently, if desperately, believe that 'Everybody's got the right to their dreams.'

A consideration of Sondheim's scores as representations of the outsider provides an entrée to discussing some of their general and specific stylistic traits. These traits create what Sondheim scholar Steven Swayne has called Sondheim's 'multiple musical voices', many of which are imitative or referential.[5] Specifically, argues Swayne, Sondheim exploits this 'range of musical voices in pursuit of his singular voice: the voice of character delineation'.[6] While Sondheim's principal purpose, therefore, is the clear depiction of individual characters, his means for achieving it are as diverse as the concepts for the shows in which those characters exist.

The introduction above of the word 'concepts' in turn demands mention of the term 'concept musical', for it is often applied to Sondheim's work in general and relates specifically to any discussion of his means of creating characters for a given show. Joanne Gordon sums up this term as follows:

> Concept, the word coined to describe the form of the Sondheim musical, suggests that all elements of the musical, thematic and presentational, are integrated to suggest a central idea or image . . . Prior to Sondheim, the musical was built around the plot . . . The book structure for Sondheim, on the other hand, means the idea. Music, lyric, dance, dialogue, design, and direction fuse to support a focal thought. A central conceit controls and shapes an entire production, for every aspect of the production is blended and subordinated to a single vision . . . Form and content cannot really be separated, for the one dictates and is dependent on the other.[7]

In other words, Gordon continues, Sondheim 'develops a new lyric, musical, and theatrical language for each work. Sondheim's music and lyrics grow out of the dramatic idea inherent in the show's concept and themselves become part of the drama.'[8]

Two compositional techniques especially facilitate Sondheim's ability to change musical languages without losing his own 'singular voice': the use of motives, or short, recognisable musical ideas that sometimes represent non-musical concepts or characters and that are often used as structural cells for lengthier musical statements; and the use of pastiche, which is the presence of music and/or musical styles from various sources in a single work. While the first of these is observable as early as *Company* and, after *Sweeney Todd* (1979), becomes increasingly important, the second appears as a recognisable trait even earlier and is variously exploited by Sondheim in nearly all his works.

Company, then, serves as an early example of one way Sondheim uses motives to define the character of an outsider. Throughout *Company*, Sondheim uses a recurring motive, the 'Robert' or 'Bobby' motive, as a cell, or building block, for much of the score, as Stephen Banfield has demonstrated.[9] (The motive, first sung to the words 'Bobby, Bobby', consists of a descending minor third followed by a descending major second. The initial pitch of each interval is the same.) What Banfield does not mention, however, is the careful utilisation of this motive in relation to Robert and the other characters, and as a musical symbol of Robert's detachment from his married friends. It is heard almost immediately at the show's beginning, and a development of it introduces the opening title song. After this, the motive is used between scenes and before, or as part of, musical numbers involving Robert and his married friends, a group from whom he is an outsider despite the mutual affection between them.

The motive does not introduce songs that involve characters or their observations without Robert, however. This is evident in 'Little Things', a commentary by the acerbic Joanne on another couple's scene as well as on marriage in general, and 'Sorry Grateful', the men's reflective answer to Robert's question, 'Are you ever sorry you got married?' The motive neither introduces nor appears in songs that involve Robert on his own or without the couples, such as 'Someone Is Waiting', or 'Barcelona', his emotionally removed duet with a flight attendant. Although these numbers do not quote the motive, they are frequently built on it, often by inverting it, as Banfield points out. Perhaps the most dramatic use of the motive is in the dance sequence 'Tick Tock', omitted from the revised version of the show. In this number, the audience hears taped dialogue of Robert and the flight attendant during sex. At a critical, post-coital moment, she says, 'I love you', and the motive is heard. It signifies what the couples all along have been wanting Robert to hear and experience; it represents their hopes fulfilled, as well as their presence in even his most intimate life. Robert, however, can only respond with 'I . . . I . . .', at which point the orchestra plays a dissonant fragment of the motive that signifies Robert's inability to express what everyone else wants him to express.

The central character's inability to respond reinforces his outsider status in the world of the married and emotionally committed. It is a telling moment, harking back to an earlier moment in the second act when, in the course of a production number, several couples perform a call-and-response tap dance break; when it is Robert's turn, there is a call but no response. Robert's motive, therefore, is expressive of the gulf between Robert and the couples, between Robert and thoughts of marriage, and between Robert and any kind of emotional commitment. On his own, Robert can only recall the motive by transforming it into something else. Woven into the show's texture, the motive and its transformations, along with the accompanying lyrics, create a web that is present in some form throughout the show, and

Plate 16 Production of *Company* in 2001 at the Missouri Repertory Theatre.

that defines Robert as a singular figure on the outside of a world of couples. This kind of motivic development is later greatly utilised by Sondheim, especially in *Sunday in the Park with George* and *Into the Woods* (1988).

Sondheim's use of pastiche appears even earlier, as noted above. In *Anyone Can Whistle* (1964), his second produced show as both composer and lyricist,[10] Sondheim made use of what he calls 'traditional musical comedy language to make points. All the numbers Angie [Angela Lansbury, one of the show's co-stars] sang in the show were pastiche – her opening number, for instance, was a Hugh Martin–Kay Thompson pastiche. The character always sang in musical comedy terms because she was a lady who dealt in attitudes instead of emotions.'[11] Interestingly, Sondheim has also said of this show that, 'Essentially the show is about, on one level, non-conformity and conformity in contemporary society.'[12] Although the show ran for only nine performances, the score is original and often memorable, and it explores subjects like sanity, depression and twentieth-century fears with a decidedly musical theatre vocabulary.

Sondheim also uses the vocabulary of the musical theatre in *Follies* (1971). Because *Follies*, in the words of director/producer Harold Prince, 'deals with the loss of innocence in the United States, using the Ziegfeld Follies … as its metaphor',[13] musical pastiche is a natural choice for realising that metaphor. Here, however, he gives resonance to characters who, unhappy with the present, look back to a past best recalled by its music and by their memory of having sung it. (The characters are former showgirls and their husbands, and the title refers to their former employment as well as to their personal delusions.) As Joanne Gordon observes, 'The work is a voyage into the collective unconscious of America's theatrical imagination. Nostalgia is not merely the mood, it is the subject matter.'[14] To this end, Sondheim writes musical numbers that recall the past eras referred to in the script and for which the characters express nostalgia, as well as numbers that are 'book' songs sung by the characters in the unhappy present. Because the script calls for the representation of the characters in their past youthful days as well as their present middle age, Sondheim sometimes combines the two styles of writing and creates a surreal blend of past and present.

The pastiche numbers, however, are most effective in the last section of the show, a kind of musical revue–nervous breakdown in which each of the four principal characters expresses his or her individual neurosis. Sally, a former chorus girl who is now unhappily married to a travelling salesman and living a nondescript suburban life in the American Southwest, expresses her long-standing love for Ben, a friend's husband whom she has quietly loved for years, in a Gershwin-like torch song. The rather mousy and decidedly unglamorous Sally stands alone in a circular spot, clad in a clinging silver gown evocative of Jean Harlow, and passionately sings 'Losing My Mind', one of Sondheim's most powerfully emotional love songs. Her husband Buddy, on the other hand, sings a patter song about loving one woman (Sally) but finding affection only in the arms of another. The upbeat and funny vaudeville quality of the song, a baggy pants routine, barely masks Buddy's desperate frustration with a lifetime of watching his wife love another man. Phyllis, Sally's former best friend and the wife of the man Sally loves, has a production number that speaks of her schizophrenia: 'The Story of Lucy and Jessie' depicts Phyllis as a young woman, warm and loving but fearful of life, and as a middle-aged woman, classy but emotionally dead. The irony is that each wants to be the other. This number recalls both Cole Porter and Kurt Weill, especially 'The Saga of Jenny' from *Lady in the Dark*.

The final number in this follies of the mind is for Ben, Phyllis's husband and the man loved by Sally. This is a top hat and tails number that also recalls Gershwin or, perhaps, the syncopated dance tunes of Irving Berlin. As Ben swaggers to the song, cane in hand and backed by the ensemble, he quite literally falls apart, forgetting his lyrics and losing control until the nightmare takes over and the revue literally explodes in a cacophony of musical fragments and shadowy images. Sondheim's choice of material to parody in this final section of the show is what makes the numbers so effectively devastating, and it is his most powerful and successful use of pastiche up to that point. His portraits of the neurotic and troubled characters are almost painful to watch, and they are created with great sympathy for the individuals who yearn for a time that was not nearly as happy, or tuneful, as they like to remember.

The complex web of relationships that forms *A Little Night Music* (1973) is one of outsiders. Of all the characters, Henrik most exemplifies this state. He goes from being a misfit at the seminary to being a misfit at home to being a misfit at Mme Armfeldt's estate. Indeed, before gathering with others at the estate for a weekend, Henrik notes that 'the devil's companions know not whom they serve, / It might be instructive to observe'. Henrik eventually does more than observe, however. Before the end of the weekend, and after contemplating suicide, he runs off with his father's young bride, who also realises her emotional and chronological distance from her husband and the others. The flight of Henrik and Anne propels the plot to its conclusion, in which the various characters rediscover their relationships and their places inside – or outside, as the case may be – the society around them. Desirée, the principal female character, compares the group of adults to clowns in 'Send in the Clowns', Sondheim's most famous song. After a statement of the song's titular command, Desirée changes her mind. 'Don't bother', she reconsiders, 'they're here'.

One of the most original creations for the musical theatre, *Sweeney Todd, The Demon Barber of Fleet Street* (1979) is filled with outsiders, colourful characters who are all dispossessed persons, outsiders in nineteenth-century London. Sweeney Todd, alias Benjamin Barker, a half-mad barber bent on revenge, comes to London to murder Judge Turpin, and when the intended victim escapes Todd's blade, Todd swears to kill all who visit his barber's chair until he cuts Turpin's throat.

In 'Epiphany' Todd's inner need for revenge is awakened to some of the angriest and most disturbing music ever written for the musical theatre. In the subsequent duet 'A Little Priest', Todd and the resourceful Mrs Lovett, who loves him, devise a plan to solve both of their problems – Todd getting rid of his murdered bodies and Mrs Lovett finding a source of meat for her pies. The cannibalistic fantasy, with its grotesque lyrics that describe how members of various professions would taste, appears as a light-hearted waltz. The counterpoint between the lyrics and the music accentuates the macabre nature of the duet.

The idea of using the waltz idiom to accompany dark and menacing lyrics was of course nothing new. Sondheim himself had used it throughout *A Little Night Music*, but in *Sweeney Todd* the style took on an even more demonic character. This would become manifest in two numbers in *Assassins*, as we shall see: the opening sequence, where 'Hail to the Chief' is transformed into a waltz, and 'Gun Song', where the carefree waltz is the musical identifier in a number that celebrates the weapon of assassination.

In the fairy-tale-based *Into the Woods* (1987), Sondheim once again has non-traditional characters as the central figures in his musical. Little Red Riding Hood, Cinderella, Jack (of beanstalk fame), Rapunzel and even Snow White appear in this musical about outsiders, all of whom have their own personal issues, working together to solve bigger problems. Encased in a larger tale of a baker and his barren wife who is under the spell of a witch, the stories of the familiar fairy tales are enhanced through their dramatic and musical treatment. Rapunzel's Prince and his brother, Cinderella's Prince, sing the waltz duet 'Agony', and the instructive ballads 'No One Is Alone' and 'Children Will Listen' have enjoyed lives of their own outside theatrical contexts. 'No One Is Alone' is a benevolent anthem to outsiders – people are never completely disconnected from others in their thoughts and actions.

Before turning our attention to *Assassins*, a veritable treasure chest of otherness that will occupy the rest of this chapter, we must acknowledge two other shows with scores by Sondheim that further demonstrate varied conditions of outsiders: *Passion* (1994) and *Bounce* (2003). The former concerns the life-altering and transformative love of a sick and physically unattractive woman – an outsider in every sense, from her physical to her emotional isolation from society – while the latter considers the troubled relationship of two entrepreneurial brothers who find it impossible to sustain themselves within the confines of society. The scores for these two shows inhabit different stylistic worlds, *Passion* rising to operatic heights through some of Sondheim's most exquisite music and *Bounce* recalling a more traditional Broadway style not unlike the earlier *Merrily We Roll Along*. Despite their being wildly different, each of these shows nonetheless provided Sondheim with additional sets of characters whose status as outsiders he could musically confirm.

It is in *Assassins*, however, that Sondheim is at his best portraying the neurotic outsider. Nowhere in Sondheim's work is this character type created with more explicit sympathy, humour or irony. *Assassins* is a troubling work that perplexed and even angered some critics and still has the power to disturb American audiences.[15] In this piece, all the characters are would-be or successful assassins of American presidents. They are also unhappy loners and, from society's perspective, losers. In *Assassins*, furthermore, Sondheim and the playwright John Weidman suggest that, with the exception of John Wilkes Booth, none of these singular figures acts out of any specific political motivation. Instead, their acts are explosive expressions of their hopeless and powerless positions in a system that seems, to them, to have been designed for the well-being of someone else. Individually and as a group, these men and women feel cheated and deprived of a happiness they view as their right. They express these feelings in one of Sondheim's most accomplished scores.

How he gives voice to these outsiders, and how his technique for doing this is unique in this work, is fascinating.

Weidman and Sondheim, who had earlier collaborated on *Pacific Overtures* (1976), created *Assassins* after the model of a vaudeville-like revue, a choice that contributed in several ways to the successful presentation of the disenfranchised titular characters. It encouraged Sondheim to exploit pastiche in new and sophisticated ways. Previously, as noted above, the composer/lyricist used familiar and traditional musical-theatre song styles to underscore aspects of situations and characters. In *Assassins*, however, the reach of Sondheim's stylistic net is much wider. The sources for his pastiche include pre-existent and often familiar pieces of music from the mid-nineteenth century to the 1980s. He also parodies familiar popular song styles from nineteenth-century parlour songs to 1980s pop love songs, as well as popular dance styles such as cakewalks, Sousa marches and hoe-downs. Non-musical sources include historical poems, lyrics, interviews and quotations. In addition, historical characters are interwoven throughout various eras to create relationships that would have been chronologically impossible. Such an extended use of historical materials, musical and textual, is unprecedented in Sondheim's work. He exploits these sources to probe the troubled psyches of deeply disturbed, and disturbing, outsiders.

By taking the familiar vocabulary of American music and using it to give voice to the disenfranchised and the desperate, moreover, Sondheim uses pastiche to particularly ironic effect. Comfortable and sometimes comforting styles of American popular music are used to depict an underside of American society, a depiction that in turn causes discomfort. Sondheim recasts or defamiliarises the comfortable styles by using them for characters who make us squirm but whose disenfranchisement, we begin to see by the show's end, is just as American as the 'comfortable' musical space it inhabits. When Sondheim uses popular song styles in ways that subvert the connotations they have carried for a century or more, he is taking a drastic stylistic step, one that cannot but disturb and unsettle American audiences. Sondheim thus creates a network of textual references to give individual numbers, and even the entire score, meanings they might otherwise lack. The whole work is a carefully spun web of various references that maintains cohesion in part through the manipulation of these references and the viewer's assumed knowledge of them. This combination of references, demonstrated below, is adroit and powerful.

The vaudeville model for *Assassins* allows each character to have his or her appropriate turn, or specialty number, each following the other in no particular order and each in a different musical style. Giuseppe Zangara sings his Sousa-inspired number strapped in an electric chair, looking as if he might at any moment make a Houdini-like escape; Charles Guiteau sings and dances a jaunty cakewalk up and down the hangman's scaffold; and Samuel Byck dictates monologues into his tape recorder as if performing stand-up comedy. This combination of seemingly unrelated styles and personalities is, of course, characteristic of American vaudeville, which was derived from, and often satirised, established genres of entertainment. The unrelated styles also allow the distinctness of each character from the others, as well as from society in general. The individual messages from the fringe are similar, but they are spoken with different musical vocabularies.

The choice of the vaudeville model no doubt also suggested the non-linear structure for *Assassins*. Like *Follies* and, especially, *Company,* the show moves smoothly but non-chronologically through time. Sometimes its dejected historical characters meet in locations non-specific to any one time period: a saloon in downtown New York City, for instance, that looks the same today as it did in 1900. Other times, however, the setting is almost painfully specific: the penultimate scene takes place in the Texas School Book Depository in Dallas, just before the assassination of President Kennedy. Sondheim also creates extended musical scenes through collections of numbers related by dramatic content and musical styles. 'How I Saved Roosevelt' is a collection of closely related but meaningfully contrasted dances. 'Gun Song' is a collection of waltzes, each of which deals with a different aspect of handguns and features a character from a different era. These waltzes are stylistically diverse, but they are connected by a refrain and preceded, as well as followed, by a sombre ballad, also a waltz. 'The Ballad of Guiteau' mixes hymn, parlour song, and cakewalk. Stephen Banfield has called these sequences 'suites'.[16]

The focus of one of these 'suites' ('How I Saved Roosevelt') is Giuseppe Zangara, an Italian immigrant who, in February 1933, attempted to kill President-elect Franklin Delano Roosevelt in Miami. He failed, but he managed to wound several others, including the Mayor of Chicago, Tony Cermak, who subsequently died from his wounds. After Cermak's death, Zangara's life sentence was changed to death by execution in the electric chair. Zangara's only political agenda was his simple if fervent anti-capitalism: he was neither an anarchist, for instance, nor a socialist nor even a communist. He bore no grudge towards any individual figure, including Roosevelt.

While 'How I Saved Roosevelt' creates a vivid portrait of Zangara, however, it also contrasts him with a group of patriotic Bystanders, as Sondheim calls them, all of whom claimed to have thwarted the assassination attempt. These individuals each received and enjoyed much attention in the press and became momentary celebrities for their claims of having saved FDR. The contrast of Zangara's passionate anti-capitalism with the all-American absorption with self-promotion and celebrity in the press creates the bipolar perspective of the musical scene. When we add to this the fact that, before Roosevelt's appearance, a band gave a concert at Bayfront Park's new bandshell,[17] we have the makings of a musical number, and it is from here that Sondheim works his magic.

Through an on-stage radio, we hear the activities at Bayfront Park: a performance of Sousa's march 'El Capitan'; an announcer's description of the festive scene, and then of the unsuccessful assassination. The announcer summarises the ensuing events, ending with, 'We take you now to a group of eyewitnesses who will tell us what they saw.' The lights come up on five Bystanders and, as the band resumes 'El Capitan', they begin singing.

Sondheim's choice of 'El Capitan' is interesting. One of Sousa's best-known marches, it, too, is a pastiche of unrelated musical numbers from Sousa's most successful operetta, also titled *El Capitan*. This lighthearted work is also concerned with political insurrection and turmoil. After opening his number with a direct quote of the march's four-bar introduction in 6/8 time, and thus emphasising the diegetic aspect of the march being played in Bayfront Park, Sondheim builds a melody related to Sousa's, albeit more of a recognisable reminiscence than a direct quote. In the third strain of the march, Sondheim changes the character through a shift to sustained quartal harmony (i.e. harmony based on fourths). This serves as Zangara's introduction into the number, and the lights come up on him confined in the electric chair. In the middle of this section, after the minor mode unambiguously appears, Zangara's music is transformed into a tarantella.

Whereas the character of the Sousa march indicates the patriotic American middle class and its capitalist system, the tarantella is, in this context, distinctly 'other' and foreign. Its heritage as a folk dance reflects Zangara's poor Italian background and provides a clear contrast to the Sousa march's more bourgeois origins. Since both are in 6/8 time, transition from one to the other is relatively simple.

After Zangara's interlude, the strains of 'El Capitan' return, and the Bystanders begin again. After they sing the same musical material as in the opening section of the number, Sondheim takes another surprise turn and introduces 'The Washington Post', another Sousa march that operates on more than one level. The first, of course, is that the 'The Washington Post' represents the establishment press to whom the Bystanders are so eagerly and self-importantly telling their stories. The other level is that of yet another dance style. After its composition in 1899, 'The Washington Post' was chosen by a group of dance instructors as suitable for a new and fashionable dance called the two-step, which in many places is still referred to as 'The Washington Post'. This dance, then, implies another contrast in social class.

When the music yet again returns to 'El Capitan', a Bystander refers to Zangara as 'Some left wing foreigner'. Zangara, however, refutes the term 'left wing' with a chilling section best described as a miniature mad scene. Here the orchestra plays dissonant snippets of the march melodies in counterpoint to Zangara's increasingly higher, and increasingly intense, vocal line. After asserting 'Zangara no foreign tool, / Zangara American! / American nothing!' Zangara begins asking about the photographers. He sings, 'And why there no photographers? / For Zangara no photographers! / Only capitalists get photographers!' Odd though it is, this ranting is based on fact: in its report of Zangara's execution in March of 1933, *Newsweek* reported that Zangara said, 'No camera man here? No one here to take picture? Lousy capitalists! No pictures! Capitalists! All capitalists! Lousy bunch! Crooks.'[18]

What Sondheim does with this outburst is particularly ingenious. Zangara's diatribe about photographers equates him with the Bystanders, who are smitten with the press and excited by their importance to it. To point out this new, if fleeting, relationship between Zangara and the Bystanders, Sondheim again quotes the second strain of 'El Capitan' and has Zangara sing a counter-melody while the Bystanders sing the original melody. Zangara's identifying tarantella, then, transforms into an integral section of the march. After Zangara asks, 'And why there no photographers? /... / Only capitalists get photographers', he comments 'No right! / No fair / Nowhere!' as the Bystanders sing, 'I'm on the front page – is that bizarre? / And all of those pictures, like a star!' The implication is that, for at least this one moment in his life, Zangara envies the capitalist middle class more than perhaps he ever dreamed possible, even as he distinguishes himself from them. Because of Zangara's presence on stage with the Bystanders, the original lyrics for this phrase in Sousa's operetta are almost eerie: 'Gaze on his misanthropic stare. / Notice his penetrating glare.' As both Zangara and the Bystanders reach the end of the number, Zangara sings, 'Pull switch!' and a hum of electricity accompanies the number's final cadence.

Sondheim again references and/or quotes other texts, musical and non-musical, in his portrayal of Charles Guiteau in 'The Ballad of Guiteau'. On the surface an affable lunatic who shot James Garfield to preserve the country and promote the sales of his book, the singular Guiteau is given a pathetic and angry underside. This is done in part through recalling writings by the character as well as subsequent folk songs about him. (Indeed, the body of extant folk songs about political assassination in fact suggests that *Assassins* is the latest in a long line of works in popular genres about this aspect of the American character.)

On the day of his execution, Charles Guiteau wrote a poem that begins, 'I am going to the Lordy; / I am so glad. / I am going to the Lordy / I am so glad. / I am going to the Lordy, / Glory Hallelujah! Glory Hallelujah! / I am going to the Lordy.'[19] This poem intrigued Sondheim, who first encountered it in the short play by Charles Gilbert that inspired *Assassins*, and he opens Guiteau's number with its first lines. They are sung hymn-like and unaccompanied, and Sondheim continues to use the line 'I am going to the Lordy' as a recurring refrain between the number's sections. The contrast of Guiteau's fervent yet hymn-like poem with the musical styles that follow it suggests Guiteau's mental imbalance, a trait the audience has already seen. He is glib, frequently charming and completely insane.

Sondheim first contrasts Guiteau's mad hymn with a parlour song in 3/4 time sung by the narrating Balladeer. The opening lines also recall the opening exhortation of the folk song mentioned above, which is, 'Come all ye Christian people, wherever you may be, / Likewise pay attention to these few lines from me.'[20] Sondheim distils this to 'Come all ye Christians, and learn from a sinner.'

Musically, Sondheim constructs a useful structure for all this textual reference. As noted above, the opening is an unaccompanied hymn sung by, and with lyrics by, Guiteau himself. Because the lights come up to reveal him at the foot of a scaffold, his reference to 'going to the Lordy' is amusing. The music, however, is a straightforward and almost austere hymn, sixteen bars of increasingly wider intervals. The initial hymn section segues into the Balladeer's triple-time parlour song, mentioned above. The parlour song leads into a sixteen-bar cakewalk refrain for Guiteau, by the end of which he has danced himself one step closer to the hangman's waiting noose. The upbeat character and tempo of the dance are reflected in Sondheim's optimistic lyrics for Guiteau. Each refrain begins 'Look on the bright side' and continues with appropriately optimistic homilies that, along with the cheerfulness of the cakewalk, provide ironic contrast to the ominous scaffold on which they are delivered. The first two statements of the refrain are upbeat, but the third is slower, more resolute and accompanied by strong chords played on the beat, and ends abruptly after only four bars. At this point, Sondheim returns to the hymn. Now, however, it is played as a resolute and forceful dance: a *danse macabre*. At the end of the forceful hymn section, the Balladeer begins his refrain, this time in the previous fast tempo, and he and Guiteau sing an extended ending. As the refrain, and the number, are finally allowed to conclude, Guiteau is blindfolded and, as the lights black out and the final chord is played, the Hangman pulls the lever that releases the trap door under Guiteau.

The implications of the cakewalk, of course, are fascinating. The dance was originally a dance of outsiders, created by plantation slaves as a means of ridiculing their white owners. It was theatrical from its conception, with its prancing, high steps, its forward and backward bowing and its practice of dressing up in costume to impersonate others. Later, when the cakewalk was included in minstrelsy, it included acknowledgement of the audience. The cakewalk was eventually accepted by all of society and it became quite popular with American and European dancers, white as well as black. Guiteau's self-consciously theatrical performance of the number recalls the cakewalk of minstrelsy and its winks and bows to the audience, and the absurdity of its urgent cheerfulness, under the circumstances of its performance, suggests Guiteau's insanity. The changing reception of the cakewalk, furthermore, suggests Guiteau's desperate desire for the respectability he thought fame and success would bring. Interestingly, the nature of the cakewalk, in its origins and later as a popular dance, was competitive. The slave who best impersonated the masters was rewarded with a prize – a cake – and later dancers also competed for prizes and acclaim. In *Assassins*, the disenfranchised seek a prize withheld by society, and their increasingly angry demand for that prize culminates in the powerful musical number 'Another National Anthem'. Guiteau's cakewalk simply and subtly drives home the idea that he, like each of the characters, is waiting for a prize, but not necessarily the noose and trap door.

The skill demonstrated in the creation of these two musical numbers suggests why Stephen Sondheim is among the most accomplished and influential composer-lyricists of the American musical theatre. His mastery of the styles that inform the score for *Assassins* is nothing less than stunning, and each musical number displays a virtuosity similar to that found in 'How I Saved Roosevelt' and 'The Ballad of Guiteau'. Even the musical interludes refer to music other than that in *Assassins* and at one point are self-referential: Samuel Byck's first monologue, a humorous if unsettling message to Leonard Bernstein dictated into a tape recorder, ends with Byck singing Sondheim's lyrics to 'America' from *West Side Story*. Sondheim then parodies Bernstein's music for 'America' to close the scene. First quoting the number and then paraphrasing it, Sondheim uses his own work as a historical source. The moment is as chilling and ironic as it is amusing. Later, before the scene in the Texas School Book Depository, Sondheim uses actual recorded music – The Blue Ridge Boys singing 'Heartache Serenade' – to give the scene an especially eerie sense of reality that is made surreal when John Wilkes Booth appears before Lee Harvey Oswald.

Drawing on the body of American popular culture to give voice to the characters as well as to make critical commentary about them, Sondheim leaves the audience with the act of assassination as a collective cultural memory that uncomfortably lingers. The bitter observations of 'Gun Song', for instance, have the capability to haunt the viewer long after the final curtain. The communal desperation of 'Another National Anthem' fades into the quieter desperation of Lee Harvey Oswald, whose violent act, still vivid in the minds of many in the audience, is the climax of the show. There is no song for Oswald because his feelings have already been anticipated and expressed: he is the culmination of all the assassins and all the songs that have gone before him. Of course, he too is the victim of assassination, an act that provokes the final chorus of 'Everybody's got the right to be happy'.

This one score, perhaps the most indigenously 'American' of all Sondheim's output given its sources, displays a master at a high point of his career. *Assassins* is representative of Sondheim's work in its use of pastiche, its experiment with form and its representation of outsiders looking at a society that, for whatever various reasons, excludes them.

In all his work, Sondheim's musical languages are varied yet identifiably his own; perhaps they are more like different accents of the same language than altogether different languages. His harmonic vocabulary is vast and he alters it somewhat with each project; but the end result is always recognisably his.[21] His musical treatment, as well as the vocabulary of the lyrics in his own scores (Sondheim has criticised some of his earlier lyrics as inappropriate),[22] display an unerring sense of character as well as theatricality, and no false note or word appears in any of his mature work. Returning to his scores again and again, the listener is continually informed, surprised and entertained by them. In *Assassins*, Sondheim's musical pastiche is a tool for revealing aspects of the American national psyche, including the American proclivity for assassinating elected leaders. The initial and nervous critical reception of *Assassins* in the United States perhaps suggests that Sondheim reveals too much too clearly. Each of his works operates in similar, although outwardly different, ways.

The sensitivity that caused the fifteen-year-old Stephen Sondheim to cry at the first-act curtain of *Carousel* is still present in his maturity. *Sweeney Todd*, *Into the Woods*, *Assassins* and *Passion* are each as heartbreaking as they are disturbing and amusing. In *Assassins*, Sondheim's outsiders find a national anthem for all the 'others' as well as for themselves in a musical score of inordinate richness. In musical after musical, Sondheim offers a moving reminder about those people who 'can't get in to the ball park', and he offers this reminder in a most American way: through the voice of America's own songs.

12 Choreographers, directors and the fully integrated musical

PAUL R. LAIRD

Can one recapture the excitement that *A Chorus Line* brought to Broadway? The Broadway musical seemed moribund in the middle of the 1970s. The big hits of the previous decade, such as *Hello, Dolly!*, *Fiddler on the Roof* and *Man of La Mancha*, had closed and the era of the great musical plays that followed the Rodgers and Hammerstein model was over. Stephen Sondheim and Hal Prince combined for major artistic successes between 1970 and 1973 with *Company*, *A Little Night Music* and *Follies*, but their appeal was limited, as can be seen by the length of their runs and their mixed commercial success. The rock musical had become a Broadway reality with *Hair*, *Two Gentlemen of Verona* and other shows, but rock was a new musical language that many in the traditional Broadway audience had not yet accepted. Creators of the musical theatre searched for a new mould that might combine new musical styles and contemporary thinking with tradition, building upon the genre's proud history. *A Chorus Line* did all of this as a veritable celebration of Broadway dance and dancers, bringing new life to the genre and taking it into the colossal hit era of six-thousand-performance runs.

Those who saw *A Chorus Line* during its original run will not easily forget it. The plot was minimal and somewhat artificial, but the characters were engrossing. We recognised types of people that we knew and with each part of their stories our fascination grew. The singing and dancing had a special immediacy because, within the world that the director Michael Bennett magically created, we knew that these characters would express themselves through music and movement.

The creators of *A Chorus Line* built upon decades of Broadway history when dance was integrated into the musical as a crucial part of character development and dramatic impact. It had taken years in the musical comedy to integrate plot and significant aspects of the music, but by the time of *Show Boat* (1927) and *Of Thee I Sing* (1931), song placement had become more careful in some shows and plots sometimes advanced during songs. Although this trend could hardly be described as linear, by the time Rodgers and Hammerstein wrote *Carousel* (1945), songs were often an important part of the plot and extended musical sequences were more common.

The integration of dance with a show's plot was a slower process. Victor Herbert, a Broadway pioneer in several areas, wrote some of the first dance musicals, such as *The Lady of the Slipper* (1912).[1] In such shows, Herbert used dance for spectacular effect and throughout entire scenes, surpassing its more common use for variety. The famous team of Vernon and Irene Castle were hired to show the latest ballroom steps, but were dismissed in Philadelphia because part of their work seemed too suggestive. During the 1920s dances would follow a song, and various stage personalities offered dance specialties that had nothing to do with the plot. For example, according to Hugh Fordin, the *Sunny* star Marilyn Miller interrupted Oscar Hammerstein II as he described the plot, wondering when she would do her specialty tap number.[2] There were a number of fine dancers on Broadway in the 1920s, including Fred and Adele Astaire, Ann Pennington and Marilyn Miller, who helped introduce dance as a way of describing their characters, but for the most part dance remained part of the musical's quest for variety. Most shows included dances added solely for entertainment; *A Connecticut Yankee* and *Show Boat* were two exceptions. Dances designed by such leading choreographers as a Busby Berkeley were fairly predictable and resulted only in the credit line 'dances by'.[3]

As Hollywood musicals appeared and confirmed the public's interest in watching stars dance (perhaps a metaphor for what could not be shown), Broadway followed suit. Ethan Mordden describes the continued development of the character dance in 'Clifton Webb's unassuming soft shoe or Tamara Geva's ballet glide' and the continued popularity of the kick line.[4] (The latter, of course, never died; *A Chorus Line* exploited the appeal of the long, shapely female leg and a line's drilled precision.) By the second half of the 1930s, however, more ambitious dances appeared in shows, first and most famously in *On Your Toes* (1936), with a score by Rodgers and Hart and direction by George Abbott. George Balanchine, the famed Russian choreographer, worked on the show and was the first honoured with the credit line 'choreography by'. His major contribution was the ballet 'Slaughter on Tenth Avenue', danced by Ray Bolger, Tamara Geva and George Church. Abbott remembered the segment as 'one of the best numbers I've ever seen in the theatre, both musically and choreographically'.[5] The show also included a ballet in the first act, 'Princess Zenobia'. The dances were part of a story about a vaudeville hoofer trying to make it in ballet. The dances were praised at the time, but, as Marian Monta Smith has noted, they were seen as an exception and the production had little immediate influence.[6] Balanchine continued to work on Broadway into the 1950s, but there are few other shows for which his choreography had a lasting influence.[7]

It seems significant that George Abbott directed *On Your Toes*, because he went on to be a major influence on the continuing integration of the musical and on two important choreographers who later became directors. As extensive use of dance became part of the musical, the director emerged as the figure who assembled the show's elements into a creative whole. By the 1960s, several of the most important directors were choreographers. Two of these, Jerome Robbins and Bob Fosse, worked with Abbott and learned to direct the book from him. The line continues with Hal Prince, who, although not a choreographer, also explored the musical's greater integration. He began his Broadway career working for Abbott in the early 1950s and learned direction from both Abbott and Robbins.

The greater integration of dance, specifically ballet, into the musical required the willing cooperation of Broadway creators and understanding talent from the ballet world, a combination that came together in *Oklahoma!*. Rodgers, Hammerstein, and the producers Theresa Helburn and Lawrence Langner of the Theatre Guild sought to make ballet part of the show's plot apparatus and hired Agnes de Mille as choreographer. She had handled western themes with her 1942 ballet *Rodeo*, with music by Aaron Copland. De Mille's work in *Oklahoma!* is legendary, from her insistence on real dancers and separate rehearsals to her battles with the director, Rouben Mamoulian.[8] Such dances as 'Laurey Makes Up Her Mind' at the end of the first act changed Broadway history. De Mille's dancers served as substitutes for most of the principal actors during the ballet and helped make convincing the notion of Laurey dreaming her way to a choice between Curly and Jud. De Mille's use of counterpoint in her ballets, with characters doing different movements at the same time, added to the visual appeal.[9]

Broadway creators are nothing if not imitative, and several immediately capitalised on the new idea of taking the highbrow art of ballet into the middlebrow world of the Broadway musical. De Mille played a major role throughout the 1940s. She next worked on *One Touch of Venus* (1943), with music by Kurt Weill and lyrics by Ogden Nash, who co-authored the book with S. J. Perelman. A show about Venus coming to life invited fanciful ballets. De Mille contributed 'Forty Minutes for Lunch' in the first act, where Venus meets New York workers in Rockefeller Center, and 'Venus in Ozone Heights' as the second act's dream ballet, where the goddess discovers suburbia. De Mille went on to *Bloomer Girl* (1944), with music by Harold Arlen and lyrics by E. Y. Harburg, where she contributed a ballet based on an 'Uncle Tom' show and a Civil War ballet in which female dancers expressed the feelings of those watching husbands and sons go off to war.

De Mille returned to work with Rodgers and Hammerstein as chore-ographer for *Carousel*, where her dances again played a major role in plot development. The opening ballet-pantomime introduces the setting and mood, and in the second-act dance, Billy Bigelow's daughter expresses her frustration. De Mille next choreographed *Brigadoon*, Lerner and Loewe's breakthrough hit, including atmospheric Scottish dances and the chase ballet in the second act. De Mille became the first choreographer-director in Rodgers and Hammerstein's *Allegro* (1947), where she tried to unify a rambling plot, a singing Greek chorus and many musical numbers calling for motion. She included a fantasy ballet where, in a manner reminiscent of *Our Town*, characters both living and dead appear. The show would have challenged any director, but it did give de Mille a chance to develop comfort with all types of stage motion.

Agnes de Mille's peers, who helped dance become a more important part of the Broadway musical, included, among others, Jack Cole, Michael Kidd and Jerome Robbins. Cole helped establish the Broadway vernacular dance tradition with his imaginative use of steps from ethnic and ballroom dances and acrobatics, often set to big band music.[10] He also added ballets to shows, such as his slow-motion softball game in *Allah Be Praised* (1944). Michael Kidd choreographed *Finian's Rainbow* (1947), *Guys and Dolls* (1950) and *Can-Can* (1953), showing an admirable range; his major success as a choreographer-director was *Li'l Abner* (1956). Jerome Robbins, one of Broadway's most important choreographers, was the first dancer to become a truly successful director.

Jerome Robbins straddled ballet and Broadway for much of his career, but worked little on Broadway from the mid-1960s to the 1980s. His first major ballet was the popular *Fancy Free* in 1944, created with the composer Leonard Bernstein. They brought the ballet's energy, references to vernacular music and dance, and a plot concerning three sailors on leave in wartime New York City to Broadway in *On the Town*, which also involved the lyricists Betty Comden and Adolph Green and director George Abbott. Much about the show was memorable (see chapter 10), especially its frenetic energy and constant motion. In her autobiography *Distant Dances*, Sono Osato, a ballet dancer who played Ivy Turnstiles, describes her work with Abbott and Robbins:[11] Abbott directed the book scenes, but Robbins had a free hand with the dances. The two major ballets were 'Miss Turnstiles' and 'Gabey in the Playground of the Rich', the latter a dream ballet near the end of the show. Both helped propel the story. Osato danced the latter ballet with a dancer substituting for the actor who played Gabey. Abbott allowed Robbins to show how dance could be incorporated in varied situations, helping lead finally to shows such as *West Side Story*.

Robbins continued to work on Broadway as well as in ballet and modern dance. In 1945 he contributed the ballet 'Interplay', with music by Morton Gould, to the vaudeville *Concert Varieties*.[12] In December of that year, *Billion Dollar Baby* opened, starring the dancer Joan McCracken with choreography by Robbins. Far more famous is Robbins' work with George Abbott during the 1947–8 season, including *High Button Shoes* (1947) and *Look, Ma, I'm*

Dancin' (1948). Abbott directed and wrote *High Button Shoes*, a fast-paced farce built around Phil Silvers. The score was Jule Styne's first for Broadway. He considered himself a songwriter, but Robbins convinced him to score the 'Mack Sennett Ballet', where leads were chased by Keystone Kops and a bear. All finally land in a pile topped by a flag-waving policeman. The number was repeated in the retrospective *Jerome Rabbins' Broadway* (1989). *Look, Ma, I'm Dancin'* was a vehicle for Nancy Walker conceived by Robbins. Walker played a brewery heiress who becomes a patron for a ballet company and finally dances with it, a hilarious possibility given her clowning skills. Robbins' 'Sleepwalker's Ballet' was one of the highlights in a show that ran for only six months because of Walker's ill health. Robbins also worked with Abbott on *Call Me Madam*, a vehicle for Ethel Merman with a score by Irving Berlin, but the show is remembered more for its star and score than for its dancing. Abbott reports that Robbins started rehearsals early to create his dances, but the major number was removed before opening night. Abbott reveals his faith in spoken materials, predictable for one of the genre's best book directors: 'Time and time again the ambitious dance effort will fail, whereas something conceived for practical purposes and on the spur of the moment will be a success. This is equally true of songs.'[13] Abbott's type of show, the fast-paced comedy, however, was in decline as dance became more an integral part of the musical.

In 1951 *The King and I* opened, a much-loved show by Rodgers and Hammerstein that included Robbins' lengthy ballet 'The Small House of Uncle Thomas', which offers interesting commentary on the plot's theme of East meeting West. The dance also appeared in *Jerome Robbins' Broadway*.

In 1954 Abbott gave Robbins billing as co-director for *The Pajama Game* (considered below), partly because of his success at working with such dancers as the star Carol Haney. The show's choreographer was Bob Fosse, and other important newcomers to Abbott's team were the producers Hal Prince and Robert E. Griffith, who later produced *West Side Story*.

Robbins earned his first full credit as a Broadway director in *Bells Are Ringing*, a show with little important dancing, music by Jule Styne, lyrics by Comden and Green and a delightful star in Judy Holliday. It ran for two years. At this point Robbins was ready to spread his wings by taking on both direction and choreography. He realised this ambition the following year with *West Side Story*.

West Side Story (1957) marks the full integration of dance into the Broadway musical and the true arrival of the choreographer-director. Plans for a modern version of *Romeo and Juliet*, involving Robbins, Bernstein and Arthur Laurents, had started as early as 1949.[14] Their original thought was that the lovers should be Catholic and Jewish and the story should occur around the time of Easter and Passover, but they were unable to work together with any consistency and the project was shelved. Bernstein and Laurents ran into each other in Beverly Hills in August 1955 and decided to move the story to New York's West Side and pit gangs of Puerto Ricans against the white 'Americans'.[15]

As director and choreographer, Robbins was responsible ultimately for the full integration of each element into a dramatic whole. He believed in method acting, dividing the cast into the two gangs and forbidding them to socialise on the set. His intensity in rehearsal was legendary. Carol Lawrence, who played Maria, remembers working with Robbins:

> You have to understand that Jerry Robbins was the motivating force in all of this. He was the eternal perfectionist. The fact that one can never attain perfection did not deter him for a second. That was what he wanted and if he ended up killing you in the interim, well that was okay too![16]

West Side Story was cast from a pool of dancers. Even the romantic leads, Carol Lawrence and Larry Kert, had extensive dance training. In effect, Robbins choreographed every movement in the show. Dance provided motion in the action sequences (such as in the 'Prologue' and 'The Rumble'), and served as an expressive device both for inarticulate characters ('Dance at the Gym' and 'Cool') and in numbers designed to release tension (such as 'I Feel Pretty' and 'Gee, Officer Krupke!').[17] How dependent the show was on dance became clear when the company arrived at the Washington theatre for its out-of-town try-out and discovered that the stage was significantly smaller than at the Winter Garden in New York, for which it was choreographed. Carol Lawrence remembers that Robbins had to rework the ballets and 'there was so much dance, almost nothing but dance in the show'.[18]

Bernstein wrote the dance numbers as well as the songs. Robbins was a close collaborator, often suggesting musical changes and at times making them himself. Bernstein showed notable command of Latin dances and various types of jazz, producing a score that still sounds contemporary. Especially effective moments include the mambo in the 'Dance at the Gym' and the rich references to cool jazz in the song 'Cool'. Bernstein uses melodies from the songs in dance sequences to great dramatic effect, such as the tune 'Maria' in the 'Maria Cha-Cha' of the 'Dance at the Gym' sequence, heard there before Tony sings the song for the first time. The song 'Somewhere' also appears in dance passages, tying the dream sequence between Tony and Maria to the show's plot.[19]

West Side Story was Bernstein's last important Broadway show, but Robbins continued to work there consistently into the mid-1960s. Two of his *West Side Story* collaborators – Arthur Laurents and Stephen Sondheim – joined the composer Jule Styne on *Gypsy* in 1959. Choreography was far less important here than in some of his previous shows, but Robbins again showed his deft staging touch, beautifully evoking vaudeville and burlesque while allowing room for one of Ethel Merman's greatest roles. His next show was *Fiddler on the Roof* (1964), another triumph of mood and atmosphere in a book musical. Along with the set designer Boris Aronson and the costume designer Patricia Zipprodt, Robbins convincingly recreated the Jewish *shtetl* of Anatevka. Robbins designed some of his most imaginative dances, using both Jewish and Russian elements to add to the show's true-to-life quality. Two memorable sequences included a joint dance by Jewish and Russian characters in the inn and the bottle dance at the wedding. Robbins' next, and last, Broadway show was the anthology *Jerome Robbins' Broadway* of 1989.

The next great choreographer-director in the line of Agnes de Mille and Jerome Robbins was Bob Fosse (1927–87), a dancer from Chicago who began his career in vaudeville and burlesque.[20] As noted above, George Abbott was important to Fosse's career development, hiring him as choreographer in *The Pajama Game* (1954). Unlike Robbins, Fosse came to Broadway through the world of ballroom and ethnic dances, showing the influence of Jack Cole's jazz-dancing techniques. Fosse's dances for *The Pajama Game*, especially in 'Hernando's Hideaway', kept up the frenetic pace popularised by Abbott and Robbins. For the star Carol Haney, with whom Fosse had worked in Hollywood, he created 'Steam Heat', which she danced with Peter Gennaro and Buzz Miller. The show bubbled over with major dance numbers, including 'Once a Year Day', '7½ Cents', and 'I'll Never Be Jealous Again'. Fosse also worked with Abbott in *Damn Yankees* (1955), which included a number of dances based upon typical baseball moves and 'Who's Got the Pain?', conceived for Gwen Verdon, Fosse's third wife and frequent collaborator. Fosse also worked on the film versions of *The Pajama Game* (1957) and *Damn Yankees* (1958). In 1956 Fosse assisted Robbins with the choreography for the Broadway show *Bells Are Ringing*, including the number 'Mu Cha Cha'. Fosse's last show with Abbott was *New Girl in Town* (1957): their break-up was caused by Abbott's moral objections to Fosse's dream ballet in a bordello. Fosse often cultivated the suggestive in his dance routines, perhaps an influence from his days in burlesque. Christine Colby Jacques, a dancer who worked with Fosse on *Dancin'*, notes that he often ironically parodied suggestive movements:

> the 'American Women' section in *Dancin'* (1978), presented three women with long-stemmed roses in their mouths. With hips thrust forward, hands on hips and elbows squeezed together in back, they took three long, exaggerated steps across the stage. Their feet came together, and looking over their shoulders out toward the audience, each woman swayed her hips

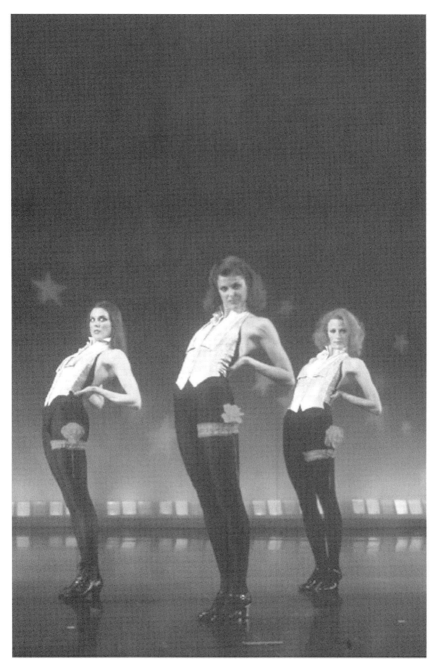

Plate 17 Ann Reinking, P. J. Mann and Christine Colby Jacques in 'Stout-Hearted Men', a dance number from Bob Fosse's *Dancin'*, in 1979.

side to side ever so slightly in an up, even tempo. The impact was a clear, yet comical comment on the pouting and sensual manner women sometimes use to manipulate men. So much of Fosse's choreography reflects a tongue-in-cheek look at ourselves, whether it's sensual movement or gestural movement . . . Fosse directed us to think of ourselves as little girls with sway backs and protruding little bellies, sucking our thumbs.[21]

Fosse became Broadway's third important choreographer-director in the late 1950s, starting with *Redhead* (1959), a vehicle for Gwen Verdon, including the dances 'Pick-Pocket Tango' and 'The Uncle Sam Rag'. Fosse shared director's credit with Abe Burrows in *How to Succeed in Business Without Really Trying* (1961), where Fosse did the 'musical staging'.

Fosse's next show was *Little Me* (1962), starring Sid Caesar. Among the dances was the effective 'Rich Kid's Rag'. His next major work was for Gwen Verdon in *Sweet Charity* (1966), which Fosse conceived, directed and choreographed. His dances included 'I'm a Brass Band' for Gwen Verdon (with the male chorus performing his trademark posture of locked ankles and a backward lean), 'Big Spender' for the hostesses at the Fandango Club, and 'The Rich Man's Frug', a satire of recent dance fads in discotheques. Fosse struggled through the film version of *Sweet Charity*, but resurrected his career by directing the highly successful film adaptation of *Cabaret* (1972), winning the Oscar for best direction. He also directed and choreographed the film *All That Jazz* (1979), which many considered Fosse's autobiography and which included brilliant dancing segments.

Fosse's last three Broadway shows included some of his most popular work. *Pippin* (1972) had a simple plot, enlivened by Fosse with characters based upon *commedia dell'arte*, clowns and several large-scale song and dance numbers, and assisted greatly by the energy and gregarious personality of Ben Vereen. *Chicago* (1975) was yet another show starring Gwen Verdon, joined by Chita Rivera. They played murderesses who form a nightclub act. Fosse's staging was lean and effective with dance an integral part, led by Verdon and Rivera, who allowed Fosse to parody their fading youth in brief costumes and suggestive poses. The show is a series of vaudeville acts, each advancing the plot, with a band on stage. Fosse's choreography made frequent use of the soft-shoe and Charleston, emphasising the 1920s setting. *Dancin'* (1978) was Fosse's answer to *A Chorus Line*: another show about dancing conceived in a workshop situation. Using music by many composers dating back to Bach, *Dancin'* includes no plot and little singing. Critics offered mixed reactions but the audience did not, propelling *Dancin'* to a run of 1,774 performances. The show was a monument to Fosse the entertainer and his eleventh Broadway hit in a row. His final Broadway show was the unsuccessful *Big Deal* (1986). A retrospective of Fosse's work, *Fosse*, ran on Broadway and in the West End and toured in the late 1990s and early 2000s. It was conceived by Richard Maltby Jr, Ann Reinking and Chet Walker with the assistance of Gwen Verdon. Reinking has had a successful career as a choreographer, for example following Fosse's work in the hit revival of *Chicago* that ran for years on Broadway (starting in 1996) and in the West End (starting in 1997).

Another of Broadway's important choreographer-directors was Gower Champion, who started as a Broadway dancer in the 1940s. He went to work in Hollywood, and then returned to Broadway as choreographer-director of *Bye Bye Birdie* (1960), a fairly simple show whose major dance was the wild 'Shriners' Ballet'. His next show was *Carnival* (1961), where Champion brought the audience into the action by dispensing with the curtain and using aisles for entrances and exits. The memorable choreography included the 'Grand Imperial Cirque de Paris'. Champion's biggest hit was *Hello, Dolly!* (1964). Although more famous for the title song and Carol Channing's inimitable presence, the show benefited enormously from Champion's staging, which included extensive business from the dancers. He made Channing the centrepiece whenever possible and crafted one of the greatest entrances in theatre history with the hilarious 'Waiter's Gallop' before Dolly Levi descends the stairs at the Harmonia Gardens (see Plate 14 on p. 187). The extensive use of choreography was also found in 'It Takes a Woman' and 'Before the Parade Passes By'. Champion's career continued for another fifteen years with both hits and flops, including *I Do! I Do!* (1966), *The Act* (1977) and *42nd Street* (1980). The latter was an unabashed return to the days of tap-dancing chorus complete with story and music from the 1933 movie by the same name. Champion died the day the show opened.

Although not a choreographer-director, Hal Prince has played a major role in the development of the musical since the 1950s.[22] Like Robbins, he learned his craft from George Abbott. He played a role in several of Abbott's shows during the 1950s and emerged from the older man's shadow when he produced *West Side Story* with Robert E. Griffith in 1957. Following Griffith's death in 1961, Prince produced such shows as *She Loves Me* (1963) and *Fiddler on the Roof* (1964). He made his directing debut with *Cabaret* (1966), a book show that he treated like a concept musical, with an inspired staging that commented on the story through the cabaret entertainment. Its run of 1,166 performances did much to establish Prince as one of the most sought-after new directors. In 1970 he began his artistically successful collaboration in concept musicals with Stephen Sondheim in *Company* (1970), *Follies* (1971) and *A Little Night Music* (1973), three shows without conventional plots where staging played a huge role. Prince pushed staging nearly to extreme limits in *Follies*, helping to create the spectacular effect of a theatre crumbling, but at the same time losing $685,000 during the one-and-a-half-year run. Since then, Prince has worked on some of Broadway's biggest successes with scores by Andrew Lloyd Webber, but his artistic vision had the most influence in the 1960s and 1970s, when he played a major role in the continuing integration of music, dance and drama in the musical. Like Robbins, he wielded great power in a production and helped make the director one of Broadway's most important figures.

The next important choreographer-director was Michael Bennett, creator of *A Chorus Line*. From a young age he showed great interest in dance and made his professional debut while still in his teens in a stock production of *West Side Story*. He later toured Europe in the show and became intimately familiar with his idol Robbins' work. Bennett became a Broadway gypsy in the early 1960s but worked in no memorable shows. He choreographed stock productions and achieved his first Broadway credit in *A Joyful Noise* (1966), which ran for twelve performances.[23] Critics praised Bennett's work, as they did his dances for *Henry, Sweet Henry* (1967), also a flop. Bennett finally worked on a hit in *Promises, Promises* (1968), directed by Robert Moore. The final version of the show included only one major dance number, but, as Ken Mandelbaum reports, 'Bennett was able to make an enormous contribution to the show by weaving scene into scene, staging marvelous "crossovers", with secretaries spinning through revolving doors in stylized movements reminiscent of ... "go-go" steps.'[24] *Promises, Promises* was the first show where Donna McKechnie was Bennett's principal female dancer. She eventually became for Bennett what Gwen Verdon was to Bob Fosse. Bennett and McKechnie were also married for a time.

Bennett's next show as choreographer was *Coco* (1969), a vehicle for Katherine Hepburn directed by Michael Benthall. With both star and director working on their first musical, Bennett's role was very large. He choreographed dances around a largely stationary, charismatic star, and worked on book scenes; Mandelbaum called *Coco* Bennett's 'unofficial directorial debut'.[25] He gained valuable experience in the concept musical *Company* (1970), working with Hal Prince. Bennett had considerable influence on the show's staging, especially in the musical numbers, such as 'You Could Drive a Person Crazy', 'Side By Side By Side', 'What We Would Do Without You', and 'Tick Tock', Donna McKechnie's memorable solo dance. Bennett wanted to direct, but worked with Prince on *Follies* (1971), this time billed as co-director. Reviewers recognised his important contribution to the show's staging, especially in numbers like 'Who's That Woman?'. Walter Kerr wrote in the *Sunday Times*: 'Michael Bennett's dazzling dance memories and perpetually musical staging are as seamlessly woven into [Sondheim's musical] personality as they are into Prince's immensely creative general direction.'[26]

Bennett had become highly regarded for his imaginative staging ideas and was ready to direct on his own. Before *A Chorus Line* he directed two non-musical plays and *Seesaw* (1973), a troubled musical that he took over in Detroit and brought to Broadway for a respectable ten-month run. Bennett received full artistic control over the show and brought in his usual assistant choreographer Bob Avian along with the dancers and choreographers Tommy Tune, Baayork Lee, Thommie Walsh and others, several of whom later worked in *A Chorus Line*. *Seesaw* had a successful national tour and made Bennett a major player in the Broadway community.

A Chorus Line started with Bennett's inspiration to do a show about dancers, a group he did not feel received its due on Broadway.[27] Along with Tony Stevens and Michon Peacock, with whom Bennett had worked in *Seesaw*, he arranged a meeting with eighteen colleagues on 18 January 1974. It was an extraordinary evening on which many felt moved to tell their life stories.[28] Bennett recorded the tales, as well as the conversations at the second such session on 8 February. After initial work with the tapes by Stevens, Peacock and the dancer-writer Nicholas Dante (whose story became the character Paul in the show), Bennett bought the rights of the raw material for *A Chorus Line*.

Bennett, Avian and Dante held more interviews and framed the show as an audition where dancers were encouraged to tell their stories. Early in the process Bennett decided to cast the show before even writing it and sold the workshop idea to Joseph Papp of the New York Shakespeare Festival. Papp agreed to pay Bennett and the dancers each $100 per week and let them work in his Newman Theater. Workshops had been used in plays for years, but *A Chorus Line* was the first musical produced through this method.

Bennett assembled his creative team. The co-writers were Bennett and Dante. Marvin Hamlisch became the composer and Edward Kleban the lyricist, both writing songs in the workshop. The first workshop, beginning in August 1974, lasted five weeks of fourteen-hour days, and after auditions included several of Bennett's favourite dancers. At the end of the workshop, however, they had only staged a few numbers. A second workshop began in late December, for which Bennett brought in writer James Kirkwood to help Dante with the script. The second workshop yielded a workable show. Kirkwood recalled the process:

> The material – book, music, lyrics, and staging concepts – changed daily … the show became structured and focused. The key to this was the invention of the character of Zach. In the first workshop, there had been an amorphous God-like figure billed only as 'Voice.' There was now an actual director character leading the audition, one who would soon be given a past involving one or more of the characters.[29]

Along with the character Zach came Cassie, his ex-lover, a small plot around which the remainder of the show could form. The workshop was highly collaborative, contributing to the final product's seamlessness. It is impossible to sort out who was responsible for each contribution. For example, Bennett often asked another dancer, such as Avian, McKechnie or Baayork Lee, to design steps that he could edit.

Formal rehearsals began in March 1975 with the first preview on 16 April 1975. The buzz around Broadway was that the show was a sure hit, and tickets at the tiny Newman Theater (299 seats) were scarce. The public remained infatuated with the show through the official off-Broadway opening on 21 May 1975 and the move to the Shubert Theatre for its Broadway opening on 19 October 1975. *A Chorus Line* ran for fifteen years, paving the way for the megamusicals of the 1980s and 1990s, but without the huge stage effects that mark many of those shows.

Bennett brought to A *Chorus Line* rich Broadway experience as a dancer, choreographer and director, and the vision to forge an unconventional show. Placing the story in the context of an audition gave the audience the feeling of peeking backstage, even though the device was essentially unrealistic. Of course no Broadway director would have cared about the life stories of auditioning dancers, but these real-life vignettes did help to give the show a sense of truth.

Although some of his signature numbers in other shows involved elaborate costumes and sets, Bennett realised that *A Chorus Line* would work best with a nearly bare stage and rehearsal clothes as costumes. He satisfied the audience's craving for Broadway glitz in the closing number, 'One', performed by the entire cast in full costume, but that seemed appropriate because the chorus had been chosen and it was time for the show to open.

The show's intensity came from its rapid pace and lack of intermission. In earlier shows Bennett had used 'cinematic' techniques of directing, fading from one scene to another through action on stage, as in the dancing secretaries between scenes in *Promises, Promises*. Such continuity and rapid pacing has long been part of the musical comedy, and was a major part of George Abbott's work in the 1930s. Prince and Bennett used the technique in *Follies*, and in *A Chorus Line* one finds its full realisation. The curtain never does go down during the show. Bennett had found success with montage scenes before, and designed his masterpiece in the long 'Hello Twelve, Hello Thirteen, Hello Love' (Martin Gottfried notes that it is one-fifth of the length of the script[30]), where the characters explore the pains of adolescence. Much of the show's action seems to occur in real time, a huge tribute to Bennett's direction.

Another major factor in the show's success is its saturation with dance and the various levels at which the audience perceives the dancing. One expects dancers to demonstrate their talent at an audition, so the audience accepts it as the show's basic language, and revels in watching those auditioning learn the steps, some succeeding and others cursing their efforts. Dance enters the characters' stories as they are told, such as the delightful tap dance 'I Can Do That', in which Mike tells of his early and natural talent. Finally, dance allows characters to express deeper feelings, especially Cassie in 'The Music and the Mirror', McKechnie's memorable solo number in which she shows that Cassie has the talent to be a solo dancer, even if that career has not worked out. Soon thereafter, the audience learns the difference between solo and chorus dancing, as Zach berates her for not dancing in unison with the others.[31]

Sometimes lost in the excitement about the show is the music, but this is partly because of the convincing way that songs and dance music are integrated with the rest of the show. In an essentially plotless musical a song cannot advance the narrative, but it can fit in with the dramatic concept of the moment, and all songs do. Most help tell a character's story, the only real exceptions being 'What I Did For Love' and 'One'. Some have criticised 'What I Did For Love' as Marvin Hamlisch's crass attempt at a hit song. The lyricist, Edward Kleban, hated it and wanted something different,[32] but the song is meaningful. After telling the most dramatic story of any of the characters, Paul falls and re-injures a knee. His career might be over. Zach asks the dancers what they will do when they can no longer dance. Diana's answer is this song, which, in the musical language of a 1970s pop anthem, answers the question by stating that one works for love of the art.

Like most Broadway scores, Hamlisch's effort in *A Chorus Line* is eclectic, including a number of styles from twentieth-century popular music. 'I Can Do That', a tap number, has the rhythmic character of 1930s jazz with melodic blues touches. 'One', in the style of a 1930s soft-shoe, is a production number from the show the dancers are auditioning for, and excerpts from it sound throughout the score. 'At the Ballet' alternates between a rock beat and a waltz with effective musical representation of speech rhythms in the rock section. The montage 'Hello Twelve, Hello Thirteen, Hello Love' is especially eclectic, befitting its length and complexity, with many characters interjecting segments of their stories. 'Nothing', part of the montage, combines an easy rock feel and the sound of a traditional Broadway ballad. The end of the montage borrows much from the sound of gospel music. 'The Music and the Mirror' provides another short tour of 1970s commercial music, moving mostly between jazz and funk.

It could be said that Hamlisch's score is firmly rooted in the 1970s (as is obvious from the instrumentation on the original cast recording), but most Broadway scores are products of their time. *A Chorus Line* probably carries the deepest meaning for Americans who grew up in the two or three decades following World War II. Bennett made a show about himself and other people willing to make sacrifices to work in their chosen fields.

Few who saw *A Chorus Line* were professional dancers, but almost everyone understands what it means to want something as badly as those dancers wanted a job. Despite his other shows, the most successful of which was *Dreamgirls* from 1981 (another masterpiece of integration of drama, music and dance), Bennett spent much of the remainder of his life overseeing *A Chorus Line*. He assembled touring companies and ensured that each company maintained the requisite energy and quality. A revival of *A Chorus Line*, directed by Bob Avian and with the choreography re-staged by Baayork Lee, opened on Broadway in October 2006.

Tommy Tune is another important Broadway choreographer-director. Born in Wichita Falls, Texas in 1939, Tune danced in a touring company of *Irma La Douce* in the early 1960s. He choreographed the touring version of *Canterbury Tales* in 1969 and appeared in films. His first major Broadway credit was the number 'It's Not Where You Start (It's Where You Finish)' in *Seesaw*, which Michael Bennett allowed Tune to choreograph. After five years without Broadway work, Tune began a string of hits as choreographer-director of *The Best Little Whorehouse in Texas* (1978), which ran for 1,584 performances. Tune's next success was sharing the choreography credit with Thommie Walsh in the New York version of the British show *A Day in Hollywood, A Night in the Ukraine* (1980). In 1982 he directed *Nine*, an adaptation of Federico Fellini's film *8 1/2*. Walsh again shared the choreography credit and Tune's innovative staging won a Tony. Tune won the Tony for best actor and shared the award for best choreography with Walsh for *My One and Only* (1983), a substantial reworking of *Funny Face* (1927). Tune then won Tonys for both choreography and direction in *Grand Hotel* (1989) and *The Will Rogers Follies* (1991). In both of these shows, Tune demonstrated his talent for mining the history of American entertainment for ideas and styles and then adding his own special energy and panache.

Choreographers and directors continue to strive to make the songs and dances of a Broadway score an integral part of the plot rather than a distraction from it. Examples of successful recent efforts were *Ragtime* (1998), directed by Frank Galati with choreography by Graciela Daniele, and *Wicked* (2003), directed by Joe Mantello with choreography by Wayne Cilento. Although *Wicked* is not a huge dancing show, Cilento's contribution to the stage movement is very important to the overall appeal. The road from Victor Herbert's *The Lady of the Slipper* to the present is long and winding, but most stops along the way were attempts to improve the artistic integration of the Broadway musical: a seminal trend in the genre's history.

13 From *Hair* to *Rent* : is 'rock' a four-letter word on Broadway?

SCOTT WARFIELD

Among the etymological legacies of the 1960s is the once ubiquitous family of musical categories distinguished by the word 'rock' somewhere within a compound name. Today one seldom hears such terms as 'jazz rock' or 'symphonic rock', but on Broadway the term 'rock musical' has retained currency, either as a show's formal subtitle or as an appellation casually used by critics and others to describe a particular work. Yet despite widespread use of the term over the past four decades, no scholarly or even semi-formal definition of the 'rock musical' has ever appeared in print. Instead, the 'rock musical' has remained an extremely pliable category, capable of embracing a wide range of characteristics.

Despite the lack of rigour with which the term has been used through the years, a number of common features identify 'rock musicals'. Virtually anyone who has written on the history of the musical has remarked – positively or negatively – on the first appearances of rock-influenced music on Broadway in the mid-1960s.[1] *Hair*, subtitled 'An American Tribal Love-Rock Musical', has been universally accepted as the first example of the genre. Almost immediately after that landmark show, other works appeared with similar subtitles, but there were also shows with rock scores that were never identified as such by their producers. In fact the latter case soon predominated, and consequently, many New York critics began to employ the term 'rock musical' to identify any stage work with even the slightest hint of popular styles.[2] Even twenty-five years after *Hair*, the closest thing to a definition of the 'rock musical' was John Rockwell's brief discussion in his article on 'Rock Opera' in *The New Grove Dictionary of Opera*. For Rockwell, both the 'rock opera' and the 'rock musical' were simply variants of their parent genres 'in which the musical idiom is rock and roll'. Following the lead of New York newspaper critics, however, Rockwell identified two Broadway shows, *Godspell* and *The Wiz*, as 'rock musicals', even though neither was ever promoted as such. Similarly, Stanley Richards' *Great Rock Musicals* lumps together a disparate group of shows – *The Wiz*, *Two Gentlemen of Verona*, *Grease*, *Jesus Christ Superstar*, *Your Own Thing*, *Hair*, *Tommy* and *Promenade* – as the leading examples of this genre.[3]

Despite the casual and often contradictory usages of the term, one can identify a number of New York productions generally associated with the 'rock musical' and from them identify a series of categories and traits that might define this genre. Avoiding temporarily the question of precisely what the music in a rock musical is like – while acknowledging that rock (at any point in its history) differs significantly from Broadway's traditional sound – four distinct categories of shows that use rock music emerge. First are those works – such as *Hair* and *Your Own Thing* – that were identified by their creators and producers as 'rock musicals' either by subtitles or in advertisements. A second category consists of works that began as concept albums – such as *Jesus Christ Superstar* – which were marketed and sold to fans of rock music before they were ever staged. The third and most arbitrary category consists of works – such as *Godspell* – that used rock styles, either in whole or in part, yet were never called 'rock musicals' by their creators. At the same time many shows that some critics label 'rock musicals' have music that is clearly not rock. Fourth are musicals – such as *Grease* – that emulate earlier styles of rock 'n' roll. This category then leads to shows that simply appropriate old songs for their nostalgic value, as in *Smokey Joe's Café*. These four types are not rigid, of course, as some shows straddle categories.

The first musical to include songs in a rock 'n' roll style was *Bye Bye Birdie* (1960). The product of Broadway newcomers Charles Strouse and Lee Adams, it revolved around the televised farewell of Conrad Birdie, a rock 'n' roll star who had been drafted into the army. The character and plot were shamelessly modelled on a conflation of Elvis Presley's own 1958 departure into the military, his staged farewell and his earlier television appearances. Although the show-within-a-show storyline included two tame rock 'n' roll numbers, *Bye Bye Birdie* owed its success to more conventional Broadway elements, including a lighthearted plot and a good variety of tunes in traditional musical comedy styles. The role of Birdie, as created by Dick Gautier in a lamé jumpsuit, was also just a caricature of Elvis, devoid of the physical and vocal sexuality that the model clearly had, and thus, despite its few rock 'n' roll elements, *Bye Bye Birdie* was not really a rock musical.

Even though *Bye Bye Birdie* proved that rock 'n' roll could be used in a musical, it was seven years before rock returned to Broadway. The reason for this gap was doubtless the declining economic conditions for New York theatres. Beginning with a strike in 1960 that raised labour costs significantly, Broadway experienced a series of disastrous seasons that reached its nadir in 1967 with the fewest new shows produced in Broadway's recorded history. In those strained financial times, essentially conservative producers grew even more so and refused to back anything but escapist fare aimed at middle-aged businessmen and theatre parties from the suburbs. Such dated material exacerbated the problem by alienating youthful customers, who felt that Broadway was disconnected from the fundamental changes then being wrought in American society.

Despite Broadway's inherent conservatism, the New York theatre community in the 1960s did include many devoted to revitalising the form and making it more relevant to modern life. One of the most innovative groups was Ellen Stewart's La Mama Experimental Theatre Club, the company that originated *Hair*.[4] Although myth would have it that *Hair* was a fluke creation by neophytes, James Rado and Gerome Ragni were both young veterans of the New York stage, and the classically trained Galt MacDermot was a successful composer of jazz and pop tunes. In 1965, Rado and Ragni found themselves drawn into the anti-war movement, which they studied in the youth culture of New York's Greenwich Village. Over the next two years they used La Mama's workshops to transform their observations into a rough script that was soon making the rounds of New York producers.

Joseph Papp agreed to mount a limited run of the music-less musical to demonstrate the social relevance of his new non-profit Public Theater. MacDermot came aboard to write songs, and in about two weeks he composed the first score of *Hair*. Gerald Freeman, the Public Theater's Artistic Director, reworked the material into a loose story that centred on the drafting of a young man named Claude and his indecision over whether to fight in Vietnam. That character stands in contrast to Berger, a high school dropout who leads a hippy commune. Instead of a logical narrative, *Hair* was more of a rambling diatribe against all authority figures and a glorification of drugs, free love, racial tolerance, respect for the individual and environmentalism. The most passionate moment came in the penultimate scene of Act 2, a stylised set piece that railed against the futility of war. The story ends with Claude accepting his call into the military, followed by his death.

When *Hair* was premiered on 2 December 1967 as the Public Theater's inaugural production, it was set for an eight-week run, but Michael Butler, a wealthy liberal with anti-war sentiments, wanted the show seen by a wider audience and thus took over as producer. The Papp production then moved uptown to a discotheque called the Cheetah for 45 additional performances and from there to the Biltmore Theatre, where it opened on 29 April 1968 and ran for 1,742 performances. Before it moved to Broadway, however, important changes were made to accommodate the production to a larger theatre and to sharpen its anti-establishment message. MacDermot composed thirteen new songs and Tom O'Horgan, one of the driving forces in La Mama, came in to direct.

Using the techniques of avant-garde theatre, O'Horgan sought to involve the audience as much as possible in the action by eliminating the proscenium's fourth wall. The stage had no curtain, and cast members were continually moving into and throughout the audience. The band, enlarged

Plate 18 The original production of *Hair* in 1968. Shelley Plimpton is on the mattress and the creators of the show, James Rado and Gerome Ragni, are in the group over her to the rear left. Jonathan Kramer is on all fours and in the foreground on the right is Hiram Keller.

from the five-piece rock group used in Papp's production by the addition of four horns, was placed on stage. To be heard above the amplified ensemble, singers used hand-held microphones that they simply passed from one performer to another. To maintain naturalness, cast members were encouraged to improvise, and everyone in the company was expected to be able to cover any role on short notice. To emphasise the lifestyle of the hippies, everyday language, including profanity, was used freely, and the first act ended with a now famous nude scene, which audience members sometimes joined. In short, there was to be no theatrical artificiality in O'Horgan's conception; rather, the show was to be more like a spontaneous 'happening'.

Hair's music was quite unlike anything that had ever appeared on Broadway. While MacDermot's songs were not cutting-edge rock, his arrangements were all in an unmistakable, amplified rock style, with prominent bass lines and strong backbeats. At the same time, nearly every song used the verse–chorus format long favoured on Broadway and eschewed the blues and other simple circular progressions from early rock 'n' roll. MacDermot also used the harmonic language of mid-1960s rock, which stood in stark contrast to the often complex and sophisticated harmonies that had been heard on Broadway for years. Remarkably, at least five songs from

Hair – 'Aquarius', 'Hair', 'Easy to Be Hard', 'Good Morning Starshine', and 'Let the Sunshine In' – all became US Top Forty hits. Indeed, 'Aquarius' became a virtual anthem for the youth movement in the late 1960s. Yet although MacDermot captured the sound of mid-1960s rock, his music remained within the bounds of what most Broadway audiences would accept, which was a remarkable achievement given the wide gap between Broadway and rock at the time. The majority of *Hair*'s songs are quite tuneful and many have remained pop standards, even if the show itself has aged poorly.[5]

The extraordinary financial success of *Hair*, which had been produced for less than a third of the typical $500,000 cost of a musical in the mid-1960s, spawned the inevitable imitations. Within a season of *Hair*'s premiere, two new rock musicals were playing off-Broadway, and by the early 1970s more than a dozen shows with pop/rock scores had been produced on Broadway. Yet only one explicitly labelled 'rock musical' lasted a full season, while a few other shows with rock-tinged scores succeeded in varying degrees.

Your Own Thing, like *Hair*, was premiered off-Broadway and remained there for its entire 933-performance run. Its plot, loosely adapted from *Twelfth Night*, concerned a marooned rock band in search of a gig, and the confusion between Shakespeare's twins was reflected in gender-crossing hairstyles and clothing. Both the cast's psychedelic costumes and the dialogue's youthful slang date the production almost to the year. The show's title, in fact, was a catchphrase of the day for an individual's right to be free from the crush of society's ways. Again as in *Hair*, an on-stage rock band provided the music. Unlike *Hair*'s score, however, the music of *Your Own Thing* – in the unmistakable electric style of late-1960s rock – was utterly lacking in individuality, and when this second rock musical closed, it vanished without a trace. *Your Own Thing* reflected its era's preoccupation with the under-thirty generation, yet with its emphasis on young love – as opposed to the serious issues confronted in *Hair* – the show was closer to the old-fashioned boy–girl musicals of the 1930s and 1940s. Finally, *Your Own Thing* cost a mere $45,000 to produce. When the New York Critics' Circle named it Best Show of 1968, producers surely noticed the substantial returns possible from the minimal investments that a rock musical required.[6]

In the five seasons after *Hair*, several other shows with rock music (or marketed as such) were premiered on or off Broadway, with those labelled explicitly as 'rock musicals' enjoying the least success. *Salvation*, New York's third rock musical, began downtown in the spring of 1969 as a loosely structured rock concert with dialogue that parodied a revival meeting. When it moved uptown that autumn, critics hailed it as the 'son of *Hair*' and Broadway's 'second rock musical' (*Your Own Thing* had meanwhile remained off-Broadway).[7] *Salvation*'s relative success enabled its co-creators, Peter

Link and C. C. Courtney, to create a fully fledged musical two seasons later. *Earl of Ruston* – billed as a 'country rock musical' – told the story of their uncle Earl, the town 'crazy' of Ruston, Louisiana. Critics faulted the story for its lack of development, and the music – played by the obligatory on-stage rock band – was considered a 'disappointment' after *Salvation*. *Earl of Ruston* folded after less than a week in May 1971.[8] The next two rock musicals suffered similar fates. *Soon*, the story of a rock musician who sells out for commercial gain, lasted just three performances in January 1971, and *Hard Job Being God*, attempting to trade on *Godspell*'s success, closed after only six shows in May 1972. Both were panned for poor music and weak books.[9]

After *Hair*, Galt MacDermot wrote three more scores for Broadway. In 1971, Joseph Papp mounted *Two Gentlemen of Verona*, another update of Shakespeare, although less explicitly contemporary than *Your Own Thing*. Critics raved about the production, but only a few singled out MacDermot's music, which Clive Barnes described as a mix of 'rock, lyricism [and] Caribbean patter' and 'more subtly shaded and more variegated than his score for *Hair*'.[10] MacDermot's two attempts in the following season, *Dude* and *Via Galactica*, both suffered from expensive, troubled productions. The score for *Dude* was praised, but the music for *Via Galactica* was seen as yet another step downward for MacDermot, who never had another Broadway hit.[11]

Following all of these failures, the designation 'rock musical' fell into disuse just as rock and pop styles began to find a place in New York's theatres. *Oh! Calcutta!*, a long-running revue first produced in 1969 and remembered now only for its gratuitous nudity, had a small on-stage band playing an eclectic mix of contemporary sounds that included rock. *The Last Sweet Days of Isaac* was a 1970 off-Broadway success that had a four-piece band playing 'soft rock'.[12] Two other shows, one a quick failure and the other a major success, demonstrated the growing symbiosis between Broadway and the recording industry. *Georgy* (1970) was an adaptation of the 1966 motion picture *Georgy Girl* and its popular title song. George Fischoff's music for the Broadway show was described as 'mediocre, an easy-listening kind of rock crammed into a show-tune style, orchestrated with disinterest', and *Georgy* closed after only four nights.[13] Burt Bacharach's score for *Promises, Promises* was certainly not rock, but the show's title song did do well on the pop charts. The production's real innovation, however, was in the pit, where every member of the band, including four female back-up singers, was miked. A sound engineer controlled the mix, which was sent out to the audience through loudspeakers on either side of the house. Audiences quickly came to expect theatrical performances to match the sound of commercial recordings.[14]

Interestingly, the only successful original rock musical that premiered in New York in the early 1970s was never explicitly promoted as one.[15] When it moved uptown in 1976, *Godspell* was roundly panned for its saccharine book, weak score, amateurish staging and lack of dance movement, but after 2,118 performances off-Broadway, the show was essentially critic-proof.[16] John-Michael Tebelak had first drafted this modernisation of the Gospel of St Matthew for his master's degree, and it was subsequently reworked at La Mama's. There the original music was discarded, and a newcomer, Stephen Schwartz, was brought in to compose a replacement score.

Tebelak had envisaged *Godspell* as something for teenagers, and the show's relentlessly upbeat tone and childlike innocence were perfect for its intended audience. The minimalist set vaguely resembled a bare schoolyard playground; the staging was just a series of sketches in which the small company acted out Biblical parables in imitations of television shows, comic strips and circus acts. The book made frequent references to current events, and the cast – costumed in brightly coloured rags and clown-like facial paint – often impersonated well-known performers of recent years. All of this also appealed to adults who might not have cared for the more realistic and scruffy hippies of *Hair.*

Schwartz's music provided a good match for the production's celebratory mood. Although the band was yet another four-piece rock ensemble, the addition of tambourines and acoustic instruments often gave the music the feel of folk-rock and even gospel. The repetitive lyrics, mirrored in the simple forms of the songs, helped to create the atmosphere of a revival meeting or a church service. 'Prepare Ye (The Way of the Lord)', for instance, is nothing but a repeated single phrase, while 'Day by Day' consists of only a few motivic fragments arranged into a standard song form. Many songs also begin slowly with quiet accompaniments, but quickly transform themselves into energetic gospel numbers through increases in tempo, the addition of drums and amplified instruments, and the use of improvisatory call-and-response patterns. The first-act finale, 'Light of the World', dispenses with the sedate opening, and instead launches itself immediately into the sound of black soul music that builds continuously until the curtain. In contrast, the strong country beat of 'We Beseech Thee' evokes the feeling of a white revival meeting, while various other easy-listening styles and even a soft-shoe number, 'All for the Best', are also part of the show. Despite this stylistic eclecticism, the score holds together well in the youthful celebration of spirituality that permeates *Godspell.*

Only a few months after *Godspell* began its off-Broadway run, a second youth-oriented rock musical with a religious theme opened in New York and thereby highlighted two emerging theatrical trends. With over two million copies of its double album sold long before its stage production opened, *Jesus Christ Superstar* (music by Andrew Lloyd Webber, lyrics by Tim Rice) abandoned the usual Broadway marketing model, in which ticket sales were the primary source of revenue and recordings only souvenirs, and instead followed the practice of pop music, in which live performances promoted recordings. *Jesus Christ Superstar* also reflected the rise of progressive rock in the late 1960s. With a sonic palette that admitted any sound source up to a symphony orchestra and an expanded harmonic vocabulary that ranged from nineteenth-century Romanticism to Stravinsky, progressive rock was able to sustain interest for the album-length works that this new style promoted. The same applied to a Broadway show.[17]

The New York production was a note-for-note rendition of the album and included all the elements of progressive rock. The heart of the show's sound is a six-piece rock ensemble, frequently augmented by a small orchestra on the recording or by synthesisers and a few horns in the theatre. The musical style, although strongly influenced by rock, already reflects Andrew Lloyd Webber's trademark eclecticism. The overture is a microcosm of his technique. Beginning with a solo electric guitar, it proceeds like any Broadway overture through a series of excerpts from the show. There are frequent shifts from rock timbres to synthesised sounds, mixtures of rock and traditional instruments, and ultimately a symphonic finale. In the show itself, a hard rock tune like 'Judas' Death' follows the campy 'King Herod's Song', which is in the style of a vaudeville number, and a soft rock tune like 'Everything's Alright' leads into a scene that includes recitative mixed with rock. One innovative element for Broadway is the frequent use of irregular metres, such as 5/4 in 'Everything's Alright' or 7/8 in 'The Temple'. In setting every bit of text to music, Lloyd Webber also went far beyond the alternation of spoken and sung passages typical of most Broadway shows, and for its use of recitative *Jesus Christ Superstar* stands closer to a rock *opera*, as the recording was billed.

The early 1970s was a high-water mark for the rock musical. The successful runs of *Godspell* and *Jesus Christ Superstar* proved that *Hair* was no fluke and thus solidified rock's position on Broadway. Beginning in the 1970s, an ever-increasing number of shows had rock-influenced scores, yet very few of them – and no commercially successful shows for nearly two decades – were ever promoted as 'rock musicals'. Simultaneously, the use of the term 'rock musical' by critics declined but never quite disappeared. Usually the term was applied to a show with a small ensemble and, presumably, music that approximated a rock or pop sound. For instance, *The Lieutenant*, a now obscure work from 1974–5 that dealt with the Vietnam War's My Lai massacre and closed after only nine performances despite much critical acclaim, was always described as either a 'rock opera' or a 'rock musical' in theatre listings, reviews and its own advertisements. Nothing was ever mentioned about the sound of its music, however.[18]

From the 1970s onwards usage of the term 'rock musical' by critics became quite inconsistent. In 1975, *The Wiz* arrived on Broadway with a score that pulsed with the sounds of soul, gospel and other black pop and rock styles, and it was followed six years later by another musical built on the Motown sound, *Dreamgirls.* Neither was ever widely identified as a 'rock musical', although a few reviews of *The Wiz* did describe its score as rock or rock-related.[19] Reviews of *Dreamgirls*, however, said almost nothing about its music, as critics chose instead to focus on the show's lavish costumes, big dance numbers and high-tech stagecraft.

Between those two productions were two 1978 shows that some critics and music theatre historians consider rock musicals, even if others hesitate to use that label. The occasional identification of *I'm Getting My Act Together and Taking It On the Road* as a rock musical may simply stem from its plot, which concerns a female singer preparing to tour with a rock band, and the fact that its soft-rock and pop score was played by a small ensemble. The other show, *Runaways*, was a story of adolescents forced to fend for themselves on the streets, and at least one reviewer compared it favourably with *Hair*, without calling it a rock musical. Its music included everything from disco and salsa to blues and country-and-western, and was performed by a six-piece ensemble that was based around a piano–guitar–drum trio.[20] Both shows, moreover, had originally been developed as limited-run off-Broadway productions by Joseph Papp.

Clearly more than just the sound of a show identified it as a rock musical. Small guitar-and-drum ensembles playing contemporary musical styles were a significant trait, and several failed rock musicals had nothing in common with *Hair* and *Jesus Christ Superstar* except for their small bands playing amplified music. At least part of a rock musical's identity seemed to derive from rock's status as an 'outsider' genre. Plots that dealt with issues important to young people in the 1970s – the Vietnam War (*Hair* and *The Lieutenant*), spiritual values (*Jesus Christ Superstar* and *Godspell*), self-identity (*The Last Sweet Days of Isaac* and *I'm Getting My Act Together*) and the problems of growing up (*Runaways*) – also marked a show as something beyond the usual Broadway fare. Such topics did not usually attract financing from established Broadway producers, and thus many rock musicals were born and nurtured in places like La Mama's and Papp's Public Theater. In contrast, *The Wiz* and *Dreamgirls* were both traditional, big-budget Broadway shows in slick productions.

The basic problem for rock musical composers was an old one, which Walter Kerr, the *New York Times*'s senior critic, summed up in a review of *Dude*:

> Rock musicals, if they are to sustain themselves as genuine theatre pieces
> rather than arena concerts, are going to have to meet the obligations earlier
> musicals have accepted, always with difficulty, often with pain. Music *is* the
> ultimate making of any musical. But the music must have something to
> stand on, something other than its own beat to move it, something to
> demand one particular song rather than another at a particular moment,
> [and] hopefully something in the way of wit to keep it company.[21]

Thus, although a few shows may have succeeded on the novelty of contemporary sounds, the key to a winning production remained the integration
of rock music with the book and the staging. Reviews of failed rock musicals in the 1970s suggest that there was often no compelling reason for
the use of rock in a particular show and, moreover, that the music itself
was frequently not very good. Admittedly, those productions usually also
had serious problems with their books, staging and other elements, but it
is almost impossible to find a failed rock musical in which critics praised
the music and condemned the rest of the show.[22] In short, the fate of a
rock musical hung chiefly on its music, which had to be both good – or at
least inoffensive – and relevant in some way to the action on stage. Some
Broadway producers, however, seemed to treat rock music as just another
element that could be grafted onto a big-budget musical, and the results
were sometimes spectacular failures.

Chess, a failure on Broadway in 1988, is a good example of a production
that appropriated rock as its musical idiom for no urgent reason. Its plot
concerns a championship chess match between an American and a Russian
during the Cold War. The work, with lyrics by Tim Rice and music by Benny
Andersson and Björn Ulvaeus (the male half of the Swedish pop vocal group
ABBA), was initially issued in 1984 as a concept album and then performed
throughout Europe in a concert version that generated two hits on European
pop charts. Two years later, a London production began a three-year run,
but in New York, *Chess* was a $6.6 million disappointment.

Although the score included a variety of musical styles, rock numbers in
ABBA's trademark style – primarily power ballads and up-tempo songs with
a strong dance beat – predominated. With no gradations in energy levels, the
result, according to Frank Rich, was that 'for three hours, the characters on
stage yell at one another to rock music'.[23] For instance, when the American,
Freddie Trumper, first meets the reporters ('Press Conference') near the
beginning of Act 1, the accompaniment is a strong rock beat, synthesisers
and snarling guitars, and his vocal line ascends regularly to its upper limits.[24]
The purpose of this scene is merely to introduce Trumper and reveal his
arrogance, but such an intense vocal display so early in the show leaves
no room for later climaxes. Despite this sort of dramatic miscalculation,
Chess contains some of the best pop/rock music ever used on the stage. 'One

Night in Bangkok' – the curtain-raiser for Act 2 in London, and a production number in Act 1 on Broadway – is a first-rate disco tune, and 'I Know Him So Well' – the show's first European hit song – is a fine rock ballad.

Such keen interest on Broadway in older, familiar rock and pop styles can be traced back to at least 1972, when *Grease,* 'a new '50's rock 'n' roll musical', premiered. The story, set in 1959, was a nostalgic look back at 'greasers' and their girls, built around a simple teenage love story. After the turbulent 1960s, *Grease* was a gentle parody of almost idyllic times, with a series of faux fifties tunes that poked fun at the teenage angst of that era. The show's success, despite mediocre reviews, was extraordinary, and *Grease* played out the decade on Broadway. Once it was apparent that imitations of old rock 'n' roll could succeed on Broadway, the genuine article came into the theatre in Tom O'Horgan's 1974 off-Broadway staging of the Beatles' album as *Sgt Pepper's Lonely Hearts Club Band on the Road,* followed by *Beatlemania* (1977), a curious mixture of concert and theatre that ran for two years on Broadway. In 1982, Dick Clark tried to mount a broader retrospective, but *Rock and Roll! The First 5,000 Years* closed in only a week. In 1989, *Buddy: The Buddy Holly Story* opened in London and a year later came to Broadway. Marketed as a 'bio-musical' and using Holly's music, the first half of the show traced his rise, while the second act recreated his final concert. Another big success in the 1990s, *Smokey Joe's Café* was an expensively produced revue of songs by Leiber and Stoller, perhaps the most famous rock 'n' roll songwriting team of the 1950s and 60s.

By the 1990s, rock – or at least a conservative form of it – was in widespread use on Broadway, making the rift between theatrical and popular music narrower than it had been at any time since just before the premiere of *Hair* in 1967.[25] It was again possible to hear songs in a Broadway theatre that were also regularly played on radio and easily available in stores, and major rock musicians were now courted by Broadway. In the mid-1990s, two veteran pop/rock songwriters of the first rank, Randy Newman and Paul Simon, each tried unsuccessfully to compose a Broadway musical. Newman's *Faust,* described as a 'rock 'n' roll travesty of Goethe's poem', died in 1996 after try-outs in San Diego and Chicago, but even before the first production was mounted, a CD was issued, with Newman joined by rock legends James Taylor, Don Henley, Linda Ronstadt and Bonnie Raitt.[26] Although eagerly anticipated on Broadway, Simon's *The Capeman* – described in one review as a 'pop-operatic retelling of a street gang murder in 1959' – struggled through its previews only to be savaged by the critics on opening night.[27] The *New York Times* called the show 'one solemn, hopelessly confused drone' and went on to comment on its twin problems of integrating pop sounds into a theatrical work and the frequent lack of stage movement. As with *Faust,* a CD, made by Simon and top session musicians, was issued before the stage premiere. Purely as a recording, *The Capeman* stands with Simon's best work, but his laid-back mix of 1950s doo-wop and Latin rhythms lacks even the occasional energetic number that might have suggested some striking stage movements.

In addition to those two well-financed failures, Broadway in the 1990s saw the frequent return of older pop and rock materials. In 1998, *Footloose*, an adaptation of the 1984 motion picture of the same name, began a nearly two-year run, and in the autumn of 1999, a stage version of the 1977 motion picture *Saturday Night Fever* premiered with music just slightly revised from the Bee Gees' film score. The following year, another relic from the 1970s, *The Rocky Horror Show*, which had played briefly and unsuccessfully on Broadway in 1975, returned to New York on the strength of its classic cult film version of nearly the same name. Yet another musical that found new life in revival is Willy Russell's *Blood Brothers*. When it first opened in London in 1983, it ran for only eight months, but successful regional productions eventually led to a 1988 London revival that was still running in the spring of 2008. A New York production opened to poor reviews in 1993, but lasted for 840 performances on the strength of its word-of-mouth.[28] *Blood Brothers* has been a quiet phenomenon with younger listeners, especially teenagers, who apparently identify with the story of twins separated at birth whose reunion years later has tragic consequences. The youthful vogue for this piece has doubtless been helped by recordings that feature such pop stars as Kiki Dee, David and Shaun Cassidy, and even the 1960s pop icon Petula Clark, despite critical opinion that Russell's music is simplistic and derivative.

Finally, the continuing popularity of ABBA's music has led to one of the most unusual musicals in Broadway's history. The book of *Mamma Mia!* – a newly invented story about a young girl's impending marriage – was written specifically to showcase twenty-seven ABBA hits from the 1970s and 80s. Less than a year after its 1999 London premiere, which recouped its costs in less than seven months, two productions were touring North America, one of which settled in October 2001 at the Winter Garden Theatre (former home of *Cats*) in New York. Five years later, one American production remained on the road, while another played in Las Vegas. Worldwide there were eleven European productions, two in South Africa, and an Asian tour on the road. Sell-out houses on the road, strong album sales and an advertising campaign that includes a state-of-the-art website suggest that *Mamma Mia!* may rival *Cats* and other Lloyd Webber shows both in longevity and financial gain.[29]

The profitability of *Mamma Mia!* has encouraged several productions in the new millennium that simply recycle old pop and rock tunes. Two of the more successful examples are *Movin' Out*, a dance revue based on the songs of Billy Joel, which won the 2003 Tony award for Twyla Tharp's choreography, and *Jersey Boys*, a well-received show built around the music of Frankie

Valli and the Four Seasons.[30] This trend of constructing shows around old pop tunes has led to the emergence in recent years of the term 'juke-box musical', often intended derisively.[31] Three expensive flops in 2005 – *All Shook Up*, based on songs popularised by Elvis Presley, the eponymous *Lennon*, and *Good Vibrations*, a show based on the music of the Beach Boys, which some critics name dubiously as the worst show in the history of Broadway – have only reinforced the low reputation of this nostalgia-driven genre.[32]

While it is doubtful that any of these shows – from *Grease* to *Mamma Mia!* to *Good Vibrations* – truly deserves the designation of 'rock musical', all of them have been described somewhere as such. This linguistic impre-cision, moreover, confirms the desire of producers to exploit the popu-larity of rock, while simultaneously suppressing its rebellious spirit and most extreme sounds. Instead of the real thing, Broadway has offered up a diluted pop sound and even an air of nostalgia that appeals to typically older theatre-goers but still draws some younger customers into theatres. In an environment where some form of watered-down pop-rock has become the *lingua franca* of Broadway,[33] one might ask if a genuine rock musical in the spirit of *Hair* is still a possibility. The answer would seem to be a qualified 'yes', if one is willing to look beyond the major theatres just north of Times Square.[34] Off-Broadway, experimental theatres and even regional companies remain vital forces for reinventing the musical, and in the late 1990s, three new works from those non-traditional milieus played in New York to excellent reviews.

Jonathan Larson's *Rent* – winner of the 1996 Pulitzer Prize for Drama, that year's Tony Award and numerous other accolades – has been com-pared to *Hair* for its similarly stunning impact on a sclerotic theatri-cal world.[35] *Rent*'s genesis, likewise, mirrors the struggles of many early rock musicals, with a beginning in an off-Broadway theatre workshop and marginal financing. Larson's death at the age of thirty-five, due to an undi-agnosed aortic aneurysm, on the eve of *Rent*'s first preview, moreover, gave the opening an air of almost gothic tragedy and generated an extraordinary amount of publicity for the show.[36] In fact, Larson's career had been on a slow but steadily upward trajectory well before *Rent*. Two awards in 1988–9 brought him to the notice of Stephen Sondheim, who then became a men-tor, and a $45,000 Richard Rodgers Development Grant in 1994 paid for the first workshop performances of *Rent*.

In retelling Puccini's *La bohème*, Larson transplanted the story of four struggling young artists to his own New York neighbourhood, the East Vil-lage, where Rado and Ragni had also found their inspiration for *Hair*. Larson based his songs and scenes on people he knew, but sentimentalised nothing. Nearly all of the principal characters are HIV positive, several are current or former drug users, and a number are also gay. Mimi, Puccini's meek, tubercular seamstress, is transformed into a dancer at a sadomasochism club, and everywhere are homeless people and other dregs of society. All of these characters are unflinchingly real, a point underscored by their ordinary clothing and an industrial grey set.[37] Despite the potential for offending an audience who had to deal regularly with these sorts of people on the streets of New York, Larson made his characters sympathetic and even attractive by focusing on how they lived with their diseases and problems, rather than on their dying. To underline that point, Mimi does not die at the end of *Rent*, as she does in *La bohème*.

The vitality of *Rent*'s characters is emphasised by the pervasive rock feel of the entire score. During pre-production, Larson insisted that a rock beat was essential for his songs, but that the words must always remain audible. Consequently, the engineer/arranger, Steve Skinner, worked hard to balance the competing needs of the singers and the five-member band.[38] The show's rock sound begins with the electric bass and drum set, which is the driving force in up-tempo tunes like 'Rent' and 'Out Tonight', and even songs with more moderate tempos, such as 'I'll Cover You', project a solid rock feel because of the strong support of bass and drums. Prominent acoustic guitars give the ballads – 'Life Support', 'Without You', 'Your Eyes' and 'Will I?' – a soft rock feel, while the influence of gospel is evident in the celebratory tones of 'La Vie Boheme' and 'Seasons of Love'. Many bits of dialogue that might have been spoken are also accompanied by rock vamps. Remarkably, virtually all of the show's songs contribute to plot or character development with a realistic text that includes justifiable use of common vulgarities. Nevertheless, Larson's word-play is often theatrically quite clever, as in the lists of 'La Vie Boheme', which obviously owe something to Sondheim's example. Larson's artistic achievement, which never resorts to artificial devices, is especially impressive when viewed against the backdrop of vacuous, big-budget entertainments dominating Broadway at the end of the century, and his use of rock music to portray these gritty characters is exactly right. It is impossible to imagine how a more conventional Broadway score could tell this story as well.

The two remaining shows could not be more different from *Rent* and also from one another, yet each exhibits a level of honesty about its subject matter seldom found on Broadway. Despite such frankness, *Hedwig and the Angry Inch* – the invented story of an East German transsexual who was the victim of a botched sex-change operation – played to audiences for two years after being premiered off-Broadway in 1998. The show was more a glam-rock concert than a traditional theatrical staging, and its hard rock music went far beyond the bounds of any previous rock musical, with several numbers that exhibit a punk sensibility. In contrast to the bizarre, adults-only world of *Hedwig, Inappropriate* dealt with the problems of teenagers in an equally direct and sometimes raw fashion. This show originated at the DeSisto School, a private boarding academy for troubled adolescents in Stockbridge, Massachusetts. Over the years their theatre programme fashioned scenes out of students' journals, which Michael DeSisto then set in musical styles ranging from rock to rap. The resulting show was performed by students from the school in a brief two-week run off-Broadway in 1999, and its success was such that a longer second run was mounted the following year. Although critics noted the production's unevenness, they also praised its honesty and noted how its expression of youthful anger, hurt and exuberance echoed the same elements in *Rent* and *Hair*.[39]

By the time the first wave of baby-boomers began approaching retirement at the end of the twentieth century, rock music had become the soundtrack of America. From television commercials selling automobiles to radio stations that programmed by the desired decade, rock was everywhere, including Broadway. While some ageing Americans might still think of rock as the music of youthful rebellion, by the late 1980s rock was a safe and respectable commodity. In its place, the hip-hop culture of black urban youths – chiefly in the form of 'gangsta rap' – had become the new sound of the disenfranchised. Similarly on Broadway, by the late 1980s middle-of-the-road rock was an unexceptional sound. No 'rap musical', however, has ever appeared in order to call attention to rock's new insider status, and thus the term 'rock musical' retains at least a tenuous connection with the rebellious traditions of early rock musicals. Still, it is almost impossible to think of a megahit from the 1980s like *Les Misérables* – described by some critics as 'the musical cum rock opera' and a 'pop opera' – as the same type of show as *Hair*.[40]

Nevertheless, at the beginning of the third millennium, there has been a modest renaissance of 'rock musicals' in the tradition of *Hair*. *Rent*, *Hedwig and the Angry Inch* and *Inappropriate* all present honest, youthful attitudes similar to those that fuelled the first rock musicals forty years ago, and while *Rent* quickly moved uptown, it was again off-Broadway that gave birth to these three shows. Beneath their vastly differing aural surfaces they speak for and to a generation that has not previously been heard on (or off) Broadway. Significantly, the generation that looks to *Rent* as its anthem are the children of the generation that embraced *Hair*. While it is too soon to say if the recent upsurge of the rock musical can or will be sustained, the odds nevertheless seem pretty good that the grandchildren of the *Hair* generation will surprise their parents with a musical of their own somewhere off-Broadway in about twenty-five years.

14 The megamusical: the creation, internationalisation and impact of a genre

PAUL PRECE AND WILLIAM A. EVERETT

Nowhere in the realm of the musical theatre is technology more evident than in the world of the megamusical. These 'larger than life' visual and aural spectacles dazzle audiences and are among the most popular musical theatre works at the beginning of the twenty-first century. *Les Misérables*, billed as 'the world's most popular musical', and *Cats*, heralded as 'now and forever', are but two shows where commercial slogans enlist, endorse and promote the genre's mass appeal.[1]

But what exactly are megamusicals? Terms such as 'through-composed popular operas' and 'poperas' have also been used to describe the phenomenon of sung-through musicals where set design, choreography and special effects are at least as important as the music. They are overtly romantic and sentimental in nature, meant to create strong emotional reactions from the audience. Stories merge aspects of human suffering and redemption with matters of social consciousness.

Aspects of the megamusical demonstrate a reinvigoration of nineteenth-century French grand opera. Whereas audiences in the late twentieth century were dazzled by stage effects such as the chandelier and underground lake in *The Phantom of the Opera*, the staircase in *Sunset Boulevard*, the barricade in *Les Misérables* and the helicopter in *Miss Saigon*, their nineteenth-century French counterparts saw the eruption of Vesuvius in Daniel-François-Esprit Auber's *La muette de Portici* (1828) and the St Bartholomew's Day Massacre in Giacomo Meyerbeer's *Les Huguenots* (1836). In both megamusicals and French grand opera, striking things happen amidst imaginative surroundings. Regarding megamusicals, dramatically effective sets range from only tables, chairs and a pair of gates in *Les Misérables* to a staircase filled with ornately costumed mannequins and live actors in *The Phantom of the Opera*.

If one central figure had to be identified as the driving creative force behind this late twentieth-century genre, it would almost certainly be the producer Cameron Mackintosh (b. 1946). His collaboration with Andrew Lloyd Webber on *Cats* in 1981 transformed the style of musical theatre. His success at creating musical theatrical experiences can be seen in many of the shows that virtually define the megamusical, including *Les Misérables*, *The Phantom of the Opera* and *Miss Saigon*. His revivals of such classics as

Oliver!, *My Fair Lady* and *Carousel* won critical praise, and the 1998 Royal Gala Performance, released on video as *Hey Mr Producer! The Musical World of Cameron Mackintosh*, was an all-star tribute to the producer. The video is self-described as 'a magical night of theatre that could only take place in your dreams . . . until now'. The pure theatricality of Mackintosh's vision – taking the aural and visual components and creating something greater than the mere sum of its parts and then marketing it with remarkable efficiency – defines so much of what makes the megamusical a critical part of today's musical theatre.

While it is Mackintosh's vision that defines the genre theatrically, parallels must be drawn between the English producer of three of the longest-running musicals of all time (*Cats*, *Les Misérables* and *The Phantom of the Opera*) and one of his nineteenth-century French predecessors, Louis Véron, director of the Paris Opera and a major force in nineteenth-century French grand opera. By definition, works in this genre related some sort of socio-political message through a grandiose medium that combined music, drama, dance, lavish costume and set designs, and special effects. It comes as no surprise that the creators of *Les Misérables*, Claude-Michel Schönberg and Alain Boublil, are French and that the original concept for 'the world's most popular musical' was in the French language. Frequently, French grand operas were set against war backgrounds; likewise, the Schönberg–Boublil musicals *La Révolution française* (1973, Paris), *Les Misérables* (1980, Paris; 1985, London; 1987, New York), *Miss Saigon* (1989, London; 1991, New York) and *Martin Guerre* (1996, London; revised 1998, London; revised 1999, West Yorkshire Playhouse) all have war settings. Sharing the desire for bringing about some sort of social change with their nineteenth-century predecessors, Schönberg and Boublil include some sort of edifying message in their shows, whether it be the power of forgiveness in *Les Misérables*, the hideous personal consequences of war in *Miss Saigon* or the repercussions of deception in *Martin Guerre*.

Schönberg–Boublil musicals have their musical basis in folk-like melodies that are given a lavish treatment, largely through orchestration. This Gallic concept permeates their three English-language shows. Pentatonicism is especially prominent, creating a sense of populist fervour in *Les Misérables*, Orientalism (Vietnam) in *Miss Saigon* and medieval French folk music in *Martin Guerre*.

Mass choral numbers, generally accompanied by inventive choreography suggesting a specific time and place, are central to the musical and dramatic structure of each show. Social injustice in the nineteenth century dominates 'At the End of the Day', 'Do You Hear the People Sing?', 'One Day More' and similar numbers in *Les Misérables*, while in *Miss Saigon*, 'The Heat Is On in Saigon' depicts Americans in Vietnam and 'The American Dream' incarnates

Plate 19 The original London cast of *Les Misérables*, Palace Theatre, 1985.

the plight of Vietnamese wanting to emigrate to America. 'Working on the Land' celebrates the sense of community in *Martin Guerre* and 'Welcome Home' acclaims the supposed return of Martin Guerre to his native village. The driving rhythms throughout the last score accentuate both the folk element and the drama of the libretto.

Because of the Gallic musical theatre tradition of audience edification, each of the shows also contains at least one song of social injustice. 'Do You Hear the People Sing?' and 'One Day More' in *Les Misérables* offer a hope for a future free from oppression of any sort. In *Miss Saigon*, the anthem 'Bui Doi', accompanied by emotional photographic images, educates the audience on the plight of children fathered by American soldiers in Vietnam. *Martin Guerre*'s 'The Impostors' is an anthem of self-reflection, the characters begging themselves and the audience to look inward and see if they are truly as forthright as they themselves claim to be.

In *Les Misérables*, Victor Hugo's immense novel receives a three-and-a-half-hour musical treatment, long for a musical, but brief considering the vast amount of source material. The human condition, the focus of the novel, is also that of the musical. Jean Valjean represents the inherent good in every person while Javert symbolises its antithesis. A single act of mercy on the part of a bishop causes Valjean to radically alter his ways, and the sacrificial deaths of Fantine, Cosette and the students for the cause of justice, personal or social, are among the most poignant moments in the show.

Recurring melodies enhance developments in the dramatic plot. Valjean and Javert share much of the same music, thus demonstrating that they represent two sides of the same human condition. For example the music of Valjean's 'Who Am I?' is the same as that of 'Javert's Suicide'. The finale includes reprises of several musical numbers, some with new texts, and ends with a 'finale ultimo' rendition of the show's central anthem, 'Do You Hear the People Sing?'

Les Misérables epitomises the pan-national production of megamusicals. The show began life as an 'arena version' at the Palais des Sports in Paris on 18 September 1980. Cameron Mackintosh heard the recording of the production and subsequently took on the task of overseeing the show's metamorphosis. The English-language result, a collaboration between Mackintosh and the Royal Shakespeare Company and first performed at the Barbican Theatre in London on 8 October 1985, was an immense success. It transferred to the Palace Theatre in the West End on 4 December 1985, and since that time has continued to draw packed houses.[2] On 9 October 2006, *Les Misérables* became the longest-running musical in the West End (as well as either in the West End or on Broadway) with its 8,372nd performance. The New York production opened on 12 March 1987 and closed on 18 May 2003, after a staggering 6,680 performances. Colm Wilkinson dazzled audiences as Jean Valjean in both London and New York, as did Frances Ruffelle as Eponine. Patti LuPone, Alun Armstrong and Michael Ball were featured in the London production, while Terrence Mann, Judy Kuhn and David Bryant appeared in New York. On 9 November 2006, just three and a half years after the initial production closed, a Broadway revival opened at the Broadhurst Theatre, giving testament to the show's continued popularity and viability as a New York tourist attraction.

Translations into many languages quickly followed. Within two years of the show's London success came performances in Hungary and Iceland in the vernacular languages of those countries. Subsequent productions opened in Norway, Austria, Poland, Sweden, the Netherlands, France, Germany, the Czech Republic, Spain, Israel, Japan, Denmark and Finland, each in the vernacular. Furthermore, recordings of the show have appeared in English, Hungarian, German, Swedish, Dutch, French, Czech, Danish, Hebrew, Japanese and Spanish. As of 2006, *Les Misérables* has played in 223 cities in thirty-eight countries in twenty-one languages and has been seen by more than fifty-one million people worldwide. The historic tenth-anniversary concert that took place in the Royal Albert Hall on 8 October 1995 included a surprise grand encore that proved the international appeal of the musical. Seventeen actors who had played Jean Valjean in various national productions processed into the hall to sing the anthem 'Do You Hear the People Sing?', each in his native tongue. Central issues associated with the megamusical – theatricality, social responsibility and international popularity – were evident in this celebratory encore.

The international popularity of the megamusical led to several of its numbers being appropriated in high-profile instances. 'One Day More' was the theme song for the Democratic Party in the US during the 1992 presidential election campaign and 'Empty Chairs and Empty Tables' became a commemorative anthem for victims of AIDS.[3] When the French team entered the stadium for the opening ceremonies of the 2000 Sydney Olympic Games, it was to the strains of 'Do You Hear the People Sing?'; the song was also featured in the opening ceremonies of the 2002 World Cup.

Following the success of *Les Misérables* came *Miss Saigon* and *Martin Guerre*. *Miss Saigon*, set in the final years of the Vietnam War, shares its plot with Puccini's opera *Madame Butterfly*. Lea Salonga and Jonathan Pryce captivated audiences and critics in both London and New York. *Martin Guerre*, yet to play in New York at the time of writing (2006) is set in sixteenth-century France against the backdrop of Protestant–Catholic religious conflicts. Its fundamentally folk-based musical style also includes sentimental ballads and dazzling dance numbers. The show has experienced numerous revisions during its existence; a 1999 cast recording made in conjunction with the West Yorkshire Playhouse documents the show's continuing evolution.

While Schönberg–Boublil musicals address broad social issues, those of Lord Andrew Lloyd Webber (b. 1948) focus on personal healing or catharsis. But there is much more to Lloyd Webber's approach to the musical theatre than this one central theme – commercialisation, pop icons and pure theatricality also loom large in his work. Although Lloyd Webber certainly has his detractors, his work has been widely recognised by both the public and theatrical professionals. He is the recipient of seven Tonys, three Grammys, six Oliviers, a London Critic's Circle Award, a Golden Globe, an Oscar, an International Emmy, and other awards. He received a knighthood in 1992 and was created an honorary life peer in 1997.

When *The Beautiful Game* (2000, London), Lloyd Webber's twelfth work, opened in September 2000, it joined its West End sisters *Cats* (1981, London; 1982, New York), *Starlight Express* (1984, London; 1987, New York), *The Phantom of the Opera* (1986, London; 1988, New York) and *Whistle Down the Wind* (1998, London). Five Lloyd Webber musicals were thus playing simultaneously in London. In August 2004, Lloyd Webber's thirteenth West End musical, *The Woman in White*, opened at the Palace Theatre, where it played for nineteen months. The diversity, popularity and longevity of Lloyd Webber's canon is staggering.

The numbers speak for themselves as far as the success of Lloyd Webber's shows is concerned. The original production of *Cats* has the distinction of being the longest-running musical in the West End and held the Broadway record of 7,485 performances until it was surpassed by another Lloyd Webber show, *The Phantom of the Opera*, on 9 January 2006. In January 2006, it was reported that *Phantom* alone had grossed more money than any other production on stage and screen (£1.7 billion/approximately $3.2 billion), surpassing huge money-making films such as *Star Wars*, *E.T.* and *Titanic*. The show has played in 120 cities in twenty-four countries and has been seen by over eighty million people.[4]

Films and video versions provide another venue for dissemination, including the theatrical films of *Jesus Christ Superstar* (1973), *Evita* (1996) and *The Phantom of the Opera* (2004), and the home video versions of *Cats* (1998), *Joseph and the Amazing Technicolor Dreamcoat* (1999) and *Jesus Christ Superstar* (2000). (See chapter 18 for a discussion of these adaptations.) Lloyd Webber – artist, businessman and visionary – is doing something right.

Norma Desmond, the Phantom, Jesus, Joseph, Evita, Grizabella and the dancing chorus of *Cats*, and Rusty and the skating Starlight trains are all Lloyd Webber prototypes that have been elevated to pop icon status, placing them firmly in the twentieth-century lexicon of musical theatre characters. As postmodern hero-protagonists they all search for immortality, deliverance and redemption from some real, imagined or self-imposed darkness. They are true 'superstars', to use the Warholian term, created and lifted to this status by Lloyd Webber's 'music of the night' and 'technicolor' imagination. His musical vision is as theatrical as it is operatic and his imaginative approach is rejuvenating and resuscitating, if not revisionist. Credited with having composed some 350 songs, Lloyd Webber, in the words of his biographer Michael Walsh, is 'a musical pack rat, salting away useful tunes in the knowledge that someday they will come in handy'.[5] He is as acutely aware of the visual possibilities of representation and the utility and potential of stage technology. Furthermore, he is cognisant of the 'really useful' need for select collaboration with creative lyricists, designers and stage directors.

Founded by Lloyd Webber in 1977, The Really Useful Group Ltd is the organisation that administers the rights to all of the composer's works from *Cats* onward. The Group has offices in London, New York, Los Angeles, Hong Kong, Singapore, Sydney, Basel and Frankfurt. In addition to involvement in management, production, recording and music publishing, the Group also owns several London theatres, including the Palace Theatre (home to *Jesus Christ Superstar*, *Les Misérables*, and *The Woman in White*), the New London Theatre (home to *Cats*), the Adelphi Theatre (where *Sunset Boulevard* played), the Palladium, the Cambridge, the Theatre Royal Drury Lane (where *Miss Saigon* enjoyed its tremendous run) and the Apollo Victoria (*Starlight Express*'s long-time home).[6] The Group also controls The Really

Useful Store, where Really Useful Merchandise is sold. The branded products carrying logos of Lloyd Webber shows comprise everything from T-shirts to thermo-reactive mugs. Production, promotion and product manufacturing and marketing are therefore all under the auspices of the same umbrella organisation.

Lloyd Webber, a baby-boomer, began composing at the age of seventeen. From an early age he had an interest in music, stagecraft and architecture and was fascinated by the musical stage and its treasures. As befits a true child of the 1950s, the evident influence of Elvis, rock 'n' roll and the Beatles intermingle with his knowledge of Prokofiev, Puccini and the classical repertory instilled largely by his father, William S. Lloyd Webber, a church organist and professor of composition at the Royal College of Music and eventually director of the London College of Music. But it was with the American musical theatre and its composers that his infatuation grew. He cites Richard Rodgers as a primary influence and reveals candidly, 'Musical theatre is the only thing that's ever made me tick.'[7]

From his early 'through-written' or 'through-composed' techno-music spectacles to his later more traditional adaptations, Lloyd Webber establishes dramatic and musical primacy and admits, 'I'm quite incapable of writing the words, but I lay out what I believe the libretto ought to be. That is one of my strongest assets.'[8] His self-confessed first rule is 'It's not the subject, it's the treatment.'[9] His librettos are cinematic, fantastic, dreamlike, sweeping, lush and conceptually rich in possibility. Whether developed from a film (*Sunset Boulevard*), a work of fiction (*The Phantom of the Opera*, *Aspects of Love*, *Whistle Down the Wind*, *The Woman in White*), a collection of poems (*Cats*), a Biblical or historical figure (*Jesus Christ Superstar*, *Joseph*, *Evita*) or simply an imaginative idea (*Starlight Express*), Lloyd Webber's (re)sources are magnified musically and theatrically.

As mentioned above, it is the search for some sort of redemption that connects all of Lloyd Webber's lead characters. Perhaps this is the influence of his father's involvement with Anglican church music and theology. Lloyd Webber's shows fall into two categories based upon subject matter: immortality musicals and intimate musicals (see Table 14.1). The immortality musicals fall into three categories: 1) those based on Biblical or historical figures, 2) those concerning some sort of competition and 3) those focusing on singular personalities who are in search of immortality.

In the Biblical musicals, *Joseph and the Amazing Technicolor Dreamcoat* and *Jesus Christ Superstar*, the title characters are imprisoned or destroyed by a group (Joseph's brothers in *Joseph*, Judas, Pontius Pilate and soldiers in *Superstar*). At the same time, a character exists in each show who looks to the protagonist for redemption (Pharaoh in *Joseph*, Mary Magdalene in *Superstar*).

Table 14.1 *Categories of musicals by Andrew Lloyd Webber*

IMMORTALITY MUSICALS

Religious/historical themes
Joseph and the Amazing Technicolor Dreamcoat (1968–72, book and lyrics by Tim Rice, video version 1999)
Jesus Christ Superstar (1971, lyrics by Tim Rice, film version 1973, video version 2000)
Evita (1978, lyrics and book by Tim Rice, film version 1996)

Competition musicals
Cats (1981, lyrics by T. S. Eliot, book based on Eliot's *Old Possum's Book of Practical Cats*, video version 1998)
Starlight Express (1984, lyrics by Richard Stilgoe, story by Andrew Lloyd Webber)

Personality shows
The Phantom of the Opera (1986, lyrics by Charles Hart, book by Richard Stilgoe, based on the novel by Gaston Leroux, film version 2004)
Sunset Boulevard (1993, lyrics and book by Don Black and Christopher Hampton, based on the Billy Wilder film)

INTIMATE MUSICALS

Retrospective musical
By Jeeves (1996, lyrics and book by Alan Ayckbourn, based on stories by P. G. Wodehouse, reworking of *Jeeves* (1975))

Personal discovery
Song and Dance (1982, lyrics by Don Black and Richard Maltby, Jr., includes *Tell Me on a Sunday* (1980, reworked in 2003) and *Variations* (1979))
Aspects of Love (1989, lyrics and book by Charles Hart and Don Black, after the novel by David Garnett)
Whistle Down the Wind (1998, lyrics by Jim Steinman, book by Patricia Knop, Gale Edwards, and Andrew Lloyd Webber, after the original novel by Mary Hayley Bell and the film by Richard Attenborough)

Societal injustice
The Beautiful Game (2000, lyrics and book by Ben Elton)
The Woman in White (2004, lyrics by David Zippel, book by Charlotte Jones, 'Freely adapted from the classic novel by Wilkie Collins')

Both *Joseph* and *Superstar* incorporate a variety of pop-rock styles, including Elvis-style and calypso numbers in *Joseph* and various rock styles in *Superstar. Joseph* began life as a 'pop cantata' for the choir of St Paul's Junior School at Colet Court, Hammersmith. It was first performed on 1 March 1968 in a concert at the Old Assembly Hall and lasted a mere fifteen minutes. It finally found life as a full-length production in 1973, after the success of *Superstar.* Further productions appeared, and the 1999 video/DVD release starring Donny Osmond, Richard Attenborough, Maria Friedman and Joan Collins made the show more accessible than ever. By contrast, *Superstar* began life as a double album. Concert tours of the rock opera followed, and a stage version ultimately emerged. The 1973 film version starred Ted Neeley and Carl Anderson, and Glenn Carter played the title role in the 2000 video/DVD version. Both shows, therefore, had origins that were atypical for canonical works in the musical theatre.

Lloyd Webber's technicolor rendition of the Old Testament story of Jacob's favourite son, *Joseph and the Amazing Technicolor Dreamcoat*, is a sung-through loosely linked series of novelty numbers. The show is circular in nature, reflected in a line from the finale, 'let us return to the beginning . . . any dream will do'. This concept of the dream reappears in *Sunset Boulevard* when Norma and her associates ponder 'new ways to dream'. *Joseph* concludes with the knowledge that a lesson has been taught and learned. It is youthful, energetic, fast-paced, lively and childlike, and its music is sweet and easily accessible, with 'Close Every Door' being the show's most haunting original tune.

Whereas *Joseph* is buoyant and lighthearted, positive and uplifting, *Jesus Christ Superstar* is brooding and imbued with a dark sense of foreboding. The last week of Jesus' life, his betrayal and Passion as seen through the eyes of Pontius Pilate, constitute the scenario. There are glorious moments of 'Hosannah' and the emblematic 'Jesus Christ Superstar' fanfare, but the Judas character defines the piece. 'King Herod's Song', a comic drag number reminiscent of 'The Pharaoh's Song' in *Joseph*, provides humorous relief but is somewhat out of keeping with the mood sustained throughout the rest of the show. In the final moments of the controversial 1971 original Tom O'Horgan Broadway production, Christ appeared crucified on an inverted triangle some twenty feet in the air and was slowly projected forward from the back wall of the stage until he loomed over the orchestra as swirling, flickering light fragments flashed through the theatre to the musical accompaniment of the signature fanfare. The show won seven Tony Awards, including Best Musical and Best Score.

The diversity of musical styles in *Joseph* and *Superstar* suggests the genre of the revue, and is a significant aspect of Lloyd Webber's overall musical language. This character-defining treatment through music would reappear in *Cats*, where each cat has its own type of music, and even more so in *The Phantom of the Opera* and *Sunset Boulevard*, where the music of the protagonist is decidedly distinct from the remainder of the score.

It was the rock opera concept of *Jesus Christ Superstar* that Lloyd Webber maintained in *Evita*, his third collaboration with Tim Rice and his third musical on a religious-historical theme. The show begins with an inventive and forceful prologue – on 26 July 1952, in a Buenos Aires cinema, the death of Eva Perón is announced. Argentina weeps, for they have lost a woman whom they considered a saint. The opera documents Eva Perón from her lowly yet ambitious beginnings to her influential position as 'the woman behind the man' of Juan Perón, president of Argentina, and her untimely death. Eva's popularity grows to the point of deification, and her youthful death immortalises her beauty and strength in the operatic tradition of the dying heroine. The moral conscience challenging her rise to power appears in the persona of the revolutionary Che Guevara. *Evita* is cinematic and sweeping, a complex immersion into the political games of Argentina in the 1940s and the sexual politics of a passionate woman and her society. The libretto lends itself to the operatic formulation of Eva Perón as both an anti-heroine and the personified conscience of a nation.

Like *Superstar*, *Evita* began its life as a concept album. The show was a turning point in the careers of both its composer and lyricist. It gave 'the first real evidence that here was not simply a minor British talent with a knack for catching a pop wave, but a serious composer of depth, talent, and technique working in tandem with a lyricist of style and substance'.[10] In *Evita*, Lloyd Webber rendered a score in 'an original, vital melodic language that stamped his music as his own – and not as a collection of disparate influences'.[11] The show received numerous Tony Awards, including one for Patti LuPone as Best Actress. 'Don't Cry for Me, Argentina' became a signature tune for LuPone, whose arm-raised final pose is one of the classic images of the musical theatre. For the 1996 film starring Madonna and Antonio Banderas, Lloyd Webber wrote a new song, 'You Must Love Me', earning him an Academy Award. Even though *Evita* was the third and perhaps crowning jewel in the Lloyd Webber–Rice collaborations, it signalled the end of their working relationship. The show solidified the reputations of both creators, and in the case of Lloyd Webber, his post-Rice works, while maintaining the fundamental approach to theatrical music, would expand his conceptual and musical horizons.

In the second type of immortality musical, competition musicals, some sort of contest takes place. In *Cats*, the winner goes to the Heaviside Layer (cat heaven) and in *Starlight Express*, the various toy train engines try to win the race to the 'Light at the End of the Tunnel'. In both shows, it is the underdog who wins – the faded Grizabella defeats her fellow felines in *Cats* and the steam engine Rusty conquers newer technologies in *Starlight Express*.

Lloyd Webber explores a variety of musical styles in both shows. *Cats* contains a wide range of songs, including an Elvis-style number. 'Memory', the show's climactic point, is a sentimental ballad that has been championed by the singers Elaine Paige and Barbra Streisand, among others. *Starlight Express* includes rock, blues and country music throughout, and concludes with a gospel finale, 'The Light at the End of the Tunnel'. In these shows, the mixture of musical styles and the search for a new life symbolised by light (a spaceship in *Cats* and the end of the tunnel in *Starlight Express*) is a shared feature, as is the transformation of the theatre into either a garbage dump (*Cats*) or a race track (*Starlight Express*).

'Cats: Now and Forever' – as the poster proclaims – proved to be more prophetic than might have been imagined by the Cameron Mackintosh team that coined it. Based on T. S. Eliot's *Old Possum's Book of Practical Cats*, this junkyard song and dance spectacle is a vaudeville/minstrel/burlesque populated by a company of colourful, dappled, tabby, be-whiskered and grizzly-coiffed felines. As a show it defies categorisation. *Cats* is an experience. The theatre itself is transformed into a junkyard, not just the stage but the house as well. Just as audiences enter the world of the Paris Opera House when they attend *Phantom*, they venture into the world of feline subculture in *Cats.* The popularity of the longest-running musical in both London and New York was further endorsed when the United States Postal Service honoured the show with a commemorative stamp in its 'Celebrate the Century' series. It was thus heralded as one of the fifteen most important events in 1980s American culture.

And if actors can be cats, why can't they be trains?

> Imagine yourself seated in a theatre which has been totally transformed into an incredible 'roller-coaster' race track. Against a background of stunning special effects, this track becomes the arena for an exciting and spectacular production. You will enjoy the thrills and spills of high speed races as they pass in front of you, behind you – and even over you! A ring-side seat at *Starlight Express* is a once-in-a-lifetime experience.[12]

Starlight Express capitalises on the formula experienced in *Cats.* The junkyard becomes a train yard and racing track. Actors on skates impersonate various types of trains – steam engines, diesels and electric engines and their coaches. Envisaged as a children's story, the production was an expensive technological spectacle. The technology of the stagecraft and the skating prowess of its athletic actors overshadowed the recorded music and over-amplified lyrics in performance except in the few quiet moments when the mayhem slowed. It has more in common with a roller-skating disco than with the musical theatre. Yet it is indeed original – another 'experience' created by the mind and music of Andrew Lloyd Webber, a 'theme park ride' of a musical. A ninety-minute version of *Starlight Express* opened in 1993 at the Las Vegas Hilton, the first major legitimate stage production to play in the famed gambling city.

The third category of immortality musicals, personality shows, includes two of Lloyd Webber's most popular shows, *The Phantom of the Opera* and *Sunset Boulevard.* Both musicals tell of an older, physically unattractive individual who searches for immortality through a younger, more beautiful one. A lush romantic operatic style with rock overtones pervades both shows. In many respects these are two versions of the same story – Norma is the Phantom in drag.

The Phantom of the Opera, Lloyd Webber's most famous score, is romantic and sweeping, dark yet seductive, and must be considered his signature composition. The 'Beauty and the Beast' tale based on the Gaston Leroux novel, set deep in the bowels of the Paris Opera House, gave Lloyd Webber the freest rein with his imagination and musical gifts. Mark Steyn asserts:

And *Phantom* has made opera hip, after half a century of being outflanked by musical comedy and the musical play. Before the First World War, *The Merry Widow* was one of the few shows to approach internationally the scale of today's Lloyd Webber mega-smashes: at one point there were over one hundred productions around the world.[13]

In *Phantom*, Lloyd Webber fuses his pop/rock sensibility with the classical models of his youth. The half-masked, caped figure appearing and disappearing accentuates the duality, the mix of old and new, in the music, the rendition and the conception. Like *Evita*, the show opens with a prologue – an auction at the Paris Opera where items, including the chandelier, are visible. As the chandelier is lit (with modern electricity), the music begins and the chandelier rises above the stalls. The magic and mystery continue as the audience passes through the mirror with the virginal young heroine and is seduced by the Phantom's 'music of the night'. *Phantom* is a modern opera played on a classical stage. The theme of unrequited and inaccessible love is as elusive and poignant as any contemporary love ballad, as classical as any opera. The fantasy transports, the music invites, the theatre technology awes. As the audience enters the doors of Her Majesty's Theatre in London, chosen specifically for *Phantom* because of its architectural features, to see the show, they pass through a portal to another world – a world of realised mystery and imagination. Michael Crawford and Sarah Brightman triumphed in the original production, the show marking a milestone in the careers of both performers.

Phantom's success is palpable. In addition to its record-breaking Broadway run, worldwide productions and tours, the 2004 film version brought renewed interest in the stage version. A new Las Vegas production opened in June 2006 – this version, running ninety-five minutes with no intermission, retains all of Lloyd Webber's songs. The production is housed in a $40 million purpose-built theatre (meant to evoke the Paris Opera House) at The Venetian Resort-Hotel-Casino and includes the largest cast of any US *Phantom* production, expanded sets and pyrotechnics, and 'an amazing chandelier experience unlike anything seen anywhere else in the world'.[14]

Sunset Boulevard commences with a musical prologue worthy of a late 1940s Hollywood movie that prepares for the story to be told in a large flashback, as with *Evita* and *Phantom*. The fast-paced motoristic fervour of 'Sunset Boulevard' is an apt overture to Lloyd Webber's faithful musical treatment of the Billy Wilder film about the fading silent movie actress longing and determined to make a comeback. The House on Sunset, Paramount Studios, Schwab's Drugstore, the Paramount backlot are the locales; Norma Desmond, Joe Gillis, Max von Mayerling, Betty Schaefer, Cecil B. DeMille and a cast of Hollywood hopeful extras are the characters. The London production starred Patti LuPone, while the Los Angeles and New York

Plate 20 Sarah Brightman and Michael Crawford in *The Phantom of the Opera,* Her Majesty's Theatre, 1986.

productions featured Glenn Close. Betty Buckley succeeded both LuPone and Close in their respective runs.

In a departure from his through-composed musicals, *Sunset Boulevard* adopts a more traditional Broadway musical structure with spoken scenes advancing the narrative. Joe is a screenwriter, Norma an actress. The presence of dialogue scenes anchors and supports the musical numbers. Norma invites Joe into her mansion and her bed proffering gifts and promises of work, success and contacts at Paramount. A phantom-like spectre, she haunts the Sunset House and fascinates the good-looking, down-on-his-luck young writer as she slowly weaves her web – she, a black widow and

Table 14.2 *Dramatic and musical parallels in* The Phantom of the Opera *and* Sunset Boulevard

Older/physically 'unattractive' character in search of immortality through a younger, beautiful one	
Phantom	Norma Desmond
Younger character	
Christine Daae	Joe Gillis
Younger character's romantic interest	
Raoul	Betty Schaefer
Ending – release from reality	
Disappearance of Phantom	Madness of Norma
Introductory musical number for the principal character	
'Angel of Music'	'With One Look'
Subsequent musical number for the principal character	
'Music of the Night'	'As If We Never Said Goodbye'
Defining musical number for younger character	
'Think of Me'	'Sunset Boulevard'

he, her prey. Her delusional hope for rejuvenation is based on the irrational belief that her conquest will assure her return to the silver screen. This is music of a much darker night. The jazzy swing and hip sounds of the Paramount people seem a world away from Norma's brooding, soulful, unresolved melodies and such telling lines as 'We taught the world new ways to dream' and her final 'I am ready for my close-up, Mr DeMille'. Her stare, her stance, her face and her eyes are etched into the lens of consciousness as she lights the darkness one last time.

The two shows, as mentioned above, have strong parallels both dramatically and musically (see Table 14.2). Both the Phantom and Norma are searching for immortality and hope to achieve this through a younger character, an apprentice of sorts. The Phantom teaches Christine to sing and star in his opera while Norma wants Joe to secure her return to the silver screen in her original version of *Salomé*. The chief protagonist is concerned about his or her physical appearance. The Phantom's facial disfigurement is covered by the iconic mask until he reveals himself to Christine. It is his physical appearance that is the root of his societal estrangement. Norma's faded physical appearance causes her great consternation, and her desire for corporeal beauty is the basis for the song 'Eternal Youth Is Worth a Little Suffering'. Both the Phantom and Norma look for youth and beauty in their apprentices.

Each of these apprentices has their own romantic interest with a young and vital person, resulting in love triangles. The ultimate result of the triangles differs in the two shows, however. In *Phantom*, Christine and Raoul are together at the final curtain while in *Sunset Boulevard*, Joe's death forbids a union with Betty.

The musicals end in a similar fashion with a release from reality. The mysterious disappearance of the Phantom into unknown regions contrasts with Norma's descent into madness at the end of *Sunset Boulevard* as she imagines herself on the set of Paramount Studios.

Lloyd Webber realises these dramatic parallels through musical means. The principal character in each show has two large-scale songs that define his or her demeanour and temperament. The first numbers, 'Angel of Music' and 'With One Look', are self-defining songs in which the characters assert their basic life views. A subsequent number illuminates their innermost desires. 'Music of the Night', a trunk song, reveals the deepest regions of the Phantom's soul through its ballad style, while 'As If We Never Said Goodbye' is an expression of Norma's sense of loss and her ardent desire to return to the world of Hollywood magic.

The younger character in each show has a solo number that defines his or her place in the drama. 'Think of Me' reveals Christine's innocence through its directness of musical expression; 'Sunset Boulevard' with its constant rhythmic underpinning depicts the angst that Joe experiences throughout his ultimately fatal relationship with Norma.

Other commonalities link the two works. A staircase figures prominently in the scenic design of both. The second act of *Phantom* opens with the New Year's Eve masquerade scene, set on a lavish staircase filled with live chorus members and mannequins. Norma Desmond's staircase in *Sunset Boulevard* is a central feature of the show. A monkey appears significantly in both musicals. In *Phantom*, a stuffed monkey is on the music box that is auctioned as the show opens. In *Sunset Boulevard*, Norma's recently deceased monkey is the subject of her mourning when Joe enters the mansion. Murders take place in both shows. The Phantom threatens or kills those who attempt to thwart his plans to make Christine a star while Joe's murder by Norma frames the plot of *Sunset Boulevard*.

Furthermore, both shows exhibit a notable conceptualisation of physical space. In *Phantom*, the lair lies beneath the Paris Opera House. In order to escape the Phantom's influence, Christine and Raoul go to the roof of the building, a physically separate location. Most of the show takes place in the Opera House, between the roof and the lair. Likewise, in *Sunset Boulevard*, Norma makes her first appearance at the top of the immense staircase. Joe, by contrast, is seen first face down in Norma's swimming pool – literally in the depths of her estate. Since the story is told in flashback, this is where Joe remains throughout the musical. The worlds of Joe and Norma are separate: the characters meet and interact on the ground floor of Norma's lavish palace – an intermediate domain between their two regions. The relationship between the physical spaces allocated to the principal characters is gender-based: female characters occupy the higher regions while male characters inhabit places physically beneath the setting of the central action.

This central mid-level dramatic location is the domain of the protagonist. Whether in the Paris Opera House or in Norma's mansion on Sunset Boulevard, the protagonists find security in their respective physical surroundings. They determine and dominate the events that take place in these domains, controlling through fear, intimidation or sheer will power all who enter these realms that are every bit as private as the Countess's boudoir in *Le nozze di Figaro.*

Finally, the performing arts backgrounds to both shows are central to their concept. The Paris Opera House and its activities provide the backdrop for *Phantom*, but Lloyd Webber also alludes to various styles of opera in the musical. Scenes from three imaginary operas appear in *Phantom*: *Hannibal* by Chalumeau, *Il muto* by Albrizzio, and *Don Juan Triumphant* by the Phantom himself. In these 'operas within an opera', Lloyd Webber pays tribute to various European operatic traditions. *Hannibal* is a French Grand Opera, complete with a scenic elephant, while *Il muto* is modelled on Italian opera buffa. *Don Juan Triumphant* is a decidedly modern work that includes musical devices such as the whole-tone scale, setting it off from the other two works. The setting for the scene from *Don Juan Triumphant* is a banquet akin to that in Mozart's *Don Giovanni.* Likewise, *Sunset Boulevard* is not only a transformation of a cinematic paragon but also homage to the lost world of silent cinema, as was the original Billy Wilder film.

The archetypal megamusical production includes lavish sets and a strong emphasis on choreography and other visual elements. In Lloyd Webber's intimate musicals, however, the lush musical style is maintained while some of the overt theatricality is eschewed.

By Jeeves is in the retrospective style of 1930s musical comedy, and its basis in P. G. Wodehouse's classic Jeeves and Wooster characters gives it a distinctively English character. Its overt Englishness was certainly a contributing factor to its lack of success in the US.

Song and Dance is an intimate two-part programme as literal as the title suggests – the first act is sung, the second is danced. Constructed from two earlier works – *Tell Me on a Sunday*, a 1979 song cycle, and *Variations for Cello and Rock Band* – it received its premiere on the BBC as a television special and subsequently played at the Palace Theatre. The idea came from Cameron Mackintosh during a conversation in which he and Lloyd Webber were trying to find a way to keep the Palace Theatre, beloved by both of them, open. Initially called 'a concert for the theatre', its billing was changed to 'a musical' after the show received good reviews in the press.[15] In 'Song' a woman sings about her relationships with several men, her experiences and her thoughts as an English girl living alone in Manhattan. 'Song' is sung through, without spoken dialogue. 'Dance', a set of variations on Paganini's 24th Caprice written for Andrew Lloyd Webber's cello-playing brother Julian, is a choreographic self-examination by one of the men mentioned in 'Song'. It consists solely of instrumental music, without either lyrics or spoken dialogue. In 2003, a new production of *Tell Me on a Sunday* (on its own) starring Denise van Outen opened at the Gielgud Theatre.

Aspects of Love is an adaptation of David Garnett's tale of intergenerational love. Here, as in *The Phantom of the Opera* and *Sunset Boulevard*, the central character uses the youth of another as a catalyst for personal transformation. Conceived as an intimate chamber piece in style and execution, it is a sung-through ballad of yearning and longing and the pains and penalties of love conquered and love lost. *Aspects* focuses on the human drama of a set of interrelated characters: Rose, an actress; Alex, a young Englishman; George, his uncle, an English painter; Giulietta, an Italian sculptress; Jenny, daughter of Rose and George; and Hugo, Rose's lover. The action takes place in France and Italy between 1947 and 1961, and is a virtual Rubik's Cube of love triangles. Michael Walsh says of the show that 'it displays Lloyd Webber's familiar melodic gifts, this time wedded to a solid technical foundation to produce moments of penetrating psychological insight and great emotional power . . . the score flows from one scene to the next, hardly stopping for breath . . . the penultimate scene . . . is the composer's finest dramatic creation'.[16] The show played for over three years in London, but its 1990 Broadway run lasted only 377 performances.

In *Whistle Down the Wind*, this idea of the transformative power of youth is combined with the religious messages of Lloyd Webber's early shows. The show opens as an electric neon billboard with the words 'Jesus Lives' hovers over a flyover where a church congregation gathers and intones a hymn, 'The Vaults of Heaven', cast in traditional Baptist mode. The minister then tells of an afterlife where there will be no more pain, loss or sorrow.

It is 1959 in a small Louisiana town and the music is that of a British composer. Lloyd Webber's adaptation of the novel and film of *Whistle Down the Wind* is a bucolic American gothic fable. The title song is a hopeful, simple anthem of hope and acceptance, and Lloyd Webber is deep in the American South, far away from Egypt, Paris and Argentina. When three siblings return home after their chores they are surprised to discover a long-haired, bleeding man hidden in the barn, sleeping in the hay. Swallow, the girl, startles the man, who, when she begins to ask who he is, responds with the expletive 'Jesus Christ'. She takes him literally, and the drama begins.

A slim premise at best, but with this *Whistle*, Lloyd Webber's imagination again takes flight. The Man is an escaped convict, an unlikely Jesus, yet the answer to months of unanswered prayers by the children. He is an object of hope and faith. The minister's exhortation is a reality in a town where racial tension, graft and passions smoulder. His appearance is a miracle of sorts, for the children, in their innocence and naivety, protect, worship and love him. The plot meanders and is fed by the hypocrisy of fundamentalism, the restlessness of youth appearing like an insidious Southern stream. A collaboration with Jim Steinman, the score includes romantic love ballads, blues, country, gospel and rock music. The eclecticism chronicled throughout this essay is again apparent in *Whistle Down the Wind*.

The musical, while demonstrating the intimate, also includes some remarkable theatrical moments such as the hydraulically lifted flyover and the head-on approach of a train in a tunnel. These visual events are at least as powerful as they are in shows such as *Phantom* because of the intimacy of the overall setting and the tone of the musical. They are not part of an awe-inspiring aesthetic but rather accentuate moments in a show conceived in a much more private manner.

The Beautiful Game, a show about Belfast footballers in 1969, may appear at first glance to be a competition musical, but Ben Elton's book and lyrics prove it to be a logical continuation of themes addressed in *Whistle*: a search for peace and the responsibility of youth to achieve a better future, this time on a societal level. The intertwined stories of two couples – the men of whom are football players – address Northern Ireland issues: the Catholic–Protestant pair (Christine and Del) who leave for America and the inter-Catholic pair (Mary and John) who are separated after John's false imprisonment and subsequent IRA involvement. Mary's solo soliloquy 'If This Is What We're Fighting For' positions the political overtones of the show squarely in focus. Her unaccompanied singing for most of the song intensifies its heartfelt lyric, as does the critical line 'No child was ever born to hate'. Ireland is celebrated in the lyrical 'God's Own Country' and the energetic opening title number endorses football as a religion every bit as powerful as the faith of the Catholic priest who coaches the team.

The Woman in White, 'freely adapted on the classic novel by Wilkie Collins', is a nearly sung-through treatment of the famous Victorian mystery thriller (first published serially in 1860), a tale of love, mistrust and greed. Several aspects of the novel were changed for the musical, including the ending (which also differs between the initial London and subsequent New York productions), the dangerous secret of the mysterious 'woman in white', and the nature of the relationship between Marian and Walter, the musical's principals. Lloyd Webber's haunting score includes recurring themes that are associated with each character (similar to operatic leitmotifs). One of the most effective use of this technique concerns 'Laura's theme'. Laura, the suffering heroine, is forced to marry the treacherous Sir Percival Glyde; at her funeral, he *dares* to sing her theme to the disgust of not only the other stage characters but also the audience. Marian and Walter ultimately work together to seek justice on Laura's behalf. Other notable uses of music include the seductive tango during which Marian and the manipulative Count Fosco attempt to outwit each other, and Fosco's delightfully sociopathic 'You Can Get Away with Anything'. William Dudley's innovative stage design consisted of video projections that created something akin to an IMAX experience. Sets were minimal, placing the focus squarely on the characters and their music. The musical fared much better in London than in New York (where it played from November 2005 to February 2006), due in large part to the novel's tremendous fame in Britain and near obscurity in the US.

In *Aspects*, *Whistle*, *Game* and *Woman*, carnal or spiritual forces challenge innocence, goodness and youth. The principals are all searching for catharsis or social justice. Like their earlier counterparts such as the Phantom or Norma, they yearn for some sort of transformation for either themselves, those they love, or society as a whole. Lloyd Webber's music, though still vaultingly romantic, is more tempered in these works, endorsing and enhancing the narrative and psychological dimensions of the librettos.

Capitalising on the high-tech staging associated with the British megamusicals are the Disney productions of the 1990s, appearing under the guise of Disney Theatricals. The live-theatre adaptations of *Beauty and the Beast* (1994) and *The Lion King* (1998) quickly became among the most popular shows in both New York and London. The transformation scene in *Beauty and the Beast* and the magical puppetry conceived by Julie Taymor for *The Lion King* took the remarkable staging and visual spectacle associated with the megamusical to new creative levels.

Like the European megamusicals, Disney productions have quickly become internationalised. In addition to English-language versions, *Beauty and the Beast* has been produced in translation in Stuttgart and Madrid and *The Lion King* has played in Tokyo and Osaka. Along these lines, the live theatrical version of *The Hunchback of Notre Dame* was first produced in Berlin in 1999 under the German title *Der Glöckner von Notre Dame*, bypassing an initial English-language version.

Disney Theatricals runs Hyperion Theatricals, whose first show was Elton John and Tim Rice's *Aida* (2000), a score that, like so many rock musicals, tried to expand the stereotypical Broadway sounds. Postmodern staging, including a vertical swimming pool, accentuated the theatrical experience.

Cameron Mackintosh and Disney Theatricals joined forces to bring *Mary Poppins* to the London stage in December 2004, followed by a Broadway transfer in autumn 2006. Billed as 'a musical based on the stories of P. L. Travers and the Walt Disney film', the stage version includes the original music and lyrics from the classic Julie Andrews–Dick Van Dyke film by Richard M. Sherman and Robert B. Sherman along with new songs by

George Stiles and Anthony Drewer. Co-created by Mackintosh, the stage version includes new settings for familiar songs, while Stiles and Drewer's new songs, such as Mary Poppins' theme 'Practically Perfect', maintain the charm and appeal of the film.

Disney returned to Broadway in May 2006 with another live-action version of a animated film, this time *Tarzan*, with music and lyrics by Phil Collins. Vine-swinging acrobats fill the stage with spectacular aerial feats and 'American Idol' veteran Josh Strickland made his Broadway debut in the title role.

The megamusical is arguably the most influential musical genre of the late twentieth century. The pioneering shows of the 1980s have a strong progeny – creating breathtaking effects for theatrical audiences has become part of the art of musical theatre thanks to the genre's profound influence. Along with spectacular visual effects, megamusicals have given their fans unashamedly romantic, lush and expansive music: *Les Misérables*, *The Phantom of the Opera* and *Beauty and the Beast*, for example, contain some of the contemporary musical theatre's most frequently heard songs. The inherent danger, however, is that these powerful blockbusters can easily overshadow other worthy efforts – impressive shows such as *Miss Saigon* and *The Woman in White* – and thus limit the reputations of their creators, individuals whose artistic visions continue to draw audiences into the theatre and whose efforts keep the great legacy of the musical theatre alive and flourishing.

15 'Something borrowed, something blue': the marriage of the musical and Europe

JUDITH SEBESTA

For those who embrace the musical as an American form – or at least as a product primarily of the English-speaking world – the phrase 'European musical' can seem an oxymoron.[1] Although, as early chapters in this volume convey, the 'musical' is an amalgamation of an almost dizzying array of forms, many European or even African-influenced, as in minstrelsy, its maturity and 'Golden Age' were largely the result of American artists, audiences and society, and through the work of such writers as Stephen Sondheim, Jeanine Tesori, David Yazbeck and Adam Guettel, the musical remains a vibrant part of American culture, both on and off Broadway.

However, the musical is becoming increasingly international, particularly through the popularity of the 'megamusical', as Prece and Everett argue in the previous chapter. As the Music Theatre International website states: 'The musical theatre is no longer the province of New York, London and the English speaking world – it is a truly multi-cultural phenomenon.'[2] This globalisation is certainly not unique to musical theatre; all forms of culture at the end of the twentieth and beginning of the twenty-first centuries are affected by the increasing interconnection of world societies and systems, an interdependency that has expanded exponentially during the past few decades through mediatised forms of communication, such as television, digital recordings, mobile phones, and perhaps most of all, the Internet. Critics of globalisation point to the breakdown of cultural specificity and nationhood; supporters applaud the levelling of world economic playing fields caused by technology. People on both sides discuss the spread of free-market capitalism that seems to have become the inevitable result of globalisation. Entertainment forms bred out of capitalism, including the musical, are a part of this phenomenon.[3]

Still, when one conducts research on musicals as increasingly international phenomena, a number of sources seem to indicate otherwise. Perusing the 2004–5 issues of *Western European Stages*, a journal published at the City University of New York that reports on the latest theatre developments in western Europe, there is little coverage of musical theatre, although the journal does cover opera. Then again, the journal fails even to cover much on *London* musical theatre, indicating a possible bias against this form. The overall effect is to give the sense that few musicals are produced in Europe. The Cardiff International Festival of Musical Theatre completed its second season in 2005 (1–17 April) in Wales – 'an exciting range of shows and events celebrating the most popular live art form – the musical', according to Simi Horwitz in *Backstage* magazine. Horwitz claims that the festival is 'designed to bring the best new musicals from around the world to the attention of producers, directors, and the public' and is 'the first – indeed, only – worldwide forum for new musicals'.[4] However, the musicals are primarily from the US (Sondheim appeared at the second festival) and British Isles, although a Czech production of *Joan of Arc* did appear the first year. Furthermore, in his introduction to the music theatre sections included in the volume on European theatre of *The Encyclopedia of Contemporary Theatre*, Horst Seeger admits the bias of the volume toward opera. While he acknowledges that 'there are many forms of music theatre to be seen in Europe today', he points toward the historical importance of opera and operetta in Europe to justify moving opera 'to the foreground of "music theatre"'.[5]

Thankfully, particularly for this author, there exist numerous sources to counteract such biases and misinformation, sources that firmly establish a growing tradition of musical theatre outside opera on the European continent. Non-English-speaking sources such as *Musical-Jahrbuch*, a German annual on musicals throughout the Western world; *Theatre Heute*, a German magazine on theatre in general; and an Austrian magazine, *Musical-Cocktail*, are quite enthusiastic in their coverage of the form. And Kurt Gänzl's *Encyclopedia of the Musical Theatre* provides a wealth of information on musical theatre in Europe.[6] These and other sources paint a picture of a growing appreciation for musicals in continental Europe. This chapter will examine recent (in the past twenty-five years or so) developments in musical theatre there, focusing primarily on Germany, Austria and France, with brief information on other countries, such as the Czech Republic. Although the British Isles are obviously a part of Europe, this chapter will discuss only musicals created and/or first produced there in their context in non-English-speaking countries. In all three countries, and others, the musical has been a bit like the old adage about traditional gifts for a bride – 'something old, something new, something borrowed, something blue' – and this chapter will be organised accordingly, if slightly out of traditional order, the reason for which should become apparent.[7]

Something old

Europe, of course, has a long history of combining music with drama or theatre, with a proud tradition of forms such as opera, operetta, ballad opera, *opéra-bouffe*, pantomime and cabaret, some of which retain their relative popularity today. The multiplicity of forms that combine music and theatre has led to considerable confusion as to how to define 'music theatre' or 'musical theatre', and an examination of the European musical is somewhat vexed by the complexities inherent in terminology. When this author, a self-professed 'musical theatre historian', participated in a seminar on 'music theatre' at the 2002 annual meeting of the International Federation for Theatre Research in Amsterdam, not being aware of the significance of the missing 'al', I was surprised to discover that most of the scholars were discussing opera.[8] Seeger argues:

> The fact is, in European and North American theatre – and in other cultures influenced by those theatres – the terms 'music theatre' and 'musical theatre' (including their German, French, Italian, and Spanish equivalents) have a wide variety of meanings and usages. No precise terminology defining the genre has, in fact, emerged.

However, Seeger goes on, accurately, to point out that 'music theatre' generally refers to work growing out of the European traditions of opera and operetta.[9] Indeed, 'musical theatre' is used more commonly to refer to works created in or influenced by American traditions. Eric Salzman, complicating things further by adding a hyphen between 'music' and 'theatre', argues in the *New York Times*:

> Opera is music-theater sung by opera singers in an opera house.
> Music-theater sung by musical-theater singers in a big Broadway or West End house is, well, musical theater. Pure music-theater must be what's left: that which is performed somewhere else by other kinds of singers. This may be as clear a definition as we're going to get.[10]

According to Salzman, then, anything not opera in Europe is 'music-theater'; he should have added Vienna, Hamburg, Berlin and/or Paris, etc., to the second sentence. Still, Salzman's admittedly somewhat unclear definitions of opera and musical theatre are particularly useful for this chapter, since opera has been defined by some as a sung-through form with little to no dialogue between songs. But since the increasing popularity of 'megamusicals', many of which are sung through, it is important to note the distinction between these, which are relatively new but increasingly popular in Europe, and opera, which, while also extremely popular in Europe, *is* a much older form.[11]

Something borrowed

Over the past twenty years, English-language musicals, either in English or in translation, have become extraordinarily popular in many European countries. The appearance of musicals from across the Atlantic *or* Channel is not new, however. For example, the Broadway-style musical was introduced to Austria in 1956 by Marcel Prawy at the Vienna Volksoper, with *Kiss Me, Kate*. *My Fair Lady* was produced in both the Netherlands and Germany in 1961, five years after its Broadway premiere. *Fiddler on the Roof* has enjoyed wide appeal in Europe; in fact, Gänzl calls it 'one of the very few English-language musical plays of its period to make a significant and enduring mark in Europe'.[12] *West Side Story* has had numerous European productions, although not until a decade after the New York premiere. *Blood Brothers*, *Cabaret*, *Chicago*, *A Chorus Line*, *Godspell*, *Grease*, *Hair*, *Rent* and other British or American shows have all enjoyed popularity in Europe.

Most popular have been the British and American 'megamusicals', from Andrew Lloyd Webber's later shows to Disney's *Beauty and the Beast*, *Lion King* and *Aida*. Prece and Everett describe the overwhelming international popularity of *Les Misérables*, often translated into the vernacular, but it is by no means the only megamusical that has taken the continent by storm. Largely responsible for this invasion is Stage Entertainment, formerly known as Stage Holding, a company based in the Netherlands that at the time of writing produces many of the most popular 'borrowed' musicals in Europe, including *Phantom*, *Aida*, *The Lion King*, *Beauty and the Beast* and *Mamma Mia!*. With twenty-two theatres, and offices in the Netherlands, Germany, Spain, Russia, Italy, New York and London, it employs more than 4,500 staff worldwide. The company was formed at the end of 1998 with a head office in Amsterdam; in six years it became one of the world's most productive and powerful live entertainment companies. Another company, Stella Management, produces such shows as *Starlight Express*, *Miss Saigon* and *Cats*.

In Germany, *We Will Rock You*, originally produced in 2002 at the Dominion Theatre in London, recently enjoyed the most successful opening in German musical theatre history at the Musical Dome in Cologne. In Stuttgart, *Miss Saigon* became the cornerstone attraction in a $333 million hotel, theatre and restaurant complex.[13] At $13 million, it is one of the most expensive German musicals ever produced. *Starlight Express* opened in a purpose-built theatre, the rather unimaginatively named 'Starlight-Halle', in Bochum in June 1988; it is still running almost seventeen years later. Munich, Dusseldorf, Essen and Aachen, among other German cities, all have musical stages. But during the past decade, Hamburg, with at least seven theatres producing musicals, has become known as the *Musicalhaupstadt* – musical capital – of Europe. The Operettenhaus, Musicaltempel-Neubau, Imperial Theater, Delphi Theater, Mobil Theater, Schmidt's Tivoli and Neue Flora all produce musicals at least once a season; for some, their stages are devoted to the form. But Berlin threatens to supplant Hamburg, with such theatres as Theater des Westens and Metropole meeting the growing demand for musicals in the post-communist city.

Glenn Loney, in an article in *Theatre Crafts International* that explores the popularity of musicals in Germany and Austria, claims accurately that 'Hamburg and Vienna are currently seen as the two poles in a kind of musical axis which meanders through Germany and Austria'.[14] As previously mentioned, the Broadway-style musical was introduced to Austria in 1956 at the Vienna Volksoper with *Kiss Me, Kate*. *Cats* ran seven years for 2,020 performances and, according to Isolde Schmid-Reiter in *The Encyclopedia of Contemporary Theatre*, 'formed the basis of Vienna's reputation as a European musical metropolis'.[15] The first foreign-language production of *Phantom of the Opera* opened at the Theater an der Wien.[16] Musical theatre gained popularity at the Theater an der Wien under the direction of Rolf Kutschera (1983–93). Even the Volksoper Wien, Europe's leading operetta house, has taken to producing musicals, opening *The Sound of Music* in February 2005. The Alliance of Vienna Stages produces many of the shows, and such venues as the Raimund, Ronacher and the Kammeroper regularly feature musicals on their stages. Outside Vienna, the Bregenz Festival, known primarily for opera, occasionally produces musicals such as *West Side Story* at its lakefront stage on the Bodensee.

The increasing popularity of Anglo-American shows in the Germanic countries is not without criticism. Some worry that these musicals will replace the native drama, that resources once reserved for German-language theatre will be shifted to support borrowed musicals due to their popularity. In their essay on contemporary German theatre in *Contemporary German Cultural Studies*, Meg Mumford and Alison Phipps argue that German-language plays are no longer the majority of repertoire in public theatres. 'Alongside the world of the canonized, German metropolis theatre centres today offer the now ubiquitous western diet of modern Anglo-American musicals, that, when taken out of context would seem to suggest the sidelining of accepted German fare by a culinary internationalized repertoire of blockbuster spectacle.'[17] Mumford and Phipps write of a crisis in German theatre, in part due to the globalisation of theatre and thus the decline of the national stage. Others view the shows more positively, such as Susanne Chambalu in her essay on Austrian theatre in *European Theatre 1960–1990: Cross-Cultural Perspectives*: 'Musicals are a fairly new and important aspect of Austrian theatre. The long run of *Cats* which started in 1983, led to the translation and production of other musicals: *A Chorus Line*, *Les Misérables*, *The Phantom of the Opera*. Sell-outs are proof of their popularity with audiences, who often come from as far away as Germany and Switzerland.' Still, Chambalu admits that some view these productions as 'alien to Vienna's cultural climate', a climate of classical music, opera, and operetta.[18]

But if some view musicals as alien to Austria, others see the form as completely anathema to France, Paris in particular. One could argue that in many cultural aspects, French and American tastes have rarely coincided, and Parisians historically have had little interest in British and American musicals. Lists of productions of the borrowed shows that have flourished in other countries, either in English or translation, rarely include Paris. But perhaps it is the notion of borrowing from other cultures that bothers the French, who, as this essay will later discuss, have contributed some major *new* musicals to the world's stages. And this seeming aversion to borrowed culture has not stopped a few French artists from adapting Anglo-American musicals. Director Jerome Savary's landmark 1986 production of *Cabaret* launched the career of German actress Ute Lemper. Savary first became famous in Paris as a director of the subversive, counter-culture theatre, Grand Magic Circus, beginning in the 1960s. Created to counteract mainstream, bourgeois high culture, the Grand Magic Circus viewed humans as sad animals who have lost the ability to express joy. The 'anything goes' atmosphere of the performances, usually in non-theatrical environments like tents or sports halls, was designed to promote the expression of animality in joyous ways. In the late 1970s Savary began to direct opera apart from the Circus, although his belief in popular theatre caused him to direct more Offenbach than Mozart. In 1988 he became director of the Théâtre National du Chaillot, where he created a large popular theatre that alternated classic with new works, specialising in musical spectacles that combined popular culture with myth, such as *Zazou* (1990). In 2000 he moved on to the financially beleaguered Opéra-Comique to continue his work in musical theatre but was replaced five years later in an attempt to return the theatre back to its eighteenth-century comic opera roots. Unfortunately, his work in musical theatre has never eclipsed his success with *Cabaret*. Swiss-born director Stefan Huber has also gained recognition for his adaptations of Anglo-American musicals, including *Cabaret*, *Les Misérables*, W*est Side Story*, *La Cage aux Folles*, *Fiddler on the Roof*, *Anything Goes*, *Grease*, *Aspects of Love* and *Singin' in the Rain.* Huber has been especially interested in producing Sondheim's musicals in Europe, including *Company*, *Sweeney Todd*, *A Funny Thing Happened on the Way to the Forum*, and the first German-language production of *Merrily We Roll Along*.

Cast members for European borrowed musicals have also largely been borrowed – from outside Europe, since most European actors lacked the appropriate training and experience. Anglo-American performers often find a goldmine of opportunity in European productions of *Phantom*, *Cats*, *Starlight*, *Les Misérables*, etc. Still, some native actors, like Ute Lemper, have gained considerable fame as musical theatre performers. German-born Lemper, who seems to channel Marlene Dietrich, began her career singing in piano bars. She then studied acting at Staatstheater Stuttgart and classical theatre at the Max Reinhardt Seminar in Vienna. Her first significant role was Grizabella in *Cats* when she was twenty-one. She is perhaps most famous for her work in *Cabaret*, *Chicago* and *Peter Pan*, as well as cabaret, particularly as an interpreter of the Kurt Weill songbook and the work of Dietrich and Edith Piaf. Other prominent European musical theatre performers include Pia Douwes, Norbert Lamla, Anne Welte, Anna Montanaro and Andreas Bieber. Of European actors, Andreas Bieber has achieved something akin to rock-star status on the continent. Like Lemper, German-born Bieber got his start in the cast of *Cats* after dance training in Vienna. He performed lead roles in productions of the original musicals *Elisabeth* and *Le Légende de Jimmy* (see the next section on 'Something new') but is perhaps most famous for playing Joseph in the German premiere of *Joseph and the Amazing Technicolor Dreamcoat*. Other productions include *Blood Brothers*, *Into the Woods*, *Grease*, *Cabaret* and *Tommy*.

No examination of European musical theatre would be complete without mentioning the work of Michael Kunze, whose name appears repeatedly on listings of Anglo-American musicals performed in Europe (and some original European musicals as well). Born in Prague in 1943 and educated in Munich, Kunze became successful in the 1970s as a songwriter and record producer, even winning a Grammy. His first adaptation of a musical for the European stage was *Evita*, for its 1981 production in Vienna at the Theater an der Wien; two years later he adapted *Cats* for the same stage. He has since adapted *Song and Dance*, *A Chorus Line*, *Little Shop of Horrors*, *The Phantom of the Opera*, *Into the Woods*, *Follies*, *Assassins*, *Kiss of the Spiderwoman*, *City of Angels*, *Sunset Boulevard* and *Aspects of Love* for German-language productions. Perhaps no other artist has had such an impact on the European musical stage.

Something new

Kunze's impact has extended beyond his translations of borrowed musicals; he has also been involved in the creation of several original musicals, one the most successful German-language musical of all time. Germany and Austria are at the forefront of the movement to create original European musicals; indeed, Gänzl argues that Germany is 'fast threatening to become the new champion of the copycat show'.[19] Besides pointing out the country's leadership in producing original shows, Gänzl's argument that the shows are 'copycats' rings true; most borrow form and style from Anglo-American megamusicals, failing to capture any distinctive Germanic quality. But at the very least, some of the musicals do attempt to draw on European subjects and themes.

In 1993, *Fletsch* opened in Saarbrücken, Germany, at Theater Arnual; about a werewolf, the show with music by Marc Schubring, lyrics by Wolfgang Adenberg and book by Holger Hauer included the unimaginatively titled song 'Ich bin ein Werwolf'. Interestingly, that same year the song 'Ich bin ein Berliner' could be heard in Munster at the Jovel Music Hall in the rock opera *JFK*. The next year *Dracula*, with music, lyrics and book all by Mathias Christian Kosel, opened in Bamberg at the ETA-Hoffman-Theater. *Ludwig II: Longing for Paradise* capitalises on tourist demand for musicals, attempting to draw them away from borrowed subjects to embrace more native themes, as well as tourists attracted to the region by Ludwig's fairy-tale castle, Neuschwanstein. Directed and produced by Stephan Barbarino, who also wrote the lyrics, and composed by Franz Hummel, the $20 million show is housed in a 1400-seat purpose-built theatre. It premiered on 7 April 2000, featuring a revolving stage and twenty-nine sets, and is presented in a mix of High German and a Bavarian dialect, with supertitles in English, Italian and Japanese, a certain internationalism competing somewhat with the Germanic themes.

The decidedly American-themed but extremely popular *Bonnie and Clyde*, written and composed by Paul Graham Brown, opened in June 2001 at the Theater Heilbronn, going on to tour Germany, Switzerland and Austria in 2003. The story of the criminal duo has captured the imagination of a number of artists recently; there have been several musicalised versions of this in the past few years, including at the 2005 NY Musical Theatre Festival. Native themes were represented in the pop/folk musical *Heidi*, based on Johanna Spyri's best-seller of the same name. Opening on 22 October 2004 in Leipzig at the Musikalische Komödie, the show featured singing pine trees and tap-dancing goats, going on to play, logically, in eastern Switzerland. Another popular novel, *The Lord of the Rings*, was recently adapted for the German musical stage as *Der Herr der Ringe*, opening in Berlin at the Mittelerde Theater Berlin. With music and book by Bernd Stromberger and lyrics by Georg Timber-Trattning, the show mirrors *Ludwig II* in its megamusical style.

Austrian artists have proved effective at the use of national themes and subjects for musicals. *Der Watzmann ruft* (The Watzmann Calls), by Wolfgang Ambros, billed itself as an Alpine rock musical. *Freudiana* treated the life of famous Austrian Sigmund Freud, including such witty tunes as 'Sects Therapy'. With music and lyrics by Eric Woolfson, *Freudiana* opened on 19 December 1990 at the Theater an der Wien. Two years later *Elisabeth*, the most successful German-language musical of all time and the most successful European musical of the post-war era, opened there. Another Stage Entertainment property, *Elisabeth* is about the much-loved nineteenth-century Austrian empress, also known as Sissi, the Princess Diana of her

Plate 21 German production of *Elisabeth*, courtesy of Stage Entertainment, Inc.

day. Michael Kunze's book of the oft-treated story begins in the underworld, where Elisabeth's assassin is explaining his crime, justifying it by saying that the empress, played in the original production by Pia Douwes, courted death her whole life. The character Death is the leading man, following Elisabeth as she deals with a domineering mother-in-law, a difficult husband, the Emperor Franz Josef, and the death of her son Rudolf (played by Andreas Bieber). The Habsburg Empire in ruins, Death takes Elisabeth.

Sylvester Levay's score combines rock, pop, jazz, and music in a more classical style. Perhaps the most appealing number is the much-reprised 'Ich gehör nur mir' (I Belong to Me), sung by Elisabeth; also memorable are Rudolf's 'Wenn ich dein Spiegel war' (I'm Just the Same as You) and the duet between Elisabeth and her husband, 'Boote in der Nacht' (Two Ships in the Night). The musical premiered at the Theater an der Wien on 3 September 1992 and totalled 1,278 productions there, closing in 1998, the centenary of the empress's death. It has achieved a kind of cult status among young people in Europe and beyond, a status akin to *Rent* in the United States, with a revival in Vienna and productions in Germany, Hungary, Sweden, the Netherlands and Japan, most recently playing in May 2005 at the Stuttgart Apollo Theatre. In a 1997 article for the *Wall Street Journal*, Ernest Beck describes some passionate audience members:

> Perched on the edge of their seats, the teenage girls stare at the stage, horror struck. They wave white hankies and dab tears with clumps of wet tissue. Some are inconsolable. 'Oh, nein!' they scream, 'It's awful' when Elisabeth, Empress of the Austro-Hungarian Empire, is murdered and the music swells.
>
>   It isn't just Austrian teens who cry for Elisabeth. Mariko Inukai is moved, too. 'I love Elisabeth,' whispers Mrs. Inukai, as her husband nods his approval. 'She's so sad, so beautiful.' The Japanese couple are in Vienna for their honeymoon and to experience 'Elisabeth'.[20]

Elisabeth fan clubs in Europe include over 1,200 members.[21]

Kunze followed *Elisabeth* with *Tanz der Vampire* (Dance of the Vampires), based on the 1967 Roman Polanski horror spoof, *The Fearless Vampire Killers*. Like such shows as *Phantom of the Opera* and *Jekyll and Hyde*, *Tanz*'s leading man is a conflicted, melodramatic anti-hero, but the show is more a dark parody, unlike the other musicals that take their themes – and spectacle – very seriously. Kunze collaborated with Jim Steinman on the German book and lyrics, Steinman composed the music, and Polanski directed the original production, which opened on 4 October 1997 at the Raimundtheater in Vienna. A hit in Vienna and elsewhere in Europe (at the time of writing the musical is playing in Hamburg), a Broadway production played for only sixty-one previews and fifty-six performances, losing its entire $12 million investment, becoming one of the costliest failures on Broadway. Still, its success in Europe likely contributed to Gänzl calling it 'undoubtedly the most complete and effective musical to have come out of central Europe in half a century'.[22]

In terms of western Europe, some might heap similar praise on musicals created by Frenchmen Alain Boublil and Claude-Michel Schönberg, particularly *Les Misérables* and *Miss Saigon*. Boublil and Schönberg's first show, *La Revolution Française* (1973), became a best-selling album and played for one season at the Palais des Sports. Seven years later, their musical version of the epic Victor Hugo novel was first produced at the Palais; however, although the album sold 260,000 copies, the production was less successful. As Richard Eyre in *Changing Stages: A View of British Theatre in the Twentieth Century* writes, *Les Misérables* 'has played successfully all over the world except, with a poetic irony, in Paris'.[23] But British producer Cameron Mackintosh heard the cast album and subsequently brought the musical to London, where he also produced their next show, *Miss Saigon*. As a result, these megamusicals could be considered as much British as French. However, they point towards two important trends in original French musical theatre: marketing and spectacle. Like Mackintosh, French producers often release a song or entire concept album well before the show's opening. And like many of the musicals Mackintosh produces, the original French musicals that are appearing in greater numbers tend to emphasise spectacle. In her essay 'The French Musicals: The Dramatic Impulse of *Spectacle*', Rebecca-Anne C. Do Rozario argues:

> The appellation increasingly applied to French musicals is *spectacle*. French musicals differ from their contemporary English and German language cousins in that their techniques and artistry come not predominantly from theatre, but from show business. In a culture that has been critically antagonistic to the musical genre over the past decade, *les spectacles musicaux* have nonetheless had extraordinary success in Europe and Canada. While the blockbuster musicals, globally produced, including *Les Misérables* (1985) and *The Phantom of the Opera* (1986), which seemed ubiquitous in the 1980s and early 90s, found no substantial audience base in France; at the turn of the century there is evidence of a substantial musical theatre originating in the French language.[24]

One of the most substantial new musicals to come out of France in the past decade is *Notre-Dame de Paris* by Riccardo Cocciante and Luc Plamondon.

Lyricist Luc Plamondon is to French musical theatre what composer Sir Andrew Lloyd Webber is to British, with a long, fairly prolific career (he is originally from Quebec). Along with composer Michael Berger, Plamondon created an early French cult musical hit, *Starmania*, although it was not a hit when it opened in Paris at the 4,000-seat Palais des Congrès in 1979. Directed by Tom O'Horgan of *Hair* and *Jesus Christ Superstar* fame, the rock opera was first produced as a concept album, and in spite of only twenty-five original performances went on to many successful remountings. As Gänzl states: 'In the otherwise modern-musical-theatre desert that is France, *Starmania* somehow lives on. And on. And on.'[25] In 1990 Plamondon and Berger collaborated again on a musical based on the life of James Dean, *Le Légende de Jimmy*, directed by Jerome Savary at the Théatre Mogador in Paris. (In 1993 a German production of the show starred Andreas Bieber.)

But Plamondon's greatest success has come with his collaboration with composer Riccardo Cocciante on *Notre-Dame de Paris*. Based on yet another Hugo novel, the musical also shares an emphasis with *Les Misérables* on spectacle, as well as a through-sung, 'Europop' sound. Introduced yet again through the recording industry, the show opened on 16 September 1998, at the Palais des Congrès, where over 500,000 people saw it between September and February; it also enjoyed a sold-out tour across France and in Canada. In London it ran for seventeen months at the Dominion Theatre. Nicolas Powell of *Variety* points out that 'once great lovers of operetta, the French in general and Parisians in particular are commonly held not to like – and not to be able to do – musicals.' But he admits that *Notre-Dame* is 'proving the greatest commercial success in French musical theater for over 20 years'.[26]

Two shows that appeared in 2001 in Paris, *Roméo & Juliette* and *Les Dix Commandements*, seemed to reaffirm the French preoccupation with epic, melodramatic, spectacular shows. However, French film composer and lyricist Michel Legrand has offered an alternative through the 1997 musical comedy, *Le Passe-Muraille*. Nearly two decades earlier, Legrand had collaborated with Jacques Demy on the adaptation of the film *Les Parapluies de Cherbourg*, for which Legrand had composed the score, to the stage. Although it originated at The Public in New York City in 1979, it was mounted later the same year in Paris at Théatre Montparnasse. *Le Passe-Muraille*, with book by Didier van Cauwelaert, ran for a year in Paris in 1997 at the Théâtre des Bouffes-Parisiens and was warmly received. Jean-Luc Jeener, of *Le Figaroscope*, gave it the ultimate compliment for a Frenchman, calling it 'a delightful musical comedy in the great French tradition, that is, original, free of any Anglo-Saxon influence'.[27] An English-language production was mounted in 2002 on Broadway as *Amour*; Alan Riding of the *New York Times* commented, 'A musical comedy that does well in France is already something of an occasion. A French musical comedy that reaches Broadway – well, "Irma la Douce" was the last to do so, in 1960.'[28] However, although the show did well in Paris, it was not so successful in New York City.

Outside France, Germany and Austria, original musicals have been created sporadically across Europe. In Italy, the songwriting team of Pietro Garinei and Sandro Giovannini are considered the godfathers of post-war musical comedy there, producing many shows at the Teatro Sistina. At the Compagnia della Rancia director Saverio Marconi has staged numerous shows, including an original production, *Dance!*, based on *Much Ado About Nothing*, as well as the first Italian version of *A Chorus Line*.[29] In pre-1956 Poland, American-style musicals were not done 'for ideological reasons' – i.e. they were viewed as symbols of capitalism. Shifts in these views after 1956 led to a fairly vital musical scene. In 1958 director Danuta Baduszkowa founded the Tatr Muzyczny (Musical Theatre) in Gdynia, focusing on contemporary Polish and foreign repertoire. The first Polish musicals were done in dramatic theatres, then in operetta theatres, Poznań, Warsaw, Gdynia and Lódź taking the lead. In 1983, Jerzy Gruza became the artistic director of Musical Theatre, staging original Polish works as well as such shows as *Fiddler* (1984), *Jesus Christ Superstar* (1987) and *Les Misérables* (1989). In Denmark, the musical *Hans Christian Anderson*, which opened in Copenhagen at the Gladsaxe Theater on 31 December 1995, has been very popular.

But just a few steps behind Germany, Austria and France in the creation of new musicals is the Czech Republic. Like Poland, communist

Czechoslovakia considered musicals at best frivolous and at worst corrupted by western capitalism, so production of western-style musicals is a relatively recent phenomenon. However, Prague now boasts several theatres producing musicals, including the GoJa Music Hall, the Spiral Theatre, the intimate Karlin Theatre, which regularly plays to near-capacity houses, and the obviously capitalist-inspired T-Mobile Arena. Two of the most notable new musicals produced in the past decade are *Rusalka Muzikál* and *Hamlet Muzikál*. The former is a rock version of 'The Little Mermaid', a story perhaps most beloved to Czech people through its manifestation as a Dvořák opera, which premiered at the National Theatre in Prague in 1901. *Rusalka Muzikál* premiered at the Milénium Theatre in Prague on 20 November 1998. The next year at the Kalich Theatre a musical based on Shakespeare's *Hamlet* ran for six hundred performances, partly due to the popularity of its creator, Janek Ledecký, a well-known Czech pop star who not only wrote the music, lyrics and libretto but also played the lead in some performances. Unfortunately, critics were not as kind as audiences; Katerina Honskusova of *The Prague Post* called it a 'McDonaldized musical version of a classic' and argued that aspects of *Hamlet Muzikál* 'would make Will turn in his grave'.[30] However, a Broadway production has been in the works.[31]

Something blue?

Admittedly, the wedding analogy breaks down a bit here at the conclusion, although at least two original European musicals have been about something 'blue': *Der blaue Engel* and *La Vie en bleu*. *Der blaue Engel* (The Blue Angel) was adapted from the 1930 von Sternberg film with Marlene Dietrich, which was the first European 'talkie'. Produced in Berlin in 1995, it starred that modern-day Dietrich, Ute Lemper. *La Vie en bleu*, a musical comedy in forty scenes about Pablo Picasso, opened in 1998 at the Théâtre Mogador in Paris. *Bleu* is an example of a musical based on European subjects and themes, created by Europeans (music by Pascal Stive and lyrics and libretto by Jean-Michel Beriat and Raymond Jeannot) for Europeans. But the European musical is not always so clearly defined. Is *Miss Saigon* a European musical, when some lyrics and 'additional material' were written by American Richard Maltby Jr, or is *Notre-Dame de Paris* when one of its creators is from Canada? Is *Les Parapluies de Cherbourg* a European musical, when it originated in New York City? Can *JFK*, *Bonnie and Clyde* and *Le Légende de Jimmy* be considered truly European, when they treat such classic American subjects?

Issues of identity are often at the heart of theatre, and they have become particularly foregrounded in the midst of globalisation, a condition that is making it difficult to define who we are as nations and cultures. What can or should the products of that culture be? Who or what should be represented? Is 'authenticity' or 'specificity' in representation important? One critic, Sheridan Morley, laments the replacement of specificity in the musical with the musical as 'event'. In his book *Spread a Little Happiness: The First Hundred Years of the British Musical*, Morley observes that big worldwide musical hits 'ask nothing of their audience beyond attendance at a certain theatre on a certain night. No language problems for foreign tourists, no demands of a shared heritage or education, no cultural barriers to be stormed'. The 'less a show is actually about', the broader appeal it will have.[32] However, just as artists and critics seem to constantly predict the death of the musical in America, only to find it not only still breathing but constantly evolving and adapting, so too will the musical survive and likely even thrive in Europe and throughout the world.[33]

16 New horizons: the musical at the dawn of the twenty-first century

BUD COLEMAN

During most of the 1960s, it was easy to see the musical as hopelessly out of touch with contemporary America. Even with three Broadway blockbusters opening in the same year (1964) – *Fiddler on the Roof*, *Hello, Dolly!*, *Funny Girl* – and the film version of *My Fair Lady* walking away with eight Academy Awards – it seemed apparent that the Golden Age of Musical Theatre had staged its own grand finale as these works neither reflected nor commented on the turmoil of the 1960s; they were escapist and nostalgic. With the assassinations of President John F. Kennedy (1963), Martin Luther King (1968) and Senator Bobby Kennedy (1968), and the escalating war in Vietnam, the world was a different place from the comparative calm of the 1950s. In 1964, the Beatles appeared on the Ed Sullivan Show for the first time, heralding with electronic chords that the British invasion was in full force, and rock 'n' roll was here to stay. As urban centres across the county fell into disrepair, many downtown theatres were abandoned (often to the wrecking ball) and the road business of touring musicals almost ceased altogether. Financially and artistically, the fabulous invalid was not in very good shape.

When *Hair* arrived on Broadway in 1968, the Great White Way at last embraced a musical whose music and sentiment reflected some of the headlines of its day, and it was staged in a way that distanced itself aesthetically light years away from other musicals playing around Times Square. With the New York premieres of Stephen Sondheim's *Company* (1970), Andrew Lloyd Webber's *Jesus Christ Superstar* (1971), Michael Bennett's *A Chorus Line* (1975), and John Kander, Fred Ebb and Bob Fosse's *Chicago* (1975), several new artists found audiences for their disparate visions of what a musical could be, sing and/or dance about. Experimentation continued as the concept musical, the jukebox musical, the revisal, the dansical and the megamusical came to be. Despite rising ticket prices, theatre attendance began to climb both in New York and on the road. While movie musicals virtually disappeared from the silver screen after *Cabaret* (1972) and *Grease* (1978), the stage musical continued to attract audiences even as it experimented with new forms and structures. Truly, rumours of its demise were grossly exaggerated.

The changes that occurred in the American musical at the end of the twentieth century made it clear that while twenty-first-century musical theatre owed much to the past, it was creating sub-genres which would have been unrecognisable to its original creators such as Cohan, Kern, Berlin, Gershwin, Hart and Fields. In order to explicate the musical at the dawn of the twenty-first century, we will first look at musical theatre genres that have their roots in the past, then move to new forms which emerged around and after 2000.[1] Finally, we will explore the changing roles of directors, choreographers, actors, and producers as musical theatre explores new options in the twenty-first century.

The operetta musical

One of the many antecedents of musical theatre is the operetta – epitomised by the work of Gilbert and Sullivan – the genre in which Rudolf Friml, Sigmund Romberg, Victor Herbert and sometimes Jerome Kern operated. (See chapters 3 and 4.) In traditional operetta, the music will be well crafted, and though the plots and even the sentiments may sometimes seem silly, the musical result is likely to be glorious. A prime requisite is well-trained semi-operatic voices. More contemporary derivations of the operetta can be heard in Raphael Crystal's *Kuni-Lemi* (1984), Frank Wildhorn's *The Scarlet Pimpernel* (1997), Jeffrey Stock's *Triumph of Love* (1997), and Michael John LaChiusa's *Marie Christine* (1999). These late twentieth-century operettas were not marketed as such, since producers no doubt wanted to avoid anything that might sound old-fashioned. Similarly, Sondheim did not label his own work thus, but *A Little Night Music* (1973), *Sweeney Todd* (1979) and *Passion* (1994) fall into this category. Opera companies often undertake revivals of these almost-an-opera musicals/operettas.

Commissioned by Philadelphia's American Music Theatre Festival in 1994, *Floyd Collins* belongs in this category, albeit a 'pocket operetta' with only thirteen performers. Based on the true story of a Kentucky man who was trapped in a cave in 1925 for sixteen days, the work featured a score by Adam Guettel and a book by Tina Landau. While one reporter visited and interviewed Collins eight times, efforts to save him failed. Before he was discovered dead, an enormous media circus sprung up outside the Sand Cave. When *Floyd Collins* opened off-Broadway at Playwrights Horizons in 1996, Ben Brantley of *The New York Times* found the work to exhibit 'good faith, moral seriousness and artistic discipline', nevertheless he also thought it 'half realized'. Responding to a 1999 revival at the Old Globe in San Diego, Rick Simas positioned Guettel with Bernstein and Sondheim – as 'one of the most innovative composers to write for the musical theatre' – and found Landau's book and direction to be 'fresh' and 'exciting'.[2]

The son of Mary Rodgers (*Once Upon a Mattress*) and grandson of Richard Rodgers, Guettel certainly enjoys the prestige of belonging to an American musical theatre dynasty. While *Floyd Collins* has its cult followers, *Love's Fire* and *Saturn Returns* (a.k.a. *Myths and Hymns*, 1998) generated more good press. Winning Tony Awards for Best Original Score and Best Orchestrations (with Bruce Coughlin and Ted Sperling) for *The Light in the Piazza* (2005) secured Guettel's place in history. In this lush, romantic score, Guettel created a soundscape much closer to *Passion* than to conventional musical theatre.

The integrated musical

Shows with a coherent, strong libretto that create a theatrical world where the focus is on story and character, and songs are constructed to further plot and character development, are alive and well. Productions such as *Ragtime* (1998), *Avenue Q* (2003), *Hairspray* (2002), and *The Drowsy Chaperone* (2006) continue this fine tradition. While the Golden Age of Musical Theatre is often seen as the maturation of the integrated book musical, musical theatre creators are still drawn to the proven efficacy of this form.

The pop/rock musical

For most of the twentieth century, musical theatre supplied many of the popular songs of the day. With the advent of rock 'n' roll, however, musical theatre composers were slow to adopt this genre as rhythm had replaced melody as the unifying element of a song, and lyrics often took back seat to percussion. For these reasons, most conventional Broadway composers veered away from rock. As a result, it is generally composers new to Broadway or the West End who write the majority of pop/rock musicals; unhappily, these writing team teams tend to create only one successful work. (See chapter 13 for more on rock musicals.) Where are the follow-up hits by Galt McDermott (*Hair*, 1968), Jim Jacobs and Warren Casey (*Grease*, 1972), Carol King (*Really Rosie*, 1980), Roger Miller (*Big River*, 1985) and others? While such musicals enjoyed long runs, they appear to be one-offs.

The exceptions to this one-hit trend are Stephen Schwartz, Elton John and David Yazbek, who have brought numerous contemporary pop musicals to the Broadway stage. Following *Godspell* (1971), Schwartz penned successful Broadway musicals – *Pippin* (1972), *The Magic Show* (1974) – and animated film musicals (*Pocahontas*, lyrics, 1995; *The Hunchback of Notre Dame*, lyrics, 1996; *The Prince of Egypt*, music and lyrics, 1997) before he wrote the blockbuster *Wicked* (2003). (See chapter 19 for more on the creation of *Wicked*.) Elton John was certainly no stranger to popular prestige, but even his most ardent fans were probably surprised by the vengeance with which he conquered the stage musical. Elton John and Tim Rice's film *The Lion King* (1994) became a phenomenal stage sensation in 1997 and then John began writing directly for the stage, starting with *Aida* (lyrics by Tim Rice) in 2000, *Billy Elliot: The Musical* (lyrics by Lee Hall) in 2005, and *Lestat* (lyrics by Bernie Taupin) in 2006. Only *Lestat* failed to connect with critics and audiences.

Having been recorded by a number of popular groups and the composer of a number of scores for television, David Yazbek came to musical theatre in 2000 by adapting for the stage the 1997 British hit film *The Full Monty*. Teaming up with veteran librettist Terrence McNally, the stage musical ran for 770 performances. Yazbek returned to Broadway with the stage musical adaptation of *Dirty Rotten Scoundrels* (2005), this time collaborating with librettist Jeffrey Lane. Along with Elton John, Yazbek is a successful pop song writer who made the transition to musical theatre, proving that he can write for character and keep his award-winning aesthetic of the engaging, contemporary pop song. Another pop song composer who has had success on Broadway is Frank Wildhorn, who had three musicals running simultaneously on Broadway in 1999 – *Jekyll and Hyde* (1997), *The Scarlet Pimpernel* (1997) and *The Civil War* (1999).[3]

Related to the pop/rock musical is the 'jukebox musical'. These revues and musicals take advantage of previously written music, as opposed to the above productions, which feature original music. Similar to the revue, the jukebox musical is an assemblage of pre-existing songs where the emphasis is clearly on the songs, not on plot and/or character. Unlike earlier elaborate revues put on by the likes of Ziegfeld and George White, late twentieth-century revues tend to focus on the music of one composer and generally do not showcase stars. With the exception of *Bubblin' Brown Sugar* (1976), *Sophisticated Ladies* (1981) and *Black and Blue* (1989) – which featured large casts, elaborate sets, and demanding choreography – most late twentieth-century jukebox musicals were small, intimate affairs, and included *Ain't Misbehavin'* (1978, music of Fats Waller), *Five Guys Named Moe* (1992, songs by Louis Jordan), *Smokey Joe's Café* (1995, songs by Jerry Leiber and Mike Stoller) and *Dream* (1997, lyrics by Johnny Mercer).

One variation of the jukebox musical/musical revue is the 'disguised pop/rock concert'. In this format a series of pop or rock hits are staged as a concert; the evening invariably ends with an uninterrupted series of numbers performed by the cast. Some of these musicals are semi-biographical:

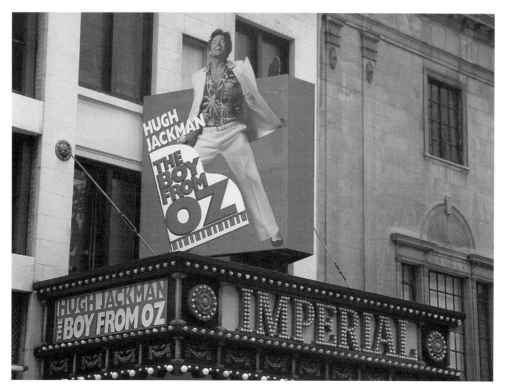

Plate 22 Imperial Theatre marquee featuring *The Boy from Oz*, summer 2004.

Beatlemania (1977, Beatles), *Eubie!* (1978, Eubie Blake), *Buddy: The Buddy Holly Story* (1990), *Leader of the Pack* (1985, Ellie Greenwich), and *Jersey Boys* (2006, Frankie Valli & The Four Seasons). Others are less concert and more biography, often using songs a singer and/or songwriter made famous, and include *The Boy from Oz* (2003, Peter Allen) and *Good Vibrations* (2005, Beach Boys).

Another genre of the jukebox musical that utilises pre-existing songs, but creates a plot around them, is the 'story album musical' or the 'anthology with a story' musical. (These contain plots where the story is not a biography of the songwriter.) Some incorporate songs written originally for musical theatre, and others use pop songs. Two of the most popular of the former variety are the 'new' Gershwin musicals *My One and Only* (1983) and *Crazy for You* (1992). *Crazy for You* contains five songs from *Girl Crazy*, four from *A Damsel in Distress*, three from the film *Shall We Dance?*, and six other Gershwin tunes. Ken Ludwig wrote a new libretto; directed by Mike Ockrent and choreographed by Susan Stroman, the musical was very popular with audiences. Similarly, two plot musicals have created new characters and contexts for songs already written by Stephen Sondheim: *Marry Me a Little* (1980) and *Putting It Together* (1999).

Jukebox musicals featuring pop songs (and non-biographical plots) include the international sensation *Mamma Mia!* (1999) and the Billy Joel/Twyla Tharp dansical, *Movin' Out* (2002). Like the biographical or rock concert jukebox musical, musicals in this niche enjoy the fact that many potential theatre patrons already know the music very well. During their ten years of existence as a band (1972–82), the Swedish group ABBA had fourteen singles in the Top 40 (four in the Top 10), and record sales that exceeded 350 million units. British playwright Catherine Johnson took twenty-two of their greatest hits and fashioned a plot around them about a young woman who wants her father to give her away at her wedding; problem is, mom doesn't know which one of three men she was seeing at the time might be Sophie's dad. *Mamma Mia!* has been performed in ten languages, in eighty-five cities, and to over twenty million people; it has become an entertainment industry in its own right. Now its fifth year (and counting) in Las Vegas, it is the longest-running full-length Broadway musical ever to play this city of chance.

Ethnic musicals

The black musical is a subdivision of the pop/rock musical, featuring music that reflects African-American jazz, blues, gospel, funk, reggae, rap or Motown. Examples are Gary Geld's *Purlie* (1970), Judd Woldin and Robert Brittan's *Raisin* (1973), Micki Grant's *Don't Bother Me, I Can't Cope* (1972) and *Your Arms Too Short to Box With God* (1976), Charlie Small's *The Wiz* (1975), Michael Butler's *Reggae* (1980), Gary Sherman's *Amen Corner* (1983), and *The Color Purple* (2005, with book by Marsha Norman and score by Brenda Russell, Allee Willis and Stephen Bray). Special mention should be made of *Mama, I Want to Sing!* (1983), which opened at the 632-seat Heckscher Theater in Harlem. Written by Vy Higginsen, Ken Wydro and Wesley Naylor, the original production ran 2,213 performances, closing after eight years only because of a lease dispute. Two sequels – *Mama, I Want To Sing II* (1990) and *Born to Sing!* (1996) – along with a six-month run on the West End of the original *Mama* in 1995 and several world tours brought the musical to millions. The original *Mama* cost $35,000 but grossed $25 million in its first five years. Higginsen (wife) and Wydro's (husband) family business earned $8.7 million in 1988; they are one of the most-successful black-owned enterprises in America.

The jukebox musical also proved to be a popular form for African-American songwriters and performers. Notable examples include *Ain't Misbehavin'* (1978), a celebration of songs by Fats Waller; *Sophisticated Ladies* (1981), showcasing the music of Duke Ellington; *Black and Blue* (1989), an

anthology of songs by African Americans that were popular in Paris between
the two world wars; and *Five Guys Named Moe* (1992), focusing on songs
by Louis Jordan. Perhaps not surprisingly, given the demographics of the
Broadway audience, few producers have attempted to bring rap music to
Broadway, the exception being *Bring in 'da Noise, Bring in 'da Funk* (1996).
Conceived and directed by George C. Wolfe, the appeal of *Funk* had more
to do with the innovative choreography and performance by Savion Glover
than the music.

New York City census information from 2000 indicates that 26.9% of the
metropolitan population was Hispanic or Latino, and that 39% of Broadway
audiences come from the New York metropolitan region.[4] Given this demo-
graphic information, it seems surprising that the Latino musical has thus far
not found an audience on Broadway. Examples include Luis Valdez's *Zoot
Suit* (1979) and Paul Simon's *Capeman* (1998). Arne Glimcher's *The Mambo
Kings* (2005) closed in San Francisco before it even came to New York.[5] More
successful have been dance-based revues such as *Tango Argentino* (1985,
revived 1999), *Flamenco Puro* (1986) and *Forever Tango* (1997, revived 2004)
and off-Broadway productions such as *El Bravo!* (1981) by José Fernandez,
Thom Schiera and John Clifton; *¡Sofrito!* (1997), a bilingual musical by
David González and Larry Harlow with a Caribbean-influenced score that
played to sold-out audiences at New York's New Victory Theater; and *Gardel:
The Musical* (2006), a bio-musical about Argentine tango music legend
Carlos Gardel. Since the only two genres of music that saw increases in CD
sales in 2004 were country and Spanish, it is only a matter of time before
savvy theatre producers move into this market. One might also expect more
examples of the Spanish light opera, or *zarzuela*, to begin to appear in the
repertoire of English and American opera companies. (See chapter 2 for
more on the *zarzuela* in North America.)

While such shows as Rodgers and Hammerstein's *Flower Drum Song*
(1958) and Boublil and Schönberg's *Miss Saigon* (1989) have given Asian-
American performers long-running hits in which to perform, there have
been very few Asian-American-authored musicals. Leon Ko and Robert
Lee's *Heading East* (1999), A. R. Rahman's *Bombay Dreams* (2004), and
Maria Maria (book and lyrics by Hye Jung Yu, music by Gyung Chan Cha,
2006) are rare exceptions. Though the original music was kept, David Henry
Hwang wrote a new libretto for *The Flower Drum Song* when it was revived
on Broadway in 2002.

In the folk/country-western music genre, there have been notable past
successes, such as Carol Hall's *The Best Little Whorehouse in Texas* (1978),
Quilters (1984) and Roger Miller's *Big River* (1985). Yet, even though country
music sales have been rising along with Spanish CD music sales, there has
yet to be a successful twenty-first-century folk or country musical.

The non-linear or 'concept' musical

In contrast to the integrated musical, the concept musical rejects a traditional storyline; instead the emphasis is on character, or on a theme or a message. And since they are 'thought pieces', concept musicals are rarely comedies. After two successful off-Broadway musicals (*First Lady Suite*, 1993; *Hello Again*, 1994), composer/lyricist Michael John LaChiusa was heralded as one of the promising musical theatre creators who were forging new forms. But the box-office failures of *The Petrified Prince* (1994), *Marie Christine* (1999), and *The Wild Party* (2000) seemed to indicate that Broadway audiences were not yet ready to embrace his experiments with the concept musical.

Joseph Moncure March's 1926 poem *The Wild Party* inspired LaChiusa and co-librettist/director George C. Wolfe to musicalise this depiction of jazz-age debauchery.[6] Produced by the New York Shakespeare Festival, the production opened on Broadway in 2000 with a top-tier cast (Eartha Kitt, Mandy Patinkin, and Toni Collette) and was nominated for seven Tony Awards. Set in the twilight of the vaudeville era, the show is conceptualised around a series of vaudeville turns, complete with signs announcing the titles of the acts. *New York Magazine*'s John Simon found the piece to be 'a fiasco' since it appeared to him to be a series of 'random incidents that refuse to mesh'.[7] Similarly, Ben Brantley (in the *New York Times*) described the evening as 'a parade of personalities in search of a missing party'.[8] Unable to find an audience, *The Wild Party* closed after sixty-eight performances, losing all of its $5 million capitalisation.

While the concept musical found a niche within the tenets of post-modernism, musical theatre audiences tended to be more conservative, preferring a linear story and hummable tunes to radical experimentation. The box-office failures of Jerry Herman's *Mack and Mabel* (1974, sixty-six performances), Stephen Sondheim's *Merrily We Roll Along* (1981, sixteen performances) and Jeanine Tesori's *Caroline, or Change* (2004, 136 performances) serve as warning beacons to those who would argue that audiences want challenging fare. Even though many critics considered each of these musicals to be some of the finest work that these creative teams in question had ever written, they failed to find a loyal audience.

One variation of the concept musical that has found appreciative audiences is the self-reflexive musical. While the 'backstage musical' has long been a popular genre – *Kiss Me, Kate* (1948), *Gypsy* (1959), *Dreamgirls* (1981), *The Producers* (2001) – the self-reflexive musical is not just about show business and/or musical theatre, it asks the audience to believe that the production of the musical which they are watching is happening in real time in front of them. Little Sally interrupts Office Lockstop as he attempts to introduce the audience to *Urinetown, the Musical* (2001). Little Sally questions why the musical has such an 'awful' title, especially when the music is so 'happy'. When she attempts to understand the seriousness of the water shortage crisis around which the musical's plot revolves, Officer Lockstock cuts her off, explaining 'nothing can kill a musical faster than too much exposition'. Similarly, in *Dirty Rotten Scoundrels* (2005) and *Spamalot* (2005), characters also often break the fourth wall. The self-reflexive musical can appear as too much of an insider phenomenon – like quoting choreography from *West Side Story* in *Urinetown* – suggesting that audiences must know a great deal about musicals in order to get all of the allusions and jokes. But musical theatre never gets tired of looking at its own reflection, as writers continue to be drawn to the backstage musical, the show-within-a-show, and the self-reflexive musical in works such as *The Musical of Musicals: The Musical* (2003), *The Drowsy Chaperone* (2006), and *Curtains!* (2007).

The 'dansical'

When *Contact* won the Tony Award for Best Musical in 2000, it was clear that the dansical had arrived, although director/choreographer Susan Stroman's work was advertised as 'a dance play'. Here the emphasis is on dance and the narrative is told through movement since there is generally no dialogue or sung lyrics. As another sign of the new supremacy of the choreographer/director (see chapter 12), the dansical often does not contain original music. Consider, for example, *Big Deal* (Bob Fosse, 1986), *Dangerous Games* (Graciela Daniele, 1989), *Chronicle of a Death Foretold* (Daniele, 1995), *Contact* (Stroman, 2000), *Movin' Out* (Twyla Tharp, 2003), and *The Times They Are A-Changin'* (Tharp, 2007). While the form is not new, Susan Stroman and Twyla Tharp can be given credit for almost single-handedly popularising the form. Some critics noted that Tharp had already been on Broadway before with an evening-long dance theatre piece *The Catherine Wheel*, which had a three-week engagement in 1981.

'Actor-musicianship'

Having worked in British regional theatres for several decades, during the belt-tightening of the 1990s, John Doyle was faced with the challenge of directing/producing musical theatre with companies who could no longer afford orchestras. At first he had actors play musical instruments when their characters were not on stage. Then he began to direct the musical in a way that the characters stayed on stage and in character, and so their playing an instrument became another facet of their characterisation. For this reason, Doyle calls his approach 'actor-musicianship' as it is 'a "multi-skilled" way of telling a story'.[9] As associate director of the Watermill Theatre, his experiments in this 220-seat theatre in Berkshire attracted critical notice. But when Doyle's *The Gondoliers* (2001) and *Sweeney Todd* (2004) transferred to the West End, more audiences were exposed to these unique revisals. *Gondoliers* was rewritten with a cast of eight actors to feature a Chicago mafia family who find themselves in a London Italian jazz café, while *Sweeney* was reduced to a cast of ten performers who all played musical instruments; neither production featured a separate orchestra. When *Sweeney Todd* moved to Broadway, Doyle won the Tony Award for Best Director of a Musical. Doyle's refashioned *Mack and Mabel* transferred to London's Criterion Theatre in 2006, the same year his Cincinnati Playhouse in the Park production of *Company* (with new orchestrations by Mary-Mitchell Campbell) moved to Broadway. In these re-imaginings of shows, the guiding hand of the auteur director (and now auteur orchestrator) is extremely visible.

The 'revisal'

A variation on the director and/or choreographer as auteur is the revival which features a new (or significantly altered) libretto. In the case of these 'revisals', the librettist is now the auteur. In 1983, Peter Stone and Timothy S. Mayer crafted a new book to create *My One and Only*, using many of the songs from George and Ira Gershwin's *Funny Face* (1927). Eventually running 767 performances, its commercial success no doubt inspired the creation of the next 'new' Gershwin musical, *Crazy for You* (1992), for which Ken Ludwig wrote a new libretto using Guy Bolton's basic storyline for the Gershwins' *Girl Crazy* (1930).

The practice of the revisal dates back centuries. When French composer Georges Bizet created *Carmen* to a libretto by Henri Meilhac and Ludovic Halévy in 1875, this *opéra-comique* contained spoken dialogue. By the time it opened in Vienna later in 1875, *Carmen* no longer featured spoken dialogue, but rather recitative devised by Ernest Guiraud, as Bizet had died three months after the opera's premiere. Oscar Hammerstein II then wrote a new libretto and lyrics in 1943 to Bizet's music, titling the new work *Carmen Jones* and setting it in World War II Alabama. The next major reiteration occurred in 1983 when Peter Brook and Jean-Claude Carrière removed the chorus to create *La Tragédie de Carmen*.

A recent, significant rewrite happened when a production of *Annie Get Your Gun* was being prepared for a 1999 Broadway revival starring Bernadette Peters. The original book by Herbert Fields and Dorothy Fields was revised by Peter Stone to remove the jokes and songs aimed at American Indians. The song 'I'm an Indian, Too' was cut and the musical's subplot was rewritten to feature an inter-racial couple. Even though Stone's alterations were made with the permission of Berlin and Fields' heirs, criticism was levelled at Stone and the revival's producers for changing a work of art. On the other hand, no one missed the racial slurs of the original 1946 show, and with Stone's new book and galvanising performances by Peters and her replacement Reba McEntire, the revisal had a very profitable run of 1,045 performances.

David Henry Hwang wrote an entirely new libretto for Joseph Fields, Richard Rodgers and Oscar Hammerstein's *Flower Drum Song*. While groundbreaking in 1958 for humanising a marginalised group in American society, the work nevertheless became perceived as sentimental, a 'minor' Rodgers and Hammerstein work. The reviews that greeted the 2001 'revisal' at the Mark Taper Forum were universally positive. *Variety* applauded Hwang's 'wholesale reconstructive surgery' to the script, calling it 'an artistic success, revealing a revitalised score and a dramatic complexion that's far richer than the original'.[10] Diane Haithman of the *Los Angeles Times* notes that Hwang's changes are not about updating a 1958 musical to twenty-first-century standards of political correctness, instead 'he plays with Asian stereotypes, rather than eliminate them'.[11] The reviews for the New York run were not as positive, and the production only managed a run of 172 performances on Broadway.

While the producers clearly marketed their productions of *My One and Only* and *Crazy for You* as 'new' Gershwin musicals (complete with quotation marks), the revisals of *Annie Get Your Gun* and *Flower Drum Song* did not have titles that distinguished them from their original incarnations. Unlike various versions of a song recorded by different artists, these revisals are not interpretations of a work of art, they are unique works of art. It is ahistorical and unethical to present a work to audiences under its old title when it contains significant alterations to its original form.

For most of the twentieth century, musical theatre writers not only supplied the nation with many of its hit songs, but also many of its top musical films as well. Indeed, perusal of the American Film Institute's (AFI) list of the twenty-five 'Greatest Movie Musicals' reveals that over half started on the Broadway stage. While the norm has been stage-to-screen transfers, there are a handful of musicals that were originally conceived and written for film that have been subsequently reconfigured for the Broadway stage. (See Table 16.1.)

The wildly acclaimed classic *The Wizard of Oz* (1939) and Rodgers and Hammerstein's television film *Cinderella* (1957) were made into popular stage properties in the 1990s, but curiously neither has ever played a

Table 16.1 *Selected stage adaptations of musical films (arranged chronologically according to the year of the stage version)*

Title	Year of film	Year of stage version
Gigi	1958	1973
42nd Street	1933	1980, 2001 revival
Singin' in the Rain	1952	1985
Meet Me in St. Louis	1944	1989
The Who's Tommy	1975	1993
Beauty and the Beast	1991	1994
Victor, Victoria	1982	1995
State Fair	1945	1996
The Lion King	1994	1997
Chitty Chitty Bang Bang	1968	2002 (London), 2005 (New York)
Mary Poppins	1964	2004 (London), 2006 (New York)

Broadway theatre. Instead, they have been performed professionally on the road and in regional theatres, and both were released for amateur productions relatively quickly. Similarly, Disney's megahit *High School Musical* (2006) went from cable television to high school productions within its first year. A New York run was once seen as an absolute imperative so a production could boast 'direct from Broadway' even if they did not have any glowing quotations from reviews to go with that claim. But these three popular productions purposefully declined a Broadway production as none of them needed the imprint of a New York production to 'validate' them.

Concerning story and characters, a minority of musicals feature an original plot; most are adaptations of source material that first existed as a novel, short story, news article, biography, ballet, or even a painting (*Sunday in the Park with George*). A recent trend – which some critics fear has become an epidemic – is the musicalisation of popular films. (See Table 16.2.)

A snapshot taken on 1 January 2006 shows thirty-eight productions on Broadway; of the twenty-nine musicals running, nineteen were either made into or from a film.

The genre of the source material is no guarantee of the critical and/or commercial success of a musical, but what the screen-to-stage musicalisation can capitalise on is name recognition. When a film like *Footloose* comes to Broadway, even a mediocre stage musical staging can run for 709 performances in New York, enjoy a long run in Las Vegas, and see numerous amateur productions. But name recognition is certainly not a reliable insurance policy: for every megahit (*Little Shop of Horrors, La Cage aux Folles, Hairspray*) there is an implosion (*The Goodbye Girl, Urban Cowboy*). In 2002, MGM created 'MGM On Stage' to develop and license films from their catalogue for stage production. Starting with *Chitty Chitty Bang Bang, Dirty Rotten Scoundrels, The Adventures of Priscilla, Queen of the Desert*

Table 16.2 *Selected stage musicals based on largely non-musical films, some of which feature significant musical sequences (arranged chronologically according to the year of the stage version)*

Title	Year of film	Year of stage musical
A Little Night Music	1955*	1973
Little Shop of Horrors	1960	1982, 2003 revival
La Cage aux Folles	1978	1983, 2004 revival
My Favorite Year	1982	1992
The Goodbye Girl	1977	1993
Sunset Boulevard	1950	1993 (London), 1994 (New York)
Passion	1981**	1994
Fame, The Musical	1980	1995
Big	1988	1996
The Full Monty	1997	2000
The Producers	1968	2001
Hairspray	1988	2002
Sweet Smell of Success	1957	2002
Thoroughly Modern Millie	1967	2002
Urban Cowboy	1980	2003
Spamalot	1975***	2005
Dirty Rotten Scoundrels	1988	2005
Billy Elliot: The Musical	2000	2005 (London), 2007 (New York)
The Wedding Singer	1988	2006
Tarzan	1999	2006
Legally Blonde	2001	2007
Young Frankenstein	1974	2007

*Based on Ingmar Bergman's *Sommarnottens leende* (Smiles of a Summer Night)
**Based on Ettore Scola's *Passione d'Amore* (Passion of Love)
***Based on *Monty Python and the Holy Grail*

(Australia, 2006), and *Legally Blonde* (2007), this division has plans to musicalise another fifteen films for the stage.

Producers

Producing changed a great deal during the last decade of the twentieth century as the days of the sole theatrical producer disappeared. Legendary solo producers, such as David Merrick and others, were known for their idiosyncratic taste, business savvy and aesthetic fingerprint. Indeed, there is a universal sentiment that with the disappearance of the solo producer there was a corresponding evaporation of much risk-taking on Broadway. These producers did not just 'discover' new musicals, they often assembled a creative team to realise an idea that they had for a musical. Historians Lawrence Maslon and Michael Kantor conclude that 'whereas once a producer was expected to have some artistic acumen, the job now was about cultivating cash'.[12] As costs to mount a new musical increased, producers beginning in the 1960s began to experiment with often bold ventures in order to secure a profit from their ventures. One of Merrick's innovations was celebrity casting. When the originating star of a musical left the show, it was the Broadway convention that that they would be replaced by an unknown (and less expensive), talented performer. Merrick's *Hello, Dolly!*, starring Carol Channing, started off with a bang, winning a record ten Tony Awards in 1964. When Channing left the show, Merrick engaged Pearl Bailey, Cab Calloway, and an all-African-American cast, which attracted new publicity and new audiences. Back to a Caucasian cast, Ginger Rogers, Martha Raye, Betty Grable, Bibi Osterwald, Phyllis Diller and then Ethel Merman essayed the role of Mrs Dolly Gallagher Levi to realise a run of 2,844 performances (almost six years). For Merrick, the idea was not to get patrons to buy a ticket once, but to create reasons for them to return. And by casting wildly different stars in the role, he also ensured different demographics might be attracted to his show. This 'revolving door' star casting ploy has been employed by producers Fran and Barry Weissler with equally impressive results in the 1994 revival of *Grease*, and later *Annie Get Your Gun*, *Wonderful Town*, and the most lucrative to date, *Chicago* (1996), which is still running in 2008.

Like Irving Berlin, Frank Loesser, and Rodgers and Hammerstein – in addition to his prodigious accomplishments as an artist – Andrew Lloyd Webber has enjoyed much success as a producer. From 1986 to 1990, Webber sought to eliminate the 'backer's audition' where the composer and lyricist sing through the score with the hopes of enticing well-heeled angels to invest in their show. Instead, he sold shares in his Really Useful Group, so that investors would be gambling that any future Webber property would be popular and run a profit, or become a blockbuster like *Cats* or *The Phantom of the Opera* and make a great deal of money. Ultimately, the strain of maintaining a publicly held company led Webber to buy back the outstanding shares in 1990. Canadian producer Garth Drabinsky similarly took his company Livent, Inc. public in 1993, but the company declared bankruptcy in 1998 amid a flurry of lawsuits.

For a 2006 London revival of *The Sound of Music*, Webber hit upon the novel idea of creating a reality television programme centred on the musical's casting. The viewing audience voted on the contestants at each stage, and the actors with the fewest votes were eliminated. Carried on BBC for eleven hours, *How Do You Solve a Problem Like Maria?* was very successful in terms of generating audience interest, as the advance ticket sales topped £10 million before opening. And while 7.7 million viewers witnessed the final showdown between the top three finalists and two million voted to extend a six-month contract to Connie Fisher, it seemed nothing more than a publicity stunt, but twenty-three-year-old Fisher received great reviews. It was inevitable that an American producer would seek to emulate this successful gimmick: *Grease: You're the One That I Want!* appeared on NBC in 2007, with viewers deciding on the casting of the leads for a Broadway revival of the classic musical.

By the 1990s, costs had begun to escalate outside the reach of the individual investor. Broadway musicals are now generally financed by teams of producers and/or corporations (Disney, 20th Century Fox, Clear Channel Entertainment, Suntory International Corporation, Warner Brothers, etc.).

Disney made their Broadway debut with little fanfare as 'The Walt Disney Studios' was listed along with James B. Freydberg, Kenneth Feld, Jerry L. Cohen, Max Weitzenhoffer, and The John F. Kennedy Center for the Performing Arts as producers of Bill Irwin's wordless masterpiece, *Largely New York* (1989). With their revitalised animated film musicals back in popularity, it was only natural that Disney began to look at its own catalogue of film musicals for possible stage transfers. The newly formed Disney Theatrical Productions made their Broadway debut in 1994 with *Beauty and the Beast*, which when it opened in London the following year was the most expensive West End show of its time (£10 million). With cross-platform advertising (television, video, web, etc.) and extensive merchandising, *Beauty and the Beast* has enormous visibility. Two additional factors contributed to the production entering its thirteenth year (five thousand plus performances) on Broadway in 2006: a reputation as 'family entertainment' and occasional star casting.

In short order, Disney decided not only to continue to produce live musicals, but to become a theatre owner as well. After a $36 million renovation, Disney reopened the New Amsterdam Theatre on 42nd Street to become the home of the next Disney blockbuster: *The Lion King*. In 1998, Disney began work on an original musical instead of adapting another one of their existing film musicals for the stage. *Elaborate Lives* was not well received in Atlanta, so Disney put the show back into rehearsal before a redesigned, rewritten, recast and retitled *Aida* opened on Broadway. Also penned by *Lion King*'s Elton John, *Aida* was another artistic triumph (four Tony Awards) and box-office success (1,852 performances). In 2004, Disney teamed up with British producer Cameron Mackintosh to bring *Mary Poppins* to the stage. Based on the stories of P. L. Travers and their own 1964 film version, this was another victory. While the stage musical version of *Tarzan* (2006, score by Phil Collins) was not well received critically, it appears to have found an audience for 486 performances.

With the disappearance of the individual producer came the increased importance of transfers arriving to Broadway not only from London but also from American regional theatres. Joseph Papp's Public Theatre has been importing productions to Broadway since *Hair* (1967) and *A Chorus Line* (1975); other musical transfers to Broadway include *Two Gentlemen of Verona* (1971), *The Pirates of Penzance* (1980 revival), *The Mystery of Edwin*

Drood (1985), and *Bring in 'da Noise, Bring in 'da Funk* (1996). Other non-profit theatres no doubt dream of replicating the success of *A Chorus Line,* which ran 6,137 performances in its original Broadway run, ultimately grossing $280 million worldwide. While Lincoln Center produces many musicals in its own theatres, it also has produced shows in traditional Broadway houses, such as *Passion* (1994) and *Sarafina!* (1987). Established in 1963, the Goodspeed Opera House in East Haddam, Connecticut, has moved seventeen productions to Broadway, including *Man of La Mancha* (1965), *Shenandoah* (1975), and *Annie* (1977). Two major theatres in California have also been successful in New York: LaJolla Playhouse with *Big River* (1985), *Thoroughly Modern Millie* (2002), *Jersey Boys* (2005) and others, and the Old Globe Theatre with *Into the Woods* (1987), *Damn Yankees* (1994 revival), *The Full Monty* (2000), and *Dirty Rotten Scoundrels* (2005).

Musicals can also come via organisations whose goals are to provide affordable New York visibility for new work; among these, the New York Musical Theatre Festival (NYMT), the New York International Fringe Festival (NYF), and the National Alliance for Musical Theatre (NAMT) are increasingly important development conduits. Established in 1999, the New York International Fringe Festival produced *Urinetown* (1999, NYF Festival; 2001, Broadway), *Debbie Does Dallas* (2001, NYF Festival; 2001, off-Broadway), and *How to Save the World and Find True Love in 90 Minutes* (2004, NYF Festival; 2006, off-Broadway). For three weeks every September, the New York Musical Theatre Festival has been presenting approximately thirty productions each season. Productions which have moved to commercial runs off-Broadway include *Altar Boyz* (2005), *The Great American Trailer Park Musical* (2005), and *Gutenberg! The Musical!* (2006). Each year eight musicals are chosen for the National Alliance for Musical Theatre annual New York conference, and are presented as forty-five-minute readings for commercial, regional, and independent producers scattered around the country. NAMT notes that 75% of their festival productions have received subsequent productions, including *The Bubbly Black Girl Sheds Her Chameleon Skin* (2000), *Thoroughly Modern Millie* (2000), *Songs for a New World* (2000), *The Drowsy Chaperone* (2006) and *I Love You Because* (2006).

The business of Broadway

While the newest technological innovations seem to make their way into the set, light, sound, and costume designs of theatrical productions, modernisation of the business of the theatre often seems to come in fits and starts. Some theatres experimented with phone reservations and credit cards in the 1960s, but it was not until 1971 that all Broadway ticket offices began to accept

American Express. By the 1980s, ticket sales were handled by centralised ticket sellers (Telecharge, Ticketmaster, Tickets.com) that allow patrons to buy tickets 24/7. Computerised ticketing meant that shows could sell further in advance than was possible with hard tickets, and by the early 1990s, patrons were able to choose their seats when ordering. The TKTS Booth opened for business in Times Square in 1973, run by the Theatre Development Fund. By selling half-price tickets the day of performance, many struggling shows were able to put paying customers in their seats, and folks of more modest means were able to attend a Broadway show. A different kind of selling tool came into being in 2001 when *The Producers* conceived the idea of premium-price ticketing in order to counteract the practice of ticket brokers buying the best seats in the house and reselling them at an enormous mark-up, a profit that did not benefit the original producers of the musical. Pricing the premium tickets at $480 meant that few seats went to resellers and that the profit from the mark-up went to the producers. While no one begrudges producers from turning a profit with their productions, this pricing scheme has not been met with universal support. According to one producer, 'The number of premium seats for the special-event shows are spiraling out of control. We're setting up a system that says, 'Hey, if you're not rich, don't even bother coming to our show.'[13]

Just as the manner of selling of tickets changed radically at the end of the twentieth century, so did advertising. Recognising that the primary strength of *Pippin* (1972) was Bob Fosse's choreography, producer Stuart Ostrow created the first television commercial to feature clips of an actual Broadway production. Running 1,944 performances, *Pippin* owed a great deal of its longevity to this commercial. While show websites were relatively modest in the 1990s, by the twenty-first century they were often elaborate affairs, selling not only tickets, but merchandise as well. Boublil and Schönberg's *The Pirate Queen* added 'castcom' to their website when the production was in previews in Chicago in 2006. Daily video blogs were posted featuring interviews with cast and crew, members of the creative team, and audience testimonials. Web viewers were invited to post comments to each entry. While most blogs and threaded discussions on musical theatre tend to focus on the negative and their pessimistic tone can be seen as damaging word of mouth, the producers of *The Pirate Queen* sought to control at least part of the web dialogue about their production. Nevertheless, the show closed quickly in New York.

Andrew Lloyd Webber's The Really Useful Group and Disney are thus far the only producing entities which group their current productions in advertising in order to build awareness in theatre-goers that there is a branding that is larger than the individual production. Otherwise, advertising for Broadway shows is done on an individual basis. Realising the strong economic impact of live theatre in New York City, the New York State Department of Commerce launched the 'I Love New York' commercials in 1978. Promoting Broadway as a must-see tourist attraction, these commercials not only increased audience attendance but are also credited with assisting the economic recovery of New York City in the 1980s. Even though the professional organisation of the League of American Theatre Owners and Producers was established in 1930, it was not until the end of the twentieth century that their mission was broadened to include promoting not specific shows, but Broadway in general. In 1997 they unveiled the 'Live Broadway' logo and advertising campaign, which is meant 'to designate genuine Broadway theatre, the highest quality form of popular entertainment'. While some are leery of any advertising scheme that attempts to promote the Ur-Broadway musical, others see a benefit to Broadway and New York to position live, professional theatre on Broadway as a unique experience.

Ultimately it does not matter whether the musical is produced by an individual or a corporation, whether it boasts an original plot or is a shameless film-to-stage transfer, whether the seats are twenty dollars off-off-Broadway or cost $480 for the Premium Broadway experience; whether the show has been in development for years or opens 'cold' on Broadway, there is no predicting unqualified success. If focus groups, talkbacks, threaded discussions, and questionnaires were one hundred per cent effective, then there would be no flops on Broadway. Yet the statistics yield a sobering fact: musical theatre remains a high-risk medium where less than one show in five breaks even. But when a show is financially successful, the economic possibilities are staggering.

As the twenty-first century gets under way, artists continue to stretch and question many of the assumptions and conventions that have guided musical theatre throughout the previous century. *The Drowsy Chaperone*'s 'Man in the Chair' explains to us the virtues of the silly (and fictional) 1928 musical we have been watching: 'It does what a musical is supposed to do. It takes you to another world, and it gives you a little tune to carry in your head when you're feeling blue.' Of course, not all musical theatre authors approach the genre with this goal. Nevertheless, whether they are writing a traditional book musical, a concept musical, a jukebox musical, a sung-through musical, a rock opera, a dansical, a film-to-stage musical, etc., all of these creators would probably agree with the director Julian Marsh when he declares his core values in *42nd Street*: 'musical comedy: the most glorious words in the English language'. The directions in which this genre will develop remain as elusive as those for creating a fail-proof show.

PART IV

Legacies and transformations

17 Why do they start to sing and dance all of a sudden? Examining the film musical

GRAHAM WOOD

Prologue

At a crucial moment in *Hedwig and the Angry Inch* (2001), our hero(ine), Hedwig, is abandoned by Sgt Luther Robinson and left to fend for him/herself in an isolated trailer park in Junction City, Kansas – a long, long way from his/her East Berlin home. Images of the Berlin Wall being torn down play on the TV and a few piano chords are heard off-screen as the TV reporter comments: 'The Germans are a patient people and good things come to those who wait.' With this indirect reminder of what might have been had Hedwig stayed at home, the camera pans from an anniversary present (a 'Wig in a Box') across the interior of the trailer and we catch a glimpse through the window of a lone immigrant musician outside playing a toy-like keyboard slung around his neck before Hedwig is revealed lying disconsolately on the couch. Though all appears to be lost, Hedwig begins to sing about the healing power of performance. The second verse adds guitar and drums to the accompaniment and the camera again pans to the window to reveal a guitarist outside. After the second chorus, a band of itinerant, Eastern European immigrant musicians (whom Hedwig will later call the 'ambassadors of Eastern Bloc Rock') file joyously through the door of the trailer brandishing guitars (though none is plugged in) and an impossibly small portable drum set and continue accompanying this song of recovery and rejuvenation. Last to enter is Yitzhak (Hedwig's future husband) carrying a fabulous new blond wig on a tray – much as one might present a lobster or flaming pancakes. The recipe: music + costume = a transformative serenade that provides the vehicle for Hedwig's rebirth as a drag performer of incredible potency. At the end of the third chorus, the side wall of the trailer suddenly bursts open and descends to reveal bright footlights as the music shifts briefly to an angry rock sound. For the fourth chorus, all six performers jostle into the frame of the trailer window to encourage some audience participation with the aid of a bouncing wig marking the lyrics. The camera then pans up and back for the lively rock coda, as if to accommodate Hedwig's phoenix-like rebirth, as the trailer-as-stage brims over with enough charisma to fill a football stadium.

An implausible transition? Possibly. An excuse for a song? Perhaps. Although unquestionably entertaining, bursting into song on screen is both the delight and difficulty of the screen musical genre. Yet surely therein lies the essence of the most popular (mis)conception of the movie musical – the spontaneous outpouring of the human spirit in song and (almost as frequently) dance in unlikely locations and for reasons which, if apparent at all, are mostly paper-thin at best. What is it about that moment where song takes over from speech that when treated with skill and finesse can seem like the most natural thing in the world, yet when carelessly done is jarring and comic in the extreme? Indeed, such is the ubiquity of this musical cliché that comedians ranging from the Monty Python team to Mel Brooks, and on television, the makers of *The Simpsons*, *South Park*, *Buffy the Vampire Slayer* and *Family Guy* have made an art of parodying this essential element of movie musicals.[1] We could only find these comic renditions amusing if we accepted, at least in part, the artificiality of someone breaking into song in the ultimate medium of documentary realism: film.

Even at this early stage in our inquiry, questions arise. Can film musicals be studied as a unique medium? Or should they be considered part of a larger repertory including musicals for the stage? Stage and screen musicals are indisputably and intimately connected in terms of their history, content and style and must be considered as such if a full picture of either genre is to emerge. Certainly, one advantage movie musicals have over stage shows is the benefit of a relatively permanent record that can be infinitely repeated and studied. Stage musicals, in contrast, truly exist only in live performance.[2] Yet the similarities and differences between screen and stage do require us to consider the specific qualities that make film musicals special, and the music in film musicals distinct from the *live* music in the theatre.

Introduction

Three discrete areas of investigation immediately present themselves as a means of examining the movie musical: 1) technology, 2) genre and 3) style. Although there is a good deal of overlap between these areas, they can serve as a useful matrix for preliminary analysis, and will be considered in turn in the sections that follow.

Under technology the principal areas of focus are advances in sound and colour, the mobility of the camera, and the way in which such changes affect the way musicals look and sound. Questions of genre explore the difference between stage transfers (those based on a pre-existing stage show) and original movie musicals (those with no stage musical precedents), different versions of a show or movie, and the sources of the music. Also important is the sub-genre of biopics, movies about the life and work of actual show-business personalities. Issues of style subdivide into three areas: musical, visual and dance. Musical style includes the notion of *diegesis* – that is, the extent to which music featured on the soundtrack could plausibly emanate from a source within the visual frame or from the narrative as a performance, a rehearsal, or some other likely musical activity. Visual style focuses on contrasts of realism, abstraction and fantasy, the comparison of spectacles that are either stage-influenced or movie-specific, and recurring iconographical symbols. Dance style considers an array of dance types – ballet, jazz, tap, folk, ballroom, etc., the use of genres such as the waltz or tango, and the scope of the performance from solos and duets to large-scale ensembles.

One notion in particular permeates all aspects of the movie musical: *self-reflexivity.* This term refers to those aspects of a musical that quote or allude to their own history – the history of musical theatre, the entertainment industry, or the process of making musicals. This might occur through plot (movies about putting on a show or making a movie), songs (including those filmed as performances or rehearsals, those with lyrics that refer to singing or other aspects of performance and/or those that quote elements of an existing song or earlier musical style), or star personae who have a prior relationship with the genre or the entertainment industry. *Singin' in the Rain* (1952) is the archetypal self-reflexive musical. The movie concerns the making of early movie musicals, shows songs in rehearsal and performance, has songs about performance and the entertainment industry ('Singin' in the Rain' and 'Make 'Em Laugh') and features an established star with a prior history in stage and screen musicals (Gene Kelly).

Allusions to other works are also not uncommon. Both *Dancer in the Dark* (2000) and *Moulin Rouge!* (2001) make multiple references to *The Sound of Music* (though to quite different effect) to make important narrative points about their central characters. In *Moulin Rouge!* it is to prove Christian's legitimacy as a inspirational scriptwriter; in *Dancer in the Dark* it is to mark Selma's increasing disconnection from the society around her.

The creative teams involved in musical production – studios, producers, directors, songwriters, actors, singers and dancers – were central to realising these visions, to formulating the combination of sights and sounds that filled the screens. Many of them frequently tapped into their experience with stage musicals and transferred, transformed or otherwise adapted the theatrical aspects of their craft to fit the film medium.

Technology

Once sound could be coordinated and then synchronised with film, the creative possibilities of the film musical genre expanded exponentially. The early successful examples of Warner Brothers' *The Jazz Singer* (1927) and Disney's animated *Steamboat Willie* (1928) demonstrated to audiences and, more importantly, to other film studios what was possible when sight and sound were combined with precision.

The next technological advance in sound concerned the way in which musical numbers were recorded. Early musicals required huge sound stages where music, singing and choreography were recorded simultaneously. The noisy camera needed to be encased in a soundproof booth, severely restricting its flexibility. Later, the sound for musical numbers was recorded separately then played back during the filming with singers lip-synching. This freed the camera from its relative immobility and soon, as Fehr and Vogel describe, 'cameras began moving more sure-footedly than ever and blending wide- and mid-angle shots with pans or dollying into close-ups at will. Film editors sped up the pace of musical films while adding variety to the visual menu.'[3] These changes challenged both silent-movie actors, who had to learn to use their voices as well as a new way of acting, and technicians, who had to rapidly master new equipment. But the manifold gains, both artistic and financial, were soon clear.

Concurrent with advances in sound was the development of colour film. In order to compete with the live spectacle of Broadway, the major studios began to use a two-strip Technicolor process, at first just in select musical sequences, but later in entire movies. Technical problems prompted continued experimentation until a three-colour process was developed in the 1930s, and from the end of the decade entire musicals in colour would become increasingly common. Unfortunately, film using the two-colour process was highly susceptible to damage and fading and many movies degraded irreversibly, some only a few years after being made. From the last decades of the twentieth century, advances in digital recording and editing have dramatically enhanced the quality of movies as well as the flexibility and control directors and technicians have over the look and sound of their projects. Computer-generated imagery (CGI), first used in movies in the 1970s, has also reached such a level of sophistication that images appear simultaneously more real and more fantastical.

Genre

The first task for any genre-based study of musical films is to distinguish them from those that are 'non-musical'. Many movies have theme songs, more have musical numbers, but not all of them qualify as true musicals. It is not so much a question of the quantity of music or the number of songs, but rather one of approach. Gerald Mast states it most succinctly: 'A play or film is a musical if its primary entertainment value and investment lie in the musical numbers themselves.'[4]

Once separated from the body of 'non-musical' films, movie musicals may then be viewed along a spectrum. At one end are the stage-to-screen transfers that recreate, to varying degrees, elements of a prior stage production. (See chapter 18 for more on screen adaptations of stage musicals.)[5] At the other end are movies originally conceived for the screen with plots based on short stories, novels, fairy tales and so forth, or on newly invented narratives, but specifically *not* on stage musicals. Examples span the whole history of the genre from *The Jazz Singer* to *Walk the Line* (2005). Some of the more outstanding examples include: *42nd Street* (1933), *Top Hat* (1935), *Snow White* (1938), *The Wizard of Oz* (1939), *Meet Me in St Louis* (1944), *Easter Parade* (1948), *An American in Paris* (1951), *Singin' in the Rain*, *Beauty and the Beast* (1991), *The Lion King* (1994), *Dancer in the Dark*, *Hedwig and the Angry Inch*, and *Moulin Rouge!*. And while the influence of theatrical conventions, styles, plots and performers is frequently felt, what distinguishes these works is the way in which they employ the medium of film.

With these generic categories now in place, the study of movie musicals should then take into account the origins of the score. Is it a newly composed set of songs written specifically for a film by a single songwriting team, or a combination of old and new songs by a variety of composers and lyricists? The songs for *Dancer in the Dark*, for example, were all written specifically for the movie by Björk and Sjón Sigurdsson. The score for *Easter Parade* contains sixteen songs, all by Irving Berlin, some newly composed, some interpolated from prior contexts. All eight of the songs for *An American in Paris* are by George and Ira Gershwin, but were assembled for the movie long after George's death. More recently, the score for *Moulin Rouge!*, in addition to including period pieces by Offenbach that reflect the late nineteenth-century Parisian setting, also includes a freewheeling array of pop songs from the 1950s to the 1990s including numbers associated with pop culture icons Marilyn Monroe, Madonna, The Beatles, David Bowie, Elton John, U2 and Sting as well as original music composed for the film by David Baerwald.

Adaptations from stage to screen might contain songs from the original stage production, new songs or a combination of the two. This seemingly arbitrary phenomenon must be understood in the context of the working methods of the studio system. Once studios realised the economic rewards to be gained from movie musicals, production increased rapidly, causing a sudden need for songs. The larger studios bought up New York publishing houses as a way of feeding their new children. Having made such an investment, the studios were subsequently reluctant to pay royalties for the use of songs they did not own. Instead, they either had staff writers in their employ compose new songs to be added to an existing score, or interpolated one or more of the many songs whose copyright they already owned. This often resulted in scores with over half a dozen different songwriters, as is the case in the movie version of *Babes in Arms* (1939). The musical and narrative effects of such composite scores have yet to be fully explored. For example, can older songs be used to evoke an earlier time period in a specific narrative framework? These and similar questions about the narrative function of songs remain to be answered.

An important subgroup of film musicals comprises biopics – movies about show-business personalities. Singers and songwriters are the typical subjects of biopics, but bandleaders, impresarios, dancers and choreographers are also occasionally featured. The biopic provides ample occasion for musical numbers as the careers of stars unfold, and also incorporates features of the backstage or 'show' musical. *De-Lovely* (2004), the second, and much more successful, screen homage to Cole Porter, contains a series of delightfully staged musical numbers and a more honest portrayal of the songwriter's personal life.[6] Kevin Kline (as Porter) sings many of the songs himself, while others are presented by an astonishing array of vocal stylists – including Robbie Williams, Sheryl Crow, Natalie Cole, Diana Krall, Alanis Morissette, and, for us older viewers, Elvis Costello. Like Porter himself, the movie is subtle and occasionally enigmatic in its style, but uses the full range of self-reflexive techniques developed over decades of backstage movie musicals. In one charming example, Porter coaches Jack – a male singer in rehearsal having difficulty with the tessitura of 'Night and Day'. 'I wrote it with you in mind,' Porter says. 'Think about the words . . . it's about obsession . . . just sing it with me' – and they begin. A rehearsal piano accompanies the verse, but as Jack reaches the chorus orchestral colours swell to reflect his growing confidence. The camera begins to circle around the duo revealing drops being flown in, off-stage business, and the empty seats of the theatre. At the second chorus, Porter asks for a key change and the camera begins its second circle with off-stage rehearsal activities once again in plain view. This time, however, as Porter turns to Monty to acknowledge Jack's grasp of the song the camera leaves the duo behind on stage. When the stage-left proscenium wall is passed for the second time, the smartly dressed opening night audience is revealed – including Porter himself plus the pit orchestra and conductor. By the time we circle back to the stage, Jack is singing in the fully staged opening-night performance. Not only is this a seamless transition from rehearsal to performance, but it is also a narrative set up for Cole's liaison with Jack later that night. Throughout the movie, each song is judiciously chosen so that in addition to its place in the surface narrative as, for example, a song that is part of Porter's latest show, its lyrics and performance style also subtly comment on the surrounding action. Other successful screen biopic subjects include Ray Charles in *Ray* (2004) and Johnny Cash in *Walk the Line.*

A further spin on this sub-genre is movies featuring charismatic performers playing characters not far removed from their stage personae in quasi-biographical scenarios. Notable examples include Elvis Presley – beginning with *Love Me Tender* (1956) – and The Beatles in *A Hard Day's Night* (1964), and *Help!* (1965). The best recent example is *8 Mile* (2002) which stars Eminem (Marshall Mathers III) playing Jimmy ('Rabbit') – a fictional Detroit rapper whose life resonates to some extent with his own. Gus Van Sant's lyrical homage to Kurt Cobain, *Last Days* (2005), also draws on elements of this sub-genre.

Biopics and other musicals provide opportunities for a particular manifestation of self-reflexivity: the foregrounding of the technology of the industry. Here, images of cameras, projectors, microphones and recording studios fill the frame, to which are frequently added audiences that observe both stage and screen performances and rehearsals. *Singin' in the Rain* has many such scenes, but there are countless other musicals that employ this device as a way of letting us in on a secret only to hide it from us at another level – we are, after all, still watching a movie.

The opening sequence of the movie version of *Evita* (1996) is an example of how deftly these self-reflexive relationships can be juggled. Over the opening black screen the names of the creators and stars of our movie appear along with sound effects and Spanish conversation. Abruptly, the screen is filled with black-and-white images – a shock since we surely expected colour. Next follows a shot of the internal audience viewing what we now realise to be the movie within our movie. For a brief moment, both external and internal audiences watch the same movie unaware of the other's presence, but when we see them, that aspect of the illusion is broken. The next shot, however, shows us both the movie screen and the projector – the source of the on-screen illusion and also the source of *our* movie. Such masterly blurring of the boundaries between on- and off-screen audiences also mirrors the blurring between the lives and personae of the two charismatic female subjects of the movie: Evita and Madonna. The stage production of *Evita* (1978) also opens inside a movie theatre, but cannot refer to itself visually in quite the same way as the movie version.

Any analysis of musical theatre and film should take into account the central importance of race and culture both in the creative process and in the final product. This area is not without its difficulties since modern audiences will continue to find the ethnic stereotyping in many older musicals distasteful, particularly the practice of 'blacking up' by both white and black actors in early musicals from *The Jazz Singer* to *Holiday Inn* (1942). Spike Lee deals head-on with this issue in *Bamboozled* (2000) in which a disillusioned TV executive tries to get himself fired by developing the most racially offensive programme he can imagine – a modern minstrel show. Ironically, the show is a hit: problems ensue. Provocative connections, however, between Yiddish theatre, minstrelsy, blacking up, Tin Pan Alley and the music of the Broadway theatre have already been noted in the literature. Surely, therefore, a consideration of the influence and impact of both Jewish and African-American culture should be an important part of the analytical and critical enterprise of musical film studies.[7]

Issues of gender and sexuality also surface regularly in this genre, to varying degrees, from the in-your-face transgender complexity of the title role in *Hedwig and the Angry Inch*, to the less challenging cross-dressing that occurs in *Victor/Victoria* (1982) and *Yentl* (1983). Also, a camp sensibility in visual and performance styles permeates the genre to such an extent that an expression of interest in musicals can be virtually synonymous with coming out as gay (at least in American culture).[8] The reception of Judy Garland as an icon for gay men has already been convincingly explored.[9] Gerald Mast has also posited a close connection between Jewish culture and gay culture as two marginalised groups that were drawn to the entertainment industry because it was a safe professional haven where they could express themselves with less fear of discrimination.[10] Our willingness to address and deal sensitively with these issues must surely be one of the priorities of future research on musical film specifically and musical theatre in general.

Visual style

The silver screen contains a fundamental dualism between realism and fantasy: realism because movies and TV report the news, war, natural disasters, sport and events that have actually occurred; fantasy because that same medium, through acting, *mise-en-scène,* creative camerawork, editing and special effects, can create entire new worlds that do not exist anywhere but on that same screen. This tension is not nearly so pronounced in the stage musical because theatre audiences have learned, over centuries, to suspend their disbelief in the illusion of reality that they observe. For movie audiences, although they can be transported to much more complete and detailed worlds of fantasy than stage audiences, the memories of wreckage from the latest plane crash or blood-soaked bodies from a terrorist shooting are never far away. For film musicals this has always presented the central problem of how to effect a smooth and convincing transition from speech into song. This dualism affects visual style in a number of ways, most obviously in the contrast between 'realism' and 'fantasy', such as Dorothy's black-and-white Kansas versus the Technicolor Oz, or the grainy textures of East Berlin compared to the garish American colour palette of *Hedwig and the Angry Inch*, or the hand-held, documentary style of the spoken scenes of *Dancer in the Dark* as opposed to the bright colours and MTV slickness of its musical numbers. But there is also a tension of visual style created by the contrast of realism and abstraction. The camerawork of Busby Berkeley is one example.

Berkeley was the dance director for three Warner Brothers productions in 1933: *42nd Street*, *Gold Diggers of 1933* and *Footlight Parade*. His now infamous and much-quoted style in these and later movies is characterised by a much more imaginative use of the camera than had ever been observed in musicals. Having choreographed the large-scale production numbers, Berkeley's camera then becomes a roving eye that reduces the multiple body parts of chorines into geometric shapes seen from all possible angles. In a sense, he caught the mood of the times by suggesting the dehumanising of his dancers as cogs in a larger visual machine while making them the voyeuristic subject of a visual spectacle – but a spectacle governed by a distinctly filmic sensibility. As Fehr and Vogel have noted, Berkeley 'elevated the movements of a chorus line to the highest imaginative level. In fact, no other artist of the period was more responsible for establishing the format of the 1930s big-budget production numbers than he … [Berkeley also] refused to accept the movie set as a West Coast proscenium. The camera was free to roam at will.'[11]

Animated musicals demonstrate the spectrum of visual styles from illusory to realistic particularly well and it may be that the role of the Disney studio has been underestimated in the history and generic development of the film musical. The opening sequence of *Dumbo* (1941), for example, shows a sky full of parachuting baby animals that bears a striking resemblance to World War II newsreel footage. Disturbing, too, are the harrowing scenes of the circus train journey through the rain that conjure up even more disquieting war-related images. Yet against this realistic background, Disney creates a striking visual contrast. When Dumbo accidentally drinks some beer, the three-dimensional depth, natural tones and realistic detail of the visual frame (talking animals and birds notwithstanding) is replaced by a flat, black background, against which surreal, garish colours play amidst logistically improbable animal mutations and abstract transformations. The pink elephant sequence is rendered all the more fantastic because its style of animation is so completely counter to the surrounding elements of the movie. The combination of highly abstract and stylised visuals and sinister minor-key music strengthens the impact of the sequence, which becomes, in effect, the show's big production number. Macabre and menacing, yet plausible because of Dumbo's alcohol-enhanced state, the sequence is also crucial to the narrative because for the first time Dumbo is able to visualise the impossible and actually fly himself – the next morning he wakes up high

in a tree with a hangover as a little piece of fantasy spills over into the real
world.

Dumbo's drunken vision is related to the dream sequences that occur in
many stage musicals such as *Betsy* (1926) and *Babes in Arms* (1937). Dream
sequences or dream ballets, as they sometimes were, transferred to some
of the screen adaptations such as Laurey's dream ballet from *Oklahoma!*
(1955), Frenchy's 'Beauty School Drop Out' from *Grease* (1978), and Leo
Bloom's 'I Want to Be a Producer' from *The Producers* (2005) and also occur
in original movie musicals such as *The Wizard of Oz, Yolanda and the Thief*
(1945), *The Pirate* (1948), *An American in Paris*, and *Dancer in the Dark*.
Most often these sequences play out the psychological dilemmas of the main
characters in fantastical worlds that are related to but far removed from their
everyday experience.[12]

Contrasting visual styles can also be combined with contrasting musical styles to enhance the narrative as in Disney's *The Lion King*. Here the
world of the African savannah is evoked by combining nature-documentary-
style visuals and 'African-sounding' pop songs by Elton John and Tim Rice.
Hans Zimmer's orchestrations effectively provide the required ethnic ambi-
ence that the songs themselves lack. Set against this overall visual style of
panoramic long shots and leaping gazelles is the occasional use of non-
realistic, stylised animation with savannah beasts doing things that you'd
never see them do on televised nature programmes. In 'I Just Can't Wait to
Be King', Simba launches into an early Michael Jackson-style number that
simultaneously abandons visual realism for hyper-real colours, flat backgrounds and abstract patterns formed by a conveniently situated chorus of
usefully marked animals. The style of Busby Berkeley immediately springs
to mind (as it does in the 'Be Our Guest' production number from *Beauty
and the Beast*), except that here it is the noble animal rather than Berkeley's
chorus girl that is visually dismembered. The good humour of the animal
play hides any apparent exploitation and once again the musical refers to its
own past. Yet, as in *Dumbo*, this musical number is crucial to the narrative
because Simba is giddy with the anticipation of regal power and the freedom
from regulations that he thinks it will provide. The number thus becomes a
space where the possibility of a positive future can be imagined. In contrast
to *Dumbo*, the sinister element in *The Lion King* is reversed. Dumbo's dream
is far more frightening than reality, whereas the party atmosphere of Simba's
production number is quite unlike the harsh reality of actually being king –
an awesome responsibility that is placed on his young shoulders after the
accidental death of his father. The terrifying realism of the wildebeest stam-
pede and destruction of the pride lands that follows sheds a darkness over
Simba's world that is entirely absent both visually and musically from his
earlier song.

Another visual device that can add to the impact of musical numbers is the use of symbols. Powerful images of steam trains occur in such movies as *The Harvey Girls* (1946), *Oklahoma!* and *Evita*. Train iconography is a vital part of the American visual landscape, as many nineteenth- and twentieth-century paintings, prints, murals and Western movies show. And aside from being a vital means of transportation for an expanding frontier, the iron horse brought along with its dirt and noise the ideas and social codes that would ultimately lead to the civilising of the continent. The song 'On the Atchison, Topeka and the Santa Fe', from *The Harvey Girls*, celebrates the railroad line that will allow the Girls to bring a feminine brand of civilisation to the West, while 'Kansas City' and 'Buenos Aires', from *Oklahoma!* and *Evita* respectively, demonstrate the potent fascination that the modern city has for rural communities. Also, these last two songs take advantage of the film medium by changing their location from the stage versions specifically in order to incorporate close-ups of real engines that powerfully reinforce the sense of urban modernity. Similarly, 'The Trolley Song' in *Meet Me in St Louis* is heading for the 1903 St Louis World's Fairground – a symbol of progress and the inescapable internationalism of the twentieth century. The family in this lavishly detailed period piece does not need to move to New York; modernity will reach them soon enough. Once again, movie musical characters are being thrust into the future through song. What these and my earlier observations illustrate is how the visual style and setting of musical numbers can affect the overall narrative framework of the movie.

The Indian film industry – both Bollywood and Anglo-Indian – has also become a more discernible presence in the English-speaking world of film musicals. This is not surprising since there is a long-standing tradition of Indian film musicals. Bollywood productions like *Lagaan: Once Upon a Time in India* (2001) have successfully played in the west and UK director Gurinder Chadha (*Bend it Like Beckham*) has ventured successfully into the genre with the delightful *Bride and Prejudice* (2004). However, the stylistic influence of such movies is most clearly felt in the production numbers and plotline of the show-within-a-show 'Spectacular Spectacular' that forms the centerpiece of *Moulin Rouge!* with its Indian characters – the beautiful courtesan, the evil Maharajah, and the penniless sitar player – and the Indian-inspired choreography, costumes, and set design of the techno production number 'Hindi Sad Diamonds'.

Musical style

No study of this rich cultural product would be complete without a treatment of the music and its relationship to surrounding elements.

Song

The basic component of the musical, the song, can be understood as a very flexible template, whose lyrics may provide narrative thrust, insight into a character's psyche or reflection on an external object. From the 1920s to the 1950s most of the popular songs used in movies exhibit a plan that consists of three discrete sections: an instrumental introduction, a verse and a chorus. Built into the pattern is the potential for repetition of the verse and the chorus. This overall plan continued to be used in later decades, but the increasing use of rock and other popular styles led to a greater variety of song patterns in musicals from the 1960s onwards.

The verse and chorus have either a single text or multiple texts that require musical repetition. Single-texted choruses may also be repeated many times. In general, the chorus carries the most musical and dramatic weight because it contains the most important musical and textual material and because of the frequency with which that material is repeated. The most common plan for choruses is four eight-bar phrases that form a thirty-two-bar pattern. Sometimes these eight-bar phrases can break down into two- and four-bar units. Thematically, choruses are most likely to fall into one of two distinct patterns that describe the eight-bar phrases: ABAC and AABA. The first pattern is the more symmetrical and has a strong half-cadence at the mid-point leading to the repeat of the A section. The second pattern has a strong half-cadence at the three-quarter point leading to the final repetition of A, giving more musical weight to the latter half of the pattern. Extensions and variations add nuance to certain phrases, but these two basic patterns form the backbone of the song repertory used in movie musicals. Rather than being abstract or arbitrary patterns, however, each has a quite different emotional effect. The ABAC pattern tends to feel more balanced and suggests restraint and elegance, whereas the AABA pattern drives more forcefully towards its final goal and, as a result, is often more passionate and direct in content and delivery. When combined with specific musical styles, time signatures and orchestrations, the choice of pattern can greatly enhance the meaning of the words and the specific dramatic context of the song itself.[13]

Diegesis

Even before the advent of the synchronised soundtrack, the movie-going experience had always been associated with the continuous playing of accompanying background music on piano, organ or even orchestra: these movies were thus never really 'silent'. After the advent of talkies and the fixing of sound to visual images, both musical and non-musical films persisted in their use of background music, or underscoring. Film scholars refer to this special category of sound as non-diegetic music, that is, music that does not clearly emanate from a performance or other sound-generating source within the visual frame. But because movie musicals frequently contain so much diegetic music – actual performances, rehearsals, recording sessions and the like – they have been able to take this technological advance and turn it to aesthetic ends. For what this phenomenon allows is a more subtle transition from non-diegetic underscoring to actual diegetic performance. Since both musical and non-musical film use orchestral underscoring, the onset of a section of orchestral background music might be perceived as underscoring for a new scene, or the non-diegetic introduction to a song. It could also be music from a diegetic orchestra playing just off-screen – something that may not be apparent until a subsequent visual edit cuts to a shot of the musicians and/or singers in a nightclub or dance hall. Transitions into environments associated with live performance or rehearsal are much easier for an audience to accept than a less obviously musical environment because we would expect music to be present even if we do not at first see the source. Thus a diegetic performance can be used to accomplish transitions from one scene to another and to smooth over visual edits. Sensitivity to this blurring of diegetic and non-diegetic music can greatly enhance the viewing experience as well as furnishing a greater understanding of musical syntax in this genre.

Transitions

The makers of movie musicals have devoted a considerable amount of attention to the problem of how to effect the transition from speech into song, often with ingenious results. For example, Fred Astaire's apparently spontaneous rendition of 'No Strings' in *Top Hat* is, in fact, very carefully prepared. Playing unobtrusively underneath Fred's banter prior to the song is non-diegetic orchestral underscoring. As the conversation turns towards marriage, the dialogue introduces the topic of the song. Since Fred's delivery of his lines is so lyrical and his singing voice so effortlessly conversational, it seems as if he has started to sing the song before we realise it. Simultaneously the underscoring becomes Fred's orchestral accompaniment. By omitting the verse and leaping directly into the chorus of the song, Fred is able to project an air of spontaneity and immediacy. Later in the same movie, when Fred and Ginger are sheltering from the rain in a bandstand, a clap of thunder cleverly sets in motion a timpani roll that allows Fred to begin the verse of 'Isn't It a Lovely Day'. Again the preceding dialogue is directly related to the first sung words of the song and its overall theme. Visual clues – a few music lyres in the background and the bandstand itself – also provide a setting ripe for music-making.

One of the more unusual approaches to solving the transition problem was the use of rhyming dialogue. Seen most effectively in two movies with scores by Richard Rodgers and Lorenz Hart, *Love Me Tonight* (1932) and *Hallelujah, I'm a Bum!* (1933), a middle zone between speech and song is created through extended passages of rhymed, rhythmical and patterned dialogue, frequently with underscoring. Sometimes these passages lead into a full-blown song, at other times they conclude with a brief antecedent–consequent phrase in arioso style that functions like a Shakespearean rhyming couplet signalling the close of an act. Although rhyming dialogue was not widely used in subsequent movies, as a unique solution it deserves further scrutiny.

A related technique is used successfully in *8 Mile* where the spontaneous breaking into rhymed rhythmical speech is a perfectly acceptable mode of discourse in a narrative about rappers. The technique proves very flexible: rapping takes place *a cappella*, to the omnipresent background beat of car radios, and in performance during the club battles. In an early scene the morning after Jimmy ('Rabbit') has choked during a battle at a local club, he is trying to fix his car with his friend Future. They mock both the banality of the diegetic background music 'Sweet Home Alabama' emerging from inside his mother's trailer and her ineffectual boyfriend Greg who sporadically, but lamely joins in. Jimmy and Future playfully sing along with the melody but then Jimmy suddenly begins to rap about Greg, his mother, the trailer and his car with a fluency that he was unable to find the previous evening. This scene, which ends symbolically with the car starting, foreshadows not only Rabbit's ultimate finding of his 'voice', but also his winning strategy in the final battle where he deconstructs himself and his life so thoroughly that his opponent, Papa Doc, has nothing left to throw at him.

Transitions out of songs also present a challenge to the movie director. Common strategies at the end of songs include a shot of the audience applauding, a view of the performer(s) from the wings of the theatre (for diegetic performances), fading to black or cutting directly to a new scene (for non-diegetic performances). Sometimes more humorous and inventive endings are fashioned. The opening number of *Gold Diggers of 1933*, for example, appears to be an electrifying live stage performance of 'We're in the Money'. It is not until the performance is interrupted that we realise this was merely a rehearsal – albeit an astonishingly well-polished one. A variant on this approach is an apparent stage performance that turns out to be a take for a movie. When someone off-screen shouts 'cut' at the end of the song, the illusion is broken.

Disney styles

The Disney Studio has dominated the production of feature-length animated musicals since *Snow White* (1938). Even when live action musicals grew scarcer from the 1970s onward, Disney continued to produce musicals on a more regular basis than anyone else. Finding renewed momentum with *The Little Mermaid* (1989), Disney has produced a string of modern classics that have earned numerous Best Song Oscars, utilise the latest computer-generated animation techniques to enhance visual splendour and are in many ways worthy successors to the classic musicals of the 1940s and 1950s.

Disney has also continued to experiment with musical style. *The Little Mermaid* and *Beauty and the Beast,* for example, both employ Broadway-style scores by Howard Ashman and Alan Menken where full-blown songs arise as a means of providing a narrative climax. In contrast, the score for *Pocahontas* (1995) by Menken and Stephen Schwartz contains several passages of singing that do not form complete or discrete songs in themselves but seem closer to the more continuous fluid style of Alain Boublil and Claude-Michel Schönberg's musicalised French epic *Les Misérables* (1987). Here, speech-like singing and smaller lyrical units are woven around more traditional musical numbers. Different again is *The Lion King* with songs by the pop megastar Elton John and the Broadway veteran Tim Rice. The rock orientation of the score combined with Hans Zimmer's stylish and slick orchestrations made the CD soundtrack of *The Lion King* considerably more marketable than earlier scores. Overall, *The Lion King* returns to the earlier format of distinctly separate numbers. This successful formula is repeated in *Tarzan* (1999), with another rock megastar, Phil Collins, writing and performing songs that are greatly enhanced through exhilarating visual effects. As the above examples show, the unique contribution of the animated Disney musicals must be included in future studies of the genre.[14]

On the other hand, alongside these fine animated examples, Disney's live-action effort *High School Musical* (2006), though astonishingly popular, pales in comparison. With bland songs that even *NSYNC might have passed on, *High School Musical* presents a thoroughly sanitised and clichéd view of American high school plausible only to naive eleven-year-olds. Drawing freely from *Grease* (1978), *Fame* (1980) and the stage version of *The Full Monty* (2000) ('Getcha Head in the Game' is surely a kid's version of 'Michael Jordan's Ball'), this movie deflates the backstage genre by reducing the anticipated opening night of the show to a mere call-back audition that is itself upstaged by the post-basketball game dance number during which all school cliques make nice. The underlying message seems to be that the gym, rather than the stage, is the true locus of teamwork and collaboration. Quite.[15]

Song migration and interpolation

An interesting phenomenon occurring in this repertory is songs that appear in more than one movie. Songwriters for stage shows have often cannibalised their own songs for reuse in later productions and the tradition of interpolating other people's songs into a show is well established. In movies, however, these practices are applied with considerably greater freedom. This is partly due to the lesser degree of control that songwriters had over the musical aspects of movies produced in a studio system. In any case, examining the different contexts of each version can be revealing. Irving Berlin's 'Blue Skies' appeared in no fewer than four movies after its initial stage appearance in Rodgers and Hart's *Betsy* (1926).[16] Belle Baker, the star of *Betsy*, was concerned about not having a show-stopping number and asked Berlin to oblige. 'Blue Skies' did stop the show – much to the consternation of the show's creators. Al Jolson's version of the song in *The Jazz Singer* is a diegetic parlour room performance to his mother in charismatic style and optimistic mood – not a cloud in sight here. 'Blue Skies' next appears in *Alexander's Ragtime Band* (1938), again as a diegetic performance – this time in a nightclub and sung by Ethel Merman. Here the mood is quite different: the tempo is slower and the performance is tinged with melancholy. The nightclub audience joins in with a spontaneous accompanying choral refrain. Bing Crosby's non-diegetic outdoor performance in *Blue Skies* (1946) is also fairly slow, but his unique crooning voice projects reassurance and optimism. Mother Nature even obliges by quelling the rainstorm before the end of the song. A fourth filmed version of 'Blue Skies' occurs in *White Christmas* (1954) and again features Crosby, this time dancing with Danny Kaye. The context is a live stage performance with an unseen but presumably diegetic orchestra. This upbeat dance number in vaudevillian style has the duo sporting straw boaters and canes and is more in the charismatic tradition of Jolson than the other versions. By tracing the progress of a song as it appears in various shows, the dramatic context for each version can be compared and contrasted, as can the orchestrations, tempos, performers and musical style. This is essentially the same song, but meaning in each case is located in the combination of a variety of factors.

The dramatic potential of interpolating popular songs that a contemporary audience might be familiar with in order to make a narrative point is demonstrated nowhere better than in *Moulin Rouge!* which includes, in part or wholly, a host of songs associated with pop icons: 'Diamonds Are a Girl's Best Friend' (Carol Channing and Marilyn Monroe), 'All You Need Is Love' (The Beatles), 'Nature Boy' (David Bowie), 'Your Song' (Elton John), 'Material Girl' and 'Like a Virgin' (Madonna) are just a few examples. The performance of both contemporary popular songs and 'old favourites' would certainly have been common practice at theatrical venues such as the Moulin Rouge. And, though anachronistic, a modern audience's familiarity with several decades of pop music and its association with megastars, divas, and dance clubs provides a sonic, pop-culture window through which the heady atmosphere of the actual Moulin Rouge can be partially glimpsed.

Singing and lyrics

The use of microphones in the making of movie musicals allowed for the possibility of a more intimate singing style. No longer did performers have to sing as if they were projecting to the back row of a theatre or filling a large auditorium with their voice. As Miles Krueger has noted, Paul Robeson chose to sing quietly with the microphone only two feet away when recording 'Ol' Man River' for the 1936 movie version of *Show Boat*.[17] The singing style of different performers also translates differently onto the screen. Compare, for example, the singing styles of Fred Astaire and Al Jolson. Jolson's personality fills the screen and his huge voice is barely contained by the soundtrack. Astaire's style, on the other hand, is more intimate and refined. Also, since vocal projection over a great distance is less crucial here, Astaire can focus on the clear diction and suave, elegant phrasing that is his forte. Technology can also affect the lyrics of songs. Before the regular use of amplified sound in theatres, lyricists developed the technique of placing long vowel sounds at the ends of lines to aid with projection ('day/free/high/show/you' etc.). But the intimacy of the recording studio allowed more complex lyrics to be fashioned that could, for example, end lines with short vowels and clipped consonants that would have been lost in a theatre environment.[18]

Dance style

A wide variety of dance styles are present in this genre, ranging from high to low, elite to popular. They may be performed by a solo dancer, a couple, or a large ensemble in a 'production number'. Contrasting styles are sometimes played off against one another – usually with the more popular styles winning out. Gene Kelly, Fred Astaire, Eleanor Powell and Ann Miller are the best of the solo dancers. Fred Astaire and Ginger Rogers set the benchmark for the special chemistry that can be generated from the couple dance in Cole Porter's 'Night and Day' from *The Gay Divorcée* (1934), a remake of the 1932 stage show *Gay Divorce*. This number established new standards of direction, design, choreography, camerawork and editing, not just for the team's subsequent dances, but for many other couples as well. In a similar way, the production numbers of Busby Berkeley greatly influenced subsequent large-scale ensemble dances. The choice of dance genre can also be an effective method of communicating aspects of the narrative as, for example, in the ironic politeness of the 'Waltz for Eva and Che' from *Evita* or the prickling tension in the 'Tango: Maureen' from *Rent*.

Concluding example

Clearly, the elements I have isolated above do not operate alone in the projection of a narrative and should, ideally, be considered in conjunction with one another. A final example attempts to bring together some of the approaches suggested above.

The example is the 'Roxanne Tango' sequence from *Moulin Rouge!*, which takes place after the final dress rehearsal of the lavish show-within-a-show, 'Spectacular Spectacular'. The Duke is unhappy with the ending and demands a rewrite and proof that Satine is really in love with him and not the penniless writer Christian. In order to save the show, Satine offers to pacify the Duke by arranging a personal meeting while the rest of the cast and crew wait anxiously for the outcome of the assignation. 'El Tango de Roxanne' is performed by off-duty performers on the large Moulin Rouge dance floor and is a composite of interpolated and newly composed material.[19]

The tango genre itself is already loaded with pessimistic notions of love and a barely contained violence-tinged physicality. After being teased by Nini, one of the Moulin Rouge dancers, Christian is warned by the Narcoleptic Argentinian: 'Never fall in love with a woman who sells herself...'. The dance begins diegetically with piano and violin. The use of a follow spotlight adds to the already theatrical *mise-en-scène*. The narrative content of the song, while abstractly about the dangers of falling in love with a prostitute (a level already present in Sting's original lyrics), is clearly directed at Christian, warning him of the pain that will inevitably ensue from his falling for Satine. There is, however, also a hint of a tortuous and broken relationship between the Argentinian and Nini with whom he dances the initial duet. As more male dancers join in provocatively flirting with Nini, and Christian sings with anguish about his situation, the dance is intercut with shots of Satine and the Duke in the cold blue-grey lighting of the Duke's castle. More dancers come to the floor and multiple couples join in the tango. Unable to contain himself, Christian makes to leave the theatre adding his own lyrical layer to the number as he slowly walks across the dance floor through the middle of the dancers – whose passionate contact is a painful reminder of the Duke's proximity to Satine. Still more dancers join the tango while the Duke offers Satine diamonds – doubly symbolic for being both Satine's stage name ('the Sparkling Diamond') and a reference to her rendition of 'Diamonds Are a Girl's Best Friend' on the night she first met both Christian and the Duke. Like the marble and stone of the Duke's room, diamonds are cold and hard and contrast to the warmer hues of the fabrics and wooden dance floor in the Moulin Rouge interior. Forlorn, Christian determinedly walks home past the elephant and looks longingly up at the balcony of the Duke's castle.

Gazing down from the balcony, Satine briefly reprises 'Come What May' – a snippet of the secret song they have agreed will remind one another of their true love. The Duke realises this and is outraged. Now, the warning of the tango is also directed at him, for he too will endure much anguish because of his love for Satine. Violence erupts: the dancers mirror the Duke's rough handling of Satine, the musical tension mounts with Astor Piazzolla-like dissonance, and the contrasting long shots and close-ups convey both the emotional intensity and physical separation of the two principal lovers. At the climax of the number, where all three male characters are virtually screaming and the rapid montage-like editing reaches its peak, the Argentinian mimes strangling Nini. Instead of Satine's parallel downfall, however, the Duke is knocked out by a single punch from Chocolat, who has crept unseen into the chamber. Thus Satine is spared.

Flashes of red (the signature colour of the movie) abound within the Moulin Rouge – the Argentinian's jacket, and the red glow from the theatre that bathes Christian as he stands in the street – suggest the true passion of these characters. These are contrasted with the icy blues, greys and blacks of the Duke's castle. On the balcony, Satine is bathed in a wash of blue, but hints of her connection to Christian are given by red light-bulbs of the ever-circling Moulin spokes (which have appeared numerous times already in the narrative, but most often when Satine and Christian are declaring their love for one another), and her red lipstick suggesting that, despite appearances to the contrary, she does indeed love him alone.

Thus colour, lighting and set design are used in combination with music, lyrics, choreography, camerawork and editing to create a powerful, emotionally charged number.[20]

Summary

Seemingly infinite access to eighty years of movie musicals through video, DVD and digital/cable/satellite TV, along with the movie-like production values of music videos and the impressively slick and continuously inventive medium of TV commercials, has broadened the niche of large-scale visual spectacle with music, dance and song of which the movie musical was once the sole occupant. Though critics might assert that some recent movie musicals have been based on successful stage productions or revivals – and thereby constitute a somewhat 'safe bet' for studios – many have not, and most have, at least in part, used the medium of film to enhance and deepen the narrative. This gives me hope that the genre will continue to reinvent itself and makes serious multidisciplinary study all the more necessary. Each time a new survey or textbook on musical theatre is published that does not discuss the unique natures of *both* stage and screen musicals diminishes the possibilities of bringing serious analytical consideration to bear on these powerful cultural artefacts. As other disciplines have already shown (film studies, cultural studies, American studies), the study of movie musicals can yield rich rewards. Again, I urge current and future scholars of musical theatre – particularly those versed in musical analysis – to continue the exploration of this magical screen counterpart.

18 Revisiting classic musicals: revivals, films, television and recordings

JESSICA STERNFELD

Broadway musicals can continue to live long after their initial productions close. They can tour, play at local community theatres, become staples of high school repertoire, and even open abroad (as discussed in chapter 15). Years later they sometimes return to Broadway, occasionally finding even greater success than when they first appeared. They can become films or television specials, and in these incarnations play to exponentially larger audiences than is possible in live performance. And thanks to recordings, these shows can be accessed wherever and whenever the necessary technology is available.

Revivals

Most successful Broadway revivals are ones that do something to the original material that is powerful, unexpected, or so deft that audiences are interested in returning to it. These shows are sometimes beloved classics filled with popular tunes and presented with a fresh interpretation and a strong cast. They can also be underappreciated, complex scores that deserve a second chance to find an audience. Yet the longest-running revival in Broadway history is a series of silly skits that generated no hit songs or complicated messages. *Oh! Calcutta!* holds a record that few revivals are ever likely to surpass: it ran for 5,959 performances between 1976 and 1989. A comedy revue featuring sketches by many writers, songs by multiple composers, and an often-nude cast, the show continued to draw audiences thanks to its novelty and air of ridiculous fun. But past this novelty of a revival, most producers, directors and performers have the same impulses when it comes to remounting a Broadway show: they wish to explore its inherent artistic possibilities and find new audiences.

The second and third longest-running revivals come from the same creative team: composer John Kander and lyricist Fred Ebb. Their two biggest hits, *Cabaret* (1966) and *Chicago* (1975), had successful initial runs and became regional theatre staples, even though the world perhaps was not quite ready for them. But when the shows returned to Broadway back-to-back in the 1990s, audiences had felt higher levels of world-weary cynicism.

Chicago arrived first, in 1996, followed two years later by *Cabaret*. The two shows became Broadway institutions, running confidently alongside the megamusicals *Les Misérables* and *The Phantom of the Opera* and Disney-produced, family-friendly shows such as *Beauty and the Beast* and *The Lion King*.

Chicago, which won Tony Awards for Best Revival, Actor (James Naughton as Billy Flynn), and Actress (Bebe Neuwirth as Velma Kelly), as well as for Director (Walter Bobbie) and Choreographer (Ann Reinking), stuck close to – indeed, took great pains to honour – its original incarnation on Broadway. Reinking, a dancer and choreographer long associated with Bob Fosse, the show's original director, choreographer and co-bookwriter, emulated her mentor's style.[1] When the revival opened, America had weathered the O. J. Simpson trial, teenager Amy Fisher's sensational shooting of her older lover's wife, the continuing dramas of Michael Jackson, and countless other strange comings-together of scandal, fame, the media and the justice system. *Chicago*, with its tale of media manipulation, now made perfect sense. Most critics praised the reduction of the production to its bare essentials: simple, stark sets; slinky uncomplicated black-and-white costumes; and intense, full-frontal performances. 'It's show biz administered through intravenous injection,' declared David Patrick Stearns.[2]

The revival of *Cabaret* opened in March 1998 at the Henry Miller Theatre, which had been remodelled and renamed the Kit Kat Klub; the audience sat at tables and became the audience for the nightclub as well as for the musical. Later that year the show moved to Studio 54, merging its mood of sleazy debauchery with that space's own lurid past. Making the audience part of the crowd at the club implied that they were complicit in the events, which culminate in the rise of the Nazis in Berlin. The innovation of directors Sam Mendes and Rob Marshall that transformed the audience into club-goers drew its inspiration from the original staging, but exaggerated and intensified the effect. (Hal Prince, in the original, used mirrors to show the audience their own faces, and to catch themselves laughing at awkward moments.) In his *New York Times* review, Ben Brantley described the new production as 'seedier, raunchier and more sinister' than either the 1966 original or the 1972 film.[3] Alan Cumming, as the Master of Ceremonies, and his girls showed enormous amounts of skin and offered many explicit, intentionally offensive gestures. But they were also a shabby lot, in tattered costumes, often wearing resigned, unsmiling expressions. Cumming, thin, angular, with big dimples and floppy hair, came across as sexually androgynous. He wore sparkling pasties over his nipples, lots of eye make-up, and a swastika on his briefly bared backside. Sally Bowles (played by Natasha Richardson) came across as more ambitious than talented, not unlike Roxie in *Chicago*; both express desperation to escape their lives and become famous at any

Plate 23 *Chicago* at the Ambassador Theatre, New York, summer 2004.

cost. In the final scene, the set and lighting disappeared and the cast emerged in prisoners' clothes, apparently in a concentration camp. The Emcee's costume included both a yellow Star of David and a pink triangle. *Cabaret* won the 1998 Tony for Best Revival, as well as Best Actor (Cumming), Actress (Richardson), and Supporting Actor (Ron Rifkin, who played Herr Schultz).

Most revivals do not last as long as those of *Chicago* and *Cabaret*. Even the fourth and fifth longest-running revivals, *42nd Street* (2001) and *Grease* (1994), each ran for less than four years. The 1992 revival of *Guys and Dolls* played less than three years and the 1999 *Annie Get Your Gun* less than two. But mounting a revival that becomes a semi-permanent tourist destination is not necessarily the goal of producers; especially since the 1980s, revivals have become a way for theatres to fill seats with safe, familiar material. They are usually considered reliable fare, likely to bring in fans familiar with the original production, the cast album, or a film version, if one exists. As pressures and prices mounted in the 1980s and many new musicals became expensive spectacles, revivals emerged as the less risky back-up plan for theatres and producers. A season-long run of a traditional staging of a classic show by Rodgers and Hammerstein, Cole Porter or Jule Styne pleased many investors. During the mid-1990s, the revival actually experienced something of a heyday on Broadway; the *New York Times* noted that between 1994 and 1999, over twenty-five revivals opened, and a fair number of them earned back their investment.[4] As proof of the significance of Broadway revivals during the decade, a Tony Award for Best Musical Revival was inaugurated in 1994.

New questions emerged. How can directors, actors and designers reinterpret the material? What new element can be highlighted, even in the most famous scores? Can a straightforward staging – one that resembles the original or a film version closely – satisfy a new audience? Will casting a famous movie or television star be enough to bring in audiences – and if not, what about using a rotating series of them? Is it acceptable to alter the classics, even if it is just a question of tone, and does this even matter?

The Golden Era's most beloved musicals have had some success in revivals, though nothing like that of *Chicago* and *Cabaret*. Rodgers and Hammerstein's first two collaborations, *Oklahoma!* and *Carousel*, have proved themselves to be relatively open to reinterpretation of tone and focus. In 2002, director Trevor Nunn (*Cats*, *Les Misérables*) brought his hit 1998 London revival of *Oklahoma!* to New York. Nunn and choreographer Susan Stroman tapped into not just the characters' youth but also their sexuality and its accompanying uncertainties. Jud (Shuler Hensley), a disturbing but somewhat under-developed character, became more central in Nunn's telling, making 'Lonely Room' (which did not even appear in the 1955 film) a powerful musical-dramatic moment. Everyone did their own dancing in Laurey's 'Dream Ballet', rather than having doubles take over as in the original, the film, and many other stagings. This Laurey (Josefina Gabrielle) morphs from adolescent tomboy to young lady; her hesitation to embrace adulthood and sexuality is underscored by her practical but unfeminine baggy overalls, which she wears until the box social forces her to put on a dress.

Oklahoma! was the second high-profile Rodgers and Hammerstein revival imported from London. In 1994, director Nicholas Hytner brought his 1992 revival of *Carousel* to New York. Though it ran for only ten months, it received a great deal of publicity, rave reviews and five Tony awards. Hytner's approach, like that of Nunn, involved focusing on the realism of the story – perhaps easier with this show than some other Rodgers and Hammerstein works, thanks to a plot involving abuse, disappointment and hopelessness. A story that had been dour was now complex and moving, thanks to Hytner, scenic designer Bob Crowley, and a cast featuring Sally Murphy (Julie Jordan), Michael Hayden (Billy Bigelow), Audra McDonald (Carrie Pipperidge) and Eddie Korbich (Enoch Snow).[5]

South Pacific has yet to have a Broadway revival, though it has had a healthy afterlife as a Hollywood film (1958), a television film adaptation (2001), a revival at London's National Theatre (2001) and a concert version, broadcast nationally on PBS's *Great Performances* (2005). *The King and I* has returned to Broadway three times since its 1951 debut with Yul Brynner and Gertrude Lawrence, most recently in 1996 with Donna Murphy and Lou Diamond Phillips.

The Sound of Music, perhaps the most well-known and beloved Rodgers and Hammerstein work (thanks to the extremely successful 1965 film), has been revived on Broadway only once since its debut in 1959. The 1998 revival starred Rebecca Luker and ran for fifteen months. Directed by Susan H. Schulman, the production featured a few added Nazi images and attempted to darken the story a bit, but mostly stuck close to the letter and spirit of both the stage version and the film (two songs dropped from the show for the film were reinstated, and the two songs written for the film were also included). The show has even entered the world of reality television; in 2006, the British series *How Do You Solve a Problem Like Maria?* found Andrew Lloyd Webber and several other producers holding a national search for the star of a new London revival of *The Sound of Music*. Potential Marias were eliminated by public voting, as in the British *Pop Idol* or its progeny *American Idol,* and the winner, Connie Fisher, appeared in the coveted role in November 2006.

Not all beloved classics have received either the reimagining or the attention of some of the Rodgers and Hammerstein revivals. Lerner and Loewe's three enduring hits, favourites in local and school theatres, have yet to make an impact as Broadway revivals. *Brigadoon*, *My Fair Lady* and *Camelot* have each returned to Broadway three times – more than most of the Rodgers and Hammerstein shows – yet most of these runs were quite brief, and none inspired critics to talk about a revitalisation of material or a fresh viewing experience. All three have the potential to become successful revivals, should a director develop an original interpretation that sparks a modern audience's interest.

Stephen Sondheim, though considered by many to be America's premier theatre composer and lyricist in recent decades, has not always found critical or financial success on Broadway. A similar reception history marks his Broadway revivals: shows like *Company, Follies, Pacific Overtures* and *Into the Woods* have all received fairly short-lived restagings. *A Funny Thing Happened On The Way To The Forum* returned to Broadway in 1996 with Nathan Lane as Pseudolus; Whoopi Goldberg took over the lead role during the run. *Assassins*, which ran off-Broadway in 1990 and had its Broadway showing postponed after 9/11, finally arrived in 2004, running for only three months but receiving strong reviews and five Tonys. John Doyle reimagined *Sweeney*

Todd: The Demon Barber of Fleet Street on Broadway in 2005, followed by *Company* in 2006, in productions that featured the actors doubling as the orchestra. (See chapter 16 for a discussion of Doyle's approach.)

Many recent revivals have centred on a single star, producers and directors hoping that the name will draw audiences. The 2003 revival of *Gypsy* pitted Broadway's reigning diva, Bernadette Peters, against the larger-than-life shadow of Ethel Merman as Rose; despite intensely negative pre-opening buzz, the production and the star received rave reviews. Another star tactic involves casting not a Broadway veteran, but a celebrity from film, television or pop music; this 'stunt casting' can be risky and is often employed not on opening night, but a year or two into a revival's run in an attempt to refresh the show and draw new audiences. When country singer Reba McEntire replaced Bernadette Peters in the 1999 revival of *Annie Get Your Gun*, she received higher praise than her predecessor and parlayed her success into a television career. Melanie Griffith, taking over as Roxie Hart in *Chicago*, received surprisingly positive reviews despite the fact that many critics agreed she could not sing or dance. Family-friendly shows often employ celebrity casting – Brooke Shields and Rosie O'Donnell in *Grease*, for example, and Joey Fatone of the boy band *NSYNC in *Rent*. Other recent revivals of note – featuring varying degrees of innovation and traditional approaches, as well as (in some cases) an array of stunt casting – include *Jesus Christ Superstar*, *Fiddler on the Roof*, *Pal Joey*, *Bells Are Ringing*, *Guys and Dolls*, *Pajama Game*, *Damn Yankees*, *Mame*, *Candide* and *A Chorus Line*, as well as the return of *Les Misérables* a mere three and a half years after its original sixteen-year run ended.

Films

Many classic stage musicals became classic – though not always perfect – films. Rodgers and Hammerstein's hits all received cinematic treatments; in most cases they remained close to their stage versions, with a few scenes rearranged or a song or two dropped. Gerald Mast applies a useful critical tool to these films by testing each one for their degree of 'opening up' the stage version. He expects a film adaptation to rethink the story and score in new and genre-appropriate ways, especially visually. For example, the film should use settings that suit film, rather than three-sided stage-derived sets. These new settings might be realistic on-location sets or they might be flights of fancy that only film can achieve, but it is not usually in a film's best interest simply to recreate the stage sets. Mast declares *The Sound of Music* (1965) to be the best of the Rodgers and Hammerstein films because it passes this critical test better than the rest; though many scholars consider the show to be old-fashioned and overwhelmingly corny, no one can deny that director Robert Wise made Salzburg and the Austrian countryside integral parts of the story and songs. *Carousel* (1956), which Mast declares 'the worst of the lot', fails in part due to its 'styleless visual void'; *South Pacific* (1958) frustrates because few characters actually engage with the gorgeous on-location scenery. *South Pacific* director Joshua Logan has also become infamous in musical theatre circles for his universally despised coloured filters. There are, nevertheless, countless things to admire about Rodgers and Hammerstein's Hollywood forays, such as the capturing of Agnes de Mille's choreography for *Oklahoma!* (1955) and the powerful performance of Yul Brynner in *The King and I* (1956).[6]

Lerner and Loewe, like Rodgers and Hammerstein, took their Broadway musicals to Hollywood with mixed results. Their stage hits – *Brigadoon* (1947), *My Fair Lady* (1956) and *Camelot* (1960) – seemed ideal material for film, but only *My Fair Lady* was generally hailed as a success. Critics agreed that *Brigadoon*, directed by Vincente Minnelli and filmed in 1954 on an MGM lot rather than on location in Scotland (as Lerner and Loewe had hoped), lost much of its magic in translation; the *New York Times* lamented that a show with such screen potential fell 'as flat as a pancake'.[7] It was especially egregious that the back-lot sets were fake-looking and dull. Star and choreographer Gene Kelly, though his talent was unimpeachable, used a modern dance style that struck many as a poor fit for the quaint country setting. Nearly half of the stage songs were cut, including hits like 'Come To Me, Bend To Me', and no new ones were added. *My Fair Lady* appeared in 1964, with non-singer Audrey Hepburn playing Eliza Doolittle, rather than Julie Andrews, who created the role on Broadway. Many were unconvinced by Hepburn as a street vendor, and Marni Nixon's dubbing for much of her singing was easily recognisable. In virtually every way except for the casting of Eliza, the film reproduces the show, for it retains the songs, book and order of events, as well as leading actor Rex Harrison as Henry Higgins. The complicated nature of the stage version of *Camelot* necessitated many changes when it was filmed for its 1967 release. The streamlining or eliminating of various subplots and secondary characters actually helped the story hold together better than it had on stage. Lerner created a new opening scene that takes place on the eve of battle; this made the rest of the movie a flashback and gave the entire show a more serious tone. One of the most successful elements of the stage version, its stellar cast – Richard Burton as Arthur, Julie Andrews as Guinevere and Robert Goulet as Lancelot – became the less well-received Richard Harris, Vanessa Redgrave and Franco Nero (whose singing voice was dubbed by the uncredited Gene Merlino).

Film adaptations of shows by creators other than Rodgers and Hammerstein or Lerner and Loewe from the 1950s to the 1970s demonstrated a variety of approaches. Frank Loesser's *Guys and Dolls* triumphed on Broadway in 1950, and then – like many other shows – underwent a somewhat inexplicable metamorphosis into a film in 1955. The explanation for casting is clear enough: studios wanted bankable movie stars. Casting non-singers Marlon Brando as Sky Masterson and Jean Simmons as Sarah Brown might seem justifiable enough, especially since they did hold their own in singing-heavy roles; but why cast Frank Sinatra as Nathan Detroit, who barely sings at all? Many have suggested that the movie would have fared better if the two male actors had been reversed. Eleven of Loesser's sixteen stage songs appear in the film, along with several new ones (such as 'Adelaide' for Sinatra). Original cast members from the stage version include Stubby Kaye as Nicely Nicely Johnson and Vivian Blaine as Adelaide, and Michael Kidd choreographed both versions.

The 1971 film version of *Fiddler on the Roof* managed to please virtually everyone: loyal fans of the stage version, the general movie-going audience and film critics. Producer and director Norman Jewison retained a great deal of Jerome Robbins' original choreography and kept the show's place-specific aesthetic. Joseph Stein, in adapting his book into a screenplay, dropped two songs but retained virtually everything else, including the extensive dialogue and every bit of the remaining songs; hence the filmed *Fiddler* lasts 180 minutes, basically the length of the stage version. Jewison filmed partly on location in and near Zagreb, Croatia, rendering the village realistic but often soft and out of focus.

Grease, the lighthearted story of teen romance and peer pressure set in the 1950s, had a successful eight-year run on Broadway starting in 1972. In 1977 John Travolta made the leap from television to film with *Saturday Night Fever*, making him a big draw for the 1978 adaptation of *Grease*, co-starring Olivia Newton-John. The book and score, by Jim Jacobs and Warren Casey, underwent radical revisions, most notably the addition of some of the film's best-loved songs such as 'Hopelessly Devoted To You', 'You're the One That I Want', and 'Grease', written by a team including Barry Gibb, John Farrar and others. Since the show is enormously popular with high schools and other local theatres, the film's songs are now often interpolated into the stage performing score. The film's somewhat troubling message – a girl should act and dress provocatively to help her boyfriend overcome the peer pressure against dating a nice girl – was entirely overshadowed by the songs, dances and comedy that were the real point. Travolta and Newton-John were part of a stellar cast, including Stockard Channing and Didi Conn, plus stars from the 1950s such as Joan Blondell, Eve Arden, Dody Goodman, Sid Caesar, Alice Ghostley and Frankie Avalon in character roles. By most accounts, *Grease* is the highest-grossing movie musical of all time. The double-album soundtrack stayed on the Billboard charts for thirty-nine weeks, at number one for twelve weeks; it featured not only the songs that the characters sing in the film, but also ones that got cut, are barely heard, or are covers of 1950s hits sung by Sha Na Na, the band that sings at Rydell High's big dance. *Grease* helped inspire a brief wave of films full of singing and/or dancing teens, including the dance-oriented *Footloose* and *Dirty Dancing*, and film musicals *Fame* and *Grease 2* (which features an even lighter plot than *Grease* but contains some excellent songs and dances).

Very few film adaptations of musicals appeared between *Grease* and *Chicago* (2002), especially compared to the constant flow that emanated from Hollywood in previous decades. Of the few that appeared, even fewer succeeded with critics or audiences. *A Chorus Line* (1975), a long-running Broadway hit, became a film box-office bomb in 1985, and in 1996, *Evita* arrived amid intense publicity and mixed reviews. The big-budget movie that starred Madonna and Antonio Banderas deftly presented Lloyd Webber and Rice's material, but did not generate enough momentum to revitalise the film musical as a genre.

The film version of *Chicago* is a milestone in the still-being-written history of film musicals. It resurrected the genre, winning the Oscar for Best Picture, but its long-term impact remains unclear. Rob Marshall, who achieved such success as the co-director of the 1998 stage revival of *Cabaret*, began his career as a choreographer, and hence was well suited to direct as well as choreograph the dance-focused *Chicago* film. The screen version is indeed filled with dancing (in a style reminiscent of original choreographer Bob Fosse, with plenty of modern touches) and retains much of the music and the book of the stage version. But Marshall made several bold moves. First, he cast three movie stars – Catherine Zeta-Jones (former vaudeville star turned murderess Velma Kelly), Renée Zellweger (fame-hungry Roxie Hart), and Richard Gere (celebrity lawyer Billy Flynn) – rather than Broadway veterans. Of these, only Zeta-Jones had training as a singer and dancer. Zellweger's character did not need to be an expert singer or dancer, she simply needed to want to be, and Zellweger's own Hollywood persona of vulnerability and stardom blended in many critics' minds with that of Roxie.[8] Since the show is about celebrity, casting three Hollywood icons seemed appropriate, even if the show's cynical tone and violent plotlines do not shed the best light on how stars achieve fame. Marshall's boldest move, though, was in his conception of the film itself. Virtually every song in the film – with the exception of Amos's 'Mr Cellophane' and a few on-stage numbers like Velma's 'All That Jazz' – takes place inside Roxie's mind. The heroine escapes from her grim reality by envisioning entire production numbers in her head. Some film critics and theatre scholars found this to be a cheap trick, a cop-out by a director afraid to let his characters burst into song during the course of their normal lives, but other critics – and movie-goers – embraced this technique as one that made the musical palatable for modern audiences not accustomed to musicals. Marshall also chose a rapid-cut editing style, filled with close-ups that never allow the viewer to see a group of dancers from a distance, nor often even an entire dancer's body. Arms curve, legs extend, but only a few numbers such as 'Razzle Dazzle' and 'Cell Block Tango' are treated like fully staged group numbers that one can take in as a whole.

The Phantom of the Opera arrived in movie theatres in December 2004. As a stage show, Phantom is lush, sweeping, full of clever effects and constant motion; indeed, it already had something of a cinematic look. The film remains largely faithful to the stage version, though some of the most complex, dissonant or recitative-like material is converted into dialogue or cut completely. Significant differences exist, particularly through the expansion of a frame story. The musical opens many years after the main action takes place with an aged Raoul recalling his encounter with the Phantom. In the film, this frame story – filmed in black and white – returns several times, including at the end. We learn, thanks to aged Raoul's journey to Christine's grave, that they had a long life together, and that the Phantom still lives, for he seems to have left a red rose on Christine's grave – the rose is his signature and its occasional appearance in the film is one of director Joel Schumacher's effective touches of detail. Emmy Rossum, only eighteen at the time, played Christine and carried the demanding part with a clear voice and a perfect porcelain-doll look. Gerard Butler's Phantom was more sympathetic than the character's portrayal in the stage version, thanks to his less shocking facial deformity and a backstory provided by Madame Giry, the ballet mistress (Miranda Richardson). His short-breathed voice conveys his stressful brooding, especially when compared to the Broadway-style tenor of Patrick Wilson as rival Raoul. Minnie Driver (whose singing was dubbed, except in a bonus song over the credits) provides comic relief in a campy performance as the diva Carlotta.

The eagerly anticipated film version of Rent opened in 2005. Six of the eight leading original cast members starred in the film, nine years after its 1996 opening, and most of the songs and story highlights remained the same. However, much of the show's cynicism – and some of its music – was cut. Almost all of the linking material, underscoring, and recitative-like sung dialogue either became spoken dialogue (over silence) or was removed. A show that was mostly sung through became a movie with a stop-and-sing format, leading to some old-fashioned and awkward song cues and the loss of some of composer/lyricist Jonathan Larson's most unpredictable material. Several songs, including 'Today 4 U', 'La Vie Boheme' and 'Light My Candle', were filmed on one set, staged and performed almost exactly as they were on stage. But director Chris Columbus also utilised the potential of the film medium. 'Seasons of Love', Rent's hit single, opens the film; the eight main characters sing it on a bare stage, in a straight line. This gives the suggestion of a frame story: these eight attractive, friendly people would like to put on a show for us. The stage version treats 'Seasons of Love' as an entr'acte, staged the same way, and interrupts a host of conflicts between the characters, who present this oratorio-style anthem to the audience. Visual montages and backstories also appear in the film; for example, Roger's 'One Song Glory' visually narrates the character's entire relationship with his dead girlfriend April. The timeline of the film differs from that of the stage version; whereas the entire first act of the stage version occurs on Christmas Eve, as it does in its source material, Puccini's *La bohème*, several days pass between the opening number 'Rent' (now with its chant-like introduction spoken) and 'La Vie Boheme' on screen. This gives two couples – Collins (Jesse L. Martin) and Angel (Wilson Jermaine Heredia), and Roger (Adam Pascal) and Mimi (Rosario Dawson) – more than a few minutes to fall in love, which either makes their relationships more realistic or less romantic, depending on one's view of opera-style love at first sight.

A radically different film adaptation of a stage show also appeared in 2005: *The Producers*. Mel Brooks took the tale from film to stage and back again. His 1968 film was not a musical, but revolved around the world of Broadway musicals and famously featured a production number from that unlikely hit, *Springtime for Hitler*, produced by con artist Max Bialystock (Zero Mostel) and wimpy accountant Leo Bloom (Gene Wilder). In 2001, Brooks and co-bookwriter Thomas Meehan refashioned *The Producers* for Broadway. It was a hit, thanks to Brooks' host of new songs, and stars Nathan Lane (Max) and Matthew Broderick (Leo). Then, a film version of the stage musical appeared, directed – like the musical – by Susan Stroman, and featuring Lane and Broderick along with original Broadway cast members Gary Beach (*Springtime*'s director Roger De Bris) and Roger Bart (De Bris's 'common-law assistant' Carmen Ghia). Film actors Will Ferrell (playwright Franz Liebkind) and Uma Thurman (secretary/actress Ulla) added Hollywood appeal.

The Producers adhered closely to its stage version, with predictable results: while fans embraced the film for capturing everything they love about the show, some critics lamented the missed opportunities to repackage the material in a filmic way. Roger Ebert, a huge fan of the 1968 film, declared this film a 'success' and enjoyed moments when it made reference to the first film (he noted that when Max promises wealth to Leo, a park fountain erupts behind them in both films – but not in the show).[9] Ebert's small observation is indicative of a larger point: whereas the show had been a homage to musical theatre past and present, the new film instead pays tribute to other films. Perhaps Brooks, Meehan and Stroman thought that their jokes about *Fiddler on the Roof*, Judy Garland, *Follies*, and the Broadway version of *The Lion King* would be lost on the movie-going audience, and indeed, Max's introductory number, 'The King of Broadway', was cut. In place of the deleted theatre jokes, Brooks offered film parodies; for example, during the end credits, Will Ferrell reprises Franz's song 'Der Guten Tag Hop-Clop' as 'The Hop-Clop Goes On'. The first version is a perky dance full of knee-slapping German folk moves, which Franz sings in the aggressive, pro-Hitler style he brings to everything he says. But in the credits, the song sneaks in first with a solo flute, and then with Franz's soft and breathy voice. It is Celine Dion's 'My Heart Will Go On' from the film *Titanic*, complete with swelling orchestra and build-to-belting refrain, and Ferrell sells it with earnest sincerity. The film musical boom continues in recent years with *Dreamgirls*, *Hairspray*, *Sweeney Todd* and *Mamma Mia!*.

Television

In the early years of television, musical theatre was a staple of network programming; original musicals and television adaptations of Broadway musicals abounded, as did musical children's shows and small-screen stagings of operas. But one need only to glance at the listings sorted by year in Joan Baxter's *Television Musicals* to see that the numbers of made-for-television musicals dropped off sharply in the 1970s, and even musical children's programmes (such as animated holiday specials) thinned in the 1980s and early 90s.[10]

By far the most famous musical for television, thanks to its star power and then-unprecedented success, was Rodgers and Hammerstein's *Cinderella*. Airing live in 1957, *Cinderella* inspired an estimated 107 million viewers to stay home; anecdotal evidence suggests that crime was down and streets were empty during the broadcast. Though aired in colour, only a black and white kinescope has survived. Twenty-one-year-old Julie Andrews received an Emmy nomination as well as rave reviews. Lesley Ann Warren recreated the role on television in 1965.

A third version of *Cinderella* aired on ABC's *The Wonderful World of Disney* in November 1997, starring pop singer and teen television star Brandy (Cinderella), Paolo Montalban (the Prince), Whoopi Goldberg and Victor Garber (the Prince's parents), Bernadette Peters (Cinderella's stepmother), Jason Alexander (the Prince's sidekick Lionel, a newly created character), and Whitney Houston (Cinderella's Fairy Godmother). Critics made much of this kingdom's racial diversity, admiring that a black queen and a white king can create a Filipino son, and that no one in the land bothers to question or even notice this. Along with this casting, *Cinderella* underwent an extensive script and score retooling. The book, adapted by Robert L. Freedman, now featured two young people looking for self-empowered independence first, and romance second. The Prince is sometimes uncomfortable being served and obeyed, and enjoys mingling incognito with his subjects. Cinderella's Fairy Godmother teaches her to follow her dreams, and Cinderella tells the Prince she wishes to be treated like a person, not a princess. The score received a major overhaul as well, gaining several interpolated songs including 'The Sweetest Sounds' from Rodgers' *No Strings* (1962) and 'Falling In Love With Love' (sung by Bernadette Peters, showing the evil stepmother's tender side) from Rodgers and Hart's *The Boys From Syracuse* (1938). In the finale, Whitney Houston sang 'There's Music In You', a song Rodgers and Hammerstein had written for Mary Martin to sing in the 1953 film *Main Street to Broadway*, and – in an interpolation within an interpolation – the middle section of Houston's song came from 'One Foot, Other Foot', borrowed from Rodgers and Hammerstein's short-lived *Allegro* (1947). While the production received mixed reviews (critics generally admired the effort and the multiracial casting but had some negative – and conflicting – things to say about the performances and the adaptation), it generated strong ratings and marked one of the highlights of the 1990s television musical boom.

A made-for-television version of *Gypsy* starring Bette Midler aired on CBS in December 1993. Critics cheered that Bette Midler succeeded in making the daunting role her own – an achievement perhaps aided by displaying the show in a new medium. It may also have helped that the production came with a vote of confidence – and even some consultation – from the entire original creative team: composer Jule Styne, lyricist Stephen Sondheim, bookwriter Arthur Laurents, and director-choreographer Jerome Robbins.

Cinderella and *Gypsy* are two examples of the boom that occurred with television musicals during the 1990s. The genre found something of a niche on ABC's *Wonderful World of Disney*. In December 1995, *Bye Bye Birdie* featured television star and long-time musical theatre performer Jason Alexander as Albert Peterson, manager of 50s rock star Conrad Birdie (Broadway regular Marc Kudisch). *Annie* appeared in November 1999 in a version directed by Rob Marshall, who infused the potentially sticky-sweet show with unflagging wit and even bite. Kathy Bates, as Miss Hannigan, surprised many with her singing and dancing, and she was surrounded by Broadway stars Victor Garber (one of the few cast members known also for his television work) as Daddy Warbucks, Audra McDonald as Grace, Alan Cumming as Rooster, and Kristin Chenoweth as Lily St Regis. Fans of the original staging could spot Andrea McArdle, Broadway's first Annie, as the would-be star just arrived in the city during the number 'NYC'. A 2001 television production of a Rodgers and Hammerstein classic, *South Pacific*, won a huge amount of media attention, thanks mostly to the popularity of its stars, Glenn Close as Nellie (she also co-executive-produced and was a driving force behind the project), and Harry Connick Jr as Lieutenant Joe Cable. Calmer than spunky Mary Martin, wiser than perky Mitzi Gaynor, Close's Nellie came across as a career military nurse whose control was shaken by her first real encounters both with true love and with racism. 'You've Got To Be Carefully Taught' becomes the central number in the show: Connick delivers it alone, in an intense, radically retooled arrangement. Gone is the rather bouncy triple metre, replaced by Connick's speech-based delivery over menacing bells. *The Music Man* came in February 2003, with Matthew Broderick, Kristin Chenoweth, Debra Monk and Victor Garber, and *Once Upon a Mattress* followed in December 2005, with Carol Burnett (who created the role of Princess Fred on Broadway) as Queen Aggravain and Tracy Ullman as Fred. With the establishment of a Sunday-night 'tradition' for television versions of esteemed musicals, a new dimension of musical theatre is emerging.

Audio and video recordings

In recent years, there has been an enormous boom in the Broadway-on-video industry. Now, some people are just as likely – perhaps even more likely – to watch a musical on DVD as to listen to it on CD. But before the advent of home video in the 1980s, the original cast album was the way that fans could remember, or imagine, the experience of seeing the show live. The full-length original Broadway cast LP phenomenon began with *South Pacific* in 1949. Its enormous success made the genre a permanent one; it is still standard procedure to record the original cast performing the score soon after a show opens and release it commercially. *South Pacific* went gold, and the release of *Oklahoma!* on LP (transferred from the 78s of its first release) quickly surpassed it in sales. In general, hit shows generate hit albums.

Soon after the original cast album became an automatic tie-in with any successful Broadway show, a new entity emerged: the studio album. Producers assembled a cast to sing the score for the purposes of a recording, without links to a live staging. These casts often included singers from different genres, especially opera, forming a sub-category known as 'crossover' recordings. Ethan Mordden cites the 1955 recording of *Carousel* with Robert Merrill and Patrice Munsel as the first of these.[11] Recordings of musicals by opera singers reached something of a peak in the mid-1980s and early 1990s. Leonard Bernstein conducted his *West Side Story* with Kiri Te Kanawa and José Carreras in 1985; Carreras returned for *South Pacific* in 1987 with Sarah Vaughan. Conductor John McGlinn released *Show Boat* (1988), *Annie Get Your Gun* (1991) and *Brigadoon* (1992) with mixes of operatic and Broadway voices in each case. Depending on one's taste, these crossover recordings can bring beautiful music and beautiful voices together, or they can feel like an awkward juxtaposition of highly trained voices singing material meant to sound more 'natural'.

The availability of musicals on video and DVD is invaluable for study, especially when one does not have the opportunity to see the show live on Broadway or wishes to compare productions. Some of the recent revivals have been released in these formats, including *Oklahoma!* and *Kiss Me, Kate*. Sondheim's shows are particularly plentiful on DVD, and include the original productions of *Sunday in the Park with George*, *Into the Woods* and *Passion*, and both the original staging and a concert version of *Sweeney Todd: The Demon Barber of Fleet Street*. Lloyd Webber released made-for-television versions of *Cats*, *Joseph and the Amazing Technicolor Dreamcoat*, and *Jesus Christ Superstar*, and Schönberg and Boublil's *Les Misérables* is available in a semi-staged concert version. In this new age, the musical theatre has changed substantially from fifty years ago when cameras were seldom allowed in a theatre. As technology and our viewing habits continue to change, one can expect that the musical theatre and the modes through which it is experienced will likewise continue to develop.

19 The creation of a Broadway musical: Stephen Schwartz, Winnie Holzman, and *Wicked*

PAUL R. LAIRD

The creation of *Wicked* began when Stephen Schwartz first encountered Gregory Maguire's fascinating retelling of *The Wizard of Oz* from the Wicked Witch of the West's viewpoint.[1] A friend told Schwartz about the novel while they were on a snorkelling trip in Hawaii.[2] The composer hears a bell when he encounters a good concept for a musical, and he reports 'that bell went off as soon as I heard the title'.[3] Back in Los Angeles, he asked his lawyer to investigate who owned the rights to *Wicked*. They followed a winding path that ended with Marc Platt, head of Universal Pictures, who owned the film rights and awaited the second draft of a screenplay.

Schwartz hoped to convince Platt that *Wicked* would make a better stage musical than a film. He recalls: 'I really believed I knew how to do it and wanted it very much.' After meetings with lower-level executives, Schwartz finally made his case to Platt personally about a year later.[4] He feels fortunate to have dealt with Platt, who liked musical theatre and had appeared in Schwartz's *Pippin* while in college. Platt asked for time to consider it; he gave the composer/lyricist permission for the project in 1997 or 1998. At one point, Platt considered doing both the stage musical and a non-musical film.[5]

Schwartz had already decided to ask Winnie Holzman to write the book. He had loved her television series *My So-Called Life*, which included convincing young female characters. With *Wicked* dominated by Elphaba and Galinda,[6] this was crucial. Schwartz had met Holzman years before when she was a student in the New York University musical theatre writing programme, for which he did masterclasses. After both had discovered *Wicked*, Disney brought Schwartz and Holzman together to discuss another project. Talk at lunch turned to the novel and Schwartz mentioned he hoped to make a musical out of it. Holzman knew of the book and had thought it would make a good movie because of its 'brilliant premise', but she abandoned the idea when she learned that Universal had the rights.[7]

About four to six months later, Schwartz called Holzman to say that Universal would produce *Wicked* as a musical. He asked her to read the book, and they began to speak by phone. Holzman was thrilled at their immediate camaraderie: 'It became kind of clear early on to both of us that we would in fact be able to work together.' She felt Schwartz drawing her into the project: 'I felt that ... *Wicked* ... was the kind of idea that comes along very rarely in life. I wanted to do this with him because I thought it would be extremely exciting to work with someone of his calibre and I felt instinctively that I was going to learn a lot.' Holzman's only previous professional experience in musical theatre had been writing the book and lyrics for *Birds of Paradise*, produced unsuccessfully in New York in the 1980s.

The focus of their discussions was a plot outline that Schwartz sent Holzman in September 1998.[8] Schwartz tends to be very involved with developing the overall structure of his shows, stating: 'I think through the years that that's been a strength of mine, the ability to give a structure and a coherent narrative to the pieces I'm working on. They're not always obvious stories.'[9] The story changed many times before the first San Francisco preview on 28 May 2003, but Schwartz remembers aspects that remained from his first outline: the Shiz students go to a dance, Galinda tricks Elphaba into wearing the peaked hat and the two then become friends. Schwartz also already knew how the show would end and that he wanted to account for all 'iconic' images famous from earlier versions of *The Wizard of Oz*: Dorothy's three friends; the Wicked Witch's hat, cape and broom; winged monkeys; and magic shoes. Schwartz and Holzman soon discovered how much assistance Marc Platt would be.[10] He read all of their drafts and was 'very helpful in pointing out where the weaknesses were in the structure and storytelling'.

Eventually, Holzman began to write scenes. Schwartz notes: 'She seemed to understand the tone immediately.' She started to invent a language for the Ozians, substituting 'incorrect' endings for words that would still be clear to the audience, such as 'rejoicify'.

Holzman spoke candidly about the novel's role in their creative process:

> I didn't worry about the story told in the book that much. We had the rights to the book and the book became a resource. You can take whatever you need out of it. It wasn't pushing you around – you're in charge of it ... We were going to recreate our own story.

Schwartz had a similar feeling about Maguire's novel: 'It is a brilliant idea for a book and a brilliant idea for a musical, but we basically just took the concept and certain situations, certain relationships, certain characters, and then went off on our own.' Schwartz says that he felt they were faithful to the novel's concept, politics, 'skewed vision', and the basic characters of Elphaba, Galinda, Fiyero, the Wizard and Madame Morrible, but he adds, 'We just told a slightly different story, and it works.' Schwartz reports that Maguire was supportive. Early in the process, the composer spoke with the author.[11] Maguire 'gave his blessing and then he basically stayed away'. The novelist came to one of the later readings and said that he thought the musical's creators had captured the essence of his story.[12]

Holzman appreciated Schwartz's vision for the show, but found the plot's details difficult to write. The novel had to be simplified to become a musical, but they still wanted the show 'to have the feeling of a journey with this girl'. Schwartz and Holzman found a good model in *The Life and Adventures of Nicholas Nickleby*, a dramatisation of Charles Dickens's novel by the Royal Shakespeare Company that ran in New York twice in the 1980s.[13] Holzman described the production: 'You felt like you were inside a big long novel and in some ways I wanted that feeling . . .'. Another goal for *Wicked* was not to 'lose the richness of the story'. Holzman believes that the musical 'still feels like a novel to some extent'.

As writing progressed, Schwartz and Holzman had no trouble finding consensus regarding the story's details. Schwartz described them as a 'terrific team . . . We really respected one another, we listened to one another; we stood firm as an authorial unit at times there was great pressure for us not to.' Much of this strain came when more collaborators joined the team. The lyricist and composer constantly gave each other ideas, with lines of dialogue becoming a song or a song turning into a brief scene that could more efficiently make the point. Holzman notes that if she had not been providing lines that turned into a song, she would not have been doing her job. For example, the opening of 'What Is This Feeling?' rose out of dialogue.[14] Holzman conceived the idea of Elphaba derisively describing Galinda in a letter to her father as a 'blonde'. Schwartz inserted the word 'respond' in an earlier line as a rhyme. Holzman also conceived the title 'For Good' for Galinda's and Elphaba's final duet, word-play that conveys the moral ambiguity that occupies *Wicked*.[15]

The first step in writing *Wicked* culminated on 23 January 2000 at the initial reading for Universal Pictures.[16] The composer strongly felt that readings were valuable experiences. This was a new experience for Holzman, who found the process 'horrifying', but she learned from Schwartz how readings could be worthwhile. They invited 'certain core people', but others such as agents or actors also came. The creative team decided what they hoped to learn, and then studied why a particular scene or song did not work. Was it the actors or the set-up? Was the song in the wrong place, or was it the wrong song? Holzman found that they must 'weigh things delicately'. She says that the actors tended to be excellent, so when a line failed, it was probably in the writing. Holzman concludes: 'That's how we made the show work, by doing these things and getting the feedback and analysing what the feedback was and moving to the next stage.'

The readings continued at irregular intervals. On 28 September 2000 they had a fuller reading in Los Angeles with Kristin Chenoweth as Galinda and Stephanie Block as Elphaba. (Block played Elphaba in San Francisco and later on tour and in New York.) Five months later, on 23 February, they did a reading of the whole show in Los Angeles, then at Universal Pictures a week later on 2 March.

Kristin Chenoweth, a remarkable actress and singer who can both belt and sing demanding coloratura, joined in *Wicked*'s creation more than two years before the San Francisco opening. Both Schwartz and Holzman described her contribution to the role of Galinda. After Chenoweth's first reading, Holzman realised 'you wanted more of her and we expanded the part'. Holzman added: 'I felt so strongly about her as an actress . . . some people just inspire you . . . you start hearing their voice in your head.' Schwartz remembers that Chenoweth 'found so many moments for us'. For example, when Glinda arrests Madame Morrible at the end, she speaks to her slowly, imitating how Madame Morrible first dealt with her. Chenoweth started to use American Sign Language as she spelled 'captivity', finding a huge, unexpected laugh.[17]

Chenoweth's contribution helped make Elphaba and Galinda equally important, symbolised by their joint bow during curtain calls. Their relationship became *Wicked*'s focal point; Holzman recalls that they repeated 'It's the girls, stupid' whenever the show started to move away from these characters. Schwartz reports that Chenoweth influenced the way he composed her music. When she came on board, he had already written 'Popular', designed to demonstrate 'the shallowness of the character with music that implied bubblegum pop'. It is belted, the way that Schwartz heard the entire character. Chenoweth also wanted to sing in her soprano register, but Schwartz told her 'you can't really sing in two different voices and be two different people'. He then realised, however, that Galinda is, in some ways, two distinct characters: the real woman who is friendly, but insecure and superficial; and the 'posed' Galinda who is the beautiful 'good witch'. Thus, as the 'real' Galinda, Chenoweth belted; as the public persona, she soared into her upper register. In her last duet with Elphaba, 'For Good', Chenoweth sang soprano on 'Because I knew you . . .', merging her two sides.

Schwartz notes that the writing team, with Platt's input, took the show as far as they could through readings in the winter of 2001;[18] it was now time to find a director. A name that was 'always on the list' was Joe Mantello, a noted Broadway actor and director. Schwartz had served with Mantello on a panel for the Jonathan Larson Foundation and had seen Mantello's production of Terrence McNally's *Corpus Christi*, remarking, 'It looked like a musical staging to me.' When they asked Mantello about *Wicked*, he had directed the opera *Dead Man Walking* (by Jack Heggie and Terrence McNally) for the San Francisco Opera and was working on a chamber musical for Lincoln Center.[19] David Stone, a theatrical producer in New York, had joined *Wicked* as another producer (besides Platt), bringing his knowledge of the New York theatre. Stone had worked with Mantello off-Broadway and confirmed that he was a good choice for *Wicked*. They spoke with Mantello and others. Once offered *Wicked*, Schwartz says that Mantello 'responded immediately, passionately, and enthusiastically'.

Schwartz reports that *Wicked*'s 'visual element' was almost entirely supervised by Mantello. He worked with the various designers: Eugene Lee for sets, Susan Hilferty for costumes and Kenneth Posner for lighting. Schwartz evinced little interest in these production elements.[20] Far more interesting for the composer were Mantello's musical contributions. For example, Schwartz reports that Holzman had the idea for a 'falling into hate' song for Galinda and Elphaba, sung after they meet. Schwartz had already written and rejected three songs for that spot when he composed 'What Is This Feeling?' as a 'Richard Rodgersesque' waltz, akin to 'Ten Minutes Ago I Saw You' from *Cinderella*. Mantello did not like the song, and he went to see *Hairspray* and was impressed with its energetic first half. He told Schwartz that he thought it was too early in the show for the lower-energy waltz, and in the next reading Mantello's suspicions were confirmed. Schwartz took the same lyrics and wrote new music for 'What Is This Feeling?' in about two days. Other such contributions from Mantello that Schwartz remembers were the deletion of a scene between 'Shiz' and 'The Wizard and I' and how he helped to delineate Fiyero's character. Holzman reports that Schwartz originally wanted to show what happens to Elphaba and Fiyero after they leave Oz, but Mantello convinced them that this was not necessary.[21]

Both Schwartz and Holzman noted the 'enormously insightful contributions'[22] that Mantello and Platt made to define Elphaba's concern for the rights of talking animals. This issue arouses her passion and drives her away from the Wizard.[23] They needed to give Elphaba a reason to care so deeply about the talking animals. Holzman said it was Mantello who suggested that they show Doctor Dillamond literally losing his ability to speak, representing what was happening to talking animals throughout Oz. Holzman and Schwartz started with Doctor Dillamond as a scientist, as in the novel, with lab scenes and a song about his belief in the similarity between animals and humans, but then they decided to make him a Shiz history professor.[24] In the song 'Something Bad', Doctor Dillamond is already beginning to bleat at times. The goat reappears in the second act, during Elphaba's second visit to the Wizard's throne room. Elphaba is about to join the Wizard, but she leaves when she discovers that Doctor Dillamond is unable to speak. This event sets the plot's final events in motion.

The first auditions for *Wicked* took place on 12 October 2001; Idina Menzel, who had been the original Maureen in *Rent*, read and sang for them on 22 October and was selected as Elphaba.[25] Holzman found Menzel to be very different from Chenoweth. She notes:

> She [Menzel] has such a different way of working. She doesn't come out with her performance for a while. She's very private . . . It takes a while to see what she's actually going to do, whereas Kristin is very polished and presentational at the beginning and you see the whole performance right away.

Holzman reports that she understood Galinda's character better than that of Elphaba, but for Schwartz it was the reverse. Holzman 'shied away' from Elphaba because of the controversy that surrounded her, and was able to see varied points of view about the character. How much they struggled with Elphaba's role will become clear when we consider the break between the San Francisco try-out and the Broadway opening.

Schwartz had written several of Elphaba's songs before Menzel won the role, including 'Defying Gravity' and 'I'm Not That Girl'. For the latter, Menzel worked extensively on her lower range, meaning that the song was not set in a key for the singer, which often happens in Broadway productions.[26] The composer had written something like the flourish with which Menzel ends 'Defying Gravity', but she made it her own in performance. Schwartz composed 'The Wizard and I' specifically for Menzel, replacing two versions of the song 'Making Good' that had been written for that moment in the show.[27]

Two readings took place in New York City on 7 and 14 December 2001, and on 17 January 2002 there was a private reading for Universal executives. The creative team then decided that major changes were necessary in the first act; this launched more than two months of work that culminated in a presentation of the new first act on 5 April. Another reading took place in New York City on 29 July. There was a choreography workshop on 30 October and a scenic presentation on 8 January 2003. They planned a June opening at the Curran Theatre in San Francisco, and rehearsals began on 31 March in New York City. Transfer to the Curran took place in the middle of May, with the dress rehearsal on 28 May, the first preview the next night and the opening on 10 June.[28]

Holzman reports that *Wicked* was a huge hit in San Francisco, something that the creative team found 'very encouraging' since they knew that they had serious problems, especially with Elphaba's character. Schwartz had suggested that *Wicked* be tested in an intimate production to test the story and music. Mantello, however, argued that *Wicked* is not a small show, and the director wanted to see a full-blown version before bringing it to Broadway. Schwartz was amenable to a full try-out, but only if they shut down production for three months before opening in New York so that they

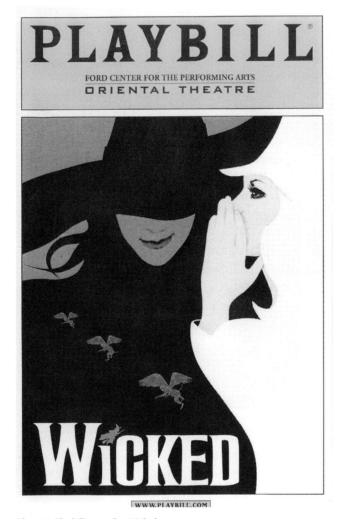

Plate 24 *Playbill* cover for *Wicked*.

could make major changes without the pressure of a running show. The scenario that Schwartz rejected has occurred often in Broadway history, but Schwartz and Holzman assert that the shutdown is the reason *Wicked* has been such a success.[29] David Stone told Schwartz that the hiatus cost the production about $1.5 million.[30]

Elphaba's persona was still the stumbling block. Schwartz notes: 'She was a difficult character to solve . . . I seemed to know how to write her musically. It took quite a while for Winnie to get the tone for her in terms of dialogue . . . and storytelling.' He estimates that eighty per cent of Elphaba's lines changed during the shutdown.[31] Holzman disagrees that the alterations were so extensive: 'It was really more delicate than that. We would change a line here, a line there.' Holzman believes that most of the changes took place at the beginning of the show, and clarified Elphaba's motivations. Once they had improved the character's set-up, many later lines did not require altering. Holzman believes that the only real change in Elphaba's lines in the second act took place in the confrontation with her sister Nessarose.

Holzman elsewhere has reported differently about work during the shutdown:[32]

> Friends of mine who saw both [the San Francisco and Broadway editions] couldn't tell what I'd rewritten. But I rewrote on every page. And Stephen wrote new songs. We rewrote very, very carefully, so as not to disturb the things that were working.

For Schwartz, the shutdown gave him a chance to bring a motivic unity to the score that did not exist in the San Francisco version. He recalls:

> That was *the* big change, to make it all come together ... Those discoveries come quite late in the process. It's really towards the end you can get a sense of the whole architecture of the piece and realise that if you just took these eight bars and use them as an intro way over here it would reflect back to something earlier and give a completeness to it.

An example of such a change was adding Elphaba's 'Unlimited' theme to the introduction of 'For Good'. The composer had planned very early in the creative process to have Elphaba sing 'Unlimited' (based on the opening of 'Somewhere Over the Rainbow' with different rhythm) early in the show and then 'I'm limited' towards the end. He had placed the latter in a song that had been cut, and Platt suggested that he move the reference to 'For Good'. Schwartz's use of the 'Unlimited' theme with the text 'I'm limited' is effective, because Elphaba has realised that she cannot accomplish her mission to save the talking animals – or Oz – alone. She must enlist Glinda's help to remove the Wizard from power.

Schwartz's other major unifying material within the score is Elphaba's theme, associated with her 'wickedness', which opens the show. Schwartz took it from the song 'As Long As You're Mine', written in the early 1970s but used in *Wicked* as the love song between Elphaba and Fiyero. The motive permeates the song, heard as the instrumental introduction and many times in the accompaniment. For Schwartz, the theme originates in musical impressions of Rachmaninov.

The composer speaks proudly of the score's musico-dramatic unity, saying that he works 'with small motifs', like opera composers. He muses: 'Does the audience hear this stuff at all? Maybe some do, but it's a fun way to write ... It's all the stuff I learned as a music student.' Concerning the entire process of writing a musical, but especially adding themes in the right places,

Schwartz notes: 'That is part of the fun. It is so satisfying to take this great, big amorphous blob and watch it slowly come to clarity and focus, the fat get trimmed away, and [find] the things that really work about it structurally and the repetitions.'

Schwartz spoke candidly about composing songs and writing a show. He sees his function as composer and lyricist to 'lead that line [of a lyric] in a way that makes it seem inevitable, but not obvious.' He usually writes lyrics and music simultaneously. Schwartz has also worked as a lyricist with other composers, including Leonard Bernstein and Alan Menken, and in those cases he usually writes words for music that already exists. When composing his own songs, Schwartz reports:

> I tend to start with a title. The title is very important to me because it helps
> to focus what the song is about. Then I might have a little piece of music or
> four lines of a lyric and then, things sort of develop together. A lot of the
> time the music gets finalised first and then I go back and work out how the
> lyric's going to fit within that, partly because I've now had so much
> experience working with other composers, and, as I said, particularly with
> Alan [Menken], that I've learned to work that way.

Schwartz might compose melody and chords first, or start with the accompaniment. Like many composers, he often begins a song with a brief, sketched idea. When looking at sketches for *Wicked* during our discussion, for example, he found the melody for 'Defying Gravity'. He notes: 'It was there before there was a title; it was before there was anything and it says something like "Elphaba's first act?"'. Schwartz also keeps a notebook of ideas for lyrics. This was an especially important part of conceiving the second-act opening, when the people of Oz spread lies about Elphaba, now called 'The Wicked Witch of the West'. Schwartz discussed such ideas with Holzman, saying, 'It's getting a lot of raw material out there without getting in my own way, and then making choices.'

Schwartz described how he tries to define emotional quality and character motivation in his songs:

> One is trying to embody the emotion the character is feeling in music.
> There's a certain sort of 'Method Acting' that comes into play where I try to
> become the character . . . and feel what the character is feeling and see
> through his or her eyes. Then, how does that express itself in music?

Schwartz finds that some of his musical and lyrical choices are conscious, but many are simply an emotional response. He looks at his work critically to make sure that it is not repetitious. He asks himself, 'Am I responding in so much the same way I always respond that it is starting to become . . . just a cliché?' From there he must try to evaluate whether his emotional response is something that the audience will understand.

Schwartz estimates that he composed fifty songs for *Wicked*, and the show includes only about twenty. He has not always worked this way. For example, the composer came into *Godspell* late in the process. The story was set, and every number that Schwartz wrote appeared in the final version. As he recalls: 'I just wrote the score because the discoveries about what the show was were already there.' For *Wicked*, the creators found the show as they went along, and some songs required five different attempts. What Schwartz revealed about the creation of representative songs appears below.[33]

After Elphaba learns that Madame Morrible appreciates her potential as sorceress, and that the Shiz headmistress might introduce her to the Wizard, the new student fantasises in 'The Wizard and I'. Schwartz remembers that the first version of the song, 'Making Good', was slower. (After hearing the earlier version, Platt was concerned that he had not yet heard an emotionally uplifting tune; Schwartz promised him that the next he wrote would be, and he composed 'One Short Day'.) Schwartz calls 'The Wizard and I' an 'I Want' song, a type that appears early in many musicals. It was his intention that the song be 'something appropriate for a teenager'.[34]

The most difficult musical sequence to finalise was 'Dancing Through Life'. They assembled the ultimate version during the shutdown. A number of songs that Schwartz wrote for the sequence were deleted. The scene carries a huge dramatic load, including: the introduction of Fiyero's character and the mutual attraction that develops between him and Galinda, the emergence of Boq and Nessarose as independent characters as Galinda brings them together, Galinda cruelly giving Elphaba the ugly black hat, and then events at the dance forcing Galinda and Elphaba together as friends. All this happens just after they all arrive at Shiz. Schwartz recalls: 'It felt like we were suddenly in *Good News!*, a show about college kids; and we had to find a way to compress all of that down, and yet there was so much storytelling to do.' Among the songs removed from the scene was Fiyero's solo 'Which Way's the Party?', a meeting duet between Fiyero and Galinda and songs at the dance, including 'The Emerald City Stomp'. Schwartz recalls that at one point the sequence was twenty-five minutes long and involved three distinct numbers. He finally wrote five versions of 'Dancing Through Life' in different musical styles, let his collaborators decide which to use, and was very pleased with their choice.[35] Schwartz did not want to cut the scene because there was so little dancing in the show. Since Mantello is not a choreographer as well as a director, like Jerome Robbins or Tommy Tune, he does not think of dancing first when deciding how to stage a scene.[36]

After Fiyero has clearly shown his preference for Galinda, Elphaba sings 'I'm Not That Girl'. The song ends with her singing a low F sharp, a note that

Menzel had to learn to place in her voice. The final chord is a dominant in the second inversion. The composer calls this a direct influence of a recording that his parents loved: folk singer Ronnie Gilbert singing 'I Know Where I'm Going'. Schwartz recalls: 'It just thrilled me that it would end on V.' He also explains that this is 'unfinished business' for Elphaba, and in the second act it is Glinda who sings the same song because Fiyero has now fallen in love with Elphaba. The song's uncertain ending left it unclear whether the audience should applaud, but Mantello and others solved that problem with lighting and changes in the orchestration.

When the girls meet the Wizard, he sings the disarming 'Sentimental Man', a fairly simple song with beautiful orchestrations. Schwartz notes that in every show he works closely with his orchestrators, encouraging them to 'write an inner line . . . stick a little French horn thing in'. The composer tries to find orchestrators 'who I know will respond to the things that I say, but also will bring me things that I don't expect'. A moment by *Wicked* orchestrator William David Brohn that Schwartz found especially effective occurs late in the show, when Elphaba and Fiyero realise that they can never return to Oz. The orchestra plays the theme to 'No One Mourns the Wicked', which Schwartz found 'icy and cold'. Alex Lacamoire and Stephen Oremus assisted with arrangements for the 'inner rhythm group' of two guitars, keyboards, bass and drums. The composer usually writes his own vocal arrangements, but Oremus also did some for *Wicked*.

In the opening of the second act, a reprise of 'No One Mourns the Wicked', the composer found his inspiration in a segment of Musorgsky's *Boris Godunov*, in what he describes as 'wind blowing on the steppes of Russia'. He told Brohn that he wanted 'fancy violin stuff and very high woodwinds', and Schwartz thinks that perhaps the concertmaster helped work out the string parts. Schwartz states: 'The fun of working with an orchestrator like Bill is that you can bring in some big Musorgsky orchestral thing and say, "Find a way to make it sound like this with twenty-three musicians."'

In the next scene, Madame Morrible, Glinda, and Fiyero are rolled out on a platform to speak to the crowd. Glinda has been declared a hero for her alleged resistance to Elphaba at the Wizard's palace (which did not happen), and the trio also announces Galinda's engagement to Fiyero, which is news to him. Schwartz wanted the song to be music for 'folk and village people', which he associates with 'slightly strange rhythms', here in the metre of 5/8. The song was originally called 'Happy Healing Day'. Glinda sings many times 'I couldn't be happier', trying to accept this deception. Schwartz set the line to an irregular rhythm with shifting metres. He reports: 'I wrote it just to really get the inner life of her expressed musically and then I worked with Kristin on it so she could kind of transfer it into her own timing and then together we sort of established what it is going to be.'

The scene in which Elphaba confronts Nessarose in the second act, 'The Wicked Witch of the East', was an especially difficult challenge. Schwartz reports that he wrote four different songs for Nessarose, but they finally decided that there was not sufficient interest in another strong female character to have her stop and sing a major solo. He then decided to have the material that Nessarose sings in this scene also appear earlier in 'Dancing Through Life' where Nessarose and Boq meet, making this statement a reprise in Act 2. So when Nessarose sings 'Finally for this one night . . .' in the first act, it was in fact one of the last parts of the score to be written. When Elphaba gives her sister the power to walk by putting a spell on the slippers, Elphaba grows excited because she has used her powers for good. Here Schwartz placed the 'Unlimited' theme in the orchestra, the only time it occurs in a major key. When she sings the words 'something good', Schwartz recalls the noodling quaver accompaniment from the first-act song 'Something Bad', emphasising the scene's ambiguity. Nessarose calls for Boq, which leads to his transformation into the Tin Man. Schwartz did not allow this musical scene to appear on the compact disc because it would give away too many plot surprises.

The next scene brings Elphaba back to the Wizard's throne room, this time to demand that the flying monkeys be released. The Wizard complies, and then sings 'Wonderful' to try to bring Elphaba back into his fold. He nearly succeeds, shown by their joint dance. Here Mantello placed a reference to *The King and I*, with Elphaba picking up her dress in one hand before they dance, just as Anna does with the King of Siam. One can hear the gasp of recognition in the audience. Schwartz admits that it is not his favourite part of the show, but knows there will be moments suggested by a collaborator that he will not like.[37] 'Wonderful' was one of only two numbers where Schwartz made use of pastiche (the other is the 'Wizomania' segment in 'One Short Day'). He wanted the Wizard's music to remind the listener of the Wizard's time from L. Frank Baum's original stories, meaning the beginning of the twentieth century. His model for the number was a Tin Pan Alley tune such as might have been written by George M. Cohan, with added tinges of ragtime. The original version of 'Wonderful' was longer and included a waltz. In the final version, Schwartz instead quotes the melody of 'The Wizard and I'.[38]

When George Hearn replaced Joel Grey as the Wizard on 20 July 2004, Schwartz rewrote 'Wonderful', mostly at the end. Being a hoofer, Grey wanted more dancing in the number. Schwartz recalls, 'When George came in, it felt unfair to saddle him with a number written for a dancer.' The composer rewrote the ending again for David Garrison, who played the role on tour (and from 4 April 2006 to 8 July 2007, on Broadway). This version used elements of both. When Ben Vereen took over as the Wizard on Broadway on 31 May 2005, Schwartz inserted the tour ending into the Broadway score.

In the song 'No Good Deed', Elphaba decides that she might as well be the wicked witch that everyone thinks she is because nothing 'good' that she has tried to do works out. Schwartz gave the title phrase a distinctive setting. Every time it occurs, it is on three consecutive crotchets, unusual for a composer who fills his songs with syncopation. Schwartz told Menzel that she needed to 'nail' those three notes because of her character's anger. The accompaniment alternates between driving semiquavers and longer chords. Schwartz calls the chords 'the classical part of it' and notes 'you just want sixty strings!' In his essay in *Wicked: The Grimmerie*, Schwartz compares the song to an opera aria and calls it the 'most ambitious' musical moment in the score.[39]

Schwartz is open about his compositional influences. He hears Leonard Bernstein in his music, especially in a 'rhythmic sense'. In *Wicked*, Bernstein's influence appears at the opening in terms of the rhythmic style and added tone chords. The show has one obvious Bernstein reference, heard at the end of the opening number and at the conclusion of the show, where the show's title is sung loudly three times in E major. Under the first two chords, an A sharp sounds in the bass, but there is no answer the third time. This tritone relationship and presentation strongly recalls the end of *West Side Story*.

After more than three decades of working on Broadway and in Holly-wood, Stephen Schwartz feels ready to write an opera. He has been writing scores with more motivic links, doing it most extensively in *Children of Eden* (1991) and *Wicked*, and he believes that the next logical step would be for him to compose for operatic voices in a contemporary style, perhaps a modern equivalent of *Porgy and Bess*. He has begun to realise this ambition by writing an opera on the 1964 film *Séance on a Wet Afternoon*, to be pre-miered by Opera Santa Barbara in 2009. He has traversed a wide field since *Godspell* and *Pippin*, primarily based upon pop music. Clearly *Wicked* is a more ambitious show and score, whose creation demonstrates a Broadway composer in the thick of framing the story with his book writer, and writing music to help advance the plot.

Notes

The publisher has used its best endeavours to ensure that the URLs for external websites referred to in this book are correct and active at the time of going to press. However, the publisher has no responsibility for the websites and can make no guarantee that a site will remain live or that the content is or will remain appropriate.

1 American musical theatre before the twentieth century

1 Edith Borroff, 'Origin of Species: Conflicting Views of American Musical Theater History', *American Music*, 2/4 (1984), p. 102.

2 Susan L. Porter, 'English–American Interaction in American Musical Theatre at the Turn of the Nineteenth Century', *American Music*, 4/1 (1986), p. 6; Anne Dhu Shapiro, 'Music in American Pantomime and Melodrama, 1730–1913', *American Music*, 2/4 (1984), p. 50.

3 Porter, 'English–American Interaction', p. 6.

4 Julian Mates, *America's Musical Stage: Two Hundred Years of Musical Theatre* (Westport, Connecticut, 1985), p. 22.

5 William Brooks, 'Good Musical Paste: Getting the Acts Together in the Eighteenth Century', in *Musical Theatre in America: Papers and Proceedings of the Conference on the Musical Theatre in America*, ed. Glenn Loney (Westport, Connecticut, 1984), p. 37.

6 Cynthia Adams Hoover, 'Music in Eighteenth-Century American Theater', *American Music*, 2/4 (1984), pp. 6–7; Brooks, 'Good Musical Paste', p. 37.

7 Shapiro, 'Music in American Pantomime', p. 56.

8 Porter, 'English–American Interaction', pp. 8–10.

9 *Ibid.*, p. 11.

10 H. Wiley Hitchcock and Stanley Sadie (eds.), *The New Grove Dictionary of American Music*, vol. Ill, *s.v.* 'Melodrama'.

11 Karl Kroeger and Victor Fell Yellin (eds.), *Early Melodrama in America: 'The Voice of Nature' and 'The Aethiop; or, The Child of the Desert'*, vol. II of *Nineteenth-Century American Musical Theater*, gen. ed. Deane L. Root (New York, 1994), p. xv.

12 *Ibid.*, p. xvi.

13 Shapiro, 'Music in American Pantomime', pp. 57–8.

14 H. Wiley Hitchcock, 'An Early American Melodrama: *The Indian Princess* of J. N. Barker and John Bray', *MLA Notes*, 12/3 (1955), p. 376.

15 Dunlap quoted in *ibid.*, p. 379; see also p. 381.

16 Anne Dhu McLucas (ed.), *Later Melodrama in America: 'Monte Cristo' (ca. 1883)*, vol. IV of *Nineteenth-Century American Musical Theater*, gen. ed. Deane L. Root (New York, 1994), p. xx.

17 *The New Grove Dictionary of American Music*, *s.v.* 'Melodrama'.

18 Mary Grace Swift, 'Celestial Queen of the Dumb Shows', in *Musical Theatre in America: Papers and Proceedings of the Conference on the Musical Theatre in America*, ed. Glenn Loney (Westport, Connecticut, 1984), pp. 291–9.

19 Katherine K. Preston, *Opera on the Road: Traveling Opera Troupes in the United States, 1825–1860* (Urbana, 1993), p. 2.

20 *Ibid.*, chapter 1.

21 *Ibid.*, pp. 101–6.

22 Sylvie Chevalley, 'Le Théâtre d'Orléans en Tournée dans les villes du nord, 1827–1833', in *Comptes rendus de l'athénée louisianais* (1955), pp. 27–71.

23 Preston, *Opera on the Road*, Chapter 3.

24 Katherine K. Preston, 'Art Music from 1800 to 1860', in *The Cambridge History of American Music*, ed. David Nicholls (Cambridge, 1998), p. 199.

25 For more information on the development of the American theatre during this period, see Alfred L. Bernheim, *The Business of the Theatre: An Economic History of the American Theatre, 1750–1932* (New York, 1932), pp. 12–25.

26 Shapiro, 'Music in American Pantomime', p. 61.

27 *The New Grove Dictionary of American Music*, *s.v.* 'Melodrama'.

28 Thomas Riis, 'The Music and Musicians in Nineteenth-Century Productions of *Uncle Tom's Cabin*', *American Music*, 4/3 (1986),

pp. 268–9; Thomas Riis (ed.), *'Uncle Tom's Cabin' (1852) by George L. Aiken and George C. Howard*, vol. V of *Nineteenth-Century American Musical Theater*, gen. ed. Deane L. Root (New York, 1994), Introduction.

29 Dale Cockrell, *Demons of Disorder: Early Blackface Minstrels and Their World* (Cambridge, 1997).

30 Dale Cockrell, 'Nineteenth-Century Popular Music', in *The Cambridge History of American Music*, ed. David Nicholls (Cambridge, 1998), pp. 158–85.

31 *Ibid.*, p. 168. See also Renee Lapp Norris, '"Black Opera": Antebellum Blackface Minstrelsy and European Opera', PhD dissertation, University of Maryland (2001) and Norris, 'Opera and the Mainstreaming of Blackface Minstrelsy', *Journal of the Society for American Music* 1/3 (2007), pp. 341–65.

32 Cockrell, 'Nineteenth-Century Popular Music', p. 174.

33 Gretchen Schneider, 'Gabriel Ravel and the Martinetti Family: The Popularity of Pantomime in 1855', in *American Popular Entertainment: Papers and Proceedings of the Conference on the History of American Popular Entertainment*, ed. Myron Matlaw (Westport, Connecticut, 1979), p. 242. This article by Schneider is almost the only source of information in this field.

34 *Ibid.*, p. 245. See also Cecil Smith and Glenn Litton, *Musical Comedy in America* (New York, 1950, 1981), pp. 5–6.

35 *The New Grove Dictionary of American Music*, vol. I, *s.v.*'Dance, II. The Nineteenth Century, 2. Ballet'.

36 Deane L. Root, *American Popular Stage Music, 1860–1880* (Ann Arbor, Michigan, 1977), pp. 70–1.

37 *Ibid.*, p. 68.

38 Rita M. Plotnicki, 'John Brougham: The Aristophanes of American Burlesque', *Journal of Popular Culture*, 12/3 (1978), p. 422.

39 *The New Grove Dictionary of American Music*, vol. I, *s.v.*'Burlesque'.

40 William C. Young, *Documents of American Theatre History*, vol. I: *Famous American Playhouses 1716–1899* (Chicago, 1973), pp. 102–3; William Brooks, 'Pocahontas, Her Life and Times', *American Music*, 2/4 (1984), pp. 19–48.

41 Preston, *Opera on the Road*, pp. 413–14, n. 9 and p. 417, n. 54.

42 See Bernheim, *Business of the Theatre*, pp. 46–63.

43 Root, *American Popular Stage Music, 1860–1880*, p. 37; Richard Kislan, *The Musical: A Look at the American Musical Theater*

(Englewood Cliffs, New Jersey, 1980), p. 67; Ethan Mordden, *Better Foot Forward: The History of American Musical Theatre* (New York, 1976), p. 25.

44 Smith and Litton, *Musical Comedy*, pp. 8–10.

45 Root, *American Popular Stage Music, 1860–1880*, p. 92.

46 *Ibid.*, p. 113.

47 Smith and Litton, *Musical Comedy*, pp. 17–18.

48 Root, *American Popular Stage Music, 1860–1880*, p. 148; Smith and Litton, *Musical Comedy*, pp. 19–23.

49 Smith and Litton, *Musical Comedy*, pp. 20–1; Richard Jackson (ed.), *Early Burlesque in America: Evangeline (1877)*, vol. XIII of *Nineteenth-Century American Musical Theater*, gen. ed. Deane L. Root (New York, 1994), pp. xiii–xiv.

50 Smith and Litton, *Musical Comedy*, 32.

51 Root, *American Popular Stage Music, 1860–1880*, pp. 49–50.

52 Smith and Litton, *Musical Comedy*, p. 34.

53 McLucas (ed.), *Later Melodrama in America*, p. xv.

54 Shapiro, 'Music in American Pantomime', p. 65.

55 David Mayer, 'The Music of Melodrama', in *Performance and Politics in Popular Drama*, ed. David Bradby, Louis James and Bernard Sharratt (Cambridge, 1980), pp. 49–50.

56 McLucas (ed.), *Later Melodrama in America*, p. xvii.

57 *Ibid.*, p. xv; see also Katherine K. Preston, 'The Music of Toga Drama', introductory essay in *'Playing Out the Empire': 'Ben Hur' and Other Toga Plays and Films, 1883–1908: A Critical Anthology*, ed. David Mayer (Oxford, 1994).

58 Cockrell, 'Nineteenth-Century Popular Music', p. 174.

59 Eileen Southern, *The Music of Black Americans: A History*, 2nd edn (New York, 1983), pp. 229–30.

60 Allen L. Woll, *Black Musical Theatre: From 'Coontown' to 'Dreamgirls'* (Baton Rouge, 1989), p. 1.

61 Thomas Riis, *Just Before Jazz. Black Musical Theater in New York, 1890–1915* (Washington DC, 1989), pp. 9–11; Eileen Southern (ed.), *African American Theater: 'Out of Bondage' (1876) and 'Peculiar Sam, or the Underground Railroad' (1879)*, vol. IX of *Nineteenth-Century American Musical Theater*, gen. ed. Deane L. Root (New York, 1994), Introduction.

62 Well, *Black Musical Theatre*, pp. 4–5.

63 Cockrell, 'Nineteenth-Century Popular Music', p. 175.

64 Katherine K. Preston, 'Between the Cracks: The Performance of English-Language Opera in Late 19th-Century America', *American Music* 21/3 (2003), pp. 349–74.

65 For more information on the Boston Ideal Opera Company, see Katherine K. Preston, "Dear Miss Ober": Musical Management and the Interconnections of Musical Culture in the United States, 1876–1883', in *European Music & Musicians in New York City, 1840–1900*, ed. John Graziano (Rochester: University of Rochester Press, 2006), pp. 273–98.

66 Root, *American Popular Stage Music, 1860–1880*, pp. 115–21.

67 For more information on German opera companies, see John Koegel, 'The Development of the German American Musical Stage in New York City, 1840–1890', in *European Music & Musicians in New York City, 1840–1900*, ed. John Graziano (Rochester: University of Rochester Press, 2006), pp. 149–81.

68 Root, *American Popular Stage Music, 1860–1880*, p. 165; see also Gerald Bordman, *American Operetta: From 'H.M.S. Pinafore' to 'Sweeney Todd'* (New York and Oxford, 1981), pp. 15–16.

69 Bordman, *American Operetta*, p. 16.

70 Root, *American Popular Stage Music, 1860–1880*, pp. 136–44; see also Charlotte Kauffman (ed.), *Early Operetta in America: 'The Doctor of Alcantara' (1879)*, vol. XII of *Nineteenth-Century American Musical Theater*, gen. ed. Deane L. Root (New York, 1994), p. xviii.

71 Paul Bierley, *The Works of John Philip Sousa* (Columbus, Ohio, 1984), p. 13.

72 Jane Stedman, ' "Then Hey! For the Merry Greenwood!": Smith and de Koven and *Robin Hood*', *Journal of Popular Culture*, 12/3 (1978), p. 433.

73 Parker Zellers, *Tony Pastor: Dean of the Vaudeville Stage* (Ypsilanti, Michigan, 1971), pp. xiii–xix. See also Gillian M. Rodger, 'Male Impersonation on the American Variety and Vaudeville Stage, 1868–1930', PhD dissertation, University of Pittsburgh, 1998.

74 *Ibid.*, p. xix.

75 American Memory Webpage, Library of Congress: The American Variety Stage: Vaudeville and Popular Entertainment, 1870–1920, http://memory.loc.gov/ammem/ammemhome.html.

76 Katherine K. Preston (ed.), *Irish American Theater: 'The Mulligan Guard Ball' (1879) and 'Reilly and the Four Hundred' (1891)*, vol. X of *Nineteenth-Century American Musical Theater*, gen. ed. Deane L. Root (New York, 1994), p. xvi. See also Jon W. Finson, ed., *David Braham: Collected Songs I (1873–1882)* and *Collected Songs II (1883–1896)*. Music of the United States of America, volume 7. (Madison: A-R Editions, 1997).

77 *Ibid.*, pp. xvi–xvii.

78 *Ibid.*, p. xix.

79 Riis, *Just Before Jazz*, p. 13; Well, *Black Musical Theatre*, pp. 68–9.

80 David Mayer, 'The Music of Melodrama', p. 49.

81 Joel H. Kaplan, 'Introduction', in *The Edwardian Theatre: Essays on Performance and the Stage*, ed. Michael R. Booth and Joel H. Kaplan (Cambridge, 1996), p. 1.

2 Non-English language musical theatre in the United States

1 While the term 'ethnic' certainly can be applied to all groups, especially as it relates to race or ethnicity, here it is used to describe those communities in the United States that had or have languages other than English as the dominant one.

2 The history of the ethnic musical theatre in the United States relates to other diasporic theatre traditions throughout the world. With their wide geographic spread and travels, musical theatre repertories and performers were highly mobile and followed lines of migration throughout the world. Yiddish theatre existed in Havana, Buenos Aires, Montréal, London, Cape Town; Spanish *zarzuela* in Mexico City, Manila, Montevideo; Chinese opera in Vancouver, Havana, Portuguese Macau, French Indochina; German theatre in Mexico, Brazil, Russia, the Baltics; French opera and operetta in Hanoi, Montréal, New Orleans; and Italian opera throughout the Americas, North Africa, and in many European colonies.

3 See *The Worlds of Mei Lanfang*, DVD documentary, Lotus Films, 2000.

4 Just as with the English-language stage, theatre buildings used by ethnic theatre troupes were continuously renamed to reflect changes in management, ownership, repertory or language.

5 The Teatro Merced in downtown Los Angeles is now part of El Pueblo de Los Angeles Historic Monument but is not used currently; it is the oldest remaining theatre building in Los Angeles and probably Southern California.

6 Freja Hall, named after the Norse goddess of love and beauty, served as a theatrical performance space in the Swedish American Hall, built in 1907 – still located on Market Street in San Francisco. See www.swedishamericanhall.com.

7 For more on the Liederkranz Hall, see www.liederkranznycity.org/history.asp. Turn Hall, at 66–68 East 4th Street and built by the Turnverein, was the site of the first performance of Yiddish theatre in the 1880s, and later was a site for Italian performances. Currently, it is the annexe of the LaMama Theatre Company. The Tivoli Turnhalle is an architectural centrepiece of the Auraria Campus, an educational centre shared by Community College of Denver, Metropolitan State College of Denver and the University of Colorado at Denver.

8 Put-in-Bay German theatre programs, 1900 (author's collection). Max Hanisch, librettist of the German version of the musical *Merry Widow* parody, *Die Lustige Witwe in zweiter Ehe/ The Merry Widow Remarried* (music by Carl von Wegern, 1909), was a well-known performer and theatre director who was active in German theatres in Columbus, Philadelphia and New York. He led the German thespians that visited Put-in-Bay in 1900. The island's charming Town Hall was built in 1887; the Opera House was on the third floor.

9 A photograph of the Los Angeles City Hall and Courthouse, with its theatrical space, appears in John Koegel, '*Canciones del país*: Mexican Musical Life in California after the Gold Rush', *California History*, 78/3 (1999), pp. 160–87, 215–19; See also Koegel, 'Mexican Musicians in California and the United States, 1910–1950', *California History*, 84/1 (2006), pp. 7–29, 64–9.

10 Ernest B. Guillet, *Un théâtre Francophone dans un Milieu Franco-Américain* (Durham, New Hampshire, 1981).

11 See John Koegel, 'Adolf Philipp and Ethnic Musical Comedy in New York's Little Germany', *American Music*, 24/3 (2006), pp. 267–319.

12 See John Koegel, 'The Development of the German American Musical Theater in New York, 1840-1890', in *European Music and Musicians in New York City, 1840–1900*, ed. John Graziano (Rochester, New York, 2006), pp. 149–81.

13 'Thalia Theatre', *New York Times*, 13 February 1886, p. 4.

14 Edna Frantz Springer, 'Dutch Pinafore – Gilbert and Sullivan in Reading', *Historical Review of Berks County*, 9/4 (1944), pp. 112–17; Albert F. Buffington, ed., *The Reichard Collection of Early Pennsylvania German Dialogues and Plays*, Pennsylvania German Society, vol. 61 (Lancaster, Pennsylvania, 1962). See also *H.M.S. Pinafore, oder, Das maedle und ihr sailor kerl n'* (Philadelphia, 1885).

15 The Brooklyn-based Kadimah Group of Hadassah, the Women's Zionist Organization of America, recorded in the 1950s abbreviated Yiddish versions for Banner Records, a Jewish music label, of both *Die Yom Bonditten* (10-inch LP, B-059) and *Der Shirz* (78 rpm disc set, B-104).

16 Compact disc recordings of all three of these Yiddish versions by The Gilbert and Sullivan Yiddish Light Opera Company are available at www.gsyiddish.com. See www.nytheatre-wire.com/yidpin.htm; Michelle Falkenstein, 'Yiddish Sails the Ocean Blue', *Hadassah Magazine*, 81/8 (April 2000), available at www.hadassah.org.

17 The earliest recordings of Mexican music (waltzes and danzas) were probably made by the United States Marine Band for the Columbia Phonograph Company of Washington, DC, circa 1890–1: 'La media noche' (José Avilés), 'Un recuerdo a Salamanca' (Luis G. Araujo), 'Carmen Waltz' and 'Over the Waves' ('Sobre las olas', Juventino Rosas). See James R. Smart, *The Sousa Band: A Discography* (Washington, DC, 1970), pp. 83–5. 'La media noche' is available at www.tinfoil.com/cm-9909.htm#c-media.

18 For recordings of Eugenia (Eugenie) Ferrer, Arturo (Arthur B.) Adiami or Antonio Vargas, see http://memory.loc.gov/ammem/berlhtml/, http://cylinders.library.ucsb.edu/; also see John Koegel, 'Crossing Borders: Mexicana, Tejana, and Chicana Musicians in the United States and Mexico', in *From Tejano to Tango: Latin American Popular Music*, ed. Walter Aaron Clark (New York, 2002), pp. 97–125.

19 See John Koegel, 'Compositores mexicanos y cubanos en Nueva York, c. 1880–1920', *Historia Mexicana*, 56/2 (2006), pp. 533–612.

20 Richard K. Spottswood, *Ethnic Music on Records: A Discography of Ethnic Recordings Produced in the United States, 1893 to 1942* (Urbana, 1990), 7 vols.

21 Hermann W. Haller, *Tra Napoli e New York: Le macchiette italo-americane di Eduardo Migliaccio* (Rome, 2006).

22 Regarding de Rosalia, see Joseph J. Accardi, 'Giovanni De Rosalia: Playwright, Poet, and Nofrio', *Italian Americana*, 19/2 (2001), pp. 176–200; www.accardiweb.com/nofrio; www.dieli.net/SicilyPage/SicilianTheatre/siculumiricani.html; Emelise Aleandri, *The Italian American Immigrant Theatre of New York*

City (Charleston, South Carolina, 1999); Aleandri, *The Italian American Immigrant Theatre of New York City, 1746–1899* (Lewiston, Maine, 2006).

23 For a recording of 'Nikolina' by Hjalmar Peterson (Olle I Skratthult), see www.emigrantregistret.s.se/tracks.htm; see also *From Sweden to America: Swedish Emigrant Songs* (Caprice compact disc CAP 21552) and Anne-Charlotte Hanes Harvey, 'Swedish American Theatre', in *Ethnic Theatre in the United States*, ed. Maxine Schwartz Seller (Westport, Connecticut, 1983), pp. 491–524.

24 The source is found at http://home.pcisys.net/~don_erickson/nikolina.htm.

25 Excerpts in Spanish translation and adaptation from these two famous Viennese operettas by Lehár and Straus were recorded for the Victor label in New York in 1931, with singers Margarita Cueto, José Moriche, and Juan Pulido, and the Mexican composer and director Eduardo Vigil y Robles as conductor; they have been re-released on compact disc in Spain on the Blue Moon label (Serie lírica): *El conde de Luxemburgo* (BMCD 7531), *El soldado de chocolate* (BMCD 7533); see www.bluemoon.es.

26 See www.tsha.utexas.edu/handbook/online/articles/EE/fes26.html

27 Many of these recordings can be heard on the Frontera Collection of Mexican American Music: http://digital.library.ucla.edu/frontera/.

28 Recording activity in the Spanish-speaking community in the United States has exploded in recent decades, and many multinational recording conglomerates take a decided interest in promoting and profiting from the music of immigrant communities.

29 See www.brandeis.edu/jewishfilm/Catalogue/ymusic.htm.

30 German musical films were shown regularly in several German movie houses in the Lincoln Park area of Chicago's predominantly German North Side even several months after the entrance of the United States into World War II, though they were advertised as 'non-political' and 'government censored' (Film programmes, dated 1940–May 1942, Little Theatre (2153 Lincoln Avenue) and German Kino (659 West North Avenue), author's collection).

3 Birth pangs, growing pains and sibling rivalry: musical theatre in New York, 1900–1920

1 'The Decline of Comic Opera', *Musical America*, 4 (13 October 1906), p. 8.

2 '"The Red Feather", Reginald De Koven's Latest Comic Opera at the Lyric', *New York Times*, 10 November 1903.

3 Armond Fields and L. Marc Fields, *From the Bowery to Broadway: Lew Fields and the Roots of American Popular Theatre* (New York and Oxford, 1993), p. 214.

4 Rennold Wolf, *New York Telegraph*, 26 December 1906.

5 Some of the following material has previously appeared in the author's 'Wien, Women and Song: *The Merry Widow* in New York', *Sonneck Society Bulletin*, 22/1 (1996), pp. 1, 8–11.

6 Richard Traubner, *Operetta: A Theatrical History* (Garden City, New York, 1983), p. 243.

7 'All New York Is "Merry Widow" Mad Now-A-Days', *Musical America*, 6 (2 November 1907), p. 21.

8 The *Oxford English Dictionary* credits the *Daily Chronicle* (9 July 1908) with the first written reference: 'The women in the galleries took off their "Merry Widow" hats, and waved them frantically.'

9 Danton Walker, unidentified clipping, c. 1945, *The Merry Widow* production folder no. 1, Museum of the City of New York.

10 Bernard Grun, *Gold and Silver: The Life and Times of Franz Lehár* (London, 1970), p. 128.

11 'London Amused by "The Merry Widow"', *Musical America*, 6 (15 June 1907), p. 7.

12 [W. J. Henderson], *New York Sun*, 22 October 1907.

13 [Richard Aldrich], *New York Times*, 22 October 1907.

14 Henry Krehbiel, *New York Tribune*, 22 October 1907.

15 *Musical Courier*, 30 October 1907, p. 22.

16 *Musical America*, 6 (26 October 1907), p. 21. The article quotes Reginald de Koven in the *New York World*, 22 October 1907.

17 *Musical America*, 6 (26 October 1907), p. 1.

18 Burns Mantle and Garrison P. Sherwood (eds.), *The Best Plays of 1899–1909* (New York, 1947), p. 554.

19 Unidentified clipping, Billy Rose Theatre Collection, New York Public Library.

20 Acton Davies, unidentified clipping, Billy Rose Theatre Collection, New York Public Library.

21 Unidentified clipping, Billy Rose Theatre Collection, New York Public Library.

22 Herbert N. Waters, *Victor Herbert: A Life in Music* (New York, 1955), p. 304.

23 H. Wiley Hitchcock and Stanley Sadie (eds.), *The New Grove Dictionary of American Music,* vol. III, *s.v.* 'Musical Theater'.

24 Charles Hamm, *Irving Berlin: Songs from the Melting Pot: The Formative Years, 1907–1914* (New York and Oxford, 1997), p. 222.
25 Gerald Bordman, *American Musical Revue* (New York and Oxford, 1985), p. 79.

4 American and British operetta in the 1920s: romance, nostalgia and adventure

1 Vesna Goldsworthy discusses this phenomenon in the realm of literature in *Inventing Ruritania: The Imperialism of the Imagination* (New Haven and London, 1998).
2 For more on *The Merry Widow* and its New York reception, see Orly Leah Krasner, 'Wien, Women and Song: *The Merry Widow* in New York', *Sonneck Society Bulletin*, 22/1 (1996), pp. 1, 8–11.
3 Geoffrey Block, *Enchanted Evenings: The Broadway Musical from 'Show Boat' to Sondheim* (New York and Oxford, 1997), p. 314.
4 For more on *Chu Chin Chow*, see William A. Everett, '*Chu Chin Chow* and Orientalist Musical Theatre in Britain', in *Portrayal of the East: Music and the Oriental Imagination in the British Empire, 1780–1940*, ed. Bennett Zon and Martin Clayton (Aldershot, 2007), pp. 277–96.
5 Stephen Banfield, 'Popular Song and Popular Music on Stage and Film', in *The Cambridge History of American Music*, ed. David Nicholls (Cambridge, 1998), p. 333.
6 For more on *Little Mary Sunshine*, especially its camp qualities, see Raymond Knapp, *The American Musical and the Performance of Personal Identity* (Princeton, 2006), pp. 40–9.

5 Images of African Americans: African-American musical theatre, *Show Boat* and *Porgy and Bess*

1 The early history of the Georgia Minstrels is discussed in Eileen Southern's article 'The Georgia Minstrels: The Early Years', *Inter-American Music Review*, 10/2 (1989), pp. 157–67.
2 Errol Hill's article 'The Hyers Sisters: Pioneers in Black Musical Comedy' is published in *The American Stage: Social and Economic Issues from the Colonial Period to the Present*, ed. Ron Engle and Tice C. Miller (Cambridge and New York, 1993).
3 For additional details on the many musicals presented during the years 1890 to 1910, see Thomas L. Riis, *Just Before Jazz: Black Musical Theater in New York, 1890–1915* (Washington, DC, 1989).
4 See Eric Ledell Smith's *Bert Williams: A Biography of the Pioneer Black Comedian* (Jefferson, North Carolina, 1992) for an excellent overview of Bert Williams's career.

5 See Robert Kimball and William Bolcom's *Reminiscing with Sissle and Blake* (New York, 1973) for an informal biography of Sissle's and Blake's careers.
6 These 1920s gatherings were associated with indigent African Americans in Harlem, who held parties in their apartments at which invited guests contributed small amounts of cash to help pay their rent. These parties often included musical entertainment to attract guests.
7 For an overview of musicals seen during the Harlem Renaissance, see John Graziano's 'Black Musical Theater and the Harlem Renaissance', in *Black Music in the Harlem Renaissance: A Collection of Essays*, ed. Samuel A. Floyd Jr (Westport, Connecticut, 1990), pp. 87–110.
8 Otto Kahn is reported to have offered Gershwin a $5,000 bonus to sign with the company (David Ewen, *George Gershwin: His Journey to Greatness* (Englewood Cliffs, New Jersey, 1970), p. 222).

6 The melody (and the words) linger on: American musical comedies of the 1920s and 1930s

1 Frederick Lewis Allen, *Only Yesterday* (New York, 1931), chapter 5.
2 Ethan Mordden, *Sing for Your Supper: The Broadway Musical in the 1930s* (New York, 2005), pp. 155–82; Alisa Roost, 'Before *Oklahoma!*: A Reappraisal of Musical Theatre during the 1930s', *Journal of American Drama and Theatre*, 16/1 (2004), pp. 1–35.
3 Malcolm Goldstein, *The Political Stage: American Drama and Theater of the Great Depression* (New York, 1974), pp. 313–15, 394–5; Ronald Sanders, *The Days Grow Short: The Life and Music of Kurt Weill* (New York, 1980), chapters 17 and 19.
4 *Cradle Will Rock*, written and directed by Tim Robbins, 1999. Tim Robbins, *Cradle Will Rock: The Movie and The Moment* (New York, 2000). See also Geoffrey Block, *Enchanted Evenings: The Broadway Musical from 'Show Boat' to Sondheim* (New York and Oxford, 1997), pp. 115–32.
5 Stanley Green (ed.), *Rodgers and Hammerstein Fact Book* (New York, 1980), pp. 12–13.
6 Stephen Banfield places *Girl Crazy* (1930) as a pivotal show that brought 'the dance-band viewpoint into the whole musical world of a stage show' (Stephen Banfield, 'Popular Song and Popular Music on Stage and Film', in *The Cambridge History of American Music*, ed. David Nicholls (Cambridge, 1998), p. 328).

7 Richard Rodgers, *Musical Stages: An Autobiography* (New York, 1995), p. 88.

8 Graham Wood, 'The Development of Song Forms in the Broadway and Hollywood Musicals of Richard Rodgers, 1919–1943', PhD diss., University of Minnesota (2000), chapter 2.

9 Rodgers, *Musical Stages*, p. 80.

10 *Ibid.*, p. 45.

11 Philip Furia, *Poets of Tin Pan Alley: A History of America's Great Lyricists* (New York, 1990), p. 126.

12 John Clum, *Something for the Boys: Musical Theater and Gay Culture* (New York, 1999).

13 *Green Book Magazine*, February 1915. Quoted in L. Bergreen, *As Thousands Cheer: The Life of Irving Berlin* (New York, 1990), p. 57.

14 B. Sobel, 'Cole Porter Admits It Gladly: He Uses a Rhyming Dictionary', *New York Herald Tribune*, 20 December 1936; also quoted in David Ewen, *The Cole Porter Story* (New York, 1965), p. 114.

15 In the last years of his career with Hart, Rodgers was responsible for the opening of 'Too Many Girls' and an unidentified number of Hart's verses. After Hammerstein's death Rodgers wrote several new lyrics as well as the music for the remake of *State Fair* and the film version of *The Sound of Music*. He also successfully composed both lyrics and music for an entire show, *No Strings*.

16 Rodgers, *Musical Stages*, pp. 101 and 103.

17 For a detailed analysis of 'My Heart Stood Still' see Allen Forte, *The American Popular Ballad of the Golden Era: 1924–1950* (Princeton, 1995), pp. 82–8.

18 'Cleverest of Our Lyricists Are Seldom Big Hit Writers', *New York Herald Tribune*, 31 May 1925. Quoted without attribution in David Ewen, *Richard Rodgers* (New York, 1957), p. 119. See also Meryl Secrest, *Somewhere For Me: A Biography of Richard Rodgers* (New York, 2001), pp. 35–6.

19 In the film short *The Makers of Melody* (1929), Rodgers and Hart re-enact the compositional process that led to 'Here In My Arms' and other songs. The Paramount film is now available in a collection entitled *Jazz Cocktails* (Kino International, 1997). See Frederick Nolan, *Lorenz Hart* (New York, 1994), pp. 127–8.

20 Ira Gershwin, *Lyrics on Several Occasions* (New York, 1959), pp. 172–4; Edward Jablonski, *George Gershwin: A Biography* (New York, 1987), pp. 83–4.

21 Banfield, 'Popular Song', p. 315; *Sondheim's Broadway Musicals* (Ann Arbor, Michigan, 1993), pp. 107–21; and 'Sondheim

and the Art That Has No Name', in *Approaches to the American Musical*, ed. R. Lawson-Peebles (Exeter, 1996), pp. 137–60.

22 According to Mordden, no fewer than fifteen (*recte* sixteen – he does not include *The Girl Friend*) of the twenty-six Broadway musicals exported to London were musical comedies. *Sally, The Blue Kitten, Lady, Be Good!, No, No, Nanette, Sunny, Tip-Toes, The Girl Friend, Oh, Kay!, Peggy-Ann, Hit the Deck, Good News!, A Connecticut Yankee, Funny Face, Hold Everything!, Heads Up!*. No musical comedies travelled in the other direction (Ethan Mordden, *Make Believe: The Broadway Musical in the 1920s* (New York and Oxford, 1997), p. 146). The only 1930s musical comedies to appear contemporaneously in London were *Gay Divorce, Anything Goes* and *On Your Toes; DuBarry Was a Lady* arrived in 1942 and *The Boys from Syracuse* in 1963 (Stanley Green, *Broadway Musicals of the 1930s* (New York, 1971), p. 368).

23 Published musical comedy librettos: *I'd Rather Be Right, Johnny Johnson, Knickerbocker Holiday, Let 'Em Eat Cake* and *Of Thee I Sing*; published musical comedy scores: *Anything Goes, Babes in Arms, The Boys from Syracuse, Girl Crazy, Johnny Johnson, Knickerbocker Holiday, Of Thee I Sing, Red, Hot and Blue!, Roberta* and *Strike Up the Band*. See Green, *Broadway Musicals of the 1930s*, pp. 372–3.

24 Allen L. Well, *Black Musical Theater: From 'Coontown' to 'Dreamgirls'* (Baton Rouge, Louisiana, 1989), pp. 58–75. 'An archival re-creation of the 1921 production featuring members of the original cast' is available on New World Records 260 (1976) with notes by Robert Kimball. See also Robert Kimball and William Bolcom, *Reminiscing with Sissle and Blake* (New York, 1973).

25 Roy Hemming, *The Melody Lingers On: The Great Songwriters and Their Movie Musicals* (New York, 1986), pp. 113–15.

26 Notes to *Good News!*. Jay Productions Ltd. CD Jay 1291 (1996), n. p.

27 In the 1963 off-Broadway revival of *The Boys from Syracuse* all that was added to George Abbott's original book was a long list of excruciating jokes (Geoffrey Block, *Yale Broadway Masters: Richard Rodgers* (New Haven, 2003)).

28 Block, *Enchanted Evenings*, pp. 41–59.

29 G. S. Kaufman, *The Cocoanuts*, in *By George: A Kaufman Collection*, comp. and ed. Donald Oliver (New York, 1979), pp. 202–58.

30 Among the *Babes in Arms* songs not included in the film are 'I Wish I Were In Love Again', 'My Funny Valentine', 'Johnny One-Note', 'Imagine' and 'The Lady Is a Tramp'.

31 Gerald Bordman, *Jerome Kern: His Life and Music* (New York, 1980), pp. 335–43; Arlene Croce, *The Fred Astaire and Ginger Rogers Book* (New York, 1972), pp. 44–53; Hemming, *The Melody Lingers On*, pp. 93–5.

32 *Anything Goes*, John McGlinn, conductor, EMI/Angel CDC 7–49848–2 (1989).

33 Tommy Krasker and Robert Kimball, *Catalog of the American Musical* (Washington, DC, 1988), pp. 184–90; Tommy Krasker, notes to *Fifty Million Frenchmen*, New World Records 80417–2 (1991), pp. 11–17.

34 Tommy Krasker, 'It's Been Fun, But I Gotta Rumrun', notes to *Oh, Kay!*, Nonesuch 79361–2 (1995), pp. 19–23.

35 Leonard Bernstein, 'American Musical Comedy', in *The Joy of Music* (New York, 1959), p. 169. The lecture was originally telecast on 7 October 1956 for the *Omnibus* series.

36 Wayne Shirley also notices the loss of meaning that resulted from the relocation of 'Someone to Watch Over Me' to the second act, but views this as a positive dramatic change (Wayne Shirley, notes to *Oh, Kay!*, Smithsonian American Musical Theater Series, RCA Special Products (1978), n.p.).

37 Tommy Krasker, '*Pardon My English*: A Tale of Two Psyches', notes to *Pardon My English*, Elektra Nonesuch 79338–2 (1994), pp. 11–16.

7 'We said we wouldn't look back': British musical theatre, 1935–1960

1 For a brief narrative of the major British shows, their creators and performers, see Andrew Lamb, *150 Years of Popular Musical Theatre* (New Haven, 2000).

2 For a study of Mayerl's significance more widely to British popular music see Peter Dickinson, *Marigold: The Music of Billy Mayerl* (Oxford, 1999).

3 For a historical placing and explanation of the meaning of the monarchy to British society in this period see David Cannadine, 'The Context, Performing and Meaning of Ritual: The British Monarchy and the "Invention of Tradition", c.1820–1977', in *The Invention of Tradition*, ed. Eric Hobsbawm and Thomas Ranger (Cambridge, 1983), pp. 101–64, esp. pp. 139–55; and Tom Nairn, 'Britain's Royal Romance', in *Patriotism: The Making and Unmaking of British National Identity*, vol. 3: *National Fictions*, ed. Raphael Samuel (London, 1989), pp. 77–86.

4 For a thorough examination of the effects of rationing on Britain see Ina Zweiniger-Bargielowska, *Austerity in Britain: Rationing, Controls and Consumption 1939–55* (Oxford, 2000).

5 For Neagle's association with the role of Queen Victoria on film see Marcia Landy, *British Genres: Cinema and Society 1930–1960* (Princeton, 1991), pp. 68–9 and Jeffrey Richards, *The Age of the Dream Palace: Cinema and Society in Britain 1930–39* (London, 1984), pp. 116–17. For a brief assessment of the importance of Neagle in British film as a performing embodiment of the best of British womanhood (and hence as an appropriate candidate for the portrayal of royalty) see Jeffrey Richards, *Films and British National Identity: From Dickens to Dad's Army* (Manchester, 1997), p. 132.

6 British Library: Lord Chamberlain's Correspondence file (7 July 1953), report of visiting inspector R. J. Hill, 28 January 1954. (The apparent discrepancy in dates is due to the fact that each Lord Chamberlain's Correspondence file is dated from the issuing of the licence for performance. After a show had received its licence and opened, there was usually little additional correspondence; in this particular case, however, extra correspondence was occasioned by a complaint from a member of the public which thus had to be investigated.) Hill begins his report by stating that 'the entire theme is promiscuity, euphemized as "having fun" ... [T]he theme as developed in dialogue is passable, but when translated into action occasionally goes a long way past the preliminaries of intercourse that ought to be acceptable for public presentation.' After a lengthy and remarkably detailed description of various actions and positions of the cast, Hill concludes 'that if anything could reconcile me to a life in Moscow, it would be the prospect of an alternative life at "Camp Karefree"'.

7 The effects of censorship by the Lord Chamberlain's Office on musicals in particular has received little attention. For a general background to its effects on theatre in Britain in the twentieth century see Nicholas de Jongh, *Politics, Prudery and Perversions: The Censoring of the English Stage 1901–1968* (London, 2000).

8 Vivian Ellis, 'Give Us a Chance', *Plays and Players* (January 1956), p. 17.

8 The coming of the musical play: Rodgers and Hammerstein

1 William G. Hyland, *Richard Rodgers* (New Haven and London, 1998), p. 104; Hugh Fordin, *Getting to Know Him: A Biography of Oscar Hammerstein II* (New York, 1977, 1995), p. 138.

2 H. Wiley Hitchcock and Stanley Sadie (eds.), *New Grove Dictionary of American Music*, vol. II, *s.v.*'Hammerstein, Oscar I'.
3 *Ibid.*, *s.v.* 'Hammerstein, Oscar II'.
4 Stanley Green (ed.), *The Rodgers and Hammerstein Fact Book* (New York, 1980), p. 502.
5 Fordin, *Getting to Know Him*, pp. 199–200.
6 For further information about various productions, tours, revivals and excerpts of reviews, see Green (ed.), *The Rodgers and Hammerstein Fact Book*; Fordin, *Getting to Know Him*, p. 202; and Richard Rodgers, *Musical Stages: An Autobiography* (New York, 1975; repr. with an introduction by Mary Rodgers, New York, 1995), p. 228.
7 Richard Rodgers and Oscar Hammerstein II, *Six Plays by Rodgers and Hammerstein* (New York, n.d.), p. 7.
8 For further discussion about the play and its Broadway run, see Hyland, *Richard Rodgers*, pp. 139–40.
9 Fordin, *Getting to Know Him*, p. 200.
10 See Geoffrey Block, *Enchanted Evenings: The Broadway Musical from 'Show Boat' to Sondheim* (New York and Oxford, 1997), pp. ix–x.
11 Philip Furia, *The Poets of Tin Pan Alley: A History of America's Great Lyricists* (London and New York, 1990), p. 181.
12 Ethan Mordden, *Rodgers and Hammerstein* (New York, 1992), p. 34.
13 Rodgers, *Musical Stages*, p. 238.
14 For a lengthy discussion of the complexity of 'The Carousel Waltz' as source material for songs in *Carousel*, see Joseph Swain, *The Broadway Musical: A Critical and Musical Survey* (New York and London, 1990), pp. 99–114.
15 Block, *Enchanted Evenings*, pp. 162–3.
16 Fordin, *Getting to Know Him*, p. 255.
17 Thomas Hischak, *Word Crazy: Broadway Lyricists from Cohan to Sondheim* (New York, 1991), p. 37.
18 Fordin, *Getting to Know Him*, p. 258.
19 *Ibid.*, p. 281.
20 Hischak, *Word Crazy*, p. 42.
21 Fordin, *Getting to Know Him*, p. 126.

9 The successors of Rodgers and Hammerstein from the 1940s to the 1960s
1 I.e. singing, dancing and acting.
2 Gerald Bordman, *American Musical Theatre: A Chronicle,* 3rd edn (New York and Oxford, 2001), p. 597.
3 Edward Jablonski, *Alan Jay Lerner: A Biography* (New York, 1996), p. 32.
4 Bordman, *American Musical Theatre*, p. 620.
5 Jablonski, *Alan Jay Lerner*, pp. 82–4.
6 *Ibid.*, pp. 101–2.

7 Alan Jay Lerner, *The Street Where I Live* (New York, 1978), pp. 43–4.
8 *Ibid.*, pp. 66–7.
9 *Ibid.*, p. 142.
10 Stanley Green, *Broadway Musicals Show by Show*, 5th edn, rev. Kay Green (Milwaukee, 1996), p. 168.
11 Bordman, *American Musical Theatre*, p. 661.
12 For more information about Arlen and his works, see Edward Jablonski, *Harold Arlen: Rhythm, Rainbows, and Blues* (Boston, 1996).
13 Lehman Engel, *The American Musical: A Consideration* (New York, 1967), pp. 76–9.
14 H. Wiley Hitchcock and Stanley Sadie (eds.), *The New Grove Dictionary of American Music*, vol. I, *s.v.*'Bock, Jerry'.
15 Bordman, *American Musical Theatre*, p. 693.
16 Joseph P. Swain, *The Broadway Musical: A Musical and Critical Survey* (New York, 1990), p. 260.
17 For more details on the film and its background, see Tim Robbins, *Cradle Will Rock: The Movie and the Moment* (New York, 2000).

10 Musical sophistication on Broadway: Kurt Weill and Leonard Bernstein
1 Quoted in David Farneth (comp. and ed.), *Lenya the Legend: A Pictorial Autobiography* (Woodstock, New York and London, 1998), p. 130.
2 Kim H. Kowalke, '*The Threepenny Opera* in America', in *Kurt Weill: The Threepenny Opera*, ed. Stephen Hinton (Cambridge, 1990), p. 79.
3 Lotte Lenya interview with David Beams, 15 and 28 February 1962, transcript of audiotape in the Weill–Lenya Research Center, New York, quoted in Farneth, *Lenya the Legend*, p. 219.
4 Benjamin Welles, 'Lyricist of "The Saga of Jenny" et al.: A History of the Life and Some of the Works of Ira Gershwin', *New York Times*, 25 May 1941.
5 Paul Green, unpublished interview with Rhoda Wynn quoted in Larry L. Lash, 'Kurt Weill's Broadway Debut', liner notes for *Music for Johnny Johnson*, The Otaré Pit Band/Joel Cohen. Erato 0630-17870-2.
6 *New York Telegraph*, 4 December 1936, quoted in Lash, 'Kurt Weill's Broadway Debut'.
7 Kurt Weill, 'Two Dreams-Come-True', undated (c. 1947), unpublished and unpaginated essay, Box 68, folder 16, Weill/Lenya Archive, Beinecke Rare Book and Manuscript Library, Yale University.
8 *Life Magazine*, 25 October 1943.

9 Brooks Atkinson, 'Walter Huston in Maxwell Anderson's Musical Comedy, "Knickerbocker Holiday"', *New York Times*, 21 October 1938.

10 bruce d. mcclung, '*Psicosi per musica*: Re-examining *Lady in the Dark*', in *A Stranger Here Myself: Kurt Weill Studien*, ed. Horst Edler and Kim H. Kowalke (Hildesheim, 1993), pp. 235–65.

11 Brooks Atkinson, 'Struck By Stage Lightning: Comments on the Theater Wonders of *Lady in the Dark* with Special Reference to Kurt Weill and Gertrude Lawrence', *New York Times*, 7 September 1941.

12 Typescript letter dated 3 April 1944 from Kurt Weill to Ira Gershwin, Gershwin Collection, Library of Congress.

13 The renaissance included a new incarnation of Johann Strauss's *Die Fledermaus*, renamed *Rosalinda* (1942), a modern version of Offenbach's *La Belle Hélène* retitled *Helen Goes to Troy* (1944) and a romanticised stage biography of Edvard Grieg entitled *Song of Norway* (1944).

14 Weill, 'Two Dreams-Come-True'.

15 Kurt Weill, 'Score for a Play', *New York Times*, 5 January 1947.

16 *Ibid.*

17 Olin Downes, 'Opera on Broadway: Kurt Weill Takes Forward Step in Setting Idiomatic American to Music', *New York Times*, 26 January 1947.

18 Alan Jay Lerner, 'Lerner's Life and *Love Life*', *P.M.*, 14 November 1948.

19 Typescript letter dated 14 November [*recte* December]1949 from Kurt Weill to Olin Downes, Weill/Lenya Archive, Yale University, partially reprinted in David Farneth, with Elmar Juchem and Dave Stein, *Kurt Weill: A Life in Pictures and Documents* (Woodstock, New York and London, 2000), p. 268.

20 Virgil Thomson, 'Kurt Weill', *New York Herald Tribune*, 9 April 1950. After a memorial concert at Town Hall in New York, however, Thomson reversed himself: 'His American work was viable but not striking, thoroughly competent but essentially conformist' ('Kurt Weill Concert', *New York Herald Tribune*, 5 February 1951).

21 'Kurt Weill Dead; Composer, Was 50', *New York Times*, 4 April 1950.

22 Maxwell Anderson, 'Kurt Weill', *Theatre Arts*, December 1950, p. 58.

23 Olin Downes, 'Memorial to Weill: Program Honoring a Man Who Aided U.S. Opera', *New York Times*, 9 July 1950.

24 Betty Comden recorded their creative principles on yellow legal pad paper, a document now in the collection of The Museum of the City of New York. For further description, see Humphrey Burton, *Leonard Bernstein* (New York, 1994), p. 130.

25 Denny Martin Flinn, *Musical!: A Grand Tour* (New York, 1997), p. 247.

26 See the title page of the accompanying booklet for the compact disc *On the Town* conducted by Michael Tilson Thomas, Deutsche Grammophon 437 516-2, 1993.

27 Joan Peyser, *Bernstein: A Biography* (New York, 1987), p. 213.

28 Olin Downes, 'Wonderful Time: Bernstein's Musical Is Brilliant Achievement', *New York Times*, 10 May 1953.

29 Peyser, *Bernstein: A Biography*, p. 248.

30 Tyrone Guthrie, *A Life in the Theatre* (New York, Toronto and London, 1959), pp. 240–1.

31 See Geoffrey Block's essay on *West Side Story* in *Enchanted Evenings: The Broadway Musical from 'Show Boat' to Sondheim* (New York and Oxford, 1997), pp. 245–73.

32 Burton, *Leonard Bernstein*, pp. 343–7.

33 *Ibid.*, pp. 374 and 379.

34 Deutsche Grammophon 289 463 448–2, 2000.

11 Stephen Sondheim and the musical of the outsider

1 Frank Rich, 'Conversations with Stephen Sondheim', *The New York Times Magazine*, 12 March 2000, p. 41.

2 *Ibid.*

3 *Ibid.*, p. 60.

4 *Ibid.*

5 Steven Robert Swayne, 'Hearing Sondheim's Voices', PhD diss., University of California, Berkeley, 1999, p. 27.

6 *Ibid.*

7 Joanne Gordon, *Art Isn't Easy: The Achievement of Stephen Sondheim* (Carbondale, Illinois, 1990), p. 7.

8 *Ibid.*

9 Stephen Banfield, *Sondheim's Broadway Musicals* (Ann Arbor, Michigan, 1993), p. 152.

10 Sondheim's first show as both composer and lyricist to open on Broadway was *A Funny Thing Happened on the Way to Forum* (1962). An earlier effort, *Saturday Night*, was slated for a production in late 1955 or early 1956, but the death of the producer, Lemuel Ayers, resulted in the cancellation of the production. *Saturday Night* finally received a New York production in February 2000.

11 Craig Zadan, *Sondheim and Co.*, 2nd edn (New York, 1989), p. 82.

12 *Ibid.*, p. 88.

13 Harold Prince, *Contradictions: Notes on Twenty-Six Years in the Theatre* (New York, 1974), p. 158.

14 Gordon, *Art Isn't Easy*, p. 78.

15 The discussion of *Assassins* is drawn from two papers by the author. The first, 'Sondheim, Sousa, and the Electric Chair', was presented at the 1997 national conference of the Sonneck Society for American Music. The second, 'Propelling the Plotless Musical: The Sondheim Solution', was presented at the 2000 national conference of the Society for American Music. Similar observations and analyses, at the time unknown to the author, were made concurrently by Steven R. Swayne in his 1999 doctoral dissertation at the University of California, Berkeley.

16 Banfield, *Sondheim's Broadway Musicals*, p. 56.

17 The large acoustical 'shell' placed behind ensembles such as bands, orchestras or choruses when they perform outdoors.

18 'Transition', *Newsweek*, 1 (25 March 1933), p. 19.

19 Patrick Donovan, *The Assassins* (New York, 1955), p. 60.

20 *Ibid.*, p. 61.

21 See Sondheim's comments on harmony in Swayne, 'Hearing Sondheim's Voices', pp. 345–6.

22 Sondheim has often recounted the story of Sheldon Harnick's criticism of the lyrics to 'I Feel Pretty' from *West Side Story*. The inner rhymes, such as 'It's alarming how charming I feel', were too sophisticated for Maria, Harnick informed Sondheim. When Sondheim simplified them, however, they were rejected, and so 'there it is to this day embarrassing me every time it's sung' (Zadan, *Sondheim and Co.*, p. 22).

12 Choreographers, directors and the fully integrated musical

1 See Ethan Mordden, *Broadway Babies: The People Who Made the Broadway Musical* (New York and Oxford, 1983), pp. 12–13.

2 Hugh Fordin, *Getting to Know Him* (New York, 1995), p. 62.

3 Marian Monta Smith, 'Six Miles to Dawn: An Analysis of the Modern American Musical Comedy', PhD diss., Cornell University, 1971, p. 105.

4 Mordden, *Broadway Babies*, p. 133.

5 George Abbott, *'Mister Abbott'* (New York, 1963), pp. 177–8.

6 Smith, 'Six Miles to Dawn', p. 105.

7 Mordden, *Broadway Babies*, p. 133.

8 See Max Wilk, *The Story of 'Oklahoma'* (New York, 1993), pp. 127ff.

9 Smith, 'Six Miles to Dawn', p. 106.

10 Martin Gottfried, *Broadway Musicals* (New York, 1984), p. 112.

11 Sono Osato, *Distant Dances* (New York, 1980), pp. 230–47.

12 For overviews of Robbins' career, see Gottfried, *Broadway Musicals*, pp. 101–9; Christine Conrad, *That Broadway Man, That Ballet Man* (London, 2000); Greg Lawrence, *Dances with Demons: The Life of Jerome Robbins* (New York, 2001); Deborah Jowitt, *Jerome Robbins: His Life, His Theater, His Dance* (New York, 2004); and Amanda Vaill, *Somewhere: The Life of Jerome Robbins* (New York, 2006).

13 Abbott, *'Mister Abbott'*, p. 227.

14 For a good overview on the making of *West Side Story*, see Keith Garebian, *The Making of 'West Side Story'* (Toronto, 1995).

15 Materials on *West Side Story*'s conception exist in several archives. The folder of notes, draft scripts and draft lyrics for *West Side Story* in the Bernstein Collection at the Library of Congress is a treasure trove concerning the show's creation, but many documents are undated. Additional papers, considered by Stephen Banfield, exist in the Stephen Sondheim Papers at the Wisconsin State Historical Society. (See Stephen Banfield, *Sondheim's Broadway Musicals* (Ann Arbor, Michigan, 1993), pp. 31–8.) What seems an early outline and synopsis in the Bernstein Collection bears the title *Gang Bang* ('working title!') and dates from when the conflict was between Jews and Italians.

Most characters still carry their Shakespearean names and adults play a larger role in the story than in the final version. For example, in Act 2, scene 2, the boy's family sits down to their *seder*, but are interrupted by police with news of the death of 'Barnard'. No similar scene occurs in the final version, where parents of the young people are never seen on stage. Bernstein's notes on *West Side Story* concerning the auditions, casting, and orchestra are found in Folder 75/5 of the Bernstein Collection at the Music Division of the Library of Congress. (For an overview of the Bernstein Collection at the Library of Congress, see Paul R. Laird, *Leonard Bernstein: A Guide to Research* (New York, 2002), pp. 230–42, and the collections website at the Library of Congress, http://memory.loc.gov/ammem/lbhtml/lbhome.html.)

The folder includes a letter of 18 October 1955 from Jerome Robbins to Bernstein and Arthur Laurents with reactions to a detailed outline they had sent. Robbins argues for two acts instead of three, objects to the description of Anita as an older and wiser, blues-singing second female lead, and insists that the audience must believe tragedy can be averted until the final moment. He states that the principals, except for the romantic leads, must be dancers. Along with this letter is the six-page synopsis to which Robbins reacts. There are other draft synopses and outlines as well. Another fascinating early document on the show in Bernstein's hand lists two acts and fifteen scenes and a short synopsis of the action in each.

16 William Westbrook Burton, *Conversations about Bernstein* (New York and Oxford, 1995), p. 171.

17 Mordden,*Broadway Babies*, p. 137.

18 Burton, *Conversations about Bernstein*, p. 179.

19 For an excellent consideration of the music of *West Side Story*, see Geoffrey Block, *Enchanted Evenings: The Broadway Musical from 'Show Boat' to Sondheim* (New York and Oxford, 1997), pp. 245–73.

20 For overviews of Fosse's career, see Gottfried, *Broadway Musicals*, pp. 111–23; Gottfried, *All His Jazz: The Life & Death of Bob Fosse* (New York, 1990); and Kevin Boyd Grubb, *Razzle Dazzle: The Life and Work of Bob Fosse* (New York, 1989).

21 Christine Colby Jacques, 'Bob Fosse' (unpublished paper), p. 6.

22 For more material on Hal Prince's Broadway career, see his autobiography, *Contradictions: Notes on Twenty-Six Years in the Theatre* (New York, 1974), and Gottfried, *Broadway Musicals*, pp.126–31. See also Foster Hirsch, *Harold Prince and the American Musical Theatre*, rev. and expanded edn (New York, 2005).

23 Ken Mandelbaum, *A Chorus Line and the Musicals of Michael Bennett* (New York, 1989), p. 43.

24 *Ibid.*

25 *Ibid.*, p. 53.

26 Quoted in *ibid.*, p. 72.

27 *Ibid.*, pp. 93ff.

28 Two other fine sources on the making of *A Chorus Line* include: Denny Martin Flinn, *What They Did for Love: The Untold Story Behind the Making of 'A Chorus Line'* (New York, 1989); Robert Viagas, Baayork Lee, Thommie Walsh with the entire original cast, *On The Line: The Creation of 'A Chorus Line'* (New York, 1990).

29 Mandelbaum, *A Chorus Line and the Musicals of Michael Bennett*, p. 127.

30 Gottfried, *Broadway Musicals*, p. 35.

31 *Ibid.*, p. 36.

32 Mandelbaum, *A Chorus Line and the Musicals of Michael Bennett*, p. 164.

13 From *Hair* to *Rent*: is 'rock' a four-letter word on Broadway?

1 See, for example, Gerald Bordman, *American Musical Theatre: A Chronicle*, 2nd edn (New York and Oxford, 1992), p. 643; Denny Martin Flinn, *Musical! A Grand Tour: The Rise, Glory, and Fall of an American Institution* (New York, 1997), chapter 18: 'The Rock Musical', pp. 315–22; and Mark Steyn, *Broadway Babies Say Goodnight: Musicals Then and Now* (New York, 1999), pp. 213–27.

2 In describing the various strains of popular music of the 1950s, 1960s and later years, the term 'rock 'n' roll' identifies musical styles that emerged in the 1950s out of the American South, while 'rock' refers to the modified pop styles that appeared in the early 1960s and carry through to the present. See H. Wiley Hitchcock and Stanley Sadie (eds.), *The New Grove Dictionary of American Music*, vol. IV, *s.v.*'Rock, I. Rock and Roll'.

3 Stanley Richards, *Great Rock Musicals* (New York: Stein and Day, 1979).

4 For the definitive study of *Hair*, see Barbara Lee Horn, *The Age of Hair: Evolution and Impact of Broadway's First Rock Musical*, Contributions in Drama and Theater Studies 42 (New York and Westport, Connecticut, 1991).

5 The 1977 revival of *Hair*, ten years after its premiere and just five years after the original run closed, was panned as a period piece whose time had passed. See Steven Suskin, *More Opening Nights on Broadway* (New York, 1997), pp. 386–90.

6 Lewis Funke, 'News of the Rialto: Will B'way Rock?', *New York Times*, 10 December 1967, noted rock's appearance in several off-Broadway productions and the inevitability of its move 'north' to Broadway.

7 See the reviews of the original off-Broadway concert, *New York Times*, 13 March 1969, and of the Broadway production, *New York Times*, 25 September 1969.

8 Judy Klemesrud, 'She Was the Perfect Grandmother for the Rock Musical Part', *New York Times*, 27 April 1971, and Clive Barnes's review, *New York Times*, 6 May 1971.

9 See the reviews of *Soon*, *New York Times*, 13 January 1971, and *Hard Job Being God*, *New York Times*, 18 May 1972.

10 *New York Times*, 2 December 1971.

11 Selected reviews in Suskin, *More Opening Nights on Broadway*, pp. 257–62, 949–53.

12 *New York Times*, 27 January 1970.

13 Selected reviews in Suskin, *More Opening Nights on Broadway*, pp. 325–9.

14 See Alan Hewitt, 'Why Can't Today's Actors Sing Out?', *New York Times*, 18 January 1970, for a description of the sound system used for *Promises, Promises* and for general commentary on the increasing use of amplification in Broadway musicals.

15 Even though its creators never labelled *Godspell* a 'rock musical', many critics clearly thought it was one, and the show's producers seemed willing to exploit this dichotomy. See, for instance, the display advertisement in the Sunday *New York Times*, 30 May 1971. About a quarter of the twenty-five quotations from various reviewers, which were undoubtedly chosen by the producers, specifically used the word 'rock' to describe *Godspell*'s music.

16 Selected reviews in Suskin, *More Opening Nights on Broadway*, pp. 334–7. *Godspell*'s Broadway run added 527 performances to make a grand total of 2,651.

17 For background on this new rock style and a descriptive analysis of one progressive rock classic, see John Covach, 'Progressive Rock, "Close to the Edge", and the Boundaries of Style', in John Covach and Graeme M. Boone, *Understanding Rock: Essays in Musical Analysis* (New York, 1997), pp. 3–32.

18 Louis Calta, 'Beset Queens Playhouse Shifts to Rock Musical', *New York Times*, 16 September 1974; review of the initial off-Broadway production, *New York Times*, 20 September 1974; 'Opening This Week' and display advertisement, *New York Times*, 9 March 1975; and 'Arts and Leisure Guide', *New York Times*, 16 March 1975.

19 Display advertisement for *The Wiz*, *New York Times*, 12 January 1975.

20 *New York Times*, 10 March 1978.

21 Quoted in Suskin, *More Opening Nights on Broadway*, p. 260; original review in *New York Times*, 22 October 1972.

22 See the reviews of the following productions, all of which were billed as 'rock musicals': *Soon* (*New York Times*, 13 January 1971); *Rockabye Hamlet* (*New York Times*, 18 February 1976); *Marlowe* (*New York Times*, 13 October 1981); *The News* (*New York Times*, 8 November 1985); *Platinum* (*New York Times*, 13 November 1978); and *Fallen Angels* (*New York Times*, 16 April 1994).

23 *New York Times*, 29 April 1988.

24 Because of significant differences between the London and Broadway versions of *Chess*, many individual numbers have different titles and lyrics, depending upon which recordings one consults. A number of websites have appeared, many of which contain guides to the multiple productions, the songs and their lyrics. As is often the case with such websites, however, one must use the information provided with a certain degree of care.

25 See Jon Pareles, 'Can Rock Play to the Broadway Crowd?', *New York Times*, 28 April 1996.

26 See *New York Times*, 24 September 1995 and 10 November 1995, for information on the album's planned release and a review. See Ben Brantley, 'Two Takes on the Devil: The Charms of the Seedy Give Way to Sunday Best', *New York Times*, 26 October 1996, for a review of the Chicago performance.

27 Ben Brantley, 'The Lure of Gang Violence to a Latin Beat', *New York Times*, 30 January 1998.

28 See the review in the *New York Times*, 23 April 1993.

29 See www.mamma-mia.com. See www.playbill.com/features/section/7.html for information on the weekly grosses of all Broadway shows, including *Mamma Mia!*.

30 See Ben Brantley, ' "Jersey Boys": From Blue-Collar Boys to Doo-Wop Sensation: A Band's Rise and Fall', *New York Times*, 7 November 2005, Blake Green, 'Four Punks from New Jersey; A New Musical Tells the Story of the Rise and Fall of The Four Seasons, Blue-Collar Kids Who Sold 175 Million Records, Then Went Their Own Ways', *Newsday*, 6 November 2005, and Michael Riedel, ' "Big 'Boys", Four Seasons Musical Quietly Beats Broadway Competition', *New York Post* (9 December 2005), for positive reviews of this show.

31 On the term ' "jukebox musical", see Jesse McKinley, 'You Can Name the Tune, But Does It Fit the Plot?', *New York Times*, 14 February 2005. On the reuse of older music and musical styles in general on Broadway, see Bruce Weber, 'Critic's Notebook; The Broadway Musical Is Changing Its Key', *New York Times*, 26 December 2003.

32 See Michael Riedel, 'Return to Sender: Shake-Up at Elvis Musical', *New York Post*, 14 September 2005, on problems in the production of *All Shook Up*. See Ben Brantley, 'Then John Met Yoko, and the Rest Is a Musical', *New York Times*, 15 August 2005, for a negative review of *Lennon*. See Michael Riedel, 'Surf's Down – It Looks Like a Wipeout for ' "Good Vibrations"', *New York Post* (4 February 2005), whose review begins with the following: ' "Good Vibrations" is the worst musical of the season, maybe even the worst musical of all time! It makes

"Footloose" (once the gold standard of awfulness) and "Dracula" look like masterpieces of the American musical theater. All three shows, by the way, were produced by Dodger Stage Holdings, the Broadway Production company that's done more damage to Western civilization than the Visigoths.' Ben Brantley, 'To Everything There Is a Purpose', *New York Times*, 3 February 2005, was equally negative, and his brief notice in '. . . And the Regrettables', *New York Times*, 22 May 2005, which ran opposite the announcement of the Tony Award nominees, was even more scathing: ' "Good Vibrations" – The show that may well be remembered (and hailed) for hastening the death of the jukebox musical, a virtuous act of euthanasia if ever there was one. The ultimate bottom-scraping example of a low form of scavenger theater, this stitched-together beach blanket of a show purged every ray of sunshine from the happy songs of the Beach Boys, as a young and firm-bodied cast modeled swimwear and drowned before our eyes.'

33 The hit show *Wicked*, which opened on 30 October 2003 and was still playing to nearly full houses in 2006, may be the best example of Broadway's current sound. The score by Stephen Schwartz, composer of *Godspell* and *Pippin*, includes numbers diverse enough to suit the operatically trained Kristin Chenoweth; the iron-lunged Idina Menzel, who debuted on Broadway as the original Maureen in *Rent*; and Broadway legend Joel Grey, whose vocal style relies more on personality than sheer power. In the pit, the orchestra starts with a standard Broadway ensemble of a small string section with a harp, pairs of trumpets, horns and trombones, and four reed players. Added to that core, however, are a set drummer, electric bass, three keyboards/synthesisers, two electric guitars and an auxiliary percussionist. On the surface, most of the numbers function and sound like traditional Broadway numbers, but at least half of the show is underlined by prominent drum and electric bass lines that can only be described as rock, pop, funk, Latin, or some combination thereof. Despite this obvious reliance on rock, the closest any critic came to calling *Wicked* a 'rock musical' was Ben Brantley, who referred to its 'swirling pop-eretta score' and described Menzel's numbers as something that 'will no doubt dazzle audience members whose musical tastes run to soft-rock stations.' ('There's Trouble In Emerald City', *New York Times*, 31 October 2003.)

34 Ben Brantley, 'Broadway Doesn't Live There Anymore', *New York Times*, 7 November 1999.
35 Ben Brantley, 'Rock Opera à la "Bohème" and "Hair"', *New York Times*, 14 February 1996.
36 Anthony Tommasini, 'A Composer's Death Echoes in His Music', *New York Times*, 11 February 1996.
37 Margo Jefferson, ' "Rent" Is Brilliant and Messy All At Once', *New York Times*, 25 February 1996.
38 Kate Giel, ed., *Rent: Book, Music and Lyrics by Jonathan Larson*, interview and text by Evelyn McDonnell with Katherine Silberger (New York, 1997).
39 Laurel Graeber, 'Family Fare: Suffering and Survival', *New York Times*, 12 March 1999; and Anita Gates, 'Smells Like Teen Spirit, or Whatever', *New York Times*, 1 January 2000.
40 A preview article (*New York Times*, 8 March 1987) used the description 'rock opera'; and a review (*New York Times*, 13 March 1987) describes the music in these words: 'Mr. Schoenberg's profligately melodious score, sumptuously orchestrated by John Cameron to straddle the eras of harpsichord and synthesizer, mixes madrigal with rock and evokes composers as diverse as Bizet (for the laborers) and Weill (for their exploiters).'

14 The megamusical: the creation, internationalisation and impact of a genre

1 'The world's most popular musical' first appeared several years into the run of *Les Misérables* and 'now and forever' was coined for the Broadway production of *Cats*. Although both shows received mixed reviews in London and seemed doomed, they were immediately embraced by the public and achieved worldwide fame.
2 The production transferred to the Queen's Theatre on 3 April 2004.
3 Edward Behr, *Les Misérables: History in the Making* (New York, 1996), p. 159.
4 *Really Useful Group* website, '*The Phantom of the Opera*', www.reallyuseful.com/rug/shows/phantom/newsDetail.htm?id=275 (accessed 2 June 2006).
5 Michael Walsh, *Andrew Lloyd Webber: His Life and Works, A Critical Biography* (New York, 1997), p. 14.
6 The Adelphi is operated in association with Nederlander International Limited. Like Lloyd Webber, Cameron Mackintosh is a theatrical owner; the producer's Delfont Mackintosh Theatres holds seven theatres in the West End (as of 2006), including The

Prince Edward, Prince of Wales, Queens and Gielgud. Lloyd Webber and Mackintosh thus collectively own over half of the theatres in the West End.

7 Mark Steyn, *Broadway Babies Say Goodnight: Musicals Then and Now* (New York, 1999), p. 286.

8 *Ibid.*, p. 280.

9 *Ibid.*, p. 276.

10 Walsh, *Lloyd Webber*, p. 97.

11 *Ibid.*

12 From a booking advertisement for *Starlight Express.*

13 Steyn, *Broadway Babies*, p. 32.

14 *Really Useful Group* website, 'Phantom – The Last Vegas Spectacular: Frequently Asked Questions', www.reallyuseful.com/rug/shows/phantom/newsDetail.htm?id=309. (accessed 2 June 2006).

15 Correspondence from Rory Runciman, archivist for Cameron Mackintosh Limited, to Emma Baxter, Cambridge University Press, 22 October 2002.

16 Walsh, *Lloyd Webber*, p. 224.

15 'Something borrowed, something blue': the marriage of the musical and Europe

1 My thanks to the editors of this volume for inviting me to contribute an essay on this topic, as well as to my research assistant, Jenny Nelson.

2 See www.mtishows.com/contact.asp.

3 For an excellent discussion of the pros and cons of globalisation, see Richard Schechner's *Performance Studies: An Introduction* (London, 2002), pp. 226–32.

4 Simi Horwitz, 'Nine Musicals Named for New International Festival', *Backstage*, 2 August 2002, p. 4.

5 Horst Seeger, 'Music Theatre', in *The Encyclopedia of Contemporary Theatre*, vol. I, ed. Don Rubin (London, 1994), p. 17.

6 Kurt Gänzl, *Encyclopedia of the Musical Theatre* (New York, 2001). Unfortunately, *Musical-Jahrbuch* was only published, by a company named Pomp, for a few years.

7 Incidentally, the complete phrase for this tradition hints at its British origins: 'Something old, something new; Something borrowed, something blue; And a silver sixpence in her shoe'. Numerous sources date it to the Victorian era.

8 I once received a posting on a listserv calling for papers for an international conference on 'Interdisciplinary Approaches to the Musical Stage'. One of the suggested paper topics was 'Problems of Genre: Opera / Music(al) Theatre'.

9 Seeger, 'Music Theatre', p. 17.

10 Eric Salzman, 'Music-Theater Defined: It's . . . Well . . . Um . . . ', *New York Times*, 28 November 1999, p. 14.

11 To add one more wrinkle, Sondheim's shows, typically book musicals, are almost exclusively produced by opera companies in Europe.

12 Gänzl, *Encyclopedia of the Musical Theatre*, p. 636.

13 Twenty-one companies have opened *Miss Saigon* in nineteen countries and 138 cities, and the show has been translated into ten languages. The *Miss Saigon* German cast recording was made a 'golden CD' in July 1998 when it sold 250,000 copies. See www.miss-saigon.com/factsandfigures/.

14 Glenn Loney, 'Germany Sings: Musical Theater Grows in Popularity in Germany and Austria', *TCI*, February 1995, pp. 10+. Infotrac. University of Arizona Library, Tucson. 11 July 2005 http://web6.infotrac.galegroup.com.ezproxy.library.arizona.edu.

15 Isolde Schmid-Reiter, 'Music Theatre: Austria', *The Encyclopedia of Contemporary Theatre*, p. 66. Tongue in cheek, Kurt Gänzl writes of the phenomenal international popularity of *Cats*: '. . . its kittens, in all sorts of languages (but always in the original production, give or take a permitted variation) have been seen all over the world from Zurich to Mexico City'. *Encyclopedia of the Musical Theatre*, p. 338.

16 *Phantom* has played more than 65,000 performances in twenty countries in 110 cities around the world to over fifty-eight million people grossing over £1.6 billion worldwide. See http://www.thephantomoftheopera.com/the_show_phantom_facts.asp.

17 Meg Mumford and Alison Phipps, 'Encountering Stories from Contemporary German Theatre', in *Contemporary German Cultural Studies*, ed. Alison Phipps (London, 2002), p. 220.

18 Susanne Chambalu, 'Austria', in *European Theatre 1960-1990: cross-cultural perspectives*, ed. Ralph Yarrow (London, 1992), p. 105.

19 Gänzl, *Encyclopedia of the Musical Theatre*, p. 128.

20 Ernest Beck, 'The Saga of Sissi: Don't Cry for Me, Austria-Hungary', *Wall Street Journal*, 8 December 1997, p. A1.

21 See www.geocities.com/Broadway/8851/vienna.htm.

22 Gänzl, *Encyclopedia of the Musical Theatre*, p. 2010.

23 Richard Eyer and Nicholas Wright, *Changing Stages: A View of British Theatre in the*

Twentieth Century (London, 2000), p. 345.

24 Rebecca-Anne C. Do Rozario, 'The French Musicals: The Dramatic Impulse of *Spectacle*', *Journal of Dramatic Theory and Criticism*, 19/1 (2004), p. 125.

25 Gänzl, *Encyclopedia of the Musical Theatre*, p. 1925.

26 Nicholas Powell, 'In Paris: Nothing Like a Dame', *Variety*, 15–21 March 1999, p. 45.

27 Quoted in Alan Riding, 'The Real Paradox: Musical Comedy Made in France', *New York Times*, 20 October 2002, sec. 2, p. 5.

28 Riding, 'The Real Paradox: Musical Comedy Made in France', p. 5.

29 See Silvia Poletti, 'Broadway Shows Keep Italian Toes Tapping', *Dance Magazine*, June 2001. Ebscohost. University of Arizona Library, Tucson. 12 July 2005 http://bll.epnet.com.ezproxy.library.arizona.edu.

30 Katerina Honskusova, 'Outrageous Misfortune', *Prague Post*, 24 November 1999. LexisNexis Academic. University of Arizona Library, Tucson. 8 Aug. 2005 http://web.lexisnexis.com.ezproxy.library.arizona.edu.

31 For more information on new developments in Czech musical theatre at the end of the twentieth century, see Delbert Unruh, 'The Musical Theatre of Prague', *TD&T (Theatre Design & Technology)*, 37/4 (2001), pp. 18–25.

32 Sheridan Morley, *Spread a Little Happiness: The First Hundred Years of the British Musical* (London, 1987), pp. 11–12.

33 As recently as August 2005, Michael John LaChiusa declared that 'The American Musical is dead' in an article for *Opera News*. See 'The Great Gray Way: Is It Prognosis Negative For The Broadway Musical?' in *Opera News*, 70/2 (2005), p. 30.

16 New horizons: the musical at the dawn of the twenty-first century

1 It is worth noting that musical theatre – like the other arts – is not governed by 'cultural Darwinism'. Musicals of the twenty-first century are not inherently better (more intellectually challenging, musically rich, directorially sophisticated, choreographically complex, etc.) than their early twentieth-century ancestors.

2 Rick A. Simas, 'Floyd Collins (review)', *Theatre Journal*, 51/4 (1999), p. 465.

3 Among the many artists who have covered Wildhorn's songs are Whitney Houston, Natalie Cole, Kenny Rogers, Sammy Davis Jr, Liza Minnelli, Freddie Jackson, Peabo Bryson, Ben Vereen, The Moody Blues, Jeffrey Osborne, Dennis DeYoung, Stacy Lattisaw, Molly Hatchet, Colm Wilkinson and Linda Eder. In the pop music field, he wrote the Number One international hit, 'Where Do Broken Hearts Go?'.

4 Jesse McKinley, 'Drawn to Broadway from Near and, Mostly, Far', *New York Times*, 13 January 2005.

5 I am not including *West Side Story* in this list since the musical is not about Puerto Ricans in New York – with the exception of 'America' – but is rather a tragic love story in a melodrama (with beautiful music).

6 Curiously, another version of *The Wild Party* also opened in 2000 in New York. Appearing off-Broadway at the Manhattan Theatre Club, this musical was written by Andrew Lippa.

7 John Simon, 'The Wild Party!', *New York Magazine*, 1 May 2000 (nymag.com/nymetro/arts/theater/reviews/29050/, accessed 3 February 2007).

8 Ben Brantley, 'Having Fun Yet, Jazz Babies?', *New York Times*, 14 April 2000.

9 Rick Pender, 'Finding the Story: An Interview with Director John Doyle', *Sondheim Review*, 12/4 (2006), p. 48.

10 Steven Oxman, 'Revival Tests "Flower" Power', *Variety*, 8–14 October 2001, p. 27.

11 Diane Haithman, 'A Different Drummer', *Los Angeles Times*, 14 October 2001.

12 Michael Kantor and Laurence Maslon, *Broadway: The American Musical* (New York, 2004), p. 376.

13 Michael Riedel, 'Odd Men In; Play's Stars Are Broadway's Highest Paid', *New York Post*, 7 July 2006.

17 Why do they start to sing and dance all of a sudden? Examining the film musical

I would like to thank Professors Phil Furia and Karal Ann Marling for teaching me how to see and hear musicals, Professor Geoffrey Block for his encouragement and trust, my editors Professors Bill Everett and Paul Laird for their patience and my friends Julia Klimek, Angie Price, Donnie Quist and Sarah Schmalenberger for invaluable additional comments.

1 If one can see beyond the political incorrectness and scatological language of *South Park: Bigger, Longer and Uncut* (1999), this addition to the animated musical catalogue is a brilliant pastiche of the entire genre of musical theatre and film. Every song is a parody of a particular musical and visual style – from the *Oklahoma!*-style opening to the monstrously over-the-top reprise-finale. The deliberately crude animation style (anti-Disney?), coupled with a highly

polished orchestral score, creates a visual and musical disjunction that is both delightfully horrifying and intoxicating.

2 The increasing availability of televised productions in DVD format has, however, enhanced scholarly access to both complete and partial stage performances: Stephen Sondheim's *Sweeney Todd, Sunday in the Park with George, Into the Woods*, and *Passion*, as well as the Royal National Theatre revival of *Oklahoma!* are just some examples. This is in addition to archival TV footage releases such as *The Best of Broadway Musicals: Original Cast Performances from the Ed Sullivan Show*, and the *Broadway's Lost Treasures* series that features televised performances from the Tony Awards ceremonies.

3 Richard Fehr and Frederick G. Vogel, *Lullabies of Hollywood: Movie Music and the Movie Musical, 1915–1992* (Jefferson, North Carolina, 1993), p. 48.

4 Gerald Mast, *Can't Help Singin': The American Musical on Stage and Screen* (New York, 1987), p. 2.

5 Movie versions of stage shows like *The Producers* (2005) closely follow the sequence of the original stage production, in this case also presenting actors who originated the two title roles (Nathan Lane and Matthew Broderick as Max Bialystock and Leo Bloom) as well as recreating the costumes and production design of the stage version. As Mast has noted, this kind of adaptation 'is not an original musical conception for cinema but a theatrical conception . . . a permanent record of an ephemeral event'. See *Can't Help Singin'*, pp. 313, 309. On the other hand, in the movie version of *Rent* (2005), director Chris Columbus takes advantage of the New York location of the musical by moving Angel and Collins' duet 'I'll Cover You' onto a bustling Manhattan sidewalk in radiant sunlight. Similarly, Roger's anthem 'One Song Glory' takes place on the rooftop of the apartment building in contrast to his and Mimi's more set-bound indoor duets 'Light My Candle' and 'Another Day'. Also, Mimi begins 'Out Tonight' as a diegetic performance number in the Cat Scratch Club that simply continues as she makes her way back to her apartment, out onto the balcony and right in through Roger's window. Columbus thus maximises the possibilities that film offers and, through creative editing and location shooting, creates a world far larger than any Broadway stage. Similarly, the movie version of *Chicago* (2002) also takes advantage of the medium of film to deepen the narrative structure of the original stage concept by using the theatrically staged

performance numbers as a musical subtext that comments on realistic events in the narrative. Songs like 'Funny Honey' and 'We Both Reached for the Gun', as well as Billy's newly inserted stage tap routine, underscore the slippery relationship between performance and reality, between 'truth' and 'illusion' that *Chicago* artfully posits. By allowing the viewer to switch between these multiple narrative levels, the movie version of *Chicago* successfully enhances the ontological playfulness of the original show in a way that is thoroughly *cinematic* in execution. For a discussion of the movie versions of *West Side Story* (1961), *The Sound of Music* (1965), *Cabaret* (1972) and *Babes in Arms* (1939), see my chapter in the first edition of *The Cambridge Companion to the Musical* (Cambridge, 2002), 'Distant Cousin or Fraternal Twin?: Analytical Approaches to the Film Musical', pp. 215–17.

6 *Night and Day* (1946) starring Cary Grant and Alexis Smith, and made during Porter's lifetime, is generally regarded as biographical travesty since it makes no mention of Porter's homosexuality. In *De-Lovely*, Cole (Kline) and Linda (Ashley Judd) attend a private screening of *Night and Day* after which Cole remarks: 'If I can survive this movie, I can survive anything.'

7 See Mast, *Can't Help Singin'*, pp. 36–7 and David Schiff, *Gershwin: 'Rhapsody in Blue'* (Cambridge, 1997), pp. 94–100.

8 See John M. Clum, *Something for the Boys: Musical Theater and Gay Culture* (New York, 1999), pp. 1–26. See also D. A. Miller, *Place for Us* (Cambridge, Massachusetts, 1998).

9 See Richard Dyer, *Heavenly Bodies: Film Stars and Society* (Basingstoke, 1986).

10 See Mast, *Can't Help Singin'*, pp. 37–8.

11 Fehr and Vogel, *Lullabies of Hollywood*, p. 101.

12 See Jane Feuer, *The Hollywood Musical*, 2nd edn (Bloomington, 1993), chapter 4: 'Dream Worlds and Dream Stages'. This technique has also been used to add a fantasy element to some stage-to-screen song adaptations, for example in the 'Waltz for Eva and Che' from *Evita* and the 'Tango: Maureen' from *Rent*.

13 For a more detailed examination of the use of these elements of songs for expressive and dramatic purposes see Graham Wood, 'The Development of Song Forms in the Broadway and Hollywood Musicals of Richard Rodgers, 1919–1943', PhD diss., University of Minnesota, 2000.

14 See Leonard Maltin, *The Disney Films* (New York, 2000).

15 How much more interesting would this movie have been if one of the leads had been black, or if Zeke had ended up with Ryan instead of his sister? Much more worthy of scrutiny and certainly bolder both visually and in its narrative is Bryan Barber's MTV-meets-*Moulin Rouge!*-styled *Idlewild* (2006). Lovers of camp might also enjoy *Reefer Madness: The Movie Musical* (2005), a deliciously trashy spoof based on the Los Angeles (1998) and Off-Broadway (2001) stage musical inspired by the (non-musical) 1936 anti-marijuana propaganda movie of the same name.

16 See also Jeffrey Magee, 'Irving Berlin's "Blue Skies": Ethnic Affiliations and Musical Transformations', *Musical Quarterly*, 84 (2000), pp. 537–80.

17 Miles Krueger, *Show Boat: The Story of a Classic American Musical* (New York, 1977), p. 117.

18 See Philip Furia, *The Poets of Tin Pan Alley: A History of America's Great Lyricists* (New York, 1990), *Ira Gershwin: The Art of the Lyricist* (New York, 1996) and *Irving Berlin: A Life in Song* (New York, 1998). See also Stephen Banfield, 'Sondheim and the Art That Has No Name', in *Approaches to the American Musical*, ed. Robert Lawson-Peebles (Exeter, 1996), pp. 137–60.

19 The 'El Tango de Roxanne (medley)' is made up of 'Roxanne', music and lyrics by Sting, and 'Le Tango du Moulin Rouge', music by Marianito Mores, lyrics by Baz Luhrmann.

20 An anlysis of 'Slap That Bass' from *Shall We Dance?* (1937) can be found in 'Distant Cousin or Fraternal Twin?', *Cambridge Companion to the Musical*, 1st edn., pp. 228–9.

18 Revisiting classic musicals: revivals, films, television and recordings

1 See Nancy Hass, 'Two Decades Later, Just Right for the Role', *New York Times*, 10 November 1996.

2 David Patrick Stearns, ' "Chicago" Comes Into Its Own', *USA Today*, 15 November 1996.

3 Ben Brantley, 'Desperate Dance at Oblivion's Brink', *New York Times*, 20 March 1998.

4 See Jesse McKinley, 'Hey, Let's Not Put On A Show!', *New York Times*, 21 August 2005.

5 See Vincent Canby, '"Carousel", A Soap Opera No Longer', *New York Times*, 3 April 1994; David Patrick Stearns, '"Carousel" Goes Up and Down: Strong Acting, Weak Musicality', *USA Today*, 25 March 1994.

6 All Mast quotations from Gerald Mast, *Can't Help Singin': The American Musical on Stage and Screen* (Woodstock, New York, 1987), pp. 216–17.

7 As quoted in James Robert Parish and Michael R. Pitts, *The Great Hollywood Musical Pictures* (Metuchen, New Jersey and London, 1992), p. 70.

8 See Stephen Hunter, 'Pure Razzmatazz; "Chicago", One Town – And a Film – That Won't Let You Down', *Washington Post*, 27 December 2002; Roger Ebert, 'Razzle-Dazzle!', *Chicago Sun-Times*, 27 December 2002; Elvis Mitchell, '"Chicago", Bare Legs And All, Makes It To Film', *New York Times*, 27 December 2002.

9 Roger Ebert, 'The Producers: Singtime for Hitler', *Chicago Sun-Times*, as reprinted on rogerebert.com, 16 December 2005.

10 Joan Baxter, *Television Musicals: Plots, Critiques, Casts and Credits for 222 Shows Written for and Presented on Television, 1944–1996* (Jefferson, North Carolina, 1997).

11 Ethan Mordden, *Rodgers & Hammerstein* (New York, 1992), p. 111.

19 The creation of a Broadway musical: Stephen Schwartz, Winnie Holzman, and *Wicked*

1 G. Maguire, *Wicked: The Life and Times of the Wicked Witch of the West* (New York, 1995).

2 Schwartz's snorkelling buddies included songwriter John Bucchino and singer Holly Near, who told him about the novel. These details are reported by D. Cote in *Wicked: The Grimmerie* (New York, 2005), p. 20.

3 Personal interview with Stephen Schwartz in New York City by the author, 22 March 2005. All quotations and information attributed to Schwartz are from this interview unless otherwise noted.

4 Cote (p. 21) reports that this meeting took place in 1997.

5 Cote, p. 21.

6 In both Maguire's novel and the show, 'Galinda' changes her name to 'Glinda' in honour of Doctor Dillamond after he is arrested. The goat professor had trouble saying 'Galinda'. In this article, I use the form of the name appropriate to the moment in the show.

7 Telephone interview with Winnie Holzman by the author, 29 March 2005. All quotations and information attributed to Holzman are from this interview unless otherwise noted.

8 Creators address Schwartz's original conception for *Wicked* in Cote, *Wicked*, pp. 36–8.

9 Telephone interview with Stephen Schwartz by the author, 23 July 2004.

10 In Cote (p. 22), Platt reports that the three worked out the story 'beat for beat' in meetings in his office that took place over a year.

11 Maguire describes the details of this meeting with Schwartz, which took place in November 1998, in Cote, pp. 21–2. Maguire comments on the adaptation in Cote, p. 35.

12 Cote (pp. 33–4) offers brief commentary on how they adapted the novel into a musical. Maguire also reports that he gave Platt five pages of notes after one workshop that he saw (Cote, p. 35).

13 *Internet Broadway Database*, www.ibdb.com, consulted 8 September 2005.

14 Schwartz interview, 22 March 2005.

15 Schwartz interview, 22 March 2005.

16 I would like to thank Stephen Schwartz and his assistant Michael Cole for making available the schedule of readings and auditions for *Wicked*. In Cote (p. 22), Schwartz reports that the first reading was of the first act at the Coronet Theatre, but says that it was in the spring of 2000.

17 Schwartz interview, 22 March 2005.

18 In Cote (p. 24), Platt recalls the 'overwhelming emotional response' generated by the first reading of the entire book at Universal in March 2001.

19 Cote, p. 25.

20 In Cote (p. 31), Schwartz mentions how difficult it is for him to look for the first time at a production in a first preview because all he can see are problems. For extensive coverage of the show's production elements with many photographs, see Cote, pp. 89–137.

21 Cote, p. 38.

22 Schwartz interview, 22 March 2005.

23 Mantello describes how this part of the plot developed in Cote, pp. 71–3.

24 Holzman interview.

25 Details on Menzel's audition and her interpretation of Elphaba appear in Cote, pp. 26–8.

26 Schwartz (Cote, p. 28) describes how Menzel also worked on her middle range for the role.

27 Schwartz interview, 22 March 2005.

28 Cote (pp. 29–31) includes commentary from principal creators on the try-out in San Francisco.

29 Schwartz interview, 22 March 2005, and Playbill.com as part of an interview with Holzman available at www.musicalschwartz.com/wicked-sf.htm, consulted 10 September 2005.

30 Schwartz interview, 22 March 2005.

31 They also worked on Elphaba's character extensively during the San Francisco runs. In Cote (p. 30), Menzel reports that her 'lines were changing every day'. She also comments on how hard she was working to understand the role.

32 Holzman interview from Playbill.com, available at www.musicalschwartz.com/wicked-sf.htm, consulted 10 September 2005.

33 All material concerning the music of *Wicked* and Schwartz's compositional process, unless otherwise noted, derives from the Schwartz interview, 22 March 2005.

34 Cote, p. 77.

35 Schwartz describes the five versions of the song in Cote, p. 78. He notes that choreographer Wayne Cilento was important in choosing the final version (modelled after songs by the pop star Sting) because it provided more opportunities for the dancers.

36 In Cote, pp. 134–6, choreographer Wayne Cilento explains that there are many types of movement in the show, even if it seems to the audience that there is not a great deal of dancing.

37 Another moment Schwartz did not favour is the reference to *Evita* when Glinda is behind the microphone early in the second act.

38 Cote, p. 85.

39 Cote, p. 86.

Select bibliography

Adler, Jacob, *A Life on the Stage*, translated and edited by Lulla Rosenfeld (New York, 1999).

Allen, Frederick Lewis, *Only Yesterday* (New York, 1931).

—— *Since Yesterday* (New York, 1940).

Alpert, Hollis, *The Life and Times of 'Porgy and Bess': The Story of an American Classic* (New York, 1990).

—— *Broadway! 125 Years of Musical Theatre* (New York, 1991).

Altman, Rick, *The American Film Musical* (Bloomington, 1987).

Aumack, Sheryl, *Song and Dance: An Encyclopedia of Musicals* (Newport Beach, California, 1990).

Bach, Steven, *Dazzler: The Life and Times of Moss Hart* (New York, 2001).

Bailey, Peter (ed.), *Music Hall: The Business of Pleasure* (Milton Keynes and Philadelphia, 1986).

Banfield, Stephen, *Sondheim's Broadway Musicals* (Ann Arbor, Michigan, 1993).

—— 'Sondheim and the Art that Has No Name', in *Approaches to the American Musical*, ed. Robert Lawson-Peebles (Exeter, 1996), pp. 137–60.

—— 'Popular Song and Popular Music on Stage and Film', in *The Cambridge History of American Music*, ed. David Nicholls (Cambridge, 1998), pp. 309–44.

—— 'Stage and Screen Entertainers in the Twentieth Century', in *The Cambridge Companion to Singing*, ed. John Potter (Cambridge, 2000), pp. 63–82.

—— 'Scholarship and the Musical: Reclaiming Jerome Kern', *Proceedings of the British Academy*, 125 (2003), pp. 183–210.

—— *Jerome Kern* (New Haven, 2006).

Barrett, Mary Ellin, *Irving Berlin: A Daughter's Memoir* (New York, 1994).

Barrios, Richard, *A Song in the Dark: The Birth of the Musical Film* (New York, 1995).

Benjamin, Ruth, and Arthur Rosenblatt, *Movie Song Catalog: Performers and Supporting Crew for the Songs Sung in 1460 Musical and Nonmusical Films, 1928–1988* (Jefferson, North Carolina, 1993).

Bennett, Robert Russell, *'The Broadway Sound': The Autobiography and Selected Essays of Robert Russell Bennett*, ed. George J. Ferencz (Rochester, New York, 1999).

Bergreen, Laurence, *As Thousands Cheer: The Life of Irving Berlin* (New York, 1990).

Bernheim, Alfred L., *The Business of the Theatre: An Economic History of the American Theatre, 1750–1932* (New York, 1932).

Bierley, Paul, *The Works of John Philip Sousa* (Columbus, Ohio, 1984).

Block, Geoffrey, 'The Broadway Canon from *Show Boat* to *West Side Story* and the European Operatic Ideal', *Journal of Musicology*, 11/4 (1993), pp. 525–44.

—— *Enchanted Evenings: The Broadway Musical from 'Show Boat' to Sondheim* (New York and Oxford, 1997).

—— *The Richard Rodgers Reader* (New York and Oxford, 2002).

—— *Richard Rodgers* (New Haven, 2003).

Bloom, Ken, *Hollywood Song: The Complete Film and Musical Companion*, 3 vols. (New York, 1995).

—— *American Song: The Complete Musical Theatre Companion*, 2nd edn, 4 vols. (New York, 1996).

—— *Routledge Guide to Broadway* (New York, 2006).

Bordman, Gerald, *American Musical Theatre: A Chronicle* (New York, 1978), 2nd edn (New York and Oxford, 1992), 3rd edn (New York and Oxford, 2001).

—— *Jerome Kern: His Life and Music* (New York and Oxford, 1980).

—— *American Operetta: From 'H. M. S. Pinafore' to 'Sweeney Todd'* (New York and Oxford, 1981).

—— *American Musical Comedy: From 'Adonis' to 'Dreamgirls'* (New York and Oxford, 1982).

—— *Days to Be Happy, Years to Be Sad: The Life and Music of Vincent Youmans* (New York and Oxford, 1982).

—— *American Musical Revue: From 'The Passing Show' to 'Sugar Babies'* (New York and Oxford, 1985).

Borroff, Edith, 'Origin of Species: Conflicting Views of American Musical Theater History', *American Music*, 2/4 (1984), pp. 101–11.

Bourne, Stephen, *Ethel Waters: Stormy Weather* (Lanham, Maryland, 2007).

Bradley, Edwin M., *The First Hollywood Musicals: A Critical Filmography of 171 Features, 1927 through 1932* (Jefferson, North Carolina, 1996).

Bristow, Eugene K., and J. Kevin Butler, '*Company*, About Face! The Show that Revolutionized the American Musical', *American Music*, 5/3 (1987), pp. 241–54.

Brockett, Oscar G., *History of the Theater*, 4th edn (Boston, 1986).

Brooks, Mel, and Tom Meehan, *The Producers* (New York, 2001).

Brooks, William, 'Good Musical Paste: Getting the Acts Together in the Eighteenth Century', in *Musical Theatre in America: Papers and Proceedings of the Conference on the Musical Theatre in America*, ed. Glenn Loney (Westport, Connecticut, 1984), pp. 37–58.

—— '*Pocahontas*, Her Life and Times', *American Music*, 2/4 (1984), pp. 19–48.

Brown, Jared, *Moss Hart: A Prince of the Theatre* (New York, 2006).

Brown, T. Allston, *A History of the New York Stage*, 3 vols. (New York, 1903).

Bowers, Dwight Blocker, *American Musical Theater: Shows, Songs, and Stars* (Washington, DC, 1989).

Burton, Humphrey, *Leonard Bernstein* (New York, 1994).

Carnovale, Norbert, *George Gershwin: A Bio-Bibliography* (Westport, Connecticut, 2000).

Chevalley, Sylvie, 'La Première Saison théâtrale française de New York', *The French Review*, 24/6 (1951), pp. 471–9.

Citron, Stephen, *The Musical from the Inside Out* (Chicago, 1992).

—— *Noel and Cole: The Sophisticates* (New York and Oxford, 1993).

—— *The Wordsmiths: Oscar Hammerstein 2nd and Alan Jay Lerner* (New York and Oxford, 1995).

—— *Sondheim and Lloyd-Webber: The New Musical* (New York and Oxford, 2001).

Clum, John M., *Something for the Boys: Musical Theater and Gay Culture* (New York, 1999).

Cockrell, Dale, *Demons of Disorder: Early Blackface Minstrels and Their World* (Cambridge, 1997).

—— 'Nineteenth-Century Popular Music', in *The Cambridge History of American Music*, ed. David Nicholls (Cambridge, 1998), pp. 158–85.

Comden, Betty, *Off Stage* (New York, 1995).

Croce, Arlene, *The Fred Astaire and Ginger Rogers Book* (New York, 1972).

Cullen, Frank, *Vaudeville, Old and New: An Encyclopedia of Variety Performers*, 2 vols. (New York, 2006).

Davis, Lee, *Scandals and Follies: The Rise and Fall of the Great Broadway Revue* (New York, 2000).

Day, Barry (ed.), *The Complete Lyrics of P. G. Wodehouse* (Lanham, Maryland, 2004).

Dickinson, Peter, *Marigold: The Music of Billy Mayerl* (Oxford and New York, 1999).

Djedje, Jacqueline Cogdell, 'African American Music to 1900', in *The Cambridge History of American Music*, ed. David Nicholls (Cambridge, 1998), pp. 103–34.

Dyer, Richard, *Heavenly Bodies: Film Stars and Society* (Basingstoke, 1986).

Engel, Lehman, *The American Musical Theatre: A Consideration* (New York, 1967).

—— *Words with Music: The Broadway Musical Libretto* (New York, 1972).

Engle, Ron, and Tice C. Miller (eds.), *The American Stage: Social and Economic Issues from the Colonial Period to the Present* (Cambridge, 1993).

Everett, William A., 'Golden Days in Old Heidelberg: The First-Act Finale of Romberg's *The Student Prince*', *American Music*, 12/3 (1994), pp. 255–82.

—— 'Sigmund Romberg and the American Operetta of the 1920s', *Arti musices*, 26/1 (1995), pp. 49–64.

—— 'King Arthur in Popular Musical Theatre and Musical Film', in *King Arthur in Music*, ed. Richard W. Barber (Woodbridge and Rochester, New York, 2002).

—— *The Musical: A Research and Information Guide* (New York, 2004).

—— *Sigmund Romberg* (New Haven, 2007).

Ewen, David, *New Complete Book of the American Musical Theater* (New York, 1958), 2nd edn (New York, 1970).

Farneth, David, with Elmar Juchem and Dave Stein, *Kurt Weill: A Life in Pictures and Documents* (Woodstock, New York and London, 2000).

Fehr, Richard, and Frederick G. Vogel, *Lullabies of Hollywood: Movie Music and the Movie Musical, 1915–1992* (Jefferson, North Carolina, 1993).

Feuer, Jane, 'The Theme of Popular vs. Elite Art in the Hollywood Musical', *Journal of Popular Culture*, 12/3 (1978), pp. 491–9.

—— *The Hollywood Musical*, 2nd edn (Bloomington, 1993).

Fields, Armond, and L. Marc Fields, *From the Bowery to Broadway: Lew Fields and the Roots of American Popular Theater* (New York and Oxford, 1993).

Finson, Jon W. (ed.), *Edward Harrigan and David Braham: Collected Songs* (Madison, 1997).

Flinn, Denny Martin, *Musical!: A Grand Tour* (New York, 1997).

Fordin, Hugh, *Getting to Know Him: A Biography of Oscar Hammerstein II* (New York, 1977, 1995).

Forte, Allen, *The American Popular Ballad of the Golden Era: 1924–1950* (Princeton, 1995).
—— *Listening to Classic American Popular Songs* (New Haven and London, 2001).
Franceschina, John, *Harry B. Smith: Dean of American Librettists* (New York, 2003).
Furia, Philip, *The Poets of Tin Pan Alley: A History of America's Great Lyricists* (New York and Oxford, 1990).
—— *Ira Gershwin: The Art of the Lyricist* (New York, 1996).
—— *Skylark: The Life and Times of Johnny Mercer* (New York, 2003).
Furia, Philip, with the assistance of Graham Wood, songography by Ken Bloom, *Irving Berlin: A Life in Song* (New York, 1998).
Furia, Philip, and Michael Lasser, *America's Songs: The Stories Behind the Songs of Broadway, Hollywood, and Tin Pan Alley* (New York, 2006).
Gänzl, Kurt, *The British Musical Theatre*, 2 vols. (London, 1986).
—— *Song and Dance: The Complete Story of Stage Musicals* (London, 1995).
—— *The Musical: A Concise History* (Boston, 1997).
—— *The Encyclopedia of the Musical Theatre*, 2nd edn, 3 vols. (New York, 2000).
Garebian, Keith, *The Making of 'West Side Story'* (Toronto, 1995).
Gershwin, Ira, *Lyrics on Several Occasions* (New York, 1959).
Giel, Kate (ed.), *Rent: Book, Music and Lyrics by Jonathan Larson*, interview and text by Evelyn McDonnell with Katherine Silberger (New York, 1997).
Gilbert, Stephen, *The Music of Gershwin* (New Haven, 1995).
Goldstein, Malcolm, *The Political Stage: American Drama and Theater of the Great Depression* (New York and Oxford, 1974).
—— *George S. Kaufman: His Life, His Theater* (New York and Oxford, 1979).
Goodhart, Sandor (ed.), *Reading Stephen Sondheim: A Collection of Critical Essays* (New York, 2000).
Gordon, Eric A., *Mark the Music: The Life and Work of Marc Blitzstein* (New York, 1989).
Gordon, Joanne, *Art Isn't Easy: The Achievement of Stephen Sondheim* (Carbondale, Illinois, 1990).
—— *Art Isn't Easy: The Theatre of Stephen Sondheim* (New York, 1992).
Gottfried, Martin, *Broadway Musicals* (New York, 1979).
—— *More Broadway Musicals: Since 1980* (New York, 1991).
—— *Sondheim* (New York, 1993).
Gottlieb, Jack, *Funny, It Doesn't Sound Jewish: How Yiddish Songs and Synagogoue Melodies Influenced Tin Pan Alley, Broadway, and Hollywood* (Albany, New York, 2004).
Graziano, John, 'Sentimental Songs, Rags, and Transformations: The Emergence of the Black Musical, 1895–1910', in *Musical Theatre in America: Papers and Proceedings of the Conference on the Musical Theatre in America*, ed. Glenn Loney (Westport, Connecticut, 1984), pp. 211–32.
—— 'Black Musical Theater and the Harlem Renaissance Movement', in *Black Music in the Harlem Renaissance: A Collection of Essays*, ed. Samuel A. Floyd Jr (Westport, Connecticut, 1990), pp. 87–110.

—— 'The Early Life and Career of the "Black Patti": The Odyssey of an African American Singer in the Late Nineteenth Century', *Journal of the American Musicological Society*, 53/3 (2000), pp. 543–96.

—— 'Vaudeville', in *The New Grove Dictionary of American Music*, ed. H. Wiley Hitchcock and Stanley Sadie.

Graziano, John (ed.), *European Music and Musicians in New York City, 1840–1900* (Rochester, New York, 2006).

Green, Stanley, *The Rodgers and Hammerstein Story* (New York, 1963).

—— *Broadway Musicals of the 30s* (New York, 1971).

—— *The World of Musical Comedy*, 4th edn (London, 1980).

—— *Encyclopedia of the Musical Film* (New York, 1981).

—— *Hollywood Musicals Year by Year* (Milwaukee, 1990).

Green, Stanley (ed.), *Rodgers and Hammerstein Fact Book* (New York, 1980).

Green, Stanley, rev. and updated by Kay Green, *Broadway Musicals Show by Show*, 5th edn (Milwaukee, 1996).

Grimsted, David, *Melodrama Unveiled: American Theater and Culture, 1800–1850* (Chicago, 1968).

Grubb, Kevin Boyd, *Razzle Dazzle: The Life and Works of Bob Fosse* (New York, 1989).

Hamm, Charles, *Yesterdays: Popular Song in America* (New York, 1979).

—— 'The Theatre Guild Production of *Porgy and Bess*', *Journal of the American Musicological Society*, 40/3 (1987), pp. 495–532.

—— *Irving Berlin: Songs from the Melting Pot: The Formative Years, 1907–1914* (New York and Oxford, 1997).

—— 'Musical Theater, III. The Tin Pan Alley Era', in *The New Grove Dictionary of American Music*, ed. H. Wiley Hitchcock and Stanley Sadie.

Happy Talk: News of the Rodgers and Hammerstein Foundation, 1993–.

Hart, Dorothy, and Robert Kimball (eds.), *The Complete Lyrics of Lorenz Hart* (New York, 1986).

Hemming, Roy, *The Melody Lingers On: The Great Songwriters and Their Movie Musicals* (New York, 1986).

Henderson, Amy, and Dwight Blocker Bowers, *Red Hot and Blue: A Smithsonian Salute to the American Musical* (Washington, DC and London, 1986).

Herman, Jerry, *Showtune: A Memoir*, with Marilyn Stasio (New York, 1996).

Heskes, Irene, 'Music as Social History: American Yiddish Theatre Music, 1882–1920', *American Music* 2/1 (1984), pp. 73–87.

Hill, Errol, 'The Hyers Sisters: Pioneers in Black Musical Comedy', in *The American Stage: Social and Economic Issues from the Colonial Period to the Present*, ed. Ron Engle and Tice L. Miller (Cambridge and New York, 1993), pp. 115–30.

Hirsch, Foster, *Hal Prince and the American Musical Theatre* (Cambridge and New York, 1989).

—— *The Boys from Syracuse: The Shuberts' Theatrical Empire* (Carbondale, Illinois, 1998).

—— *Kurt Weill on Stage: From Berlin to Broadway* (New York, 2002).

Hirschhorn, Clive, *The Hollywood Musical* (New York, 1981).

Hischak, Thomas S., *Say It with Music: An Encylopedic Guide to the American Musical Theatre* (Westport, Connecticut, 1993).

—— *Film It with Music: An Encyclopedic Guide to the American Movie Musical* (Westport, Connecticut and London, 2001).

Hitchcock, H. Wiley, 'An Early American Melodrama: *The Indian Princess* of J. N. Barker and John Bray', *MLA Notes*, 12/3 (1955), pp. 375–88.

Hoare, Philip, *Noël Coward: A Biography* (London, 1995).

Hoover, Cynthia Adams, 'Music in Eighteenth-Century American Theater', *American Music*, 2/4 (1984), pp. 6–18.

Horn, Barbara Lee, *The Age of 'Hair': Evolution and Impact of Broadway's First Rock Musical* (New York and Westport, Connecticut, 1991).

Horowitz, Mark Eden, *Sondheim on Music: Minor Details and Major Decisions* (Lanham, Maryland, 2003).

Hummel, David. *The Collector's Guide to the American Musical Theatre*, 2nd edn (Grawn, Michigan, 1978).

Hyland, William G., *The Song is Ended: Songwriters and American Music, 1900–1950* (New York and Oxford, 1995).

—— *Richard Rodgers* (New Haven, 1998).

Ilson, Carol, *Harold Prince: From 'Pajama Game' to 'Phantom of the Opera'* (Ann Arbor, Michigan, 1989).

Internet Movie Database, http://us.imdb.com

Jablonski, Edward, *Gershwin: A Biography* (New York, 1987).

—— *Harold Arlen: Rhythm, Rainbows, and Blues* (Boston, 1996).

—— *Irving Berlin: American Troubadour* (New York, 1999).

Jackson, Arthur, *The Best Musicals from 'Show Boat' to 'A Chorus Line': Broadway, Off-Broadway, London* (New York, 1977).

Jessel, George, *A Pictoral History of Vaudeville* (New York, 1961).

Jones, John Bush, *Our Musicals, Ourselves: A Social History of the American Musical* (Hanover, New Hampshire, 2003).

Jones, Tom, *Making Musicals: An Informal Introduction to the World of Musical Theatre* (New York, 1998).

Kander, John, and Fred Ebb, as told to Greg Lawrence, *Colored Lights: Forty Years of Words and Music, Show Biz, Collaboration and All That Jazz* (New York, 2003).

Kanellos, Nicolás, *A History of Hispanic Theatre in the United States: Origins to 1940* (Austin, Texas, 1990).

Kantor, Michael, and Laurence Maslon, *Broadway: The American Musical*, based on the documentary film by Michael Kantor (New York, 2004).

Kaplan, Joel H., 'Introduction', in *The Edwardian Theatre: Essays on Performance and the Stage*, ed. Michael R. Booth and Joel H. Kaplan (Cambridge, 1996).

Kaufman, Gerald, *Meet Me in St. Louis* (London, 1994).

Kennedy, Michael Patrick, and John Muir, *Musicals* (Glasgow, 1997).

Kilroy, David Michael, 'Kurt Weill on Broadway: The Postwar Years (1945–1950)', Ph.D. diss., Harvard University, 1992.

Kimball, Robert (ed.), *The Complete Lyrics of Cole Porter* (New York, 1984).

—— *The Complete Lyrics of Ira Gershwin* (New York, 1993).

Kirle, Bruce, *Unfinished Business: Broadway Musicals as Works-in-Progress* (Carbondale, Illinois, 2005).

Kislan, Richard, *The Musical: A Look at the American Theater* (Englewood Cliffs, New Jersey, 1980).

Kmen, Henry, *Music in New Orleans: The Formative Years, 1791-1841* (Baton Rouge, Louisiana, 1966)

Knapp, Raymond, *The American Musical and the Formation of National Identity* (Princeton, 2005).

—— *The American Musical and the Performance of Personal Identity* (Princeton, 2006).

Koegel, John, 'Adolf Philipp and Musical Comedy on the German-American Stage in New York, 1890–1918,' *American Music* 24/3 (2006), pp. 267–319.

Kowalke, Kim, 'The Threepenny Opera in America', in *Kurt Weill: The Threepenny Opera*, ed. Stephen Hinton (Cambridge, 1990), pp. 78–120.

—— 'Formerly German: Kurt Weill in America', in *A Stranger Here Myself: Kurt Weill Studien*, ed. Kim Kowalke and Horst Edler (Hildesheim, 1993), pp. 35–57.

—— 'Kurt Weill, Modernism, and Popular Culture: Öffentlichkeit als Stil', *Modernism/Modernity*, 2/1 (1995), pp. 27–69.

Kowalke, Kim H. (ed.), *A New Orpheus: Essays on Kurt Weill* (New Haven, 1986).

Kowalke, Kim H., and Horst Edler (eds.), *A Stranger Here Myself: Kurt Weill Studien* (Hildesheim, 1993).

Krasker, Tommy, *Catalog of the American Musical* (Washington, DC, 1988).

—— Notes to *Fifty Million Frenchmen*, New World Records 80417-2 (1991), pp. 11–17.

—— 'What Price Cheese?' and 'Two Strikes, Two Hits, and One Man Out', notes to *Strike Up the Band*, Elektra Nonesuch 79273-2 (1991), pp. 17–22 and 37–41.

—— 'A Wonderful Party: *Lady, Be Good!*', notes to *Lady, Be Good!*, Elektra Nonesuch 79308-2 (1992), pp. 15–19.

—— '*Pardon My English*: A Tale of Two Psyches', notes to *Pardon My English*, Elektra Nonesuch 79338-2 (1994), pp. 11–16.

—— 'It's Been Fun, But I Gotta Rumrun', notes to *Oh, Kay!*, Nonesuch 79361-2 (1995), pp. 19–23.

Krasner, Orly Leah, 'Reginald de Koven (1859–1920) and American Comic Opera at the Turn of the Century', PhD diss., City University of New York, 1995.

—— 'Wien, Women and Song: *The Merry Widow* in New York', *Sonneck Society Bulletin*, 22/1 (1996), pp. 1, 8–11.

Kreuger, Miles, *Show Boat: The Story of a Classic American Musical* (New York and Oxford, 1977).

—— 'Some Words about *Anything Goes*', notes to *Anything Goes*, EMI/Angel CDC 7-49848-2 (1989), pp. 9–17.

—— 'Some Words about *Girl Crazy*', notes to *Girl Crazy*, Elektra Nonesuch 75559-79250-2 (1990), pp. 15–24.

Laird, Paul R., *Leonard Bernstein: A Guide to Research* (New York, 2002).

Lamb, Andrew, *Jerome Kern in Edwardian London* (New York, 1985).

—— *150 Years of Popular Musical Theatre* (New Haven and London, 2000).

Larkin, Colin (ed.), *The Guinness Who's Who of Stage Musicals* (Enfield, 1994).

Laufe, Abe, *Broadway's Greatest Musicals* (New York, 1973).

Laurents, Arthur, *Original Story by Arthur Laurents: A Memoir of Broadway and Hollywood* (New York, 2000).

Lawrence, Greg, *Dance with Demons: The Life of Jerome Robbins* (New York, 2001).

Lawson-Peebles, Robert (ed.), *Approaches to the American Musical* (Exeter, 1996).

Lee, Joanna, Edward Harsh, and Kim Kowalke (eds.), *'Street Scene': A Sourcebook*, 2nd edn (New York, 1996).

Lerner, Alan Jay, *The Street Where I Live* (New York and London, 1978).

—— *The Musical Theatre: A Celebration* (New York, 1986).

Levine, Lawrence W., *Highbrow/Lowbrow: The Emergence of Cultural Hierarchy in America* (Cambridge, Massachusetts, 1988).

Lifson, David S., *The Yiddish Theatre in America* (New York, 1965).

Londré, Felicia Hardison, and Daniel J. Watermeier, *The History of North American Theater: The United States, Canada and Mexico: From Pre-Columbian Times to the Present* (New York and London, 2000).

Loney, Glenn (ed.), *Musical Theatre in America: Papers and Proceedings of the Conference on the Musical Theatre in America* (Westport, Connecticut, 1984).

Lott, Eric, *Love and Theft: Blackface Minstrelsy and the American Working Class* (New York, 1993).

Magee, Jeffrey, 'Irving Berlin's "Blue Skies": Ethnic Affiliations and Musical Transformations', *Musical Quarterly* 84/4 (2000), pp. 537–80.

—— '"Everybody Step": Irving Berlin, Jazz, and Broadway in the 1920s', *Journal of the American Musicological Society*, 59/3 (2006), pp. 697–732.

Mahar, William J., *Behind the Burnt Cork Mask: Early Blackface Minstrelsy and Antebellum American Popular Culture* (Urbana, Illinois, 1999).

Maltin, Leonard, *The Disney Films*, 4th edn (New York, 2000).

Mandelbaum, Ken, *Not Since Carrie: 40 Years of Broadway Musical Flops* (New York, 1991).

Marmorstein, Gary, *Hollywood Rhapsody: Movie Music and its Makers, 1900–1975* (New York, 1997).

Mast, Gerald, *Can't Help Singin': The American Musical on Stage and Screen* (Woodstock, New York, 1987).

Mates, Julian, *The American Musical Stage before 1800* (New Brunswick, New Jersey, 1962).

—— *America's Musical Stage: Two Hundred Years of Musical Theatre* (Westport, Connecticut, 1985).

Mayer, David, 'The Music of Melodrama', in *Performance and Politics in Popular Drama*, ed. David Bradby, Louis James and Bernard Sharratt (Cambridge, 1980), pp. 49–63.

Mayer, David, and Matthew Scott (eds.), *Four Bars of 'Agit': Incidental Music for Victorian and Edwardian Melodrama* (London, 1983).

McBrien, William, *Cole Porter: A Biography* (New York, 1998).

McCabe, John, *George M. Cohan: The Man Who Owned Broadway* (Garden City, New York, 1973).

mcclung, bruce d., 'American Dreams: Analyzing Moss Hart, Ira Gershwin, and Kurt Weill's *Lady in the Dark*', PhD diss., University of Rochester, 1995.

—— 'Life after George: The Genesis of *Lady in the Dark*'s Circus Dream', *Kurt Weill Newsletter*, 14/2 (1996), pp. 4–8.

—— '*Lady in the Dark*': *Biography of a Musical* (Oxford, 2007).

mcclung, bruce d., Joanna Lee, and Kim Kowalke (eds.), '*Lady in the Dark*': *A Sourcebook*, 2nd edn (New York, 1997).

McConachie, Bruce A., *Melodramatic Formations: American Theatre and Society, 1820–1870* (Iowa City, 1992).

McGlinn, John, 'The Original *Anything Goes* – A Classic Restored', notes to *Anything Goes*, EMI/Angel CDC 7-49848-2 (1989), pp. 29–34.

—— 'Finding the Bliss', notes to *Sitting Pretty*, New World Records 80387-2 (1990), pp. 10–16.

McMillin, Scott, *The Musical as Drama* (Princeton, 2006).

McNamara, Brooks, *The Shuberts of Broadway* (New York and Oxford, 1990).

Meyerson, Harold, and Ernie Harburg, *Who Put the Rainbow in 'The Wizard of Oz'?: Yip Harburg, Lyricist* (Ann Arbor, Michigan, 1993).

Miller, Scott, *From 'Assassins' to 'West Side Story': The Director's Guide to Musical Theatre* (Portsmouth, New Hampshire, 1996).

—— *Deconstructing Harold Hill: An Insider's Guide to Musical Theatre* (Portsmouth, New Hampshire, 2000).

—— *Rebels with Applause: Broadway's Groundbreaking Musicals* (Portsmouth, New Hampshire, 2001).

—— *Strike Up the Band: A New History of Musical Theatre* (Portsmouth, New Hampshire, 2007).

Moody, Richard, 'Introduction: *Po-ca-hon-tas; or, the Gentle Savage*', in *Dramas from the American Theatre, 1762–1909*, ed. Richard Moody (New York, 1966), pp. 397–421.

Mordden, Ethan, *Better Foot Forward: The History of the American Musical Theatre* (New York, 1976).

—— *Broadway Babies: The People Who Made the American Musical* (New York and Oxford, 1983).

—— '"Show Boat" Crosses Over', *New Yorker* (3 July 1989), pp. 79–94.

—— *Rodgers and Hammerstein* (New York, 1992).

—— *Make Believe: The Broadway Musical in the 1920s* (New York and Oxford, 1997).

—— *Coming Up Roses: The Broadway Musical in the 1950s* (New York and Oxford, 1998).

—— *Beautiful Mornin': The Broadway Musical in the 1940s* (New York and Oxford, 1999).

—— *Open a New Window: The Broadway Musical in the 1960s* (New York, 2001).

—— *One More Kiss: The Broadway Musical in the 1970s* (New York, 2003).

—— *The Happiest Corpse I've Ever Seen: The Last Twenty-Five Years of the Broadway Musical* (New York, 2004).

—— *Sing For Your Supper: The Broadway Musical in the 1930s* (New York, 2005).

Morley, Sheridan, *Spread a Little Happiness: The First Hundred Years of the British Musical* (London, 1986).

Morley, Sheridan, and Ruth Leon, *Hey Mr Producer! The Musical World of Cameron Mackintosh* (London, 1998).

Most, Andrea, *Making Americans: Jews and the Broadway Musical* (Cambridge, Massachusetts, 2004).

Mundy, John, *Popular Music on Screen: From the Hollywood Musical to Music Video* (Manchester, 1999).

Myers, Paul, *Leonard Bernstein* (London, 1998).

Newsletter of the Stephen Sondheim Society, 1993–.

Noble, Peter, *Ivor Novello, Man of the Theatre* (London, 1951).

Nolan, Frederick, *Lorenz Hart* (New York and Oxford, 1994).

Norris, Renee Lapp, 'Opera and the Mainstreaming, of Blackface Minstrelsy', *Journal of the Society for American Music* 1/3(2002), pp. 341–65.

Norton, Elliot, *Broadway Down East: An Informal Account of the Plays, Players and Playhouses of Boston from Puritan Times to the Present* (Boston, 1978).

Norton, Richard C., *A Chronology of American Musical Theatre*, 3 vols. (New York, 2002).

Odell, George C. D., *Annals of the New York Stage*, 15 vols. (New York, 1927–41).

Oja, Carol, 'Marc Blitzstein's *The Cradle Will Rock* and Mass-Song Style of the 1930s', *Musical Quarterly*, 73/4 (1989), pp. 445–75.

Ohl, Vicki, *Fine and Dandy: The Life and Work of Kay Swift* (New Haven, 2004).

Oland, Pamela Phillips, *The Art of Writing Great Lyrics* (New York, 2001).

Paskman, Dailey, and Sigmund Spaeth, *'Gentlemen, Be Seated!': A Parade of the Old-Time Minstrels* (Garden City, New York, 1928).

Peterson, Bernard L., Jr, *A Century of Musicals in Black and White* (Westport, Connecticut, 1993).

—— *Profiles of African American Stage Performers and Theatre People, 1816–1960* (Westport, Connecticut and London, 2001).

Peyser, Joan, *Bernstein: A Biography* (New York, 1987, 1998).

—— *The Memory of All That: The Life of George Gershwin* (New York, 1993).

Plotnicki, Rita M., 'John Brougham: The Aristophanes of American Burlesque', *Journal of Popular Culture*, 12/3 (1978), pp. 422–31.

Pohly, Linda, *The Barbra Streisand Companion: A Guide to Her Vocal Style and Repertoire* (Westport, Connecticut, 2000).

Pollack, Howard, *George Gershwin: His Life and Work* (Berkeley, 2006).

Portantiere, Michael, ed., *The Theater Mania Guide to Musical Theater Recordings* (New York, 2004).

Porter, Susan L., 'English–American Interaction in American Musical Theater at the Turn of the Nineteenth Century', *American Music*, 4/1 (1986), pp. 6–19.

—— *With an Air Debonair: Musical Theatre in America, 1785–1815* (Washington, DC, 1991).

Preston, Katherine K., *Opera on the Road: Traveling Opera Troupes in the United States, 1825–1860* (Urbana, Illinois, 1993).

—— 'Art Music from 1800 to 1860', in *The Cambridge History of American Music*, ed. David Nicholls (Cambridge, 1998), pp. 186–213.

—— 'Between the Cracks: The Performance of English-Language Opera in Late 19th Century America', *American Music* 21/3 (2003).

Rao, Nancy Yunhwa, 'Songs of the Exculsion Era: New York's Chinatown's Opera Theatres in the 1920s," *American Music* 20/4 (2002), pp. 399–445.

Rice, Tim, *Oh, What a Circus* (London, 1999).

Riddle, Peter H., *The American Musical: History & Development* (Oakville, Ontario, 2003).

Riis, Thomas L., 'The Music and Musicians in Nineteenth-Century Productions of *Uncle Tom's Cabin*', *American Music*, 4/3 (1986), pp. 268–86.

——*Just Before Jazz: Black Musical Theater in New York, 1890–1915* (Washington, DC, 1989).

——*More Than Just Minstrel Shows: The Rise of Black Musical Theatre at the Turn of the Century* (New York, 1992).

——*Frank Loesser* (New Haven, 2008)

Riis, Thomas L. (ed.), *The Music and Scripts of 'In Dahomey'* (Madison, 1996).

Robbins, Tim, *'Cradle Will Rock': The Movie and the Moment* (New York, 2000).

Rodger, Gillian M. 'Male Impersonation on the American Variety and Vaudeville Stage, 1868–1930', PhD diss., University of Pittsburgh, 1998.

Rodgers, Richard, *Musical Stages: An Autobiography* (New York, 1975; repr. with an introduction by Mary Rodgers, New York, 1995).

Rogers, David A. II, 'Murder, Schtick, and Jazz: An Exploration of Realism in the Broadway Musical *Chicago*', M.M. thesis, University of Missouri–Kansas City, 1998.

Root, Deane L., *American Popular Stage Music, 1860–1880* (Ann Arbor, Michigan, 1981).

Root, Deane L., and John Graziano, 'Burlesque', in *The New Grove Dictionary of American Music*, ed. H. Wiley Hitchcock and Stanley Sadie.

Root, Deane L. (gen. ed.), *Nineteenth-Century American Musical Theater* (New York).

Vol. I. *British Opera in America: 'Children in the Wood' (1795) and 'Blue Beard' (1811)*, ed. Susan L. Porter (1994).

Vol. II. *Early Melodrama in America: 'The Voice of Nature' (1803) and 'The Aethiop' (1813)*, ed. Karl Kroeger and Victor Fell Yellin (1994).

Vol. III. *Italian Opera in English: 'Cinderella' (1831)*, ed. John Graziano (1994).

Vol. IV. *Later Melodrama in America: 'Monte Cristo' (ca. 1883)*, ed. Anne Dhu McLucas (1995).

Vol. V. *'Uncle Tom's Cabin' 1852 by George L. Aiken and George C. Howard*, ed. Thomas Riis (1994).

Vol. VI. *The Collected Works of John Hill Hewitt*, ed. N. Lee Orr and Lynn Wood Bertrand (1994).

Vol. VII. *The Collected Works of Alfred B. Sedgwick*, ed. Michael Meckna (1994).

Vol. VIII. *Pasticcio and Temperance Plays in America: 'Il Pesceballo' (1862) and 'Ten Nights in a Bar-Room' (1890)*, ed. Dale Cockrell (1994).

Vol. IX. *African American Theater: 'Out of Bondage' (1876) and 'Peculiar Sam, or The Underground Railroad' (1879)*, ed. Eileen Southern (1994).

Vol. X. *Irish American Theater: 'The Mulligan Guard Ball' (1879) and 'Reilly and the Four Hundred' (1891)*, ed. Katherine K. Preston (1994).

Vol. XI. *Yiddish Theater in America: 'David's Violin' (1897) and 'Shloyme Gorgl' (189–)*, ed. Mark Slobin (1994).

Vol. XII. *Early Operetta in America: 'The Doctor of Alcantara' (1879)*, ed. Charlotte Kaufman (1994).

Vol. XIII. *Early Burlesque in America: 'Evangeline' (1877)*, ed. Richard Jackson (1994).

Vol. XIV. *Later Operetta in America, Part I: 'El capitan' (1896)*, ed. Paul E. Bierley (1994).

Vol. XV. *Later Operetta in America, Part II: 'The Highwayman' (1897)*, ed. Orly Leah Krasner (1994).

Vol. XVI. *Grand Opera in America: 'The Scarlet Letter' (1896)*, ed. Elise K. Kirk (1994).

Rosenberg, Bernard, and Ernest Harburg, *The Broadway Musical: Collaboration in Commerce and Art* (New York, 1993).

Rosenberg, Deena, *Fascinating Rhythm: The Collaboration of George and Ira Gershwin* (New York, 1991).

Sanders, Ronald, *The Days Grow Short: The Life and Music of Kurt Weill* (New York, 1980).

Scheuer, Timothy E., 'The Beatles, The Brill Building, and the Persistence of Tin Pan Alley in the Age of Rock', *Popular Music and Society*, 20 (1996), pp. 89–102.

Schiff, David, *Gershwin: 'Rhapsody in Blue'* (Cambridge, 1997).

Schneider, Gretchen, 'Gabriel Ravel and the Martinetti Family: The Popularity of Pantomime in 1855', in *American Popular Entertainment: Papers and Proceedings of the Conference on the History of American Popular Entertainment*, ed. Myron Matlaw (Westport, Connecticut, 1979), pp. 241–58.

Schuster-Craig, John, 'Stravinsky's *Scènes de Ballet* and Billy Rose's *The Seven Lively Arts*: The Abravanel Account', in *Music in the Theater, Church, and Villa: Essays in Honor of Robert Lamar Weaver and Norma Wright Weaver*, ed. Susan Parisi (Warren, Michigan, 2000), pp. 285–90.

Secrest, Meryle, *Stephen Sondheim: A Life* (New York, 1998).

Seeley, Robert, and Rex Bunnett, *London Musical Shows on Record, 1889–1989* (Harrow, 1989).

Seller, Maxine (ed.), *Ethnic Theatre in the United States* (Westport, Connecticut, 1984).

Sennett, Ted, *Song and Dance: The Musicals of Broadway* (New York, 1998).

Shapiro, Anne Dhu, 'Melodrama', in *The New Grove Dictionary of American Music*, ed. H. Wiley Hitchcock and Stanley Sadie.

—— 'Music in American Pantomime and Melodrama, 1730–1913', *American Music*, 2/4 (1984), pp. 49–72.

Sharland, Elizabeth, *The British on Broadway: Backstage and Beyond – The Early Years* (Watchet, 1999).

Sheppard, W. Anthony, *Revealing Masks: Exotic Influences and Ritualized Performance in Modernist Musical Theatre* (Berkeley, 2001).

Shirley, Wayne, Notes to *Oh, Kay!*, Smithsonian American Musical Theater Series, RCA Special Products (1978).

Shout, John D., 'The Musical Theater of Marc Blitzstein', *American Music*, 3 (1985), pp. 413–28.

Show Music, 1981–2002.

Shubert Archive, Staff of (Maryann Chach, Reagan Fletcher, Mark Swartz and Sylvia Wang), *The Shuberts Present: 100 Years of American Theater* (New York, 2001).

Smith, Cecil, and Glenn Litton, *Musical Comedy in America* (New York, 1950, 1981).

Smith, Marian Monta, 'Six Miles to Dawn: An Analysis of the Modern American Musical Comedy', PhD diss., Cornell University, 1971.

Snelson, John, *Andrew Lloyd Webber* (New Haven, 2004).

Snyder, Linda June, 'Leonard Bernstein's Works for the Musical Theatre: How the Music Functions Dramatically', DMA thesis, University of Illinois at Urbana–Champaign, 1982.

Southern, Eileen, *The Music of Black Americans : A History*, 2nd edn (New York, 1983).

—— 'The Georgia Minstrels: The Early Years', *Inter-American Music Review*, 10/2 (1989), pp. 157–67.

Spottswood, Richard K., *Ethnic Music on Records: A Discography of Ethnic Recordings Produced in the United States, 1893 to 1942*, (Urbana, Illinois, 1990). 7 vols.

Stedman, Jane, '"Then Hey! For the Merry Greenwood!": Smith and de Koven and Robin Hood', *Journal of Popular Culture*, 12/3 (1978), pp. 432–5.

Stempel, Larry, 'The Musical Play Expands', *American Music*, 10 (1992), pp. 136–69.

Sternfeld, Jessica, *The Megamusical* (Bloomington, Indiana, 2006).

Steyn, Mark, *Broadway Babies Say Goodnight: Musicals Then and Now* (New York, 1999).

Sturman, Janet L., *Zarzuela: Spanish Operetta, American Stage* (Urbana and Chicago, 2000).

Suskin, Steven, *Berlin, Kern, Rodgers, Hart, and Hammerstein: A Complete Song Catalogue* (Jefferson, North Carolina and London, 1990).

—— *Opening Night on Broadway: A Critical Quotebook of the Golden Era of the Musical Theatre* (New York, 1990).

—— *More Opening Nights on Broadway: A Critical Quotebook of the Musical Theatre 1965 through 1981* (New York, 1997).

—— *Show Tunes: The Songs, Shows, and Careers of Broadway's Major Composers*, rev. and expanded 3rd edn (New York and Oxford, 2000).

Swain, Joseph P., *The Broadway Musical: A Critical and Musical Survey* (New York and Oxford, 1990).

Swartz, Mark Evan, *Oz Before the Rainbow* (Baltimore and London, 2000).

Swayne, Steven Robert, 'Hearing Sondheim's Voices', PhD diss., University of California, Berkeley, 1999.

—— *How Sondheim Found His Sound* (Ann Arbor, Michigan, 2005).

Swift, Mary Grace, 'Celestial Queen of the Dumb Shows', in *Musical Theatre in America: Papers and Proceedings of the Conference on the Musical Theatre in America*, ed. Glenn Loney (Westport, Connecticut, 1984), pp. 291–9.

Taymor, Julie, *The Lion King: Pride Rock on Broadway* (New York, 1997).

Thorne, Kathleen Hegarty, *The Story of Starlight Theatre: The History of Kansas City's Delightful Musical Theatre under the Stars* (Eugene, Oregon, 1993).

Thornhill, William, 'Kurt Weill's *Street Scene*', PhD diss., University of North Carolina, Chapel Hill, 1990.

Traubner, Richard, *Operetta: A Theatrical History* (Garden City, New Jersey, 1983; 2nd edn, New York, 1989).

Turk, Edward Baron, *Hollywood Diva: A Biography of Jeanette MacDonald* (Berkeley, 1998).

Valance, Tom, *The American Musical* (London, 1970).

Viagas, Robert, Baayork Lee, Thommie Walsh and the entire original cast, *On the Line: The Creation of 'A Chorus Line'* (New York, 1990; 2nd edn, Pompton Plains, New Jersey, 2006).

Walsh, Michael, *Andrew Lloyd Webber: His Life and Works, A Critical Biography* (rev. and enlarged edn, New York, 1997).

Waters, Edward N., *Victor Herbert: A Life in Music* (New York, 1955).

Webb, Paul, *Ivor Novello: A Portrait of a Star* (London, 1999).

Weill, Kurt, and Lotte Lenya, *Speak Low (When You Speak Love): The Letters of Kurt Weill and Lotte Lenya*, trans. and ed. Lys Symonette and Kim H. Kowalke (Berkeley and London, 1996).

Wilder, Alex, *American Popular Song: The Great Innovators 1900–1950* (New York and Oxford, 1972).

Wilk, Max, *OK!: The Story of 'Oklahoma!'* (New York, 1993).

—— *The Making of 'The Sound of Music'* (New York, 2006).

Wilson, Sandy, *I Could Be Happy* (London, 1975).

Woll, Allen L. *Black Musical Theatre: From 'Coontown' to 'Dreamgirls'* (Baton Rouge, Louisiana, 1989).

Wollman, Elizabeth L., *The Theater Will Rock: A History of the Rock Musical, from 'Hair' to 'Hedwig'* (Ann Arbor, Michigan, 2006).

Wood, Graham, 'The Development of Song Forms in the Broadway and Hollywood Musicals of Richard Rodgers, 1919–1943', Ph.D. diss., University of Minnesota, 2000.

—— 'Distant Cousin or Fraternal Twin? Analytical Approaches to the Film Musical', in *The Cambridge Companion to the Musical*, ed. William A. Everett and Paul R. Laird (Cambridge and New York, 2002), pp. 212–30.

Wyatt, Robert, and John Andrew Johnson, eds., *The George Gershwin Reader* (Oxford, 2004).

Yellin, Victor Fell, 'Rayner Taylor's Music for *The Aethiop*, Part I: Performance History', *American Music*, 4 (1986), pp. 249–67.

Young, William C., *Documents of American Theatre History*, vol. I. *Famous American Playhouses 1716–1899* (Chicago, 1973).

Zadan, Craig, *Sondheim and Co.* (New York, 1986, 1989).

Zellers, Parker, *Tony Pastor: Dean of the Vaudeville Stage* (Ypsilanti, Michigan, 1971).

Index

Shows, sources of shows, songs, and dances are listed by title, not under author's names. Titles in italics with no parenthetical identification are staged musicals or operas. Song titles are in single quotation marks.

'A Woman's Touch', 122
ABBA, 244, 246, 289
Abbott, Emma, 22
Abbott, George, 107, 160, 169, 173, 178, 197–8, 221–4, 226, 229, 232
Abyssinia, 96, 99
Ace of Clubs, 129, 139
Acheson, Dean, 141
Act, The, 229
Adam, Adolphe, 15
Adamini, Arturo, 48
Adams, Lee, 181–2, 236
'Adelaide', 332
Adenberg, Wolfgang, 277
Adler, Jacob P., 43
Adler, Richard, 173, 178
Adventures of Harlequin and Scaramouche, The, 4
Adventures of Priscilla, The (film), 295
Adventures of Priscilla, The (show), 295
Africaine, L', 90
After the Ball (show), 129, 132
'After the Ball', 100
Agee, James, 199
'Agony', 212
Aguglia, Mimi, 49
'Ah! Sweet Mystery of Life', 66, 87
Aida (show), 268, 273, 287, 298
Aimée, Marie, 24
Ain't Misbehavin', 287, 289
'Ain't It Romantic?', 122
Albini, Felix, 72
Alboni, Marietta, 16
Aldrich, Richard, 63
Aleichem, Sholom, 186
Alexander, Jason, 336–7
Alexander's Ragtime Band (film), 320
'Alexander's Ragtime Band', 68, 109
'All for the Best', 241
All Shook Up, 247
All That Jazz (film), 228
'All That Jazz', 333
'All the Things You Are', 149
'All Through the Night', 119
'All You Need is Love', 320
Allah Be Praised, 223
'Allah's Holiday', 74

Allegro, 156–7, 160, 169, 189, 223, 337
Allen, Frederick Lewis, 103
Allen, Peter, 288
Allyson, June, 118
Alt Heidelberg (play), 77
Altar Boyz, 299
Altman, Robert, 129
Amberg, Gustav, 45
Ambros, Wolfgang, 277
Amen Corner, 289
'America', 200, 218
'American Dream, The', 251–2
American in Paris, An (film), 309, 314
'American Women', 226–8
Amerikaner Shadkhn, 51
America's Sweetheart, 106
'Amores chicanos', 50
Amour, 281
Anderson, Carl, 257
Anderson, Maxwell, 103, 107–8, 192–3, 196–7
Andersson, Benny, 244
Andrews, Julie, 160, 176, 183, 268, 331, 336
Androcles and the Lion, 162
'Angel of Music', 263–4
'Ankunft der Grünhorner, Die', 49
Anna and the King of Siam, 159
Annie (show), 182, 299
Annie (television version), 337
Annie Get Your Gun, 110, 133–4, 139, 156, 168, 293–4, 297, 327, 330, 338
'Another Day', 369 n.5
'Another National Anthem', 218
'Another Op'nin', Another Show', 140, 172
Anouilh, Jean, 199
Anstey, F., 194
'Any Old Place with You', 109
'Anvil Chorus, The', 92
'Any Time's Kissing Time', 85
Anyone Can Whistle, 209
Anything Goes (film), 119
Anything Goes (show), 104, 107, 110–11, 118, 120, 122–3, 171, 275, 359 n.22, 359 n.23
'Anything You Can Do', 168
Applause, 182
'Aquarius', 239
Arc de Triomphe, 131–2
Archers, The, 6

Arden, Eve, 332
Ariadne Abandoned by Theseus in the Isle of Naxos, 7
Arlen, Harold, 167, 178–9, 222
Armstrong, Alun, 253
Armstrong, Louis, 103, 109, 186, 190
Arne, Thomas, 9
Arnold, Samuel, 6
Aronson, Boris, 226
Arthur, Daniel V., 57, 69
'As If We Never Said Goodbye', 263–4
'As Long As You're Mine', 347
As Thousands Cheer, 108, 111
Asche, Oscar, 84–5
Ashman, Howard, 87, 319
Askey, Arthur, 133
Aspects of Love (novel), 256–7, 266
Aspects of Love (show), 257, 266, 268, 275–6
Assassins, 196, 206–7, 211–19, 276, 329
Astaire, Fred, 113, 119–20, 171, 317, 321
Astaire, Fred and Adele, 61, 68, 221
'At a Georgia Camp Meeting', 101
At Home Abroad, 111
'At the Ball, That's All', 97
'At the Ballet', 233
'At the End of the Day', 251
Atkinson, Brooks, 171, 176, 193–4, 196–7, 199
Attaché d'ambassade, L' (play), 60
Attenborough, Richard, 257
Auber, Daniel François-Esprit, 8, 9, 14, 15, 16, 23, 250
Audran, Edmond, 24, 44
'Auf Wiedersehn', 75
Austin, Elizabeth, 9
'Auto-da-fé', 200
'Automobile Song, The', 67
Avalon, Frankie, 332
Avenue Q, 286
Avian, Bob, 231–2, 234
Ay Jalisco . . . no te rajes!, 52
Ayckbourn, Alan, 257

Babes in Arms (film), 119, 310, 369 n.5
Babes in Arms (show), 104, 107, 108, 123, 147, 314, 359 n.23, 359 n.30
Babes in Toyland, 55, 56
Babes on Broadway (film), 171
Babette, 55, 58
'Baby, Talk to Me', 181
Bach, Johann Sebastian, 228
Bacharach, Burt, 240
Baduszkowa, Danuta, 281
Bailey, Pearl, 167, 187, 297
Baker, Belle, 320
Baker, Josephine, 117
Baker, Thomas, 18
Balanchine, George, 118, 154, 221
Balfe, Michael W., 15, 23, 90

'Bali Ha'i', 158
Balkan Princess, The, 72
Ball, Michael, 253
Ball at the Savoy, 148
'Ballad of Guiteau, The', 214, 216–18
Balle, Ernest, 49
'Ballet at the Village Vortex', 199
Bamboozled (film), 311–12
Banderas, Antonio, 259, 333
Banfield, Stephen, 87, 115, 208, 214, 363 n.15
Barbarino, Stephen, 277
'Barcelona', 208
Barker, J. N., 8
Barnes, Clive, 240
Barnes, James, 90
Baron Trenck, 72
Barrie, J. M., 198
Bart, Lionel, 143, 145
Bart, Roger, 335
Bartók, Béla, 199
Bates, Kathy, 337
'Battle Hymn of the Republic, The', 79
'Baubles, Bangles, and Beads', 177
Baum, L. Frank, 351
Baxter, Joan, 336
Be Good!, 359 n.22
'Be Our Guest', 314
Beach, Amy, 97
Beach, Gary, 335
Beach Boys, 247, 288, 365 n.32
Beatlemania, 245, 288
Beatles, The, 245, 256, 284, 288, 309, 311, 320
Beaton, Cecil, 176
Beautiful Game, The, 254, 257, 267–8
Beauty and the Beast (film), 295, 309, 314
Beauty and the Beast (show), 87, 268–9, 273, 295, 298, 319, 326
'Beauty of the Nile, or Doomed by Fire, The', 91
Beauty Prize, The, 105
'Beauty School Drop Out', 314
Beck, Ernest, 279
Beethoven, Ludwig van, 23
'Before the Parade Passes By', 229
Beggar Student, The, 24
Beggar's Opera, The, 3
'Begin the Beguine', 114
Begum, The, 25
Bell, Mary Hayley, 257
Belle Hélène, La, 361–2 n.13
Belle of New York, The, 56, 63, 164
Belle Paree, La, 69
Bellini, Vincenzo, 9, 15, 16, 23
Bells Are Ringing, 179, 224, 226, 330
Bend It Like Beckham (film), 315
Benedict, Julius, 23
Bennett, Michael, 220, 230–4, 284
Bennett, Robert Russell, 121
Benthall, Michael, 230

Berger, Michael, 280
Beriat, Jean-Michel, 282
Berkeley, Busby, 221, 313–14, 321
Berlin, Irving, 27, 67–9, 107–15, 119, 133, 156, 166, 168, 170, 172–3, 178, 210, 224, 285, 294, 297, 309, 320
Bernard, Crystal, 168
Bernstein, Leonard, 122, 166, 173, 178, 190–2, 197–201, 206, 218, 223, 225, 285, 338, 348, 352, 363 n.15
Berté, Heinrich, 75, 85
Besoyan, Rick, 87
Best Little Whorehouse in Texas, The, 234, 290
'Best Things in Life Are Free, The', 118
Betsy, 106, 147, 314, 320
Bieber, Andreas, 276, 278, 280
Big (film), 296
Big (show), 296
Big Deal, 228, 292
Big River, 286, 290, 299
'Big Spender', 228
Bigley, Isobel, 140
Billion Dollar Baby, 223
Billy Elliot: The Musical (film), 296
Billy Elliot: The Musical (show), 287, 296
Birds of Paradise, 341
Bishop, Anna, 16
Bitter Sweet (film version), 83
Bitter Sweet (show), 72, 86, 129–30, 133
Bizet, Georges, 23, 149, 197, 293
Black, Don, 257
Black and Blue, 287, 289–90
Black Crook, The, 3, 18–19, 177
Black Hussar, The, 24
Black Patti's Troubadours, 93
Blackbirds, 99
'Blackville Derby, The', 92
Blaine, Vivian, 332
Blake, Eubie, 94, 99, 105, 117, 288
Blaue Engel, Der, 282
Bless the Bride, 134–6, 138–9
Blitzstein, Marc, 107–18, 190, 197
Block, Stephanie, 343
Blondell, Joan, 332
Blood Brothers, 246, 273, 276
'Bloody Mary', 158
Bloomer, Amelia ('Dolly'), 167
Bloomer Girl, 167, 222
'Blow, Gabriel Blow', 119
Blue Eyes, 106
Blue Kitten, The, 359 n.22
Blue Ridge Boys, 218
Blue Skies (film), 320
'Blue Skies', 320
Blyth, Ann, 83
Blossom Time, 74–6, 85
Blossom, Henry, 58
Blue Paradise, The, 74–5

Bobbie, Walter, 326
Bock, Jerry, 173, 180–1, 186
Bohème, La, 36, 247–8, 335
Bohemian Girl, The, 23
Boieldieu, François-Adrien, 9
Boles, John, 83
Bolger, Ray, 173, 221
Bolton, Guy, 68–70, 105–6, 109, 117, 293
Bombay Dreams, 71, 290
'Bon Voyage', 200
Bonnie and Clyde, 277, 282
'Boote in der Nacht', 278
Booth, John Wilkes, 212, 218
Booth, Junius Brutus, 9
Bordman, Gerald, 25, 69, 172, 185–6
Boris Godunov, 350
Born to Sing, 289
Borodin, Alexander, 177
Boroff, Edith, 3
Boublil, Alain, 251–4, 279, 290, 300, 319
Boulanger, Nadia, 182
Bounce, 212
'Bowery, The', 20
Bowie, David, 309, 320
Boy Friend, The, 127, 141–3
'Boy Friend Back Home, The', 122
Boy from Oz, The, 288
'Boy Like That/I Have a Love, A', 200
Boys from Syracuse, The (film), 119–20
Boys from Syracuse, The (show), 107, 123, 147, 337, 359 n.22, 359 n.23, 359 n.27
'Braavleis', 139
Bradford, Joseph, 89
Braham, Dave, 26–7
Brando, Marlon, 332
Brandy, 336
Brantley, Ben, 285, 291, 326
Braun, Carl, 49
Bravo!, El, 290
Bray, John, 8
Bray, Stephen, 289
Brayton, Lily, 84
Brecht, Bertolt, 188, 190, 192, 201
Brent, Romney, 107
Brice, Fanny, 67, 185–6
Bricusse, Leslie, 188
Bride and Prejudice (film), 315
Brigadoon (film), 331
Brigadoon (show), 166, 170–1, 175, 195, 222–3, 329, 338
Brightman, Sarah, 261–2
Bring in 'da Noise, Bring in 'da Funk, 290, 299
Brisson, Frederick, 178
Brittan, Robert, 289
'Brivele der Mamen, A', 38–9
'Brivele dem Taten, A', 38–41
Broderick, Matthew, 175, 335, 338
Brohn, William David, 350

Brook, Peter, 293
Brook, The, 19–20
Brooks, Mel, 87, 306, 335–6
Brooks, William, 5
Brougham, John, 15
Brown, Lew, 104, 106–7, 117–18
Brown, Paul Graham, 277
Bryan, Wayne, 118
Bryant, David, 253
Brynner, Yul, 329, 331
Bubblin' Brown Sugar, 287
Bubbly Black Girl Sheds Her Chameleon Skin, The, 299
Buchanan, Jack, 137
Buckley, Betty, 262
Buddy: The Buddy Holly Story, 245, 288
'Buddy Beware', 122
'Buenos Aires', 315
Buffy the Vampire Slayer, 306
'Bui Doi', 252
Burger, Seppel, 49
Burnett, Carol, 338
Burnside, Robert Hubber Thorne, 105
Burrows, Abe, 173–4, 177, 228
Burton, Richard, 183, 331
Butcher aus der Erste Avenue, Der, 45
Butler, Gerard, 334
Butler, Michael, 237, 289
'Butterfly Ballet, The', 70
By Jeeves, 257, 265
Byck, Samuel, 214, 218
Bye Bye Birdie (show), 181–2, 189, 229, 236
Bye Bye Birdie (television version), 337

Cabaret (film), 228, 284, 369 n.5
Cabaret (show), 188, 196, 229, 273, 275–6, 325–8, 333
Cabaret Girl, The, 105
Cabin in the Sky, 167
Caesar, Irving, 104–6
Caesar, Sid, 228, 332
Cage aux Folles, La (film), 296
Cage aux Folles, La (show), 275, 295–6
Cahill, Marie, 57, 69
Cahn, Sammy, 169
Cairo, 85
Caldwell, Anne, 105–6
Call Me Madam, 110, 138–41, 172–3, 224, 360 n.6
Call Me Mister, 166
Calloway, Cab, 297
Camelot (film), 331
Camelot (show), 170, 183–4, 329, 331
Campbell, Mary-Mitchell, 293
Can-Can, 176–7, 223
'Can't Help Lovin' Dat Man', 100
Candide, 182, 190, 197, 199–200, 330
Canterbury Pilgrims, The, 59

Canterbury Tales, 234
Cantor, Eddie, 67
Capitan, El, 25, 215
'Capitan, El' (march), 215–16
Capeman, The, 245–6, 290
Capote, Truman, 178
Careless Rapture, 129
Carmen, 149, 197, 293
Carmen Jones, 149, 156, 167, 205, 293
'Carnegie Hall Pavane (Do-Do-Re-Do)', 198
Carnival, 184, 229
Caroline, or Change, 291
Carousel (film), 160, 331
Carousel (show), 139, 155–8, 162, 165, 168, 172, 174, 182–3, 205, 219, 220, 222, 251, 328, 338
'Carousel Waltz, The', 156
Carr, Benjamin, 5, 6
Carreras, José, 338
'Carried Away', 198
Carrière, Jean-Claude, 293
Carter, Desmond, 105
Carter, Glenn, 257
Casey, Warren, 286, 332
Cassidy, David, 246
Cassidy, Shaun, 246
Castle, Irene, 69
Castle, Vernon and Irene, 61, 68, 221
Cat and the Fiddle, The, 104
Catherine Wheel, The, 292
Cats (show), 71, 246, 250–1, 254–5, 257–60, 273–6, 297, 328, 367 n.15
Cats (video), 255, 257, 339
Cavalcade, 132
'Cell Block Tango', 334
Cellini, Benvenuto, 194
Century Girl, The, 68
Cermak, Tony, 214
Cha, Gyung Chan, 290
Chadha, Gurinder, 315
Chadwick, George Whitfield, 25, 97
Chagall, Marc, 186
Chalía, Rosalía, 48
Chambalu, Susanne, 274
Champion, Gower, 181, 184–5, 187, 229
Channing, Carol, 169, 187–8, 199, 229, 297, 320
Channing, Stockard, 332
Charley's Aunt (play), 44, 173
Charnin, Martin, 162
Chee-Chee, 106, 147
Chenoweth, Kristin, 337–8, 342–3, 345, 350–1
Cherry Blossoms, 79
Chess, 244–5, 365 n.24
Chicago (film), 333–4, 369 n.5
Chicago (show), 196, 229, 273, 276, 284, 297, 325–8
Children in the Wood, The, 6

Children of Eden, 352
Children of the Sun, The, 98
'Children Will Listen', 212
'Chismitos de vecindad', 50
Chitty-Chitty Bang Bang (film), 295
Chitty-Chitty Bang Bang (show), 295
Chocolate Soldier, The, 50, 65, 72, 356 n.25
Chodorov, Jerome, 198
Chopin, Frédéric, 73
Chorus Line, A (film), 333
Chorus Line, A (show), 189, 196, 220–1, 228, 230–4, 273–4, 276, 281, 284, 298–9, 330
Chow Chow, or A Tale of Pekin, 90
Christians, Rudolf, 43, 45
'Christopher Street', 199
Chronicle of a Death Foretold, 292
Chu Chin Chow, 84–5, 131
Church, George, 221
Cilento, Wayne, 234
Cinderella (show), 294–5
Cinderella (television version), 160, 294, 336–7, 344
City of Angels, 276
Civil War, The, 287
'Clap Yo' Hands', 119
Clark, Dick, 245
Clark, Petula, 246
Clifton, John, 290
Clorindy, or the Origin in the Cakewalk, 21, 93–4
Close, Glenn, 162, 262, 337–8
'Close Every Door', 258
Clum, John, 114
Clurman, Harold, 192
Clutsam, G. H., 85
Cobain, Kurt, 311
'Cobbler's Song, The', 85
Cocciante, Riccardo, 280
Cochran, C. B., 135
Coco, 230
Cocoanuts, The, 104, 111, 119
Cody, Buffalo Bill, 168
Cohan, George M., 27, 55, 56, 60, 69, 70, 108, 109, 164, 174, 285, 351
Cohen, Jerry L., 298
Cole, Jack, 223, 226
Cole, Natalie, 310
Cole, Robert (Bob), 21, 94, 96–7, 99
Collette, Toni, 291
Collins, Floyd, 103
Collins, Joan, 257
Collins, Jose, 85
Collins, Phil, 269, 298, 319
Collins, Wilkie, 257, 267
Color Purple, The, 289
'Colorado Love Call', 87
Columbus, Chris, 334–5, 369 n.5
Comden, Betty, 118, 173, 179, 184, 197–9, 201, 223–4, 362 n.24

'Come Rain or Come Shine', 167
'Come to Me, Bend to Me', 331
'Come Up to My Place', 198
'Come What May', 323
Company, 189, 196, 206–9, 214, 220, 229–30, 284, 293, 329–30
Comte de Monte-Cristo, Le, 20
Concert Varieties, 223
Conesa, María, 50
'Conga!', 199
Conn, Didi, 332
Connecticut Yankee, A, 104, 106, 110, 113, 147, 221, 359 n.22
Connick, Harry, Jr., 338
Conried, Heinrich, 45
Contact, 292
Cook, Will Marion, 21, 93–4, 96, 99
'Cool', 200, 225
Cooper, James Fenimore, 8
Copland, Aaron, 103, 153, 182, 198, 222
Corner Grocer aus der Avenue A, Der, 45
Corpus Christi (play), 343
Costello, Elvis, 310
Cotrelly, Mathilde, 45
Coughlin, Bruce, 198, 286
Count of Luxembourg, The, 50, 65, 356 n.25
Courted into Court, 94
Courtneidge, Cicely, 138–40
Courtney, C. C., 240
Coward, Noël, 86, 127, 129–30, 132–3, 139, 143, 145, 175
Cradle Will Rock, The, 107–8, 123, 197
Crawford, Cheryl, 175
Crawford, Joan, 83
Crawford, Michael, 261–2
Crazy for You, 118, 288, 293–4
Creole Burlesque Co., The, 21, 91
Crest of the Wave, 129, 138
Criss-Cross, 106
Crosby, Bing, 119, 320
Crossey, J. S., 25
Crouse, Russel, 107, 138
Crow, Sheryl, 310
Crowley, Bob, 328
Cry the Beloved Country (novel), 196
Crystal, Raphael, 285
Cullen, Countee, 167
Cumming, Alan, 326–7, 337
Curtains!, 292
Curti, Carlos, 50
Czárdásfürstin, Die, 70

Daly, Tyne, 180
Damn Yankees (film), 226
Damn Yankees (show), 178, 226, 299, 330
Damsel in Distress, A, 288
Dance!, 281
'Dance at the Gym, The', 200–1, 225

Dancer in the Dark, 307, 309, 313–14
Dancin', 226–8
'Dancing Through Life', 349, 351
Dancing Years, The, 129–32
Dangerous Games, 292
Daniele, Graciela, 234, 292
Dante, Nicholas, 231
Darin, Bobby, 190
Darktown Follies, 97
'Darktown Is Out Tonight', 94
'Darktown Outing at Blackville Park', 93
Davies, Acton, 65
Davies, Harry Parr, 131, 138–9
Davis, John, 9
Davis, Luther, 177
Davis, Owen, 106
Davis, Sammy, Jr, 170, 182
Dawson, Rosario, 335
'Day by Day', 241
Day in Hollywood, A Night in the Ukraine, A, 234
Dead Man Walking, 343
Dear Miss Phoebe, 138–9
Dearest Enemy, 104–5, 115, 147
Debbie Does Dallas, 299
'Deep in My Heart, Dear', 77
De Koven, Reginald, 25, 55, 59–60, 63–4, 67, 97
Delibes, Léo, 90
De-Lovely, 310, 369 n.6
De Mille, Agnes, 153, 156–7, 167, 171, 175, 182, 194, 222–3, 226, 331
Dee, Kiki, 246
'Defying Gravity', 345, 348
Demy, Jacques, 281
'Den of Iniquity', 144
Desert Song, The (show), 72, 76–80, 85, 86, 87, 131, 148–9, 156
Desert Song, The (film versions), 82–3
'Desert Song, The', 78
DeSisto, Michael, 249
DeSylva, B. G., 104–7, 117–18
Deval, Jacques, 192
Diamond, David, 182
'Diamonds Are a Girl's Best Friend', 169, 320, 322
Dibdin, Charles, 9
Dickens, Charles, 71, 342
Dietrich, Marlene, 275–6, 282
Dietz, Howard, 166, 175
Dieu et la bayardère, Le, 14
Diller, Phyllis, 187, 297
Dillingham, C. B., 68, 70
Dion, Celine, 336
Dirty Dancing (film), 333
Dirty Rotten Scoundrels (film), 295–6
Dirty Rotten Scoundrels (show), 287, 292, 295–6, 299
'Dites-moi', 158
Dix Commandements, Les, 281

Do I Hear a Waltz?, 162, 184–5
'Do I Hear a Waltz?', 114
Do Rozario, Rebecca-Anne C., 280
'Do You Ever Dream of Vienna?', 87
'Do You Hear the People Sing?', 251–4
Do Re Mi, 184
'Do-Re-Mi', 114
Doctor of Alcantara, 25
'Doin' the Reactionary', 108
'Doin' What Comes Natur'lly', 168
Dollar Princess, The, 65, 69
Dolly Varden, 65
Don Giovanni, 15, 265
Don Quixote, 45
'Don't Ask', 122
Don't Bother Me, I Can't Cope, 289
'Don't Cry for Me, Argentina', 259
Donaldson, Walter, 117
Donizetti, Gaetano, 15, 16, 23
Donnelly, Dorothy, 77, 85
'Door of My Dreams, The', 75–6
Dors, Diana, 143
Douglass, Stephen, 178
Douwes, Pia, 276, 278
'Down with Everybody But Us', 122
Downes, Olin, 195–7, 199
Doyle, John, 292–3, 329–30
D'Oyly Carte, Richard, 24
Dr Beans from Boston, 97
Drabinsky, Garth, 297
Dracula, 277, 365 n.32
Dream, 287
'Dream Ballet' (*Oklahoma!*), 153, 165, 222, 314, 328
Dream City, 65
Dreamgirls, 234, 243, 291
Dressler, Marie, 57
Dreigroschenoper, Die, see *The Threepenny Opera*
Dreimäderlhaus, Die, 75, 85
'Drinking Song', 77, 87
Drewer, Anthony, 269
Driver, Minnie, 334
Drowsy Chaperone, The, 286, 292, 299, 301
Du bist mein Gluck, 51
DuBarry Was a Lady, 104, 107–8, 110–11, 133, 359 n.22
DuBois, W. E. B., 98
Dude, 240, 243–4
Dudley, Sherman H., 97
'Duet for One', 201
'Dulcinea', 188
Dumas, Alexandre, 20, 81
Dumbo (film), 313–14
Dumont, Margaret, 119
Dunbar, Paul Laurence, 93–4
Dunlap, William, 7–8
Dunne, Irene, 120

Durante, Jimmy, 120
Durbin, Deanna, 168
Dvořák, Antonín, 73, 282

E.T. (film), 255
'Eagle and Me, The', 167
Earl of Ruston, 240
East Wind, 81, 148
Easter Parade (film), 309
'Eastern and Western Love', 79
'Easy to Be Hard', 239
'Easy to Remember', 147
Ebb, Fred, 188, 284, 325–6
Ebert, Roger, 335
'Echoes of the Jazz Age', 103
Eddy, Nelson, 66, 83–4, 87
Edens, Roger, 119
Edward VII (king of England), 61
Edward VIII (king of England, subsequently
    Duke of Windsor), 141
Edwards, Gale, 257
Edwards, Julian, 65, 67
Edwards, Sherman, 188
Edwin and Angelina, 6
Eichberg, Julius, 23, 25
8 1/2, 234
8 Mile (film), 311, 318
Elaborate Lives, see Aida
Eliot, T. S., 257, 259
Elisabeth, 276–9
Elisir d'amore, L', 23
Elizabeth II (queen of England), 140
Elliott, Madame Celeste Keppler, 8, 14
Ellington, Duke, 103, 289
Ellis, Mary, 130, 132
Ellis, Vivian, 134–5, 139, 143, 145
Elssler, Fanny, 14
Elton, Ben, 257, 267
'Embraceable You', 113
'Emerald City Stomp, The', 349
Emney, Fred, 140
'Empty Chairs and Empty Tables', 254
Engel, Lehman, 174, 181, 189
'England Is a Lovely Place', 138
Engländer, Ludwig, 25, 27, 67
Eminem (Marshall Mathers III), 311
'Epiphany', 211
Escalona, Beatriz, 43, 50
'Escándolos en la Cámara De Diputados y en
    las calles de la Ciudad de México', 50
Eternal Road, The, 191
'Eternal Youth Is Worth a Little Suffering', 263
Eubie!, 288
Evangeline; or the Belle of Acadie, 3, 18, 19
'Every Day Is Ladies' Day with Me', 58
'Evelina', 167
Ever Green, 106
Everett, William A., 270, 273

'Everything Reminds Me of You', 99
'Everything's Alright', 242
Evita (film), 255, 257, 311, 315, 321, 333, 369
    n.12
Evita (show), 256–9, 261, 276, 311
Exception and the Rule, The, 201
Express Bongo, 136, 141, 144
Eyre, Richard, 279
Eysler, Edmund, 74–5

Fabray, Nanette, 169, 196
Face the Music, 107–8
Fall, Leo, 65, 69
Fall of a Nation, The (film), 56
Fallen Angels, 365 n.22
'Falling in Love with Love', 114, 337
Fame (film), 296, 319, 333
Fame, The Musical (show), 296
Family Guy (television show), 306
Fancy Free (ballet), 197, 223
Fanfaron, El, 52
Fantasticks, The, 182–3
'Farmer and the Cowman, The', 139
'Farmer's Daughter, The', 82
Farrar, John, 332
'Fascinating Rhythm', 109, 115
Fatinitza, 24
Fatone, Joey, 330
Faust, 18, 245
Faye, Alice, 169
Fearless Vampire Killers, The (film), 279
Fechter, Charles, 20
Fehr, Richard, 308, 313
Feigay, Paul, 197
Feld, Kenneth, 298
Fellini, Federico, 234
Femme à Papa, La, 67
Ferber, Edna, 99, 179
Fernández, José, 290
Ferrell, Will, 335–6
Ferrer, Eugenia, 48
Feuer, Cy, 173
'Few Minutes with Sissle and Blake, A', 99
Fiddler on the Roof (film), 332
Fiddler on the Roof (show), 181, 186, 220, 226,
    229, 273, 275, 281, 284, 330, 335
Fields, Dorothy, 120, 168, 293–4
Fields, Gracie, 131
Fields, Herbert, 105–7, 119, 122–3, 168, 285,
    293–4
Fields, Joseph, 198, 294
Fields, Lew, 55–9, 64, 68–9
Fields, W. C., 67
Fifty Million Frenchmen, 106, 110, 122, 171
Fine and Dandy, 106
Fings Ain't Wot They Used T'Be, 143, 145
Finian's Rainbow, 166, 171, 195, 223
Fiorello!, 174, 180–1

Firbank, Ronald, 143
Firebrand, The (play), 194
Firebrand of Florence, The, 194
Firefly, The, 66, 73–5, 79, 86
First Lady Suite, 291
First Life Guards at Brighton, The, 25
Fischoff, George, 240
Fisher, Amy, 326
Fisher, Connie, 297, 329
Fitzgerald, Ella, 190
Fitzgerald, F. Scott, 73, 103
Fitzjames, Natalie, 14
Five Guys Named Moe, 287, 290
Flamenco Puro, 290
'Flash-Bang-Wallop', 145
Fledermaus, Die, 361–2 n.13
Fletcher, Percy, 85
Fletsch, 277
'Flight of the Sylphide, The', 14
Flinn, Denny Martin, 198
Flora, or, Hob in the Wall, 4
Flora, the Red Menace, 188
Flotow, Friedrich von, 23, 90
Flower Drum Song, 160, 178, 290, 294
Floyd Collins, 285
Flying High, 106, 110–11
Flynn, Errol, 137
Foerster, Therese, 56
Follies (general reference to Ziegfeld's shows), 67–71, 97, 111, 209, 335
Follies (Sondheim's show), 87, 206, 209–11, 214, 220, 229–30, 232, 276, 329
Follies of 1907, The, 67
Follies of 1910, The, 67
Follies of 1915, The, 67
Follies of 1918, The, 70
Follies of 1919, The, 69, 70
Follow the Fleet (film), 119
Follow the Girls, 133
Follow Thru, 104, 106
Footlight Parade, 313
Footloose (film), 333
Footloose (show), 246, 295, 365 n.32
'For Good', 342–3, 347
Forbidden Broadway, 71
Fordin, Hugh, 221
Forever Tango, 290
Forrest, George, 166, 177
Fortune Teller, The, 25, 56
'Forty Minutes for Lunch', 222
42nd Street (film), 295, 309, 313
42nd Street (show), 229, 295, 301, 327
Forty-Five Minutes from Broadway, 69, 110
Fosse, 228–9
Fosse, Bob, 178, 222, 224, 226–30, 284, 292, 300, 326, 333
Foy, Eddie, Jr, 178
Fra Diavolo, 23

Frau im Hermelin, Die, 85
Frederick, Pauline, 57
Free as Air, 143
Free for All, 148
Freedman, Robert L., 336
Freeman, David, 106
Freeman, Gerald, 237
Freischütz, Der, 18
French Spy; or, the Siege of Constantina, The, 8
'French Marching Song', 79
Freud, Sigmund, 277
Freudiana, 277
Freydberg, James B., 298
Friedman, Maria, 257
'Friendship', 110
Friml, Rudolf, 66, 73–84, 104, 148, 285
Fritchie, Barbara, 79
From Dixie to Broadway, 99
Fryer, Robert, 198
Fuchs, Leo, 51
Full Monty, The (film), 296
Full Monty, The (show), 287, 296, 299, 319
Funny Face (film), 119
Funny Face (show), 104, 106, 110, 118, 234, 293, 359 n.22
Funny Girl, 185–6
'Funny Honey', 369 n.5
Funny Thing Happened on the Way to the Forum, A, 275, 329, 362 n.10
Furia, Philip, 114

'Gabey in the Playground of the Rich', 223
Gabrielle, Josefina, 328
Gaiety Girl, The, 18
Galati, Frank, 234
Gang's All Here, The, 148
Gänzl, Kurt, 271, 273, 276, 279–80
Garber, Victor, 336–8
Garbo, Greta, 177
García, Manuel, 9
Gardel, Carlos, 80, 290
Gardel: The Musical, 290
Garden, Mary, 56, 131
Garfield, James, 216
Garinei, Pietro, 281
Garland, Judy, 117, 119, 312, 335
Garland, Robert, 156
Garnet, David, 257, 266
Garrick Gaieties, The, 111, 147
Garrison, David, 351–2
Gasparone, 51
'Gaston', 87
Gaunt, Percy, 20
Gautier, Dick, 236
Gaxton, William, 110–11, 119
Gay, Noel, 127
Gay Divorce, The, 107, 118, 171, 321, 359 n.22
Gay Divorcée, The (film), 118, 321

Gay Hussars, The, 69
Gay's the Word, 136, 139–40
Gaynor, Mitzi, 119, 338
'Gee, Officer Krupke!', 206, 225
Geistinger, Marie, 43
Geld, Gary, 289
Genée, Ottilie, 42
Genée, Richard, 63
Gennaro, Peter, 226
Gensler, Louis E., 148
Gentlemen Prefer Blondes, 169–70
George White Scandals, 68–9, 111, 113
Georgy, 240
Georgy Girl (film), 240
Gere, Richard, 333
Gershe, Leon, 119
Gershwin, Ira, 101–2, 104–9, 114–16, 120, 122,
    170, 180, 193–4, 293, 309
Gershwin, George, 27, 68, 79, 101–2, 104–16,
    118–19, 121–3, 147, 165, 167, 171, 180, 210,
    285, 288, 293–4, 309
Gershwin, Lenore, 120
'Getcha Head in the Game', 319
Getchell, E. S., 89
'Getting to Know You', 159
Geva, Tamara, 221
Ghostley, Alice, 332
'Gianina Mia', 74
Gibb, Barry, 332
Gigi (film), 170, 295
Gigi (show), 295
Gigli, Beniamino, 51
Gilbert, Charles, 217
Gilbert, James, 143
Gilbert, Jean, 85
Gilbert, Ronnie, 350
Gilbert, William S. (*see also* Gilbert and
    Sullivan), 23–5, 47, 54, 55, 59, 64, 90
Gilbert and Sullivan, 23–5, 47, 54, 59, 64, 90,
    134, 193, 197, 285, 356 n.16
Gilfrey, Rodney, 86
Giovannini, Sandro, 281
Girl Called Jo, The, 139
Girl Crazy, 106, 110, 113, 118, 288, 293, 359
    n.23
Girl Friend, The, 106, 147, 359 n.22
Girl from Utah, The, 109
Girl of the Golden West, The (film), 83
'Girl That I Marry, The', 139
Giroflá, 44
Giroflé, 44
'Give Me Your Tired, Your Poor', 169
'Give My Regards to Broadway', 55
'Glad to Be Unhappy', 114
Glamorous Night, 127, 129
Glaser, Lulu, 65
Glimcher, Arne, 290
'Glitter and Be Gay', 200

Glöckner von Notre Dame, Der, 268
Glorious Days, The, 140
Glover, Savion, 290
'Go While the Goin' is Good', 58
'God's Own Country', 267
Godoy, María, 48
Godspell, 235–6, 240–3, 273, 287, 349, 352, 364
    n.15
Goethe, Johann Wolfgang von, 18, 37, 245
Goetschius, Percy, 112
Gogorza, Emilio de, 48
Gold Diggers of 1933 (film), 313, 318
Goldberg, Whoopi, 329, 336
Golden Boy, 182
Golden City, 139
'Golden Days', 77
Gondoliers, The, 293
González, David, 290
Good Morning Dearie, 105
'Good Morning Sunshine', 239
Good News! (film), 118
Good News! (show), 104, 106, 117–18, 349, 359
    n.22
Good Vibrations, 247, 288, 365 n.32
'Good-a-bye, John!', 58
'Good-bye Becky Cohen', 67
Goodbye Girl, The (film), 296
Goodbye Girl, The (show), 295–6
'Goodbye My Lady Love', 101
Goodman, Dody, 332
'Good-night, My Someone', 180
Goodwin, John Cheever, 19
Gordon, Joanne, 207, 210
'Gorgeous Alexander', 80
Göritz, Otto, 49
Gosford Park (film), 129
Gottfried, Martin, 232
Gould, Morton, 223
Goulet, Robert, 331
Gounod, Charles, 23
Governor's Son, The, 27
Grab Me a Gondola, 143
Grable, Betty, 187, 297
Graham, Harry, 85
'Grand Amazonian March', 91
Grand Hotel, 234
'Grand Imperial Cirque de Paris', 229
Grande Duchesse de Gerolstein, La, 24, 25, 89
Grant, Micki, 289
Graupner, Gottlieb, 5
Gravet, Fernand, 83
Gray, Dolores, 133
Grayson, Kathryn, 82–3
Grease (film), 284, 332–3
Grease (show), 235–6, 245, 247, 273, 276, 286,
    297–8, 314, 319, 327, 330
'Grease', 332
Grease 2 (film), 333

Great American Trailer Park Musical, The, 299
Great Gatsby, The, 73
'Great Lover Displays Himself, The', 198
Green, Adolph, 118, 173, 179, 184, 197–9, 201, 223–4
Green, Joseph, 51
Green, Paul, 107–8, 192
Green, Stanley, 185
'Green Carnations', 86
Green Grow the Lilacs, 148
Green Pastures, The, 167
'Green Violinist, The' (painting), 186
Greenwich, Ellie, 288
Greenwich Village Follies, 111
Grever, María, 50
Grey, Clifford, 81, 105–6, 117
Grey, Joel, 188, 351
Grieg, Edvard, 361–2 n.13
Griffith, Melanie, 330
Griffith, Robert E., 178, 224, 229
Grisi, Giulia, 16
Grossmith, George, Jr., 105
Gruza, Jerzy, 281
Guettel, Adam, 270, 285–6
Guevara, Che, 258
Guiraud, Ernest, 293
Guiteau, Charles, 213–14, 216–18
Guízar, Tito, 51, 52
'Gun Song', 211, 214, 218
'Guten Tag Hop-Clop, Der' ('The Hop-Clop Goes On'), 336
Gutenberg! The Musical!, 299
Guthrie, Tyrone, 199
Guys and Dolls (film), 332
Guys and Dolls (show), 139–40, 173, 175, 223, 327, 330
Gypsy (show), 110, 180, 185, 206, 225–6, 291, 330
Gypsy (television version), 337
Gypsy Baron, The, 51
'Gypsy Blues', 99

'Hail to the Chief', 211
Hair, 220, 235–43, 245, 247, 249, 273, 280, 284, 286, 298
'Hair', 239
Hairspray (film), 296
Hairspray (show), 286, 295–6, 344
Haithman, Diane, 294
Halévy, Ludovic, 293
Half a Sixpence (film), 137
Half a Sixpence (show), 145
Hall, Adelaide, 117
Hall, Carol, 290
Hall, Juanita, 167
Hall, Lee, 287
'Hallelujah', 119
Hallelujah, I'm a Bum! (film), 318

Hamlet Muzikál, 282
Hamlin, Fred, 56–7
Hamlisch, Marvin, 231, 233
Hamm, Charles, 65
Hammerstein, Arthur, 66, 73, 148
Hammerstein I, Oscar, 56, 148
Hammerstein II, Oscar (*see also* Rodgers and Hammerstein), 75, 77, 79, 87, 99–101, 104, 107–8, 114–15, 117, 120, 147–63, 165, 167, 181–2, 184–5, 195, 205, 221, 293, 358 n.15
Hammerstein, William, 148
Hampton, Christopher, 257
Haney, Carol, 224, 226
Hans Christian Andersen, 281
Hapgood, Hutchins, 36
Happy as a King, 140
'Happy Healing Day', 350
Happyland, 59
Harbach (Hauerbach), Otto, 66, 74, 75, 77, 104–7, 113, 148
Harburg, E. Y., 166–7, 171, 175, 222
Hard Day's Night, A (film), 311
Hard Job Being God, 240
Harlow, Jean, 210
Harlow, Larry, 290
Harnick, Sheldon, 363 n.22
Harrigan and Hart, 17, 26–7
Harrigan, Ned, 27
Harris, Charles K., 100
Harris, Richard, 331
Harris, Sam H., 69, 193
Harrison, Lou, 36
Harrison, Rex, 116, 176, 183, 331
Hart, Charles, 257
Hart, Lorenz (*see also* Rodgers and Hart), 83, 104–8, 114–15, 147–9, 154, 162, 166, 170, 285, 358 n.15
Hart, Moss, 107–8, 183, 192–3
Harte, Bret, 175
Harvey Girls, The (film), 315
'Hashkiveinu', 191
Hassall, Christopher, 138
Hauer, Holger, 277
Hayden, Michael, 328
Haymes, Dick, 168
Hayward, Leland, 180
Heading East, 290
Heads Up!, 106, 147, 359 n.22
Hearn, George, 351
'Heartache Serenade', 218
'Heat Is On in Saigon, The', 251
Hecht, Ben, 107
Hedwig and the Angry Inch (film), 248–9, 305, 309, 312–13
Heggie, Jake, 343
Heidi, 277
Helburn, Theresa, 148, 156, 222
Held, Anna, 66–7, 70

Helen Goes to Troy, 361–2 n.13
Hellman, Lillian, 199–200
Hello, Again, 291
Hello, Dolly!, 186–7, 220, 229, 284, 297
'Hello, Dolly!', 187
'Hello Twelve, Hello Thirteen, Hello Love',
   232–3
Hellzapoppin', 112, 192
Help! (film), 311
Hemingway, Ernest, 103
Henderson, Fletcher, 109, 167
Henderson, Ray, 104, 106, 117–18, 147
Henderson, W. J., 61–3
Heneker, David, 144–5
Henley, Don, 245
Henry, Sweet Henry, 230
Hensley, Shuler, 328
Hepburn, Audrey, 176, 331
Hepburn, Katherine, 230
Her Excellency, 138–40
Herbert, A. P., 134–5
Herbert, Victor, 25, 54, 55, 56–60, 64, 65–6,
   67, 68, 70, 73, 76, 79, 87, 109, 193, 221,
   234, 285
"Here In My Arms', 115, 359 n.19
Heredia, Wilson Jermaine, 335
Herman, Jerry, 186–8, 291
Hermanos Areu, Los, 50
'Hernando's Hideaway', 178, 226
Hérold, Ferdinand, 14
Herr der Ringe, Der, 277
Hervé, 24, 67
Herzig, Sid, 167
Heuberger, Victor, 74
Hewitt, James, 5, 6
'Hey, There, You With the Stars in Your Eyes',
   178
Hey Mr Producer! The Musical World of
   Cameron Mackintosh, 252
Heyer, Georgette, 132
Heyward, Dorothy and Dubose, 101–2, 104
Hicks, Charles B., 89
Higgensen, Vy, 289
High Button Shoes, 169, 223–4
High Jinks, 74
High School Musical (show), 295, 319
High School Musical (video), 295
High Tor, 192
'Highwayman Love', 132
Highwayman, The, 59
Hilferty, Susan, 344
Hill, J. Leubrie, 97
Hindemith, Paul, 199
'Hindi Sad Diamonds', 315
History of New York by Diedrich Knickerbocker,
   The, 192
Hit the Deck (film), 119
Hit the Deck (show), 106, 119, 359 n.22

Hitchy-Koo, 111
Hitler, Adolf, 154
HMS Pinafore, 24–5, 47
Hobart, George V., 64
Hogan, Ernest, 94, 97
Hoity-Toity, 56
Hold Everything!, 104, 106, 359 n.22
Holiday Inn (film), 311
Holliday, Judy, 179, 224
Holloway, Stanley, 176
Holly, Buddy, 245, 288
Holm, Celeste, 167
Holzman, Winnie, 340–8
'Honey Bun', 158
Honskusova, Katerina, 282
Hood, Basil, 60
Hooker, Brian, 81, 104
Hope, Anthony, 72
Hope, Bob, 120
'Hopelessly Devoted to You', 332
Hopper, De Wolf, 59
Horne, Lena, 179
Horner, Harry, 193
Horwitz, Simi, 271
'Hosanna', 258
House of Flowers, 178–9
Houston, Whitney, 336–7
'How About You', 171
'How Are Things in Glocca Morra', 171
'How I Saved Roosevelt', 214–16, 218
'How Long Has This Been Going On', 119
How Newtown Prepared, 98
How to Save the World and Find True Love in 90
   Minutes, 299
How to Success in Business Without Really Trying
   (film), 175
How to Success in Business Without Really Trying
   (show), 174–5, 228
'How Ya' Gonna Keep 'Em Down on the Farm',
   117
Howard, Joseph, 101
Hoym, Otto, 45
Hoyos, Rodolfo, 43, 50
Hoyt, Charles H., 20
Huber, Stefan, 275
Huckleberry Finn, 196
Hughes, Langston, 195
Hugo, Victor, 252, 279–80
Huguenots, Les, 250
Hummel, Franz, 277
Hunchback of Notre Dame, The (film), 287
Hunchback of Notre Dame, The (show), 268
Hwang, David Henry, 290, 294
Hyers, Anna Madah and Emma Louise, 21,
   89–90, 92
Hyers, Samuel B., 89
Hyman, Dick, 190
Hytner, Nicholas, 328

'I Am Chu Chin Chow of China', 85
'I Am Easily Assimilated', 200
'I Cain't Say No', 153
'I Can Do That', 232
'I Can Give You the Starlight', 131
I Do! I Do!, 185, 229
'I Feel Like I'm Not Out of Bed Yet', 198
'I Feel Pretty', 200, 225, 363 n.22
'I Get a Kick Out of You', 119, 122
'I Got Rhythm', 110, 113–14
'I Had Myself a True Love', 167
'I Just Can't Wait to Be King', 314
'I Know Him So Well', 245
'I Know Where I'm Going', 350
'I Leave My Heart in an English Garden', 138
'I Love Paris', 177
'I Love Thee So', 85
I Love You Because, 299
I Married an Angel (film), 83
I Married an Angel (show), 107
I Remember Mama (play), 156
I Remember Mama (musical), 162
'I Talk to the Trees', 175
'I Want to be a Producer', 314
'I Want What I Want When I Want It', 58
'I Was Never Kissed Before', 135
'I Wish I Were in Love Again', 359 n.30
'I Whistle a Happy Tune', 159
'I Won't Dance', 120
'I Worship You', 122
'Ich bin ein Berliner', 277
'Ich bin ein Werwolf', 277
'Ich gehör nur mir', 278
'I'd be Hard to Handle', 110
I'd Rather Be Right, 104, 107, 359 n.23
'I'd Rather Charleston', 109
'I'll Be Hard to Handle', 120
'I'll Build a Stairway to Paradise', 68, 113
'I'll Cover You', 248, 369 n.5
'I'll Never Be Jealous Again', 226
'I'll See You Again', 86
'I'm a Brass Band', 228
'I'm an Indian, Too', 294
'I'm Falling in Love With Someone', 66
I'm Getting My Act Together and Taking It On the Road, 243
'I'm Just Wild about Harry', 99, 117
'I'm Not That Girl', 345, 349–50
'I'm Simply Full of Jazz', 99
'I've Told Every Little Star', 149
'Idyll of Miss Sarah Brown, The', 173–4
'If Ever I Would Leave You', 183
'If I Loved You', 155–6
'If I Were a Rich Man', 186
If I Were King, 81
'If I Were on the Stage', 58
'If Love Were All', 86
'If Only He'd Looked My Way', 140

'If This Is What We're Fighting For', 267
'If You've Never Been Vamped by a Brownskin', 99
'Imagine', 359 n.30
'Impossible Dream, The', 188
'Imposters, The', 252
In Dahomey, 96, 99, 164
Inappropriate, 249
'Indian Love Call', 75–7, 87
Indian Princess, ou, La Belle Sauvage, The, 8
Indy, Vincent d', 112
Infante, Pedro, 52
Ingram, Rex, 167
'Interplay', 223
'Interrupted Trio', 80
Into the Woods, 116, 209, 212, 218, 276, 299, 329, 339, 368 n.2
Irene, 104
Iris, Esperanza, 43, 50
Irma La Douce, 234, 281
Irving, Washington, 192
Irwin, Bill, 298
Irwin, May, 57, 94
Isham, John W., 91–4
'Isn't It a Lovely Day', 317
'Isn't It a Pity?', 123
'Isn't It Romantic', 147
'It Ain't Necessarily So', 101
It Happened in Nordland, 57–9, 65
'It Might as Well Be Spring', 154–5
'It Takes a Woman', 229
'It's a Grand Night for Singing', 154
'It's a Great Occasion', 139
'It's a Scandal! It's an Outrage!', 160
'It's Got to Be Love', 114
'It's Love, My Darling, It's Love', 139
'It's Not Where You Start (It's Where You Finish)', 234
'Italian Street Song', 66
Ixion, or the Man at the Wheel, 19

Jack, Sam T., 91, 93–4
Jackson, Ethel, 61, 63
Jackson, Michael, 314, 326
Jacobs, Jim, 286, 332
Jacoby, Elliott, 198
Jacques, Christine Colby, 226–8
Jamaica, 179
James, Paul, 106
Janney, Russell, 81
'Javert's Suicide', 253
Jazz Singer, The, 308–9, 311, 320
Jeannot, Raymond, 282
Jeener, Jean-Luc, 281
Jeeves, 257
Jekyll and Hyde, 279, 287
Jerome Robbins' Broadway, 224, 226
Jersey Boys, 246–7, 288, 299

Jesus Christ Superstar (film), 255, 257
Jesus Christ Superstar (show), 235–6, 241–3,
    255–9, 280–1, 284, 330
Jesus Christ Superstar (video), 255, 257, 339
'Jesus Christ Superstar', 258
Jesusita en Chihuahua, 52
'Jet Song', 200
Jewison, Norman, 332
JFK, 277, 282
Jiranek, Josef, 73
Joan of Arc, 271
Joel, Billy, 246, 289
John, Elton, 268, 286–7, 298, 309, 314, 319–20
John, Graham, 106
Johnny Johnson, 107–8, 123, 192–3, 359 n.23
'Johnny One-Note', 359 n.30
'Johnny's Song', 192
Johnson, Bill, 133
Johnson, Billy, 94
Johnson, Catherine, 289
Johnson, J. Rosamond, 96–7, 99
Johnson, James Weldon, 96–7
Jolson, Al, 69, 74, 109, 320–1
Jones, Charlotte, 257
Jones, Shirley, 162
Jones, Sissieretta, 93
Jones, Tom, 183, 185
Joplin, Scott, 94
Jordan, Louis, 287, 290
Joseph and the Amazing Technicolor Dreamcoat
    (show), 256–8, 276
Joseph and the Amazing Technicolor Dreamcoat
    (video), 255, 257, 339
Joyful Noise, A, 230
Jubilee, 104, 107
Juch, Emma, 22
'Judas' Death', 242
Jumbo (film), 120
Jumbo (show), 104, 107, 113, 147, 173
'Just in Time', 179

Kahn, Gus, 83, 106
Kaiser, George, 192
Kalich, Bertha, 43, 48
Kálmán, Emmerich, 69, 70
Kalmar, Bert, 106
Kander, John, 188, 284, 325–6
Kanin, Garson, 184
'Kansas City', 153, 315
Kantor, Michael, 296
Kaplan, Joel, 28
Katinka, 74
Kaufman, George S., 106–8, 119, 193–4
Kay, Hershy, 198
Kaye, Danny, 320
Kaye, Stubby, 140, 332
Kean, Edmund, 9
Keel, Howard, 83

Keene, Laura, 14, 18
'Keep the Home Fires Burning', 128
Keith, B. F., 26
Kellogg, Clara Louise, 22
Kelly, Gene, 307, 321, 331
Kemble, Charles, 9
Kennedy, Jacqueline, 183
Kennedy, John F., 183, 214, 284
Kennedy, Robert F., 284
Kerker, Gustave, 56, 63, 67
Kern, Jerome, 55, 67, 68–70, 99–101, 104–9,
    112–13, 115–17, 120, 128, 148, 154, 171, 285
Kerr, Walter, 230, 243–4
Kersands, Billy, 90
Kert, Larry, 225
Kessler, David, 42, 48
Kidd, Michael, 223, 332
'Kiddush', 191
'Kids', 181
Kilenyi, Edward, 113
King and I, The, 139–40, 159, 162, 174–6, 178,
    224, 329, 351
'King Herod's Song', 242, 258
'King of Broadway, The', 336
'King of Cannibal Islands, The', 15
King's Rhapsody, 135–7, 139
King, Billy, 101
King, Carlotta, 83
King, Carol, 286
King, Dennis, 83
King, Martin Luther, Jr, 284
King, Wallace, 90
Kirkwood, James, 231
Kismet, 139, 177
'Kiss Me Again', 58
Kiss Me, Kate, 139, 166, 171–2, 273–4, 291, 339
Kiss of the Spiderwoman, 276
Kitt, Eartha, 291
Klaw and Erlanger, 67, 70
Kleban, Edward, 231, 233
Klein Deutschland, 45–6
Kline, Kevin, 310
Knickerbocker Holiday, 107–8, 123, 193, 359
    n.23
Knoblock, Edward, 177
Knop, Patricia, 257
Ko, Leon, 290
Kobler, Arthur, 141
Kollo, Walter, 74
Korbich, Eddie, 328
Kosel, Mathias Christian, 277
Krall, Diana, 310
Krasker, Tommy, 120–3
Krehbiel, Henry E., 63
Krueger, Miles, 321
Kudisch, Marc, 337
Kuhn, Judy, 253
Kuni-Lemi, 285

Kunze, Michael, 276, 278–9
Kutschera, Rolf, 274

Lacamoire, Alex, 350
'Là ci darem la mano', 15
La! La! Lucille, 109
LaChiusa, Michael John, 285, 291
Ladd, Cheryl, 168
Lady Be Good (film), 115
Lady, Be Good! (show), 105, 109, 123
Lady in the Dark, 193–4, 200, 210
'Lady Is a Tramp, The', 359 n.30
Lady of the Rose, The, 85
Lady of the Slipper, The, 221, 234
Lagaan: Once Upon a Time in India (film), 315
La Guardia, Fiorello, 180
Lahr, Bert, 110–11
Lakmé, 90
Lamas, Fernando, 83
'The Lambeth Walk', 130
Lamla, Norbert, 276
Landau, Tina, 285–6
'Ländler', 162
Landon, Margaret, 159
Lane, Burton, 166, 171, 188
Lane, Jeffrey, 287
Lane, Lupino, 130, 136
Lane, Nathan, 329, 335
Lanfang, Mei, 36
Langner, Lawrence, 148, 156, 222
Lansbury, Angela, 180, 187–8, 209
Lanza, Mario, 83
Largely New York, 298
Lark, The, 199
Larson, Jonathan, 247–8, 334–5
Last Days (film), 311
Last Sweet Days of Isaac, The, 240, 243
'Last Time I Saw Paris, The', 115
LaTouche, John, 199
Laurents, Arthur, 162, 180, 200, 224–5, 337, 363 n.15
'Laurie Makes Up Her Mind', see 'Dream Ballet' (Oklahoma!)
Lawford, Peter, 118
Lawrence of Arabia, 78
Lawrence, Carol, 225
Lawrence, Gertrude, 121–2, 159, 193, 329
Lawrence, Vincent, 106
Leader of the Pack, 288
'Leaning on a Lamppost', 130
Leave It to Me!, 107–8, 110
Lecocq, Alexandre Charles, 23, 24, 44, 63
Ledecky, Janek, 282
Lederer, Charles, 177
Lee, Baayork, 231–2, 234
Lee, Eugene, 344
Lee, Gypsy Rose, 180
Lee, Robert, 290

Lee, Spike, 311–12
Lee, W. H., 89
Legally Blonde (film), 296
Legally Blonde (show), 296
Légende de Jimmy, Le, 276, 280, 282
Legrand, Michel, 281
Lehár, Franz, 50, 60–6, 72, 74, 109, 130–1, 356 n.25
Leigh, Mitch, 188
Leiber, Jerry, 245, 287
Leigh, Rowland, 107
Lemper, Ute, 275–6, 282
Lennon, 247
Lenya, Lotte, 190–1, 201
León, Victor, 60
Leoncavallo, Ruggero, 23
Leonhardt, Robert, 49
Leonowens, Anna, 159
Lerdo de Tejada, Miguel, 50
Lerner, Alan Jay (see also Lerner and Loewe), 166, 170, 175, 183–4, 188, 195–6, 201
Lerner and Loewe, 144, 166, 170–1, 175, 183–4, 222–3, 331
Leroux, Gaston, 257, 260
Leslie, Lew, 99
Lessing, Gotthold Ephraim, 37
Lestat, 287
Let 'Em Eat Cake, 107–8, 110, 359 n.23
'Let the Sunshine In', 239
'Let's Begin', 120
'Let's Do It', 114
Let's Face It, 133
'Let's Step Out', 122
Levay, Sylvester, 278
Levene, Sam, 140
Levy, Benn, 106
Levy, Ethel, 55
Lewis, Hallam, 4, 5
Lewis, Sinclair, 103
Li'l Abner, 223
Lido Lady, 106
Lieutenant, The, 242–3
Life and Adventures of Nicholas Nickleby, The (play), 342
'Life is Happiness Indeed', 200
'Life Support', 248
'Light at the End of the Tunnel', 259
Light in the Piazza, The, 286
'Light My Candle', 334, 369 n.5
'Light of the World', 241
'Like a Virgin', 320
Lilac Time, 85
Liliom (play), 155
Lindbergh, Charles, 103–4
Lindsay, Howard, 107, 138
Link, Peter, 239–40
Linley, Thomas, 9
Lion King, The (film), 295, 309, 314

Lion King, The (show), 268, 273, 287, 295, 298, 319, 326, 336
Lisbon Story, The, 131
Liszt, Franz, 73
Little Duchess, The, 67
'Little Jazz Bird', 109
Little Johnny Jones, 3, 27, 55, 57, 59, 69, 164
Little Mary Sunshine, 87
Little Me, 228
Little Mermaid, The (film), 319
Little Millionaire, The, 69
Little Night Music, A, 211, 220, 229, 285, 296
'Little Priest, A', 211
Little Shop of Horrors (film), 296
Little Shop of Horrors (show), 276, 295–6
'Little Things', 208
Little Tycoon, The, 25
Littlewood, Joan, 143
Llera, Felipe, 50
Lloyd Webber, Andrew, 127, 145, 229, 242, 246, 250, 254–69, 273, 280, 284, 297, 329, 333
Lloyd Webber, William S., 256
Locke, Alain, 98
Loesser, Frank, 166, 169, 173–4, 178, 182, 297, 332
Loewe, Frederick (*see also* Lerner and Loewe), 166, 170–1, 175, 178, 183–4
Logan, Joshua, 141, 157–8, 331
Lohengrin, 65
'Lonely Room', 151, 153, 160, 205, 328
'Lonely Town', 198
'Lonely Town: Pas de Deux', 198
Loney, Glenn, 274
Longfellow, Henry Wadsworth, 19
Lonsdale, Frederick, 85
Look, Ma, I'm Dancin'!, 223–4
Look Back in Anger (play), 143
'Look For the Silver Lining', 70, 117
'Look to the Rainbow', 171
Lord of the Rings, The (novel), 277
Lorelei, 169
'Lorelei', 131
'Losing My Mind', 210
Lost in the Stars, 196–7
'Lot of Livin' to Do, A', 181
Love Call, The, 79
'Love is Like a Firefly', 74
'Love is My Reason', 132
Love Laughs –, 127
Love Life, 195–6, 201
Love Me Tender (film), 311
Love Me Tonight (film), 318
'Love Me Tonight', 81
'Love Will Find a Way', 85, 99
Love's Fire, 286
'Lovely to Look At', 120
'Lover, Come Back to Me', 80, 82–3
'Lowdown Blues', 99

Luana, 81
Lube, Max, 43
Luca, John, 90
Lucas, Sam, 91, 94
Luchow, August, 43
Luders, Gustav, 54
Ludwig II: Longing for Paradise, 277
Ludwig, Ken, 288, 293
Luker, Rebecca, 329
'Lumberjack Song, The', 87
LuPone, Patti, 253, 259, 261
Lyle, Willie, 90
Lyles, Aubrey, 98, 101, 105, 111
Lynde, Paul, 181

McArdle, Andrea, 337
MacArthur, Charles, 107
McCarthy, Justin, 81
McCarthy, Joseph P., 199
McCauley, Jack, 169
McCracken, Joan, 167, 223
MacDermot, Galt, 237–40, 286
McDonald, Audra, 328, 337
MacDonald, Jeanette, 66, 83–4
MacDonough, Glen, 56
McEntire, Reba, 168, 294, 330
McGlinn, John, 120–2, 338
McGowan, John, 106
McGuire, William Anthony, 81, 106
McHugh, Jimmy, 120
McKayle, Donald, 182
McKechnie, Donna, 230, 232–3
McKenney, Ruth, 198
Mackintosh, Cameron, 250–1, 253, 259, 265, 268, 279–80, 298
MacLaine, Shirley, 178
McNally, Terrence, 287, 343
McPherson, Aimée Semple, 104
MacRae, Gordon, 82–3
Macready, William Charles, 9
'Ma Belle', 81
Mack and Mabel, 291, 293
'Mack Sennett Ballet', 224
'Mack the Knife', 190
Madama, Mark, 118
Madame Butterfly, 254
'Madame Toussante L'Ovature's Reception', 92–3
Madeleine, 56
Madonna, 259, 309, 320, 333
Maeder, James G., 15
Magic Knight, The, 65
Magic Show, The, 287
Maguire, Gregory, 340–2
Maid of the Mountains, The, 84–5, 131
Main Street to Broadway (film), 337
'Make Believe', 100
'Make 'Em Laugh', 307

'Make Someone Happy', 184
'Make Your Garden Grow', 200
Makers of Melody (film), 359 n.19
'Making Good', 345, 349
Malibran, María, 9
Maltby, Richard, Jr, 229, 257, 282
Mama, I Want to Sing, 289
Mama, I Want to Sing II, 289
Mambo Kings, The, 290
Mame, 187–8, 330
Mamma Mia!, 71, 246–7, 273, 289
Mam'zelle Nitouche, 67
Mamoulian, Rouben, 156, 167, 222
'Man I Love, The', 113
Man of La Mancha, 188, 220, 299
Mandel, Frank, 77, 79, 105–6
Mandelbaum, Ken, 230
'Manhattan', 111, 147
Mann, P. J., 227
Mann, Terrence, 253
Manning, Irene, 82–3
Mantello, Joe, 234, 343–5, 349–51
Marbury, Elisabeth, 70
March, Joseph Moncure, 291
'March of the Musketeers', 81
'March of the Siamese Children', 159
Marconi, Saverio, 281
Maretzek, Max, 16, 25
Margaret Rose, Princess, 141, 144
'Maria', 200–1, 225
'Maria Cha Cha', 201, 225
Marie Christine, 285, 291
Maria Maria, 290
'Marianne', 80
Mario, Giovanni Matteo, 16
Marion, Dave, 93
Marion, George, Jr., 107
Marlowe, 365 n.22
Marriage of Figaro, The, 23, 265
Marry Me a Little, 288
Mars Attacks! (film), 87
Marshall, Rob, 326, 333, 337
Martha, 23
Martin, Ernest, 173
Martin, Hugh, 209
Martin, Jesse L., 335
Martin, Mary, 132, 158, 169, 185, 194, 337–8
Martin Guerre, 251–2, 254
Marvenga, Ilse, 78, 86
Marx Brothers, 111, 119, 194
Mary Poppins (film), 268–9, 295
Mary Poppins (show), 268–9, 295, 298
Mascagni, Pietro, 23
Mascotte, La, 44
Maslon, Lawrence, 296
Mast, Gerald, 308–9, 312, 330–1
Matchmaker, The, 186
'Matchmaker, Matchmaker', 186

'Material Girl', 320
Mates, Julian, 5
'Matter of Minutes, A', 140
Maurier, Daphne du, 132
May Wine, 81, 148
Mayer, David, 20, 28
Mayer, Edwin Justus, 194
Mayer, Timothy S., 293
Mayerl, Billy, 127, 130
'Mayor of Dixie, The', 98
Maytime (film), 83
Maytime (show), 74–5, 86
'Me', 144
Me and My Girl, 127, 130–1, 136
Me and Juliet, 160, 189
Medford, Kay, 181
Meehan, Thomas, 335
Meet Me in St. Louis (film), 295, 309, 315
Meet Me in St. Louis (show), 295
Meilhac, Henri, 60, 293
Meilziner, Jo, 160
Me ha de comer esa tuna, 52
'Memory', 145, 259
Mendes, Sam, 326
Mendoza, Lydia, 43
Menken, Alan, 87, 319, 348
Menzel, Idina, 344–5, 349–50, 352
Menzies, Archie, 138
Mercadante, Saverio, 15
Mercer, Johnny, 167, 287
Merlino, Gene, 331
Merman, Ethel, 110–11, 119, 122, 133, 168–9,
    171–2, 180, 187, 224, 226, 297, 320, 330
Merrick, David, 180, 185, 296–7
Merrill, Bob, 173, 184–5
Merrill, Robert, 338
Merrily We Roll Along, 212, 275, 291
Merry War, The, 24
Merry Widow, The, 60–6, 68, 71, 72, 109,
    130–1, 261, 355 n.8
Merry Widow and the Devil, The, 64
Merry Widow Remarried, The, 355 n.8
Messel, Oliver, 179
Mesta, Perle, 172
Meyer-Foerster, Wilhelm, 77
Meyerbeer, Giacomo, 23, 90, 250
'Mi compadre en Santa Anita', 50
'Michael Jordan's Ball', 319
Michener, James, 157
Middleton, Ray, 196
Midler, Bette, 337
Migliaccio, Eduardo ('Farfariello'), 48–9
Mikado, The, 24–5, 47, 90
Milk and Honey, 186
'Milkmaid's Flirtations, The', 92
Miller, Ann, 321
Miller, Buzz, 226
Miller, Flournoy, 98, 101, 105, 111

Miller, Marilyn, 70, 79, 110, 117, 221
Miller, Roger, 286, 290
Millöcker, Karl, 24, 51, 63
Mills, Florence, 117
Mills, Kerry, 101
Minnelli, Liza, 117, 188
Minnelli, Vincente, 331
Minstrel, Der, 45
Misérables, Les (novel), 252, 279
Misérables, Les (show), 249–55, 269, 273–5,
    279–81, 319, 326, 328, 330, 366 n.40
Misérables, Les (video), 339
'Misery', 100
Miss Liberty, 168
Miss 1917, 68
Miss Saigon, 250–2, 254–5, 269, 273, 279, 282,
    290, 367 n.13
'Miss Turnstiles', 223
Mr Wonderful, 170
Mitchell, Julian, 56, 67
Mitchell, William, 15
Mitropoulos, Dimitri, 201
Mlle Modiste, 58
'Mob Song, The', 87
Mojica, José, 51, 52
'Molly Dolly', 48
Molnár, Ferenc, 155
Mongkut (king of Siam), 159
Monk, Debra, 338
Monroe, Marilyn, 309, 320
Montalban, Paolo, 336
Montanaro, Anna, 276
Monte Cristo, 20
Monty Python and the Holy Grail (film), 296
'Moon Is on the Sea, The', 122
Moore, Grace, 82–3
Moore, Victor, 110–11, 119
Moral, Jorge del, 50
Mordden, Ethan, 221, 338
Moreno, Rita, 84
Morgan, Dennis, 82–3
Morgan, Merlin, 85
Morissette, Alanis, 310
Morley, Sheridan, 283
Most Happy Fella, The, 174
Mostel, Zero, 186, 335
Moulin Rouge! (film), 307, 309, 315, 320–3
'Mountain Greenery', 114
Mountaineers, The, 6
'Mounties, The', 75–6, 81, 87
Movin' Out, 246, 289, 292
Mozart, Wolfgang Amadeus, 9, 15, 23, 116,
    265, 275
'Mr Cellophane', 333
Mr Jinks, 89
'Mu Cha Cha', 226
Much Ado About Nothing, 281
Muette de Portici, La, 250

Mulligan Guard, The, 26–7
Mumford, Meg, 274
Munsel, Patrice, 338
Murphy, Donna, 329
Murphy, Sally, 328
'Music and the Mirror, The', 233
Music Box Revues, 69, 111
Music in the Air, 148–9
'Music of the Night', 145, 263–4
Music Man, The (show), 116, 180
Music Man, The (television version), 338
Musical of Musicals: The Musical, The, 292
Musorgsky, Modest, 350
'My Cousin in Milwaukee', 123
'My Dearest Dear', 131
'My Dreams', 81
My Fair Lady (film), 284, 331
My Fair Lady (show), 116, 144, 170, 175–6,
    183–4, 251, 273, 329
My Favorite Year (film), 296
My Favorite Year (show), 296
'My Funny Valentine', 359 n.30
'My Heart Belongs to You', 131
'My Heart Stood Still', 113–15
'My Heart Will Go On', 336
'My Man's Gone Now', 101–2
My Maryland, 76–7, 79
My One and Only, 118, 234, 288, 293–4
My Princess, 79
'My Romance', 113
'My Ship', 193
My Sister Eileen, 198
My So-Called Life (television show), 340
'My Sword and I', 81
Mystery of Edwin Drood, The, 298–9

Nash, N. Richard, 185
Nash, Ogden, 194, 222
Natoma, 56, 76
'Nature Boy', 320
Naughton, James, 326
'Naughty, Naughty Nancy', 87
Naughty Marietta (film), 83
Naughty Marietta (show), 66, 73, 79, 87, 109
Naylor, Wesley, 289
Neagle, Anna, 83, 137, 140
Neeley, Ted, 257
Negrete, Jorge, 52
Nelson, Baby Face, 104
Nero, Franco, 331
Neuendorff, Adolf, 45–6
Neuwirth, Bebe, 326
New Girl in Town, 226
New Moon (film), 82–3
New Moon, The (film), 83
New Moon, The (show), 72, 76–7, 79–80, 86,
    87, 148–9, 156
'New York, New York', 198

New York bei Nacht, 45
New York in Wort und Bild, 45
New Yorkers, The, 106
New Yorker Brauer und seine Familie, Der, 45
Newley, Anthony, 188
Newman, Randy, 245
News, The, 365 n.22
Newton-John, Olivia, 332
'Nice Work If You Can Get It', 114
Nicholas, Harold and Fayard, 167
'Nicolina', 49
Nielsen, Alice, 56
Night and Day (film), 369 n.6
'Night and Day', 114, 118, 310, 321
Night Boat, The, 105
The Night is Young, 149
Nina Rosa, 81
Nine, 234
Ninety in the Shade, 69
Niniche, 67
Ninotchka, 177
Nixon, Marni, 331
'No Coon Can Come Too Black for Me', 21
'No Good Deed', 352
'No One is Alone', 212
'No One Mourns the Wicked', 350
No Song, No Supper, 6
No Strings, 162, 184, 337, 358 n.15
'No Strings', 317
No, No, Nanette, 104–5, 118, 123, 359 n.22
'Nobody', 96
Noll, Christiane, 86
Norman, Marsha, 289
Norman, Monty, 144
Norton, Frederic, 84–5
'Nothing', 233
Notre-Dame de Paris, 280–2
Novarro, Ramón, 51
Novello, Ivor, 127–32, 135–40, 143, 145
Nozze di Figaro, Le, see *Marriage of Figaro, The*
*NSYNC, 319, 330
Nunn, Trevor, 328
'NYC', 337
Nymph Errant, 107

Oakley, Annie, 168
O'Connor, Donald, 119
O'Donnell, Rosie, 330
O'Horgan, Tom, 237–8, 245, 258, 280
O'Neill, Eugene, 103
Ockrent, Mike, 288
Octoroons, 21, 91–2
Odets, Clifford, 182
Of Thee I Sing, 104, 107–8, 110–11, 174, 180, 220, 359 n.23
Offenbach, Jacques, 16, 23–5, 44, 54, 63, 89, 275, 309, 361–2 n.13
Oh, Boy!, 70

Oh! Calcutta!, 240, 325
Oh, Kay!, 104, 106, 110, 119, 121–3, 359 n.22
'Oh, How I Hate to Get Up in he Morning', 69
'Oh, I Got Plenty O' Nuttin'', 101
'Oh, What a Beautiful Mornin'', 151–3
Oklahoma! (film), 160, 315, 328
Oklahoma! (show), 87, 116–17, 133–4, 137, 139, 149–58, 162, 164–8, 171–2, 177, 179, 181–2, 185, 194, 197, 205, 222, 314, 328, 331, 338–9, 368 n.1, 368 n.2
'Oklahoma!', 139, 143, 154
'Ol' Man River', 99, 321
'Old Black Joe and Uncle Tom', 99
Old Chelsea, 131
'Old Devil Moon', 171
Old Possum's Book of Practical Cats, 257, 259
Oliver! (film), 137
Oliver! (show), 143, 145, 251
On a Clear Day You Can See Forever, 188
'On Emancipation Day', 96
'On the Atchison, Topeka and the Santa Fe', 315
On the Town, 166, 197–8, 223
On Your Toes, 104, 107, 118, 123, 147, 165, 221, 359 n.22
'Once a Year Day', 226
Once and Future King, The (novel), 183
Once Upon a Mattress (show), 286
Once Upon a Mattress (television version), 338
'One', 232–3
'One Alone', 78–9
'One Day More', 251–2, 254
'One Flower Grows Alone in Your Garden', 79
'One Foot, Other Foot', 337
'One Hand, One Heart', 200
'One Hundred Easy Ways', 199
'One Kiss', 80, 81, 82
'One More Kiss', 87
'One Night in Bangkok', 244–5
'One Short Day', 349, 351
'One Song Glory', 335, 369 n.5
110 in the Shade, 185
One Touch of Venus, 194, 198, 222
'Only a Rose', 81
'Oom Pah Pah', 145
Operette, 129
Oremus, Stephen, 350
Oreste, 83–4
Oriental America, 92
Osato, Sono, 198, 223
Osborne, John, 143
Osmond, Donny, 257
Osterwald, Bibi, 297
Ostrow, Stuart, 300
Oswald, Lee Harvey, 218
Our Town (play), 223
Out of Bondage, 89–90
'Out Tonight', 248, 369 n.5
Oysher, Moishe, 51

Pabst, Frederick, 42
Pacific 1860, 129, 132–3
Pacific Overtures, 213, 329
Paige, Ellen, 259
Paige, Janet, 178
Paine, John Knowles, 63
Paint Your Wagon, 140, 170, 175
Pajama Game, The (film), 226, 330
Pajama Game, The (show), 178, 224, 226
Pal Joey, 139, 144, 147–8, 160, 170, 181, 189, 205, 330
Panama Hattie, 133, 171
'Papa, Won't You Dance with Me', 169
Papa's Wife, 56, 67
Papp, Joseph, 231, 237–8, 240, 243, 298–9
Parapluies de Cherbourg, Les, 281–2
Pardon My English, 107, 123
Parepa-Rosa, Euphrosyne, 22
Paris, 106
Parker, Dorothy, 199
Parodi, Teresa, 16
Partch, Harry, 36
'Party's Over, The', 179
Pascal, Adam, 335
Pascal, Gabriel, 175
Passe-Muraille, Le, 281
Passing Show, The, 27, 68–9, 74
Passion (show), 116, 212, 219, 285–6, 296, 299, 339, 368 n.2
Passione d'Amore (film), 296
Pastor, Tony, 26
Pastorela, La, 37
Pastores, Los, 37
Patinkin, Mandy, 291
Paton, Alan, 196
Pawnbroker von der Eastside, Der, 45
Pawnbroker von Harlem, Der, 45
Peacock, Michon, 231
Peggy-Ann, 106, 147, 359 n.22
Pelissier, Victor, 5, 6, 7
Penner, Joe, 120
Pennington, Ann, 68, 221
'People', 185
'People Will Say We're in Love', 139, 152–3
Perchance to Dream, 132
Perelman, S. J., 194, 222
Perón, Eva, 258–9
Perón, Juan, 258
Pet of the Petticoats, The, 18
Peter Ibbetson, 102
Peter Pan (play), 198
Peter Pan (show), 179, 276
Peters, Bernadette, 168, 293–4, 330, 336–7
Peterson, Hjalmar, 49
Petrified Prince, The, 291
Phantom of the Opera, The (film), 255, 257, 334
Phantom of the Opera, The (novel), 256–7, 260

Phantom of the Opera, The (show), 71, 250–1, 254–8, 260–5, 267, 269, 273–6, 279–80, 297, 326
'Pharaoh's Song, The', 258
Philipp, Adolf, 42, 43, 44, 45–6
Phillips, Lou Diamond, 329
Phipps, Alison, 274
'Phrenologist Coon, The', 95
Piaf, Edith, 276
Piazzolla, Astor, 323
Picasso, Pablo, 282
'Pick-Pocket Tango', 228
'Pickaninny Shoes', 99
Picon, Molly, 43, 48, 51
Pins and Needles, 108, 112, 192
Pinza, Ezio, 158
Pipe Dream, 160
Pippin, 228, 287, 300, 340, 352
Pirate, The (film), 314
'Pirate Jenny', 190–1
Pirate Queen, The, 300
Pirates of Penzance, The, 23–4, 47, 298
Plamondon, Luc, 280
Planquette, Robert, 23, 24
Platinum, 365 n.22
Platt, Marc, 340–1, 343–4, 347, 349
'Please Don't Make Me Be Good', 122
Please Teacher!, 127
Po-ca-hon-tas; or, the Gentle Savage, 15
Pocahontas (film), 287, 319
Polanski, Roman, 279
Pollard, Michael, 181
'Polovtsian Dances', 177
Poor Little Ritz Girl, 109–10, 147
Poor Soldier, The, 6
'Pore Jud Is Daid', 151–2
'Popular', 343
Porgy (novel and play), 101
Porgy and Bess (opera), 101–2, 104, 113, 123, 165, 167, 192, 194, 205, 352
Porter, Cole, 27, 104–9, 111–12, 114–16, 118–19, 133, 166, 171–2, 175–8, 210, 310, 321, 328, 369 n.6
Porter, Susan, 6
Posford, George, 139
Posner, Kenneth, 344
Post, W. H., 81
Powell, Eleanor, 321
Powell, Nicolas, 280–1
'Practically Perfect', 269
'Praise the Lord and Pass the Ammunition', 173
Prawy, Marcel, 273
Prece, Paul, 270, 273
'Prepare Ye (The Way of the Lord)', 241
Present Arms, 106, 147
Presley, Elvis, 181, 236, 247, 256–7, 311
'Press Conference', 244
Preston, Robert, 116, 185

'Prettiest Girl in Town, The', 139
'Pretty Girl is Like a Melody, A', 69
Primrose (Gershwin show), 105
'Primrose' (Novello song), 131
Prince, Faith, 179
Prince, Harold (Hal), 178, 186, 200, 209, 220, 222, 224, 229–30, 232, 326
Prince Igor, 177
Prince of Egypt, The, 287
Prince of Pilsen, The, 54
'Princess Zenobia', 221
Prinz Waldmeister, 45
Prisoner of Zenda, The, 72
Pritchett, John, 139
Producers, The (film), 296, 335–6, 369 n.5
Producers, The (show), 291, 296, 300, 314, 335
Prokofiev, Sergei, 256
'Prologue' (*West Side Story*), 200, 225
'Prologue (The Carousel Waltz)', 155–6
Promenade, 235
Promises, Promises, 230, 232, 240
Pryce, Jonathan, 254
Puccini, Giacomo, 23, 36, 155, 247–8, 254, 256, 335
Purcell, Harold, 138
Purdom, Edward, 83
Purlie, 289
'Put On a Happy Face', 181
Putting It Together, 288
'Puzzlement, A', 174
Pygmalion, 175

Queen of the Desert (film), 295–6
Queen of the Desert (show), 295–6
'Queen of Terre Haute, The', 122
Queen's Lace Handkerchief, The, 24
Quilters, 290

Rachmaninov, Sergei, 347
Rado, James, 237, 247
Ragni, Gerome, 237, 247
Ragtime, 234, 286
Rahman, A. R., 290
Rainbow, 154
Rainmaker, The (play), 185
Raisin, 289
Raitt, Bonnie, 245
Raitt, John, 178
Rank, Bernhard, 43
Rattenfänger von Hameln, Die, 45
Ravel, Gabriel, 13–14, 18
Ray (film), 311
Raye, Martha, 120, 187, 297
'Razzle Dazzle', 334
Really Rosie, 286
Red, Hot and Blue!, 104, 107, 110, 359 n.23
Red Feather, The, 55
Red Mill, The, 58–9

Red Moon, The, 96–7
Red Petticoat, The, 109
Redgrave, Vanessa, 331
Redhead, 228
Reefer Madness: The Movie Musical, 369 n.15
Reggae, 289
Reinagle, Alexander, 5, 6
Reinhardt, Max, 276
Reinking, Ann, 181, 227, 229, 326
'Reise nach der alten Heimat, Ein', 49
Rent (film), 321, 334–5, 369 n.5, 369 n.12
Rent (show), 247–9, 273, 278, 330, 344
'Rent', 248, 335
'Reuben and Cynthia', 20
Reutter, Otto, 49
Révolution française, La, 251, 279
Rex, 162
Reynolds, Dorothy, 141
Rhapsody in Blue, 109
Rice, Edward Everett, 19
Rice, Elmer, 194–5
Rice, Tim, 242, 244, 257–9, 268, 287, 314, 319, 333
Rich, Frank, 205, 244
'Rich Kid's Rag', 228
'Rich Man's Frug, The', 228
Richard, Cliff, 144
Richards, Stanley, 235
Richardson, Miranda, 334
Richardson, Natasha, 326–7
Richings, Caroline, 22
Richings, Peter, 9
Riding, Alan, 281
'Riff Song, The', 78, 81
Rifkin, Ron, 327
Riggs, Lynn, 148, 150
'Right as the Rain', 167
Ring, Blanche, 57–8, 65
Rip Van Winkle, 59
Rivera, Chita, 181, 228
Riverdance, 71
Riviera Girl, The, 70
Roar of the Greasepaint – The Smell of the Crowd, The, 188
Rob Roy, 59
'Robbers of the Woods', 85
Robbins, Jerome, 142, 153, 168–9, 178, 180, 186, 197–201, 222–6, 229–30, 332, 337, 349
Roberta (film), 120
Roberta (show), 107, 109–10, 113, 120, 359 n.23, 363 n.15
Robeson, Paul, 117, 321
Robin, Leo, 106
Robin Hood, 25, 59, 63
Robinson Crusoe, Jr., 74
Rock and Roll! The First 5,000 Years, 245
'Rock Me in the Cradle of Love', 97
Rockabye Hamlet, 365 n.22

Rockwell, John, 235
Rocky Horror Show, The, 246
Rodeo, 153, 222
Rodgers and Hammerstein, 87, 111, 114, 116,
    118, 133, 147–76, 181–6, 189, 201, 220,
    222–4, 290, 294, 297, 328–31, 336–7
Rodgers and Hart, 83, 104–9, 115–16, 119–20,
    147–9, 154, 160, 162, 165–6, 170, 173, 221,
    318, 320, 337, 359 n.19
Rodgers, Mary, 286
Rodgers, Richard (*see also* Rodgers and Hart
    and Rodgers and Hammerstein), 83, 87,
    104–8, 110–15, 140, 143, 147–63, 165–6,
    170, 177–8, 182–5, 247, 256, 286, 337, 344,
    358 n.15
Rogers, Ginger, 119–20, 187, 297, 321
Rogue Song, The (film), 82
'Romance', 78
Romberg, Sigmund, 54, 59, 66, 67, 73–85, 106,
    109–10, 119, 131, 148, 168,
    193, 285
Rome, Harold, 108, 141, 166
Roméo & Juliette, 281
Romeo and Juliet, 224
Ronstadt, Linda, 245
Rooke, William Michael, 15
Rooney, Mickey, 119
Roosevelt, Franklin D., 104, 108, 193, 214–15
Rosalia, Giovanni de, 49
Rosalie (film), 119
Rosalie (show), 79, 104, 106, 110
Rosalinda, 361–2 n.13
Rose, Billy, 147
Rose of Araby, The, 85
'Rose of England', 138, 145
Rose Marie (film), 83–4
Rose Marie (show), 72, 75–7, 81, 85–7, 131,
    148, 156
'Rose Marie', 75
'Rose's Turn', 206
'Rosin the Bow', 15
Rosina, 6
Ross, Adrian, 60, 85
Ross, Charlie, 65
Ross, Jerry, 173, 178
Rossini, Gioacchino, 9, 15, 16, 23
Rossum, Emmy, 334
Rousset sisters, 14
Royal, Ted, 198
Royal Wedding (film), 171
Rubens, Paul, 72
Ruby, Harry, 106
Ruffelle, Frances, 253
'Rumble, The', 200, 225
Rumshinsky, Joseph, 48
Runaways, 243
Runyon, Damon, 173
Rusalka Muzikál, 282

Russell, Brenda, 289
Russell, Rosalind, 198–9
Russell, Willy, 246
Ryskind, Morrie, 106–8, 123

'Sabre Song, The', 78
Saddler, Donald, 199
'Saga of Jenny, The', 210
Saidy, Fred, 167, 175
St Louis Woman, 167–8
Salad Days, 127, 141–3
Sally, 70, 104–5, 110, 117, 359 n.22
Salonga, Lea, 254
Salsbury, Nate, 19
Salvation, 239–40
Salvi, Lorenzo, 16
Salvini, Tommaso, 37
Salzman, Eric, 272
'Same Silver Moon, The', 79
Sarafina!, 299
Saratoga, 179
Saturday Night, 362 n.10
Saturday Night Live (film), 332
Saturday Night Live (show), 246
Saturn Returns (*Myths and Hymns*), 286
Satz, Ludwig, 48, 51
Savage, Henry, 64
Savary, Jerome, 275, 280
Scarlet Pimpernel, The, 285, 287
Scheff, Fritzi, 58
Schiera, Thom, 290
Schildkraut, Rudolf, 43
Schiller, Johann Christoph Friedrich von, 37
Schillinger, Joseph, 113
Schmid-Reiter, Isolde, 274
Schmidt, Harvey, 183
Schmitz, Eugenie, 43
Schneitzhoeffer, Jean, 14
Schoenberg, Arnold, 113
Schönberg, Claude-Michel, 251–4, 279, 290,
    300, 319, 366 n.40
Schubert, Franz, 74–5, 115
Schubring, Marc, 277
Schulman, Susan H., 329
Schumacher, Joel, 334
Schwab, Laurence, 77, 79, 105–7
Schwartz, Arthur, 147, 166, 173, 175
Schwartz, Maurice, 48
Schwartz, Stephen, 241, 286–7, 319, 340–52,
    366 n.33
Scott, Randolph, 120
Séance on a Wet Afternoon, 352
'Seasons of Love', 248, 334–5
'Sects Therapy', 277
See America First, 109
Seeger, Horst, 271–2
Seesaw, 230, 234
Seguin, Anne, 9, 15

Seguin, Edward (Ned), 9, 15
'Send in the Clowns', 211
'Sentimental Man', 350
'September Song', 193
'Serenade' ('Overhead the moon is beaming'),
    77
Serenade, The, 25
'Serenade Blues', 99
'7–11–77', 93
'7 ¹/₂ Cents', 226
1776, 188
'Seventy-Six Trombones' 180
*Sgt Pepper's Lonely Hearts Club Band on the
    Road*, 245
Shakespeare, William, 13, 36, 37, 171–2,
    239–40, 282, 318
Shall We Dance (film), 288
'Shall We Dance?', 159
'Shalom', 186
Shapiro, Anne Dhu, 11
Sharaff, Irene, 160
Shaw, George Bernard, 175
Shenandoah, 299
Sherman, Gary, 289
Sherman, Richard M. and Robert B., 268
Sherwood, Robert, 168
She Loves Me, 229
She's My Baby, 106, 147
Shield, William, 6, 9
Shields, Brooke, 330
Shirley, Wayne, 359 n.36
Shirreff, Jane, 9
'Shiz', 344
Shoo-Fly Regiment, The, 96–7
Show Boat (1936 film), 120, 148
Show Boat (novel), 99
Show Boat (show), 3, 70, 79, 99–102, 104, 108,
    110, 117, 120, 123, 131, 148–51, 154, 156,
    168, 205, 220–1, 321, 338
Show Girl, 106
'Shriner's Ballet', 181, 229
Shubert brothers, 59, 68, 69, 74–5
Shuffle Along, 98–9, 105, 117
Shuffle Along: Keep Shufflin', 117
Shuffle Along of 1933, 117
'Side By Side By Side', 230
Sigurdsson, Björk and Sjón, 309
Silk Stockings, 176–7
Silvers, Phil, 169, 184, 224
Silvers, Sid, 81
Simas, Rick, 285
Simmons, Jean, 332
Simon, John, 291
Simon, Paul, 245–6, 290
Simple Simon, 106
Simpson, Harold, 85
Simpson, O. J., 326
Simpsons, The (television show), 306

Sinatra, Frank, 190, 332
Sinbad, 74, 109
Sing-along Sound of Music, The, 162–3
Singin' in the Rain (film), 295, 307, 309, 311
Singin' in the Rain (show), 275, 295
'Singin' in the Rain', 307
Sissle, Noble, 98–99, 105, 117
Sitting Pretty, 105, 109, 120
Six, Les (group of composers), 81
1600 Pennsylvania Avenue, 201
Skin of Our Teeth, The, 201
Skinner, Steve, 248
Slade, Julian, 127, 141–3
'Slap that Bass', 113
'Slaughter on Tenth Avenue', 221
'Sleepwalker's Ballet', 224
Sleepy Hollow, or the Headless Horseman, 25
'Small House of Uncle Thomas, The', 159, 224
Small, Charlie, 289
Smith, Harry B., 67, 69
Smith, Marian Monta, 221
Smith, Oliver, 183, 197
Smith, Paul Gerard, 106
'Smoke Gets in Your Eyes', 110, 113, 120
Smokey Joe's Café, 71, 236, 245, 287
Smulewitz, Solomon, 38
Snow White (film), 309, 318
'So in Love', 172
Sobre las olas, 52
¡Sofrito!, 290
'Softly, As in a Morning Sunrise', 80
'Soliloquy', 156
'Some Enchanted Evening', 140
'Somebody Loves Me', 68, 113
'Someday My Heart Will Awake', 137, 145
'Someone is Waiting', 208
'Someone to Watch Over Me', 121–2, 359 n.36
'Something Bad', 344
'Something Had to Happen', 120
'Something's Coming', 200
'Sometimes I'm Happy', 119
'Somewhere', 200–1, 225
'Somewhere Over The Rainbow', 347
Sommarnottens leende (film), 296
Sondheim, Stephen, 87, 116, 162, 173, 180,
    184–5, 200, 205–20, 225, 229–30, 247–8,
    270–1, 275, 284–5, 288, 291, 329–30, 337,
    339, 363 n.22, 363 n.15, 368 n.2
Song and Dance, 257, 265–6, 276
'Song of Love', 75
Song of Norway, 133, 166, 194, 361–2 n.13
'Song of the Vagabonds', 81
Songs for a New World, 299
Sonnambule, La, 14
Sons of Ham, 95–6
Sontag, Henriette, 16
Soon, 365 n.22
Sophisticated Ladies, 287, 289

'Sorry Grateful', 208
Sound of Music, The (film), 329–30, 358 n.15, 369 n.5
Sound of Music, The (show), 160–3, 182–3, 274, 297, 307, 329
Sousa, John Philip, 25, 100, 213, 215
South Pacific (film), 160, 329
South Pacific (show), 87, 139, 157–9, 162, 173–4, 178, 329, 331
South Pacific (television version), 162, 329, 337–8
South Park (television show), 306, 368 n.1
Southerners, The, 99
Spamalot, 292, 296
'Speak Low', 194
'Spectacular Spectacular', 315, 322
Spencer, Willard, 25
Sperling, Ted, 286
Spewack, Bella and Samuel, 107–8, 171–2
Spialek, Hans, 118, 121
'Sporty Coon, The', 92
Spottswood, Richard K., 48
Spring is Here, 106
Spyri, Johanna, 277
Star Wars (film), 255
Starlight Express, 254–7, 259–60, 273, 275
Starmania, 280
State Fair (film), 154–5, 295, 358 n.15
State Fair (show), 295
'State Fair', 154
'Steam Heat', 178, 226
Steamboat Willie, 308
Stearns, Daniel Patrick, 326
Stein, Joseph, 332
Stein, Leo, 60
Steinbeck, John, 160
Steinman, Jim, 257, 267, 279
Steinway, William, 43
Stepping Stones, The, 105
Stevens, Tony, 231
Stewart, David Ogden, 106
Stewart, Ellen, 237
Stewart, Michael, 181
Steyn, Mark, 260
Stiles, George, 269
Stilgoe, Richard, 257
'Still the World Goes On', 93
Sting, 309
Stive, Pascal, 282
Stock, Jeffrey, 285
Stoller, Mike, 245, 287
Stone, David, 343–4, 346
Stone, Peter, 162, 293–4
Stop the World – I Want to Get Off, 188
Storace, Stephen, 6
'Story of Lucy and Jessie, The', 210
Stothart, Herbert, 82
'Stouthearted Men', 80–2, 87, 227

Stowe, Harriet Beecher, 11, 89–90, 159
Strakosch, Maurice, 16
Strakosch, Max, 16
'Stranger in Paradise', 177
Straus, Oscar, 50, 65, 72, 356 n.25
Strauss, Johann, 24, 51, 60, 63–4, 361–2 n.13
Stravinsky, Igor, 199, 242
Street Scene (opera), 194–5
Street Scene (play), 194–5
'Streets of New York, The', 58
Streisand, Barbra, 169, 185, 188, 259
Strickland, Josh, 269
Strike Up the Band, 106, 108, 118, 359 n.23
Stroman, Susan, 288, 292, 328, 335
Stromberger, Bernd, 277
Strouse, Charles, 178, 181–2, 236
Student Gypsy, The, 87
Student King, The, 59
Student Prince, The (film), 83–4
Student Prince, The (show), 59, 72, 75–8, 80, 86–7
'Students' Marching Song', 77
Styne, Jule, 166, 169–70, 173, 178–80, 184–5, 206, 224–5, 329, 337
Sullivan, Arthur, 23–5, 47, 54, 59, 63–4, 90
Sullivan, Ed, 284
'Summertime', 101
Sunday in the Park With George, 116, 206, 209, 295, 339, 368 n.2
'Sunday Morning in England', 138
Sunny, 104–5, 110, 117, 148, 221, 359 n.22
'Sunrise, Sunset', 186
Sunset Boulevard (film), 256–8, 261, 296
Sunset Boulevard (show), 250, 255–8, 260–5, 276, 296
'Sunset Boulevard', 261, 263–4
Suppé, Franz von, 24
'Supper Time', 108
'Surrey with the Fringe on Top, The', 152–3
Swann, Donald, 139
'Swanee', 109
Swayne, Steven, 207
Sweeney Todd, 71, 116, 207, 211, 219, 275, 285, 293, 329–30, 339, 368 n.2
Sweet: Little Devil, 105
Sweet Adeline, 148
Sweet Charity (film), 228
Sweet Charity (show), 228
'Sweet Home Alabama', 318
Sweet Smell of Success (film), 296
Sweet Smell of Success (show), 296
'Sweetest Sounds, The', 337
Sweethearts (film), 83
Sweethearts (show), 66
Swift, Kay, 106
'Swing', 199
'Swing Along', 96
Sylphide, La, 13–14

'Sympathy', 74
Symphony no. 3 ('Kaddish' – Bernstein), 191

'Ta-Ra-Ra-Boom-De-Ay', 86
Tabasco, 25
Tag im Paradis, Ein, 74
Taglioni, Paul, 13
Take a Chance, 107
'Take Care of this House', 201
Talavera, Mario, 50
'Tale of the Oyster, The', 122
Tales of the South Pacific (short stories collection), 157–8
Taming of the Shrew, The, 171
Tamiris, Helen, 168
Tammany; or, the Indian Chief, 6
'Tango: Maureen', 321, 369 n.12
Tango Argentina, 290
'Tango de Roxanne, El', 322–3
Tanz der Vampire, 279
Tarzan (film), 296, 319
Tarzan (show), 269, 296, 298
Tate, James, 85
Tauber, Richard, 131
Taupin, Bernie, 287
Taylor, Deems, 102
Taylor, Dwight, 107
Taylor, James, 245
Taylor, Rayner, 5, 6
Taylor, Samuel, 162
Taymor, Julie, 268
Te Kanawa, Kiri, 338
Tebelak, John-Michael, 241
'Telephone Hour, The', 182
Tell Me More!, 105
Tell Me on a Sunday, 257, 265–6
'Temple, The', 242
Temple, Shirley, 169
Templeton, Fay, 120
'Ten Minutes Ago I Saw You', 344
'Tenderloin Coon, A', 93
Tesori, Jeanine, 270, 291
'Tevye and His Daughters', 186
'That's Him', 194
Tharp, Twyla, 246, 289, 292
Theodore & Co, 128
'There Is Nothin' Like a Dame', 158
'There Once Was a Man', 178
'There's No Business Like Show Business', 168, 172
'They Call the Wind Maria', 175
'They Can't Take That Away', 113
'They Didn't Believe Me', 109
'They Say It's Wonderful', 168
'They'll Always Be a Lady Fair', 119
'Think of Me', 263–4
'30 Minutes Around the Operas', 92
'This Can't Be Love', 114, 120

This is the Army, 166
Thomas, Ambroise, 23
Thomashefsky, Boris, 43, 48
Thompson, Fred, 105–6
Thompson, Kay, 209
Thompson, Lydia, 19
Thomson, Virgil, 196, 362 n.20
Thoroughly Modern Millie (film), 296
Thoroughly Modern Millie (show), 296, 299
'Thou Swell', 113
Three Dance Episodes from 'On the Town', 198
Three Musketeers, The, 72, 76, 81
Three Sisters, 107, 120
Threepenny Opera, The, 190–1
Thurber, Jeanette, 23
Thurman, Uma, 335
Tibbett, Lawrence, 82–3
'Tick Tock', 208, 230
Till the Clouds Roll By, 117
'Till There Was You', 180
Timber-Trattning, Georg, 277
'Times Square: 1944', 198
Times They Are A-Changin', The, 292
Tinted Venus, The, 194
Tip Toes, 104–5, 359 n.22
Tirado, Romualdo, 43, 50
Titanic (film), 255, 336
'Today 4 U', 334
Todd, Mike, 168
Tommy (film), 295
Tommy (show), 235, 276
'Tonight', 200
'Too Late Now', 171
Too Many Girls, 107–8
'Too Many Girls', 358 n.15
Top Hat (film), 110, 309, 317
Toré, John, 139
Tormé, Mel, 118
Tostée, Lucille, 24
'Totem Tom Tom', 76–7
'Touch of Your Hand, The', 120
Tough at the Top, 135, 138
Tours, Frank, 69
Toye, Wendy, 135
'Tradition', 186
Tragédie de Carmen, La, 293
'Tramp! Tramp! Tramp!', 66
Trapp, Captain von, 162
Trapp, Maria von, 162
Traubel, Helen, 160
Travers, P. L., 268, 298
Treasure Girl, 106
Trentini, Emma, 66, 73–4
Tres García, Los, 52
Trip to Chinatown, A, 20, 94–95
Trip to Coontown, A, 21
Triumph of Love, 285
'Triumphs of Spring, The', 132

'Trolley Song, The', 315
'Tropical Revelries', 91
Trouble in Tahiti, 190, 198
Truman, Harry, 117, 172
'Try to Remember', 183
Tunbridge, Joseph, 127
Tune, Tommy, 181, 231, 234, 349
Turner, J. H., 106
Tutt, J. Homer, 97–8, 102
Tweed, Boss, 168
Twelfth Night, 239
Twenty to One, 127–8, 130–1
Twirly-Whirly, 56
Two by Two, 162
Two Gentlemen of Verona, 220, 235, 240, 298

U2, 309
Ullman, Bernard, 16
Ullman, Tracy, 338
Ulmer, Edgar G., 51
Ulvaeus, Björn, 244
'Uncle Sam Rag, The', 228
Uncle Tom's Cabin, 11–12, 89–90, 99, 159
Up in Central Park, 168
Urban, Joseph, 67, 68–9
Urban Cowboy (film), 296
Urban Cowboy (show), 295–6
Urinetown: The Musical, 291–2, 299
Urlina, The African Princess, 89–90

Vagabond King, The (film), 83–4
Vagabond King, The (show), 76, 81, 86, 104
Valdez, Luis, 290
Valentina, La, 52
Valentino, Rudolf, 78
Valli, Frankie, 246–7, 288
Valmouth, 143
van Cauwelaert, Didier, 281
Van Dyke, Dick, 181, 268
Van Sant, Gus, 311
Varèse, Edgard, 81, 103
Vargas, Antonio, 48
Variations for Cello and Rock Band, 257, 265–6
'Varsity Drag, The', 118
Vaughan, Sarah, 338
'Vaults of Heaven, The', 266
'Venus in Ozone Heights', 222
Verdi, Giuseppe, 16, 23, 90, 199
Verdon, Gwen, 177–8, 226, 228–30
Vereen, Ben, 228, 352
Véron, Louis, 251
Very Warm for May, 107, 149
Via Galactica, 241
Victor/Victoria (film), 295, 312
Victor/Victoria, (show), 295
Victory at Sea (television show), 160
'Vie Boheme, La', 248, 334–5
Vie en bleu, La, 282

'Violet', 179
'Vitality', 140
Vogel, Frederick G., 308, 313
Voice of Nature, The, 7, 8
von Sternberg, Josef, 282

Wagner, Richard, 23, 36, 63, 65, 199, 201
'Waiter's Gallop', 229
Wake Up and Dream, 106
Walk the Line (film), 309, 311
Walker, Chet, 229
Walker, Don, 198
Walker, George, 67, 95–7
Walker, James J., 108, 180
Walker, Nancy, 184, 198, 224
Wallace, Vincent, 15
Waller, Fats, 287, 289
Waller, Jack, 127
Walsh, Michael, 255, 266
Walsh, Thommie, 231, 234
Walston, Ray, 178
Waltz Dream, A, 72
'Waltz for Eva and Che', 321, 369 n.12
'Waltz of My Heart', 130, 145
'Wanting You', 80, 82
Warren, Lesley Anne, 336
'Washington Post March', 100–1, 215
Watch Your Step, 68, 109
Water Gypsies, The, 139
Watzmann Ruft, Der, 277
Wayhighman, The, 59
'We Beseech Thee', 241
'We Both Reached for the Gun', 369 n.5
'We Said We Wouldn't Look Back', 142
We Will Rock You, 273
'We'll Gather Lilacs', 132
Webb, Clifton, 221
Weber, Carl Maria von, 15, 18, 23
Weber, Joseph, 55, 59, 64–5, 68
Wedding Singer, The (film), 296
Wedding Singer, The (show), 296
Weidman, John, 212–13
Weill, Kurt, 107–8, 178, 188, 190–8, 200–1,
   210, 222, 276, 362 n.20
Weissler, Fran and Barry, 297
Weitzenhoffer, Max, 298
'Welcome Home', 252
Wells, William K., 105
Welte, Anne, 276
'Wenn ich dein Spiegel war', 278
Wept of Wish-Ton-Wish, The, 8
'We're in the Money', 318
Werfel, Franz, 192
West Side Story (film), 369 n.5
West Side Story (show), 101, 142, 165, 180, 190,
   197, 200–1, 206, 223–5, 229, 230, 273–5,
   292, 338, 352, 363 n.22, 363 n.15, 368 n.5
Westley, Helen, 120

'What I Did For Love', 233
'What Is This Feeling?', 342, 344
'What We Would Do Without You', 230
'What'll I Do?', 69
Wheeler, Hugh, 200
'When I Grow Too Old to Dream', 149
'When My Dreams Come True', 119
'When Our Ship Comes Sailing In', 122
'Where or When', 119
Where's Charley?, 173
'Which Way's the Party?', 349
Whistle Down the Wind (film), 257
Whistle Down the Wind (novel), 256–7
Whistle Down the Wind (show), 254, 256–7, 266–8
'Whistle It', 58
White Fawn, The, 18
White, George, 27, 68, 70, 111, 287
White, Miles, 156
White, T. H., 183
White Christmas (film), 320
White House Cantata, A, 201
Whiteman, Paul, 173
Whiting, Richard A., 107, 148
Whitman, Slim, 87
Whitney, Salem Tutt, 97–8, 102
'Who', 117
'Who Am I?', 253
'Who Dat Say Chicken in Dis Crowd', 94
'Who's Got the Pain?', 226
'Who's That Woman?', 230
Who's Tommy, The, see *Tommy*
Whoop-de-Doo, 56
'Why Can't I?', 120
Wicked (novel), 340–2
Wicked (show), 234, 287, 340–52, 366 n.33
'Wicked Witch of the East, The', 351
Widow Jones, The, 94
'Widow Machree', 15
Wie Einst im Mai, 74
'Wig in a Box', 305
Wilbur, Richard, 199
Wild Party, The, 291
Wild Thyme, 139
Wilder, Billy, 257, 261
Wilder, Gene, 335
Wilder, Thornton, 186, 201
Wildflower, 148
Wildhorn, Frank, 285, 287
Wilkinson, Colm, 253
'Will I?', 248
Will Rogers Follies, The, 234
'Will You Remember?' ('Sweethearts, Sweethearts'), 75
Williams, Bert, 67, 95–7
Williams, Robbie, 310
Willis, Allee, 289
Willson, Meredith, 180

Wilson, John, 9
Wilson, Patrick, 334
Wilson, Sandy, 127, 141–3, 145
Winston Churchill – The Valiant Years, 162
Wise, Robert, 331
Wish You Were Here, 140–1
'With One Look', 263–4
'Without You', 248
Wiz, The, 235, 243, 289
'Wizard And I, The', 344–5, 349, 351
The Wizard of Oz (1939 film), 110, 179, 294–5, 309, 312, 314, 340–1
Wizard of Oz, The (1903 stage show), 56
Wizard of the Nile, The, 3, 25
Wodehouse, P. G., 68, 70, 81, 105–6, 109, 257, 265
Woldin, Judd, 289
Wolf, Rennold, 59
Wolfe, George C., 290–1
Woll, Alfred, 21
Woman in White, The (novel), 256–7
Woman in White, The (show), 254–5, 257, 267–9
'Wonderful', 351
Wonderful Town, 139, 190, 197–9, 297
Wood, Joseph, 9
Wood, Mary Anne Paton, 9
Woolfson, Eric, 277
'Working on the Land', 252
Wright, Robert, 166, 177
'Wrong Note Rag', 199
'Wunderbar', 172
Wydro, Ken, 289
Wynn, Ed, 67, 106

'Yankee Doodle Boy, The', 55, 164
'Yankele', 48
Yazbeck, David, 270, 286–7
Yentl (film), 312
'Yesterdays', 113, 120
Yidl mitn fidl, 51
'Yigdal', 191
Yip, Yip, Yaphank, 69
Yolanda and the Thief (film), 314
'You Are Too Beautiful', 147
'You Can Get Away with Anything', 268
'You Could Drive A Person Crazy', 230
'You Must Love Me', 259
You Never Know, 107
Youmans, Irving, 104–6, 119, 147–8
Young Frankenstein (film), 296
Young Frankenstein (show), 87, 296
Your Arms Too Short to Box With God, 289
'Your Eyes', 248
'Your Land and My Land', 79, 81
Your Own Thing, 235–6, 239–40
'Your Song', 320
'You're Devastating', 120

'You're the One I Want', 332
'You're the Top', 119
'You've Got to Be Carefully Taught', 159, 338
Yu, Hye Jung, 290

Zangara, Giuseppe, 213–16
Zazou, 275
Zellweger, Renée, 333
Zeta-Jones, Catherine, 333

Ziegfeld, Florenz, 19, 27, 56, 66–71, 79, 97, 111, 287
'Zigainer Madel, Dus', 48
'Zigeuner', 86
Zimmer, Hans, 314, 319
Zip Goes a Million, 139
Zippel, David, 257
Zipprodt, Patricia, 226
Zoot Suit, 290

Cambridge Companions to Music

Topics
The Cambridge Companion to Ballet
Edited by Marion Kant

The Cambridge Companion to Blues and Gospel Music
Edited by Allan Moore

The Cambridge Companion to the Concerto
Edited by Simon P. Keefe

The Cambridge Companion to Conducting
Edited by José Antonio Bowen

The Cambridge Companion to Electronic Music
Edited by Nick Collins and Julio D'Escriván

The Cambridge Companion to Grand Opera
Edited by David Charlton

The Cambridge Companion to Jazz
Edited by Mervyn Cooke and David Horn

The Cambridge Companion to the Lied
Edited by James Parsons

The Cambridge Companion to the Musical, second edition
Edited by William Everett and Paul Laird

The Cambridge Companion to the Orchestra
Edited by Colin Lawson

The Cambridge Companion to Pop and Rock
Edited by Simon Frith, Will Straw and John Street

The Cambridge Companion to the String Quartet
Edited by Robin Stowell

The Cambridge Companion to Twentieth-Century Opera
Edited by Mervyn Cooke

Composers
The Cambridge Companion to Bach
Edited by John Butt

The Cambridge Companion to Bartók
Edited by Amanda Bayley

The Cambridge Companion to Beethoven
Edited by Glenn Stanley

The Cambridge Companion to Berg
Edited by Anthony Pople

The Cambridge Companion to Berlioz
Edited by Peter Bloom

The Cambridge Companion to Brahms
Edited by Michael Musgrave

The Cambridge Companion to Benjamin Britten
Edited by Mervyn Cooke

The Cambridge Companion to Bruckner
Edited by John Williamson

The Cambridge Companion to John Cage
Edited by David Nicholls

The Cambridge Companion to Chopin
Edited by Jim Samson

The Cambridge Companion to Debussy
Edited by Simon Trezise

The Cambridge Companion to Elgar
Edited by Daniel M. Grimley and Julian Rushton

The Cambridge Companion to Handel
Edited by Donald Burrows

The Cambridge Companion to Haydn
Edited by Caryl Clark

The Cambridge Companion to Liszt
Edited by Kenneth Hamilton

The Cambridge Companion to Mahler
Edited by Jeremy Barham

The Cambridge Companion to Mendelssohn
Edited by Peter Mercer-Taylor

The Cambridge Companion to Mozart
Edited by Simon P. Keefe

The Cambridge Companion to Ravel
Edited by Deborah Mawer

The Cambridge Companion to Rossini
Edited by Emanuele Senici

The Cambridge Companion to Schubert
Edited by Christopher Gibbs

The Cambridge Companion to Schumann
Edited by Beate Perrey

The Cambridge Companion to Sibelius
Edited by Daniel M. Grimley

The Cambridge Companion to Verdi
Edited by Scott L. Balthazar

Instruments
The Cambridge Companion to Brass Instruments
Edited by Trevor Herbert and John Wallace

The Cambridge Companion to the Cello
Edited by Robin Stowell

The Cambridge Companion to the Clarinet
Edited by Colin Lawson

The Cambridge Companion to the Guitar
Edited by Victor Coelho

The Cambridge Companion to the Organ
Edited by Nicholas Thistlethwaite and Geoffrey Webber

The Cambridge Companion to the Piano
Edited by David Rowland

The Cambridge Companion to the Recorder
Edited by John Mansfield Thomson

The Cambridge Companion to the Saxophone
Edited by Richard Ingham

The Cambridge Companion to Singing
Edited by John Potter

The Cambridge Companion to the Violin
Edited by Robin Stowell